TEACH YOURSELF BOOKS

LATIN DICTIONARY

NTC Publishing Group

TEACH YOURSELF BOOKS

LATIN DICTIONARY

Alastair Wilson

B.A.

NTC Publishing Group

Long-renowned as *the* authoritative source for self-guided
learning – with more than 30 million copies sold worldwide –
the *Teach Yourself* series includes over 200 titles in the fields
of languages, crafts, hobbies, sports, and other leisure activities.

DEC 13 1993

This edition was first published in 1992 by NTC Publishing Group,
4255 West Touhy Avenue, Lincolnwood (Chicago), Illinois 60646 –
1975 U.S.A. Originally published by Hodder and Stoughton Ltd.

Library of Congress Catalog Card Number: 92 80874

Printed in England

CONTENTS

INTRODUCTION

THE chief benefit that a knowledge of Latin confers is the ability to read the works of the Roman authors, particularly those of the Golden and Silver Ages of Latin Literature, i.e. 60 B.C.–A.D. 100. This Dictionary has been compiled with this in mind, and also with an eye to the "non-specialist". To this end, the equivalents in the Latin–English section of the Dictionary have been presented in as simple and "modern" a form as possible, while at the same time the most important distinctions in meaning which each Latin word bears have been indicated. The vocabulary has been based on that commonly used by the authors of the period mentioned above, and a person who is acquainted with Latin grammar and the common forms of the Latin language should be able, with a little help from this Dictionary, to read them without much difficulty. For those not so acquainted, for those whose memory may have dimmed with the passage of time, and for those who have never been fully conversant with a highly inflected language like Latin, a Concise Latin Grammar has been provided. This contains, in tabulated form and with simple explanations, all the basic regular and irregular word-forms needed for translation from the commoner Latin authors.

In the English–Latin section, the Latin equivalent given is that which represents the best *general* meaning of the English, and which is used in that sense by a Classical author. Occasionally, however, where no exact Latin equivalent for an English word exists, it has been necessary to give a short circumlocution: in this case the phrase given is always translated into English, e.g. disinterested, neutri favens (favouring neither side). Where several different meanings are borne by the same word, or where ambiguity may occur, care has been taken to differentiate between the various meanings, e.g. order, *nn*, (arrangement), ordo, *m*; (in —), *adj*, dispŏsĭtus; (command, direction), iussum, *n*; (class, rank), ordo, *m*; (in — to), ut.

Where fuller information is required about any of the words given in the Dictionary, reference should be made to the following standard works upon the subject: A Latin Dictionary by Charlton T. Lewis and Charles Short and Smaller English–Latin Dictionary by Dr. William Smith.

ADVICE ON LEARNING VOCABULARY

If you are gifted with a good memory, you will find it particularly easy to learn Latin vocabulary, especially if you try to link in your mind new Latin words and any English derivatives of them which you can think of, e.g. mare—sea—marine; nauta—ship—nautical. A high proportion of Latin words have quite common English derivatives. If you do this, not only will your interest in both languages grow, but you will begin to form an impression of the debt which our language owes to that of the Romans.

If on the other hand, you are one of those who find it "difficult to make words stick" in schoolboy phraseology, then here is a piece of simple advice —not to be despised because of its simplicity—which might help you to retain words in your memory. To learn a new word it is not only essential to find out and to understand its meaning, but also to see it working in relationship to other words, and to "meet" it as many times as possible immediately after first acquaintance. It is therefore advisable to *re-read* the piece in which you originally met the word two or three times after you have learned it, and to make an effort to find the same word again within a day or two of first meeting it, otherwise you may find, on ultimately seeing it again, that it has "gone". Above all, try to maintain your interest in learning new vocabulary, for without such interest no learning of real or lasting nature can take place.

ABBREVIATIONS USED

( ) Brackets are used to indicate alternative forms.

a, um, see adj.

abl. ablative case; see page 295.

acc. accusative case; see page 295.

acis }
atis } genitive singular ending of nouns indicating that they belong to the third declension.

adj. adjective, **a, um era, erum** after an adjective indicates that it belongs to the First Class, "e" that it belongs to the Second Class; see page 297.

adv. adverb. The adverb ending is often given, e.g. **e, iter, nter, um, o,** and should be attached to the *stem* of the adjective, e.g. **abditus** (*adj*); **abdite** (*adv*). See page 316.

ae. genitive singular ending of a noun, indicating that it belongs to the first declension.

arum, genitive plural ending, indicating that the noun belongs to the first declension.

auxil. auxiliary verb.

c. common gender.

c. comp. comparative adjective or adverb, see pages 299–316.

conj. conjunction; see p. 315.

cris, cre. nominative feminine and neuter endings, indicating that an adjective belongs to the Second Class; see page 298.

cl. clause.

dat. dative case; see page 295; also some verbs take a dative case after them.

defect. a defective verb, i.e. it has not all its parts; see page 312.

demonst. demonstrative pronoun.

dep, see v. dep.

e. see adj.

ei. genitive singular ending of noun, indicating that it belongs to the fifth declension.

enis }
etis } genitive singular endings of nouns indicating that they belong to the third declension.

exclam. exclamation.

f. feminine gender.

f.pl. feminine plural.

fut. future.

i, ii. genitive singular ending of noun, indicating that it belongs to the second declension.

icis }
inis } genitive singular endings of nouns indicating that they belong to the third declension.

impers. impersonal verb; see page 311.

indecl. indeclinable.

inf. infinitive.

interj. interjective.

interr. interrogative.

irreg. irregular verb; see pages 307–310.

is. genitive singular of noun, indicating that it belongs to the third declension.

iter, see adv.

itis. genitive singular ending of noun, indicating that it belongs to the third declension.

ium. genitive plural ending of noun, indicating that it belongs to the third declension.

m. masculine gender.

m.pl. masculine plural.

n. neuter gender.

nn. noun.

nter, see adv.

ntis. genitive singular ending of some nouns and adjectives of the third declension.

num. numeral.

n.pl. neuter plural.

onis } genitive singular noun ending, indicating that the noun belongs to the
oris } third declension.

orum. genitive plural ending, indicating that a noun belongs to the second declension.

partic. participle.

pass. a passive verb, conjugated in the passive voice only.

perf. perfect.

pers. personal.

phr. phrase.

pl. plural.

poss. possessive.

prep. preposition; see page 314: the case taken by the preposition is usually indicated.

pres. present.

pron. pronoun; see pages 312–314.

pron. adj. pronominal adjective; a pronoun which declines and agrees like an adjective.

reflex. reflexive.

rel. relative.

semi-dep. semi-deponent; verbs which are deponent in some of their tenses.

sup(erl). superlative adjective or adverb.

tis } genitive singular ending of some nouns and adjs. of the third declension.
tris }

um. genitive plural ending of noun, indicating that it belongs to the third declension.

ūs. genitive singular ending of noun, indicating that it belongs to the fourth declension.

v. vb. verb. The conjugation to which a verb belongs is indicated by the figure 1, 2, 3, or 4; see page 299. In the case of 3rd conjugation verbs, and other verbs whose Perfect stem and Supine are not regular, these are given with the verb, e.g. **aboleo, evi, itum.** If none of these parts are given, it may be assumed that the verb is regularly conjugated; if some, but not all parts are given, it may be assumed that the ones not given are not in regular use.

v. dep. verb deponent; see page 310.

v.i. verb intransitive, i.e. a verb which does not have a direct object.

v. impers. verb impersonal; see page 311.

v.i.t. a verb which can be used intransitively or transitively. The separate uses are indicated by the use of the semi-colon, e.g. **abhorreo,** *v.i.t.* 2, to shrink back (intransitive); to disagree with (transitive).

voc. vocative case, see page 295.

v.t. verb transitive, i.e. a verb which has a direct object.

LATIN – ENGLISH

For List of Abbreviations used, turn to pages 3, 4

A

ā, ăb, *prep. with abl*, by (agent); from (place, time); in, at (position); since

ăbăcus, ĭ, *m*, sideboard, counting or gaming board, slab

ăbăliēno, *v.t.* 1, to estrange, make a legal transfer

ăbăvus, ĭ, *m*, great-great-grandfather, ancestor

abdĭcātĭo, ōnis, *f*, renunciation of office

abdĭco, *v.t.* 1, to resign

abdīco, xi, ctum, *v.t.* 3, to refuse assent

abdĭtus, a, um, *adj, adv*, ē, hidden, secret

abdo, didi, dĭtum, *v.t.* 3, to conceal

abdōmĕn, inis, *n*, belly

abdūco, xi, ctum, *v.t.* 3, to lead away

ăbĕo, *v.i.* 4, to go away

ăberro, *v.i.* 1, to go astray

ăbhinc, *adv*, ago

ăbhorrĕo, *v.i.t.* 2, to shrink back; disagree with

ăbi, see ăbĕo

ăbĭcĭo, iēci, iectum, *v.t.* 3, to throw away

abiectus, a, um, *adj, adv*, ē, downcast

ăbiēgnus, a um, *adj*, made of fir

ăbiēs, ĕtis, *f*, fir

ăbĭgo, ĕre, ēgi, actum, *v.t.* 3, to drive away

ăbĭtĭo, ōnis, *f*, departure

ăbĭtus, ūs, *m*, departure

abiūdico, *v.t.* 1, to deprive by legal sentence

abiungo, nxi, nctum, *v.t.* 3, to unyoke

abiūro, *v.t.* 1, to deny on oath

ablātus, a, um, *adj*. from aufĕro, taken away

ablēgātĭo, ōnis, *f*, banishment

ablēgo, *v.t.* 1, to send away

ablŭo, ŭi, ūtum, *v.t.* 3, to wash away

ablūtĭo, ōnis, *f*, ablution, washing

abnĕgo, *v.t.* 1, to refuse

abnormis, e, *adj*, irregular

abnŭo, ŭi, ūtum, *v.i.t.* 3, to refuse

ăbŏlĕo, ēvi, ĭtum, *v.t.* 2, to destroy

ăbŏlesco, ēvi, *v.i.* 3, to decay

ăbŏlĭtĭo, ōnis, *f*, abolition

ăbolla, ae, *f*, cloak

ăbōmĭnor, *v.t.* 1, *dep*. to wish away (being ominous)

ăbŏrīgĭnes, um, *m.pl*, natives

ăbortĭo, ōnis, *f*, miscarriage

ăbortus, ūs, *m*, abortion

abrādo, si, sum, *v.t.* 3, to scrape off

abrĭpĭo, ŭi, reptum, *v.t.* 3, to drag away

abrōdo, si, sum, *v.t.* 3, to gnaw away

abrŏgātĭo, ōnis, *f*, repeal

abrŏgo, *v.t.* 1, to repeal

abrumpo, rūpi, ruptum, *v.t.* 3, to break off

abruptus, a, um, *adj*, steep

abscēdo, cessi, cessum, *v.i.* 3, to go away

abscīdo, cīdi, scīsum, *v.t.* 3, to cut off

abscindo, scĭdi, scissum, *v.t.* 3, to tear away

abscīsus, a, um, *adj, adv*, ē, steep

absconditus, a, um, *adj, adv*, ē, hidden

abscondo, di, dĭtum, *v.t.* 3, to conceal

absens, entis, *adj*, absent

absentĭa, ae, *f*, absence

absĭlĭo, *v.i.* 4, to jump away

absĭmĭlis, e, *adj*, unlike

absinthĭum, ii, *n*, absinth

absisto, stĭti, *v.i.* 3, to stand aloof

absŏlūtĭo, ōnis, *f*, acquittal

absŏlūtus, a, um, *adj, adv*, ē, complete

absolvo, vi, sŏlūtum, *v.t.* 3, to unfasten, acquit

absŏnus, a, um, *adj, adv*, ē, discordant

absorbĕo, bŭi, ptum, *v.t.* 2, to swallow up

absquĕ, *prep. with abl*, without

abstēmĭus, a, um, *adj*, sober

abstergĕo, rsi, rsum, *v.t.* 2, to wipe off

absterrĕo, *v.t.* 2, to frighten away

abstĭnens, ntis, *adj, adv*, nter, temperate

abstĭnentĭa, ae, *f*, self-restraint

abstĭnĕo, ŭi, tentum, *v.i.t.* 2, to abstain from; restrain

abstrăho, xi, ctum, *v.t.* 3, to drag away

abstrūdo, si, sum, *v.t.* 3, to push away

abstrūsus, a, um, *adj*, *adv*, ē, hidden
absum, esse, abfui (afui), *v.i. irreg*, to be absent
absūmo, mpsi, mptum, *v.t.* 3, to take away, use up
absurdus, a, um, *adj*, *adv*, ē, stupid, tuneless
ābundans, ntis, *adj*, *adv*, nter, plentiful
ābundantīa, ae, *f*, plenty
ābundo, *v.i.* 1, to overflow
ābūtor, ī, usus sum, *v.* 3, *dep. with abl*, to use up, abuse
āc, *conj*, and
ācācia, ae, *f*, acacia
ācādēmīa, ae, *f*, academy
accēdo, cessi, cessum, *v.i.* 3, to approach
accēlēro, *v.i.t.* 1, to hurry; quicken
accendo, ndi, nsum, *v.t.* 3, to set on fire
accensēo, ūi, nsum, *v.t.* 2, to add to
accensus, i, *m*, attendant
accentus, ūs, *m*, accentuation
acceptīo, ōnis, *f*, acceptance
acceptum, i, *n*, receipt
acceptus, a, um, *adj*, agreeable
accessīo, ōnis, *f*, approach, increase
accessus, ūs, *m*, approach
accīdo, cīdi, cīsum, *v.t.* 3, to cut
accido, cīdi, *v.i.* 3, to fall upon, happen
accingo, nxi, nctum, *v.t.* 3, to equip, put on
accīo, *v.t.* 4, to summon
accīpīo, cēpi, ceptum, *v.t.* 3, to receive
accīpiter, tris, *m*, hawk
accītus,ūs, *m*, summons
acclāmātīo, ōnis, *f*, shout
acclāmo, *v.t.* 1, to shout at
acclīnis, e, *adj*, leaning on
acclīno, *v.t.* 1, to lean
acclīvis, e, *adj*, uphill
acclīvitas, ātis, *f*, ascent
accōla, ae, *c*, neighbour
accōlo, cōlui, cultum, *v.t.* 3, to live near
accommōdātus, a, um, *adj*, *adv*, ē, suitable
accommōdātīo, ōnis, *f*, compliance
accommōdo, *v.t.* 1, to adapt
accommōdus, a, um, *adj*, suitable
accresco, crēvi, crētum, *v.i.* 3, to grow
accrētīo, ōnis, *f*, increase
accūbitīo, ōnis, *f*, reclining
accūbo, *v.i.* 1, to lie near, recline at table
accumbo, cūbūi, cūbitum, *v.i.* 3, to lie near, recline at table
accūmūlo, *v.t.* 1, to heap up
accūro, *v.t.* 1, to take care of
accūrātus, a, um, *adj*, *adv*, ē, prepared carefully, precise

accurro, curri, cursum, *v.i.* 3, to run to
accūsātīo, ōnis, *f*, accusation
accūsātor, ōris, *m*, accuser
accūso, *v.t.* 1, to accuse
ācer, cris, e, *adj*, *adv*, iter, keen
ācer, ēris, *n*, maple tree
ācerbitas, ātis, *f*, bitterness
ācerbo, *v.t.* 1, to embitter
ācerbus, a, um, *adj*, bitter, keen
ācernus, a, um, *adj*, made of maple
ācerra, ae, *f*, incense-box
ācervo, *v.t.* 1, to heap up
ācervus, i, *m*, heap
ācētārīa, ōrum, *n.pl*, salad
ācētum, i, *n*, vinegar
ācīdus, a, um, *adj*, *adv*, ē, sour
ācīes, ēi, *f*, edge, pupil of eye, battle-line, keenness
ācīnāces, is, *m*, scimitar
ācīnus, i, *m* (um, i, *n*), berry
ācīpenser, ēris, *m*, sturgeon
aclys, ydis, *f*, small javelin
ācōnītum, i, *n*, aconite
acquiesco, ēvi, ētum, *v.i.* 3, to rest, aquiesce
acquiro, sīvi, sītum, *v.t.* 3, to procure
ācrimōnia, ae, *f*, sharpness
ācriter, *adv*, keenly
acia, ōrum, *n.pl*, acts, records
actīo, ōnis, *f*, act, legal action
actor, ōris, *m*, driver, plaintiff, performer
actūārīus, a, um, *adj*, swift
actūārīus, i, *m*, notary
actum, i, *n*, deed
actus, a, um, see ăgo
actus, ūs, *m*, impulse, act (of drama)
ācūlēātus, a, um, *adj*, prickly
ācūlēus, i, *m*, sting
ācūmēn, ĭnis, *n*, point, sting
ācūo, ūi, ūtum, *v.t.* 3, to sharpen
ācus, ūs, *f*, needle, pin
ācūtus, a, um, *adj*, *adv*, ē, sharp
ad, *prep. with acc*, to, towards, near (place), about (time), for (purpose)
ādaequo, *v.i.t.* 1, to be equal; to make equal
ādāmas, ntis, *m*, steel, diamond
ādāmo, *v.t.* 1, to love deeply
ādāpērīo, ūi, rtum, *v.t.* 4, to open fully
ādaugēo, xi, ctum, *v.t.* 2, to increase
addīco, xi, ctum, *v.t.* 3, to assent, award
addictīo, ōnis, *f*, adjudication
addictus, a, um, *adj*, dedicated
addo, dĭdi, dĭtum, *v.t.* 3, to add to
addūbito, *v.i.t.* 1, to doubt
addūco, xi, ctum, *v.t.* 3, to lead to, influence
ādemptīo, ōnis, *f*, seizure

ădĕo, *v.i.* 4, to approach, attack
ădĕo, *adv*, so much, so long
ădeps, ĭpis, *c*, fat
ădeptĭo, ōnis, *f*, attainment
ădēquĭto, *v.i.* 1, to gallop up
ădhaerĕo, si, sum, *v.i.* 2, to cling to
ădhaeresco, si, sum, *v.i.* 3, to cling to
ădhĭbĕo, *v.t.* 2, to apply, invite
ădhortātĭo, ōnis, *f*, encouragement
ădhortor, *v.t.* 1, *dep*, to encourage
ădhuc, *adv*, still
adiăcĕo, *v.i.* 2, to adjoin
adicĭo, iēci, iectum, *v.t.* 3, to throw to, add to
ădīgo, ēgi, actum, *v.t.* 3, to drive to, compel
ădīmo, ēmi, emptum, *v.t.* 3, to take away
ădĭpiscor, eptus, *v.t.* 3, *dep*, to obtain
ădĭtus, ūs, *m*, approach
adiūdĭco, *v.t.* 1, to assign
adiūmentum, i, *n*, assistance
adiunctĭo, ōnis, *f*, union
adiungo, xi, ctum, *v.t.* 3, to join to
adiūro, *v.t.* 1, to swear, confirm
adiūtor, ōris, *m*, helper
adiūvo, iūvi, iūtum, *v.t.* 1, to help
admātūro, *v.t.* 1, to precipitate
admētĭor, mensus, *v.t.* 4, *dep*, to measure out
admĭnĭcŭlum, i, *n*, prop
admĭnister, tri, *m*, servant
admĭnistrātĭo, ōnis, *f*, aid, management, arrangement
admĭnistro, *v.t.* 1, to assist, manage
admīrābĭlis, e, *adj*, *adv*, ĭter, wonderful
admīrātĭo, ōnis, *f*, admiration
admīror, *v.t.* 1, *dep*, to wonder at
admiscĕo, scŭi, xtum, *v.t.* 2, to mix with
admissārĭus, ii, *m*, stallion
admissĭo, ōnis, *f*, reception
admissum, i, *n*, fault
admitto, mīsi, ssum, *v.t.* 3, to let in, let go, incur, commit
admixtĭo, ōnis, *f*, mixture
admŏdum, *adv*, up to the limit, very much, nearly
admŏnĕo, *v.t.* 2, to remind
admŏnĭtĭo, ōnis, *f*, warning
admŏnĭtus, ūs, *m*, suggestion
admordĕo, di, sum, *v.t.* 2, to bite at
admōtĭo, ōnis, *f*, application
admŏvĕo, mōvi, mōtum, *v.t.* 2, to conduct, assault
admurmŭrātĭo, ōnis, *f*, murmur
admurmŭro, *v.i.* 1, to murmur at
adn- see ann-
ădŏlĕo, ŭi, ultum, *v.i.* 3, to grow up
ădŏlescens, ntis, *adj*, young

ădŏlescens, ntis, *c*, young person
ădŏlescentĭa, ae, *f*, youth
ădŏlescentŭlus, i, *m*, very young man
ădŏlesco, ēvi, ultum, *v.i.*3, to grow up
ădŏpĕrĭo, ŭi, rtum, *v.t.* 4, to cover up
ădoptātĭo, ōnis, *f*, adoption
ădoptĭo, ōnis, *f*, adoption
ădoptīvus, a, um, *adj*, adoptive
ădopto, *v.t.* 1, to choose, adopt
ădor, ōris, *n*, grain
ădōrātĭo, ōnis, *f*, adoration
ădōrĕa, ae, *f*, reward for bravery
ădōrĭor, ortus, *v.t.* 4, *dep*, to attack, undertake
ădorno, *v.t.* 1, to equip, decorate
ădōro, *v.t.* 1, to worship, entreat
adrādo, si, sum, *v.t.* 3, to shave
adsum, esse, adfui, *v.i*, *irreg*, to be near
ads . . . see ass . . .
ădūlātĭo, ōnis, *f*, flattery
ădūlātor, ōris, *m*, flatterer
ădūlor, *v.t.* 1, *dep*, to flatter
ădulter, ĕri, *m*, adulterer
ădultĕra, ae, *f*, adulteress
ădultĕrātĭo, ōnis, *f*, adulteration
ădultĕrīnus, a, um, *adj*, false
ădultĕrĭum, ii, *n*, adultery
ădultĕro, *v.i.t.* 1, to commit adultery; to falsify, pollute
ădultus, a, um, *adj*, grown up
ădumbrātĭo, ōnis, *f*, sketch
ădumbro, *v.t.* 1, to sketch
ăduncus, a, um, *adj*, hooked
ădurgĕo, *v.t.* 2, to press
ădūro, ssi, stum, *v.t.* 3, to scorch
ădusque. *prep. with acc*, right up to
ădusta, ōrum, *n.pl*, burns
ădustus, a, um, *adj*, burnt
advĕho, xi, ctum, *v.t.* 3, to carry to
advĕna, ae, *c*, stranger
advĕnĭo, vēni, ventum, *v.t.* 4, to reach
advento, *v.i.* 1, to approach
adventus, ūs, *m*, arrival
adversārĭus, ii, *m*, opponent
adversārĭus, a, um, *adj*, opposite, opposing
adversor, *v.* 1, *dep. with dat*, to oppose
adversus, a, um, *adj*, opposite; (of winds) contrary
adversus, *prep. with acc*, opposite
adversum, *adv*, opposite
adverto, ti, sum, *v.t.* 3, to direct towards
advespĕrascit, avit, *v. impers*, evening approaches
advĭgĭlo, *v.i.* 1, to keep watch
advŏcātĭo, ōnis, *f*, summons, legal assistance
advŏcātus, i, *m*, legal adviser
advŏco, *v.t.* 1, to call, summon help

For List of Abbreviations used, turn to pages 3, 4

advŏlo, v.i. 1, to fly towards
advolvo, vĭ, ūtum, v.t. 3, to roll, grovel before
ădўtum, ĭ, n, sanctuary
aedēs, is, f, temple, house
aedicŭla, ae, f, shrine, niche
aedificātor, ōris, m, builder
aedificium, ii, n, building
aedificātĭo, ōnis, f, constructing
aedifico, v.t. 1, to build
aedĭlĭcĭus, a, um, adj, of an aedile
aedīlis, is, m, aedile—Roman magistrate
aedīlĭtas, ātis, f, aedileship
aedĭtŭus, ĭ, m, verger
aeger, ra, rum, adj, ill, sad
aegis, ĭdis, f, shield
aegrĕ, adv, with difficulty, scarcely, amiss, with displeasure
aegresco, v.i. 3, to fall ill
aegrĭtūdo, ĭnis, f, illness, grief
aegrōtātĭo, ōnis, f, sickness
aegrōto, v.i. 1, to be ill
aegrōtus, a, um, adj, ill
aemŭlātĭo, ōnis, f, rivalry
aemŭlor, v.t. 1, dep, to rival, envy
aemŭlus, a, um, adj, rivalling
aēnĕus, a, um, adj, of bronze
aenigma, ătis, n, riddle
aequābĭlis, e, adj, adv, ĭter, similar, uniform
aequābĭlĭtas, ātis, f, equality
aequaevus, a, um, adj, of equal age
aequālis, e, adj, adv, ĭter, level, contemporary
aequālĭtas, ātis, f, uniformity
aequē, adv, equally, justly
aequĭlĭbrĭum, ii, n, horizontal position
aequĭnoctĭum, ĭ, n, equinox
aequĭpăro, v.i.t. 1, to equal; compare
aequĭtas, ātis, f, equality, fairness, calmness
aequo, v.i.t. 1, to equalize; match, raze
aequor, ōris, n, even surface, sea
aequum, i, n, plain, justice
aequus, a, um, adj, flat, friendly, equal, reasonable
āēr, ris, m, air
aerārĭa, ae, f, mine
aerārĭum, i, n, treasury
aerārĭus, a, um, adj, of bronze, of the treasury
aerātus, a, um, adj, bronze-covered
aerĕus, a, um, adj, of bronze
aerĭpes, ĕdis, adj, bronze-footed
āērĭus, a, um, adj, lofty
aerūgo, ĭnis, f, rust, envy
aerumna, ae, f, suffering

aerumnōsus, a, um, adj, wretched
aes, aeris, n, copper, money
aescŭlētum, i, n, oak-forest
aescŭlĕus, a, um, adj, oaken
aescŭlus, i, f, oak
aestas, ātis, f, summer
aestĭfer, ĕra, ĕrum, adj, hot, sultry
aestĭmābĭlis, e, adj, valuable
aestĭmātĭo, ōnis, f, valuation
aestĭmātor, ōris, m, valuer
aestimo, v.t. 1, to value, assess
aestīva, ōrum, n.pl, summer-camp
aestīvus, a, um, adj, adv, ē, summerlike
aestŭārĭum, ii, n, creek, air-hole
aestŭo, v.i. 1, to seethe, glow
aestŭōsus, a, um, adj, adv, ē, sweltering
aestus, ūs, m, heat, tide, rage, excitement
aetas, ātis, f, age, life-time
aetātŭla, ae, f, tender age
aeternĭtas, ātis, f, eternity
aeternus, a, um, adj, adv, um, everlasting
aether, ĕris, m, upper air, heaven
aethĕrĭus, a, um, adj, celestial
Aethĭops, ŏpis, m, Aethiopian, negro
aethra, ae, f, upper air
aevum, i, n, lifetime, generation
affābĭlis, e, adj, adv, ĭter, courteous
affātim, adv, enough
affātus, partic. from affor
affectātĭo, ōnis, f, pretension, whim
affectātus, a, um, adj, far-fetched
affectĭo, ōnis, f, disposition, whim
affecto, v.t. 1, to strive after
affectus, ūs, m, mood, sympathy
affĕro, afferre, attŭli, allātum, v.t, irreg, to bring to, announce, help, produce, confer
afficĭo, affēci, ctum, v.t. 3, to influence, seize
affīgo, xi, xum, v.t. 3, to fasten to
affingo, nxi, ictum, v.t. 3, to add to, fabricate
affīnis, e, adj, neighbouring, related
affīnĭtas, ātis, f, kinship
affirmātē, adv, explicitly
affirmātĭo, ōnis, f, assertion
affirmo, v.t. 1, to assert
affixus, a, um, adj, fastened to
afflātus, ūs, m, breath, blast
afflicto, v.t. 1, to trouble, shatter
afflictus, a, um, adj, damaged, prostrate
afflīgo, xi, ctum, v.t. 3, to dash to the ground, damage

afflo, *v.t.* 1, to breathe on, inspire
afflüens, ntis, *adj, adv,* nter, rich in
afflüo, xi, xum, *v.i.* 3, to flow towards, flock in
affor, *v.t.* 1, *dep,* to speak to, accost
affulgëo, ulsi, *v.i.* 2, to shine on
affundo, üdi, üsum, *v.t.* 3, to pour on, in
Afrïcus (ventus), S.W. wind
äfui, see absum
ägäso, önis, *m,* groom
ägë!, come on!
ägellus, i, *m,* small field
ägens, ntis, *adj,* powerful
äger, gri, *m,* field, territory
agger, ëris, *m,* mound, rampart
aggëro, ssi, stum, *v.t.* 3, to convey
aggëro, *v.t.* 1, to heap up
agglömëro, *v.t.* 1, to add to
aggrävo, *v.t.* 1, to make heavier or worse
aggrëdïor, grössus, *v.t.* 3, *dep,* to approach, attack, undertake
aggrëgo, *v.t.* 1, to adhere, join
aggressus, see aggrëdior
ägilis, e, *adj, adv,* iter, active
ägilïtas, ätis, *f,* activity
ägïtätio, önis, *f,* quick movement, contemplation
ägïtätor, öris, *m,* charioteer
ägïtätus, a, um, *adj,* driven, dogged
ägïto, *v.t.* 1, to drive, shake, swing, torment, mock, consider
agmen, ïnis, *n,* marching column
agna, ae, *f,* ewe lamb
agnätus, a, um, *adj,* related (male line)
agnïtio, önis, *f,* recognition
agnömen, ïnis, *n,* surname, additional name
agnosco, növi, ïtum, *v.t.* 3, to recognize, acknowledge
agnus, i, *m,* lamb
ägo, ëgi, actum, *v.t.* 3, to drive, steal, bring, do, negotiate, pass (time), act, lead (life)
ägrärïus, a, um, *adj,* agrarian
ägrärii, örum, *m.pl,* land reformers
ägrestis, is, *m,* peasant
ägrestis, e, *adj,* rural, coarse
agricöla, ae, *m,* farmer, countryman
agricultüra, ae, *f,* agriculture
äio (parts only), to assert
äla, ae, *f,* wing, armpit, porch
äläcer, cris, e, *adj, adv,* iter, brisk, vigorous
äläcrïtas, ätis, *f,* briskness
äläpa, ae, *f,* slap
älauda, ae, *f,* lark
albärïum, ii, *n,* whitewash
albätus, a, um, *adj,* clothed in white

albëo, *v.i.* 2, to be white
albesco, *v.i.* 3, to become white
album, i, *n,* whiteness, register
albus, a, um, *adj,* white
alces, is, *f,* elk
alcëdo, ïnis, *f,* kingfisher
alcÿon, önis, *f,* kingfisher
alcÿonëus, a, um, *adj,* halcyon
älëa, ae, *f,* gambling, a game with dice, chance, hazard
älëätor, öris, *m,* gambler
älës, ïtis, *adj,* winged
älës, ïtis, *c,* bird
alga, ae, *f,* sea-weed
algëo, si, *v.i.* 2, to feel cold
algïdus, a, um, *adj,* cold
algor, öris, *m,* coldness
älïä, adv, in a different way
älïäs . . . älïäs, adv, at one time . . . at another time, otherwise
älïbi, adv, elsewhere
älïcübi, adv, somewhere
älïcunde, adv, from somewhere
älïënätïo, önis, *f,* transfer, aversion, delirium
älïënätus, a, um, *adj,* alienated
älïënïgëna, ae, m, foreigner
älïëno, *v.t.* 1, to transfer, estrange
älïënus, a, um, *adj,* someone else's, strange, hostile, unsuitable
älïënus, i, m, stranger
älïënum, i, n, stranger's property
äliger, ëra, ërum, adj, winged
älii, see ällus
älïmentum, i, n, nourishment
älïmönïum, ii, n, nourishment
älïö, ulu, to another place
älïöquï(n), adv, in other respects
älïpës, ëdis, adj, wing-footed
älïquä, adv, somehow
älïquamdïu, adv, for some time
älïquando, adv, at some time
älïquantus, a, um, adj, adv, ö, um, somewhat, some
älïqui, qua, quod, pron, adj, some, any
älïquis, quid, pron, someone, something
älïquö, adv, to some place
älïquot, adv, several
älïquötïes, adv, at different times
älïter, adv, otherwise
älïunde, adv, from elsewhere
älïus, a, ud, pron, adj, other, different
alläbor, psus, v. 3, *dep,* to glide, flow towards
allapsus, üs, m, stealthy approach
allätro, v.t. 1, to bark at
allecto, v.t. 1, to entice
allëgo, v.t. 1, to commission
allëgo, ëgi, ectum, v.t. 3, to elect

allēgŏrĭa, ae, f, allegory

allĕvātĭo, ōnis, f, raising up

allĕvo, v.t. 1, to lift up, relieve

allĭcĭo, exi, ectum, v.t. 3, to attract

allīdo, si, sum, v.t. 3, to strike

allĭgo, v.t. 1, to bind, fasten

allīno, ēvi, ĭtum, v.t. 3, to bedaub

allĭum, i, n, garlic

allŏcūtĭo, ōnis, f, address

allŏquĭum, ii, n, exhortation

allŏquor, lŏcūtus, v.t. 3, dep, to speak to, exhort, console

allūdo, si, sum, v.i.t. 3, to play, joke; sport with

allŭo, ŭi, v.t. 3, to wash against, bathe

allŭvĭes, ēi, f, pool

allŭvĭo, ōnis, f, inundation

almus, a, um, adj, nourishing, kind

alnus, i, f, alder

ălo, ŭi, altum, v.t. 3, to nourish, cherish, encourage

alŏē, ēs, f, aloe

alpīnus, a, um, adj, Alpine

alsĭus, a, um, adj, cold, chilly

alsus, a, um, adj, cold, chilly

altāre, altāris, n, high altar

altārĭa, ĭum, n.pl, high altar

alter, ĕra, ĕrum, adj, one or the other of two, second

altercātĭo, ōnis, f, dispute

altercor, v.i. 1, dep, to quarrel

alterno, v.i.t. 1, to hesitate; alternate

alternus, a, um, adj, alternate

altĕrŭter, ra, rum, adj, one or the other, either

altĭlis, e, adj, fattened, rich

altĭsŏnus, a, um, adj, high sounding

altĭtūdo, ĭnis, f, height, depth

altor, ōris, m, foster-father

altrix, īcis, f, foster-mother

altum, i, n, the deep (sea)

altus, a, um, adj, high, deep, great

ālūcĭnor, v.i. 1, dep, to wander in the mind

ălumna, ae, f, foster-child

ălumnus, i, m, foster-child

ălūta, ae, f, soft leather

alvĕārĭum, ii, n, beehive

alvĕus, i, m, salver, channel, canoe

alvus, i, f, belly, stomach

ămābĭlis, e, adj, adv, ĭter, lovable, amiable

ămando, v.t. 1, to remove

ămans, ntis, adj, fond

ămans, ntis, m, lover

ămārĭtĭes, ēi, f, bitterness

ămārus, a, um, adj, bitter

ămātor, ōris, m, lover

ămātōrĭum, ii, n, love-philtre

ămātōrĭus, a, um, adj, amatory

ambactus, i, m, vassal

ambāges, is, f, roundabout way

ambĭgo, v.i. 3, to waver, go about

ambĭgŭĭtas, ātis, f, double sense

ambĭgŭum, i, n, uncertainty

ambĭgŭus, a, um, adj, adv, ē, doubtful, changeable

ambĭo, v.i.t. 4, to go round; solicit

ambĭtĭo, ōnis, f, canvassing

ambĭtĭōsus, a, um, adj, adv, ē, embracing, fawning

ambĭtus, ūs, m, going round, circuit, bribery

ambō, ae, ō, adj, both

ambrŏsĭa, ae, f, food of the gods

ambrŏsĭus, a, um, adj, immortal

ambŭlātĭo, ōnis, f, walk

ambŭlātor, ōris, m, walker

ambŭlo, v.i. 1, to walk, lounge

ambūro, ssi, stum, v.t. 3, to singe

ambustum, i, n, burn

amellus, i, m, star-wort

āmens, ntis, adj, out of one's mind

āmentĭa, ae, f, madness

āmentum, i, n, strap

āmĕs, ĭtis, m, pole, shaft

ămēthystus, i, f, amethyst

ămīca, ae, f, mistress

ămĭcĭo, ŭi, ctum, v.t. 4, to wrap

ămīcĭtĭa, ae, f, friendship

ămictus, ūs, m, cloak

ămīcŭlum, i, n, cloak

ămīcus, i, m, friend

ămīcus, a, um, adj, adv, ē, friendly

āmissĭo, ōnis, f, loss

ămīta, ae, f, paternal aunt

āmitto, misi, missum, v.t. 3, to let go, dismiss, lose

amnis, is, m, river

ămo, v.t. 1, to love, like

ămoenĭtas, ātis, f, pleasantness

ămoenus, a, um, adj, adv, ē, charming

āmōlĭor, v.t. 4, dep, to remove, refute

ămor, ōris, m, love, desire

āmŏvĕo, mōvi, tum, v.t. 2, to remove

amphĭthĕātrum, i, n, amphitheatre

amphŏra, ae, f, two-handled jar

amplector, xus, v.t. 3, dep, to embrace

amplexus, ūs, m, embrace

amplĭfĭcātĭo, ōnis, f, enlargement

amplĭfĭco, v.t. 1, to enlarge

amplĭo, v.t. 1, to enlarge

amplĭtūdo, ĭnis, f, width, size

amplĭus, comp. adv, more

amplus, a, um, adj, adv, ē, ĭter, spacious, great, glorious

ampulla, ae, f, bottle

ampŭtātĭo, ōnis, f, pruning

ampŭto, v.t. 1, to cut away

ămurca, ae, f, dregs of oil

ămȳlum, ī, *n*, starch

ăn, *conj*, or: also used to introduce a question

ănăphŏră, ae, *f*, recurrence

ănăs, ătis, *f*, duck

ănătĭcŭla, ae, *f*, duckling

anceps, cĭpĭtĭs, *adj*, two-headed, doubtful

ancīle, is, *n*, oval shield

ancilla, ae, *f*, maidservant

ancŏra, ae, *f*, anchor

ancŏrāle, is, *n*, cable

ānellus, ī, *m*, small ring

anfractus, ūs, *m*, circuitous route, digression

angīna, ae, *f*, quinsy

angĭportus, ūs, *m*, alley

ango, xī, ctum, *v.t.* 3, to strangle, torment

angor, ōris, *m*, strangling, distress

anguilla, ae, *f*, eel

anguĭnĕus, a, um, *adj*, snaky

anguĭpēs, ĕdis, *adj*, snake-footed

anguis, is, *c*, snake

angŭlātus, a, um, *adj*, angular

angŭlāris, e, *adj*, angular

angŭlus, ī, *m*, corner

angustiae, ārum, *f.pl*, defile, straits, difficulties

angustus, a, um, *adj*, *adv*, ē, narrow, difficult

ānhēlĭtus, ūs, *m*, panting, vapour

ānhēlo, *u.i.* 1, to pant, exhale

ānhēlus, a, um, *adj*, panting

ănĭcŭla, ae, *f*, little old woman

ănīlis, e, *adj*, *adv*, iter, old womanish

ănĭma, ae, *f*, breeze, breath, life, soul

ănĭmadversĭo, ōnis, *f*, attention, reproof

ănĭmadverto, tī, sum, *v.t.* 3, to pay attention to, notice, punish

ănĭmăl, ālis, *n*, animal

ănĭmālis, e, *adj*, *adv*, iter of air, living

ănĭmans, ntis, *adj*, living

ănĭmātus, a, um, *adj*, disposed, courageous

ănĭmo, *v.i.t.* 1, to have life; revive, give life to

ănĭmōsus, a, um, *adj*, *adv*, ē, bold

ănĭmōsus, a, um, *adj*, gusty, living, spirited

ănĭmus, ī, *m*, soul, mind, memory, opinion, anger, purpose, courage, attitude

annāles, ĭum, *m.pl*, chronicles

annālis, e, *adj*, annual

annĕ—introduces a question

annecto, xŭi, xum, *v.t.* 3, to fasten to, add

annĭtor, nīsus (nixus), *v.i.* 3, *dep*, to lean against, exert oneself

ănnĭversārĭus, a, um, *adj*, anniversary

anno, *v.i.* 1, to swim to

annon, *conj*, or not

annōna, ae, *f*, annual produce, grain price

annōsus, a, um, *adj*, old

annŏtātĭo, ōnis, *f*, annotation, note

annŏto, *v.t.* 1, to note down

annŭa, ōrum, *n.pl*, annuity

annŭmĕro, *v.t.* 1, to pay, include

annŭo, ŭi, ūtum, *v.i.* 3, to nod, assent

annus, ī, *m*, year

annŭus, a, um, *adj*, annual, yearly

ănōmălĭa, ae, *f*, anomaly

anquīro, sīvi, sītum, *v.t.* 3, to search for

ansa, ae, *f*, handle, opportunity

anser, ĕris, *m*, goose

antĕ, *prep. with acc*, before, in front of

antĕ (antĕā), *adv*, before

antĕcēdo, ssi, ssum, *v.i.t.* 3, to distinguish oneself; precede

antĕcello, *v.i.t.* 3, to be outstanding; surpass

antĕcessĭo, ōnis, *f*, antecedent

antĕcursor, ōris, *m*, advanced guard

antĕ-ĕo, *v.i.* 4, to go before, excel

antĕfĕro, ferre, tŭli, lātum, *v.t.*, *irreg*, to carry in front, prefer

antĕgrĕdĭor, gressus, *v.t.* 3, *dep*, to go in front

antĕhāc, *adv*, previously

antĕlūcānus, a, um, *adj*, before daybreak

antĕmĕrīdĭānus, a, um, *adj*, before midday

antĕmitto, mīsi, missum, *v.t.* 3, to send on

antenna, ae, *f*, sail-yard

antĕpōno, pŏsŭi, ĭtum, *v.t.* 3, to place in front

antĕquam, *conj*, before

antĕris, idis, *f*, buttress (*pl.*)

antes, ĭum, *m.pl*, ranks

antĕsignānus, ī, *m*, in front of the standard, selected soldier

antesto, ĕti, *v.i.* 1, to stand before, excel

antestor, *v.* 1, *dep*, to call a witness

antĕverto, tī, sum, *v.t.* 3, to precede, anticipate

anthrōpŏphăgus, ī, *m*, cannibal

antĭcus, a, um, *adj*, foremost

anticĭpo, *v.t.* 1, to anticipate

antĭdŏtum, ī, *n*, remedy

antĭpŏdes, um, *m.pl*, antipodes

antīquĭtas, ātis, *f*, age, olden times

antīqui, ōrum, *m.pl*, old writers

antĭquus, a, um, *adj, adv,* ē, old
antistĕs, ĭtis, *m, f,* high priest
antistĭta, ae, *f,* high priestess
antlĭa, ae, *f,* pump
antrum, i, *n,* cave
ānŭlus, i, *m,* ring
ānus, ūs, *f,* old woman
anxĭetas, ātis, *f,* anxiety
anxĭus, a, um, *adj, adv,* ē, troubled
ăpăgĕ!, *interj,* begone!
ăper, pri, *m,* wild boar
ăpĕrĭo, rŭi, rtum, *v.t.* 4, to open, explain
ăpertus, a, um, *adj, adv,* ē, open, frank
ăpex, ĭcis, *m,* summit, crown
ăpis, is, *f,* bee
ăpiscor, aptus, *v.t.* 3, *dep,* to reach for, acquire
ăpĭum, ii, *n,* parsley
āplustre, is, *n,* stern
āpo, — aptum, *v.t.* 3, to fasten
ăpŏcha, ae, *f,* receipt
ăpŏthēca, ae, *f,* store-place
appărātĭo, ōnis, *f,* preparation
appărātus, a, um, *adj, adv,* ē, ready, elaborate
appărātus, ūs, *m,* preparation, apparatus, pomp
appārĕo, *v.i.* 2, to appear
appărĭtĭo, ōnis, *f,* service
appārĭtor, ōris, *m,* public servant
appăro, *v.t.* 1, to prepare
appellātĭo, ōnis, *f,* calling, appeal, title
appellātor, ōris, *m,* appellant
appellātus, a, um, *adj,* called
appello, ŭli, ulsum, *v.t.* 3, to drive towards, land
appello, *v.t.* 1, to speak to, appeal to, name
appendix, ĭcis, *f,* supplement
appendo, ndi, nsum, *v.t.* 3, to weigh
appĕtens, ntis, *adj, adv,* nter, eager for
appĕtentĭa, ae, *f,* desire
appĕtĭtĭo, ōnis, *f,* desire
appĕtĭtus, ūs, *m,* attack, passion
appĕto, ii, ĭtum, *v.i.t.* 3, to approach; strive after
applĭcātĭo, ōnis, *f,* inclination
applĭco, *v.t.* 1, to affix, attach, steer
appōno, pŏsŭi, sĭtum, *v.t.* 3, to put near, apply, add
apporto, *v.t.* 1, to conduct
appŏsĭtus, *adj, adv,* ē, bordering, suitable
apprĕhendo, di, sum, *v.t.* 3, to seize, understand

apprīmus, a, um, *adj, adv,* ē, very first
apprŏbātĭo, ōnis, *f,* sanction
apprŏbo, *v.t.* 1, to approve, make satisfactory
apprŏpĕro, *v.i.t.* 1, to hurry; speed up
apprŏpinquātĭo, ōnis, *f,* approach
apprŏpinquo, *v.i.* 1, to approach
appulsus, ūs, *m,* landing, approach
ăprīcātĭo, ōnis, *f,* sunning
ăprīcor, *v.i.* 1, *dep,* to sun oneself
ăprīcus, a, um, *adj,* sunny
Aprīlis (mensis), April
aptātus, a, um, *adj,* suitable
apto, *v.t.* 1, to adjust
aptus, a, um, *adj, adv,* ē, suitable
ăpŭd, *with acc,* at the house of, in the works of, amongst, near
ăqua, ae, *f,* water, rain; *pl.* spa
ăquaeductus, ūs, *m,* aqueduct
ăquālis, is, *c,* wash-basin
ăquārĭus, ii, *m,* water-bearer, a Sign of the Zodiac
ăquātĭcus, a, um, *adj,* watery
ăquātĭlis, e, *adj,* aquatic
ăquātĭo, ōnis, *f,* water-fetching
ăquător, ōris, *m,* water-carrier
ăquila, ae, *f,* eagle, standard
ăquilĭfer, ĕri, *m,* standard-bearer
ăquilīnus, a, um, *adj,* aquiline
ăquĭlo, ōnis, *m,* north wind, north
ăquilōnāris, e, *adj,* northern
ăquor, *v.i.* 1, *dep,* to fetch water
ăquōsus, a, um, *adj,* moist, rainy
āra, ae, *f,* altar
ărānĕa, ae, *f,* spider, web
ărānĕus, i, *m,* spider, web
ărātĭo, ōnis, *f,* cultivation
ărător, ōris, *m,* ploughman
ărātrum, i, *n,* plough
arbĭter, tri, *m,* witness, umpire
arbĭtrātus, ūs, *m,* free-will
arbĭtrĭum, ii, *n,* verdict, power, inclination
arbĭtror, *v.i.* 1, *dep,* to think, decide
arbor, ōris, *f,* tree
arbŏrĕus, a, um, *adj,* tree-like
arbustum, i, *n,* plantation
arbŭtum, i, *n,* wild strawberry
arbŭtus, i, *f,* wild strawberry tree
arca, ae, *f,* box, dungeon
arcānus, a, um, *adj, adv,* ō, secret
arcĕo, *v.t.* 2, to confine, keep off
arcessītus, a, um, *adj,* sent for, farfetched
arcesso, sīvi, sĭtum, *v.t.* 3, to send for
architector, *v.t.* 1, *dep,* to design
architectūra, ae, *f,* architecture
architectus, i, *m,* architect

arcĭtĕnens, ntis, *adj*, armed with bow

arctŏs, i, *f*, Bear, North Pole

arctūrus, i, *m*, chief star in constellation Boötes

arcŭla, ae, *f*, small box

arcŭo, *v.t.* 1, to bend

arcus, ūs, *m*, rainbow, arch

ardĕa, ae, *f*, heron

ardens, ntis, *adj*, *adv*, nter, burning, eager

ardĕo, arsĭ, sum, *v.i.* 2, to burn, be eager

ardesco, arsĭ, *v.i.* 3, to catch fire

ardor, ōris, *m*, blaze, desire

ardŭus, a, um, *adj*, high, difficult

ārĕa, ae, *f*, open space, threshing-floor

ārēna, ae, *f*, sand, arena

ārēnātum, ĭ, *n*, mortar, plaster

ārēnōsus, a, um, *adj*, sandy

ārens, ntis, *adj*, parched

ūrŏo, *v.i.* 2, to be dry

āresco, ŭi, *v.i.* 3, to dry up

argentāria, ae, *f*, bank, silver-mine

argentārius, ii, *m*, banker, broker

argentātus, a, um, *adj*, silver-plated

argentĕus, a, um, *adj*, silver

argentum, ĭ, *n*, silver, money

argilla, ae, *f*, white clay

argūmentātĭo, ōnis, *f*, proof

argūmentor, *v.i.* 1, *dep*, to prove

argūmentum, ĭ, *n*, proof, content, artistic aim

argŭo, ŭi, ūtum, *v.t.* 3, to prove, accuse, convict

argŭtiae, ārum, *f.pl*, liveliness

argūtus, a, um, *adj*, *adv*, ō, clear, witty, rattling

ārĭdĭtas, ātis, *f*, dryness

ārĭdum, ĭ, *n*, dry land

ārĭdus, a, um, *adj*, dry

ārĭēs, tis, *m*, ram, battering-ram

ārista, ae, *f*, ear of corn

ārĭthmētĭca, ōrum, *n.pl*, arithmetic

arma, ōrum, *n.pl*, armour, shield, weapons, army, equipment

armāmenta, ōrum, *n.pl*, gear, tackle

armāmentārĭum, ii, *n*, arsenal

armāmentum, ĭ, *n*, ship's tackle

armārĭum, ii, *n*, cupboard

armātura, ae, *f*, equipment, (light-) armed troops

armātus, a, um, *adj*, equipped

armentārĭus, ii, *m*, herdsman

armentum, ĭ, *n*, plough-animal, herd

armĭfer, ĕra, ĕrum, *adj*, warlike, armoured

armĭger, ĕra, ĕrum, *adj*, warlike, armoured

armilla, ae, *f*, bracelet

armĭpŏtens, ntis, *adj*, valiant

armĭsŏnus, a, um, *adj*, with clashing armour

armo, *v.t.* 1, to arm, equip

armus, ĭ, *m*, shoulder, side

ăro, *v.t.* 1, to plough

arquātus, a, um, *adj*, bent

arrectus, a, um, *adj*, steep

arrēpo, psi, ptum, *v.i.* 3, to creep towards

arrha, ae, *f*, money given as a pledge

arrīdĕo, si, sum, *v.i.* 2, to laugh at, favour

arrĭgo, rexi, rectum, *v.t.* 3, to erect, excite

arrĭpĭo, ŭi, reptum, *v.t.* 3, to seize, indict

arrŏgans, ntis, *pres. partic*, *adj*, *adv*, nter, haughty

arrŏgantĭa, ae, *f*, haughtiness

arrŏgo, *v.t.* 1, to claim, confer

ars, tis, *f*, art, skill, theory, habit, stratagem

artē, *adv*, closely

arthrītĭcus, a, um, *adj*, arthritic

artĭcŭlātim, *adv*, piece by piece

artĭcŭlo, *v.t.* 1, to articulate

artĭcŭlus, i, *m*, joint, movement

artĭfex, fĭcis, *m*, artist, author

artĭfĭcĭōsus, a, um, *adj*, *adv*, ē, skilful

artĭfĭcĭum, ii, *n*, trade, skill; (*pl*) intrigue

arto, *v.t.* 1, to compress

artus, ūs, *m*, limb

artus, a, um, *adj*, *adv*, ō, confined

ārun, ārus ... see hărun, hărus ..

arvīna, ae, *f*, grease

arvum, ĭ, *n*, cultivated land

arvus, a, um, *adj*, ploughed

arx, cis, *f*, citadel

as, assis, *m*, pound weight, coin

ascendo, ndi, nsum, *v.i.t.* 3, to climb

ascensus, ūs, *m*, ascent

ascĭa, ae, *f*, adze

ascĭo, *v.t.* 4, to receive

ascĭsco, īvi, ītum, *v.t.* 3, to admit

ascītus, ūs, *m*, reception

ascrībo, psi, ptum, *v.t.* 3, to insert, enrol, attribute

ascriptīvus, a, um, *adj*, supernumerary

ascriptus, a, um, *adj*, appointed

ăsella, ae, *f*, small ass

ăsellus, i, *m*, small ass

ăsĭnus, i, *m*, ass, simpleton

aspectābĭlis, e, *adj*, visible

aspecto, *v.t.* 1, to look at eagerly

aspectus, ūs, *m*, look, sight

asper, ĕra, ĕrum, *adj*, *adv*, ē, rough, bitter, austere, adverse

aspĕrĭtas, ātis, *f*, roughness

aspĕrum, ĭ, *n*, rough ground

aspergo, si, sum, *v.t.* 3, to scatter, sprinkle, defile
aspergo, inis, *f,* sprinkling, spray
aspēritas, ātis, *f,* roughness
aspernātio, ōnis, *f,* disdain
aspernor, *v.t.* 1, *dep,* to despise
aspēro, *v.t.* 1, to roughen, rouse
aspersio, ōnis, *f,* sprinkling
aspicio, exi, ectum, *v.t.* 3, to look at
aspīrātio, ōnis, *f,* exhalation
aspīro, *v.i.t.* 1, to aspire to; breathe on
aspis, idis, *f,* adder
asporto, *v.t.* 1, to carry away
assēcla, ae, *c,* attendant
assectātio, ōnis, *f,* attendance
assectātor, ōris, *m,* follower
assector, *v.t.* 1, *dep,* to wait upon
assensio, ōnis, *f,* approval
assensus, ūs, *m,* approval
assentātio, ōnis, *f,* flattery
assentātor, ōris, *m,* flatterer
assentior, sus, *v.* 4, *dep. with dat,* to agree with
assentor, *v.* 1, *dep. with dat,* to flatter
assēquor, sēcūtus, *v.t.* 3, *dep,* to pursue, overtake, comprehend
asser, ēris, *m,* stake
assēro, rūi, sertum, *v.t.* 3, to claim, set free
assertor, ōris, *m,* protector
asservo, *v.t.* 1, to keep, guard
assessor, ōris, *m,* assessor
assēvērātio, ōnis, *f,* assertion
assēvēro, *v.t.* 1, to assert
assidēo, sēdi, sessum, *v.i.* 2, to sit by, wait upon, blockade, resemble
assidūitas, ātis, *f,* constant presence
assidūus, a, um, *adj, adv, ē,* constantly present
assignātio, ōnis, *f,* allotment
assigno, *v.t.* 1, to distribute
assilio, ūi, sultum, *v.i.* 4, to spring upon
assimilis, e, *adj, adv, iter,* like
assimŭlo, *v.i.t.* 1, to resemble; imitate
assimŭlātus, a, um, *adj,* similar
assisto, astiti, *v.i.* 3, to stand near, aid
assōlĕo, *v.i.* 2, to be in the habit of doing
assuĕfăcio, fēci, factum, *v.t.* 3, to make someone used to
assuesco, ēvi, ētum, *v.i.t.* 3, to become used to; familiarise
assuētūdo, inis, *f,* habit
assuētus, a, um, *adj,* customary
assulto, *v.t.* 1, to jump on, attack
assultus, ūs, *m,* attack
assūmo, mpsi, mptum, *v.t.* 3, to take up, adopt
assŭo, *v.t.* 3, to sew on

assurgo, surrexi, rectum, *v.i.* 3, to rise, stand up
assŭla, ae, *f,* splinter, chip
assus, a, um, *adj,* roasted; **assa, ōrum,** *n.pl,* turkish bath
ast, see at
astipŭlātor, ōris, *m,* assistant
astipŭlor, *v.* 1, *dep. with dat.* to bargain with
asto, stiti, *v.i.* 1, to stand near
astrĕpo, *v.i.t.* 3, to make a noise; applaud
astringo, nxi, ctum, *v.t.* 3, to bind, fasten, cool, limit
astrictus, a, um, *adj, adv, ē,* tight, concise
astrŏlŏgia, ae, *f,* astronomy
astrŏlŏgus, i, *m,* astronomer
astrum, i, *n,* star, constellation
astrŭo, xi, ctum, *v.t.* 3, to build near, add
astŭpĕo, *v.i.* 2, to be astonished
astus, ūs, *m,* dexterity, craft
astūtia, ae, *f,* dexterity, slyness
astūtus, a, um, *adj, adv, ē,* shrewd, sly
asȳlum, i, *n,* place of refuge
at, *conj,* but, on the other hand
ătăvia, ae, *f,* ancestor
ătăvus, i, *m,* ancestor
āter, tra, trum, *adj,* black, deadly
āthĕōs, i, *m,* atheist
athlēta, ae, *c,* wrestler, athlete
ătŏmus, i, *f,* atom
atque, *conj,* and, and also
atqui, *conj,* but, nevertheless
ātrāmentum, i, *n,* ink, varnish
ātrātus, a, um, *adj,* in mourning
ātriensis, is, *m,* house-steward
ātriŏlum, i, *n,* ante-room
ātrium, ii, *n,* hall, forecourt
ātrōcitas, ātis, *f,* harshness, cruelty
ātrox, ōcis, *adj, adv, iter,* horrible, fierce, stern
attactus, ūs, *m,* touch
attāmen, *adv,* but nevertheless
attendo, di, tum, *v.t.* 3, to stretch out, give attention to
attentio, ōnis, *f,* attention
attento, *v.t.* 1, to try, attack
attentus, a, um, *adj, adv, ē,* engrossed, frugal
attĕnŭo, *v.t.* 1, to impair, reduce
attĕro, trīvi, trītum, *v.t.* 3, to rub away, exhaust
attinĕo, ūi, tentum, *v.i.t.* 2, to stretch, concern; retain
attingo, tigi, tactum, *v.t.* 3, to touch, reach, attack
attollo, *v.t.* 3, to raise
attondĕo, di, sum, *v.t.* 2, to shear

attŏnĭtus, a, um, *adj*, *adv*, ē, astonished

attŏno, ŭi, ĭtum, *v.t.* 1, to stun

attorquĕo, *v.t.* 2, to hurl

attrăho, xi, ctum, *v.t.* 3, to drag towards, attract

attrecto, *v.t.* 1, to handle

attrĭbŭo, ŭi, ūtum, *v.t.* 3, to assign

attrĭbūtum, i, *n*, predicate

attrītus, ūs, *m*, rubbing against

auceps, ŭpis, *c*, bird-catcher, eavesdropper

auctĭo, ōnis, *f*, auction, increase

auctiōnor, *v.i.* 1, *dep*, to hold an auction

auctor, ōris, *c*, creator, master, witness, supporter, author

auctōrĭtas, ātis, *f*, influence, power

auctumnālis, e, *adj*, autumnal

auctumnus, a, um, *adj*, autumnal

auctumnus, i, *m*, autumn

auctus, a, um, *adj*, enlarged

auctus, ūs, *m*, increase

aucŭpĭum, ii, *n*, bird-catching

aucŭpor, *v.i.t.* 1, *dep*, to go bird-catching; pursue, watch for

audācĭa, ae, *f*, boldness, insolence

audax, ācis, *adj*, *adv*, cter, bold, rash

audens, ntis, *adj*, *adv*, nter, bold

audentĭa, ae, *f*, boldness

audĕo, ausus, *v.i.t.* 2 (*semi-dep.*), to dare

audĭentĭa, ae, *f*, hearing, audience

audĭo, *v.t.* 4, to hear, understand, obey

audĭtĭo, ōnis, *f*, a hearing, report

audĭtor, ōris, *m*, hearer, pupil

audĭtus, ūs, *m*, sense of hearing

aufĕro, ferre, abstŭli, ablātum, *v.t*, *irreg*, to take away, rob, obtain

aufŭgĭo, fūgi, ĭtum, *v.i.* 3, to run away

augĕo, xi, ctum, *v.i.t.* 2, to grow; enlarge

augesco, *v.i.* 3, to grow

augur, ŭris, *c*, diviner, prophet

augŭrālis, e, *adj*, prophetic

augŭrātus, ūs, *m*, office of augur

augŭrĭum, ii, *n*, omen, augury

augŭrĭus, a, um, *adj*, augural

augŭror, *v.t.* 1, *dep*, to prophesy, suppose

augustus, a, um, *adj*, *adv*, ē, venerable

aula, ae, *f*, palace, court

aulaeum, i, *n*, curtain

aulĭcus, i, *m*, courtier

aura, ae, *f*, air, soft breeze, sky, publicity, gleam

aurārĭa, ae, *f*, gold mine

aurātus, a, um, *adj*, gilded

aurĕus, i, *m*, gold piece

aurĭcŏmus, a, um, *adj*, golden-haired

aurĭcŭla, ae, *f*, ear

aurĭfer, ēra, ērum, *adj*, gold-producing

aurĭfex, ficis, *m*, goldsmith

aurīga, ae, *c*, charioteer

aurĭger, ēra, ērum, *adj*, bearing gold

auris, is, *f*, ear

aurītus, a, um, *adj*, long-eared

aurōra, ae, *f*, dawn

aurum, i, *n*, gold

ausculto, *v.i.t.* 1, to listen

auspex, ĭcis, *c*, diviner

auspĭcātō, *adv*, after taking the auspices

auspĭcĭum, ii, *n*, divination

auspĭcor, *v.i.t.* 1, *dep*, to take the auspices, begin

auster, tri, *m*, south wind

austērus, a, um, *adj*, *adv*, ē, harsh, severe

austrālis, e, *adj*, southern

austrīnus, a, um, *adj*, southern

ausum, i, *n*, bold attempt

aut, *conj*, or, aut ... aut, either ... or

autem, *conj*, but

autumnālis, *adj*, autumnal

autumnus, a, um, *adj*, autumnal

autŭmo, *v.i.* 1, to assert

auxĭlĭa, ōrum, *n.pl*, auxiliary troops

auxĭlĭāris, o, *adj*, helping

auxĭlĭāres, ĭum, *m.pl*, auxiliary troops

auxĭlĭor, *v.* 1, *dep. with dat.* to help

auxĭlĭum ii, *n*, help

ăvārĭtĭa, ae, *f*, greediness

ăvārus, a, um, *adj*, *adv*, ē, greedy

ăve! (*pl*, ăvete), hail! farewell!

ăvĕho, vexi, ctum, *v.t.* 3, to carry away

ăvello, velli, vulsum, *v.t.* 3, to tear away

ăvēna, ae, *f*, oats, shepherd's pipe

ăvēnācĕus, a, um, *adj*, oaten

ăvĕo, *v.t.* 2, to long for

ăvĕo, *v.i.* 2, to be well

ăversor, *v.t.* 1, *dep*, to turn away from, avoid

ăversor, ōris, *m*, embezzler

ăversus, a, um, *adj*, backwards, hostile

ăverto, ti, sum, *v.t.* 3, to push aside, steal, estrange

ăvĭa, ae, *f*, grandmother

ăvĭārĭum, ii, *n*, bird-haunts

ăvĭdĭtas, ātis, *f*, eagerness, desire

ăvĭdus, a, um, *adj*, *adv*, ē, greedy

ăvis, is, *f*, bird

ăvītus, a, um, *adj*, ancestral

ăvĭum, ii, *n*, pathless place

ăvĭus, a, um, *adj*, pathless

ăvŏcātĭo, ōnis, *f*, calling away, distraction

For List of Abbreviations used, turn to pages 3, 4

ăvŏco, *v.t.* 1, to call away
ăvŏlo, *v.i.* 1, to fly away
ăvuncŭlus, ĭ, *m*, uncle
ăvus, ĭ, *m*, grandfather
axis, is, *m*, axle, chariot, region

B

bāca, ae, *f*, berry
bācātus, a, um, *adj*, pearl-set
baccar, ăris, *n*, fox-glove
baccha, ae, *f*, bacchanal
bacchānālĭa, ĭum, *n.pl*, orgies of Bacchus
bacchātĭo, ōnis, *f*, orgy
bacchor, *v.i.* 1, *dep*, to rave
bācĭfer, ĕra, ĕrum, *adj*, berry-bearing
bācĭllum, ĭ, *n*, stick
bācŭlum, ĭ, *n*, stick, sceptre
bāiŭlo, *v.t.* 1, to carry a load
bāiŭlus, ĭ, *m*, porter
bālaena, ae, *f*, whale
bălănus, ĭ, *f*, acorn
bălătro, ōnis, *m*, comedian
bālātus, ūs, *m*, bleating
balbus, a, um, *adj*, *adv*, ē, stammering
balbūtĭo, *v.i.t.* 4, to stammer
ballista, ae, *f*, artillery engine
balnĕae, ārum, *f.pl*, baths
balnĕātor, ōris, *m*, bath-keeper
balnĕum, ĭ, *n*, bath
bālo, *v.i.* 1, to bleat
balsămum, ĭ, *n*, balm
baltĕus, ĭ, *m*, belt, sword-belt
bărāthrum, ĭ, *n*, abyss
barba, ae, *f*, beard
barbărĭa, ae, *f*, foreign country, rudeness
barbărus, ĭ, *m*, foreigner, stranger
barbărus, a, um, *adj*, *adv*, ē, foreign, rude, savage
barbātus, a, um, *adj*, bearded
barbĭtos, *m*, *f*, (*pl*, a), lute, lyre
bardus, a, um, *adj*, stupid
bāro, ōnis, *m*, blockhead
barrus, ĭ, *m*, elephant
băsĭlĭca, ae, *f*, town-hall
băsĭlĭcus, a, um, *adj*, royal
băsĭo, *v.t.* 1, to kiss
băsis, is, *f*, pedestal, base
băsĭum, ĭĭ, *n*, kiss
battŭo, ŭi, *v.i.t.* 3, to fence; beat
bĕātĭtas, ātis, *f*, happiness
bĕātĭtūdo, ĭnis, *f*, happiness
bĕātus, a, um, *adj*, *adv*, ē, happy, fortunate
bellans, see bello
bellārĭa, ōrum, *n.pl*, dessert

bellātor, ōris, *m*, warrior
bellātrix, īcis, *f*, female-warrior
bellē, *adv*, prettily
bellĭcōsus, a, um, *adj*, warlike
bellĭcum, ĭ, *n*, signal for march or attack
bellĭcus, a, um, *adj*, military
bellĭger, ĕra, ĕrum, *adj*, warlike
bellĭgĕro, *v.t.* 1, to wage war
bellis, ĭdis, *f*, daisy
bello, *v.i.* 1 (bellor, *v.* 1, *dep*), to make war
bellum, ĭ, *n*, war
bellus, a, um, *adj*, pretty
bēlŭa, ae, *f*, beast
bĕnē, *adv*, well, very
bĕnēdīco, xi, ctum, *v.i.t.* 3, to praise
bĕnēdictĭo, ōnis, *f*, blessing
bĕnēfăcĭo, fēci, factum, *v.t.* 3, to do well, oblige
bĕnēfactum, ĭ, *n*, good deed
bĕnēfĭcentĭa, ae, *f*, kind treatment
bĕnēfĭcĭārĭi, ōrum, *m.pl*, privileged soldiers (excused fatigues)
bĕnēfĭcĭum, ĭi, *n*, a kindness
bĕnēfĭcus, a, um, *adj*, obliging
bĕnēvŏlentĭa, ae, *f*, good will
bĕnēvŏlus, a, um, *adj*, *adv*, ē, well-disposed
bĕnignē, *adv*, thank you; no thank you; courteously
bĕnignus, a, um, *adj*, kind, fruitful
bĕnignĭtas, ātis, *f*, kindness
bĕo, *v.t.* 1, to bless, enrich
bes, bessis, *m*, eight ounces
bestĭa, ae, *f*, wild beast
bestĭārĭus, ĭi, *m*, wild-beast fighter
bestĭŏla, ae, *f*, small animal
bēta, ae, *f*, beet
bĕtŭla, ae, *f*, birch
biblĭa, ōrum, *n.pl*, the Bible
biblĭŏpōla, ae, *m*, bookseller
biblĭŏthēca, ae, *f*, library
biblĭŏthēcārĭus, ĭi, *m*, librarian
bĭbo, bĭbi, ĭtum, *v.t.* 3, to drink
bĭbŭlus, a, um, *adj*, given to drink, porous
bĭceps, cĭpĭtis, *adj*, two-headed
bĭcŏlor, ōris, *adj*, two-coloured
bĭcornis, e, *adj*, two-horned
bĭdens, ntis, *adj*, two-pronged
bĭdens, ntis, *m*, hoe
bĭdŭum, ĭi, *n*, space of two days
biennĭum, ĭi, *n*, space of two years
bĭfārĭam, *adv*, in two ways
bĭfer, ĕra, ĕrum, *adj*, blooming or fruiting twice a year
bĭfĭdus, a, um, *adj*, cut in two

bĭfŏris, e, *adj,* with double opening

bĭformis, e, *adj,* two-shaped

bĭfrons, ntis, *adj,* two-headed

bĭfurcus, a, um, *adj,* two-pronged

bĭgae, ārum, *f.pl,* pair of horses, two-horsed chariot

bĭgātus, a, um, *adj,* stamped with a two-horsed chariot (of coins)

bĭiŭgus, a, um, *adj,* yoked two together

bĭlībris, e, *adj,* weighing two pounds

bĭlinguis, e, *adj,* bilingual

bĭliōsus, a, um, *adj,* bilious

bĭlis, is, *f,* bile

bĭmāris, e, *adj,* lying between two seas

bĭmārītus, i, m, bigamist

bĭmembris, e, *adj,* half-man, half-beast

bĭmestris, e, *adj,* two months old

bĭmus, a, um, *adj,* two years old

bīni, ae, a, *adj,* two each, a pair

bĭpartĭo, *v.t.* 4, to bisect

bĭpartīto, *adv,* in two ways

bĭpĕdālis, e, *adj,* measuring two feet.

bĭpennĭfer, ĕra, ĕrum, *adj,* carrying a double-edged axe

bĭpennis, e, *adj,* double-edged

bĭpēs, ĕdis, *adj,* two-legged

bĭrēmis, e, *adj,* two-oared

bĭrēmis, is, *f,* a galley with two banks of oars

bis, *adv,* twice

bĭsextĭlis, e, *adj* (of years) leap

bĭsulcus, a, um, *adj,* cloven

bĭtūmen, ĭnis, n, bitumen

bĭvĭum, ii, n, cross-road

bĭvĭus, a, um, *adj,* going in two directions

blaesus, a, um, *adj,* stammering

blandĭmentum, i, n, flattery

blandĭor, v. 4, dep. with dat, to flatter

blandĭtĭa, ae, f, flattery

blandus, a, um, *adj, adv,* **ē,** smooth-tongued, enticing

blasphēmo, v.t. 1, to revile

blătĕro, v.t. 1, to babble

blătĕro, ōnis, m, gabbler

blatta, ae, f, cockroach, moth

bŏārius, a, um, *adj,* of cattle

bōlētus, i, m, mushroom

bombyx, ȳcis, m, silk, silk-worm

bŏnĭtas, ātis, f, excellence

bŏna, ōrum, n.pl, goods, property

bŏnum, i, n, goodness, profit

bŏnus, a, um, *adj,* good

bŏrĕas, ae, m, north wind

bŏrĕus, a, um, *adj,* northern

bōs, bŏvis, c, ox; *pl,* cattle

bŏvārĭus, see **boārius**

brācae, ārum, f.pl, trousers

brācātus, a, um, *adj,* wearing trousers, foreign

bracchĭum, ii, n, fore-arm, branch, dike

bractĕa, ae, f, thin metal plate

branchĭae, ārum, f.pl, fish-gills

brassĭca, ae, f, cabbage

brĕvī, adv, in a short time, in a few words

brĕvĭārĭum, ii, n, summary

brĕvis, e, *adj, adv,* **ĭter,** short, brief

brĕvĭtas, ātis, f, conciseness, shortness

brūma, ae, f, shortest day, winter

brūmālis, e, *adj,* wintry

brūtus, a, um, *adj,* unwieldy, dull

būbo, ōnis, m, owl

būbulcus, i, m, ploughman

būbŭlus, a, um, *adj,* of cattle

bucca, ae, f, the cheek

buccŭla, ae, f, small mouth, helmet

būcĭna, ae, f, trumpet

būcŭla, ae, f, heifer

būfo, ōnis, m, toad

bulbus, i, m, bulb

bulla, ae, f, bubble, knob, amulet

bullo, v.i. 1, to bubble

būmastus, i, f, grape which grows in large bunches

būris, is, m, plough-beam

bustum, i, n, funeral pyre, grave

bŭtȳrum, i, n, butter

buxĭfer, ĕra, ĕrum, *adj,* growing box-trees

buxum, i, n, box-wood

buxus, i, f, box-tree

byssus, i, f, cotton

C

căballus, i, m, pack-horse

căcăbus, i, m, saucepan

căchinnātĭo, ōnis, f, guffaw

căchinno, v.i. 1, to laugh aloud

căchinnus, i, m, laughter, jeering

căcūmen, ĭnis, n, extremity, peak

căcūmĭno, v.t. 1, to make into a point

cădāver, ĕris, n, corpse

cădo, cĕcĭdi, cāsum, v.i. 3, to fall, wane, occur, decay

cādūcĕātor, ōris, m, herald

cādūcĕum, i, n (us, i, m), herald's staff, Mercury's wand

cādūcĭfer, ĕra, ĕrum, *adj,* carrying a herald's staff (Mercury)

cādūcus, a, um, *adj,* falling, doomed

cādus, i, m, large jar (for liquids)

caecĭtas, ātis, f, blindness

caeco, v.t. 1, to blind

caecus, a, um, *adj,* blind, hidden

caedēs, is, f, slaughter

caedo, cĕcīdi, caesum, *v.t.* 3, to cut, strike, slaughter
caelātor, ōris, *m*, engraver
caelātūra, ae, *f*, carving
caelebs, lībis, *adj*, unmarried
caelĕs, ĭtis, *adj*, heavenly
caelĭtes, um, *pl*, gods
caelestĭa, ĭum, *n.pl.*, the heavenly bodies
caelestis, e, *adj*, heavenly
caelestis, is, *m*, god
caelĭbātus, ūs, *m*, celibacy
caelĭcŏla, ae, *m. f*, inhabitant of heaven
caelĭfer, ĕra, ĕrum, *adj*, supporting the heavens (Atlas)
caelo, *v.t.* 1, to engrave
caelum, ĭ, *n*, heaven, climate
caelum, ĭ, *n*, chisel
caementum, ĭ, *n*, quarry-stone
caenum, ĭ, *n*, dirt
caepa, ae, *f* (e, is, *n*), onion
caerĭmōnĭa, ae, *f*, religious ceremony, awe
caerŭlĕus(lus), a, um, *adj*, dark blue
caesărĭēs, ēi, *f*, the hair
caesim, *adv*, by cutting
caesĭus, a, um, *adj*, green or grey-eyed
caespĕs, ĭtis, *m*, a turf
caestus, ūs, *m*, boxing-glove
caetra, ae, *f*, native shield
călămister, tri, *m*, curling-iron; *pl*, flourishes
călămĭtas, ātis, *f*, disaster
călămĭtōsus, a, um, *adj*, *adv*, ē, destructive, unhappy
călămus, ĭ, *m*, cane, reed-pen
călăthus, ĭ, *m*, basket
calcăr, āris, *n*, spur, stimulus
calcĕāmentum, ĭ, *n*, shoe
calcĕo, *v.t.* 1, to shoe
calcĕus, ĭ, *m*, shoe
calcĭtrātus, ūs, *m*, kicking
calcĭtro, *v.i.* 1, to kick, resist
calco, *v.t.* 1, to tread on, oppress
calcŭlātor, ōris, *m*, accountant
calcŭlus, ĭ, *m*, pebble, calculation, vote, piece (chess, draughts)
călĕfăcio, fēci, factum. *v.t.* 3, to heat, excite
călĕo, *v.i.* 2, to be warm, roused
călesco, *v.i.* 3, to become warm
călĭdus, a, um, *adj*, warm, hot, hot-headed
călĭga, ae, *f*, leather boot
călĭgātus, a, um, *adj*, wearing soldier's boots
călĭgĭnōsus, a, um, *adj*, obscure
călīgo, ĭnis, *f*, mist, gloom

cālīgo, *v.i.* 1, to steam, be dark
călix, ĭcis, *m*, cup
calyx, see calix
callĕo, *v.i.t.* 2, to be callous, insensible; to know by experience
callĭdĭtas, ātis, *f*, skill, cunning
callĭdus, a, um, *adj*, *adv*, ē, skilful, sly
callis, is, *m*, footpath
callum, ĭ, *n*, hard or thick skin
cālo, ōnis, *m*, soldier's servant, menial
călor, ōris, *m*, heat, ardour
caltha, ae, *f*, marigold
călumnĭa, ae, *f*, trickery, libel
călumnĭātor, ōris, *m*, slanderer
călumnĭor, *v.t.* 1, *dep*, to blame or accuse unjustly
calva, ae, *f*, scalp
calvārĭa, ae, *f*, skull
calvĭtĭum, ĭ, *n*, baldness
calvus, a, um, *adj*, bald
calx, cis, *f*, heel
calx, cis, *f*, limestone, chalk
cămēlŏpardălis, is, *f*, giraffe
cămēlus, ĭ, *m*, camel
cămēna, ae, *f*, muse
cămēra, ae, *f*, vault
cămīnus, ĭ, *m*, forge, furnace
campester, tris, e, *adj*, on level ground
campestre, is, *n*, wrestling trunks
campus, ĭ, *m*, plain, open country, opportunity, scope
cămŭr, ŭra, ŭrum, *adj*, curved inwards
cănālis, is, *m*, pipe, groove
cancelli, ōrum, *m.pl*, railings
cancer, cri, *m*, crab
candēla, ae, *f*, candle
candēlābrum, ĭ, *n*, candlestick
candens, ntis, *adj*, shining white, glowing hot
candĕo, *v.i.* 2, to shine, glow
candesco, ŭi, *v.i.* 3, to glisten
candĭdātus, ĭ, *m*, candidate
candĭdus, a, um, *adj*, *adv*, e, dazzling white, beautiful, honest
candor, ōris, *m*, whiteness, beauty, honesty
cānens, ntis, *adj*, grey, white
cānĕo, *v.i.* 2, to be white, grey
cānesco, *v.i.* 3, to grow white
cănīcŭla, ae, *f*, small dog, Dog-star
cănīnus, a, um, *adj*, dog-like
cănis, is, *c*, dog, Dog-star
cănistrum, ĭ, *n*, open basket
cānĭties, (*no genitive*) *f*, grey hair, old age
canna, ae, *f*, reed, flute
cannăbis, is, *f*, hemp

căno, cĕcĭni, cantum, *v.i.t.* 3, to sing, play; prophesy
cănor, ōris, *m*, tune
cănōrus, a, um, *adj*, melodious
cantērius, see canthērius
cantātor, ōris, *m*, singer
canthăris, ĭdis, *f*, beetle
canthărus, i, *m*, tankard
canthērius, ii, *m*, mule, rafter
cantĭcum, i, *n*, song
cantĭlēna, ae, *f*, hackneyed song
canto, *v.i.t.* 1, to sing, act; predict
cantor, ōris, *m*, singer, actor
cantus, ūs, *m*, music, prophecy, singing
cānus, a, um, *adj*, white, old
căpācĭtas, ātis, *f*, capacity
căpax, ācis, *adj*, roomy, capable
căpella, ae, *f*, she-goat
căper, pri, *m*, goat
căpesso, ĭvi, ĭtum, *v.t.* 3, to seize, undertake, reach for
căpillāmentum, i, *n*, wig
căpillāre, is, *n*, hair-oil
căpillātus, a, um, *adj*, hairy
căpillus, i, *m*, the hair
căpĭo, cōpi, captum, *v.t.* 3, to take, capture, tempt, choose, obtain, undertake, hold, grasp
căpistrum, i, *n*, halter
căpĭtālis, e, *adj*, of life and death, criminal, dangerous
capra, ae, *f*, she-goat
căprĕa, ae, *f*, wild she-goat, roe
căprĕŏlus, i, *m*, roebuck, prop
căprĭcornus, i, *m*, capricorn
căprĭfĭcus, i, *f*, wild fig-tree
căprĭgĕnus, a, um, *adj*, goat-born
căprīnus, a, um, *adj*, of a goat
capsa, ae, *f*, box, satchel
captātor, ōris, *m*, fortune-hunter
captĭo, ōnis, *f*, fraud, quibble
captīvĭtas, ātis, *f*, captivity
captīvus, a, um, *adj* (i, *m*), prisoner
capto, *v.t.* 1, to chase, entice
captus, ūs, *m*, grasp, capacity
captus, a, um, *adj*, taken, disabled
căpŭlus, i, *m*, tomb, handle
căpŭt, ĭtis, *n*, head, person, chief, origin, summit, status, paragraph, chapter
carbăsĕus, a, um, *adj*, made of flax, linen
carbăsus, i, *f*, flax, linen
carbo, ōnis, *m*, charcoal, coal
carbuncŭlus, i, *m*, ruby, carbuncle
carcer, ĕris, *m*, prison, jail-bird
carchēsĭum, ii, *n*, goblet, mast-head
cardĭăcus, a, um, *adj*, dyspeptic
cardo, ĭnis, *m*, hinge, crisis

cardŭus, i, *m*, thistle
cărĕo, *v.i.* 2 (*with abl.*), to lack
cărex, ĭcis, *f*, reed-grass
cărĭes, (*no genitive*) *f*, decay
cărĭca, ae, *f*, dried fig
cărīna, ae, *f*, hull, keel, boat
cărĭōsus, a, um, *adj*, decayed
cārĭtas, ātis, *f*, costliness, affection
carmen, ĭnis, *n*, song, poem
carnārĭum, ii, *n*, larder
carnĭfex, ĭcis, *m*, executioner
carnĭfĭcīna, ae, *f*, execution, torment
carnĭfĭco, *v.t.* 1, to execute
carnĭvŏrus, a, um, *adj*, carnivorous
carnōsus, a, um, *adj*, fleshy
căro, carnis, *f*, flesh, meat
carpentum, i, *n*, chariot
carpo, psi, ptum, *v.t.* 3, to pluck, graze, slander, weaken, pass over
carptim, *adv*, separately
carrus, i, *m*, two-wheeled cart
cartilāgo, ĭnis, *f*, cartilage
cārus, a, um, *adj*, *adv*, ē, dear
căsa, ae, *f*, cottage, hut
cāsĕus, i, *m*, cheese
căsĭa, ae, *f*, cinnamon (tree)
casses, ĭum, *m.pl*, hunting-net, spider's web
cassis, ĭdis, *f*, helmet
cassĭda, ae, *f*, helmet
cassus, a, um, *adj*, empty, vain
castănĕa, ae, *f*, chestnut
castē, *adv*, purely
castellum, i, *n*, stronghold
castīgātĭo, ōnis, *f*, punishment
castīgātor, ōris, *m*, critic
castīgo, *v.t.* 1, to correct, punish
castĭmōnĭa, ae, *f*, purity
castĭtas, ātis, *f*, chastity
castor, ōris, *m*, beaver
castra, ōrum, *n.pl*, camp
castrensis, e, *adj*, of the camp, military
castro, *v.t.* 1, to castrate
castrum, i, *n*, fort
castus, a, um, *adj*, pure, virtuous
cāsū, *adv*, accidentally
cāsus, ūs, *m*, fall, chance, mishap
catăpulta, ae, *f*, catapult
cătăracta, ae, *f*, waterfall, portcullis
cătellus, i, *m* (a, ae, *f*), puppy
cătēna, ae, *f*, chain, fetter
cătēnātus, a, um, *adj*, chained
căterva, ae, *f*, crowd, company
cătervātim, *adv*, by companies
căthēdra, ae, *f*, chair
cătillus, i, *m*, dish
cătīnus, i, *m*, bowl, dish
cătŭlus, i, *m*, puppy, young animal
cătus, a, um, *adj*, *adv*, ē, intelligent, sly

For List of Abbreviations used, turn to pages 3, 4

cauda, ae, *f,* tail
caudex, ĭcis, *m,* tree-trunk, ledger
caulae, ārum, *f.pl,* hole, enclosure
caulis, is, *m,* stem, cabbage
caupo, ōnis, *m,* retailer, innkeeper
caupōna, ae, *f,* shop, inn
caupōnor, *v.t.* 1, *dep,* to trade
causa, ae, *f,* reason, cause, motive; *abl.* **causā** for the sake of
causĭdĭcus, i, *m,* counsel
causor, *v.i.t.* 1, *dep,* to make excuses; plead
cautē, *adv,* cautiously
cautēs, is, *f,* crag, rock
cautĭo, ōnis, *f,* precaution
cautus, a, um, *adj,* safe, cautious
căvĕa, ae, *f,* den, coop
căvĕo, cāvi, cautum, *v.i.t.* 2, to be on one's guard; stipulate
căverna, ae, *f,* cave, ship's hold
căvillātĭo, ōnis, *f,* jeering
căvillor, *v.i.t.* 1, *dep,* to jeer; taunt, quibble
căvo, *v.t.* 1, to hollow out
căvum, i, *n* (us, i, *m*), hole
căvus, a, um, *adj,* hollow
cēdo, cessi, cessum, *v.i.t.* 3, to move, yield, happen; befall
cēdo, *imperative,* here! say! give!
cĕdrus, i, *f,* cedar (wood, tree, oil)
cĕlĕbĕr, ĕbris, ĕbre, *adj,* much frequented, crowded, famous
cĕlĕbrātĭo, ōnis, *f,* crowd, festival,
cĕlĕbrātus, a, um, *adj,* popular, usual, well-known
cĕlĕbrĭtas, ātis, *f,* crowd, fame
cĕlĕbro, *v.t.* 1, to frequent, use, celebrate, praise, proclaim, solemnize
cĕlĕr, ĕris, ĕre, *adj, adv,* ĭter, swift, lively, rash
cĕlĕrĭtas, ātis, *f,* speed
cĕlĕro, *v.i.t.* 1, to hurry; quicken
cella, ae, *f,* store-room
cellārĭus, i, *m,* butler
cēlo, *v.t.* 1, to conceal
cēlox, ōcis, *f,* yacht
celsus, a, um, *adj,* high, eminent
cēna, ae, *f,* dinner
cēnācŭlum, i, *n,* attic, refectory
cēnātĭo, ōnis, *f,* dining-room
cēnātus, a, um, *adj,* having dined
cēno, *v.i.t.* 1, to dine; eat
censĕo, ŭi, censum, *v.t.* 2, to assess, give an opinion
censor, ōris, *m,* censor
censōrĭus, a, um, *adj,* censorial
censūra, ae, *f,* censorship

census, ūs, *m,* census, wealth
centaurēum, i, *n,* herb (centaury)
centaurus, i, *m,* a Centaur
centēni, ae, a, *adj,* a hundred each
centēsĭmus, a, um, *adj,* hundredth
centĭens (centĭes), *adv,* a hundred times
centĭmănus, a, um, *adj,* hundred-handed
cento, ōnis, *m,* patchwork
centum, a hundred
centumgĕmĭnus, a, um, *adj,* a hundredfold
centumpondĭum, ĭi, *n,* weight of a hundred pounds
centŭplex, plĭcis, *adj,* hundredfold
centŭrĭa, ae, *f,* division, century
centŭrĭātim, *adv,* by hundreds
centŭrĭo, ōnis, *m,* centurion
centŭrĭo, *v.t.* 1, to divide into centuries
cēnŭla, ae, *f,* small dinner
cēra, ae, *f,* wax, writing-tablet
cĕrāsus, i, *f,* cherry (tree)
cerdo, ōnis, *m,* handicraftsman
cĕrēbrōsus, a, um, *adj,* hot-headed
cĕrēbrum, i, *n,* brain, understanding
cērĕus, a, um, *adj,* of wax
cērĕus, i, *m,* wax taper
cerevisia, ae, *f,* beer
cērintha, ae, *f,* wax-flower
cerno, crēvi, crētum, *v.t.* 3, to perceive, decide
cernŭus, a, um, *adj,* headfirst
cēro, *v.t.* 1, to smear with wax
cerrītus, a, um, *adj,* frantic, crazy
certāmen, ĭnis, *n,* struggle
certātim, *adv,* eagerly
certātĭo, ōnis, *f,* contest
certē, *adv,* undoubtedly
certĭōrem făcĭo, to inform
certō, *adv,* certainly
certo, *v.i.t.* 1, to struggle; contest
certus, a, um, *adj,* certain, fixed
cērussa, ae, *f,* white lead
cerva, ae, *f,* doe
cervĭcal, ālis, *n,* pillow
cervīnus, a, um, *adj,* of a deer
cervisia, see cerevisia
cervix, īcis, *f,* neck
cervus, i, *m,* deer
cessātĭo, ōnis, *f,* loitering
cessātor, ōris, *m,* idler
cessātrix, īcis, *f,* idler
cesso, *v.i.t.* 1, to loiter, cease; fail
cētārĭum, ĭi, *n,* fish-pond
cētārĭus, ĭi, *m,* fishmonger
cētĕrōqui, *adv,* in other respects

cētĕrum, *adv.* otherwise, but yet
cētĕrus, a, um, *adj, adv,* um, the rest, remainder
cētus, i, *m,* sea-monster, whale
ceu, *adv.* as, just as
chălybs, ȳbis, *m,* steel
charta, ae, *f,* writing paper
chĕlȳdrus, i, *m,* water-snake
chĕrăgra, ae, *f,* gout in the hand
chīrŏgrăphum, i, *n,* handwriting
chīrurgĭa, ae, *f,* surgery
chīrurgus, i, *m,* surgeon
chlămys, ȳdis, *f,* military cloak
chorda, ae, *f,* string of a musical instrument
chŏrēa, ae, *f,* dance
chŏrus, i, *m,* dance, chorus, group
Christus, i, *m,* Christ
Christĭānus, a, um, *adj,* Christian
cibārĭa, ōrum, *n.pl,* food
cibārĭus, a, um, *adj,* of food
cibŏrĭum, ĭi, *n,* drinking-cup
cĭbus, i, *m,* food
cĭcāda, ae, *f,* grasshopper
cĭcātrix, īcis, *f,* scar
cĭcer, ĕris, *n,* chick pea
cĭcīnus, a, um, *adj,* of the cici tree
cĭcōnĭa, ae, *f,* stork
cĭcur, ŭris, *adj,* tame
cĭcūta, ae, *f,* hemlock
cĭĕo, cīvi, cĭtum, *v.t.* 2, to rouse, move, summon
cĭlĭcĭum, ĭi, *n,* coarse cloth
cīmex, īcis, *m,* bug
cincinnātus, a, um, *adj,* with ringlets
cincinnus, i, *m,* lock of hair
cinctus, ūs, *m,* girdle
cĭnĕrĕus, a, um, *adj,* ash-coloured
cingo, nxi, nctum, *v.t.* 3, to enclose, encircle, fasten on, crown, besiege
cingŭla, ae, *f,* (um, i, *n*), girdle
cĭnis, ĕris, *m,* ashes, death
cippus, i, *m,* stake
circā, *adv. and prep. with acc,* round about
circenses, ĭum, *m.pl,* The Games
circĭnus, i, *m,* pair of compasses
circĭter, *adv. and prep. with acc,* round about, near
circĭtor, ōris, *m,* patrol
circŭĭtĭo, ōnis, *f,* patrolling
circŭĭtus, ūs, *m,* circuit
circŭlor, *v.i.* 1, *dep,* to form a group
circŭlus, i, *m,* circle, orbit
circum, *adv. and prep. with acc,* around, near
circŭmăgo, ēgi, actum, *v.t.* 3, to wheel, drive round, pass (time)
circumcīdo, cīdi, cīsum, *v.t.* 3, to cut around, reduce

circumcīsus, a, um, *adj,* cut off
circumclūdo, si, sum, *v.t.* 3, to shut in, surround
circumdătus, a, um, *adj,* surrounded
circumdo, dĕdi, dătum, *v.t.* 1, to put around, shut in, surround
circumdūco, xi, ctum, *v.t.* 3, to lead around
circŭmĕo, circŭĭtum, *v.i.t.* 4, to go around; surround, canvass
circumfĕro, ferre, tŭli, lātum, *v.t., irreg,* to carry or pass around
circumflecto, xi, xum, *v.t.* 3, to bend, turn round
circumflŭo, xi, ctum, *v.i.t.* 3, to flow round; overflow with
circumfŏrānĕus, a, um, *adj,* movable
circumfundo, fūdi, fūsum, *v.t.* 3, to pour around, envelop, hem in
circumgrĕdĭor, gressus, *v.i.t.* 3, *dep,* to go around
circumĭcĭo, iēci, ctum, *v.t.* 3, to throw or set round
circumĭectus, a, um, *adj,* surrounding
circumlĭgo, *v.t.* 1, to tie round
circumlĭno,—itum, *v.t.* 3, to besmear
circummitto, mīsi, missum, *v.t.* 3, to send around
circummūnĭo, *v.t.* 4, to fortify round
circumplector, xus, *v.t.* 3, *dep,* to embrace, surround
circumplĭco, *v.t.* 1, to wind round
circumrōdo, di, *v.t.* 3, to nibble round
circumscrībo, psi, ptum, *v.t.* 3, to draw a line round, restrict, deceive
circumscriptĭo, ōnis, *f,* circle, outline
circumsĕdĕo, sedi, sessum, *v.t.* 2, to surround, blockade
circumsisto, stĕti, *v.i.t.* 3, to stand around; surround
circumsŏno, *v.i.t.* 1, to resound; fill with sound
circumspecto, *v.i.t.* 1, to look round; survey carefully
circumspectus, a, um, *adj.* guarded, considered
circumspectus, ūs, *m,* contemplation, spying
circumspĭcĭo, spexi, ctum, *v.i.t.* 3, to look around, take care; survey, search for
circumsto, stĕti, *v.i.t.* 1, to stand around; surround, besiege
circumtextus, a, um, *adj,* woven round
circumtŏno, ŭi, *v.t.* 1, to thunder around
circumvādo, si, *v.t.* 3, to envelop
circumvallo, *v.t.* 1, to surround with a wall, blockade

circumvector, v. 1, dep, to ride around
circumvěhor, vectus, v.i.t. 3, dep, to ride around
circumvěnio, věni, věntum, v.t. 4, to surround
circumvŏlito, v.i.t. 1, to flit; fly around
circumvŏlo, v.t. 1, to fly around
circumvolvo—vŏlūtum, v.t. 3, to roll around
circus, i, m, circle, ring
cīris, is, f, sea-bird
cirrus, i, m, curl
cis, prep, with acc, on this side of, within
cisium, ii, n, two-wheeled vehicle
cista, ae, f, box, chest
cisterna, ae, f, cistern
cītātus, a, um, adj, urged on, quick
cītěrior, comp. adj, on this side
cithăra, ae, f, guitar, lute
cithărista, ae, m, guitar-player
cithăroedus, i, m, a singing guitar-player
cito, adv, soon, quickly
cito, v.t. 1, to incite, call
citrā, adv. and prep. with acc, on this side (of)
citrěus, a, um, adj, of citrus-wood, of the citrus tree
citro, adv. (with ultro), to and fro, backwards and forwards
citrus, i, f, citrus-tree
citus, a, um, adj, swift, quick
civicus, a, um, adj, of a citizen, civic, civil
civilis, e, adj, adv, iter, of a citizen, civic, civil
civis, is, c, citizen
civitas, ātis, f, citizenship, the state, the citizens
clādes, is, f, disaster, massacre
clam, adv. and prep. with acc, secretly; unknown to
clāmito, v.i.t. 1, to call out
clāmo, v.i.t. 1, to shout; declare
clāmor, ōris, m, shout, applause
clāmōsus, a, um, adj, noisy, bawling
clandestīnus, a, um, adj, adv, o, secret, hidden, furtive
clangor, ōris, m, noise, clash
clārěo, v.i. 2, to shine, be famous
clāresco, clārŭi, v.i. 3, to become clear or famous
clāritas, ātis, f, brightness, renown
clārĭtūdo, ĭnis, f, renown
clārus, a, um, adj, adv, e, clear, bright, plain, famous
classiārii, ōrum, m. pl, marines
classicum, i, n, battle-signal

classis, is, f, fleet, class or muster of citizens
claudĕo, v.i. 2 (no perf), to limp, be lame
claudico, v.i. 1, to limp, be lame
claudĭcātio, ōnis, f, limping
claudo, si, sum, v.t. 3, to shut, cut off, enclose, blockade
claudus, a, um, adj, lame
claustra, ōrum, n. pl, lock, bolt, barricade
clausŭla, ae, f, conclusion, end
clausum, i, n, enclosed space
clāva, ae, f, club, cudgel
clāviger, ěra, ěrum, adj, club-armed
clāviger, ěri, m, key-bearer
clāvis, is, f, key
clāvŭlus, i, m, small nail
clāvus, i, m, nail, tiller, stripe
clēmens, ntis, adj, adv, nter, gentle, mild, merciful
clēmentia, ae, f, mildness, mercy
clēpo, psi, ptum, v.t. 3, to steal
clepsydra, ae, f, water-clock
cliens, ntis, c, retainer, follower
clientēla, ae, f, patronage, train of dependants
clīpěus, i, m, Roman round shield
clitellae, ārum, f. pl, saddle-bags
clīvōsus, a, um, adj, hilly
clīvus, i, m, slope, hill
clōāca, ae, f, sewer, drain
clūnis, is, m, f, buttock, haunch
cŏăcervo, v.t. 1, to pile together
cŏactor, ōris, m, money-collector
cŏactum, i, n, a thick covering
cŏactus, a, um, adj, adv, e, forced
cŏaequo, v.t. 1, to level, equalize
cŏagmento, v.t. 1, to join together
cŏagŭlo, v.t. 1, to coagulate
cŏālesco, ălŭi, ălĭtum, v.i. 3, to grow together, combine
cŏargŭo, ŭi, v.t. 3, to convict, refute, demonstrate
cŏarto, v.t. 1, to compress
coccĭněus, a, um, adj, scarlet
coccum, i, n, scarlet colour
cochlěa, ae, f, snail, spiral
cŏclěa, ae, f, snail, spiral
cŏclěar, āris, n, spoon
coctĭlis, e, adj, baked, burned
cŏcus, i, m, cook
cōdex, ĭcis, m, tree-trunk, ledger
cōdĭcilli, ōrum, m. pl, note-book
cŏěmo, ēmi, emptum, v.t. 3, to buy up
coenum, i, n, dirt
cŏěo, v.i. 4, to assemble, unite, encounter, conspire
(coepio) coepi, coeptum, v.i.t. 3, defect, to begin

coeptum, i, *n*, attempt

coeptus, ūs, *m*, undertaking

cŏercĕo, *v.t.* 2, to confine, curb

cŏercitĭo, ōnis, *f*, coercion, restraint

coetus, ūs, *m*, meeting, crowd

cōgĭtātĭo, ōnis, *f*, thought, reflection, purpose

cōgĭtātum, i, *n*, idea, thought

cōgĭtātus, a, um, *adj*, thought out

cōgĭto, *v.t.* 1, to consider, think, be disposed towards, plan

cognātĭo, ōnis, *f*, blood relationship, family

cognātus, a, um, *adj*, related by birth; (*as a noun*) blood-relative

cognĭtĭo, ōnis, *f*, study, knowledge, recognition, idea, trial

cognĭtor, ōris, *m*, legal representative

cognĭtus, a, um, *adj*, known, approved

cognōmen, ĭnis, *n*, surname

cognōmĭnis, e, *adj*, of the same name

cognosco, gnōvi, gnĭtum, *v.t.* 3, to learn, understand, inquire

cōgo, cŏēgi, cŏactum, *v.t.* 3, to collect, compel, restrict

cŏhaerens, see cohaerĕo

cŏhaerĕo, si, sum, *v.i.* 2, to cling together, agree with

cŏhērĕs, ēdis, *o*, fellow heir

cŏhĭbĕo, *v.t.* 2, to hold together, confine, restrain

cŏhonesto, *v.t.* 1, to honour

cŏhorresco, horrŭi, *v.i.* 3, to shudder

cŏhors, tis, *f*, company of soldiers ($\frac{1}{10}$ of a legion); enclosure

cŏhortālis, e, *adj*, of the poultry-farm

cŏhortātĭo, ōnis, *f*, encouragement

cŏhortor, *v.t.* 1, *dep*, to encourage

cŏĭtĭo, ōnis, *f*, meeting, conspiracy

cŏĭtus, ūs, *m*, meeting, crowd, sexual intercourse

cŏlăphus, i, *m*, blow, cuff

collăbĕfacto, *v.t.* 1, to dislodge

collăbĕfīo, fĭeri, factus, *v. irreg*, to be overthrown, disabled

collābor, psus, *v.i.* 3, *dep*, to fall, faint, decay

collăcrĭmo, *v.i.t.* 1, to weep; deplore

collactĕus, i, *m*, (a, ae, *f*.) foster-brother (sister)

collātĭo, ōnis, *f*, collection, encounter, comparison

collaudo, *v.t.* 1, to praise highly

collēga, ae, *m*, partner, colleague

collēgĭum, ii, *n*, organization, body of officials

collĭbet, *v. impers*, 2, it is agreeable

collīdo, si, sum, *v.t.* 3, to beat or strike together

collĭgo, lēgi, ctum, *v.t.* 3, to collect, compress, consider

collĭgo, *v.t.* 1, to tie together

collīno, lēvi, lĭtum, *v.t.* 3, to besmear, defile

collīnus, a, um, *adj*, hilly

collis, is, *m*, hill, high ground

collŏcātĭo, ōnis, *f*, setting up, giving in marriage

collŏco, *v.t.* 1, to arrange, give in marriage, invest, employ

collŏquĭum, ii, *n*, conversation

collŏquor, cūtus, *v.i.* 3, *dep*, to hold a conversation, discuss

collūcĕo, *v.i.* 2, to shine

collūdo, si, sum, *v.i.* 3, to play with, be in collusion with

collum, i, *n*, neck, throat

collumna, see columna

collŭo, lŭi, lūtuma, *v.t.* 3, to rinse

collūsĭo, ōnis, *f*, collusion

collūsor, ōris, *m*, playmate

collustro, *v.t.* 1, to illumine

collŭvĭo, ōnis, *f*, heap of rubbish

collŭvĭes, —, *f*, heap of rubbish

cŏlo, ŭi, cultum, *v.t.* 3, to cultivate improve, worship, study

cōlo, *v.t.* 1, to filter

cōlŏcāsĭa, ae, *f*, marsh-lily

cōlon, i, *n*, colon

cŏlōna, ae, *f*, farmer's wife

cŏlōnĭa, ae, *f*, Roman outpost, colonial settlement, farm

cŏlonus, i, *m*, farmer, colonist

cŏlor, ōris, *m*, colour, dye, beauty

cŏlōrātus, a, um, *adj*, coloured

cŏlōro, *v.t.* 1, to colour, dye

cŏlossus, i, *m*, gigantic statue

cŏlŭber, bri, *m* (bra, ae, *f*), snake

cōlum, i, *n*, strainer, colander

cŏlumba, ae, *f*, (us, i, *m*), dove

cŏlumbārĭum, ĭi, *n*, dove-cot

cŏlumbīnus, a, um, *adj*, of a dove, dove-coloured

cŏlŭmella, ae, *f*, small pillar

cŏlūmen, ĭnis, *n*, summit, prop

cŏlumna, ae, *f*, pillar, post

cŏlurnus, a, um, *adj*, of hazel

cŏlus, ūs, *f*, distaff

cōma, ae, *f*, hair, crest, foliage

cōmans, ntis, *adj*, hairy

cōmātus, a, um, *adj*, long-haired

combĭbo, bĭbi, *v.t.* 3, to drink up

combūro, ussi, ustum, *v.t.* 3, to burn, consume completely

cŏmĕdo, ēdi, ēsum, *v.t.* 3, to eat up, waste

cōmes, ĭtis, *c*, companion, attendant

cōmētes, ae, *m*, comet

cōmĭcus, a, um, *adj*, *adv*, ē, comic

For List of Abbreviations used, turn to pages 3, 4

cŏmĭcus, ĭ, *m*, comedian

cōmis, e, *adj, adv,* ĭter, courteous, obliging

cōmissātĭo, ōnis, *f*, drinking-party

cōmissātor, ōris, *m*, reveller

cōmissor, *v.i.* 1, *dep*, to have a party

cōmĭtas, ātis, *f*, affability

cōmĭtātus, a, um, *adj*, accompanied

cōmĭtātus, ūs, *m*, escort, retinue

cōmĭtĭa, ōrum, *n.pl*, Roman assembly for electing magistrates

cōmĭtĭālis, e, *adj*, of the elections; (with morbus) epilepsy

cōmĭtĭum, ii, *n*, assembly place for voting

cōmĭtor, *v.t.* 1, *dep*, to accompany

commăcŭlo, *v.t.* 1, to stain

commĕātus, ūs, *m*, expedition, leave of absence, convoy, supplies

commĕmŏrātĭo, ōnis, *f*, mention

commĕmŏro, *v.t.* 1, to remember, relate

commendātĭcĭus, a, um, *adj*, commendatory

commendātĭo, ōnis, *f*, recommendation

commendo, *v.t.* 1, to entrust, recommend

commentārĭus, ii, *m* (ium, ii, *n*), notebook, record

commentātĭo, ōnis, *f*, careful study

commentĭcĭus, a, um, *adj*, thought-out, imaginary, false

commentor, *v.i.t.* 1, *dep*, to study

commentor, ōris, *m*, inventor

commentum, ĭ, *n*, fabrication

commĕo, *v.i.* 1, to come and go, frequent

commercĭum, ii, *n*, commerce, trade, a relationship with

commĕrĕo, *v.t.* 2, to deserve fully, be guilty of

commigro, *v.t.* 1, to migrate

commīlĭtĭum, ii, *n*, comradeship

commīlĭto, ōnis, *m*, comrade

commĭnātĭo, ōnis, *f*, threats

commĭnĭscor, mentus, *v.t.* 3, *dep*, to devise, invent

commĭnor, *v.t.* 1, *dep*, to threaten

commĭnŭo, ŭi, ūtum, *v.t.* 3, to crush, lessen, weaken

commĭnus, *adv*, at close quarters

commiscĕo, scŭi, xtum, *v.t.* 2, to mix together

commĭsĕror, *v.t.* 1, *dep*, to pity

commissĭo, ōnis, *f*, opening of the games, prepared speech

commissum, ĭ, *n*, offence, secret

commissūra, ae, *f*, knot, joint

committo, mīsi, ssum, *v.t.* 3, to connect, engage in, begin, entrust, do something wrong, bring together in combat

commŏdātum, ĭ, *n*, loan

commŏdē, *adv*, appropriately, just in time

commŏdĭtas, ātis, *f*, benefit

commŏdo, *v.t.* 1, to adjust, lend, be kind to, oblige

commŏdum, ĭ, *n*, convenient time or opportunity, advantage

commŏdus, a, um, *adj*, suitable, obliging, advantageous

commŏnĕfăcĭo, fēci, factum, *v.t.* 3, to remind, impress upon

commŏnĕo, *v.t.* 2, to impress upon

commonstro, *v.t.* 1, to point out

commŏrātĭo, ōnis, *f*, delay

commŏror, *v.i.t.* 1, *dep*, to wait, stay

commŏtĭo, ōnis, *f*, commotion, excitement

commōtus, a, um, *adj*, aroused

commŏvĕo, mōvi, mōtum, *v.t.* 2, to shake, move, arouse, disturb

commūnĭcātĭo, ōnis, *f*, communication

commūnĭco, *v.t.* 1, to share with another, consult, unite, partake

commūnĭo, *v.t.* 4, to fortify strongly

commūnĭo, ōnis, *f*, partnership

commūnē, is, *n*, community, state

commūnis, e, *adj, adv,* ĭter, common, general

commūnĭtas, ātis, *f*, fellowship

commūtābĭlis, e, *adj*, changeable

commūtātĭo, ōnis, *f*, change

commūto, *v.t.* 1, to change, exchange

cōmo, mpsi, mptum, *v.t.* 3, to arrange comb, braid, adorn

cōmoedĭa, ae, *f*, comedy

cōmoedus, a, um, *adj*, comic

cōmoedus, ĭ, *m*, comic actor

compactum, ĭ, *n*, agreement

compactus, a, um, *adj*, thick-set

compāges, is, *f*, joint, structure

compār, ăris, *adj*, equal, like

compār, ăris, *m*, companion

compărātĭo, ōnis, *f*, comparison, preparation

compărātīvus, a, um, *adj*, comparative

compārĕo, *v.i.* 2, to be evident

compăro, *v.t.* 1, to pair off, compare, make ready, provide

compello, pŭli, pulsum, *v.t.* 3, to collect, compel

compello, *v.t.* 1, to address, rebuke

compendiārĭus, a, um, *adj*, short

compendĭum, ĭi, *n*, gain, saving, abbreviation

compensātĭo, ōnis, *f*, compensation

compenso, *v.t.* 1, to make things balance, compensate

compĕrendĭno, *v.t.* 1, to remand

compĕrĭo, pĕri, pertum, *v.t.* 4, to ascertain

compertus, a, um, *adj*, proved

compēs, ēdis, *f*, chain, shackle for the feet

compesco, scŭi, *v.t.* 3, to restrain

compĕtītor, ōris, *m*, rival

compĕto, īvi, ītum, *v.i.* 3, to correspond, coincide

compīlo, *v.t.* 1, to plunder

compingo, pēgi, pactum, *v.t.* 3, to construct, fasten together

compĭtum, ĭ, *n*, cross-road

complāno, *v.t.* 1, to level

complector, xus, *v.t.* 3, *dep*, to embrace, value, enclose, understand

complēmentum, ĭ, *n*, complement

complĕo, ēvi, ētum, *v.t.* 2, to fill up, supply

complexĭo, ōnis, *f*, combination

complexus, ūs, *m*, embrace, love

complĭco, *v.t.* 1, to fold up

complōrātĭo, ōnis, *f*, lamentation

complōrātus, ūs, *m*, lamentation

complōro, *v.t.* 1, to lament

complūres, a, *pl. adj*, several

compōno, posŭi, posĭtum, *v.t.* 3, to put together, unite, build, arrange, compare, put to sleep, adjust, pretend, agree upon

comporto, *v.t.* 1, to bring together

compōs, ōtis, *adj*, *with genit. or abl*, having control of

compŏsĭtĭo, ōnis, *f*, arranging

compŏsĭtus, a, um, *adj*, *adv*, ē, well-arranged, suitable: ex compŏsĭto, by previous agreement

comprĕhendo, di, sum, *v.t.* 3, to seize, perceive, recount, understand

comprĕhensĭo, ōnis, *f*, arrest

comprĭmo, pressi, pressum, *v.t.* 3, to press together, restrain

comprŏbo, *v.t.* 1, to approve, prove

comptus, a, um, *m*, *adj*, dressed-up

compulsus, a, um, *adj*, collected, driven

compungo, nxi, nctum, *v.t.* 3, to prick, sting

compŭto, *v.t.* 1, to calculate

cōnāmen, ĭnis, *n*, effort

cōnāta, ōrum, *n.pl*, undertaking

cōnātum, ĭ, *n*, attempt

cōnātus, ūs, *m*, effort, enterprise

concăvus, a, um, *adj*, hollow, arched

concēdo, cessi, ssum, *v.i.t.* 3, to go away, yield; permit

concĕlĕbro, *v.t.* 1, to frequent, celebrate, notify

concentus, ūs, *m*, harmony

conceptĭo, ōnis, *f*, comprehension, conception

conceptus, ūs, *m*, gathering

concertātĭo, ōnis, *f*, dispute

concerto, *v.t.* 1, to dispute

concessĭo, ōnis, *f*, permission

concessu (*abl*), by permission

concessus, a, um, *adj*, yielded, confirmed

concha, ae, *f*, shell-fish, oyster-shell, Triton's trumpet

conchȳlium, ĭi, *n*, shell-fish

concĭdo, cĭdi, *v.i.* 3, to collapse

concīdo, cīdi, cīsum, *v.t.* 3, to cut up, kill, annihilate

concĭĕo, īvi, ītum, *v.t.* 2, to bring together

concĭlĭābŭlum, ĭ, *n*, assembly-place

concĭlĭātĭo, ōnis, *f*, union

concĭlĭātor, ōris, *m*, promoter

concĭlĭo, *v.t.* 1, to unite, win over, bring about

concĭlĭum, ĭi, *n*, meeting, assembly

concinnĭtas, ātis, *f*, elegance

concinnus, a, um, *adj*, *adv*, ē, well-adjusted, graceful

concĭno, nŭi, *v.i.t.* 3, to harmonize; celebrate

concĭpĭo, cēpi, ceptum, *v.t.* 3, to take hold of, become pregnant, understand, formulate, designate

concīsus, a, um, *adj*, *adv*, ē, cut short

concĭtātĭo, ōnis, *f*, quick motion

concĭtātus, a, um, *adj*, *adv*, ē, swift, roused

concĭto, *v.t.* 1, to stir up, rouse

conclāmo, *v.i.t.* 1, to shout out; call upon

conclāve, is, *n*, room

conclūdo, si, sum, *v.t.* 3, to enclose, include, conclude

concoctĭo, ōnis, *f*, digestion

concŏlor, ōris, *adj*, similar in colour

concŏquo, xi, ctum, *v.t.* 3, to boil together, digest, put up with

concordĭa, ae, *f*, agreement

concordo, *v.i.* 1, to agree

concors, cordis, *adj*, *adv*, ĭter, of the same mind

concrēdo, dĭdi, dĭtum, *v.t.* 3, to entrust

concrĕmo, *v.t.* 1, to burn up

concrĕpo, ŭi, ĭtum, *v.i.t.* 3, to creak, crack; 2 rattle, clash concresco, crēvi, tum, *v.i.* 3, to grow together, harden

concrētus, a, um, *adj*, hardened

concŭbīna, ae, *f*, concubine

concŭbīus, a, um, *adj*, (with nox) at dead of night

conculco, *v.t.* 1, to trample on

concŭpisco, cŭpīvi, ītum, *v.t.* 3, to long for, strive after

concurro, curri, cursum, *v.i.* 3, to rush together, assemble, join battle

concursātio, ōnis, *f*, running together

concursio, ōnis, *f*, running together

concurso, *v.i.t.* 1, to run, travel about, skirmish; frequent

concursus, ūs, *m*, rush, collision

concŭtio, cussi, ssum, *v.t.* 3, to shake, disturb, terrify, examine

condemno, *v.t.* 1, to convict

condenso, *v.t.* 1, to condense

condensus, a, um, *adj*, thick

condĭcio, ōnis, *f*, agreement, proposition, terms, alliance, rank, situation

condīmentum, i, *n*, seasoning

condĭo, *v.t.* 4, to pickle

condiscĭpŭlus, i, *m*, school-friend

condisco, dĭdĭci, *v.t.* 3, to learn carefully

condĭtor, ōris, *m*, builder, author, founder

condĭtus, a, um, *adj*, fashioned, composed

condĭtus . a, um, *adj*, savoury

condo, dĭdi, dĭtum, *v.t.* 3, to construct, found, store up, hide, thrust in

condŏlesco, lŭi, *v.i.* 3, to suffer pain

condōno, *v.t.* 1, to present, give up, surrender, pardon

condūco, xi, ctum, *v.i.t.* 3, to be useful; collect, connect, hire

conductio, ōnis, *f*, hiring

conductor, ōris, *m*, tenant, contractor

conductum, i, *n*, tenement

conductus, a, um, *adj*, hired

cōnecto, xŭi, xum, *v.t.* 3, to tie together, involve

confarrēātio, ōnis, *f*, marriage

confectio, ōnis, *f*, arrangement, completion

confectus, a, um, *adj*, completed, exhausted

confercio, (*no perf.*) fertum, *v.t.* 4, to cram, stuff together

confĕro, ferre, tŭli, collātum, *v.t*, *irreg*, to bring together, contribute, confer, talk about, engage, fight, compare, condense, convey, postpone; (*reflex.*) to betake oneself, go

confertus, a, um, *adj*, *adv*, ē, crowded

confessio, ōnis, *f*, confession

confessus, a, um, *adj*, admitted

confestim, *adv*, immediately

confĭcio, fēci, fectum, *v.t.* 3, to complete, produce, exhaust, kill

confīdens, ntis, *adj*, *adv*, nter, bold, impudent

confidentia, ae, *f*, boldness

confido, fīsus sum, *v.i.* 3, *semi-dep*, to feel confident; *with dat*, to trust

configo, xi, xum, *v.t.* 3, to nail, fasten together, transfix

confingo, nxi, ctum, *v.t.* 3; to fashion, invent

confinis, e, *adj*, adjoining

confinĭum, ii, *n*, border

confirmātio, ōnis, *f*, encouragement, confirming

confirmātus, a, um, *adj*, resolute

confirmo, *v.t.* 1, to strengthen, encourage, prove

confisus, a, um, *adj*, trusting

confĭtĕor, fessus, *v.t.* 2, *dep*, to acknowledge, own

conflāgro, *v.i.* 1, to burn

conflicto, *v.t.* 1, to strike or dash together, ruin, harass

conflīgo, xi, ctum, *v.i.t.* 3, to fight, struggle; strike or dash together

conflo, *v.t.* 1, to kindle, cause

conflŭens, ntis, *m*, confluence of rivers

conflŭo, xi, *v.i.* 3, to flow together, unite, come in crowds

confōdio, fōdi, fossum, *v.t.* 3, to dig thoroughly, stab, pierce

conformātio, ōnis, *f*, shaping

conformo, *v.t.* 1, to form, fashion

confrāgōsus, a, um, *adj*, broken

confringo, frēgi, fractum, *v.t.* 3, to smash up

confŭgio, fūgi, *v.i.* 3, to run away for help, take refuge

confundo, fūdi, sum, *v.t.* 3, to pour together, confuse

confūsio, ōnis, *f*, blending, disorder

confūsus, a, um, *adj*, *adv*, ē, disorderly

confūto, *v.t.* 1, to repress, silence

congĕlo, *v.i.t.* 1, to freeze; thicken

congĕmino, *v.t.* 1, to redouble

congĕmo, ŭi, *v.i.t.* 3, to sigh; mourn

congĕries, ēi, *f*, heap

congĕro, ssi, stum, *v.t.* 3, to bring together, accumulate

congestus, ūs, *m*, heap

congiārium, ii, *n*, gratuity

congius, ii, *m*, 6-pint measure

conglŏbo, *v.t.* 1, to gather, press into a ball

conglūtĭno, *v.t.* 1, to glue or cement together, unite

congrĕdĭor, gressus, *v.i.* 3, *dep*, to meet, encounter

congrĕgātĭo, ōnis, *f*, assembly

congrĕgo, *v.t.* 1, to collect into a flock, unite

congressus, ūs, *m*, meeting, combat

congrŭens, ntis, *adj*, *adv*, nter, appropriate, proper, consistent

congrŭentĭa, ae, *f*, agreement

congrŭo, ŭi, *v.i.* 3, to meet, coincide

cōnĭcĭo, iēci, iectum, *v.t.* 3, to hurl, infer, drive

conĭecto, *v.t.* 1, to hurl, foretell

conĭectūra, ae, *f*, inference

conĭectus, ūs, *m*, throwing, heap

conĭectus, a, um, *adj*, thrown together

cōnĭfer, ĕra, ĕrum, *adj*, cone-bearing

cōnĭtor, nisus (nixus), *v.i.* 3, *dep*, to strive, struggle towards

cōnīvĕo, nīvi, *v.i.* 2, to wink, blink

conĭūgĭum, ii, *n*, union, marriage

conĭunctĭo, ōnis, *f*, uniting, junction

conĭunctus, a, um, *adj*, *adv*, e, near, connected, allied

conĭungo, nxi, nctum, *v.t.* 3, to join together, marry

conĭunx, iŭgis, *m*, *f*, husband, wife

conĭūrātĭo, ōnis, *f*, conspiracy

conĭūrātus, i, *m*, conspirator

conĭūro, *v.t.* 1, to conspire, band together

conl . . . see coll . . .

connecto, . . . see cōnecto

connīvĕo, see cōnīvĕo

connŭbĭum, ii, *n*, marriage

cōnōpēum, i, *n*, gauze-net

cōnor, *v.t.* 1, *dep*, to try, undertake

conquĕror, questus, *v.i.t.* 3, *dep*, to complain (of)

conquĭesco, quiēvi, quiētum, *v.i.* 3, to rest, pause

conquīro, quīsīvi, sītum, *v.t.* 3, to search for

conquīsītĭo, ōnis, *f*, search

conquīsītus, a, um, *adj*, sought after

consălūto, *v.t.* 1, to greet

consānesco, ŭi, *v.i.* 3, to heal

consanguĭnĕus, a, um, *adj*, related by blood

consanguĭnĭtas, ātis, *f*, blood-relationship

conscendo, di, sum, *v.i.t.* 3, to embark; mount

conscĭentĭa, ae, *f*, joint knowledge, moral sense

conscindo, ĭdi, issum, *v.t.* 3, to tear in pieces

conscisco, scīvi, ītum, *v.t.* 3, to make a joint resolution, decree, inflict

conscĭus, a, um, *adj*, sharing knowledge of, (with sibi) conscious of

conscĭus, i, *m*, accomplice

conscrībo, psi, ptum, *v.t.* 3, to enroll, enlist, compose

conscriptus, i, *m*, senator

consĕco, cŭi, ctum, *v.t.* 1, to cut up

consecrātĭo, ōnis, *f*, consecration

consecro, *v.t.* 1, to dedicate, doom

consector, *v.t.* 1, *dep*, to pursue eagerly, imitate

consĕnesco, nŭi, *v.i.* 3, to grow old or weak

consensĭo, ōnis, *f*, agreement, plot

consensus, ūs, *m*, agreement, plot

consentānĕus, a, um, *adj*, suited

consentĭo, sensi, sum, *v.i.t.* 4, to agree, conspire, resolve; plot

consĕquens, ntis, *adj*, according to reason, fit

consĕquor, secūtus, *v.t.* 3, *dep*, to follow, pursue, overtake, attain, obtain

consĕro, sēvi, sĭtum (sătum), *v.t.* 3, to plant, sow

consĕro, rŭi, rtum, *v.t.* 3, to fasten together

consertus, a, um, *adj*, *adv*, ē, joined, close, serried

conservātĭo, ōnis, *f*, maintenance

conservo, *v.t.* 1, to maintain, keep safe

conservus, i, *m*, fellow-slave

consessus, ūs, *m*, assembly

consīdĕrātus, a, um, *adj*, *adv*, e, well-considered, cautious, discreet

consīdĕrātĭo, ōnis, *f*, consideration

consīdĕro, *v.t.* 1, to examine, contemplate

consīdo, sēdi, sessum, *v.i.* 3, to sit down, take up position, subside

consigno, *v.t.* 1, to seal, certify

consĭlĭarĭus, ii, *m*, adviser

consĭlĭor, *v.i.* 1, *dep*, to consult

consĭlĭum, ii, *n*, plan, deliberation, policy, advice, assembly, wisdom

consĭmĭlis, e, *adj*, quite like

consisto, stĭti, stĭtum, *v.i.* 3, to stand, halt, take up position, endure, exist, settle

consōbrīnus, i, *m* (a, ae, *f*), cousin

consōcĭātus, a, um, *adj*, united

consōcĭo, *v.t.* 1, to share, unite

consōlātĭo, ōnis, *f*, comfort

consōlātor, ōris, *m*, comforter

consōlor, *v.t.* 1, *dep*, to comfort

consŏnans, ntis (with littera), consonant

For List of Abbreviations used, turn to pages 3, 4

consŏno, ŭi, v.i. 1, to resound, harmonize, agree

consŏnus, a, um, adj, adv, ē, fit, harmonious

consōpio, v.t. 4, to put to sleep

consors, rtis, adj, partner

consortĭo, ōnis, f, association

conspectus, ūs, m, look, sight, view, presence

conspectus, a, um, adj, distinguished, visible

conspergo, si, sum, v.t. 3, to sprinkle

conspicĭo, spexi, ctum, v.t. 3, to look at, understand

conspicor, v.t. 1, dep, to catch sight of

conspicŭus, a, um, adj, visible, striking

conspīrātĭo, ōnis, f, agreement, plot

conspīro, v.i. 1, to agree, plot

consponsor, ōris, m, joint surety

conspŭo, —, ūtum, v.t. 3, to spit on, cover

constans, ntis, adj, adv, nter, firm, resolute, consistent

constantĭa, ae, f, firmness, consistency

constat, v. impers, it is agreed

consternātĭo, ōnis, f, dismay

consterno, strāvi, strātum, v.t. 3, to cover over

consterno, v.t. 1, to alarm, provoke

constitŭo, ŭi, ūtum, v.t. 3, to put, place, draw up, halt, establish, arrange, determine, decide

constitūtĭo, ōnis, f, arrangement, establishment

constitūtum, i, n, agreement

constitūtus, a, um, adj, arranged

consto, stĭti, stātum, v.i. 1, to agree with, endure, be established, exist, consist of, cost

constrātus, a, um, adj, covered

constringo, nxi, ctum, v.t. 3, to tie up, restrain

construŭo, xi, ctum, v.t. 3, to heap up, build

constŭpro, v.t. 1, to ravish

consŭēfăcĭo, fēci, factum, v.t. 3, to accustom

consŭesco, sŭēvi, sŭētum, v.i.t. 3, to be accustomed; train

consŭētūdo, ĭnis, f, habit, custom, intimacy

consŭētus, a, um, adj, customary

consŭl, ŭlis, m, consul (highest Roman magistrate)

consŭlāris, e, adj, of a consul

consŭlātus, ūs, m, consulship

consŭlo, ŭi, sultum, v.i.t. 3, to consider, consult; with dat. promote the interests of

consulto, v.i.t. 1, to deliberate; consult

consultor, ōris, m, adviser, client

consultum, i, n, decision, decree

consultus, a, um, adj, adv, e, o, well-considered

consummātĭo, ōnis, f, summing-up, completion

consūmo, mpsi, mptum, v.t. 3, to use, eat up, consume, waste, destroy

consumptĭo, ōnis, f, wasting, use

consurgo, surrexi, surrectum, v.i. 3, to stand up, rise

contăbŭlātĭo, ōnis, f, flooring

contăbŭlo, v.t. 1, to board over

contactus, ūs, m, touch, contact, contagion

contāgĭo, ōnis, f, touch, contact, contagion

contāmĭnātus, a, um, adj, impure

contāmĭno, v.t. 1, to blend, stain

contēgo, xi, ctum, v.t. 3, to cover up, hide

contemnendus, a, um, adj, contemptible

contemno, mpsi, mptum, v.t. 3, to despise

contemplātĭo, ōnis, f, observation

contemplor, v.t. 1, dep, to observe

contemptor, ōris, m, despiser

contemptus, ūs, m, contempt

contemptus, a, um, adj, despicable

contendo, di, tum, v.i.t. 3, to strive, march, fight, stretch; compare, make a bid for

contentĭo, ōnis, f, struggle, effort, contrast, dispute

contentus, a, um, adj, strained

contentus, a, um, adj, satisfied

contermĭnus, a, um, adj, bordering on

contĕro, trīvi, trītum, v.t. 3, to grind, wear away, waste

conterrĕo, v.t. 2, to frighten

contestor, v.t. 1, dep, to call to witness

contexo, ŭi, xtum, v.i.t. 3, to weave together; build, compose

contextus, ūs, m, connection

contĭcesco, tĭcŭi, v.i. 3, to be silent, cease

contignātĭo, ōnis, f, wooden floor

contĭgŭus, a, um, adj, adjoining

contĭnens, ntis, f, continent

contĭnens, ntis, adj, adv, nter, moderate, adjacent, unbroken

contĭnentĭa, ae, f, self-restraint

contĭnĕo, ŭi, tentum, *v.t.* 2, to keep together, contain, enclose, restrain

contingo, tĭgi, tactum, *v.i.t.* 3, to happen; touch, border on, reach

contĭnŭātĭo, ōnis, *f*, succession

contĭnŭō, *adv*, immediately

contĭnŭo, *v.t.* 1, to connect, to do one thing after another

contĭnŭus, a, um, *adj*, unbroken

contĭō, ōnis, *f*, meeting, speech

contĭōnātor, ōris, *m*, demagogue

contĭōnor, *v.* 1, *dep*, to expound

contorquĕo, torsi, tortum, *v.t.* 2, to twist, brandish, hurl

contortĭo, ōnis, *f*, twisting, intricacy

contortus, a, um, *adj*, *adv*, ē, energetic, complicated

contrā, *adv*, *prep. with acc*, opposite, facing, contrary to

contractĭo, ōnis, *f*, contraction

contractus, a, um, *adj*, compressed

contrādīco, xi, ctum, *v.t.* 3, to reply

contrādictĭo, ōnis, *f*, reply

contrāho, xi, ctum, *v.t.* 3, to bring together, shorten, produce, check

contrārĭum, ii, *n*, the contrary

contrārĭus, a, um, *adj*, *adv*, ē, opposite, injurious

contrecto, *v.t.* 1, to handle, feel

contrēmĭsco, mŭi, *v.i.t.* 3, to quake; tremble at

contrĭbŭo, ŭi, ūtum, *v.t.* 3, to incorporate, unite

contristo, *v.t.* 1, to sadden, cloud

contrītus, a, um, *adj*, worn out

contrōversĭa, ae, *f*, dispute

contrōversus, a, um, *adj*, questionable

contrūcīdo, *v.t.* 1, to slash

contŭbernālis, is, *c*, messmate

contŭbernĭum, ii, *n*, companionship

contŭĕor, *v.t.* 2, *dep*, to survey

contŭmācĭa, ae, *f*, obstinacy

contŭmax, ācis, *adj*, *adv*, ĭter, stubborn, insolent

contŭmēlĭa, ae, *f*, insult

contŭmēlĭōsus, a, um, *adj*, abusive

contŭmŭlo, *v.t.* 1, to bury

contundo, tŭdi, tūsum, *v.t.* 3, to grind, crush, subdue

conturbo, *v.t.* 1, to confuse

contus, i, *m*, pole

contūsum, i, *n*, bruise

cōnūbĭum, ii, *n*, marriage

cōnus, i, *m*, cone, helmet-tip

convălesco, lŭi, *v.i.* 3, to regain strength or health

convallis, is, *f*, valley

convecto, *v.t.* 1, to collect

convĕho, xi, ctum, *v.t.* 3, to bring together

convello, velli, vulsum, *v.t.* 3, to tear up

convĕnĭens, ntis, *adj*, *adv*, nter, consistent, appropriate

convĕnĭentĭa, ae, *f*, consistency, symmetry

convĕnĭo, vēni, ventum, *v.i.t.* 4, to assemble, agree with; meet

convĕnit, *impers*, it is agreed, it is right, it suits

conventum, i, *n*, agreement

conventus, ūs, *m*, meeting, assizes

conversĭo, ōnis, *f*, revolution

conversus, a, um, *adj*, reversed, turned, transposed

converto, ti, sum, *v.i.t.* 3, to turn; change, alter

convexus, a, um, *adj*, arched

convīcĭum, ii, *n*, outcry, squabbling, abuse

convictor, ōris, *m*, close friend

convictus, ūs, *m*, intimacy

convinco, vīci, victum, *v.t.* 3, to conquer, prove

convīva, ae, *c*, guest

convīvĭum, ii, *n*, dinner-party

convīvor, *v.i.* 1, *dep*, to banquet

convŏco, *v.t.* 1, to call together

convŏlo, *v.i.* 1, to flock together

convolvo, volvi, vŏlūtum, *v.t.* 3, to roll up, interweave

convulsĭo, ōnis, *f*, convulsion

convulsus, a, um, *adj*, torn-up

cōŏpĕrĭo, rŭi, rtum, *v.t.* 4, to cover up, overwhelm

cōŏptātĭo, ōnis, *f*, election

cōŏpto, *v.t.* 1, to nominate, elect

cōŏrĭor, ortus, *v.i.* 4, *dep*, to arise, break out

cŏphĭnus, i, *m*, wicker basket

cōpĭa, ae, *f*, abundance, power, supply, opportunity; (*pl*) forces

cōpĭōsus, a, um, *adj*, *adv*, ē, wellsupplied, eloquent

cōpŭla, ae, *f*, thong, grappling-iron

cōpŭlo, *v.t.* 1, to link, join

cŏquo, xi, ctum, *v.t.* 3, to cook, burn, ripen, devise, harass

cŏquus, i, *m*, cook

cŏr, cordis, *n*, heart, mind

cŏrālĭum, ii, *n*, coral

cōram, *adv. and prep. with abl*, in the presence of, openly

corbis, is, *c*, basket

corbīta, ae, *f*, merchant ship

cordātus, a, um, *adj*, shrewd

cŏrĭārĭus, ii, *m*, tanner

cŏrĭum, ii, *n*, skin, hide, leather, layer, stratum

cornĕus, a, um, *adj*, horny

cornĕus, a, um, *adj,* of cornel-wood
cornĭcen, ĭnis, *m,* horn-player
cornĭcŭla, ae, *f,* jackdaw
cornĭcŭlum, ĭ, *n,* little horn, feeler
cornĭger, ĕra, ĕrum, *adj,* horned
cornĭpēs, ĕdis, *adj,* hoofed
cornix, ĭcis, *f,* crow
cornū, ūs, *n,* horn, hoof, beak, tributary, promontory, knob, wing of army, bow, trumpet, drinking horn
cornum, ĭ, *n,* cornel-cherry
cornus, ĭ, *f,* cornel-cherry tree, cornel-wood javelin
cŏrōna, ae, *f,* garland, wreath, crown, ring, circle, crowd
cŏrōno, *v.t.* 1, to crown, encircle
corpŏrĕus, a, um, *adj,* physical
corpŭlentus, a, um, *adj,* corpulent
corpus, ŏris, *n,* body
correctĭo, ōnis, *f,* improvement
corrector, ōris, *m,* reformer
correpo, psi, *v.i.* 3, to creep
corrĭgĭa, ae, *f,* shoe-lace
corrĭgo, rexi, ctum, *v.t.* 3, to put right, improve
corrĭpĭo, pŭi, reptum, *v.t.* 3, to snatch, plunder, attack, shorten
corrōbŏro, *v.t.* 1, to strengthen
corrūgo, *v.t.* 1, to wrinkle
corrumpo, rūpi, ptum, *v.t.* 3, to destroy, corrupt, spoil
corrŭo, ŭi, *v.i.t.* 3, to collapse; overthrow
corruptēla, ae, *f,* corruption
corruptor, ōris, *m,* corruptor, seducer
corruptus, a, um, *adj, adv,* ē, spoiled, damaged, tainted
cortex, ĭcis, *m,* bark, rind
cortīna, ae, *f,* kettle, cauldron
cŏrusco, *v.i.t.* 1, to glitter; shake
cŏruscus, a, um, *adj,* glittering, vibrating
corvus, ĭ, *m,* raven
cŏrўlus, ĭ, *f,* hazel shrub
cŏrymbus, ĭ, *m,* cluster of fruit or flowers
cŏrўtŏs, ĭ, *m,* quiver
cōs, cōtis, *f,* flintstone
costa, ae, *f,* rib, wall
cōthurnus, ĭ, *m,* hunting-boot, buskin (worn by tragic actors)
cottīdĭānus, a,. um, *adj, adv,* ō, daily, usual
cottīdĭē, *adv,* daily
cŏturnix, īcis, *f,* quail
**coxendix, ĭcis,. f,* hip
crabro, ōnis, *m,* hornet
crambē, es, *f,* cabbage, kale
crāpŭla, ae, *f,* intoxication
crās, *adv,* tomorrow

crassĭtūdo, ĭnis, *f,* thickness
crassus, a, um, *adj, adv,* ē, thick, fat, solid
crastīnus, a, um, *adj,* of tomorrow
crātēr, ĕris, *m,* mixing-bowl, basin
crātēra, ae, *f,* mixing-bowl, basin
crātīcŭla, ae, *f,* gridiron
crātis, is, *f,* wicker-work, hurdle
crĕātĭo, ōnis, *f,* appointing
crĕātor, ōris, *m,* founder, creator
crĕātrix, īcis, *f,* mother
crēber, bra, brum, *adj, adv,* o, thick, numerous, repeated
crēbresco, brŭi, *v.i.* 3, to become frequent, gain strength
crēdens, ntis, *c,* believer
crēdĭbĭlis, e, *adj, adv,* īter, credible, probable
crēdĭtor, ōris, *m,* creditor
crēdo, dĭdi, dĭtum, *v.t.* 3, to lend, entrust, trust, believe in (*with dat*); suppose
crēdŭlĭtas, ātis, *f,* credulity
crēdŭlus, a, um, *adj,* ready to believe
crĕmo, *v.t.* 1, to burn
crĕo, *v.t.* 1, to produce, appoint
crĕpīda, ae, *f,* sandal
crĕpīdo, ĭnis, *f,* pedestal, dike
crĕpĭtācŭlum, ĭ, *n,* rattle
crĕpĭto, *v.i.* 1, to rattle, rustle
crĕpĭtus, ūs, *m,* rattling, clashing, cracking
crĕpo, ŭi, ĭtum, *v.i.t.* 1, to rattle, creak, jingle; prattle about
crĕpundĭa, ōrum, *n.pl,* child's rattle
crĕpuscŭlum, ĭ, *n,* twilight, dusk
cresco, crēvi, crētum, *v.i.* 3, to arise, grow, appear, thrive
crēta, ae, *f,* chalk
crētus, a, um, *adj,* arisen, born of
crībro, *v.t.* 1, to sift
crībrum, ĭ, *n,* sieve
crīmen, ĭnis, *n,* accusation, offence
crīmĭnātĭo, ōnis, *f,* accusation, calumny
crīmĭnor, *v.t.* 1, *dep,* to accuse
crīmĭnōsus, a, um, *adj, adv,* ē, slanderous, culpable
crīnālis, e, *adj,* of the hair
crīnis, is, *m,* the hair
crīnītus, a, um, *adj,* long-haired
crispo, *v.i.t.* 1, to curl; brandish
crispus, a, um, *adj,* curled, quivering
crista, ae, *f,* crest, plume
cristātus, a, um, *adj,* crested
crītĭcus, ĭ, *m,* critic
crŏcĕus, a, um, *adj,* of saffron or yellow
crŏcĭo, *v.i.* 4, to croak
crŏcŏdīlus, ĭ, *m,* crocodile

crŏcus, i, *m* (um, i, *n*), crocus
crŭciātus, ūs, *m*, torture, pain
crŭcio, *v.t.* 1, to torture
crūdēlis, e, *adj, adv*, īter, cruel
crūdēlĭtas, ātis, *f*, cruelty
crūdesco, dŭi, *v.i.* 3, to get worse
crūdĭtas, ātis, *f*, indigestion
crūdus, a, um, *adj*, raw, fresh, unripe, cruel
crŭento, *v.t.* 1, to stain with blood
crŭentus, a, um, *adj*, blood-stained, blood-thirsty
crŭmēna, ae, *f*, small purse
crŭor, ōris, *m*, blood (from a wound), murder
crūs, ūris, *n*, leg, shin
crusta, ae, *f*, crust, bark, mosaic
crustŭlārius, ii, *m*, confectioner
crustŭlum, i, *n*, confectionery
crustum, i, *n*, confectionery
crux, ŭcis, *f*, cross
crypta, ae, *f*, cloister, vault
crystallum, i, *n*, crystal
cŭbĭcŭlārius, ii, *m*, chamber-servant
cŭbĭcŭlum, i, *n*, bedroom
cŭbĭcus, a, um, *adj*, cubic
cŭbīle, is, *n*, bed, lair
cŭbĭtăl, ālis, *n*, cushion
cŭbĭtum, i, *n*, elbow
cŭbĭtus, i, *m*, elbow
cŭbĭtum, see cŭbo
cŭbo, ŭi, ĭtum, *v.i.* 1, to lie down, sleep, lie ill, slant
cŭcullus, i, *m*, hood
cŭcŭlus, i, *m*, cuckoo
cŭcŭmis, ĕris, *m*, cucumber
cŭcurbĭta, ae, *f*, oup
cŭdo, *v.t.* 3, to beat, strike, stamp
cŭius, a, um, *interr. adj*, whose?
cŭius, *genit*, of qui, quis
culcīta, ae, *f*, mattress, cushion
cŭlex, ĭcis, *m*, gnat, mosquito
cŭlīna, ae, *f*, kitchen, food
cullĕus, i, *m*, leather bag
culmen, ĭnis, *n*, summit, roof
culmus, i, *m*, stem, stalk
culpa, ae, *f*, blame, fault, weakness
culpābĭlis, e, *adj*, culpable
culpandus, a, um, *adj*, culpable
culpo, *v.t.* 1, to blame
culter, tri, *m*, knife, ploughshare
cultor, ōris, *m*, cultivator, supporter, inhabitant
cultrix, ĭcis, *f*, female inhabitant
cultūra, ae, *f*, cultivation, care
cultus, a, um, *adj*, cultivated, elegant
cultus, ūs, *m*, farming, education, culture-pattern, reverence, dress
cŭlullus, i, *m*, drinking-cup
cum, *conj*, when, whenever, since, al-

though, cum ... tum, both ... and, not only ... but also
cum, *prep. with abl*, with, together with; *it is attached to the abl. case of personal prons*, e.g. mecum, with me
cumba, ae, *f*, small boat
cŭmĕra, ae, *f*, box, chest
cŭmĭnum, i, *n*, cumin (plant)
cumque, *adv*, however, whenever
cŭmŭlātus, a, um, *adj, adv*, ē, full, increased
cŭmŭlo, *v.t.* 1, to heap up, complete
cŭmŭlus, i, *m*, heap, "last straw"
cūnābŭla, ōrum, *n.pl*, cradle
cūnae, ārum, *f. pl*, cradle
cunctans, ntis, *adj, adv*, nter, loitering, sluggish
cunctātio, ōnis, *f*, delay, doubt
cunctātor, ōris, *m*, loiterer, cautious person
cunctor, *v.i.* 1, *dep*, to hesitate, delay
cunctus, a, um, *adj*, all together
cŭnĕātim, *adv*, wedge-shaped
cŭnĕo, *v.t.* 1, to fasten with wedges
cŭnĕus, i, *m*, wedge, wedge-shaped block of theatre-seats or troop-formation
cŭnĭcŭlum, i, *n*, tunnel, mine
cŭnĭcŭlus, i, *m*, rabbit
cūpa, ae, *f*, barrel, cask
cūpēdĭa, ōrum, *n.pl*, delicacies
cŭpĭdē, *adv*, eagerly
cŭpĭdĭtas, ātis, *f*, desire, longing
cŭpīdo, ĭnis, *f*, lust, greed
cŭpĭdus, a, um, *adj*, eager, longing for, greedy, passionate
cŭpiens, ntis, *adj, adv*, nter, eager or longing for
cŭpĭo, īvi, ĭtum, *v.t.* 3, to desire
cŭpressus, i, *f*, cypress tree
cūr, *adv*, why
cūra, ae, *f*, care, attention, management, anxiety
cūrātio, ōnis, *f*, administration, cure
cūrātor, ōris, *m*, manager
cūrātus, a, um, *adj*, urgent
curcŭlio, ōnis, *m*, weevil
cūria, ae, *f*, senate-house, city-ward
cūriālis, e, *adj*, of the same ward
cūriōsus, a, um, *adj, adv*, e, careful, inquisitive
cūro, *v.t.* 1, to take care of; *with acc. and gerundive*, to see to it that ... to arrange, command
currĭcŭlum, i, *n*, race-course, chariot, racing, career
curro, cŭcurri, cursum, *v.i.* 3, to run
currus, ūs, *m*, chariot
cursim, *adv*, swiftly

For List of Abbreviations used, turn to pages 3, 4

curso, *v.i.* 1, to run to and fro
cursor, ōris, *m,* runner, courier
cursus, ūs, *m,* running, journey, speed, direction
curtus, a, um, *adj,* shortened, humble
curūlis, e, *adj,* of a chariot; **sella curūlis,** ivory chair of office used by high magistrates
curvāmen, inis, *n,* curve
curvo, *v.t.* 1, to bend
curvus, a, um, *adj,* bent, stooping
cuspis, idis, *f,* point, lance, spit, sting
custōdia, ae, *f,* watch, guard, imprisonment, guard-room
custōdio, *v.t.* 4, to guard, watch, keep, preserve
custos, ōdis, *c,* guardian, goaler
cutis, is, *f,* skin, surface
cyathus, i, *m,* small ladle
cycnēus, a, um, *adj,* of a swan
cycnus, i, *m,* swan
cylindrus, i, *m,* roller, cylinder
cymba, ae, *f,* small boat
cymbalum, i, *n,* cymbal, bell
cymbium, ii, *n,* bowl, basin
Cynicus, i, *m,* a Cynic philosopher
cyparissus, i, *f,* cypress tree

D

dactylus, i, *m,* dactyl (metrical foot consisting of 1 long and 2 short syllables)
daedālus, a, um, *adj,* skilful
daemōnium, ii, *n,* demon
damma (dāma), ae, *f,* deer
damnātio, ōnis, *f,* condemnation
damnātōrius, a, um, *adj,* condemnatory
damnātus, a, um, *adj,* guilty
damno, *v.t.* 1, to condemn
damnōsus, a, um, *adj, adv,* e, destructive
damnum, i, *n,* damage, loss, fine
daps, dapis, *f,* formal banquet
dātio, ōnis, *f,* distribution
dātor, ōris, *m,* giver
dē, *prep. with abl,* from, down from, about, concerning, on account of
dea, ae, *f,* goddess
dealbo, *v.t.* 1, to whitewash
deambūlo, *v.i.* 1, to take a walk
dearmo, *v.t.* 1, to disarm
dēbacchor, *v.i.* 1, *dep,* to rage
dēbellātor, ōris, *m,* conqueror
dēbello, *v.i.t.* 1, to finish a war; subdue
dēbeo, *v.i.t.* 2, to be indebted; owe, (one) ought

dēbilis, e, *adj,* disabled, weak
dēbilitas, ātis, *f,* weakness
dēbilitātio, ōnis, *f,* maiming, enervating
dēbilito, *v.t.* 1, to cripple, weaken
dēbitor, ōris, *m,* debtor
dēbitum, i, *n,* debt
dēbitus, a, um, *adj,* owed
dēcanto, *v.i.* 1, to sing repeatedly
dēcēdo, ssi, ssum, *v.i.* 3, to go away, cease, yield, resign
dĕcem, *indecl. adj,* ten
December (mensis), December
dĕcempēda, ae, *f,* measuring rod (ten feet long)
dĕcempēdātor, ōris, *m,* surveyor
dĕcemvirālis, e, *adj,* of the decemviri
dĕcemvirātus, ūs, *m,* the rank of decemvir
dĕcemviri, ōrum, *m.pl,* commission of ten (early rulers of Rome)
dĕcens, ntis, *adj, adv,* nter, proper, graceful
dĕcentia, ae, *f,* comeliness
dēceptus, a, um, *adj,* deceived
dēcerno, crēvi, crētum, *v.i.t.* 3, to decide, resolve; fight
dēcerpo, psi, ptum, *v.t.* 3, to pluck, gather
dēcertātio, ōnis, *f,* struggle
dēcerto, *v.i.t.* 1, to fight it out; struggle for
dēcessio, ōnis, *f,* departure
dēcessus, ūs, *m,* departure
dĕcet, cuit, *v. 2, impers,* it is becoming or proper
dēcido, cidi, *v.i.* 3, to fall down, die, perish
dēcido, cidi, cīsum, *v.t.* 3, to cut off, settle
dĕciēs (dĕciens), *adv,* ten times
dĕcima, ae, *f,* tenth part, tithe
dĕcimānus, a, um, *adj,* of tithes, of the tenth legion; **porta dĕcimāna,** main camp-gate
dĕcimo, *v.t.* 1, to punish every tenth man, decimate
dĕcimus, a, um, *adj,* tenth
dēcipio, cēpi, ptum, *v.t.* 3, to deceive
dēcisio, ōnis, *f,* decision
dēclāmātio, ōnis, *f,* practice in public speaking
dēclāmātor, ōris, *m,* speech-expert
dēclāmātōrius, a, um, *adj,* rhetorical
dēclāmo, *v.i.* 1, to practise speaking
dēclāro, *v.t.* 1, to make clear
dēclīnātio, ōnis, *f,* avoidance, bending
dēclīno, *v.i.t.* 1, to turn aside

dēclīve, is, *n*, slope

dēclīvis, e, *adj*, sloping downwards

dēclīvitas, ātis, *f*, slope

dēcoctor, ōris, *m*, bankrupt

dēcoctus, a, um, *adj*, boiled, refined

dēcŏlor, ōris, *adj*, discoloured

dēcŏlōro, *v.t.*, to discolour

dēcŏquo, xi, ctum, *v.t.* 3, to boil down, go bankrupt

dēcor, ōris, *m*, elegance

dēcŏro, *v.t.* 1, to adorn

dēcōrum, i, *n*, decency

dēcōrus, a, um, *adj*, *adv*, ē, becoming, proper, elegant

dēcrĕpĭtus, a, um, *adj*, decrepit

dēcresco, crēvi, tum, *v.i.* 3, to diminish, wane

dēcrētum, i, *n*, decree, decision

dēcūma, dēcūmānus, see decim . . .

dēcumbo, cŭbŭi, *v.i.* 3, to lie down, lie ill

dēcŭrĭa, ae, *f*, section of ten

dēcŭrĭo, *v.t.* 1, to divide into sections

dēcŭrĭo, ōnis, *m*, the head of ten, superintendent

dēcurro, cŭcurri, cursum, *v.i.* 3, to run down, complete a course, manoeuvre, have recourse to

dēcursus, ūs, *m*, descent, course, manoeuvre, attack

dēcus, ōris, *n*, ornament, splendour

dēcussātĭo, ōnis, *f*, intersection

dēcŭtĭo, cussi, ssum, *v.t.* 3, to shake off, beat off

dēdĕcet, cŭit, *v.* 2, *impers*, it is unbecoming

dēdĕcŏro, *v.t.* 1, to disgrace

dēdĕcus, ōris, *n*, disgrace, shame

dēdĭcātĭo, ōnis, *f*, dedication

dēdĭco, *v.t.* 1, to dedicate

dēdignor, *v.t.* 1, *dep*, to disdain

dēdisco, dĭdĭci, *v.t.* 3, to forget

dēdītĭcĭus, ii, *m*, prisoner-of-war

dēdĭtĭo, ōnis, *f*, surrender

dēdĭtus, a, um, *adj*, addicted to

dēdo, dēdĭdi, dĭtum, *v.t.* 3, to give up, surrender, devote

dēdŏcĕo, *v.t.* 2, to teach one not to . . .

dēdŏlĕo, *v.i.* 2, to stop grieving

dēdūco, xi, ctum, *v.t.* 3, to bring, lead down, withdraw, conduct, escort, mislead, subtract, launch

dēductĭo, ōnis, *f*, diversion, transplanting, inference

dēductus, a, um, *adj*, fine-spun

dēerro, *v.i.* 1, to go astray

dēfătīgātĭo, ōnis, *f*, exhaustion

dēfătīgo, *v.t.* 1, to exhaust

dēfectĭo, ōnis, *f*, rebellion, failure, eclipse

dēfectus, ūs, *m*, rebellion, failure, eclipse

dēfectus, a, um, *adj*, worn out

dēfendo, di, sum, *v.t.* 3, to repel, defend, support

dēfensĭo, ōnis, *f*, defence

dēfensor, ōris, *m*, protector

dēfĕro, ferre, tŭli, lātum, *v.t. irreg*, to bring down or away, convey, refer, announce, indict, offer

dēfervesco, fervi, *v.i.* 3, to cool down

dēfessus, a, um, *adj*, weary

dēfĕtiscor, fessus, *v.i.* 3, *dep*, to grow tired

dēfĭcĭo, fēci, fectum, *v.i.t.* 3, to fail, disappear, revolt; desert

dēfīgo, xi, xum, *v.t.* 3, to fasten down, astound

dēfingo, nxi, *v.t.* 3, to shape

dēfīnĭo, *v.t.* 4, to mark off, restrict, define

dēfīnītĭo, ōnis, *f*, definition

dēfīnītus, a, um, *adj*, *adv*, ē, precise

dēfīxus, a, um, *adj*, fixed

dēflăgrātĭo, ōnis, *f*, destruction by fire

dēflăgro, *v.i.* 1, to burn out

dēflecto, xi, xum, *v.i.t.* 3, to swerve; divert

dēflĕo, ēvi, ētum, *v.t.* 2, to deplore

dēflōresco, rŭi, *v.i.* 3, to wither

dēflŭo, xi, xum, *v.i.* 3, to flow down, vanish

dēfŏdĭo, fōdi, ssum, *v.t.* 3, to dig deep, bury

dēfŏre, *fut. infinitive* (dēsum)

dēformis, e, *adj*, deformed, ugly

dēformitas, ātis, *f*, ugliness

dēformo, *v.t.* 1, to shape

dēformo, *v.t.* 1, to disfigure

dēfossus, a, um, *adj*, buried

dēfraudo, *v.t.* 1, to cheat

dēfrĭco, cŭi, ctum, *v.t.* 1, to rub hard

dēfringo, frēgi, fractum, *v.t.* 3, to break up, break off

dēfrūtum, i, *n*, syrup

dēfŭgĭo, fūgi, *v.i.t.* 3, to escape; avoid

dēfunctus, a, um, *adj*, having finished, deceased

dēfundo, fūdi, fūsum, *v.t.* 3, to pour out

dēfungor, functus, *v.* 3, *dep. with abl*, to bring to an end

dēgĕner, ĕris, *adj*, unworthy of one's birth, ignoble

dēgĕnĕro, *v.i.t.* 1, to deteriorate; impair

dēgo, dēgi, *v.i.t.* 3, to live; spend

dēgrandinat, *v. impers*, it is hailing, ceasing to hail

dēgrăvo, *v.t.* 1, to weigh down

dēgrĕdĭor, gressus, *v.i.* 3, *dep,* to step down, dismount

dēgusto, *v.t.* 1, to taste, graze

dēhinc, *adv,* from here, hence, next, afterwards

dēhisco, hīvi, *v.i.* 3, to split open, gape

dēhŏnesto, *v.t.* 1, to disgrace

dēhortor, *v.t.* 1, *dep,*.to dissuade

dēicĭo, iēci, iectum, *v.t.* 3, to throw down, drive out, lower

dēiectus, a, um, *adj,* downcast

dēiectus, ūs, *m,* descent, felling

dēin, *adv,* from there, after that, afterwards

dēindĕ, *adv,* from there, after that, afterwards

dēinceps, *adv,* in succession

dēlābor, lapsus, *v.i.* 3, *dep,* to fall, sink, glide down

dēlasso, *v.t.* 1, to tire out

dēlātĭo, ōnis, *f,* accusation

dēlātor, ōris, *m,* informer

dēlectābĭlis, e, *adj,* delightful

dēlectātĭo, ōnis, *f,* delight, pleasure

dēlecto, *v.t.* 1, to allure, charm

dēlectus, a, um, *adj,* chosen

dēlectus, ūs, *m,* choice, selection, levy

dēlectum hăbēre, to hold a levy

dēlēgo, *v.t.* 1, to dispatch, assign, attribute

dēlēnĭmentum, i, *n,* allurement

dēlēnĭo, *v.t.* 4, to soothe, charm

dēlĕo, lēvi, lētum, *v.t.* 2, to destroy, finish

dēlībĕrātĭo, ōnis, *f,* careful thought

dēlībĕrātus, a, um, *adj,* settled

dēlībĕro, *v.t.* 1, to consider, consult, resolve

dēlībo, *v.t.* 1, to taste, pluck, detract from

dēlībūtus, a, um, *adj,* smeared

dēlĭcātus, a, um, *adj, adv,* e, charming, luxurious

dēlĭcĭae, ārum, *f. pl,* pleasure, luxury, sweetheart, pet

dēlictum, i, *n,* crime, offence

dēlĭgo, lēgi, lectum, *v.t.* 3, to pick, choose, gather

dēlĭgo, *v.t.* 1, to tie down

dēlinquo, līqui, lictum, *v.i.* 3, to fail, offend

dēlīrātĭo, ōnis, *f,* silliness

dēlīrĭum, ii, *n,* delirium

dēlīro, *v.i.* 1, to be out of one's mind

dēlīrus, a, um, *adj,* crazy

dēlĭtesco, tŭi, *v.i.* 3, to lurk

delphīnus, i, *m,* dolphin

dēlūbrum, i, *n,* sanctuary

dēlūdo, si, sum, *v.t.* 3, to mock

dēmando, *v.t.* 1, to entrust

dēmens, ntis, *adj, adv,* nter, out of one's mind

dēmensum, i, *n,* ration

dēmentĭa, ae, *f,* insanity

dēmĕrĕo, *v.t.* 2, to deserve, oblige

dēmergo, si, sum, *v.t.* 3, to immerse, sink

dēmētĭor, mensus, *v.t.* 4, *dep,* to measure off

dēmĕto, messŭi, ssum, *v.t.* 3, to mow, reap, gather

dēmigro, *v.i.* 1, to emigrate

dēmĭnŭo, ŭi, ūtum, *v.t.* 3, to lessen, infringe

dēmĭnūtĭo, ōnis, *f,* decrease

dēmīror, *v.t.* 1, *dep,* to wonder

dēmissĭo, ōnis, *f,* abasement

dēmissus, a, um, *adj, adv,* ē, low-lying, drooping, downcast, shy

dēmitto, mīsi, ssum, *v.t.* 3, to send down, lower, descend, enter upon, lose heart

dēmo, mpsi, mptum, *v.t.* 3, to take away, remove

dēmōlĭor, *v.t.* 4, *dep,* to pull down, destroy

dēmonstrātĭo, ōnis, *f,* indication

dēmonstro, *v.t.* 1, to point out

dēmŏrĭor, mortŭus, *v.i.* 3, *dep,* to die

dēmŏror, *v.i.t.* 1, *dep,* to loiter; restrain

dēmŏvĕo, mōvi, mōtum, *v.t.* 2, to remove, put aside

dēmum, *adv,* at last, not until then, only

dēmūto, *v.i.t.* 1, to change

dēnārĭus, ii, *m,* small Roman silver coin

dēnăto, *v.i.* 1, to swim down

dēnĕgo, *v.t.* 1, to deny completely

dēni, ae, a, *adj,* ten each, ten

dēnīque, *adv,* and then, at last, in short

dēnōmĭno, *v.t.* 1, to name

dēnormo, *v.t.* 1, to disfigure

dēnŏto, *v.t.* 1, to mark out, point out

dens, ntis, *m,* tooth, prong

denso, *v.t.* 1, to thicken, close up

densus, a, um, *adj,* thick, frequent

dentālĭa, ium, *n.pl,* plough-beam

dentātus, a, um, *adj,* with teeth

dentĭfrĭcĭum, ii, *n,* tooth-powder

dentĭo, *v.i.* 4, to teethe

dentĭtĭo, ōnis, *f,* teething

dentiscalpĭum, ii, *n,* toothpick

dēnūbo, psi, ptum, *v.i.* 3, to marry

dēnūdo, *v.t.* 1, to lay bare

dēnuntĭātĭo, ōnis, *f,* declaration

dēnuntĭo, *v.t.* 1, to announce, command, warn

dēnŭō, *adv*, anew, again

dĕorsum, *adv*, downwards

dēpāciscor, see dēpēciscor

dēpasco, pāvi, pastum, *v.t.* 3, to feed on, consume

dēpēciscor, pectus (pactus), *v.t.* 3, *dep*, to bargain for

dēpēcŭlor, *v.t.* 1, *dep*, to plunder

dēpello, pŭli, pulsum, *v.t.* 3, to drive away, dissuade

dēpendĕo, *v.i.* 2, to hang down, depend on

dēpendo, di, sum, *v.t.* 3, to spend, pay

dēperdo, dĭdi, dĭtum, *v.t.* 3, to destroy, lose

dēpērĕo, *v.i.* 4, to perish completely, die with love for

dēpingo, pinxi, pictum, *v.t.* 3, to paint, portray, sketch

dēplōro, *v.i.t.* 1, to lament; deplore

dēpōno, pōsŭi, pōsĭtum, *v.t.* 3, to put aside, entrust, bet, get rid of

dēpōpŭlātĭo, ōnis, *f*, pillaging

dēpōpŭlor, *v.t.* 1, *dep*, to plunder

dēporto, *v.t.* 1, to carry down, carry away, banish, earn

dēposco, pōposci, *v.t.* 3, to demand, challenge

dēpōsĭtum, i, *n*, deposit, trust

dēprāvātĭo, ōnis, *f*, corruption

dēprāvo, *v.t.* 1, to pervert, corrupt

dēprĕcātĭo, ōnis, *f*, pleading, intercession

dēprĕcātor, ōris, *m*, pleader

dēprĕcor, *v.t.* 1, *dep*, to avert by prayer, beseech, plead for

dēprĕhendo, di, sum, *v.t.* 3, to catch, overtake, discover

dēpressus, a, um, *adj*, low-lying

dēprĭmo, pressi, pressum, *v.t.* 3, to press down, sink, suppress

dēproelior, *v.i.* 1, *dep*, to battle fiercely

dēprōmo, mpsi, mptum, *v.t.* 3, to fetch out

dēprŏpĕro, *v.i.t.* 1, to hasten; prepare hastily

dēpugno, *v.i.* 1, to fight it out

dēpulsĭo, ōnis, *f*, warding off

dēpŭto, *v.t.* 1, to prune

dērēlinquo, līqui, lictum, *v.t.* 3, to abandon completely

dērĭdĕo, si, sum, *v.t.* 2, to mock

dērĭgesco, gŭi, *v.i.* 3, to stiffen

dērĭpĭo, rĭpŭi, reptum, *v.t.* 3, to tear off, pull down

dērīsor, ōris, *m*, scoffer

dērīvātĭo, ōnis, *f*, turning off

dērīvo, *v.t.* 1, to divert water

dērŏgo, *v.t.* 1, to remove, restrict

dērōsus, a, um, *adj*, nibbled

dēruptus, a, um, *adj*, broken, steep

dēsaevĭo, *v.i.* 4, to rage

dēscendo, di, sum, *v.i.* 3, to go down, come down, go into battle, penetrate, resort to

dēscensus, ūs, *m*, descent

dēscisco, īvi, ītum, *v.i.* 3, to revolt, desert, degenerate

dēscrībo, psi, ptum, *v.t.* 3, to transcribe, describe, define, arrange

dēscripta, ōrum, *n.pl*, records

dēscriptĭo, ōnis, *f*, sketch, description, arrangement

dēsĕco, cŭi, ctum, *v.t.* 1, to cut off

dēsĕro, rŭi, rtum, *v.t.* 3, to abandon

dēserta, ōrum, *n.pl*, desert

dēsertor, ōris, *m*, deserter

dēsertus, a, um, *adj*, abandoned

dēservĭo, *v.i.* 4, to serve wholeheartedly

dēses, ĭdis, *adj*, indolent

dēsĭdĕo, sēdi, *v.i.* 2, to sit idle

dēsīdērĭum, ĭi, *n*, longing, grief, request

dēsīdĕro, *v.t.* 1, to miss, crave for

dēsĭdĭa, ae, *f*, idleness

dēsĭdĭōsus, a, um, *adj*, lazy

dēsīdo, sēdi, *v.i.* 3, to sink down

dēsignātĭo, ōnis, *f*, description, arrangement

dēsignātor, ōris, *m*, master of ceremonies, undertaker

dēsignātus, a, um, *adj*, elect

dēsigno, *v.t.* 1, to mark out, indicate, appoint

dēsĭlĭo, sĭlŭi, sultum, *v.i.* 4, to jump down

dēsĭno, sĭi, ĭtum, *v.i.t.* 3, to cease; put an end to

dēsĭpĭo, *v.i.* 3, to be foolish

dēsisto, stĭti, stĭtum, *v.i.* 3, to leave off, halt

dēsōlātus, a, um, *adj*, forsaken

dēsōlo, *v.t.* 1, to abandon

dēspecto, *v.t.* 1, to look down on

dēspectus, ūs, *m*, view down on

dēspectus, a, um, *adj*, despicable

dēspērātĭo, ōnis, *f*, hopelessness

dēspērātus, a, um, *adj*, past hope

dēspēro, *v.i.t.* 1, to despair; give up as lost

dēspĭcĭo, exi, ctum, *v.i.t.* 3, to look down; despise

dēspŏlĭo, *v.t.* 1, to plunder

dēspondĕo, di, nsum, *v.t.* 2, to promise (in marriage)

dēspūmo, *v.t.* 1, to skim off

dēspŭo, *v.i.t.* 3, to spit; reject

dēstillo, *v.i.* 1, to trickle, drip

dēstĭnātĭo, ōnis, *f*, purpose

For List of Abbreviations used, turn to pages 3, 4

dēstĭnātum, ĭ, *n*, aim, intention

dēstĭnātus, a, um, *adj*, fixed

dēstĭno, *v.t.* 1, to secure, intend

dēstĭtŭo, ŭi, ūtum, *v.t.* 3, to place, desert

dēstĭtūtus, a, um, *adj*, abandoned

dēstringo, nxi, ctum, *v.t.* 3, to strip off, unsheath, graze

dēstrŭo, xi, ctum, *v.t.* 3, to demolish

dēsŭesco, sŭēvi, sŭētum, *v.i.t.* 3, to become unused; cease to use

dēsŭētus, a, um, *adj*, disused

dēsultor, ōris, *m*, acrobat on horseback

dēsum, dĕesse, dēfŭi, *v.i*, to be lacking, fail, desert

dēsūmo, mpsi, mptum, *v.t.* 3, to select

dēsŭpĕr, *adv*, from above

dēsurgo, *v.i.* 3, to rise from

dētĕgo, xi, ctum, *v.t.* 3, to expose

dētentus, a, um, *adj*, kept back

dētergĕo, si, sum, *v.t.* 2, to wipe clean

dētĕrĭor, ĭus, *adj*, lower, worse

dētĕrĭus, *adv*, worse, less

dētermĭno, *v.t.* 1, to fix limits

dētĕro, trīvi, trītum, *v.t.* 3, to rub or wear away, impair

dēterrĕo, *v.t.* 2, to discourage

dētestābĭlis, e, *adj*, detestable

dētestātĭo, ōnis, *f*, cursing

dētestor, *v.t.* 1, *dep*, to curse, loathe, ward off

dētexo, xŭi, xtum, *v.t.* 3, to weave, finish

dētĭnĕo, tĭnŭi, tentum, *v.t.* 2, to keep back, delay, lengthen

dētŏno, ŭi, *v.i.* 1, to thunder, cease thundering

dētorquĕo, si, tum, *v.t.* 2, to turn aside, distort

dētrăho, xi, ctum, *v.t.* 3, to pull down, remove, deprecate

dētrecto, *v.t.* 1, to reject, detract from

dētrīmentum, ĭ, *n*, loss, damage, defeat

dētrūdo, si, sum, *v.t.* 3, to push down, dislodge

dētrunco, *v.t.* 1, to lop off

dēturbo, *v.t.* 1, to throw down

dēūro, ussi, ustum, *v.t.* 3, to burn

dĕus, ĭ, *m*, god

dēvasto, *v.t.* 1, to devastate

dēvĕho, xi, ctum, *v.t.* 3, to carry down, carry away

dēvĕnĭo, vēni, ventum, *v.i.* 4, to come down, arrive at

dēversor, *vi.* 1, *dep*, to lodge

dēversor, ōris, *m*, lodger

dēversōrĭum, ĭi, *n*, inn

dēverto, ti, sum, *v.i.t.* 3, to lodge, stay; turn aside

dēvexus, a, um, *adj*, sloping down

dēvia, ōrum, *n.pl*, lonely places

dēvincĭo, nxi, nctum, *v.t.* 4, to tie up, endear

dēvinco, vīci, ctum, *v.t.* 3, to conquer completely

dēvinctus, see dēvincĭo

dēvĭto, *v.t.* 1, to avoid

dēvĭus, a, um, *adj*, out-of-the-way

dēvŏco, *v.t.* 1, to call away

dēvŏlo, *v.i.* 1, to fly down

dēvolvo, volvi, vŏlūtum, *v.t.* 3, to roll down

dēvŏro, *v.t.* 1, to gulp down

dēvōtĭo, ōnis, *f*, consecration

dēvōtus, a, um, *adj*, devoted

dēvŏvĕo, vōvi, vōtum, *v.t.* 2, to dedicate, doom, devote

dexter, tĕra, tĕrum (tra, trum), *adj*, on the right, skilful, suitable

dextĕra (dextra), ae, *f*, right hand

dextĕrĭtas, ātis, *f*, dexterity

dextrorsum, *adv*, to the right

di, *pl.* of dĕus

diădēma, ătis, *n*, crown, diadem

diăgōnālis, e, *adj*, diagonal

diălecticus, a, um, *adj*, of debate

diălŏgus, ĭ, *m*, conversation

diāria, ōrum, *n.pl*, rations

dīca, ae, *f*, lawsuit

dĭcācĭtas, ātis, *f*, wit

dĭcax, ācis, *adj*, witty

dĭcĭo, ōnis, *f*, dominion, power

dīco, *v.t.* 1, to dedicate, devote

dīco, xi, ctum, *v.t.* 3, to say, tell, appoint

dicta, see dictum

dictāta, ōrum, *n.pl*, written exercises

dictātĭo, ōnis, *f*, dictation

dictātor, ōris, *m*, dictator (Roman magistrate appointed in emergencies)

dictātūra, ae, *f*, dictatorship

dictĭo, ōnis, *f*, speaking, style

dictĭto, *v.t.* 1, to repeat, dictate, compose

dicto, *v.t.* 1, to declare, dictate

dictum, ĭ, *n*, saying, proverb, order

dictus, a, um, *adj*, said, told

dīdo, dīdĭdi, dīdĭtum, *v.t.* 3, to distribute

dīdūco, xi, ctum, *v.t.* 3, to divide, scatter

dĭēs, dĭēi, *m*, *f*, day

diffĕro, differre, distŭli, dīlātum, *v.i.t.*, *irreg*, to differ; scatter, publish, defer

differtus, a, um, *adj,* crowded

diffībŭlo, *v.t.* 1, to unbuckle

difficĭlis, e, *adj, adv,* **ē, ĭter,** difficult, surly

difficultas, ātis, *f,* difficulty, obstinacy

diffīdens, ntis, *adj,* distrustful

diffīdentĭa, ae, *f,* mistrust, despair

diffīdo, fīsus sum, *v.i.* 3, *semi-dep. with dative,* to mistrust, despair

diffindo, fīdi, fīsum, *v.t.* 3, to split, divide

diffingo, *v.t.* 3, to re-shape

diffĭtĕor, *v.t.* 2, *dep,* to deny

difflŭo, *v.i.* 3, to flow away

diffūgĭo, fūgi, *v.i.* 3, to disperse

diffundo, fūdi, fūsum, *v.t.* 3, to pour out, scatter

diffūsus, a, um, *adj, adv,* **ē,** spread out, wide

dīgĕro, gessi, gestum, *v.t.* 3, to separate, arrange, interpret

dīgesta, ōrum, *n.pl,* digest of writings

dīgĭtus, i, *m,* finger, toe, inch

dīglādĭor, *v.i.* 1, *dep,* to fight fiercely

dignātĭo, ōnis, *f,* reputation

dignĭtas, ātis, *f,* worthiness, rank, authority

dignor, *v.t.* 1, *dep,* to consider someone worthy

dignus, a, um, *adj, adv,* **ē,** *with abl,* worthy, suitable

dīgrĕdĭor, gressus, *v.i.* 3, *dep,* to go away

dīgressĭo, ōnis, *f,* digression

dīgressus, ūs, *m,* departure

dĭiūdĭco, *v.t.* 1, to decide

dĭiun . . . see **dĭsiun . . .**

dīlābor, lapsus, *v.i.* 3, *dep,* to dissolve, scatter, perish

dīlăcĕro, *v.t.* 1, to tear apart, or to pieces

dīlănĭo, *v.t.* 1, to tear apart, or to pieces

dīlātĭo, ōnis, *f,* delay

dīlāto, *v.t.* 1, to enlarge

dīlātor, ōris, *m,* delayer

dīlātus, a, um, *adj,* scattered

dīlectus, a, um, *adj,* beloved

dīlĭgens, ntis, *adj, adv,* **nter,** scrupulous, thrifty

dīlĭgentĭa, ae, *f,* care, economy

dīlĭgo, lexi, lectum, *v.t.* 3, to value highly

dīlūcesco, luxi, *v.i.* 3, to grow light, dawn

dīlūcĭdus, a, um, *adj,* clear

dīlūcŭlum, i, *n,* dawn

dīlŭo, ŭi, ūtum, *v.t.* 3, to wash away, dilute, drench, weaken

dīlūtum, i, *n,* solution

dīlŭvĭes, ēi, *f* **(. . . ĭum, ii,** *n),* flood, destruction

dīmētĭor, mensus, *v.t.* 4, *dep,* to measure out

dīmĭcātĭo, ōnis, *f,* struggle

dīmĭco, *v.i.* 1, to struggle

dīmĭdĭātus, a, um, *adj,* halved

dīmĭdĭum, ii, *n,* a half

dīmĭdĭus, a, um, *adj,* half

dīmissĭo, ōnis, *f,* sending out

dīmitto, mīsi, missum, *v.t.* 3, to send away, break up, disband, throw away, give up

dīmŏvĕo, mōvi, mōtum, *v.t.* 2, to divide, part, remove

dīnŭmĕro, *v.t.* 1, to count up

diplōma, ātis, *n,* official letter of recommendation

dīra, ōrum, *n.pl,* curses

dīrectus, a, um, *adj, adv,* **ē,** straight, level

dīreptĭo, ōnis, *f,* plundering

dīreptor, ōris, *m,* plunderer

dīrĭgo, rexi, ctum, *v.t.* 3, to put in a straight line, arrange

dīrĭmo, ēmi, emptum, *v.t.* 3, to part, divide, interrupt

dīrĭpĭo, ŭi, reptum, *v.t.* 3, to tear apart, plunder

dīrumpo, rūpi, plum, *v.t.* 3, to break in pieces, sever

dīrŭo, ŭi, ūtum, *v.t.* 3, to destroy

dīrus, a, um, *adj,* fearful, ill-omened

discēdo, cessi, cessum, *v.i.* 3, to depart, abandon, gape, deviate

disceptātĭo, ōnis, *f,* discussion

discepto, *v.t.* 1, to debate

discerno, crēvi, tum, *v.t.* 3, to separate, distinguish between

discerpo, psi, ptum, *v.t.* 3, to tear in pieces

discessus, ūs, *m,* departure

discĭdĭum, ii, *n,* separation

discinctus, a, um, *adj,* casually-dressed, slovenly

discindo, cĭdi, cissum, *v.t.* 3, to cut to pieces, divide

discingo, nxi, nctum, *v.t.* 3, to take off or undo (clothing)

disciplīna, ae, *f,* teaching, knowledge, system, tactics

discĭpŭlus, i, *m,* pupil

disclūdo, si, sum, *v.t.* 3, to keep apart, separate

disco, dĭdĭci, *v.t.* 3, to learn

discŏlor, ōris, *adj,* of different colours

discordĭa, ae, *f,* disagreement

discordo, *v.i.* 1, to differ

discors, dis, *adj,* disagreeing

discrĕpantĭa, ae, *f,* discrepancy

discrĕpo, ŭi, v.i. 1, to differ
discrībo, scrīpsi, ptum, v.t. 3, to distribute
discrīmen, ĭnis, n, division, distinction, crisis, danger
discrīmĭno, v.t. 1, to divide
discrūcĭo, v.t. 1, to torture
discumbo, cŭbŭi, cŭbĭtum, v.i. 3, to recline at table
discurro, curri, cursum, v.i. 3, to run about
discursus, ūs, m, bustle, activity
discus, i, m, discus, quoit
discŭtĭo, cussi, ssum, v.t. 3, to shatter, disperse
dīsertus, a, um, adj, adv, ē, fluent, clear
dīsicĭo, iēci, ctum, v.t. 3, to scatter, destroy
disiunctus, a, um, adj, adv, ē, distant, abrupt
disiungo, nxi, nctum, v.t. 3, to separate, unyoke
dispar, ăris, adj, unlike, unequal
dispăro, v.t. 1, to divide
dispello, pŭli, pulsum, v.t. 3, to drive away, scatter
dispendĭum, ii, n, expense, cost
dispenso, v.t. 1, to pay out, distribute, manage
disperdo, dĭdi, dĭtum, v.t. 3, to spoil, ruin
dispĕrĕo, v.i. 4, to perish
dispergo, si, sum, v.t. 3, to scatter about
dispertĭo, v.t. 4, to distribute
dispĭcĭo, spexi, ctum, v.i.t. 3, to look around; discern, reflect on
displĭcĕo, v.i. 2, to displease
dispōno, pŏsŭi, pŏsĭtum, v.t. 3, to arrange, dispose
dispŏsĭtus, a, um, adj, arranged
dispungo, xi, ctum, v.t. 3, to check
dispŭtātĭo, ōnis, f, debate, dispute
dispŭtātor, ōris, m, debater
dispŭto, v.i.t. 1, to theorise; examine, discuss
dissēmĭno, v.t. 1, to spread about
dissensĭo, ōnis, f, disagreement
dissentĭo, si, sum, v.i. 4, to disagree, differ
dissĕrēnat, v. impers. 1, to be clear
dissĕro, rŭi, rtum, v.t. 3, to discuss, argue
dissĭdĕo, ēdi, essum, v.i. 2, to differ, disagree
dissilĭo, ŭi, v.i. 4, to leap apart, split
dissimĭlis, e, adj, adv, ĭter, unlike, different
dissĭmĭlĭtūdo, ĭnis, f, unlikeness

dissĭmŭlātus, a, um, adj, disguised
dissĭmŭlo, v.t. 1, to disguise, hide
dissĭpātĭo, ōnis, f, scattering, destruction
dissĭpo, v.t. 1, to scatter, rout
dissŏcĭābĭlis, e, adj, dividing
dissŏcĭo, v.t. 1, to estrange
dissŏlūtĭo, ōnis, f, break-up, destruction
dissŏlūtus, a, um, adj, loose
dissolvo, solvi, sŏlūtum, v.t. 3, to unloose, separate, pay, annul, destroy
dissŏnus, ă, um, adj, discordant
dissuādĕo, si, sum, v.t. 2, to advise against
dissulto, v.i. 1, to burst apart
distans, ntis, adj, distant
distendo, di, tum, v.t. 3, to stretch out, distend, torture
distentus, a, um, adj, full
distentus, a, um, adj, busy
distinctĭo, ōnis, f, difference
distinctus, a, um, adj, adv, ē, separate, clear, adorned
distĭnĕo, tĭnŭi, tentum, v.t. 2, to keep apart, perplex, hinder
distinguo, nxi, nctum, v.t. 3, to separate, discriminate, adorn
disto, v.i. 1, to be distant, differ
distorquĕo, rsi, rtum, v.t. 2, to twist, distort, torture
distortĭo, ōnis, f, distortion
distortus, a, um, adj, deformed
distractĭo, ōnis, f, division
distractus, a, um, adj, bewildered
distrăho, xi, ctum, v.t. 3, to pull apart, divide, distract, perplex
distrĭbŭo, ŭi, ūtum, v.t. 3, to distribute
distrĭbūtē, adv, methodically
distrĭbūtĭo, ōnis, f, distribution
districtus, a, um, adj, busy, strict
distringo, nxi, ctum, v.t. 3, to stretch tight, distract the attention
disturbo, v.t. 1, to disturb, demolish, frustrate
dīto, v.t. 1, to enrich
dĭū, adv, a long time
dĭurnus, a, um, adj, daily
dĭurna, ōrum, n.pl, records
dĭūtĭnus, a, um, adj, long-lasting
dĭūtĭus, comp. adv, longer
dĭūturnĭtas, ātis, f, long duration
dĭūturnus, a, um, adj, adv, ē, long-lasting
dīva, ae, f, goddess
dīvello, velli, vulsum, v.t. 3, to tear to pieces, destroy
dīvendo, (no perfect), ĭtum, v.t. 3, to retail
dīverbĕro, v.t. 1, to cut

dīversĭtas, ātis, *f*, disagreement

dīversus, a, um, *adj, adv*, ē, opposite, contrary, hostile, separate, different

dīverto, ti, sum, *v.i.* 3, to diverge

dīves, ĭtis, *adj*, rich

dīvīdo, vīsi, sum, *v.t.* 3, to separate, distribute, destroy

dīvĭdŭus, a, um, *adj*, divisible

dīvīnĭtas, ātis, *f*, divinity

dīvīnĭtus, *adv*, providentially

dīvīno, *v.t.* 1, to prophesy

dīvīnus, a, um, *adj, adv*, ē, divine, prophetic, superhuman

dīvīnus, i, *m*, prophet

dīvīsio, ōnis, *f*, division

dīvīsor, ōris, *m*, distributor of bribes to electors

dīvĭtĭae, ārum, *f.pl.* wealth

dīvortĭum, ii, *n*, separation

dīvulgo, *v.t.* 1, to make known

dīvum, i, *n*, sky

dīvus, a, um, *adj*, divine

dīvus, i, *m* (a, ae, *f*), god, (goddess)

do, dĕdi, dătum, *v.t.* 1, to give

dŏcĕo, ŭi, doctum, *v.t.* 2, to teach, inform

dŏcĭlis, e, *adj*, easily taught

doctor, ōris, *m*, teacher

doctrīna, ae, *f*, teaching, education, learning

doctus, a, um, *adj, adv*, ē, learned, skilled

dŏcŭmentum, i, *n*, lesson, example

dōdrans, ntis, *m*, three quarters

dogma, ătis, *n*, doctrine, dogma

dŏlābra, ae, *f*, pick-axe

dŏlĕo, *v.i.t.* 2, to suffer pain; grieve, deplore

dŏlĭum, ii, *n*, large jar

dŏlo, *v.t.* 1, to chop, beat

dŏlor, ōris, *m*, pain, sorrow

dŏlōsus, a, um, *adj*, deceitful

dŏlus, i, *m*, fraud, trick

dŏmābĭlis, e, *adj*, tamable

dŏmestĭcus, a, um, *adj*, of the home

dŏmestĭci, ōrum, *m. pl*, family, servants, escort

dŏmi, *adv*, at home

dŏmĭcĭlĭum, ii, *n*, dwelling place

dŏmĭna, ae, *f*, mistress, lady

dŏmĭnans, ntis, *adj*, ruling

dŏmĭnātĭo, ōnis, *f*, absolute rule

dŏmĭnātus, ūs, *m*, absolute rule

dŏmĭnĭum, ii, *n*, banquet, property-ownership

dŏmĭnor, *v.i.* 1, *dep*, to reign

dŏmĭnus, i, *m*, master, owner

dŏmĭto, *v.t.* 1, to tame

dŏmĭtor, ōris, *m*, tamer

dŏmĭtus, a, um, *adj*, tamed

dŏmo, ŭi, ĭtum, *v.t.* 1, to tame, conquer

dŏmus, ūs, *f*, house, home

dōnārĭum, ii, *n*, altar, sanctuary

dōnātĭo, ōnis, *f*, donation

dōnātus, a, um, *adj*, presented

dōnĕc, *conj*, while, until

dōno, *v.t.* 1, to present, remit

dōnum, i, *n*, gift, present

dorcas, ădis, *m*, gazelle

dormĭo, *v.i.* 4, to sleep

dormīto, *v.i.* 1, to fall asleep

dorsum, i, *n*, the back, ridge, ledge

dōs, dōtis, *f*, dowry

dōtālis, e, *adj*, of a dowry

dōtātus, a, um, *adj*, endowed

dōto, *v.t.* 1, to endow

drachma, ae, *f*, small Greek silver coin

drăco, ōnis, *m*, water-snake

drŏmas, ădis, *m*, dromedary

dryas, ădis, *f*, wood-nymph

dŭbĭe, *adv*, doubtfully

dŭbĭtātĭo, ōnis, *f*, doubt, uncertainty

dŭbĭto, *v.i.t.* 1, to hesitate; doubt

dŭbĭum, ii, *n*, doubt

dŭbĭus, a, um, *adj*, doubtful, dangerous

dŭcēni, ae, a, *adj*, two hundred each

dŭcenti, ae, a, *adj*, two hundred

dūco, xi, ctum, *v.t.* 3, to lead, marry, construct, receive, prolong, consider

ductĭlis, e, *adj*, moveable, malleable

ductor, ōris, *m*, leader

ductus, ūs, *m*, bringing, leadership

dūdum, *adv*, some time ago, formerly

dulcĕ, *adv*, sweetly

dulcēdo, ĭnis, *f*, sweetness, charm

dulcĭtūdo, ĭnis, *f*, sweetness, charm

dulcis, e, *adj, adv*, ĭter, sweet, pleasant, dear

dum, *conj*, while, until, provided that

dūmētum, i, *n*, thicket

dummŏdo, *adv*, as long as

dūmōsus, a, um, *adj*, bushy

dūmus, i, *m*, bramble

dumtaxat, *adv*, in so far as, merely, at least

dŭŏ, ae, ŏ, *adj*, two

dŭŏdĕcĭes, *adv*, twelve times

dŭŏdĕcim, *adj*, twelve

dŭŏdĕcĭmus, a, um, *adj*, twelfth

dŭŏdēni, ae, a, *adj*, twelve each

dŭŏdēvīcensĭmus, a, um, *adj*, eighteenth

dŭŏdēvīginti, *adj*, eighteen

dŭŏvĭri, ōrum, *m.pl*, board or commission of two men

dŭplex, ĭcis, *adj, adv*, ĭter, double, deceitful

For List of Abbreviations used, turn to pages 3, 4

dŭplĭco, *v.t.* 1, to double

dŭplus, a um, *adj*, double

dūra, ōrum, *n.pl*, hardship

dūrābĭlis, e, *adj*, durable

dūrātus, a, um, *adj*, hardened

dūrē, *adv*, roughly

dūresco, rŭi, *v.i.* 3, to harden

dūrĭtĭa, ae, *f*, hardness, strictness, austerity

dūro, *v.i.t.* 1, to be hard, endure; harden

dūrus, a, um, *adj*, *adv*, ē, ĭter, hard, rough, harsh, stern

dux, dŭcis, *m*, leader, commander

dȳnastes, ae, *m*, chieftain

dȳsentĕrĭa, ae, *f*, dysentery

dyspnoea, ae, *f*, asthma

E

ē, *prep. with abl*, out of, from, since

ĕa, see is

ĕādem, see idem

ĕātĕnus, *adv*, so far

ĕbĕnus, i, *f*, ebony (tree)

ēbĭbo, bi, bĭtum, *v.t.* 3, to drink up, absorb, squander

ēblandĭor, *v. t.* 4, *dep*, to obtain by flattery

ēbrĭĕtas, ātis, *f*, drunkenness

ēbrĭōsus, a, um, *adj*, addicted to drink

ēbrĭus, a, um, *adj*, drunk

ēbullĭo, *v.t.* 4, to boast about

ēbŭlum, i, *n*, dwarf-elder

ĕbŭr, ŏris, *n*, ivory

ĕburnĕus, a, um, *adj*, of ivory

ecce, *demonstrative adv*, see!

ĕchīnus, i, *m*, hedgehog, sea-urchin, rinsing bowl

ēchō, ūs, *f*, echo

ecquando, *interr. adv*, at any time?

ecqui, ae, od, *interr. pron, adj*, any? anyone?

ecquis, id, *interr. pron*, anyone? anything?

ēdācĭtas, ātis, *f*, gluttony

ēdax, ācis, *adj*, greedy

ēdentŭlus, a, um, *adj*, toothless

ēdīco, xi, ctum, *v.t.* 3, to publish, declare

ēdictum, i, *n*, proclamation

ēdisco, dĭdĭci, *v.t.* 3, to learn by heart, study

ēdissĕro, rŭi, rtum, *v.t.* 3, to explain in full

ēdĭtĭo, ōnis, *f*, bringing out, publishing

ēdĭtus, a, um, *adj*, high, raised, brought out

ĕdo, ēdi, ēsum, *v.t.* 3, to eat

ēdo, dĭdi, dĭtum, *v.t.* 3, to produce, bring out, declare, cause, erect

ēdŏcĕo, cŭi, ctum, *v.t.* 2, to teach thoroughly

ēdŏmo, ŭi, ĭtum, *v.t.* 1, to subdue

ēdŭcātĭo, ōnis, *f*, bringing up, education

ēdūco, xi, ctum, *v.t.* 3, to lead or bring out, summon, educate, erect

ēdŭco, *v.t.* 1, to bring up (child)

ĕdūlis, e, *adj*, eatable

effātus, a, um, *adj*, established

effectĭo, ōnis, *f*, doing, performing

effectus, a, um, *adj*, completed

effectus, ūs, *m*, accomplishment

effēmĭnātus, a, um, *adj*, effeminate

effĕrātus, a, um, *adj*, wild

effĕro, efferre, extŭli, ēlātum, *v.t. irreg*, to bring out, bury, declare, raise; *in passive or with* se, to be haughty

effĕro, *v.t.* 1, to brutalize

effĕrus, a, um, *adj*, savage

effervesco, ferbŭi, *v.i.* 3, to boil up, rage

effervo, *v.i.* 3, to boil over

effētus, a, um, *adj*, exhausted

efficax, ācis, *adj*, efficient

efficiens, ntis, *adj*, *adv*, nter, efficient

efficĭo, fēci, fectum, *v.t.* 3, to bring about, complete, produce

effictus, a, um, *adj*, fashioned

effĭgĭes, ēi, *f*, portrait, copy

effingo, nxi, ctum, *v.t.* 3, to shape, fashion, portray

efflāgĭto, *v.t.* 1, to request urgently

efflo, *v.t.* 1, to breathe out

efflōresco, rŭi, *v.i.* 3, to bloom

efflŭo, xi, *v.i.* 3, to flow out, vanish

effŏdĭo, fōdi, fossum, *v.t.* 3, to dig out, dig up

effor, *v. t.* 1, *dep*, to speak out

effrēnātus, a, um, *adj*, unruly

effrēnus, a, um, *adj*, unrestrained

effringo, frēgi, fractum, *v.t.* 3, to break open, smash

effŭgĭo, fūgi, *v.i.t.* 3, to escape; flee from, avoid

effŭgĭum, ii, *n*, escape

effulgĕo, si, *v.i.* 2, to gleam

effundo, fūdi, fūsum, *v.t.* 3, to pour out, let loose, squander; *in pass. or with reflexive*, to rush out

effūsĭo, ōnis, *f*, outpouring, profusion

effūsus, a, um, *adj*, *adv*, ē, poured out, spread out, wide, loosened

effūtĭo, *v.t.* 4, to blurt out

ēgĕlĭdus, a, um, *adj*, cool

ĕgens, ntis, *adj*, in want of
ĕgēnus, a, um, *adj*, in want of
ĕgĕo, *v.i.* 2, *with abl*, to be in need of
ĕgĕro, ssi, stum, *v.t.* 3, to bring out
ĕgestas, ātis, *f*, poverty
ĕgŏ, *pers. pron*, I
ĕgŏmet, *pron*, I myself
ĕgrĕdĭor, gressus, *v.i.t.* 3, *dep*, to go or
   come out; leave, exceed
ĕgrĕgĭus, a, um, *adj*, *adv*, ē, distinguished
ĕgressus, ūs, *m*, departure, passage
ĕheu! alas!
ēĭā! hey! I say!
ēĭācŭlor, *v. t.* 1, *dep*, to shoot out
ēĭcĭo, ĭēci, ĭectum, *v.t.* 3, to drive out,
   expel, wreck; *with reflexive*, to rush
   out
ēĭecto, *v.t.* 1, to vomit
ēĭūro, *v.t.* 1, to reject on oath,
   abandon
ēĭus, *genit. of* is, ea, id
ēĭusmŏdĭ, in such a manner
ēlābor, lapsus, *v.i.* 3, *dep*, to slip away,
   escape
ēlābŏrātus, a, um, *adj*, elaborate
ēlābŏro, *v.i.t.* 1, to make an effort;
   take pains with
ēlanguesco, gŭi, *v.i.* 3, to grow feeble
ēlātĭo, ōnis, *f*, lifting up, passion
ēlātro, *v.t.* 1, to bark loudly
ēlātus, a, um, *adj*, raised, lofty
ēlectĭo, ōnis, *f*, selection
ēlectrum, i, *n*, amber
ēlectus, a, um, *adj*, selected
ēlĕgans, ntis, *adj*, *adv*, nter, refined,
   tasteful
ēlĕgantĭa, ae, *f*, refinement
ēlĕgi, ōrum, *m. pl*, elegy
ēlĕgĭa, ae, *f*, elegy
ēlĕmentum, i, *n*, element, first principle; *pl*, rudiments
ēlĕphantus, i, *m*, elephant, ivory
ēlĕvo, *v.t.* 1, to lift up, weaken, disparage
ēlĭcĭo, cŭi, cĭtum, *v.t.* 3, to lure out,
   call out
ēlīdo, si, sum, *v.t.* 3, to knock or force
   out, shatter
ēlĭgo, lēgi, ctum, *v.t.* 3, to choose
ēlinguis, e, *adj*, speechless
ēlixus, a, um, *adj*, boiled
ellychnĭum, ii, *n*, lampwick
ēlŏco, *v.t.* 1, to let (a farm)
ēlŏcūtĭo, ōnis, *f*, expression, elocution
ēlŏgĭum, ii, *n*, saying, inscription
ēlŏquens, ntis, *adj*, eloquent
ēlŏquentĭa, ae, *f*, eloquence
ēlŏquor, ēlŏcūtus, *v. t.* 3, *dep*, to speak
   out, declare

ēlūcĕo, xi, *v.i.* 2, to shine out
ēluctor, *v.i.t.* 1, *dep*, to struggle out;
   struggle out of
ēlūdo, si, sum, *v.t.* 3, to evade, cheat,
   frustrate
ēlūgĕo, xi, *v.t.* 2, to mourn for
ēlŭo, ŭi, ūtum, *v.t.* 3, to wash off,
   clean
ēlūtus, a, um, *adj*, insipid
ēlŭvies, *no genit*, *f*, inundation
ēlŭvĭo, ōnis, *f*, inundation
ēmancĭpo, *v.t.* 1, to set free, transfer,
   sell
ēmāno, *v.i.* 1, to flow out, arise from
embŏlĭum ii, *n*, interlude
ēmendātĭo, ōnis, *f*, correction
ēmendātor, ōris, *m*, corrector
ēmendātus, a, um, *adj*, faultless
ēmendo, *v.t.* 1, to correct
ēmentĭor, *v. t.* 4, *dep*, to assert falsely
ēmercor, *v. t.* 1, *dep*, to purchase
ēmĕrĕo, *v.t.* 2 (ēmĕrĕor, *v.t.* 2, *dep*), to
   deserve, earn, complete one's military service
ēmergo, si, sum, *v.i.* 3, to come out,
   escape
ēmĕrĭtus, a, um, *adj*, worn out
ēmētĭor, mensus, *v.t.* 4, *dep*, to measure
   out, travel over
ēmĭco, ŭi, ātum, *v.f.* 1, to spring out,
   appear
ēmĭgro, *v.i.* 1, to depart
ēmĭnens, ntis, *adj*, projecting, distinguished
ēmĭnentĭa, ae, *f*, prominence
ēmĭnĕo, *v. i.* 2, to stand out, excel
ēmĭnus, *adv*, from or at a distance
ēmissārĭum, ii, *n*, drain, vent
ēmissārĭus, ii, *m*, spy
ēmissĭo, ōnis, *f*, sending out, hurling
   (of missiles)
ēmitto, mīsi, ssum, *v.t.* 3, to send out,
   produce, publish; *with manū*, to
   set free
ēmo, ēmi, emptum, *v.t.* 3, to buy
ēmŏdŭlor, *v. t.* 1, *dep*, to sing
ēmollĭo, *v.t.* 4, to soften
ēmŏlŭmentum, i, *n*, effort, profit
ēmŏrĭor, mortuus, *v.i.* 3, *dep*, to die
ēmŏvĕo, mōvi, tum, *v.t.* 2, to remove,
   shake
empīrĭcus, a, um, *adj*, empirical
emplastrum, i, *n*, plaster
empŏrĭum, ii, *n*, market
emptĭo, ōnis, *f*, purchase
emptor, ōris, *m*, buyer
ēmunctus, a, um, *adj*, clean, shrewd
ēmungo, nxi, nctum, *v.t.* 3, to wipe the
   nose
ēmūnĭo, *v.t.* 4, to fortify

ēn! see! come!

ēnarro, v.t. 1, to expound

ēnascor, nātus, v. i. 3, dep, to spring up, be born

ēnăto, v.i. 1, to swim away

ēnectus, a, um, adj, killed

ēnĕco, ŭi, ctum, v.t. 1, to kill, exhaust

ēnervo, v.t. 1, to weaken

ēnim, conj, for, indeed

ēnimvēro, conj, certainly

ēnīsus, a, um, adj, strenuous

ēnĭtĕo, v.i. 2, to shine out

ēnĭtesco, tŭi, v.i. 3, to shine out

ēnītor, nīsus (nixus), v. i. t. 3, dep, to struggle upwards, climb, strive; give birth to, ascend

ēnixus, a, um, adj, adv, ē, strenuous, earnest

ēno, v.i. 1, to swim out or away

ēnōdātĭo, ōnis, f, explanation

ēnōdis, e, adj, smooth, clear

ēnōdo, v.t. 1, to elucidate

ēnormis, e, adj, enormous, shapeless

ēnormĭtas, ātis, f, shapelessness

ēnŏto, v.t. 1, to note down

ensĭger, ĕra, ĕrum, adj, carrying a sword

ensis, is, m, sword

ēnūclĕātus, a, um, adj, adv, ē, pure, clear, simple

ēnŭmĕrātĭo, ōnis, f, counting, recapitulation

ēnŭmĕro, v.t. 1, to count, relate

ēnuntĭo, v.t. 1, to disclose, declare

ĕo, īre, īvi (ii), ĭtum, v.i. irreg, to go; with pedibus, to vote for

ĕō, adv, to that place, to such an extent, so long, besides

eo . . . quo, (with comparatives) the more . . . the more

ĕōdem, adv, to the same place, to the same point or purpose

ĕōus, i, m, (a, um, adj), east

ĕphēbus, i, m, a youth

ĕphippĭum, ii, n, saddle

ĕphŏrus, i, m, Spartan magistrate

ĕpĭcus, a, um, adj, epic

ĕpiscŏpus, i, m, bishop

ĕpĭgramma, ătis, n, inscription

ĕpistŏla, ae, f, letter

ĕpistŏmĭum, ii, n, valve

ĕpĭtŏmē (ĕpĭtŏma), ēs, f, abridgement

ĕpōs, n, epic poem

ēpōto, pōtum, v.t. 1, to drink up

ēpŭlae, ārum, f. pl, food, banquet

ēpŭlor, v.i.t. 1, dep, to banquet; eat

ĕqua, ae, f, mare

ĕquārĭa, ae, f, stud of horses

ĕques, ĭtis, m, horseman, Knight

ĕquester, tris, tre, adj, of a horseman, of cavalry

ĕquĭdem, adv, indeed, of course, for my part

ĕquīnus, a, um, adj, of horses

ĕquĭtātĭo, ōnis, f, riding on horseback

ĕquĭtātus, ūs, m, cavalry

ĕquĭto, v.i. 1, to ride

ĕquŭlĕus, i, m, colt, the rack

ĕquus, i, m, horse

ēra, ae, f, lady of the house

ērādīco, v.t. 1, to root out

ērādo, si, sum, v.t. 3, to scrape out, abolish

ērectus, a, um, adj, upright, noble, haughty, resolute

ērēpo, psi, v.i.t. 3, to creep out; creep over

ergā, prep. with acc, towards

ergastŭlum, i, n, detention centre

ergō, adv, therefore; prep. following genit, on account of

ērigo, rexi, rectum, v.t. 3, to raise up, encourage

ērīlis, e, adj, of the master, or mistress

ērĭpĭo, rĭpŭi, reptum, v.t. 3, to snatch, take away; with reflexive, to escape

ērŏgātĭo, ōnis, f, paying out

ērŏgo, v.t. 1, to pay out, squander

errābundus, a, um, adj, wandering

errātĭcus, a, um, adj, rambling

errātum, i, n, mistake

erro, v.i. 1, to stray, err

erro, ōnis, m, wanderer

error, ōris, m, straying, mistake

ērŭbesco, bŭi, v.i. 3, to blush, feel ashamed

ērūca, ae, f, caterpillar

ēructo, v.t. 1, to belch, emit

ērŭdĭo, v.t. 4, to polish, instruct

ērŭdītĭo, ōnis, f, learning

ērŭditus, a, um, adj, adv, ē, learned, skilled

ērumpo, rūpi, ptum, v.i.t. 3, to break out; burst

ērŭo, ŭi, ŭtum, v.t. 3, to throw out, dig out, destroy, rescue

ēruptĭo, ōnis, f, break-out

ĕrus, i, m, master of the house

ervum, i, n, wild pea

esca, ae, f, food, bait

escendo, di, sum, v.i. 3, to climb

escensĭo, ōnis, f, ascent

escŭlentus, a, um, adj, eatable

esse, see sum

essĕdārĭus, i, m, chariot-fighter

essĕdum, i, n, war-chariot

ēsŭrĭens, ntis, adj, hungry

ēsŭrĭo, *v.i.t.* 4, to be hungry; long for

ĕt, *conj*, and, as

ĕtĕnim, *conj*, and indeed

ĕtĭam, *conj*, also, even, still

ĕtĭamnum, ĕtĭamnunc, *adv*, even then, till now

etsi, *conj*, although, even if

eu!, well done!

eurĭpus, i, *m*, canal

eurōus, a, um, *adj*, eastern

eurus, i, *m*, east wind

ēvādo, si, sum, *v.i.t.* 3, to go out, escape; leave behind

ēvăgor, *v.i.t.* 1, *dep.* to stray; overstep

ēvălesco, lŭi, *v.i.* 3, to grow strong, to be able

ēvānesco, nŭi, *v.i.* 3, to vanish

ēvānĭdus, a, um, *adj*, vanishing

ēvasto, *v.t.* 1, to devastate

ēvĕho, xi, ctum, *v.t.* 3, to carry out; *in passive*, to ride or move out

ēvello, velli, vulsum, *v.t.* 3, to tear out, eradicate

ēvĕnĭo, vēni, ventum, *v.i.* 4, to come out, turn out, result

ēventum, i, *n*, occurrence, result, fortune

ēventus, ūs, *m*, occurrence, result, fortune

ēverbĕro, *v.t.* 1, to strike hard

ēverro, verri, versum, *v.t.* 3, to sweep out

ēversĭo, ōnis, *f*, destruction

ēversor, ōris, *m*, destroyer

ēversus, a, um, *adj*, overthrown

ēverto, ti, sum, *v.t.* 3, to overthrow, ruin

ēvĭdens, ntis, *adj*, apparent

ēvĭgĭlo, *v.i.t.* 1, to wake up; keep awake, keep watch through

ēvincĭo, nxi, nctum, *v.t.* 4, to bind round

ēvinco, vīci, ctum, *v.t.* 3, to conquer completely, succeed

ēviscĕro, *v.t.* 1, to tear apart

ēvĭto, *v.t.* 1, to avoid

ēvŏcāti, ōrum, *m. pl*, reservists

ēvŏco, *v.t.* 1, to call out

ēvŏlo, *v.i.* 1, to fly away

ēvolvo, vi, vŏlūtum, *v.t.* 3, to unroll (and read a book), disclose

ēvŏmo, ŭi, ĭtum, *v.t.* 3, to spit out, vomit

ēvulsĭo, ōnis, *f*, pulling out

ex(ē), *prep. with abl*, out of, from, after, since, on account of, according to, made of

exăcerbo, *v.t.* 1, to irritate

exactĭo, ōnis, *f*, debt or tax collecting, expelling

exactor, ōris, *m*, expeller, superintendent, tax-collector

exactus, a, um, *adj*, accurate

exăcŭo, ŭi, ūtum, *v.t.* 3, to sharpen, stimulate

exadversum (. . . us), *adv. and prep. with acc*, opposite

exaedĭfĭco, *v.t.* 1, to construct

exaequo, *v.t.* 1, to place equal

exaestŭo, *v.i.* 1, to seethe

exaggĕro, *v.t.* 1, to heap up

exăgĭto, *v.t.* 1, to disturb

exalbesco, bŭi, *v.i.* 3, to turn pale

exāmen, ĭnis, *n*, crowd, swarm

exāmĭno, *v.t.* 1, to weigh, test

exănĭmātĭo, ōnis, *f*, terror

exănĭmatus, a, um, *adj*, out of breath

exănĭmis, e, *adj*, lifeless

exănĭmus, a, um, *adj*, lifeless

exănĭmo, *v.t.* 1, to deprive of breath, kill, terrify

exardesco, arsi, sum, *v.i.* 3, to be inflamed

exāresco, rŭi, *v.i.* 3, to dry up

exāro, *v.t.* 1, to plough, write

exaspĕro, *v.t.* 1, to roughen, provoke

exauctōro, *v.t.* 1, to discharge honourably or dishonourably from army

exaudĭo, *v.t.* 4, to hear, grant

cxcandcsco, dŭi, *v.i.* 3, to glow

excēdo, ssi, ssum, *v.i.t.* 3, to depart, die; leave, exceed

excellens, ntis, *adj*, *adv*, nter, distinguished, excellent

excello, cellŭi, lsum, *v.i.* 3, to be eminent, excel

excelsus, a, um, *adj*, distinguished

exceptĭo, ōnis, *f*, restriction

excepto, *v.t.* 1, to catch

excerno, crēvi, crētum, *v.t.* 3, to separate

excerpo, psi, ptum, *v.t.* 3, to select

excessus, ūs, *m*, departure

excidĭum, ii, *n*, destruction

excĭdo, cĭdi, *v.i.* 3, to fall from, escape, disappear, slip the memory, fail in

excīdo, cīdi, cīsum, *v.t.* 3, to cut down, destroy

excĭo, *v.t.* 4, to call or bring out.

excĭpĭo, cēpi, ceptum, *v.t.* 3, to take out, make an exception, receive, capture, follow after, overhear, intercept

excĭtātus, a, um, *adj*, roused, vigorous

excĭto, *v.t.* 1, to rouse up, excite

exclāmātĭo, ōnis, *f*, exclamation

exclāmo, *v.i.t.* 1, to call out

exclūdo, si, sum, *v.t.* 3, to shut out, drive out, remove, hinder, hatch

exclūsĭo, ōnis, *f*, exclusion

For List of Abbreviations used, turn to pages 3, 4

excōgĭto, *v.t.* 1, to think out

excŏlo, cŏlŭi, cultum, *v.t.* 3, to cultivate, improve, refine

excŏquo, xi, ctum, *v.t.* 3, to boil away, purify

excors, dis, *adj*, stupid

excresco, crēvi, crētum, *v.i.* 3, to grow up

excrētus, a, um, *adj*, full grown

excrētus, a, um, *adj*, separated

excrŭcio, *v.t.* 1, to torture

excŭbiae, ārum, *f. pl*, watch, guard

excŭbĭtor, ōris, *m*, watchman

excŭbo, ŭi, ĭtum, *v.i.* 1, to sleep out of doors, keep watch

excūdo, di, sum, *v.t.* 3, to hammer out

exculco, *v.t.* 1, to trample down

excurro, cŭcurri, cursum, *v.i.* 3, to run out, make a sortie, extend

excursĭo, ōnis, *f*, attack, invasion, sally

excursus, ūs, *m*, attack, invasion, sally

excūsābĭlis, e, *adj*, excusable

excūsātĭo, ōnis, *f*, excuse

excūso, *v.t.* 1, to excuse, plead in excuse

excŭtĭo, cussi, cussum, *v.t.* 3, to shake off, get rid of, hurl, examine

exĕdo, ēdi, ēsum, *v.t.* 3, to eat up

exemplar, āris, *n*, copy, model

exemplum, i, *n*, copy, model, precedent, warning, example

exemptus, a, um, *adj*, removed

exĕo, *v.i.t.* 4, to depart, run out (time), die; cross, avoid

exercĕo, *v.t.* 2, to keep busy, train, exercise, pester

exercĭtātĭo, ōnis, *f*, practice

exercĭtātus, a, um, *adj*, trained

exercĭtor, ōris, *m*, trainer

exercĭtus, ūs, *m*, army

exercĭtus, a, um, *adj*, trained, harrassed

exhālātĭo, ōnis, *f*, exhalation

exhālo, *v.t.* 1, to breathe out

exhaurĭo, si, stum, *v.t.* 4, to draw out, exhaust, empty

exhaustus, a, um, *adj*, drained, worn out

exhērēdo, *v.t.* 1, to disinherit

exhĭbĕo, *v.t.* 2, to present, display, procure, cause

exhĭbĭtus, a, um, *adj*, produced

exhĭlăro, *v.t.* 1, to delight

exhorresco, rŭi, *v.i.t.* 3, to tremble; shrink from, dread

exhortor, *v. t.* 1, *dep*, to encourage

exiens, see exeo

exĭgo, ēgi, actum, *v.t.* 3, to drive out, enforce, demand, complete, examine, estimate, spend (time)

exĭgŭĭtas, ātis, *f*, small size

exĭgŭus, a, um, *adj*, *adv*, ē, small, short

exīlis, e, *adj*, *adv*, ĭter, small, thin, feeble, insignificant

exĭlĭum, ii, *n*, exile

exĭmĭus, a, um, *adj*, *adv*, ē, unusual, distinguished

exĭmo, ēmi, emptum, *v.t.* 3, to take away, free, waste

exĭnānĭo, *v.t.* 4, to empty

exindē (exin), *adv*, from there, then, next, accordingly

existĭmātĭo, ōnis, *f*, opinion, reputation, character

existĭmātor, ōris, *m*, critic

existĭmo, *v.t.* 1, to estimate, think

exĭtĭābĭlis, e, *adj*, fatal, deadly

exĭtĭālis, e, *adj*, fatal, deadly

exĭtĭōsus, a, um, *adj*, destructive

exĭtĭum, ii, *n*, destruction

exĭtus, ūs, *m*, departure, outlet, conclusion, result, death

exŏlesco, ŏlēvi, lētum, *v.i.* 3, to grow up, disappear

exŏnĕro, *v.t.* 1, to unload

exoptātus, a, um, *adj*, longed for

exopto, *v.t.* 1, to long for

exōrābĭlis, e, *adj*, easily persuaded

exordĭor, orsus, *v. t.* 4, *dep*, to begin, weave

exordĭum, ii, *n*, beginning, introduction

exŏrĭor, ortus, *v. i.* 4, *dep*, to spring up, arise, appear

exornātĭo, ōnis, *f*, decoration

exorno, *v.t.* 1, to equip, adorn

exōro, *v.t.* 1, to prevail upon

exorsus, a, um, *adj*, begun

exortus, ūs, *m*, rising

exōsus, a, um, *adj*, hating, detested

expăvesco, pāvi, *v.i.t.* 3, to be afraid; dread

expect, see exspect

expēdĭo, *v.t.* 4, to set free, prepare, arrange, explain; *impers*, it is expedient

expēdītĭo, ōnis, *f*, campaign

expēdītē, *adv*, promptly

expēdītus, a, um, *adj*, ready

expēdītus, i, *m*, soldier in light-marching-order

expello, pŭli, pulsum, *v.t.* 3, to drive away

expendo, di, sum, *v.t.* 3, to pay out, consider, pay the penalty expergĕfăcĭo, fēci, factum, v.t. 3, to arouse

expergiscor, perrectus, v.i. 3, dep. to awake

expĕrĭens, ntis, adj, enterprising

expĕrĭentĭa, ae, f, experiment, practice

expĕrīmentum, i, n, proof, experience

expĕrĭor, pertus, v. t. 4, dep, to prove, test, try; perf, know from experience

expers, rtis, adj, devoid of

expertus, a, um, adj, proved

expĕto, īvi (ii), ītum, v.t. 3, to long for, aim at, reach

expĭātĭo, ōnis, f, atonement

expīlo, v.t. 1, to plunder

expīlātĭo, ōnis, f, plundering

expingo, nxi, ctum, v.t. 3, to paint

expĭo, v.t. 1, to atone for

expiscor, v. t. 1, dep, to search out

explānātĭo, ōnis, f, explanation

explāno, v.t. 1, to explain

explĕo, ēvi, ētum, v.t. 2, to fill up, fulfil, finish

explētĭo, ōnis, f, satisfying

explētus, a, um, adj, full, complete

explĭcātĭo, ōnis, f, unfolding, explanation

explĭcātus, a, um, adj, spread-out, plain

explĭco, v.t. 1, (or ... ŭi ... ītum) to unfold, spread out, deploy, arrange, explain

explōdo, si, sum, v.t. 3, to hiss off the stage, disapprove

explōrātor, ōris, m, spy, scout

explōrātus, a, um, adj, adv, ē, established, certain

explōro, v.t. 1, to search out, spy, test

expŏlĭo, v.t. 4, to polish

expōno, pŏsŭi, pŏsĭtum, v.t. 3, to expose, put on shore, explain

exporto, v.t. 1, to carry away

exposco, pŏposci, v.t. 3, to implore, require

expŏsĭtĭo, ōnis, f, elucidation

expŏsĭtus, a, um, adj, accessible

expostŭlātĭo, ōnis, f, complaint

expostŭlo, v.t. 1, to demand, upbraid, complain

expressus, a, um, adj, clear

exprĭmo, pressi, pressum, v.t. 3, to press out, model, extort

exprŏbrātĭo, ōnis, f, reproach

exprŏbro, v.t. 1, to reproach

exprōmo, mpsi, mptum, v.t. 3, to fetch out, display, explain

expugnātĭo, ōnis, f, capture by assault

expugno, v.t. 1, to storm, capture

expurgo, v.t. 1, to purify, justify

exquīro, sīvi, sītum, v.t. 3, to search out

exquīsītus, a, um, adj, adv, ē, choice, excellent

exsanguis, e, adj, bloodless, weak

exsātĭo, v.t. 1, to satisfy

exsātŭro, v.t. 1, to satiate

exscensĭo, ōnis, f, landing

exscindo, ĭdi, issum, v.t. 3, to destroy completely

exscrībo, psi, ptum, v.t. 3, to write out, copy

exsĕco, cŭi, ctum, v.t. 1, to cut out, cut off

exsĕcrābĭlis, e, adj, accursed

exsĕcrātĭo, ōnis, f, curse

exsĕcrātus, a, um, adj, accursed

exsĕcror, v. i.t. 1, dep, to take an oath; curse,

exsĕcūtĭo, ōnis, f, execution

exsĕquĭae, ārum, f. pl, funeral

exsĕquor, sĕcūtus, v.t. 3, dep, to pursue, follow, carry out, describe, avenge

exsĕro, rŭi, rtum, v.t. 3, to put out, uncover, protrude

exserto, v.t. 1, to stretch out

exsicco, v.t. 1, to dry up

exsĭlĭo, ĭlŭi, v.i. 4, to leap out, jump up

exsĭlĭum, ĭi, n, exile

exsisto, stĭti, stĭtum, v.i. 3, to come out, appear, arise, exist

exsolvo, solvi, sŏlūtum, v.t. 3, to unloose, free, discharge

exsomnis, e, adj, sleepless

exsorbĕo, v.t. 2, to suck up

exsors, rtis, adj, specially chosen, deprived of

exspātĭor, v.i. 1, dep, to digress, launch out

exspectātĭo, ōnis, f, expectation

exspectātus, a, um, adj, desired

exspecto, v.t. 1, to look out for, wait for, hope for

exspergo (spargo), no perfect, spersus v.t. 3, to scatter

exspīrātĭo, ōnis, f, breathing out

exspīro, v.i.t. 1, to rush out, expire, cease; breathe out

exspŏlĭo, v.t. 1, to plunder

exstĭmŭlo, v.t. 1, to goad on

exstinctor, ōris, m, destroyer

exstinctus, a, um, adj, destroyed, extinct

exstinguo, nxi, nctum, v.t. 3, to quench, kill, destroy

exstirpo, v.t. 1, to uproot

exsto, *v.i.* 1, to project, be conspicuous, exist

exstructio, ōnis, *f*, structure

exstrŭo, xi, ctum, *v.t.* 3, to heap up, build up

exsūdo, *v.t.* 1, to toil or sweat at

exsul (exul), ŭlis, *c*, an exile

exsŭlo (exulo), *v.i.* 1, to live in exile

exsultans, ntis, *adj*, boastful

exsultātio, ōnis, *f*, rapture

exsultim, *adv*, friskingly

exsulto, *v.i.* 1, to jump about, run riot, boast

exsŭpĕrābilis, e, *adj*, surmountable

exsŭpĕro, *v.i.t.* 1, to get the upper hand; pass over, exceed

exsurdo, *v.t.* 1, to deafen, dull

exsurgo, surrexi, *v.i.* 3, to rise, stand up

exsuscĭto, *v.t.* 1, to awaken

exta, ōrum, *n.pl*, the inwards

extemplō, *adv*, immediately

extendo, di, tum, *v.t.* 3, to stretch out, enlarge, prolong

extentus, a, um, *adj*, extensive

extĕnŭātio, ōnis, *f*, attenuation

extĕnŭo, *v.t.* 1, to diminish, weaken

exter (extĕrus), ĕra, ĕrum, *adj*, external, strange, foreign

extergĕo, si, sum, *v.t.* 2, to plunder

extĕrĭor, us, *comp. adj*, outer

extermĭno, *v.t.* 1, to expel

externus, a, um, *adj*, external, foreign

extĕro, trĭvi, trītum, *v.t.* 3, to rub off, wear away

exterrĕo, *v.t.* 2, to frighten

extĭmesco, mŭi, *v.i.t.* 2, to be afraid; to dread

extollo, sustŭli, *v.t.* 3, to raise

extorquĕo, si, sum, *v.t.* 2, to wrench away from, extort

extorris, e, *adj*, exiled

extrā, *adv. and prep. with acc.* outside, beyond, except

extrăho, xi, ctum, *v.t.* 3, to drag out, release, prolong

extrānĕus, i, *m*, stranger

extrăordĭnārius, a, um, *adj*, extraordinary

extrēma, ōrum, *n.pl*, last resort

extrēmĭtas, ātis, *f*, extremity

extrēmum, i, *n*, the end

extrēmum, *adv*, for the last time, finally

extrēmus, a, um, *adj*, furthest, the end of, or extremity of

extrĭco, *v.t.* 1, to disentangle

extrinsĕcus, *adv*, from, or on, the outside

extrūdo, si, sum, *v.t.* 3, to push out

extundo, tŭdi, tūsum, *v.t.* 3, to force out, hammer out

exturbo, *v.t.* 1, to drive away

exūbĕro, *v.i.* 1, to be abundant

exul, see exsul

exulcĕro, *v.t.* 1, to aggravate

exŭlŭlo, *v.i.* 1, to howl

exundo, *v.i.* 1, to overflow

exŭo, ŭi, ūtum, *v.t.* 3, to strip, deprive of, discard

exūro, ussi, ustum, *v.t.* 3, to burn up, consume

exustio, ōnis, *f*, conflagration

exŭviae, ārum, *f. pl*, stripped-off clothing or equipment

F

făba, ae, *f*, bean

fābella, ae, *f*, short story

făber, bri, *m*, smith, carpenter

făbrica, ae, *f*, workshop, a trade, a skilled work

făbricātio, ōnis, *f*, structure

făbricātor, ōris, *m*, maker

făbricor, *v.t.* 1, *dep* (fabrico, *v.t.* 1), to construct, form

făbrīlis, e, *adj*, of a craftsman

făbŭla, ae, *f*, story, play

fābŭlor, *v.t.* 1, *dep*, to talk, chat

fābŭlōsus, a, um, *adj*, legendary

făcesso, cessi, ītum, *v.i.t.* 3, to depart; perform, cause

făcētiae, ārum, *f. pl*, witticisms

făcētus, a, um, *adj*, *adv*, ē, courteous, elegant, witty

făcies, ēi, *f*, face, shape, appearance

făcĭlē, *adv*, easily

făcĭlis, e, *adj*, easy, quick, goodnatured

făcĭlitas, ātis, *f*, ease, affability

făcĭnus, ŏris, *n*, deed, crime

făcĭo, fēci, factum, *v.i.t.* 3, to do, act, to side with (cum, ab), or against (contra), to be useful; to make, do, produce, assert, pretend, practise (trade)

factio, ōnis, *f*, faction, party

factiōsus, a, um, *adj*, mutinous

factito, *v.t.* 1, to keep doing

factum, i, *n*, deed

făcultas, ātis, *f*, power, opportunity, supply

făcundia, ae, *f*, eloquence

făcundus, a, um, *adj*, *adv*, ē, eloquent

faecŭla, ae, *f*, wine-dregs

faenĕrātio, ōnis, *f*, money-lending

faenĕrātor, ōris, *m*, money-lender

faenĕrātōrius, a, um, *adj*, usurious

faeneror, v.t. 1, dep (faenero, v.t. 1), to lend on interest
faenilia, ium, n. pl, hay-loft
faenum, i, n, hay
faenus, ŏris, n, interest, profit
faex, cis, f, dregs, sediment
fāgīnĕus (nus), a, um, adj, of beech
fāgus, i, f, beech-tree
fălārīca, ae, f, burning missile
falcātus, a, um, adj, armed with scythes, curved
falcīfer, ĕra, ĕrum, adj, holding a sickle
falco, ŏnis, m, falcon
fallācĭa, ae, f, trick, deceit
fallax, ācis, adj, adv, ĭter, deceitful, fallacious
fallo, fĕfelli, falsum, v.t. 3, to deceive, betray, escape the notice of, appear
falsum, i, n, falsehood
falsus, a, um, adj, adv, ē, or o, false, counterfeit, deceptive
falx, cis, f, scythe, hook
fāma, ae, f, rumour, public opinion, reputation, fame
fāmes, is, f, hunger, famine
fămĭlĭa, ae, f, domestic servants, family property, crowd or set
fămĭliāris, o, adj, adv, ĭter, domestic, intimate
fămĭliāris, is, m, friend
fămĭliārĭtas, ătis, f, friendship
fāmōsus, a, um, adj, notorious
fămŭla, ae, f, maid-servant
fămŭlātus, ūs, m, servitude
fămŭlor, v.i. 1, dep, to serve, wait on
fămŭlus, i, m, servant
fănātĭcus, a, um, adj, inspired, frantic
fandus, a, um, adj, lawful
fānum, i, n, temple, shrine
fār, farris, n, grain, corn
farcīmen, ĭnis, n, sausage
farcio, rsi, rtum, v.t. 4, to cram
fărīna, ae, f, flour
farrāgo, ĭnis, f, hotchpotch
fartor, ōris, m, poultry-farmer
fartum, i, n, stuffing
fartūra, ae, f, cramming, padding
fās, n (indeclinable), divine law, right
fascēs, ium, m. pl, bundle of rods and axes; symbol of magistrates' power of scourging and beheading
fascĭa, ae, f, band, head-band
fascĭcŭlus, i, m, small bundle
fascĭnātĭo, ōnis, f, bewitching
fascĭno, v.t. 1, to charm, enchant
fascĭnum, i, n, lucky charm
fascĭŏla, ae, f, small bandage

fascis, is, m, bundle, pack
fassus, a, um, participle, having acknowledged
fasti, ōrum, m. pl, working days, calendar
fastīdĭo, v.i.t. 4, to be disgusted; to loathe
fastīdĭōsus, a, um, adj, adv, ē, scornful, squeamish, disagreeable
fastīdĭum, ii, n, loathing, scorn
fastīgātus, a, um, adj, adv, e, sloping
fastīgĭum, ii, n, gable, top, bottom, slope
fastīgo, v.t. 1, to make jointed
fastus, a, um (diēs), court-day
fastus, ūs, m, arrogance
fātālis, e, adj, adv, ĭter, destined, deadly
fătĕor, fassus, v.t. 2, dep, to admit confess
fātĭdĭcus, a, um, adj, prophetic
fātĭfer, ĕra, ĕrum, adj, deadly
fătīgātĭo, ōnis, f, exhaustion
fătīgātus, a, um, adj, exhausted
fătīgo, v.t. 1, to weary, harass, torment
fătisco, v.i. 3, to fall apart
fătŭĭtas, ātis, f, foolishness
fātum, i, n, destiny, calamity, prophetic saying
fătŭus, a, um, adj, foolish
faucēs, ium, f. pl, throat, narrow passage
faustus, a, um, adj, adv, ē, fortunate
fautor, ōris, m, supporter
fautrix, īcis, f, patroness
făvĕo, favi, fautum, v.i. 2, with dat; to favour, befriend
făvilla, ae, f, embers
făvor, ōris, m, good-will, applause
făvōrābilis, e, adj, popular
făvus, i, m, honey-comb
fax, făcis, f, torch, stimulus
febrĭcŭlōsus, a, um, adj, feverish
fĕbris, is, f, fever
Fēbrŭārĭus (mensis), February
fēbrŭum, i, n, atonement
fēcundĭtas, ātis, f, fertility
fēcundo, v.t. 1, to fertilize
fēcundus, a, um, adj, fertile, abundant
fel, fellis, n, gall-bladder, poison, bitterness
fēles, is, f, cat
fēlīcĭtas, ātis, f, happiness
fēlix, īcis, adj, adv, ĭter, happy, fortunate, abundant
fēmĭna, ae, f, woman
fēmĭnĕus, a, um, adj, feminine
fēmur, ŏris (ĭnis), n, thigh
fēn... see faen

For List of Abbr viations used, turn to pages 3, 4

fĕnestra, ae, *f*, window
fĕra, ae, *f*, wild animal
fĕrālis, e, *adj*, of the dead
fĕrax, ācis, *adj*, fertile
fercŭlum, i, *n*, barrow, dish
fĕrē, *adv*, almost, nearly, usually
fĕrentārĭus, ii, *m*, light-armed soldier
fĕrĕtrum, i, *n*, bier
fĕrĭae, ārum, *f. pl*, holidays
fĕrĭātus, a, um, *adj*, on holiday
fĕrīnus, a, um, *adj*, of wild animals
fĕrĭo, *v.t.* 4, to strike, kill; with foedus, to make a treaty
fĕrĭtas, ātis, *f*, wildness
fermē, *adv*, almost, usually
fermentum, i, *n*, yeast, beer
fĕro, ferre, tŭli, lātum, *v.t. irreg*, to bear, bring, move, produce, plunder, offer, tolerate, show, assert; fertur, ferunt, it is said
fĕrōcĭa, ae, *f*, high spirits, ferocity
fĕrōcĭtas, ātis, *f*, high spirits, ferocity
fĕrōcĭter, *adv*, bravely, fiercely
fĕrox, ōcis, *adj*, brave, fierce
ferrāmentum, i, *n*, iron tool
ferrātus, a, um, *adj*, iron-clad
ferrĕus, a, um, *adj*, made of iron
ferrūgĭnĕus, a, um, *adj*, rusty, dark red
ferrūgo, ĭnis, *f*, rust, dark red
ferrum, i, *n*, iron, sword
ferrūmen, ĭnis, *n*, cement, glue, solder
ferrūmĭno, *v.t.* 1, to cement, solder
fertĭlis, e, *adj*, fertile
fertĭlĭtas, ātis, *f*, fertility
fĕrŭla, ae, *f*, stalk, rod
fĕrus, a, um, *adj*, wild, cruel
fĕrus, i, *m*, wild animal
fervĕfăcĭo, fēci, factum, *v.t.* 3, to heat, melt
fervens, ntis, *adj*, *adv*, nter, burning, boiling, hot
fervĕo, bŭi, *v.i.* 2, to boil, burn, rage, swarm
fervĭdus, a, um, *adj*, burning, impetuous
fervor, ōris, *m*, heat, passion
fessus, a, um, *adj*, tired
festīnans, ntis, *adj*, *adv*, nter, in haste
festīnātĭo, ōnis, *f*, haste
festīno, *v.i.t.* 1, to hurry
festīnus, a, um, *adj*, quick
festīvĭtas, ātis, *f*, humour
festīvus, a, um, *adj*, *adv*, ē, witty, lively, cheerful
festum, i, *n*, holiday, banquet
festus, a, um, *adj*, festive, gay
fētĕo, *v.i.* 2, to stink

fētĭāles, ĭum, *m*, *pl*, college of priests concerned with war-ceremonies
fētĭdus, a, um, *adj*, stinking
fētor, ōris, *m*, stench
fētūra, ae, *f*, bearing of young, young brood
fētus, ūs, *m*, bearing of young, young brood
fētus, a, um, *adj*, pregnant, fruitful, newly delivered
fībra, ae, *f*, fibre, nerve
fībŭla, ae, *f*, brooch, pin
fībŭlo, *v.t.* 1, to fasten
fictĭlis, e, *adj*, made of clay
fictĭle, is (ia, ĭum), *n*, earthen pottery
fictor, ōris, *m*, designer
fictus, a, um, *adj*, imagined
fīcus, i, or, ūs, *f*, fig-tree
fĭdēlis, e, *adj*, *adv*, ĭter, faithful, true, sure
fĭdēlĭtas, ātis, *f*, faithfulness
fīdens, ntis, *adj*, *adv*, nter, self-confident
fīdentĭa, ae, *f*, confidence
fĭdes, ĕi, *f*, trust, faith, confidence, honesty, promise
fĭdes, ĭum, *f. pl*, lute, guitar
fĭdĭcen, ĭnis, *m*, lute-player
fīdo, fīsus sum, *v.* 3, *semi-dep. with dat*; to trust
fīdūcĭa, ae, *f*, confidence
fīdus, a, um, *adj*, trustworthy
fĭĕri, see flo
fīgo, xi, xum, *v.t.* 3, to fix, fasten, transfix
fĭgŭlāris, e, *adj*, of a potter
fĭgŭlus, i, *m*, potter
fĭgūra, ae, *f*, shape, phantom, atom, nature
fĭgūrātus, a, um, *adj*, shaped
fĭgūro, *v.t.* 1, to shape
fīlĭa, ae, *f*, daughter
fīlĭŏla, ae, *f*, little daughter
fīlĭŏlus, i, *m*, little son
fīlĭus, i, *m*, son
fĭlix, ĭcis, *f*, hair, fern
fīlum, i, *n*, thread, texture
fimbrĭae, ārum, *f. pl*, threads, fringe
fĭmus, i, *m*, manure
findo, fĭdi, ssum, *v.t.* 3, to split
fīnes, ĭum, *m. pl*, territory
fingo, nxi, ctum, *v.t.* 3, to shape, adorn, imagine, devise
fīnĭo, *v.t.* 4, to enclose, limit, prescribe, end, die
fīnis, is, *m*, boundary, limit, end
fīnĭtĭmus, a, um, *adj*, adjoining
fīnĭtĭmi, ōrum, *m. pl*, neighbours

finitor, ōris, *m*, surveyor
fio, fiĕri, factus sum, *v*, *irreg*, to become, happen
firmāmen, ĭnis, *n*, prop, support
firmāmentum, ĭ, *n*, prop, support
firmĭtas, ātis, *f*, strength, firmness
firmĭtūdo, ĭnis, *f*, strength, firmness
firmo, *v.t.* 1, to strengthen, encourage, promise
firmus, a, um, *adj*, *adv*, ē, ĭter, strong, stable, constant, true
fiscella, ae, *f*, small basket, muzzle
fiscĭna, ae, *f*, small basket
fiscus, ĭ, *m*, purse, imperial treasury
fissĭlis, e, *adj*, breakable
fissum, ĭ, *n*, cleft, chink
fissūra, ae, *f*, split, chink
fistūca, ae, *f*, rammer
fistŭla, ae, *f*, pipe, tube
fistŭlātor, ōris, *m*, piper
fīsus, a, um, *adj*, trusting, relying on
flābellum, ĭ, *n*, small fan
flābra, ōrum, *n*. *pl*, gusts
flaccĭdus, a, um, *adj*, flabby
flăgello, *v.t.* 1, to whip
flăgellum, ĭ, *n*, whip, thong
flăgĭtātĭo, ōnis, *f*, demand
flăgĭtĭōsus, a, um, *adj*, *adv*, e, disgraceful
flăgĭtĭum, ĭi, *n*, disgraceful conduct, shame
flăgĭto, *v.t.* 1, to demand
flăgrans, ntis, *adj*, burning
flăgro, *v.i.* 1, to blaze, glow
flăgrum, ĭ, *n*, whip
flāmen, ĭnis, *m*, priest
flāmen, ĭnis, *n*, blast
flāmĭnĭum, ĭi, *n*, priesthood
flamma, ae, *f*, flame, blaze
flammĕum, ĭ, *n*, bridal-veil
flammĕus, a, um, *adj*, flaming
flammĭfer, ĕra, ĕrum, *adj*, flame-carrying
flammo, *v.i.t.* 1, to burn
flātus, ūs, *m*, blowing, bluster
flāvens, ntis, *adj*, yellow
flāvĕo, *v.i.* 2, to be golden, yellow
flāvesco, *v.i.* 3, to turn golden
flāvus, a, um, *adj*, golden, yellow
flēbĭlis, e, *adj*, *adv*, ĭter, lamentable, tearful
flecto, xi, xum, *v.i.t.* 3, to turn; bend, curve, wheel, persuade
flĕo, ēvi, tum, *v.i.t.* 2, to weep; mourn
flētus, ūs, *m*, weeping
flexĭbĭlis, e, *adj*, flexible
flexĭo, ōnis, *f*, curve
flexŭōsus, a, um, *adj*, crooked
flexus, ūs, *m*, bend, turning
flictus, ūs, *m*, collision

flō, *v.i.t.* 1, to blow
floccus, ĭ, *m*, lock of wool
flōrens, ntis, *adj*, shining, flourishing
flōrĕo, *v.i.* 2, to bloom, flourish
flōresco, *v.i.* 3, to come into flower, flourish
flōrĕus, a, um, *adj*, made of flowers
flōrĭdus, a, um, *adj*, blooming
flōs, ōris, *m*, flower, ornament
floscŭlus, ĭ, *m*, small flower
fluctŭo, *v.i.* 1, to ripple, undulate, hesitate
fluctŭōsus, a, um, *adj*, billowy
fluctus, ūs, *m*, wave
flŭens, ntis, *adj*, lax, fluent
flŭentum, ĭ, *n*, stream, flood
flŭĭdus, a, um, *adj*, flowing, slack
flŭĭto, *v.i.* 1, to flow, float
flūmen, ĭnis, *n*, river, flood
flūmĭnĕus, a, um, *adj*, of a river
flŭo, xi, xum, *v.i.* 3, to flow, wave, vanish
flŭvĭālis, e, *adj*, of a river
flŭvĭus, ĭi, *m*, river
flŭxĭo, ōnis, *f*, flowing
flŭxus, a, um, *adj*, fluid, slack
fōcāle, is, *n*, neck-tie
fōcŭlus, ĭ, *m*, brazier
fōcus, ĭ, *m*, fire-place, home
fŏdĭco, *v.t.* 1, to dig, nudge, stab
fŏdĭo, fōdi, fossum, *v.i.t.* 3, to dig; dig up, prick, stab
foedĕrātus, a, um, *adj*, allied
foedĭtas, ātis, *f*, filthiness
foedo, *v.t.* 1, to disfigure, disgrace, stain
foedus, a, um, *adj*, *adv*, ē, filthy, shameful
foedus, ĕris, *n*, treaty, contract
foet . . . see fet . . .
fŏlĭum, ĭi, *n*, leaf
follĭcŭlus, ĭ, *m*, small bag
follis, is, *m*, pair of bellows
fōmentum, ĭ, *n*, poultice, comfort
fōmes, ĭtis, *m*, firewood
fons, ntis, *m*, fountain, origin
fontĭcŭlus, ĭ, *m*, small fountain
for, *v.i.t.* 1, *dep*, to speak; say, predict
fŏrāmen, ĭnis, *n*, hole
fŏrās, *adv*, out-of-doors
forceps, ĭpis, *m*, *f*, tongs, pincers
fŏrĕ = futurum esse see esse
fŏrem = essem,
fŏrensis, e, *adj*, concerning the courts of law
fŏres, um, *f*. *pl*, door, entrance
forfex, ĭcis, *f*, scissors (*usually in pl.*)
fŏrĭca, ae, *f*, public convenience

fŏrĭcŭlae, ārum, f. pl, shutters
fŏris, is, f, door, entrance
fŏris, adv, outside, from outside
forma, ae, f, form, shape, beauty
formīca, ae, f, ant
formīdābĭlis, e, adj, fearful
formīdo, v.i.t. 1, to be afraid; fear
formīdo, ĭnis, f, fear, terror
formīdŭlōsus, a, um, adj, adv, ē, dreadful, fearful
formo, v.t. 1, to shape
formōsus, a, um, adj, beautiful
formŭla, ae, f, rule, principle, agreement, lawsuit
fornax, ācis, f, oven
fornix, ĭcis, m, arch, vault
fors, rtis, f, chance, luck
fors, adv, perhaps
forsan, adv, perhaps
forsĭtan, adv, perhaps
fortassē, adv, perhaps
fortē, adv, by chance
fortis, e, adj, adv, ĭter, strong, brave
fortĭtūdo, ĭnis, f, bravery
fortŭĭtō(ŭ), adv, by chance
fortŭĭtus, a, um, adj, accidental
fortūna, ae, f, luck, fate, fortune (good or bad), circumstances, property
fortūnātus, a, um, adj, adv, ē, lucky, happy
fortūno, v.t. 1, to enrich, bless
fŏrum, i, n, market-place, business
fŏrus, i, m, gangway, passage, row of seats
fossa, ae, f, ditch
fossĭo, ōnis, f, excavation
fossor, ōris, m, digger, miner
fŏvĕa, ae, f, pit, pitfall
fŏvĕo, fŏvi, fōtum, v.t. 2, to warm, caress, love
fractūra, ae, f, fracture
fractus, a, um, adj, weak, feeble
frāga, ōrum, n. pl, strawberries
frăgĭlis, e. adj, brittle, frail
frăgĭlĭtas, ātis, f, frailty
fragmen, ĭnis, n, fracture, splinter
fragmentum, i, n, fragment
frăgor, ōris, m, crash
frăgōsus, a, um, adj, rugged, crashing
frăgro, v.i. 1, to smell
frāgum, i, n, strawberry plant
frango, frēgi, fractum, v.t. 3, to break, crush, weaken
frāter, tris, m, brother
frāternĭtas, ātis, f, brotherhood
frāternus, a, um, adj, adv, ē, brotherly
frātrĭcīda, ae, m, a fratricide
fraudātĭo, ōnis, f, deceit
fraudātor, ōris, m, deceiver

fraudo, v.t. 1, to cheat, defraud
fraudŭlentus, a, um, adj, deceitful
fraus, dis, f, deceit, crime, mistake, injury
fraxĭnĕus, a, um, adj, of ash
fraxĭnus, i, f, ash-tree
frĕmĭtus, ūs, m, murmur, roar
frĕmo, ŭi, ĭtum, v.i.t. 3, to roar, murmur, howl; grumble at
frĕmor, ōris, m, murmuring
frendĕo, ŭi, frēsum, v.i. 2, to gnash the teeth, crush
frēno, v.t. 1, to bridle, curb
frēnum, i, n, bridle, restraint
frĕquens, ntis, adj, adv, nter, usual, repeated, crowded
frĕquentātĭo, ōnis, f, frequency
frĕquentĭa, ae, f, crowd
frĕquento, v.t. 1, to frequent, repeat, crowd, celebrate
frĕtum, i, n, channel, strait
frĕtus, a, um, adj. with abl, relying on
frico, cŭi, ctum, v.t. 1, to rub
frictus, a, um, adj, rubbed, (frico); roasted (frigo)
frīgĕo, v.i. 2, to be cold or languid, to be slighted
frīgesco, frixi, v.i. 3, to grow cold, become languid
frīgĭdus, a, um, adj, cold, stiff, feeble, spiritless
frīgĭda, ae, f, cold water
frīgo, xi, ctum, v.t. 3, to roast
frīgus, ōris, n, cold, winter
fringilla, ae, f, small bird, robin, chaffinch
frondātor, ōris, m, pruner
frondĕo, v.i. 2, to be in leaf
frondesco, dŭi, v.i. 3, to come into leaf
frondĕus, a, um, adj, leafy
frondōsus, a, um, adj, leafy
frons, dis, f, foliage, leaf
frons, ntis, f, forehead, front, appearance
fructŭōsus, a, um, adj, fruitful, advantageous
fructus, ūs, m, enjoyment, fruit, profit
frūgālis, e, adj, adv, ĭter, thrifty, careful
frūgālĭtas, ātis, f, thrift, worth
frūges, um, f. pl, see frux
frūgi, indecl. adj, worthy, useful
frūgĭfer, ĕra, ĕrum, adj, fertile
frūmentārĭus, a, um, adj, of corn
frūmentor, v.i. 1, dep, to fetch corn
frūmentum, i, n, corn
frŭor, fructus, v. 3, dep. with abl, to enjoy

frustrā, *adv*, in vain

frustrātĭo, ōnis, *f*, deception, frustration

frustror, *v.t.* 1, *dep*, to deceive

frustum, i, *n*, piece

frŭtex, ĭcis, *m*, bush

frŭtĭcētum, i, *n*, thicket

frŭtĭcōsus, a, um, *adj*, bushy

frux, frūgis, *f*, fruit, crops, value, result

fūcātus, a, um, *adj*, painted, counterfeit

fūco, *v.t.* 1, to paint, dye

fūcōsus, a, um, *adj*, coloured, spurious

fūcus, i, *m*, rouge, disguise

fūcus, i, *m*, drone

fŭga, ae, *f*, flight, exile

fŭgax, ācis, *adj*, runaway, swift

fŭgĭens, ntis, *adj*, fleeing

fŭgĭo, fūgi, fŭgĭtum, *v.i.t.* 3, to run away; flee from, avoid

fŭgĭtīvus, a, um, *adj*, fugitive

fŭgĭtīvus, i, *m*, runaway slave, deserter

fŭgĭto, *v.t.* 1, to flee, avoid

fŭgo, *v.t.* 1, to rout, chase

fulcĭo, fulsi, fultum, *v.t.* 4, to prop up, strengthen

fulcrum, i, *n*, foot (of couch)

fulgens, ntis, *adj*, shining

fulgĕo, lsi, *v.i.* 2, to flash, shine

fulgĭdus, a, um, *adj*, flashing, shining

fulgor, ōris, *m*, lightning, gleam, splendour

fulgur, ūris, *n*, lightning

fulgŭrat, *v*, *impers*, it lightens

fŭlĭca, ae, *f*, moor-hen

fūlīgo, ĭnis, *f*, soot

fūlīgĭnōsus, a, um, *adj*, sooty

fulmen, ĭnis, *n*, thunderbolt, lightning

fulmĭnĕus, a, um, *adj*, of lightning, destructive, brilliant

fulmĭno, *v.i.* 1, to thunder

fultūra, ae, *f*, prop, tonic

fulvus, a, um, *adj*, deep yellow

fūmĕus, a, um, *adj*, smoky

fūmĭdus, a, um, *adj*, smoky

fūmĭfer, ĕra, ĕrum, *adj*, smoking, steaming

fūmĭfĭcus, a, um, *adj*, smoking, steaming

fūmĭgo, *v.t.* 1, to smoke out, fumigate

fūmo, *v.i.* 1, to smoke

fūmōsus, a, um, *adj*, smoky, smoke-dried

fūmus, i, *m*, smoke

fūnāle, is, *n*, cord, torch

functĭo, ōnis, *f*, performing

functus, a, um, *partic. adj*, *with abl*, having completed

funda, ae, *f*, sling, missile

fundāmen, ĭnis, *n*, foundation

fundāmentum, i, *n*, foundation

fundĭtor, ōris, *m*, slinger

fundĭtus, *adv*, from the bottom, completely

fundo, fūdi, fūsum, *v.t.* 3, to pour out, spread out, scatter, overthrow, produce

fundo, *v.t.* 1, to found, fix

fundus, i, *m*, the bottom, a farm

fundus, i, *m*, guarantor

fūnĕbris, e, *adj*, of a funeral

fūnĕrĕus, a, um, *adj*, of a funeral

fūnĕro, *v.t.* 1, to bury, kill

fūnesto, *v.t.* 1, to pollute

fūnestus, a, um, *adj*, fatal, sad

fungor, functus, *v.* 3, *dep*, *with abl*, to perform, complete

fungus, i, *m*, mushroom, fungus

fūnis, is, *m*, rope

fūnus, ĕris, *n*, funeral, death, ruin

fūr, fūris, *c*, thief, rogue

fūrax, ācis, *adj*, light-fingered

furca, ae, *f*, two-pronged fork or pole for punishment

furcĭfer, ĕri, *m*, gallows-bird

furcilla, ae, *f*, small fork

furcŭla, ae, *f*, fork-shaped prop, ravine

fūrens, ntis, *adj*, raging

furfur, ūris, *m*, bran

fŭriae, ārum, *f. pl*, rage, frenzy, avenging Furies

fŭrĭālis, e, *adj*, *adv*, iter, raging, wild

fŭrĭbundus, a, um, *adj*, raging

fŭrĭo, *v.t.* 1, to enrage

fŭrĭōsus, a, um, *adj*, raging

furnus, i, *m*, oven

fŭro, ŭi, *v.i.* 3, to rage, be mad

fūror, *v.t.* 1, *dep*, to steal

fŭror, ōris, *m*, rage, fury

furtim, *adv*, stealthily

furtīvus, a, um, *adj*, stolen, secret

furtum, i, *n*, theft, trick

furtō, *adv*, secretly

fūruncŭlus, i, *m*, pilferer, sore, boil

furvus, a, um, *adj*, gloomy, swarthy

fuscĭna, ae, *f*, trident

fusco, *v.t.* 1, to blacken, darken

fuscus, a, um, *adj*, dark, swarthy

fūsĭlis, e, *adj*, fluid, soft

fustis, is, *m*, cudgel, club

fūsus, a, um, *adj*, spread out, wide

fūsus, i, *m*, spindle

futtĭlis (fūtĭlis), e, *adj*, worthless

futtĭlĭtas (fūtĭlĭtas), ātis, *f*, worthlessness

fŭtūra, ōrum, *n. pl*, the future

fŭtūrum, i, *n*, the future

fŭtūrus, a, um, *adj,* future

G

gaesum, i, *n,* heavy Gallic javelin
galbĭnus, a, um, *adj,* greenish-yellow
gălĕa, ae, *f,* helmet
gălĕo, *v.t.* 1, to issue with helmets
gălērum, i, *n* (us, i, *m*), hat
galla, ae, *f,* oak-apple
gallīna, ae, *f,* hen
gallīnārĭŭm, ii, *n,* hen-house
gallus, i, *m,* cock
gānĕa, ae, *f,* eating-house
gānĕo, ōnis, *m,* glutton
gannĭo, *v.i.* 4, to bark, snarl
gannītus, ūs, *m,* chattering
garrĭo, *v.t.* 4, to chatter
garrŭlĭtas, ātis, *f,* chattering
garrŭlus, a, um, *adj,* talkative
gărum (garon), i, *n,* fish-sauce
gaudĕo, gāvīsus, *v.i.t.* 2, *semi-dep,* to rejoice
gaudĭum, ii, *n,* joy, delight
gausăpa, ae, *f,* rough cloth
gāvĭa, ae, *f,* sea-bird
gāza, ae, *f,* treasure (of Persia)
gĕlĭdus, a, um, *adj, adv,* ē, ice-cold, frosty
gĕlo, *v.i.t.* 1, to freeze
gĕlum, i (gĕlu, ūs), *n,* frost, cold
gĕmellus, a, um, *adj,* (us, i, *m*), twin
gĕmĭno, *v.t.* 1, to double, pair
gĕmĭnus, a, um, *adj,* twin
gĕmĭni, ōrum, *m. pl,* twins
gĕmĭtus, ūs, *m,* lamentation
gemma, ae, *f,* bud, jewel, goblet, signet-ring
gemmārĭus, ii, *m,* jeweller
gemmātus, a. um *adj,* set with jewels
gemmĕus, a, um, *adj,* set with jewels
gemmo, *v.i.* 1, to come into bud
gĕmo, ·ŭi, ĭtum, *v.i.t.* 3, to groan, creak; deplore
gĕna, ae, *f,* the cheek
gĕner, ĕri, *m,* son-in-law
gĕnĕrālis, e, *adj,* of a certain kind, general
gĕnĕrātim, *adv,* in classes, in general
gĕnĕrātor, ōris, *m,* breeder
gĕnĕro, *v.t.* 1, to create, produce, be born (passive)
gĕnĕrōsus, a, um, *adj, adv,* ē, of noble birth, generous
gĕnesta, ae, *f,* small shrub with yellow flowers, broom
gĕnĕtīvus, a, um, *adj,* inborn
gĕnĕtrix, īcis, *f,* mother

gĕnĭālis, e, *adj, adv,* ĭter, bridal, cheerful
gĕnĭtālis, e, *adj,* of birth, fruitful
gĕnĭtor, ōris, *m,* father
gĕnĭus, ii, *m,* guardian angel
gens, ntis, *f,* clan, race, descendant, nation
gentĭlĭcĭus, a, um, *adj,* of the same clan
gentīlis, e, *adj,* of the same clan
gentīlis, is, *c,* relative
gĕnu, ūs, *n,* knee
gĕnŭĭnus, a, um, *adj,* innate
gĕnŭĭnus, a, um, *adj,* of the cheek or jaw
gĕnus, ĕris, *n,* birth, race, kind, type, descendant
gĕōgrăphĭa, ae, *f,* geography
gĕōmĕtres, ae, *m,* mathematician
gĕōmĕtrĭa, ae, *f,* geometry
germānĭtas, ātis, *f,* brotherhood
germānus, a, um, *adj,* own
germānus, i, *m* (a, ae, *f*), brother, (sister)
germen, ĭnis, *n,* bud, sprig
germĭno, *v.i.* 1, to bud
gĕro, gessi, stum, *v.t.* 3, to bear, wear, bring, produce, behave, display, carry on, honour
gerrae, ārum, *f.pl,* nonsense
gĕrŭlus, i, *m,* porter
gestāmen, ĭnis, *n,* load
gestātĭo, ōnis, *f,* riding, driving
gestĭo, *v.i.* 4, to be joyful, desire passionately
gesto, *v.t.* 1, to carry, wear, have
gestus, ūs, *m,* posture, gesture
gestus, a, um, *adj,* achieved, carried
gibber, ĕris, *m,* hump; *as adj,* hunch-backed
gibbus, i, *m,* hump; *as adj,* hunch-backed
gĭgantĕus, a, um, *adj,* of giants
gĭgās, ntis, *m,* giant
gigno, gĕnŭi, gĕnĭtum, *v.t.* 3, to give birth to; (*passive*) be born
gilvus, a, um, *adj,* pale yellow
gingīva, ae, *f,* gum
glăber, bra, brum, *adj,* bald
glăcĭālis, e, *adj,* frozen
glăcĭes, ēi, *f,* ice
glăcĭo, *v.t.* 1, to freeze
glădĭātor, ōris, *m,* gladiator
glădĭātōrĭus, a, um, *adj,* gladiatorial
glădĭus, ii, *m,* sword
glaeba (glēba), ae, *f,* clod
glans, ndis, *f,* acorn, bullet
glārĕa, ae, *f,* gravel

glaucus, a, um, *adj*, blue-grey
gleba, see glaeba
glis, gliris, *m*, dormouse
glisco,–*v.i.* 3, to swell, grow
globosus, a, um, *adj*, spherical
globus, i, *m*, ball, crowd
glomero, *v.t.* 1, to gather into a heap, crowd together
glomus, eris, *n*, ball of thread
gloria, ae, *f*, glory, boasting
gloriatio, onis, *f*, boasting
glorior, *v.i.t.*1, *dep*, to boast
gloriosus, a, um, *adj*, *adv*, e, famous, conceited
glossarium, ii, *n*, glossary
gluten, inis, *n*, glue
glutinator, oris, *m*, bookbinder
glutino, *v.t.* 1, to glue
gluttio, *v.t.* 4, to gulp
gnarus, a, um, *adj. with genit*, acquainted with, expert in
gnatus, a, um, *adj*, born
gnav . . . see nav . . .
gossypium, ii, *n*, cotton
gracilis, e, *adj*, slender
gracilitas, atis, *f*, slenderness
graculus, i, *m*, jackdaw
gradatim, *adv*, gradually
gradatio, onis, *f*, gradation, climax
gradior, gressus, *v.i.* 3, *dep*, to walk, go, move
gradus, us, *m*, pace, step, rank, position,-station, stair, plait
graecor, *v.i.* 1, *dep*, to live like the Greeks
grallae, arum, *f. pl*, stilts
gramen, inis, *n*, grass
gramineus, a, um, *adj*, grassy
grammatica, ae, *f*, grammar
grammaticus, i, *m*, grammarian
granaria, orum, *n. pl*, granary
granatus, a, um, *adj*, with many seeds
grandaevus, a, um, *adj*, old
grandiloquus, a, um, *adj*, boastful
grandinat, *v.* 1, *impers*, it is hailing
grandis, e, *adj*, full-grown, large, old, strong, noble
grando, inis, *f*, hail, hail-storm
granum, i, *n*, grain, seed
granosus, a, um, *adj*, seedy
grassator, oris, *m*, idler, footpad
grassor, *v.i.* 1, *dep*, to hang about, attack, rage
grate, *adv*, gratefully, willingly
grates, *f. pl*, thanks
gratia, ae, *f*, esteem, friendship, charm, beauty, kindness, favour, gratitude; *in abl*, for the sake of; gratiis (gratis), as a favour; *pl*, thanks

gratificatio, onis, *f*, doing favours
gratificor, *v.* 1, *dep*, to do as a favour, oblige
gratiosus, a, um, *adj*, popular
grator, *v. i.t.* 1, *dep*, to congratulate
gratuitus, a, um, *adj*, voluntary
gratulatio, onis, *f*, rejoicing
gratulor, *v.i.t.* 1, *dep*, to congratulate
gratus, a, um, *adj*, pleasing, grateful
gravate, *adv*, unwillingly
gravedo, inis, *f*, cold, catarrh
graveolens, ntis, *adj*, stinking
gravesco, *v.i.* 3, to grow heavy
gravidus, a, um, *adj*, pregnant
gravis, e, *adj*, *adv*, iter, heavy, loaded, low, pregnant, severe, unpleasant, serious, urgent, important
gravitas, atis, *f*, weight, heaviness, severity, dignity, urgency
gravo, *v.t.* 1, to load, oppress
gravor, *v.i.t.* 1, *dep*, to be irritated or reluctant; not to tolerate
gregalis, e, *adj*, of the herd, gregarious
gregarius, a, um, *adj*, common
gregatim, *adv*, in herds
gremium, ii, *n*, bosom, lap
gressus, us, *m*, step, way
grex, gregis, *m*, flock, herd
grumus, i, *m*, hillock
grunnio, *v.i.* 4, to grunt
grunnitus, us, *m*, grunt
grus, gruis, *m*, *f*, crane
gryllus, i, *m*, grasshopper
gryps, gryphis, *m*, griffin
gubernaculum, i, *n*, rudder
gubernatio, onis, *f*, management
gubernator, oris, *m*, steersman
guberno, *v.t.* 1, to, steer, manage
gula, ae, *f*, throat, appetite
gulosus, a, um, *adj*, gluttonous
gummi, *n*, (*indecl.*), gum
gurges, itis, *m*, whirlpool, abyss
gustatio, onis, *f*, taste
gustatus, us, *m*, sense of taste
gusto, *v.t.* 1, to taste
gustus, us, *m*, tasting, snack
gutta, ae, *f*, drop, spot
guttur, uris, *n*, throat
gutus (guttus), i, *m*, flask
gymnasium, ii, *m*, gymnasium
gymnicus, a, um, *adj*, gymnastic
gypsatus, a, um, *adj*, covered with lime
gypso, *v.t.* 1, to plaster
gypsum, i, *n*, white lime
gyrus, i, *m*, circuit, ring

H

habena, ae, *f*, thong, rein

hăbĕo, *v.t.* 2, to have, keep, be able, render, esteem, use, deal with, know; with in animo, to intend

hăbĭlis, e, *adj,* convenient, expert

hăbĭtābĭlis, e, *adj,* habitable

hăbĭtātĭo, ōnis, *f,* residence

hăbĭto, *v.i.t.* 1, to live; inhabit

hăbĭtus, ūs, *m,* condition, bearing, state, dress, shape

hāc, *adv,* by this way, here

hactĕnus, *adv,* up to this point

haec, see hĭc

haedus, i, *m,* young goat

haemorrhăgĭa, ae, *f,* haemorrhage

haerĕo, si, sum, *v.i.* 2, to hang, cling, hesitate

haesĭtans, ntis, *adj,* hesitant

haesĭtantĭa, ae, *f,* stammering

haesĭtātĭo, ōnis, *f,* embarrassment

haesĭto, *v.i.* 1, to hesitate

hālĭtus, ūs, *m,* breath, steam

hālo, *v.i.t.* 1, to breathe; exhale

hāma, ae, *f,* bucket

hāmātus, a, um, *adj,* hooked

hāmus, i, *m,* hook, fish-hook

hăra, ae, *f,* coop, pen, sty

hărēna, ae, *f,* sand, arena

hărēnārĭus, a, um, *adj,* of sand

hărēnōsus, a, um, *adj,* sandy

hărĭŏlor, *v.i,* 1, *dep,* to foretell

hărĭŏlus, i, *m,* prophet

harmŏnĭa, ae, *f,* harmony

harpăgo, ōnis, *m,* grappling-hook

hărundo, ĭnis, *f,* reed, fishing-rod, shaft, shepherd's pipe

hăruspex, ĭcis, *m,* clairvoyant

hasta, ae, *f,* spear, lance

hastāti, ōrum, *m. pl,* pike-men; front line of a Roman army

hastīle, is, *n,* spear-shaft

haud (haut), *adv,* not at all

haudquāquam, *adv,* by no means

haurĭo, si, stum, *v.t.* 4, to draw up, drink in, drain, exhaust

haustus, ūs, *m,* a drink, draught

hav ... see av ...

hĕbĕnus, i, *f,* ebony

hĕbĕo, *v.i.* 2, to be dull

hĕbes, ĕtis, *adj,* blunt, dull

hĕbesco, *v.i.* 3, to grow dull

hĕbĕto, *v.t.* 1, to blunt

hĕdĕra, ae, *f,* ivy

hei, *interj,* ah! alas!

hellŭo, ōnis, *m,* glutton

hellŭor, *v.* 1, *dep, with abl,* to squander

hem! (em!), *interj,* ah! indeed!

hēmĭcyclĭum, ii, *n,* semi-circle

hēmisphaerĭum, ii, *n,* hemisphere

hĕra, ae, *f,* lady of the house

herba, ae, *f,* grass, plant

herbārĭus, a, um, *adj,* of plants

herbĭdus, a, um, *adj,* grassy

herbōsus, a, um, *adj,* grassy

hercŭle (hercle)! by Hercules!

hĕrĕ, *adv,* yesterday

hērēdĭtārĭus, a, um, *adj,* inherited

hērēdĭtas, ātis, *f,* inheritance

hēres, ēdis, *c,* heir, heiress

hĕri, *adv,* yesterday

hĕrīlis, e, *adj,* of the master or mistress

hernĭa, ae, *f,* rupture

hērōĭcus, a, um, *adj,* heroic

hēros, ōis, *m,* demigod

hērus, i, *m,* master of the house

hespĕris, ĭdis, *adj,* western

hespĕrĭus, a, um, *adj,* western

hesternus, a, um, *adj,* yesterday's

heu!, *interj,* oh! alas!

heus!, *interj,* hallo there!

hexămĕter, tri, *m,* a verse metre consisting of six feet

hĭans, see hĭo

hĭātus, ūs, *m,* aperture

hīberna, ōrum, *n.pl,* winter-quarters

hībernācŭla, ōrum, *n.pl,* tents to spend winter in

hīberno, *v.i.* 1, to spend the winter

hībernus, a, um, *adj,* of winter

hĭbrĭda, ae, *c,* cross-breed

hĭc, haec, hōc, *pron,* this

hĭc, *adv,* here

hĭĕmālis, e, *adj,* of winter

hĭĕmo, *v.i.t.* 1, to spend the winter; freeze

hĭems (hĭemps), hĭĕmis, *f,* winter, stormy weather

hĭlăris, e, *adj, adv,* ē, cheerful

hĭlărĭtas, ātis, *f,* gaiety

hĭlăro, *v.t.* 1, to cheer up

hillae, ārum, *f. pl,* sausage

hinc, *adv,* from here, hence

hinnĭo, *v.i.* 4, to neigh

hinnītus, ūs, *m,* neighing

hinnŭlĕus, i, *m,* young stag

hĭo, *v.i.* 1, to gape open

hippŏpŏtāmus, i, *m,* hippopotamus

hircīnus, a, um, *adj,* of a goat

hircus, i, *m,* goat

hirsūtus, a, um, *adj,* shaggy

hirtus, a, um, *adj,* rough, shaggy

hĭrūdo, ĭnis, *f,* leech

hĭrundĭnīnus, a, um, *adj,* of swallows

hĭrundo, ĭnis, *f,* a swallow

hisco,– *v.i.t.* 3, to gape; whisper

hispĭdus, a, um, *adj,* rough, shaggy

histŏrĭa, ae, *f,* story, account

histŏrĭcus, a, um, *adj,* historical

histŏrĭcus, i, *m,* historian

histrĭo, ōnis, *m,* actor

hĭulcus, a, um, *adj,* gaping; (of speech) badly connected

hoc, see hic
hŏdĭē, *adv*, today
hŏdĭernus, a, um, *adj*, of today
hŏlus, ĕris, *n*, vegetables
hŏluscŭlum, i, *n*, small vegetable
hŏmĭcīda, ae, *c*, murderer
hŏmĭcīdĭum, ii, *n*, homicide
hŏmo, ĭnis, *c*, human being
hŏmullus, i, *m*, puny man
hŏmuncŭlus, i, *m*, puny man
hŏnestas, ātis, *f*, honour, good name, integrity
hŏnesto, *v.t.* 1, to honour, adorn
hŏnestum, i, *n*, integrity
hŏnestus, a, um, *adj*, *adv*, ē, respectable, esteemed, eminent
hŏnor (hŏnos), ōris, *m*, esteem, public office, reward, charm
hŏnōrārĭus, a, um, *adj*, honorary
hŏnōrātus, a, um, *adj*, respected
hŏnōrĭfĭous, a, um, *adj*, *adv*, ō, complimentary
hŏnōro, *v.t.* 1, to honour, respect, adorn
hŏnos, see hŏnor
hŏnus . . . see ōnus . . .
hōra, ae, *f*, hour, time, season
hōrārĭum, ii, *n*, hour-glass
hordĕŏlus, i, *m*, sty (eye)
hordĕum, i, *n*, barley
hŏrĭŏla, ae, *f*, fishing-boat
hornōtĭnus, a, um, *adj*, this year's
hornus, a, um, *adj*, this year's
hōrōlŏgĭum, ii, *n*, clock
horrendus, a, um, *adj*, terrible
horrĕo, *v.i.t.* 2, to bristle, tremble; dread
horresco, horrŭi, *v.i.* 3, to become ruffled or frightened
horrĕum, i, *n*, barn, warehouse
horrĭbĭlis, e, *adj*, terrible
horrĭdŭlus, a, um, *adj*, rough
horrĭdus, a, um, *adj*, *adv*, ē, rough, bristly, wild, uncouth
horrĭfer, ĕra, ĕrum, *adj*, dreadful
horrĭfĭco, *v.t.* 1, to ruffle, terrify
horrĭfĭcus, a, um, *adj*, terrible
horrĭsŏnus, a, um, *adj*, with fearful sounds
horror, ōris, *m*, bristling, trembling, chill, terror
hortāmen, ĭnis, *n*, encouragement
hortātĭo, ōnis, *f*, encouragement
hortātor, ōris, *m*, encourager
hortātus, ūs, *m*, encouragement
hortor, *v. t.* 1, *dep*, to encourage, urge, cheer on
hortŭlus, i, *m*, little garden
hortus, i, *m*, garden
hospĕs, ĭtis, *m*, (hospĭta, ae, *f*), host(ess), guest, stranger

hospĭtālis, e, *adj*, hospitable
hospĭtĭum, ii, *n*, hospitality, friendship, lodgings
hostĭa, ae, *f*, sacrificial victim
hostĭcus, a, um, *adj*, of the enemy
hostīlis, e, *adj*, *adv*, ĭter, hostile
hostis, is, *c*, enemy, stranger
hūc, *adv*, to this place or point
huĭ!, *interj*, oh!
huĭus, *genitive of* hic
hūiuscĕmŏdi, hūiusmŏdi, *pron. adj*, (indecl.) of this sort
hūmāna, ōrum, *n.pl*, human affairs
hūmānē, *adv*, like a reasonable human being, courteously
hūmānĭtas, ātis, *f*, humanity, gentleness, refinement
hūmānĭter, *adv*, see hūmānē
hūmānus, a, um, *adj*, human, mortal, humane, gentle, kind
hūmecto, *v.t.* 1, to moisten
hūmĕo, *v.i.* 2, to be wet
hūmĕrus, i, *m*, shoulder, arm
hūmi, *adv*, on or to the ground
hūmĭdus, a, um, *adj*, damp, wet
hūmĭlis, e, *adj*, *adv*, ĭter, low, humble, abject
hūmĭlĭtas, ātis, *f*, lowness, insignificance, meanness
hūmo, *v.t.* 1, to bury
hūmor, ōris, *m*, liquid
hūmus, i, *f*, the ground, region
hyăcinthus(os), i, *m*, blue iris
hyaena, ae, *f*, hyena
hyălus, i, *m*, glass
hybrĭda, ae, *c*, cross breed
hȳdra, ae, *f*, seven-headed watersnake
hydrĭa, ae, *f*, jug
hydrops, ōpis, *m*, dropsy
hydrus, i, *m*, water-snake
hȳmen, mĕnis, *m*, marriage
hȳperbŏlē, es, *f*, exaggeration, hyperbole
hystrix, ĭcis, *f*, porcupine

I

ĭambēus, a, um, *adj*, iambic
ĭambus, i, *m*, iambic foot (2 syllables, short followed by long)
ĭanthĭnus, a, um, *adj*, violet in colour
ĭāpyx, ĭapўgis, *m*, West-North-West wind
ĭaspis, ĭdis, *f*, jasper
ĭbī, *adv*, there, then
ĭbīdem, *adv*, in that same place, at that very moment
ĭbis, ĭdis, *f*, sacred bird, ibis
īcĭo (īco), īci, ictum, *v.t.* 3, to hit, strike (a bargain)

For List of Abbreviations used, turn to pages 3, 4

ictus, ūs, *m*, blow, stroke, shot
id, see is
idcirco, *adv*, for that reason
idem, ěădem, idem, *pron*, the same
identidem, *adv*, repeatedly
iděo, *adv*, for that reason
idiōta, ae, *m*, layman
idōněus, a, um, *adj*, suitable, capable, sufficient
idus, ŭum, *f. pl*, the Ides, 13th or 15th day of the month
idyllium, ii, *n*, idyll
igitur, *adv*, therefore, then
ignārus, a, um, *adj*, unaware
ignāvia, ae, *f*, laziness, cowardice
ignāvus, a, um, *adj*, *adv*, ē, lazy, cowardly
ignesco, *v.i.* 3, to catch fire
ignēus, a, um, *adj*, burning
igniculus, i, *m*, spark
ignifer, ěra, ěrum, *adj*, fiery
ignis, is, *m*, fire, glow
ignōbilis, e, *adj*, unknown, obscure
ignōbilitas, ātis, *f*, obscurity
ignōminia, ae, *f*, disgrace
ignōminiōsus, a, um, *adj*, shameful
ignōrans, ntis, *adj*, unaware
ignōrantia, ae, *f*, ignorance
ignōrātio, ōnis, *f*, ignorance
ignōro, *v.i.t.* 1, to be unaware (of)
ignosco, nōvi, nōtum, *v.t.* 3 (*with dat. of person*), to forgive
ignōtus, a, um, *adj*, unknown, of low birth
ii, see is
ilex, icis, *f*, evergreen oak
ilia, ium, *n.pl*, groin, flank
ilicet, *adv*, immediately
ilico, *adv*, immediately
ilignus, a, um, *adj*, of oak
illa, see ille
illăběfactus, a, um, *adj*, unbroken
illābor, psus, *v.i.* 3, *dep*, to slip, glide, fall
illac, *adv*, on that side
illācessitus, a, um, *adj*, unprovoked
illācrimābilis, e, *adj*, unlamented
illācrimo, *v.i.* 1, to weep over
illaesus, a, um, *adj*, unhurt
illaetābilis, e, *adj*, gloomy
illāquěo, *v.t.* 1, to ensnare
illātus, see infero
ille, a, ud, *pron*, *adj*, that, he, she, it
illěcěbra, ae, *f*, charm, allurement, bait
illěcěbrōsus, a, um, *adj*, alluring
illěpidus, a, um, *adj*, ill-mannered, rude
illex, icis, *c*, decoy

illībātus, a, um, *adj*, unimpaired
illībērālis, e, *adj*, mean
illic, *adv*, there, over there
illicio, lexi, ctum, *v.t.* 3, to allure, entice
illicitus, a, um, *adj*, forbidden
illico, *adv*, there, immediately
illido, si, sum, *v.t.* 3, to strike, dash, beat
illigo, *v.t.* 1, to tie, fasten
illinc, *adv*, from there
illino, lēvi, litum, *v.t.* 3, to smear, spread
illittěrātus, a, um, *adj*, illiterate
illius, *genitive of* ille
illō, *adv*, to that place
illōtus, a, um, *adj*, dirty
illūc, *adv*, to that place
illūcesco, luxi, *v.i.* 3, to grow light, dawn, shine
illud, see ille
illūdo, si, sum, *v.i.t.* 3, to play; mock, ridicule
illūmino, *v.t.* 1, to light up
illustris, e, *adj*, lighted up, distinct, distinguished
illustro, *v.t.* 1, to elucidate, make famous
illŭvies, ēi, *f*, dirt
imāgo, inis, *f*, statue, picture, copy, echo, conception
imbēcillitas, ātis, *f*, weakness
imbēcillus, a, um, *adj*, weak
imbellis, e, *adj*, unwarlike
imber, bris, *m*, rain, shower
imberbis, e, *adj*, beardless
imbibo, bibi, *v.t.* 3, to drink in
imbrex, icis, *f*, gutter, tile
imbrifer, ěra, ěrum, *adj*, rainy
imbŭo, ŭi, ŭtum, *v.t.* 3, to soak, infect, instil, train
imitābilis, e, *adj*, easily imitated
imitātio, ōnis, *f*, imitation
imitātor, ōris, *m*, imitator
imitātrix, icis, *f*, imitator
imitor, *v.t.* 1, *dep*, to imitate
immădesco, dŭi, *v.i.* 3, to become wet
immānia, ium, *n.pl*, horrors
immanis, e, *adj*, *adv*, ē, iter, enormous, frightful, savage
immānitas, ātis, *f*, enormity, barbarism, vastness
immansuētus, a, um, *adj*, untamed
immātŭrus, a, um, *adj*, untimely, immature
immědicābilis, e, *adj*, incurable
imměmor, ōris, *adj.* heedless
imměmŏrātus, a, um, *adj*, unmentioned

immensĭtas, ātis, *f*, immensity
immensum, i, *n*, immensity
immensus, a, um, *adj*, measureless, endless
immĕrens, ntis, *adj*, undeserving, innocent
immergo, si, sum, *v.t.* 3, to dip, plunge, immerse
immĕrĭtus, a, um, *adj*, undeserved
immētātus, a, um, *adj*, unmeasured
immĭgro, *v.i.* 1, to go into
immĭnĕo, *v.i.* 2, to overhang, overlook, threaten, strive for
immĭnŭo, ŭi, ūtum, *v.t.* 3, to reduce, weaken, destroy
immĭnūtĭo, ōnis, *f*, weakening
immĭnūtus, a, um, *adj*, unabated
immiscĕo, scŭi, xtum, *v.t.* 2, to mix in, blend, unite
immĭsĕrābĭlis, e, *adj*, unpitied
immĭsĕrĭcoors, oordis, *adj*, merciless
immissĭo, ōnis, *f*, admission
immītis, e, *adj*, harsh, rough
immitto, mīsi, ssum, *v.t.* 3, to send in, let fly, incite, allow to grow wild
immo, *adv*, on the contrary
immōbĭlis, e, *adj*, immovable
immōbĭlĭtas, ātis, *f*, immobility
immŏdĕrātus, a, um, *adj*, *adv*, ē, excessive
immŏdĭcus, a, um, *adj*, excessive
immŏlātĭo, ōnis, *f*, sacrifice
immŏlo, *v.t.* 1, to coorifioo, kill
immŏrior, mortŭus, *v.i.* 3, *dep*, to die, die away
immortāles, ĭum, *m*, *pl*, the gods
immortālis, e, *adj*, immortal
immortālĭtas, ātis, *f*, immortality
immōtus, a, um, *adj*, unmoved
immŭgĭo, *v.i.* 4, to roar, resound
immundus, a, um, *adj*, dirty
immūnis, e, *adj*, exempt, idle, devoid of
immūnĭtas, ātis, *f*, exemption
immūnītus, a, um, *adj*, unfortified
immurmŭro, *v.i.* 1, to murmur at
immūtābĭlis, e, *adj*, unchangeable
immūtātĭo, ōnis, *f*, interchange
immūto, *v.t.* 1, to change, alter
impācātus, a, um, *adj*, unsubdued
impar, ăris, *adj*, *adv*, ĭter, unequal, uneven
impărātus, a, um, *adj*, unprepared
impastus, a, um, *adj*, hungry
impătĭens, ntis, *adj*, impatient
impăvĭdus, a, um, *adj*, fearless
impeccābĭlis, e, *adj*, faultless
impēdīmenta, ōrum, *n.pl*, luggage
impēdīmentum, i, *n*, obstacle
impēdĭo, *v.t.* 4, to hinder, entangle, hamper

impēdītus, a, um, *adj*, difficult; (soldiers) in full marching-kit
impēdītĭo, ōnis, *f*, obstruction
impello, pŭli, pulsum, *v.t.* 3, to strike upon, drive on, urge, overthrow
impendens, ntis, *adj*, overhanging
impendĕo, *v.i.t.* 2, to overhang; threaten
impendĭum, ii, *n*, cost, expense
impendo, di, sum, *v.t.* 3, to expend, devote
impĕnĕtrābĭlis, e, *adj*, impenetrable
impensa, ae, *f*, cost, expense
impensus, a, um, *adj*, *adv*, ē, large, strong, expensive
impĕrātor, ōris, *m*, general
impĕrātōrius, a, um, *adj*, of a general
impĕrātum, i, *n*, order
imperfectus, a, um, *adj*, incomplete
impĕrĭōsus, a, um, *adj*, powerful, mighty, tyrannical
impĕrītĭa, ae, *f*, inexperience
impĕrīto, *v.i.t.* 1, to command
impĕrītus, a, um, *adj*, *with genit*, unskilled, or inexperienced in
impĕrĭum, ii, *n*, power, command, control, dominion
impermissus, a, um, *adj*, forbidden
impĕro, *v.t.* 1, *with dat. of person*, to command, impose on, demand, requisition, rule
impertĭo, *v.t.* 4, to share
imporvĭuo, a, um, *adj*, imporvĭouo
impĕtĭbĭlis, e, *adj*, intolerable
impĕtrābĭlis, e, *adj*, attainable
impĕtro, *v.t.* 1, to obtain, get
impĕtus, ūs, *m*, attack, impetuosity, impulse
impexus, a, um, *adj*, uncombed
impĭĕtas, ātis, *f*, lack of respect for duty, disloyalty
impĭger, gra, grum, *adj*, energetic
impingo, pēgi, pactum, *v.t.* 3, to thrust, drive, strike (something) against
impĭus, a, um, *adj*, undutiful, unpatriotic, disloyal, wicked
implācābĭlis, e, *adj*, implacable
implācātus, a, um, *adj*, unsatisfied
implācĭdus, a, um, *adj*, rough
implecto, xi, xum, *v.t.* 3, to plait, interweave
implĕo, ēvi, ētum, *v.t.* 2, to fill, complete, fulfil
implĭcātĭo, ōnis, *f*, entwining, complication
implĭcātus, a, um, *adj*, entangled, confused
implĭco, *v.t.* 1, to entangle, involve, grasp, unite
implōrātĭo, ōnis, *f*, entreaty

implōro, *v.t.* 1, to implore, beg for

implūmis, e, *adj*, unfledged, callow

implŭvĭum, ii, *n*, rain-tank in floor of atrium of Roman house

impŏlītus, a, um, *adj*, unpolished

impōno, pŏsŭi, pŏsĭtum, *v.t.* 3, to place in or on, impose, assign

importo, *v.t.* 1, to carry in, import, cause

importūnĭtas, ātis, *f*, insolence

importūnus, a, um, *adj*, *adv*, ē, inconvenient, unsuitable, troublesome, rude

impŏtens, ntis, *adj*, powerless, weak, violent, headstrong

impŏtentĭa, ae, *f*, violence

impransus, a, um, *adj*, fasting

imprĕcātĭo, ōnis, *f*, imprecation, curse

imprĕcor, *v.t.* 1, *dep*, to pray for something for someone

impressĭo, ōnis, *f*, imprint, onset

impressus, a, um, *adj*, stamped, printed

imprīmis, *adv*, especially

imprĭmo, pressi, ssum, *v.t.* 3, to stamp, imprint, engrave

imprŏbĭtas, ātis, *f*, wickedness

imprŏbo, *v.t.* 1, to disapprove

imprŏbus, a, um, *adj*, *adv*, ē, bad, wicked, violent, enormous, shameless

imprōvĭdus, a, um, *adj*, not anticipating

imprōvīsus, a, um, *adj*, *adv*, o, unexpected

imprūdens, ntis, *adj*, *adv*, nter, unsuspecting, unaware

imprūdentĭa, ae, *f*, lack of foresight

impūbes, is, *adj*, youthful

impŭdens, ntis, *adj*, shameless

impŭdentĭa, ae, *f*, impudence

impŭdīcĭtĭa, ae, *f*, shameful behaviour

impŭdīcus, a, um, *adj*, shameless, lewd, disgusting

impugno, *v.t.* 1, to attack

impulsor, ōris, *m*, instigator

impulsus, ūs, *m*, pressure, impulse, suggestion

impūnē, *adv*, without punishment

impūnĭtas, ātis, *f*, impunity

impūnītus, a, um, *adj*, unpunished

impūrus, a, um, *adj*, filthy

impŭto, *v.t.* 1, to reckon, ascribe, impute

īmus, a, um, *adj*, lowest, last

in, *prep. with abl*, in, on, within, among; *with acc*, into, towards, till, against

ĭnaccessus, a, um, *adj*, inaccessible

ĭnaedĭfĭco, *v.t.* 1, to build on

ĭnaequābĭlis, e, *adj*, uneven, unlike

ĭnaequālis, e, *adj*, uneven, unlike

ĭnaequālĭtas, ātis, *f*, inequality

ĭnaestĭmābĭlis, e, *adj*, inestimable

ĭnāmābĭlis, e, *adj*, hateful

ĭnāmāresco, *v.i.* 3, to become bitter

ĭnambŭlo, *v.i.* 1, to walk up and down

ĭnāne, is, *n*, emptiness

ĭnānĭmus, a, um, *adj*, lifeless

ĭnānis, e, *adj*, *adv*, ĭter, empty, useless, vain

ĭnānĭtas, ātis, *f*, emptiness

ĭnărātus, a, um, *adj*, unploughed

ĭnardesco, arsi, *v.i.* 3, to catch fire, glow

ĭnassŭētus, a, um, *adj*, unaccustomed

ĭnaudax, ācis, *adj*, timid

ĭnaudĭo, *v.t.* 4, to hear

ĭnaudītus, a, um, *adj*, unheard of

ĭnaugŭro, *v.i.t.* 1, to divine omens; to consecrate, inaugurate

ĭnaurātus, a, um, *adj*, golden

ĭnauro, *v.t.* 1, to cover with gold

ĭnauspĭcātus, a, um, *adj*, without good omens

ĭnausus, a, um, *adj*, unattempted

incaedŭus, a, um, *adj*, uncut

incălesco, călŭi, *v.i.* 3, to grow hot, glow

incallĭdus, a, um, *adj*, stupid

incandesco, dŭi, *v.i.* 3, to grow hot, glow

incānesco, nŭi, *v.i.* 3, to grow grey or white

incanto, *v.t.* 1, to chant, bewitch

incānus, a, um, *adj*, grey, white

incassum, *adv*, in vain

incastīgātus, a, um, *adj*, unpunished

incautus, a, um, *adj*, *adv*, ē, rash, careless, unexpected

incēdo, cessi, ssum, *v.i.* 3, to advance, appear, enter

incendĭārĭus, ii, *m*, an incendiary

incendĭum, ii, *n*, fire, heat

incendo, cendi, censum, *v.t.* 3, to burn, excite, irritate

incensus, a, um, *adj*, unregistered

incensus, a, um, *adj*, burning, excited

inceptĭo, ōnis, *f*, an attempt, undertaking

inceptum, i, *n*, an attempt; undertaking

incertum, i, *n*, uncertainty

incertus, a, um, *adj*, uncertain, hesitating, doubtful

incesso, cessīvi, *v.t.* 3 to attack, accuse

incessus, ūs, *m*, walk, pace, approach

incesto, *v.t.* 1, to pollute

incestum, i, *n*, adultery, incest

incestus, a, um, *adj*, impure

incĭdo, cĭdi, cāsum, *v.i.* 3, to fall into or upon, meet, happen, occur
incīdo, cīdi, sum, *v.t.* 3, to cut into, carve, interrupt
incingo, nxi, nctum, *v.t.* 3, to encircle
incĭpĭo, cēpi, ceptum, *v.i.t.* 3, to begin; undertake
incīsĭo, ōnis, *f,* an incision
incĭtāmentum, i, *n,* incentive
incĭtātĭo, ōnis, *f,* instigation, energy
incīsūra, ae, *f,* cutting, incision
incĭtātus, a, um, *adj,* swift
incĭto, *v.t.* 1, to urge on, rouse, excite, inspire
incĭtus, a, um, *adj,* swift
inclāmo, *v.i.t.* 1, to cry out; call out, to rebuke, abuse
inclēmens, ntis, *adj,* **nter,** harsh, severe
inclēmentĭa, ae, *f,* harshness
inclīnātĭo, ōnis, *f,* leaning, tendency
inclīno, *v.i.t.* 1, to sink, yield; bend, turn, change
inclīnātus, a, um, *adj,* bent, disposed
inclĭtus, a, um, *adj,* famous
inclūdo, si, sum, *v.t.* 3, to shut in, include, finish
inclūsĭo, ōnis, *f,* confinement
inclŭtus, a, um, *adj,* famous
incoctus, a, um, *adj,* uncooked
incognĭtus, a, um, *adj,* unknown
incŏhātus, a, um, *adj,* incomplete
incŏho, *v.i.t.* 1, to begin; undertake
incŏla, ae, *c,* inhabitant
incŏlo, lŭi, *v.i.t.* 3, to settle; inhabit
incŏlŭmis, e, *adj,* safe, sound
incŏlŭmĭtas, ātis, *f,* safety
incŏmĭtātus, a, um, *adj,* unaccompanied
incommŏdĭtas, ātis, *f,* unsuitability
incommŏdo, *v.i.* 1, to be annoying
incommŏdum, i, *n,* disadvantage
incommŏdus, a, um, *adj, adv,* **ē,** troublesome, unsuitable
incompertus, a, um, *adj,* unknown
incompŏsĭtus, a, um, *adj,* badly-arranged
incomptus, a, um, *adj,* unadorned
inconcessus, a, um, *adj,* illicit
inconcinnus, a, um, *adj,* awkward
incondĭtus, a, um, *adj,* irregular, confused, rude
inconsīdĕrātus, a, um, *adj, adv,* **ē,** thoughtless, inconsiderate
inconsōlābilis, e, *adj,* inconsolable
inconstans, ntis, *adj, adv,* **nter,** inconsistent, fickle
inconstantĭa, ae, *f,* inconstancy
inconsultus, a, um, *adj, adv,* **ē,** without advice, indiscreet

inconsumptus, a, um, *adj,* unconsumed
incontāmĭnātus, a, um, *adj,* uncontaminated
incontĭnens, ntis, *adj, adv,* **nter,** immoderate
incŏquo, xi, ctum, *v.t.* 3, to boil, dye
incorruptus, a, um, *adj,* unspoiled
incrēbresco, brŭi, *v.i.* 3, to increase, become prevalent
incrēdĭbĭlis, e, *adj, adv,* **ĭter,** incredible, unbelievable
incrēdŭlus, a, um, *adj,* unbelieving
incrēmentum, i, *n,* increase
increpĭto, *v.t.* 1, to rebuke
increpo, ŭi, ĭtum, *v.i.t.* 1, to rattle, clatter; blare out, rebuke, reprimand
incresco, ēvi, *v.i.* 3, to grow
incrŭentus, a, um, *adj,* bloodless
incrusto, *v.t.* 1, to coat over
incŭbo, ŭi, ĭtum, *v.i.* 1, to lie in or on, rest on, fall upon
inculco, *v.t.* 1, to trample on, cram in, force on, obtrude
incultus, a, um, *adj, adv,* **ē,** uncultivated, unpolished
incumbo, cŭbŭi, ĭtum, *v.i.* 3, to lean or lie on, overhang, fall upon, take pains over, influence
incūnābŭla, ōrum, *n.pl,* cradle, birthplace, origin, swaddling-clothes
incūrĭa, ae, *f,* neglect
incūrĭōsus, a, um, *adj, adv,* **ē,** indifferent
incurro, curri, cursum, *v.i.t.* 3, to run at, happen; attack
incursĭo, ōnis, *f,* raid, attack
incurso, *v.i.t.* 1, to run to; attack, strike
incursus, ūs, *m,* attack
incurvo, *v.t.* 1, to bend
incurvus, a, um, *adj,* bent
incūs, ūdis, *f,* anvil
incūso, *v.t.* 1, to accuse, blame
incustōdītus, a, um, *adj,* unguarded
incŭtĭo, cussi, cussum, *v.t.* 3, to strike upon, hurl, inflict
indāgātĭo, ōnis, *f,* investigation
indāgo, *v.t.* 1, to track down
indāgo, ĭnis, *f,* enclosing
indĕ, *adv,* from there, then
indēbĭtus, a, um, *adj,* not due
indĕcor, ōris, *adj,* disgraceful
indĕcŏro, *v.t.* 1, to disgrace
indĕcōrus, a, um, *adj, adv,* **ē,** unbecoming, unsightly, disgraceful
indēfensus, a, um, *adj,* undefended
indēfessus, a, um, *adj,* unwearied
indēlēbĭlis, e, *adj,* indestructible
indēlĭbātus, a, um, *adj,* untouched

For List of Abbreviations used, turn to pages 3, 4

indemnātus, a, um, *adj*, unsentenced

indēprensus, a, um, *adj*, unnoticed

index, icis, *m*, *f*, forefinger, informer, sign, list

indĭcĭum, ii, *n*, information, evidence, proof, indication

indĭco, *v.t.* 1, to show, indicate, give evidence

indīco, xi, ctum, *v.t.* 3, to announce, appoint, impose

indictus, a, um, *adj*, unsaid

indidem, *adv*, from the same place

indies, *adv*, from day to day

indifferens, ntis, *adj*, indifferent

indĭgĕna, ae, *adj*, native

indĭgĕo, *v.i.* 2, to need, want

indĭgestus, a, um, *adj*, confused

indignans, ntis, *adj*, enraged

indignātĭo, ōnis, *f*, indignation

indignĭtas, ātis, *f*, shameful behaviour, unworthiness

indignor, *v.t.* 1, *dep*, to be indignant at, scorn

indignus, a, um, *adj*, *adv*, ē, unworthy, shameful, cruel

indĭgus, a, um, *adj*, needing

indīligens, ntis, *adj*, *adv*, nter, careless

indīligentĭa, ae, *f*, carelessness

indiscrētus, a, um, *adj*, unseparated

indĭsertus, a, um, *adj*, at a loss for words

indīvĭdŭus, a, um, *adj*, indivisible

indo, dĭdi, dĭtum, *v.t.* 3, to put or place upon or into, attach

indŏcĭlis, e, *adj*, unteachable, untaught

indoctus, a, um, *adj*, untaught

indōles, is, *f*, inborn abilities

indŏlesco, lŭi, *v.i.* 3, to be in pain, to be troubled

indŏmĭtus, a, um, *adj*, untamed

indormĭo, *v.i.* 4, to fall asleep over

indōtātus, a, um, *adj*, without a dowry, poor

indŭbĭto, *v.i.* 1, to distrust

indŭbĭus, a, um, *adj*, not doubtful

indūco, xi, ctum, *v.t.* 3, to lead in, conduct, exhibit, spread over, put on (clothes), induce, resolve, cancel

inductĭo, ōnis, *f*, introduction, exhibition, intention

indulgens, ntis, *adj*, *adv*, nter, kind, indulgent, fond

indulgentĭa, ae, *f*, indulgence

indulgĕo, si, tum, *v.i.t.* 2, *with dat*, to be kind to; permit, grant

indŭo, ŭi, ūtum, *v.t.* 3, to put on (garment), assume

indūro, *v.t.* 1, to harden

indūsĭum, ii, *n*, woman's petticoat

industrĭa, ae, *f*, diligence; *with* de *or* ex, on purpose

industrĭus, a, um, *adj*, diligent

indūtĭae, ārum, *f*. *pl*, truce

indūtus, a, um, *adj*, clothed

inēdĭa, ae, *f*, fasting

inēlĕgans, ntis, *adj*, *adv*, nter, unrefined

inēluctābĭlis, e, *adj*, unavoidable

inemptus, a, um, *adj*, unbought

inēnarrābĭlis, e, *adj*, indescribable

inĕo, *v.i.t.* 4, to begin; enter, calculate, estimate, contrive

ineptĭae, ārum, *f*. *pl*, absurdities

ineptus, a, um, *adj*, *adv*, ē, improper, inept, foolish

inermis, e, *adj*, unarmed

iners, rtis, *adj*, unskilful, idle, sluggish

inertĭa, ae, *f*, ignorance, idleness

inērŭdĭtus, a, um, *adj*, illiterate

inēvĭtābĭlis, e, *adj*, unavoidable

inexcūsābĭlis, e, *adj*, inexcusable

inexercĭtātus, a, um, *adj*, untrained

inexhaustus, a, um, *adj*, inexhaustible

inexōrābĭlis, e, *adj*, inexorable

inexpectātus, a, um, *adj*, unexpected

inexpertus, a, um, *adj*, inexperienced, untried

inexpĭābĭlis, e, *adj*, irreconcilable

inexplēbĭlis, e, *adj*, insatiable

inexplētus, a, um, *adj*, unsatisfied

inexplĭcābĭlis, e, *adj*, inexplicable

inexplōrātus, a, um, *adj*, unexplored

inexpugnābĭlis, e, *adj*, impregnable

inexstinctus, a, um, *adj*, imperishable

inextrĭcābĭlis, e, *adj*, inextricable

infăbrē, *adv*, unskilfully

infăcētus, a, um, *adj*, coarse

infāmĭa, ae, *f*, disgrace

infāmis, e, *adj*, disreputable

infāmo, *v.t.* 1, to disgrace

infandus, a, um, *adj*, unutterable

infans, ntis, *adj*, speechless

infans, ntis, *c*, child, baby

infantĭa, ae, *f*, speechlessness, infancy

infătŭo, *v.t.* 1, to make a fool of

infaustus, a, um, *adj*, unfortunate

infector, ōris, *m*, dyer

infectus, a, um, *adj*, unfinished

infēcundus, a, um, *adj*, unfruitful

infēlix, īcis, *adj*, unhappy, unfortunate, barren

infensus, a, um, *adj*, enraged

infĕri, ōrum, *m*. *pl*, the dead

infĕrĭae, ārum, *f*. *pl*, sacrifices in honour of the dead

infĕrĭor, ĭus, *adv*, lower, later, younger, inferior

infĕrius, *adv*, lower
infernus, **a**, **um**, *adj*, lower, underground
infĕri, **ōrum**, *m. pl*, inhabitants of the
underworld, the dead
infero, **inferre**, **intŭli**, **illātum**, *v.t.
irreg*, to bring to or against, attack,
produce, inflict
infĕrus, **a**, **um**, *adj*, below, lower
infervesco, **ferbŭi**, *v.i.* 3, to boil
infesto, *v.t.* 1, to attack, molest
infestus, **a**, **um**, *adj*, *adv*, **ē**, dangerous,
hostile, unsafe
inficio, **fēci**, **fectum**, *v.t.* 3, to stain,
dye, taint, corrupt
infidēlis, **e**, *adj*, untrustworthy
infidēlitas, **ātis**, *f*, treachery
infidus, **a**, **um**, *adj*, treacherous
infigo, **xi**, **xum**, *v.t.* 3, to fix into, drive
in, imprint
infimus, **a**, **um**, *adj*, lowest
infindo, **fidi**, **fissum**, *v.t.* 3, to cut into
infinitas, **ātis**, *f*, endlessness
infinitus, **a**, **um**, *adj*, *adv*, **ē**, unlimited,
endless
infirmātio, **ōnis**, *f*, weakening
infirmitas, **ātis**, *f*, weakness
infirmo, *v.t.* 1, to weaken, annul
infirmus, **a**, **um**, *adj*, *adv*, **ē**, weak
infit, *v. defect*, he (she, it) begins
infitias **ĕo** (ire, ii), to deny
infitiātio, **ōnis**, *f*, denial
infitiātor, **ōris**, *m*, bad debtor
infitior, *v.t.* 1, *dep*, to deny
inflammātio, **ōnis**, *f*, inflammation,
setting on fire
inflammo, *v.t.* 1, to set on fire
inflātus, **ūs**, *m*, blast
inflātus, **a**, **um**, *adj*, puffed up,
haughty, inflated
inflecto, **xi**, **xum**, *v.t.* 3, to bend
inflētus, **a**, **um**, *adj*, unmourned
inflexibilis, **e**, *adj*, inflexible
inflexio, **ōnis**, *f*, bending
infligo, **xi**, **ctum**, *v.t.* 3, to strike (something) against
inflo, *v.t.* 1, to blow into
influo, **xi**, **xum**, *v.i.* 3, to flow into,
crowd in
infodio, **fodi**, **fossum**, *v.t.* 3, to dig in,
bury
informātio, **ōnis**, *f*, outline
informis, **e**, *adj*, shapeless
informo, *v.t.* 1, to shape, sketch,
educate
infortūnātus, **a**, **um**, *adj*, unfortunate
infrā, *adv*, *and prep. with acc*, below,
under
infractio, **ōnis**, *f*, breaking
infractus, **a**, **um**, *adj*, broken, exhausted

infrĕmo, **ŭi**, *v.i.* 3, to growl
infrendĕo, *v.i.* 2, to gnash the teeth,
threaten
infrēnis, **e** (**us**, **a**, **um**), *adj*, unbridled
infrēno, *v.t.* 1, to bridle, curb
infrĕquens, **ntis**, *adj*, rare, not well
filled
infrĕquentia, **ae**, *f*, scantiness
infringo, **frēgi**, **fractum**, *v.t.* 3, to break
off, crush, weaken
infula, **ae**, *f*, head-band, ribbon
infundibulum, **i**, *n*, funnel
infundo, **fūdi**, **fūsum**, *v.t.* 3, to pour
out, lay before, impart
infusco, *v.t.* 1, to darken, stain
infūsus, **a**, **um**, *adj*, streaming or falling over
ingĕmino, *v.i.t.* 1, to increase; repeat,
redouble
ingĕmisco, **mŭi**, *v.i.* 3, to sigh
ingĕmo, **ŭi**, *v.i.t.* 3, to groan; lament,
mourn
ingĕnĕro, *v.t.* 1, to produce
ingĕniōsus, **a**, **um**, *adj*, *adv*, **ē**, talented,
adapted to
ingĕnium, **ii**, *n*, natural disposition,
abilities, intelligence
ingens, **ntis**, *adj*, huge, famous
ingĕnuitas, **ātis**, *f*, good birth, gentlemanly character
ingĕnuus, **a**, **um**, *adj*, *adv*, **ē**, natural,
in-born, free-born, frank, honour-
able
ingĕnuus, **i**, *m* (**a**, **ae**, *f*), free-born man
or woman
ingĕro, **gessi**, **gestum**, *v.t.* 3, to carry,
throw or thrust into
ingigno, **gĕnui**, **gĕnitum**, *v.t.* 3, to implant, produce
inglōrius, **a**, **um**, *adj*, inglorious
ingluvies, **ēi**, *f*, gizzard, maw
ingrātiis, *adv*, unwillingly
ingrātus, **a**, **um**, *adj*, *adv*, **ē**, unpleasant, ungrateful
ingrăvesco, *v.i.* 3, to become heavy or
worse
ingrăvo, *v.t.* 1, to aggravate
ingrĕdior, **gressus**, *v.i.t.* 3, *dep*, to
advance; enter, upon
ingressio, **ōnis**, *f*, entering, pace
ingressus, **ūs**, *m*, entrance, inroad,
commencement
ingruo, **ŭi**, *v.i.* 3, to attack
inguen, **inis**, *n*, groin, abdomen
ingurgīto, *v.t.* 1, (*with* **se**) to gorge,
addict one's self to
inhăbilis, **e**, *adj*, unwieldy, incapable
inhăbitābilis, **e**, *adj*, uninhabitable
inhaerĕo, **si**, **sum**, *v.i.* 2, to cling to,
adhere to

inhaeresco, haesi, haesum, *v.i.* 3, to cling to, adhere to
inhĭbĕo, *v.t.* 2, to restrain
inhĭo, *v.i.* 1, to gape, gaze
inhŏnestus, a, um, *adj*, shameful
inhŏnōrātus, a, um, *adj*, unhonoured
inhorrĕo, *v.i.* 2, to bristle, shiver
inhorresco, *v.i.* 3, to bristle, shiver
inhospĭtālis, e, *adj*, inhospitable
inhospĭtus, a, um, *adj*, inhospitable
inhūmānĭtas, ātis, *f*, barbarity, niggardliness
inhūmānus, a, um, *adj*, *adv*, ē, ĭter, savage, uncivilized, rude
inhūmātus, a, um, *adj*, unburied
inĭbi, *adv*, there
inĭcĭo, iēci, iectum, *v.t.* 3, to throw into, seize, inspire
inĭmīcĭtĭa, ae, *f*, enmity
inĭmīco, *v.t.* 1, to make into enemies
inĭmīcus, a, um, *adj*, *adv*, ē, unfriendly, hostile
inĭmīcus, i, *m* (a, ae, *f*), enemy
inīquĭtas, ātis, *f*, unevenness, difficulty, injustice
inīquus, a, um, *adj*, *adv*, ē, uneven, unfair, unfortunate, hostile, disadvantageous
inĭtĭo, *v.t.* 1, to initiate
inĭtĭō, *adv*, in the beginning
inĭtĭum, ii, *n*, beginning, origin; (*in pl*) first principles, sacred rites
inĭūcundus, a, um, *adj*, *adv*, ē, unpleasant
inĭungo, nxi, nctum, *v.t.* 3, to join on to, inflict, impose
inĭūrātus, a, um, *adj*, without taking an oath
inĭūrĭa, ae, *f*, injury, wrong
inĭūrĭōsus, a, um, *adj*, wrongful
inĭussu, *adv*, without orders
inĭussus, a, um, *adj*, of one's accord
inĭustĭtĭa, ae, *f*, injustice
inĭustus, a, um, *adj*, *adv*, ē, unjust, wrongful, harsh
innascor, nātus, *v.i.* 3, *dep*, to be born in, grow up in
innăto, *v.t.* 1, to swim, float in
innātus, a, um, *adj*, innate
innāvĭgābĭlis, e, *adj*, unnavigable
innecto, xŭi, xum, *v.t.* 3, to tie, fasten, attach, contrive
innītor, nixus (nīsus), *v.* 3, *dep*, *with dat. or abl*, to lean on
inno, *v.i.* 1, to swim, float in
innŏcens, ntis, *adj*, harmless, blameless
innŏcentĭa, ae, *f*, integrity
innŏcŭus, a, um, *adj*, harmless
innoxĭus, a, um, *adj*, harmless, innocent, unhurt

innŭbus, a, um, *adj*, unmarried
innŭmĕrābĭlis, e, *adj*, countless
innŭmĕrus, a, um, *adj*, countless
innŭo, ŭi, ūtum, *v.i.* 3, to nod, hint
innuptus, a, um, *adj*, unmarried
inobservātus, a, um, *adj*, unperceived
inoffensus, a, um, *adj*, untouched, uninterrupted
inŏlesco, lēvi, lĭtum, *v.i.* 3, to grow in, take root
inŏpĭa, ae, *f*, lack, need
inŏpīnans, ntis, *adj*, unaware
inŏpīnātus, a, um, *adj*, *adv*, ē, ō, unexpected
inŏpīnus, a, um, *adj*, unexpected
inopportūnus, a, um, *adj*, unfitting, inopportune
inops, ŏpis, *adj*, helpless, needy
inordĭnātus, a, um, *adj*, in disorder
inornātus, a, um, *adj*, unadorned
inquam, *v. irreg*, I say
inquĭes, ētis, *f*, restlessness
inquĭētus, a, um, *adj*, restless
inquĭlīnus, i, *m*, lodger
inquĭnātus, a, um, *adj*, filthy
inquĭno, *v.t.* 1, to stain, corrupt
inquīro, sīvi, sītum, *v.t.* 3, to search for, examine
inquīsītĭo, ōnis, *f*, legal investigation
insălūbris, e, *adj*, unhealthy
insălūtātus, a, um, *adj*, without saying goodbye
insānābĭlis, e, *adj*, incurable
insānĭa, ae, *f*, madness, folly
insānĭo, *v.i.* 4, to be insane, to rage
insānĭtas, ātis, *f*, disease
insānus, a, um, *adj*, *adv*, ē, insane, frantic, excessive
insătĭābĭlis, e, *adj*, insatiable
inscĭens, ntis, *adj*, unaware
inscĭentĭa, ae, *f*, ignorance, inexperience
inscītĭa, ae, *f*, ignorance, inexperience
inscītus, a, um, *adj*, *adv*, ē, ignorant, stupid
inscĭus, a, um, *adj*, unaware
inscrībo, psi, ptum, *v.t.* 3, to write on, attribute
inscriptĭo, ōnis, *f*, title
insculpo, psi, ptum, *v.t.* 3, to engrave
insĕco, cŭi, ctum, *v.t.* 1, to cut up
insectātĭo, ōnis, *f*, pursuit
insectātor, ōris, *m*, pursuer
insector, *v.t.* 1, *dep*, to pursue, reproach
insectum, i, *n*, insect
insĕnesco, nŭi, *v.i.* 3, to grow old at
insĕpultus, a, um, *adj*, unburied
insĕquor, sĕcūtus, *v.i.t.* 3, *dep*, to follow; pursue, reproach
insĕro, sēvi, sĭtum, *v.t.* 3, to implant, ingraft

insĕro, rŭi, rtum, *v.t.* 3, to put in, introduce

inserto, *v.t.* 1, to insert

inservio, *v.i.* 4, to serve, be submissive to, attend to

insīdĕo, sēdi, sessum, *v.i.t.* 2, to sit upon, be fixed; occupy, inhabit

insĭdĭae, ārum, *f. pl,* ambush, plot; *with* **ex** *or* **per,** craftily

insĭdior, *v.* 1, *dep, with dat,* to lie in ambush

insĭdĭōsus, a, um, *adj, adv,* **ē,** cunning, dangerous

insīdo, sēdi, sessum, *v.i.t.* 3, to settle on or in; occupy

insigne, is, *n,* mark, sign, costume, signal, ornament

insignio, *v.t.* 4, to make distinguished

insignis, e, *adj,* conspicuous, famous, distinguished

insĭlĭo, ŭi, *v.i.* 4, to spring upon

insĭmŭlo, *v.t.* 1, to accuse

insincērus, a, um, *adj,* tainted

insĭnŭo, *v.i.t.* 1, to penetrate; insinuate

insĭpĭens, ntis, *adj,* foolish

insĭpĭentĭa, ae, *f,* folly

insisto, stĭti, *v.i.t.* 3, to step, stand, begin, halt; devote oneself to

insĭtus, a, um, *adj,* inborn

insŏlens, ntis, *adj, adv,* **nter,** unusual, unaccustomed, haughty

insŏlentĭa, ae, *f,* strangeness, novelty, affectation, arrogance

insŏlĭtus, a, um, *adj,* unaccustomed, unusual

insomnĭa, ae, *f,* sleeplessness

insomnis, e, *adj,* sleepless

insomnĭum, ĭi, *n,* dream

insŏno, ŭi, *v.i.* 1, to resound

insons, ntis, *adj,* innocent, harmless

inspecto, *v.t.* 1, to look at

inspērans, ntis, *adj,* not hoping

inspērātus, a, um, *adj,* unhoped for, unexpected

inspergo, si, sum, *v.t.* 3, to sprinkle

inspĭcio, spexi, spectum, *v.t.* 3, to examine, consider

inspĭro, *v.t.* 1, to breathe on, inspire

instăbĭlis, e, *adj,* unsteady, changeable

instans, ntis, *adj,* present

instar, *n, indecl,* resemblance, appearance, value; *with genit,* as big as, like

instauro, *v.t.* 1, to renew

insterno, strāvi, strātum, *v.t.* 3, to spread or cover over

instĭgo, *v.t.* 1, to incite

instillo, *v.t.* 1, to instil

instĭmŭlo, *v.t.* 1, to spur on

instinctus, ūs, *m,* impulse

instinctus, a, um, *adj,* incited

institor, ōris, *m,* commercial-traveller

instĭtŭo, ŭi, ūtum, *v.t.* 3, to set up, appoint, undertake, resolve, arrange, train

instĭtūtĭo, ōnis, *f,* arrangement, custom, education

instĭtūtum, i, *n,* purpose, plan, custom

insto, stĭti, stātum, *v.i.* 1, to stand over, harass, impend, urge on, pursue

instructus, a, um, *adj,* arranged, provided with

instrūmentum, i, *n,* tool, stores

instrŭo, xi, ctum, *v.t.* 3, to erect, arrange, provide, teach

insŭāvis, e, *adj,* unpleasant

insuesco, ēvi, ētum, *v.i.t.* 3, to become accustomed; to accustom

insuētus, a, um, *adj,* unaccustomed to, unusual

insŭla, ae, *f,* island, block of flats

insŭlānus, i, *m,* islander

insulsĭtas, ātis, *f,* silliness

insulsus, a, um, *adj, adv,* **ē,** tasteless, silly

insulto, *v.i.t.* 1, to jump, leap; to spring at, abuse

insum, inesse, infŭi, *v.i, irreg,* to be in, be contained in

insūmo, mpsi, mptum, *v.t.* 3, to employ, expend

insŭo, ŭi, ūtum, *v.t.* 3, to sew on

insŭper, *adv, and prep. with acc,* moreover, besides; above

**inoŭpŏrābĭlis, o, adj,* insurmountable

insurgo, surrexi, rectum, *v.i.* 3, to arise, rise to

insŭsurro, *v.i.t.* 1, to whisper

intābesco, bŭi, *v.i.* 3, to waste away

intactus, a, um, *adj,* untouched, unattempted, chaste

intāmĭnātus, a, um, *adj,* pure

intectus, a, um, *adj,* uncovered

intĕger, gra, grum, *adj, adv,* **ē,** untouched, perfect, blameless, unspoiled, undecided

intĕgo, xi, ctum, *v.t.* 3, to cover

intĕgrĭtas, ātis, *f,* completeness, uprightness

intĕgro, *v.t.* 1, to renew, refresh

intĕgŭmentum, i, *n,* covering, disguise

intellĕgens, ntis, *adj,* understanding

intellĕgentĭa, ae, *f,* understanding

intellĕgo, xi, ctum, *v.t.* 3, to understand, perceive

intĕmĕrātus, a, um, *adj,* pure

intempĕrans, ntis, *adj,* extravagant

intempĕrantĭa, ae, *f,* extravagance

For List of Abbreviations used, turn to pages 3, 4

intempĕrĭes, ĕi, *f,* inclement weather, violence

intempestīvus, a, um, *adj, adv,* **ē,** untimely, inconvenient

intempestus, a, um, *adj,* unseasonable, unhealthy; (with **nox**) the dead of night

intendo, dĭ, tum (sum), *v.t.* 3, to stretch or spread out, aim, direct, threaten, concentrate, intend

intentātus, a, um, *adj,* untried

intentĭo, ōnis, *f,* tension, effort, application

intentus, a, um, *adj, adv,* **ē,** stretched, bent, intent

intĕpesco, pŭi, *v.i.* 3, to grow warm

inter, *adv, and prep. with acc,* among, between, during

intercēdo, cessi, ssum, *v.i.* 3, to go between, intervene, occur

intercessĭo, ōnis, *f,* veto, intervention

intercessor, ōris, *m,* mediator, surety, user of the veto

intercīdo, dĭ, sum, *v.t.* 3, to cut up

intercĭdo, dĭ, *v.i.* 3, to happen, fall down, perish

intercĭpĭo, cēpi, ceptum, *v.t.* 3, to intercept, seize, steal

interclūdo, si, sum, *v.t.* 3, to block, cut off, hinder, separate, blockade

intercurro, curri, cursum, *v.i.* 3, to run between, intercede

interdīco, dixi, dictum, *v.t.* 3, to prohibit, banish

interdictum, i, *n,* prohibition

interdĭu, *adv,* in the daytime

interdum, *adv,* sometimes

intĕrĕā, *adv,* meanwhile

intĕrĕo, ĭi, ĭtum, *v.i.* 4, to perish, die, become lost

interest, see **intersum**

interfector, ōris, *m,* murderer

interfĭcĭo, fēci, fēctum, *v.t.* 3, to kill, destroy

interflŭo, xi, *v.i.* 3, to flow between

interfūsus, a, um, *adj,* poured between, interposed, stained

intĕrim, *adv,* meanwhile

intĕrĭmo, ēmi, emptum, *v.t.* 3, to take away, destroy, kill

intĕrĭor, ĭus, *comp. adj,* inner

intĕrĭus, *adv,* inside

intĕrĭtus, ūs, *m,* annihilation

interiăcĕo, *v.i.* 2, to lie between

intericĭo, iēci, iectum, *v.t.* 3, to put or throw between

interiectus, a, um, *adj,* interposed

interlābor, lapsus, *v.i.* 3, *dep,* to glide or flow between

interlĕgo, lēgi, lectum, *v.t.* 3, to pluck, pick

interlūcĕo, luxi, *v.i.* 2, to shine out, appear

interlŭo, *v.t.* 3, to flow between

intermĭnātus, a, um, *adj,* endless

intermiscĕo, scŭi, xtum, *v.t.* 2, to intermix

intermissĭo, ōnis, *f,* interruption, cessation

intermitto, mīsi, missum, *v.i.t.* 3, to cease; neglect, omit, stop, pause, interrupt

intermortŭus, a, um, *adj,* lifeless

internĕcīnus, a, um, *adj,* deadly, internecine

internĕcĭo, ōnis *f,* massacre

internecto, *v.t.* 3, to bind up

internosco, nōvi nōtum, *v.t.* 3, to distinguish between

internuntĭus, ii, *m,* negotiator

internus a, um *adj,* internal

interpellātĭo, ōnis, *f,* interruption

interpello, *v.t.* 1, to interrupt

interpŏlo, *v.t.* 1, to furbish

interpōno, pŏsŭi, ĭtum, *v.t.* 3, to put between, introduce; with **se,** to interfere; with **fidem,** to pledge

interpŏsĭtĭo, ōnis, *f,* insertion

interprĕs, ĕtis, *c,* negotiator

interprĕtātĭo, ōnis, *f,* explanation

interprĕtor, *v.t.* 1, *dep,* to explain

interpunctĭo, ōnis, *f,* punctuation

interpungo, nxi, ctum, *v.t.* 3, to punctuate

interquĭesco, quĭēvi, quĭētum, *v.i.* 3, to rest for a while

interregnum, i, *n,* vacancy in the kingship or high office

interrex, rēgis, *m,* regent

interrĭtus, a, um, *adj,* fearless

interrŏgātor, ōris, *m,* questioner

interrŏgātum, i, *n,* question

interrŏgo, *v.t.* 1, to inquire

interrumpo, rūpi, ruptum, *v.t.* 3, to break up, interrupt

intersaepĭo, psi, ptum, *v.t.* 4, to hedge in, cut off

interscindo, scĭdi, scissum, *v.t.* 3, to tear down, divide

intersĕro, rŭi, rtum, *v.t.* 3, to interpose

intersum, esse, fŭi, *v.i, irreg,* to lie between, differ, take part in; **interest,** *v. impers,* it concerns, it is of importance

intertexo, xŭi, xtum, *v.t.* 3, to intertwine

intervallum, i, *n,* space, pause

intervĕnĭo, vēni, ventum, *v.i.* 4, to interrupt, happen, prevent

interventus, ūs, *m*, intervention

intervīso, si, sum, *v.t.* 3, to inspect, visit occasionally

intestābĭlis, e, *adj*, abominable

intestīna, ōrum, *n.* pl, intestines

intestīnus, a, um, *adj*, internal

intexo, xŭi, xtum, *v.t.* 3, to interlace

intĭmus, a, um, *adj*, inmost

intŏlĕrābĭlis, e, *adj*, intolerable

intŏlĕrandus, a, um, *adj*, intolerable

intŏlĕrans, ntis, *adj, adv*, nter, impatient, intolerable

intŏno, ŭi, *v.i.* 1, to thunder

intonsus, a, um, *adj*, unshaven

intorquĕo, si, sum, *v.t.* 2, to twist, sprain, hurl

intrā, *adv, and prep. with acc*, on the inside, within

intractābĭlis, e, *adj*, unmanageable

intractātus, a, um, *adj*, untried

intrĕmo, ŭi, *v.i.* 3, to tremble

intrĕpĭdus, a, um, *adj*, fearless

intrō, *adv*, within, inside

intro, *v.i.t.* 1, to enter

intrōdūco, xi, ctum, *v.t.* 3, to lead in, introduce

intrōductĭo, ōnis, *f*, introduction

intrōĕo, *v.i.* 4, to enter

intrōfĕro, ferre, tŭli, lātum, *v.t, irreg*, to bring in

intrōgrĕdĭor, gressus, *v.i.* 3, *dep*, to enter

intrōĭtus, ūs *m*, entrance

intrōmitto, mī si, ssum, *v.t.* 3, to send in

introrsum (us), *adv*, within

intrōspĭcĭo, spexi, spectum, *v.t.* 3, to look into, examine

intŭĕor, *v.t.* 2, *dep*, to look at

intŭmesco, mŭi, *v.i.* 3, to swell

intus, *adv*, within, inside

intūtus, a, um, *adj*, unguarded

inultus, a, um, *adj*, unavenged

inumbro, *v.t.* 1, to shade

inundātĭo, ōnis, *f*, flooding

inundo, *v.i.t.* 1, to overflow; flood

inungo, nxi, unctum, *v.t.* 3, to anoint

inurbānus, a, um, *adj*, rude

inūro, ssi, stum, *v.t.* 3, to brand

inūsĭtātus, a, um, *adj, adv*, ē, unusual, strange

inūtĭlis, e, *adj*, useless

inūtĭlitas, ātis, *f*, uselessness

invādo, si, sum, *v.i.t.* 3, to enter; attack, invade, seize

invălĭdus, a, um, *adj*, weak

invĕho, xi, ctum, *v.t.* 3, to carry, bring to; *passive or reflex*, to ride, drive, attack (with words)

invĕnĭo, vēni, ventum, *v.t.* 4, to find, meet with, devise

inventĭo, ōnis, *f*, invention

inventor, ōris, *m*, inventor

inventum, i, *n*, invention

invĕnustus, a, um, *adj*, unattractive

invĕrēcundus, a, um, *adj*, immodest

invergo, *v.t.* 3, to pour on

inversus, a, um, *adj*, inverted, perverted

inverto, ti, sum, *v.t.* 3, to turn upside down, exchange

invespĕrascit, *v. impers*, evening is approaching

investĭgātĭo, ōnis, *f*, investigation

investīgo, *v.t.* 1, to search for

invĕtĕrasco, rāvi, *v.i.* 3, to grow old, become permanent

invĕtĕrātus, a, um, *adj*, old-established

invĕtĕro, *v.t.* 1, to endure

invĭcem, *adv*, alternately

invictus, a, um, *adj*, unconquered, invincible

invĭdĕo, vīdi, vīsum, *v.t.* 2, *with dat*; to envy, grudge

invĭdĭa, ae, *f*, envy, ill-will

invĭdĭōsus, a, um, *adj, adv*, ē, jealous, enviable

invĭdus, a, um, *adj*, envious

invĭgĭlo, *v.i.* 1, to be watchful

invĭŏlātus, a, um, *adj*, unharmed

invīso, si, sum, *v.t.* 3, to visit

invīsus, a, um, *adj*, hated

invīsus, a, um, *adj*, unseen

invītātĭo, ōnis, *f*, challenge, invitation

invīto, *v.t.* 1, to invite, challenge, tempt

invītus, a, um, *adj*, unwilling

invĭus, a, um, *adj*, pathless

invŏcātus, a, um, *adj*, uninvited

invŏco, *v.t.* 1, to appeal to

invŏlĭto, *v.i.* 1, to hover

invŏlo, *v.i.t.* 1, to fly at; attack

invŏlūcrum, i, *n*, wrapper

invŏlūtus, a, um, *adj*, intricate

involvo, volvi, vŏlūtum, *v.t.* 3, to roll on, wrap up, envelop

invulnĕrābĭlis, e, *adj*, invulnerable

ĭō, *interj*, oh! ah! ho!

ipse, a, um (*genit*, ipsius, *dat*, ipsi), *emphatic pron*, himself, herself, itself, precisely, just

īra, ae, *f*, anger

īrācundĭa, ae, *f*, rage, temper

īrācundus, a, um, *adj*, irritable

īrascor, īrātus, *v.* 3, *dep. with dat*, to be angry with

īrātus, a, um, *adj*, angry

ĭre, see ĕo

īris, ĭdis, *f*, iris

īrōnĭa, ae, *f*, irony

irpex, ĭcis, m, harrow
irrĕmĕābĭlis, e, adj, irretraceable
irrĕpĕrābĭlis, e, adj, irrecoverable
irrĕpertus, a, um, adj, undiscovered
irrēpo, psi, ptum, v.t. 3, to creep in, insinuate oneself
irrēquiētus, a, um, adj, restless
irrētĭo, v.t. 4, to entangle
irrētortus, a, um, adj, not turned back
irrĕvŏcābĭlis, e, adj, irrevocable
irrīdĕo, si, sum, v.i.t. 2, to joke, jeer; mock, ridicule
irrĭgātĭo, ōnis, f, irrigation
irrĭgo, v.t. 1, to water, refresh
irrĭgŭus, a, um, adj, well-watered, moistening
irrīsĭo, ōnis, f, mockery
irrīsus, ūs, m, mockery
irrīsor, ōris, m, scoffer
irrītābĭlis, e, adj, irritable
irrītāmen, ĭnis, n, incentive
irrītāmentum, i, n, incentive
irrīto, v.t. 1, to provoke
irrĭtus, a, um, adj, invalid, unsuccessful
irrŏgo, v.t. 1, to propose (against someone), inflict
irrŏro, v.t. 1, to bedew
irrumpo, rūpi, ptum, v.i.t. 3, to break in; attack, interrupt
irrŭo, ŭi, v.i. 3, to rush in, seize
irruptus, a, um, adj, unbroken
is, ĕa, id, demonst. pron, he, she, it, that
ischĭas, ădis, f, sciatica
iste, a, ud, demonst. pron, that
isthmus, i, m, isthmus
istīc, adv, there
istinc, adv, from there
istūc, adv, to that place
ĭtă, adv, in such a way, so
ĭtăque, conj, and so, therefore
ĭtem, adv, likewise, also
ĭter, ĭtĭnĕris, n, route, journey, march
ĭtĕrātĭo, ōnis, f, repetition
ĭtĕro, v.t. 1, to repeat
ĭtĕrum, adv, again
ĭtĭdem, adv, in the same way
ĭtĭo, ōnis, f, travelling

J (consonantal i)

iăcĕo, v.i. 2, to lie (recumbent), lie sick
iăcĭo, iēci, iactum, v.t. 3, to throw, lay down
iactans, ntis, pres. part, adj, boastful
iactantĭa, ae, f, ostentation
iactātĭo, ōnis, f, tossing, bragging
iactātor, ōris, m, braggart
iacto, v.t. 1, to throw about, boast

iactūra, ae, f, throwing overboard, sacrifice
iactus, ūs, m, throw, shot
iăcŭlātor, ōris, m, thrower
iăcŭlātrix, ĭcis, f, huntress
iăcŭlor, v.t. 1, dep, to hurl
iăcŭlum, i, n, javelin
iam, adv, already, now
iamdūdum, adv, a long time ago
iamprīdem, adv, for a long time now
iānĭtor, ōris, m, doorkeeper
iānŭa, ae, f, door, entrance
Iānŭārĭus (mensis), January
iĕcur, ŏris, n, liver
iēiūnĭtas, ātis, f, meagreness
iēiūnĭum, ii, n, fast, hunger
iēiūnus, a, um, adj, hungry, barren
ientācŭlum, i, n, breakfast
iento, v.i. 1, to breakfast
iŏcātĭo, ōnis, f, joke
iŏcor, v.i.t. 1, dep, to joke
iŏcōsus, a, um, adj, humorous
iŏcŭlārĭs, e, adj, amusing
iŏcŭlātor, ōris, m, joker
iŏcus, i, m, joke
iŭba, ae, f, mane, crest
iŭbar, ăris, n, radiance
iŭbĕo, iussi, iussum, v.t. 2, to order, tell
iūcundĭtas, ātis, f, pleasantness
iūcundus, a, um, adj, pleasant
iūdex, ĭcis, m, judge
iūdĭcĭalis, e, adj, judicial
iūdĭcatĭo ōnis, f, judgement
iūdĭcĭum, ii, n, trial, verdict, court discretion, judgement
iūdĭco, v.t. 1, to judge, decide
iŭgālis, e, adj, yoked together
iŭgāles, m. pl, chariot-horses
iūgĕrum, i, n, acre (approx.)
iūgis, e, adj, perpetual
iūglans, dis, f, walnut
iŭgo, v.t. 1, to marry, connect
iŭgōsus, a, um, adj, mountainous
iŭgŭlo, v.t. 1, to cut the throat
iŭgum, i, n, yoke, bench, mountain-ridge
Iūlĭus (mensis), July
iūmentum, i, n, pack-animal
iuncĕus, a, um, adj, made of rushes
iuncōsus, a, um, adj, full of rushes
iunctĭo, ōnis, f, junction
iunctūra, ae, f, joint
iuncus, i, m, bullrush
iungo, nxi, nctum, v.t. 3, to join
iūnĭor, comp. adj, from iŭvĕnis, younger
iūnĭpĕrus, i, f, juniper tree
Iūnĭus (mensis), June
iūrātor, ōris, m, commissioner of oaths

iūrātus, a, um, *adj,* bound by oath
iurgĭum, ii, *n,* quarrel
iurgo, *v.i.t.* 1, to quarrel; upbraid
iūris consultus, i, *m,* lawyer
iūris dictĭo, ōnis, *f,* jurisdiction
iūro, *v.i.t.* 1, to take an oath; to swear
  by
iūs, iūris, *n,* law, legal status, right,
  authority
iūs, iūris, *n,* soup
iusiūrandum, i, *n,* oath
iussum, i, *n,* order
iusta, ōrum, *n.pl,* due ceremonies
iustē, *adv,* rightly
iustitĭa, ae, *f,* justice
iustitĭum, *n,* holiday for lawcourts,
  public mourning
iustum, i, *n,* fairness
iustus, a, um, *adj,* fair, lawful
iŭvĕnālis, e, *adj,* youthful
iŭvenca, ae, *f,* heifer
iŭvencus, i, *m,* bullock
iŭvĕnesco, nŭi, *v.i.* 3, to reach youth
iŭvĕnīlis, e, *adj,* youthful
iŭvĕnis, is, *m, f,* young person; (*adj*)
  young
iŭvĕnor, *v.i.* 1, *dep,* to act youthfully
iŭventa, ae, *f,* the age of youth
iŭventas, ātis, *f,* the age of youth
iŭventus, ūtis, *f,* the age of youth
iŭvo, iūvi, iūtum, *v.t.* 1, to help,
  gratify; iŭvat (*impers. with acc*), it
  pleases, It is of use
iuxtā, *adv, and prep. with acc,* near
iuxtim, *adv, and prep. with acc,* next
  to

K

Kalendae, ārum, *f. pl,* the Kalends,
  the first day of the month

L

lăbĕfăcĭo, fēci, factum, *v.t.* 3, to
  shake, loosen, overthrow
lăbĕfacto, *v.t.* 1, to shake, destroy
lăbellum, i, *n,* a lip
lăbellum, i, *n,* tub, basin
lābes, is, *f,* sinking, downfall
lābes, is, *f,* spot, blemish
lābo, *v.i.* 1, to totter, waver
lābor, lapsus, *v.i.* 3, *dep,* to slip, slide,
  glide, pass away, be mistaken
lăbor, ōris, *m,* work, toil, workmanship, distress
lăbōrĭōsus, a, um, *adj, adv,* ē, laborious, industrious
lăbōro, *v.i.t.* 1, to strive, be in trouble
  or difficulty; to make, prepare
lăbrum, i, *n,* lip

lābrum, i, *n,* tub, basin
lăbўrinthus, i, *m,* labyrinth
lac, lactis, *n,* milk
lăcer, ĕra, ĕrum, *adj,* mangled
lăcerna, ae, *f,* cloak
lăcĕrātĭo, ōnis, *f,* laceration
lăcĕro, *v.t.* 1, to tear, rend, censure,
  destroy
lăcerta, ae, *f* (us, i, *m*), lizard
lăcertōsus, a, um, *adj,* brawny
lăcertus, i, *m,* arm, strength
lăcertus, i, *m,* lizard, newt
lăcesso, īvi, ītum, *v.t.* 3, to provoke,
  attack, irritate, urge
lăcinĭa, ae, *f,* edge of garment
lăcrima, ae, *f,* tear
lăcrimābilis, e, *adj,* mournful
lăcrimo, *v.i.* 1, to weep
lăcrimōsus, a, um, *adj,* tearful
lactens, ntis, *f,* very young (un-
  weaned) animal
lactĕus, a, um, *adj,* milky
lacto, *v.i.t.* 1, to have milk; suck
lactūca, ae, *f,* lettuce
lăcūna, ae, *f,* ditch, pond, gap
lăcūnar, āris, *n,* ceiling
lăcus, ūs, *m,* lake, tank, tub
laedo, si, sum, *v.t.* 3, to injure, offend
laena, ae, *f,* cloak
laetābilis, e, *adj,* joyful
laetĭfĭco, *v.t.* 1, to delight
laetitĭa, ae, *f,* joyfulness
laetor, *v.i.* 1, *dep,* to rejoice
laetus, a, um, *adj, adv,* ē, glad, cheerful, willing, pleased, prosperous,
  beautiful
laeva, ae, *f,* the left hand
laevus, a, um, *adj,* on the left side,
  unfortunate, foolish
lăgănum, i, *n,* a cake
lăgēna, ae, *f,* wine-jar
lăgōis, idis, *f,* grouse
lăgōpūs, ōdis, *f,* grouse
lăguncŭla, ae, *f,* small bottle
lambo, bi, bĭtum, *v.t.* 3, to lick
lāmentābilis, e, *adj,* mournful
lāmentātĭo, ōnis, *f,* mourning
lāmentor, *v.i.t.* 1, *dep,* to weep; mourn
lāmenta, ōrum, *n.pl,* moaning
lămĭa, ae, *f,* witch, vampire
lāmĭna, ae, *f,* thin metal plate
lampas, ădis, *f,* torch
lāna, ae, *f,* wool
lancĕa, ae, *f,* lance, spear
lānĕus, a, um, *adj,* woollen
languens, ntis, *adj,* faint, weak
languĕo, *v.i.* 2, to be faint or listless
languesco, gŭi, *v.i.* 3, to become faint
  or listless
languĭdus, a, um, *adj,* faint, weary,
  sluggish

For List of Abbreviations used, turn to pages 3, 4

languor, ōris, *m*, weakness, weariness, sluggishness
lănĭātus, ūs, *m*, laceration
lānĭcĭum, ii, *n*, wool
lănĭēna, ae, *f*, butcher's stall
lānĭfĭcus, a, um, *adj*, weaving
lānĭger, ĕra, ĕrum, *adj*, fleecy
lānĭo, *v.t.* 1, to mutilate
lănista, ae, *m*, fencing-master
lănĭus, ii, *m*, butcher
lanterna, ae, *f*, lamp, torch
lānūgo, ĭnis, *f*, down, hair
lanx, ncis, *f*, dish, plate
lăpăthus, i, *f*, sorrel
lăpĭcīda, ae, *m*, quarryman
lăpĭcīdīnae, ārum, *f. pl*, stone-quarries
lăpĭdātĭo, ōnis, *f*, stoning
lăpĭdĕus, a, um, *adj*, of stone
lăpĭdōsus, a, um, *adj*, stony
lăpillus, i, *m*, pebble, grain
lăpis, ĭdis, *m*, stone, milestone, jewel
lappa, ae, *f*, a bur
lapso, *v.i.* 1, to slip, stumble
lapsus, a, um, *adj*, fallen, sinking, ruined
lapsus, ūs, *m*, fall, slip, gliding
lăquĕar, āris, *n*, ceiling
lăquĕātus, a, um, *adj*, panelled
lăquĕus, i, *m*, noose, snare
lar, āris, *m*, guardian deity of a house, home
largĭor, *v.t.* 4, *dep*, to lavish, give
largĭtas, ātis, *f*, abundance
largītĭo, ōnis, *f*, generous distribution, bribery
largītor, ōris, *m*, briber, generous giver
largus, a, um, *adj*, *adv*, ē, iter, abundant, lavish, large
lārĭdum (lardum), i, *n*, lard
lārix, ĭcis, *f*, larch
larva, ae, *f*, ghost, mask
lascīvĭa, ae, *f*, playfulness
lascīvĭo, *v.i.* 4, to frolic
lascīvus, a, um, *adj*, playful, licentious
lassĭtūdo, ĭnis, *f*, weariness
lasso, *v.t.* 1, to tire, fatigue
lassus, a, um, *adj*, exhausted
lātē, *adv*, far and wide
lătĕbra, ae, *f*, hiding-place, subterfuge
lătĕbrōsus, a, um, *adj*, full of hiding-places, secret
lătens, ntis, *adj*, *adv*, nter, hidden, secret
lătĕo, *v.i.* 2, to lie hidden, keep out of sight
lăter, ĕris, *m*, brick, tile, ingot
lătērĭcĭus, a, um, *adj*, made of bricks
lătex, ĭcis, *m*, liquid
lătĭbŭlum, i, *n*, hiding-place

Lătīnē, *adv*, in Latin
lătĭto, *v.i.* 1, to lie hidden
lătĭtūdo, ĭnis, *f*, breadth
lātor, ōris, *m*, proposer of a law
lātrātor, ōris, *m*, a barker
lātrātus, ūs, *m*, barking
lātrīna, ae, *f*, water-closet
lātro, *v.i.t.* 1, to bark; bark at
lătro, ōnis, *m*, robber
lătrōcĭnĭum, ii, *n*, robbery, fraud, robber-band
lătrōcĭnor, *v.i.* 1, *dep*, to practise high-way robbery
lătruncŭlus, i, *m*, robber
lătus, a, um, *adj*, *adv*, ē, wide
lătus, ĕris, *n*, the side, flank, lungs
laudābilis, e, *adj*, praiseworthy
laudātĭo, ōnis, *f*, praises, eulogy
laudātor, ōris, *m*, praiser
laudātus, a, um, *adj*, praiseworthy
laudo, *v.t.* 1, to praise, name
laurĕa, ae, *f*, laurel (tree)
laurĕātus, a, um, *adj*, crowned with laurel (of victory)
laurĕus, a, um, *adj*, of laurel
laurus, i, *f*, laurel
laus, dis, *f*, praise, merit
lautē, *adv*, elegantly
lautĭtĭa, ae, *f*, elegance
lautŭmĭae, ārum, *f. pl*, stone-quarry
lautus, a, um, *adj*, elegant, splendid, noble
lăvātĭo, ōnis, *f*, ablution, washing
lăvo, lāvi, lautum, *v.i.t.* 1 or 3, to wash or wet
laxĭtas, ātis, *f*, spaciousness
laxo, *v.t.* 1, to enlarge, loosen, relax, relieve, weaken
laxus, a, um, *adj*, wide, loose
lĕa, ae, *f*, lioness
lĕaena, ae, *f*, lioness
lĕbes, ētis, *m*, copper basin
lectīca, ae, *f*, sedan, litter
lectĭo, ōnis, *f*, selection, reading aloud
lector, ōris, *m*, reader
lectŭlus, i, *m*, sofa, couch
lectus, a, um, *adj*, chosen, excellent
lectus, i, *m*, bed, couch
lectus, ūs, *m*, reading
lēgātĭo, ōnis, *f*, delegation
lēgātum, i, *n*, legacy
lēgātus, i, *m*, ambassador, delegate, lieutenant-general
lēges, see lex
lēgĭfer, ĕra, ĕrum, *adj*, law-giving
lēgĭo, ōnis, *f*, Roman legion (4,000–6,000 soldiers)
lĕgĭōnārĭus, a, um, *adj*, of a legion

lēgĭtĭmus, a, um, *adj*, legal, legitimate, proper, right

lēgo, *v.t.* 1, to send with a commission, appoint as a deputy, leave as a legacy

lĕgo, lēgi, lectum, *v.t.* 3, to read, gather, select, steal, pass through, sail by, survey

lĕgūmen, ĭnis, *n*, pulse, beans

lembus, i, *m*, yacht, cutter

lēmŭres, um, *m. pl*, ghosts, spirits

lēna, ae, *f*, bawd

lēnĭmen, ĭnis, *n*, alleviation, palliative

lēnĭmentum, i, *n*, alleviation, palliative

lēnĭo, *v.t.* 4, to soften, soothe

lēnis, e, *adj*, *adv*, ĭter, soft, smooth, gentle, calm

lēnĭtas, ātis, *f*, gentleness

lēno, ōnis, *m*, pimp, seducer

lēnōcĭnĭum, ĭi, *n*, pandering, ornamentation

lēnōcĭnor, *v.i*, *dep*, *with dat*, to flatter, promote

lens, ntis, *f*, lentil

lentesco, *v.i.* 3, to become soft or sticky

lentīgo, ĭnis, *f*, freckle

lentĭtūdo, ĭnis, *f*, apathy, sluggishness

lento, *v.t.* 1, to bend

lentus, a, um, *adj*, *adv*, ē, slow, flexible, sticky, tedious, calm (of character)

lēnuncŭlus, i, *m*, boat

lĕo, lōnis, *m*, lion

lĕpĭdus, a, um, *adj*, *adv*, ē, charming, elegant, pleasant

lĕpor (lĕpos), ōris, *m*, charm, pleasantness, wit

lĕpŏrārĭum, ĭi, *n*, warren

leprae, ārum, *f. pl*, leprosy

lĕprōsus, a, um, *adj*, leprous

lĕpus, ŏris, *m*, a hare

lĕpuscŭlus, i, *m*, leveret

lētālis, e, *adj*, fatal

lēthargĭcus, a, um, *adj*, lethargic

lēthargus, i, *m*, stupor

lētĭfer, ĕra, ĕrum, *adj*, deadly

lētum, i, *n*, death

lĕvāmen, ĭnis, *n*, consolation, comfort

lĕvāmentum, i, *n*, consolation, comfort

lĕvātĭo, ōnis, *f*, raising

lĕvis, e, *adj*, *adv*, ĭter, light, mild, light-armed, agile, trivial, unreliable

lēvis, e, *adj*, smooth, soft

lĕvĭtas, ātis, *f*, inconstancy

lēvĭtas, ātis, *f*, smoothness

lĕvo, *v.t.* 1, to raise, relieve, take away, support, soothe, release

lēvo, *v.t.* 1, to smooth

lex, lēgis, *f*, law, condition

lībāmen, ĭnis, *n*, drink-offering

lībāmentum, i, *n*, drink-offering

lībella, ae, *f*, small coin

lĭbellus, i, *m*, small book, pamphlet, diary

lībens, ntis, *adj*, *adv*, nter, with pleasure, willing

līber, ĕra, ĕrum, *adj*, *adv*, ē, free, frank

1. līber, ĕri, *m*, wine

2. līber, ĕri, *m*, child

lĭber, brī, *m*, book, tree-bark

lībĕrālis, e, *adj*, *adv*, ĭter, honourable, generous

lībĕrālĭtas, ātis, *f*, generosity

lībĕrātĭo, ōnis, *f*, release

lībĕrātor, ōris, *m*, liberator

lībĕri, ōrum, *m. pl*, children

lībĕro, *v.t.* 1, to release, free from slavery, acquit

lībertas, ātis, *f*, freedom

lībertīnus, i, *m*, freedman

lībertīnus, a, um, *adj*, of a freedman

lībertus, i, *m*, a freedman

lĭbet, lĭbuit, lĭbĭtum est, *v.* 2, *impers*, it is agreeable

lībīdĭnōsus, a, um, *adj*, lecherous

lībīdo, ĭnis, *f*, desire, passion, whim

lībo, *v.t.* 1, to taste, touch, pour out an offering of wine

lībra, ae, *f*, Roman pound (12 oz.), pair of scales

lībrāmentum, i, *n*, a weight

lībrārĭus, i, *m*, secretary

lībrārĭus, a, um, *adj*, of books

lībrātus, a, um, *adj*, balanced

lībrīlis, e, *adj*, weighing a pound

lībro, *v.t.* 1, to balance, hurl

lībum, i, *n*, pancake

līburna, ae, *f*, fast sailing-ship

līcenter, *adv*, without restraint

līcentĭa, ae, *f*, freedom, licence

līcĕo, *v.i.* 2, to be for sale, be valued at

līcĕor, *v.t.* 2, *dep*, to bid (for)

līcet, cŭit, cĭtum est, *v.* 2, *impers*, it is allowed, one may

līcet, *conj*, although

līcĭtus, a, um, *adj*, permitted

līcĭtātĭo, ōnis, *f*, bidding

līcĭum, ĭi, *n*, a thread

līctor, ōris, *m*, official attendant of high magistrates

līēn, ēnis, *m*, spleen

līgāmen, ĭnis, *n*, bandage

līgāmentum, i, *n*, ligament

līgnārĭus, ĭi, *m*, carpenter, joiner

līgnātĭo, ōnis, *f*, wood-gathering

līgnātor, ōris, *m*, wood-cutter

līgnĕus, a, um, *adj*, wooden

līgnor, *v.i.* 1, *dep*, to collect wood

lignum, i, n, wood
ligo, v.t. 1, to tie, bind
ligo, ōnis, m, hoe
ligŭla, ae, f, small tongue (of land);
tongue of a shoe
ligŭrio, v.t. 4, to lick, desire
ligustrum, i, n, a plant, privet
lilium, ii, n, lily
lima, ae, f, file
limax, ācis, f, slug
limbus, i, m, border, edge
limen, inis, n, door-step, door, lintel
limĕs, itis, m, boundary, track
limo, v.t. 1, to file, polish, finish
limōsus, a, um, adj, slimy, muddy
limpĭdus, a, um, adj, clear, bright
limus, a, um, adj, aslant
limus, i, m, slime, mud
limus, i, m, apron
lināmentum, i, n, linen, lint
linĕa, ae, f, thread, string, line, end,
goal
linĕāmentum, i, n, line, feature
linĕus, a, um, adj, linen
lingo, nxi, v.t. 3, to lick
lingua, ae, f, tongue, speech, language
liniger, ĕra, ĕrum, adj, clothed in
linen
lino, lēvi, litum, v.t. 3, to daub, smear
over
linquo, līqui, v.t. 3, to leave
lintĕo, ōnis, m, linen-weaver
linter, tris, f, boat, tray
lintĕum, i, n, linen
lintĕus, a, um, adj, of linen
linum, i, n, flax, linen, thread, rope,
net
lippĭtūdo, inis, f, inflammation of the
eyes
lippus, a, um, adj, blear-eyed
liquĕfăcio, fēci, factum, v.t. 3, to melt,
dissolve
liquĕfactus, a, um, adj, molten
liquens, ntis, adj, liquid
liquĕo, liqui, v.i. 2, to be clear
liquesco, licŭi, v.i. 3, to melt
liquĭdus, a, um, adj, liquid, flowing,
clear
liquo, v.t. 1, to melt, filter
liquor, v.i. 3, dep, to melt, flow
liquor, ōris, m, a liquid
lis, tis, f, dispute, lawsuit
litĭgĭōsus, a, um, adj, quarrelsome
litigo, v.i. 1, to quarrel
lito, v.i.t. 1, to make a sacrifice with
favourable omens; appease
litŏrĕus, a, um, adj, of the sea-shore
littĕra, ae, f, a letter of the alphabet
littĕrae, ārum, f. pl, a letter, document, literature, learning
littĕrātus, a, um, adj, educated

littĕrŭla, ae, f, small letter, moderate
literary knowledge
litūra, ae, f, smear, erasure
litus, ōris, n, sea-shore
litŭus, i, m, augur's staff, trumpet
livens, ntis, adj, bluish
livĕo, v.i. 2, to be black and blue
livĭdus, a, um, adj, bluish, black and
blue, envious
livor, ōris, m, leaden colour, envy,
malice
lixa, ae, m, camp-follower
lōca, ōrum, n.pl, a region
lōcātĭo, ōnis, f, placing, arrangement,
lease
lōco, v.t. 1, to place, arrange, give in
marriage, lease, contract for
lōcŭlāmentum, i, n, box
lōcŭlus, i, m, satchel, purse
lōcŭplēs, ētis, adj, wealthy
lōcŭplēto, v.t. 1, to enrich
lŏcus, i, m, place, position, topic, subject, cause, reason
lōcusta, ae, f, locust
lōcūtĭo, ōnis, f, speaking, pronunciation, phrase
lōdix, icis, f, blanket
lŏgĭca, ōrum, n.pl, logic
lŏgĭcus, a, um, adj, logical
lōlīgo, inis, f, cuttle-fish
lōlium, ii, n, darnel
longaevus, a, um, adj, ancient
longē, adv, far off, greatly
longinquĭtas, ātis, f, duration, distance
longinquus, a, um, adj, distant,
strange, prolonged
longitūdo, inis, f, length
longŭrius, ii, m, long pole
longus, a, um, adj, long, tall, vast,
distant, tedious
lŏquācĭtas, ātis, f, talkativeness
lŏquax, ācis, adj, adv, iter, talkative,
babbling
lŏquēla, ae, f, speech, discourse
lŏquor, lŏcūtus, v.i.t. 3, dep, to speak;
tell, mention, declare
lōrīca, ae, f, breastplate
lōripēs, pĕdis, adj, bandy-legged
lōrum, i, n, strap, whip
lōtos (lōtus), i, f, lotus-tree
lŭbens, lŭbet, see libens, libet
lūbrĭcus, a, um, adj, slippery, dangerous, deceitful
lŭcellum, i, n, slight profit
lūcĕo, xi, v.i. 2, to shine
lūcet, v. impers, day breaks
lūcerna, ae, f, lamp
lūcesco, v.i. 3, to dawn
lūcĭdus, a, um, adj, bright, clear
lūcĭfer, ĕrum, adj, light-bringing;
lūcĭfer ĕri, m, morning-star

lūcifŭgus, a, um, *adj*, retiring
lŭcrātīvus, a, um, *adj*, profitable
lŭcror, *v.t.* 1, *dep*, to gain, win
lŭcrum, i, *n*, profit, advantage
luctāmen, inis, *n*, wrestling, struggle
luctātio, ōnis, *f*, wrestling, struggle
luctātor, ōris, *m*, wrestler
luctīficus, a, um, *adj*, woeful
luctor, *v.i.* 1, *dep*, to struggle
luctŭōsus, a, um, *adj*, sorrowful
luctus, ūs, *m*, grief, mourning (clothes)
lūcŭbrātio, ōnis, *f*, night-work
lūcŭlentus, a, um, *adj*, bright
lūcus, i, *m*, wood, grove
lūdĭbrium, ii, *n*, mockery, jest, laughing-stock
lūdibundus, a, um, *adj*, playful
lūdicer, īcra, īcrum, *adj*, sportive, theatrical
lūdĭcrum, i, *n*, public show or games, a play
lūdĭfĭcātio, ōnis, *f*, mocking
lūdĭfĭcor, *v.i.t.* 1, *dep* (lūdĭfĭco, *v.t.* 1), to mock, deceive
lūdĭmăgister, tri, *m*, schoolmaster
lūdius, ii, *m*, pantomine-actor
lūdo, si, sum, *v.i.t.* 3, to play, frolic; mock, deceive
lūdus, i, *m*, a play, game, public games, school, joke
lŭes, is, *f*, an epidemic
lūgĕo, xi, ctum, *v.i.t.* 2, to mourn
lūgŭbris, e, *adj*, lamentable, disastrous
lumbus, i, *m*, loin
lūmen, inis, *n*, light, lamp, gleam, life, eye, glory
lūna, ae, *f*, moon
lūnāris, e, *adj*, lunar
lūnātus, a, um, *adj*, crescent-shaped
lūno, *v.t.* 1, to bend into a crescent-shape
lŭo, lŭi, *v.t.* 3, to pay a debt or penalty, undergo, atone for
lŭpāta, ōrum, *n.pl*, horse-bit
lŭpātus, a, um, *adj*, jagged
lŭpīnus, a, um, *adj*, of the wolf
lŭpīnus, i, *m*, lupin (plant)
lŭpus, i, *m*, wolf, pike (fish), a jagged bit, hook
lūridus, a, um, *adj*, lurid, sallow
luscĭnia, ae, *f*, nightingale
lūsor, ōris, *m*, player, mocker
lustrālis, e, *adj*, expiatory
lustrātio, ōnis, *f*. purification by sacrifice
lustro, *v.t.* 1, to purify by sacrifice, wander over, review
lustrum, i, *n*, den, wood
lustrum, i, *n*, purificatory sacrifice, period of five years

lūsus, ūs, *m*, play, sport, game
lūtĕŏlus, a, um, *adj*, yellow
lūtĕus, a, um, *adj*, golden-yellow
lūtĕus, a, um, *adj*, muddy, worthless
lūtra, ae, *f*, otter
lūtŭlentus, a, um, *adj*, filthy
lūtum, i, *n*, yellow
lŭtum, i, *n*, mud, clay
lux, lūcis, *f*, light, dawn, day, life, brightness, glory
luxŭria, ae, *f*, luxuriance, extravagance
luxŭrio, *v.i.* 1 (luxŭrior, *v.* 1, *dep*), to be overgrown, to have in excess, run riot
luxŭriōsus, a, um, *adj*, luxuriant, excessive
luxus, ūs, *m*, extravagance, pomp
lychnūcus, i, *m*, lamp-stand
lychnus, i, *m*, light, lamp
lympha, ae, *f*, water
lymphātus, a, um, *adj*, frenzied
lyncēus, a, um, *adj*, sharp-eyed
lynx, cis, *c*, lynx
lyra, ae, *f*, lute, poetry, song
lyricus, a, um, *adj*, of the lute, lyric

M

măcellum, i, *n*, food-market
măcer, cra, crum, *adj*, lean, thin
măcēria, ac, *f*, wall
măcĕro, *v.t.* 1, to soften, weaken, torment
māchina, ae, *f*, engine, machine, battering-ram, trick, plan
māchinālis, e, *adj*, mechanical
māchinātio, ōnis, *f*, contrivance, machine, trick
māchinātor, ōris, *m*, engineer, inventor
māchinor, *v.t.* 1, *dep*, to design, plot
măcies, ēi, *f*, thinness, poverty
macte or macti (*voc. of* mactus), good luck! well done!
macto, *v.t.* 1, to sacrifice a victim, reward, honour, destroy
mactus, a, um, *adj*, worshipped
măcŭla, ae, *f*, spot, stain, fault, mesh
măcŭlo, *v.t.* 1, to stain, disgrace
măcŭlōsus, a, um, *adj*, spotted, dishonoured
mădĕfăcio, fēci, factum, *v.t.* 3, to soak, drench
mădens, ntis, *adj*, moist, drunk
mădĕo, *v.i.* 2, to be moist, to drip, to be boiled, softened
mădesco, dŭi, *v.i.* 3, to become wet
mădidus, a, um, *adj*, soaked
maena, ae, *f*, small salted fish

For List of Abbreviations used, turn to pages 3, 4

maeniānum, i, *n*, balcony
maerens, ntis, *adj*, mourning
maerĕo, *v.i.t.* 2, to mourn; bewail
maeror, ōris, *m*, grief, mourning
maestitĭa, ae, *f*, sadness
maestus, a, um, *adj*, sad
māga, ae, *f*, witch
māgālĭa, ĭum, *n.pl*, huts
māgĭcus, a, um, *adj*, magic
māgis, *comp. adv* (magnus), more, rather
māgister, tri, *m*, master, leader, director, teacher
māgistērĭum, ii, *n*, president's position
māgistra, ae, *f*, mistress
māgistrātus, ūs, *m*, magistracy, magistrate
magnānĭmĭtas, ātis, *f*, magnanimity
magnānĭmus, a, um, *adj*, great-hearted
magnes, ētis, *m*, magnet
magnētĭcus, a, um, *adj*, magnetic
magni, see magnus
magnĭfĭcentĭa, ae, *f*, nobleness, splendour, boasting
magnĭfĭcus, a, um, *adj*, *adv*, ē, noble, distinguished, sumptuous, bragging
magnĭlŏquentĭa, ae, *f*, high-sounding language
magnĭtūdo, ĭnis, *f*, size
magnŏpĕrē, *adv*, very much
magnus, a, um, *adj*, large, great; magni or magno, at a high price
māgus, i, *m*, magician
Māius (mensis), May
māiestas, ātis, *f*, greatness, grandeur, sovereignty, treason
māior, *comp. adj*, larger, greater; māiōres, um, *m. pl*, ancestors, the Senate; maior nātu, older
māla, ae, *f*, cheek-bone, jaw
mālācĭa, ae, *f*, a calm at sea
mālagma, ătis, *n*, poultice
mălē, *adv*, badly, exceedingly; often reverses the meaning of an adj: male sānus, deranged
mălēdĭcens, ntis, *adj*, abusive
mălēdīco, xi, ctum, *v.i.* 3, to abuse, slander
mălēdictĭo, ōnis, *f*, abuse
mălēdictum, i, *n*, abusive word
mălēdĭcus, a, um, *adj*, abusive
mălēfĭcĭum, ii, *n*, wrongdoing
mălēfĭcus, a, um, *adj*, evil-doing
mălēsuādus, a, um, *adj*, persuading towards wrong
mălēvŏlens, ntis, *adj*, spiteful
mălēvŏlentĭa, ae, *f*, malice
mălēvŏlus, a, um, *adj*, spiteful

mălignus, a, um, *adj*, malicious
mălitĭa, ae, *f*, malice
mālitĭōsus, a, um, *adj*, wicked
mallĕus, i, *m*, hammer
mālo, malle, mālŭi, *v.t. irreg*, to prefer
mālŏbăthrum, i, *n*, a costly ointment
mālum, i, *n*, apple, fruit
mălum, i, *n*, evil, misfortune
mălus, a, um, *adj*, bad, harmful
mālus, i, *m*, mast
malva, ae, *f*, the mallow
mamma, ae, *f*, breast, teat
manceps, cipis, *m*, contractor
mancĭpĭum, ii, *n*, legal purchase, right of ownership, slave
mancĭpo, *v.t.* 1, to sell, transfer
mancus, a, um, *adj*, maimed
mandātum, i, *n*, order, commission
mandātus, ūs, *m*, order, commission
mando, *v.t.* 1, to order, commission, commit
mandūco, *v.t.* 1, to chew
māne, *indecl. n*, morning; *adv*, in the morning
mănĕo, nsi, nsum, *v.i.t.* 2, to stay, remain, continue; await
mānes, ĭum, *m. pl*, deified ghosts of the dead
mănĭcae, ārum, *f. pl*, glove, gauntlet, handcuff
mănĭfestus, a, um, *adj*, *adv*, ō, clear, apparent
mănĭpŭlāris, e, *adj*, belonging to a company (a soldier)
mănĭpŭlus, i, *m*, handful, bundle, company of soldiers
mannus, i, *m*, coach-horse, pony
māno, *v.i.t.* 1, to flow, trickle; pour out
mansĭo, ōnis, *f*, a stay, inn
mansŭēfăcĭo, fēci, factum, *v.t.* 3, to tame, civilize
mansŭesco, sŭēvi, sŭētum, *v.i.* 3, to grow tame or gentle
mansŭētus, a, um, *adj*, gentle
mansŭētūdo, ĭnis, *f*, gentleness
mansūrus, a, um, *adj*, lasting
mantēle, is, *n*, towel, cloth
mantĭca, ae, *f*, suit-case
mănūbĭae, ārum, *f. pl*, money from the sale of booty
mănūbrĭum, ii, *n*, handle
mănūmissĭo, ōnis, *f*, the freeing of a slave
mănūmitto, mīsi, missum, *v.t.* 3, to set free a slave
mănus, ūs, *f*, hand, bravery, combat, violence, grappling-iron, armed band
māpālĭa, ĭum, *n. pl*, African huts

MAP 73 MEN

mappa, ae, f, towel, napkin

marceo, v.i. 2, to be weak

marcesco, v.i. 3, to wither

marcidus, a, um, adj, decayed

mare, is, n, the sea

marga, ae, f, marl

margarita, ae, f, pearl

margo, inis, m, f, edge, border

marinus, a, um, adj, of the sea

marita, ae, f, wife

maritalis, e, adj, matrimonial

maritimus, a, um, adj, of the sea

maritus, a, um, adj, matrimonial

maritus, i, m, husband

marmor, oris, n, marble, statue; in pl, surface of the sea

marmoreus, a, um, adj, of marble

martialis, e, adj, sacred to Mars

martius, a, um, adj, sacred to Mars

Martius (mensis), March

martyr, yris, o, martyr

martyrium, ii, n, martyrdom

mas, maris, adj, male

masculus, a, um, adj, male, bold

massa, ae, f, lump, mass

matellio, onis, m, pot

mater, tris, f, mother

materfamilias, matrisfamilias, f, mistress of the house

materia, ae, f, timber, materials, topic, opportunity

materis, is, f, Celtic javelin

maternus, a, um, adj, maternal

matertera, ae, f, maternal aunt

mathematica, ae, f, mathematics

mathematicus, a, um, adj, mathematical

matricida, ae, c, murderer of his (her) mother

matrimonium, ii, n, marriage

matrona, ae, f, married woman

matronalis, e, adj, of a married woman

mature, adv, at the proper time, soon, quickly

maturesco, rui, v.i. 3, to ripen

maturitas, atis, f, ripeness

maturo, v.i.t. 1, to ripen, hurry; bring to maturity

maturus, a, um, adj, mature, ripe, early

matutinus, a, um, adj, of the morning

maxilla, ae, f, jawbone, jaw

maxime, adv, especially, very

maximus, a, um, sup. adj, very large or great

mazonomus, i, m, dish

me, acc. or abl. of ego (1)

meatus, us, m, motion, course

medeor, v. 2, dep. with dat, to heal, remedy, amend

mediastinus, i, m, drudge

medica, ae, f, a kind of clover

medicabilis, e, adj, curable

medicamen, inis, n, remedy, drug

medicamentum, i, n, remedy, drug

medicamentarius, a, um, adj, of drugs

medicina, ae, f, the art of medicine, remedy

medico, v.t. 1, to heal, sprinkle, dye

medicor, v.t. 1, dep, to heal

medicus, a, um, adj, healing

medicus, i, m, doctor, surgeon

medimnum, i, n, bushel

mediocris, e, adj, adv, iter, ordinary, insignificant

mediocritas, atis, f, a middle state, insignificance

meditatio, onis, f, contemplation, preparation

meditatus, a, um, adj, considered

mediterraneus, a, um, adj, inland

meditor, v.i.t. 1, dep, to consider, muse; study, intend, practise

medium, ii, n, middle, the public

medius, a, um, adj, middle, neutral

medius, i, m, mediator

medulla, ae, f, kernel, marrow

meio, v.i. 3, to urinate

mel, mellis, n, honey

melancholicus, a, um, adj, melancholic

meles, is, f, badger

melimela, orum, n. pl, honey apples

mellor, us, comp. adj, better

melisphyllum, i, n, balm

melius, comp. adv, better

mellifer, era, erum, adj, honey-producing

mellifico, v.t. 1, to make honey

mellitus, a, um, adj, of honey

melo, onis, m, melon

melos, i, n, tune, song

membrana, ae, f, skin, parchment

membratim, adv, piece by piece

membrum, i, n, limb, division

memini, isse, v.i. defective, to remember

memor, oris, adj, remembering, mindful

memorabilis, e, adj, memorable

memorandus, a, um, adj, memorable

memoratus, a, um, adj, renowned

memoria, ae, f, memory, posterity, historical account, tradition

memoro, v.t. 1, to mention

menda, ae, f, defect

mendacium, ii, n, a lie

mendax, acis, adj, lying, false

mendicitas, atis, f, poverty

mendico, v.i. 1, to beg

mendicus, a, um, adj, needy

mendicus, i, m, beggar

mendōsus, a, um, *adj, adv,* ē, faulty, false

mendum, ǐ, *n,* blunder, defect, mistake

mens, ntis, *f,* mind, intellect, understanding, intention, courage

mensa, ae, *f,* table, course; sěcunda mensa, dessert

mensārius, ǐǐ, *m,* banker

mensis, is, *m,* month

mensor, ōris, *m,* valuer, surveyor

menstrǔus, a, um, *adj,* monthly

mensūra, ae, *f,* measurement, quantity

mensus, a, um, *adj,* measured off

menta, ae, *f,* mint

mentǐo, ōnis, *f,* recollection, mention

mentǐor, *v.i.t.* 4, *dep,* to lie, cheat; counterfeit, imitate

mentītus, a, um, *adj,* counterfeit

mentum, ǐ, *n,* chin

měo, *v.i.* 1, to go

měrācus, a, um, *adj,* unmixed

mercātor, ōris, *m,* wholesaler

mercātūra, ae, *f,* trade

mercātus, ūs, *m,* trade, market

mercēdǔla, ae, *f,* small wages

mercēnārius, a, um, *adj,* hired

merces, ēdis, *f,* pay, wages, rent, interest, reward

merces (*pl*), see merx

mercor, *v.t.* 1, *dep,* to buy

měrens, ntis, *adj,* deserving

měrěo, *v.t. dep)* 2, to deserve, earn; with stipendǐa, to serve as a soldier

měrětrīcius, a, um, *adj,* of prostitutes

měrětrix, trīcis, *f,* prostitute

merges, ǐtis, *f,* sheaf

mergo, sǐ, sum, *v.t.* 3, to immerse

mergus, ǐ, *m,* sea-bird (diver)

měrīdiānus, a, um, *adj,* of midday

měrīdies, ēi, *m,* midday, south

měrītōrius, a, um, *adj,* bringing in money

měrǐtum, ǐ, *n,* reward, benefit, fault, blame

měrǐtus, a, um, *adj, adv,* ō, deserved, deserving

měrops, ǒpis, *m,* bee-eating bird

merso, *v.t.* 1, to immerse, drown

měrǔla, ae, *f,* blackbird

měrum, ǐ, *n,* pure wine

měrus, a, um, *adj,* pure, only, genuine

merx, cis, *f,* goods, commodities

messis, is, *f,* harvest, crops

messor, ōris, *m,* harvester

mēta, ae, *f,* winning-post, end, cone

mětallǐcus, a, um, *adj,* metallic

mětallǐcus, ǐ, *m,* miner

mětallum, ǐ, *n,* mine, metal

mētātor, ōris, *m,* surveyor

mētǐor, mensus, *v.t.* 4, *dep,* to measure, distribute, traverse, estimate, value

mēto, ssǔi, ssum, *v.t.* 3, to mow, gather, cut down

mētor, *v.t.* 1, *dep,* to measure, mark out, traverse

mětrǐcus, a, um, *adj,* metrical

mětǔendus, a, um, *adj,* formidable

mětǔo, ǔi, ūtum, *v.i.t.* 3, to be afraid; to fear

mětus, ūs, *m.* fear, awe

měus, a, um, *adj,* my, mine: měǐ, ōrum, *m. pl,* my relatives

mīca, ae, *f,* crumb

mǐco, ǔi, *v.i.* 1, to tremble, sparkle

mǐgrātǐo, ōnis, *f,* migration

mǐgro, *v.i.* 1, to depart, change

mīlēs, ǐtis, *c,* soldier, army

mīlia, see mille

mīliārǐum, ǐǐ, *n,* mile-stone

mīlǐtāris, e, *adj,* military

mīlǐtāris, is, *m,* soldier

mīlǐtǐa, ae, *f,* military service, warfare

mīlǐto, *v.i.* 1, to serve as a soldier

mīlǐum, ǐǐ, *n,* millet

mille (*pl,* mīlia, with *genit.*), a thousand; mille passus, or passuum, a mile

millēsǐmus, a, um, *adj,* the thousandth

millǐes (millǐens), *adv,* a thousand times

milǔīnus, a, um, *adj,* kite-like

milǔus, ǐ, *m,* kite, gurnard

mīmǐcus, a, um, *adj,* farcical

mīmus, ǐ, *m,* mime, mimic actor

mǐna, ae, *f,* Greek silver coinage

mǐnae, ārum, *f. pl,* threats

mǐnax, ācis, *adj, adv,* ǐter, threatening, projecting

mǐnǐmē, *sup. adv,* very little

mǐnǐmus, a, um, *sup. adj,* very small

mǐnǐster, trǐ, *m,* mǐnǐstra, ae, *f,* servant, assistant

mǐnǐstērǐum, ǐǐ, *n,* service, occupation

mǐnǐstrātor, ōris, *m,* servant

mǐnǐstro, *v.t.* 1, to wait upon, serve, manage

mǐnǐtor, *v.i.t.* 1, *dep,* to threaten

mǐnǐum, ǐǐ, red-lead

mǐnor, *v.i.t.* 1, *dep,* to threaten

mǐnor, us, *comp. adj,* smaller

mǐnǔo, ǔi, ūtum, *v.i.t.* 3, to ebb; to reduce, weaken, chop up

mǐnus, *comp. adv,* less

mǐnuscǔlus, a, um, *adj,* rather small

mǐnūtal, ālis, *n,* mincemeat

mǐnūtātim, *adv,* little by little

mǐnūtus, a, um, *adj, adv,* ē, small

mīrābǐlis, e, *adj, adv,* ǐter, wonderful, strange

mīrācŭlum, i, *n*, a wonder, marvel

mirandus, a, um, *adj*, wonderful

mirātĭo, ōnis, *f*, surprise

mirātor, ōris, *m*, admirer

mirĭfĭcus, a, um, *adj*, *adv*, ē, marvellous, extraordinary

mĭror, *v.i.t.* 1, *dep*, to be amazed; to marvel at, admire

mīrus, a, um, *adj*, *adv*, ē, marvellous, extraordinary

miscĕo, scŭi, xtum, *v.t.* 2, to mix, unite, disturb

misellus, a, um, *adj*, wretched

miser, ĕra, ĕrum, *adj*, *adv*, ē, wretched, pitiable, worthless

mĭsĕrābĭlis, e, *adj*, *adv*, ĭter, pitiable, sad

mĭsĕrandus, a, um, *adj*, pitiable

mĭsĕrātĭo, ōnis, *f*, pity

mĭsĕrĕor, *v.* 2, *dep*, *with gen*, to pity

mĭsĕret (me, te, etc.), *v.* 2, *impers*, it distresses (me), I pity, am sorry for

mĭsĕresco, *v.i.* 3, to feel pity

mĭsĕrĭa, ae, *f*, misfortune, wretchedness

mĭsĕrĭcordĭa, ae, *f*, pity

mĭsĕrĭcors, dis, *adj*, merciful

mĭsĕror, *v.t.* 1, *dep*, to lament, pity

missĭle, is, *n*, missile, javelin

missĭlis, e, *adj*, that is thrown

missĭo, ōnis, *f*, throwing, discharge, release

missus, ūs, *m*, dispatching, throwing, shot

mĭtella, ae, *f*, turban, bandage

mĭtesco, *v.i.* 3, to grow mild or soft or ripe

mītĭgātĭo, ōnis, *f*, mitigation

mītĭgo, *v.t.* 1, to make soft or ripe, to tame, soothe

mītis, e, *adj*, mild, ripe, calm

mītra, ae, *f*, head-band

mitto, mīsi, missum, *v.t.* 3, to send, announce, cease, release, throw, escort

mītŭlus, i, *m*, sea-mussel

mixtūra, ae, *f*, mixture

mixtus, a, um, *adj*, mixed

mōbĭlis, e, *adj*, *adv*, ĭter, movable, agile, flexible, fickle

mōbĭlĭtas, ātis, *f*, speed, inconstancy

mŏdĕrāmen, ĭnis, *n*, rudder, management

mŏdĕrātĭo, ōnis, *f*, moderation, restraint

mŏdĕrātor, ōris, *m*, manager

mŏdĕrātus, a, um, *adj*, *adv*, ē, moderate

mŏdĕror, *v.t.* 1, *dep*, to restrain, govern

mŏdestĭa, ae, *f*, moderation, discretion, modesty

mŏdestus, a, um, *adj*, *adv*, ē, modest, gentle

mŏdĭcus, a, um, *adj*, *adv*, ē, modest, ordinary

mŏdĭfĭcātus, a, um, *adj*, measured

mŏdĭus, ii, *m*, peck, measure

mŏdŏ, *adv*, only, but, just, lately; non mŏdŏ, not only; mŏdŏ... mŏdŏ, at one time... at another time

mŏdŭlātor, ōris, *m*, musician

mŏdŭlor, *v.t.* 1, *dep*, to sing, play

mŏdŭlātus, a, um, *adj*, sung, played

mŏdŭlus, i, *m*, a small measure

mŏdus, i, *m*, measure, quantity, rhythm, limit, restriction, end, method, way

moechus, i, *m*, adulterer

moenĭa, ĭum, *n.pl*, ramparts

mŏla, ae, *f*, millstone, grain mixed with salt to be sprinkled on sacrificial animals

mŏlāris, is, *m*, millstone

mōles, is, *f*, mass, bulk, dam, pier, power, difficulty

mŏlestĭa, ae, *f*, trouble, affectation

mŏlestus, a, um, *adj*, *adv*, ē, troublesome, affected

mōlīmen, ĭnis, *n*, undertaking, attempt

mōlīmentum, i, *n*, undertaking, attempt

mōlĭor, *v.i.t.* 4, to strive, depart; to rouse, construct, attempt

mŏlĭtor, ōris, *m*, miller

mōlĭtor, ōris, *m*, contriver

mollesco, *v.i.* 3, to grow soft

mollĭo, *v.t.* 4, to soften, restrain

mollis, a, *adj*, *adv*, ĭter, soft, supple, tender, effeminate

mollĭtĭa, ae, *f*, softness, weakness

mollĭtĭes, ēi, *f*, softness, weakness

mollĭtūdo, ĭnis, *f*, softness, weakness

mŏlo, ŭi, ĭtum, *v.t.* 3, to grind

mōmentum, i, *n*, movement, motion, moment, instant, cause, influence, importance

mŏnăcha, ae, *f*, nun

mŏnastērĭum, ii, *n*, monastery

mŏnĕdŭla, ae, *f*, jackdaw

mŏnĕo, *v.t.* 2, to warn, advise, remind, instruct, tell

mŏnēta, ae, *f*, the mint, coin

mŏnētālis, e, *adj*, of the mint

mŏnīle, is, *n*, necklace, collar

mŏnĭtĭo, ōnis, *f*, warning

mŏnĭtor, ōris, *m*, adviser, instructor

mŏnĭtum, i, *n*, advice

mŏnĭtus, ūs, *m*, warning, omen

For List of Abbreviations used, turn to pages 3, 4

mŏnŏcĕros, ōtis, m, unicorn
mŏnŏpōlĭum, ii, n, monopoly
mons, ntis, m, mountain
monstrātĭo, ōnis, f, showing, pointing out
monstrātor, ōris, m, teacher
monstro, v.t. 1, to show, tell
monstrum, i, n, omen, monster
monstrŭōsus, a, um, adj, strange, monstrous
montānus, a, um, adj, of a mountain, mountainous
montĭcŏla, ae, c, mountain-dweller
montīvăgus, a, um, adj, wandering in the mountains
montŭōsus, a, um, adj, mountainous
mŏnŭmentum, i, n, monument, memorial, written record
mŏra, ae, f, delay, hindrance
mōrālis, e, adj, moral
mōrātus, a, um, adj, mannered;
mŏrātus partic. from mŏror, having delayed
morbĭdus, a, um, adj, diseased
morbus, i, m, illness, disease
mordax, ācis, adj, biting, stinging
mordĕo, mŏmordi, morsum, v.t. 2, to bite, clasp, sting
mordĭcus, a, um, adj, by biting
mōres, see mos
mōrētum, i, n, salad
mŏrĭbundus, a, um, adj, dying
mŏrĭens, ntis, adj, dying
mŏrĭor, mortŭus, v.i. 3, dep, to die
mŏror, v.i.t. 1, dep, to delay
mōrōsĭtas, ātis, f, fretfulness
mōrōsus, a, um, adj, fretful, fastidious
mors, mortis, f, death
morsus, ūs, m, bite, pungency
mortālis, e, adj, mortal, human, temporary
mortālis, is, c, human being
mortālĭtas, ātis, f, mortality
mortārĭum, ii, n, a mortar
mortĭfer, ĕra, ĕrum, adj, fatal
mortŭus, a, um, adj, dead
mortŭus, i, m, a dead person
mōrum, i, n, blackberry
mōrus, i, f, blackberry-bush
mos, mōris, m, custom, manner, habit, fashion; in pl, character
mōtăcilla, ae, f, wagtail
mōtĭo, ōnis, f, motion
mōto, v.t. 1, to move about
mōtus, ūs, m, motion, movement, impulse, emotion, rebellion
mŏvĕo, mōvi, mōtum, v.t. 2, to move, stir, excite, cause
mox, adv, soon, immediately

mūcĭdus, a, um, adj, musty
mūcor, ōris, m, mouldiness
mūcōsus, a, um, adj, mucous
mūcro, ōnis, m, sword's point
mūgil, is, m, mullet
mūgĭnor, v.i. 1, dep, to hesitate
mūgĭo, v.i. 4, to low, bellow, groan, crash
mūgītus, ūs, m, bellowing, roaring
mūla, ae, f, she-mule
mulcĕo, si, sum, v.t. 2, to stroke, soothe
mulco, v.t. 1, to maltreat
mulctra, ae, f, milk-bucket
mulctrārium, ii, n, milk-bucket
mulgĕo, si, sum, v.t. 2, to milk
mŭlĭĕbris, e, adj, adv, ĭter, female, effeminate
mūlier, ĕris, f, woman, wife
mŭlĭercŭla, ae, f, girl
mūlĭo, ōnis, m, mule-driver
mullus, i, m, mullet
mulsum, i, n, honey-wine
multa, ae, f, penalty, fine
multātĭo, ōnis, f, penalty, fine
multi, see multus
multĭfārĭam, adv, on many sides
multĭplex, ĭcis, adj, with many windings, numerous, many
multĭplĭcātĭo, ōnis, f, multiplication
multĭplĭco, v.t. 1, to multiply
multĭtūdo, ĭnis, f, crowd, great number
multō, adv, a great deal
multo, v.t. 1, to punish
multum, adv, very much, greatly
multus, a, um, adj, much; pl, many
mūlus, i, m, mule
mundĭtĭa, ae, f, cleanliness, neatness
mundĭtĭes, ēi, f, cleanliness, neatness
mundo, v.t. 1, to cleanse
mundus, a, um, adj, clean, elegant
mundus, i, m, world, universe, ornaments
mūnĕro, v.t. 1 (mūnĕror, v.t. 1, dep.), to reward, honour
mūnĭa, ōrum, n.pl, duties
mūnĭceps, cĭpis, c, citizen
mūnĭcĭpālis, e, adj, municipal
mūnĭcĭpĭum, ii, n, self-governing town
mūnĭfĭcentĭa, ae, f, generosity
mūnĭfĭcus, a, um, adj, adv, ē, generous
mūnĭmen, ĭnis, n, rampart, protection
mūnĭmentum, i, n, rampart, protection
mūnĭo, v.t. 4, to fortify, secure, make a way

mūnītĭo, ōnis, *f*, fortification

mūnītor, ōris, *m*, engineer

mūnītus, a, um, *adj*, fortified

mūnus, ĕris, *n*, service, duty, employment, post, tax, gift, public show

mūnuscŭlum, i, *n*, small present

mūrālis, e, *adj*, of a wall

mūrex, ĭcis, *m*, purple fish, purple dye, pointed rock

mūrĭa, ae, *f*, brine, pickle

murmur, ūris, *n*, murmur, crash

murmŭro, *v.i.* 1, to murmur, roar

murra, ae, *f*, myrrh (tree)

murrĕus, a, um, *adj*, perfumed with myrrh

mūrus, i, *m*, wall, defence

mūs, mūris, *c*, mouse

mūsa, ae, *f*, goddess of the arts

musca, ae, *f*, a fly

muscĭpŭlum, i, *n*, mouse-trap

muscōsus, a, um, *adj*, mossy

muscŭlus, i, *m*, little mouse, mussel, muscle, military shed

muscus, i, *m*, moss

mūsēum, i, *n*, museum

mūsĭca, ae, *f*, music

mūsĭcus, a, um, *adj*, musical

mūsĭcus, i, *m*, musician

musso, *v.i.* 1, to mutter, be silent, be in doubt

mustēla, ae, *f*, weasel

mustum, i, *n*, new wine

mūtābĭlis, e, *adj*, changeable

mūtābĭlĭtas, ātis, *f*, changeableness

mūtātĭo, ōnis, *f*, alteration

mūtĭlo, *v.t.* 1, to cut off, maim

mūtĭlus, a, um, *adj*, maimed

mūto, *v.i.t.* 1, to alter, change

mūtŭlus, i, *m*, bracket

mūtŭō, *adv*, in turns

mūtŭor, *v.t.* 1, *dep*, to borrow

mūtus, a, um, *adj*, dumb, mute

mūtŭum, i, *n*, loan

mūtŭus, a, um, *adj*, borrowed, mutual

mȳrīca, ae, *f*; mȳrīce, es, *f*, a shrub, tamarisk

myrr ... see murr ...

myrtētum, i, *n*, myrtle-grove

myrtĕus, a, um, *adj*, of myrtle

myrtum, i, *n*, myrtle-berry

myrtus, i, *f*, myrtle-tree

mysta (es), ae, *f*, priest of Ceres' mysteries

mystērĭum, ii, *n*, secret rites

mystĭcus, a, um, *adj*, mystical

N

naevus, i, *m*, wart, mole

Nāĭăs, ădis, *f*, water-nymph

nam, *conj*, for

namque, *conj*, for indeed

nanciscor, nactus, *v.t.* 3, *dep*, to obtain, meet with, find

nānus, i, *m*, dwarf

nāpus, i, *m*, turnip

narcissus, i, *m*, narcissus

nardus, i, *f*, perfumed balm

nāris, is, *f*, nostril; *pl*, nose

narrātĭo, ōnis, *f*, narrative

narrātor, ōris, *m*, narrator

narro, *v.t.* 1, to tell, relate

narthēcĭum, ii, *n*, medicine-chest

nascor, nātus, *v.i.* 3, *dep*, to be born, rise, proceed

nasturtĭum, ii, *n*, cress

nāsus, i, *m*, nose

nāsūtus, a, um, *adj*, large-nosed

nāta, ae, *f*, daughter

nātālĭcĭus, a, um, *adj*, birthday

nātālis, e, *adj*, of birth

nātālis, is, *m*, birthday

nātantes, um, *f. pl*, fish

nātātĭo, ōnis, *f*, swimming

nātātor, ōris, *m*, swimmer

nātĭo, ōnis, *f*, race, nation

nātis, is, *f*, buttock

nātīvus, a, um, *adj*, created, inborn, natural

năto, *v.i.* 1, to swim, float, waver

nătrix, ĭcis, *f*, water-snake

nātūra, ae, *f*, nature

nātūrālis, e, *adj*, *adv*, ĭter, by birth, natural

nātus, ūs, *m*, birth

nātus, i, *m*, son

nātus, a, um, *adj*, born, aged

nauarchus, i, *m*, ship's master

naufrăgĭum, ii, *n*, shipwreck

naufrăgus, a, um, *adj*, shipwrecked

naumăchĭa, ae, *f*, mock sea-fight

nausĕa, ae, *f*, sea-sickness

nausĕābundus, a, um, *adj*, sea-sick

nausĕo, *v.i.* 1, to be sea-sick

nauta, ae, *m*, sailor

nautĭcus, a, um, *adj*, nautical

nāvālĭa, ĭum, *n.pl*, dockyard

nāvāle, is, *n*, dockyard

nāvālis, e, *adj*, naval

nāvĭcŭla, ae, *f*, boat

nāvĭcŭlārĭus, ii, *m*, ship-owner

nāvĭfrăgus, a, um, *adj*, ship-wrecking

nāvĭgābĭlis, e, *adj*, navigable

nāvĭgātĭo, ōnis, *f*, sailing

nāvĭger, ĕra, ĕrum, *adj*, navigable

nāvĭgĭa, ōrum, *n.pl*, ships, shipping

nāvĭgĭum, ii, *n*, ship, boat

nāvĭgo, *v.i.t.* 1, to sail; navigate

nāvis, is, *f*, ship; nāvis longa, warship

nāvĭta, ae, *m* (nauta), sailor

nāvĭter, *adv*, completely

nāvo, *v.t.* 1, to do vigorously
nāvus, a, um, *adj*, hard-working
nē, *conj*, lest; nē ... quidem, not even ...
-nē, attached to the first word of a sentence to form a question
nē, *interj*, indeed, truly
nēbŭla, ae, *f*, mist, fog, smoke
nēbŭlo, ōnis, *m*, rascal, wretch
nēbŭlōsus, a, um, *adj*, misty
nēc, *adv*, not; *conj*, and not; nēc ... nēc, neither ... nor
necdum, *conj*, not yet
nēcessārius, a, um, *adj*, *adv*, ō, unavoidable, necessary, related
nēcessārius, ii, *m*, relative
nēcesse, *indecl. adj*, unavoidable
nēcessĭtas, ātis, *f*, necessity, compulsion, destiny
nēcessĭtūdo, ĭnis, *f*, necessity, relationship
necnĕ, *adv*, or not
nec-non, and also
nĕco, *v.t.* 1, to kill
nēcŏpīnans, ntis, *adj*, unaware
nēcŏpīnātus, a, um, *adj*, *adv*, ō, unexpected
nēcŏpīnus, a, um, *adj*, unexpected
nectar, ăris, *n*, the drink of the gods
nectărĕus, a, um, *adj*, of nectar
necto, xŭi, xum, *v.t.* 3, to tie, fasten together
nēcŭbi, *adv*, so that nowhere
nēdum, *conj*, still less
nēfandus, a, um, *adj*, abominable, heinous, wrong
nēfārius, a, um *adj*, heinous, wrong
nēfas, *n*, *indecl*, wrong, sin
nēfastus, a, um, *adj*, with dies, a day on which neither trials nor public meetings could be held, wicked, unlucky
nēgātĭo, ōnis, *f*, denial
nēgĭto, *v.t.* 1, to persist in denying
neglectus, a, um, *adj*, despised
neglĕgens (neglĭgens), ntis, *adj*, careless, indifferent
neglĕgentĭa, ae, *f*, carelessness
neglĕgo, xi, ctum, *v.t.* 3, to neglect, slight, despise
nēgo, *v.i.t.* 1, to say no (not); refuse
nēgōtĭātĭo, ōnis, *f*, wholesale-business, banking
nēgōtĭātor, ōris, *m*, wholesaler, banker
nēgōtĭor, *v.i.* 1, *dep*, to carry on business, trade or banking
nēgōtĭōsus, a, um, *adj*, busy
nēgōtĭum, ii, *n*, business, occupation, difficulty
nēmo, ĭnis, *m*, *f*, nobody
nēmŏrālis, e, *adj*, woody

nēmŏrōsus, a, um, *adj*, woody
nempĕ, *conj*, certainly
nēmus, ŏris, *n*, wood, grove
nēnĭa, ae, *f*, funeral hymn, sad song, popular song
nĕo, nēvi, nētum, *v.t.* 2, to spin
nēpa, ae, *f*, scorpion
nēpos, ōtis, *m*, *f*, grandson (... daughter), descendant, spendthrift
neptis, is, *f*, grand-daughter
nēquam, *indecl. adj*, *adv*, nēquĭter, worthless, bad
nēquāquam, *adv*, not at all
nēque, *adv*, not; *conj*, and not; nēque ... nēque, neither ... nor
nēquĕo, īvi (ĭi), ĭtum, *v.i.* 4, to be unable
nēquīquam, *adv*, in vain
nēquĭtĭa, ae, *f*, worthlessness, idleness, extravagance
nervōsus, a, um, *adj*, *adv*, ē, sinewy, energetic
nervus, i, *m*, sinew, string of musical instrument or bow
nescĭo, *v.t.* 4, not to know, to be unable
nescĭus, a, um, *adj*, unaware
neu, *adv*, and so that ... not
neuter, tra, trum, *adj*, neither the one nor the other
neutĭquam, *adv*, not at all
neutrō, *adv*, neither way
nēve, *adv*, and so that ... not
nex, nĕcis, *f*, death, slaughter
nexĭlis, e, *adj*, tied together
nexum, i, *n*, slavery for debt, obligation
nexus, ūs, *m*, tying together
nĭ, *conj*, unless
nictātĭo, ōnis, *f*, winking
nicto, *v.i.* 1, to wink, blink
nĭdor, ōris, *m*, steam, smell
nīdŭlus, i, *m*, little nest
nīdus, i, *m*, nest, home; *in pl*, nestlings
nĭger, gra, grum, *adj*, black, dark, ill-omened, funereal
nĭgrans, ntis, *adj*, black
nĭgresco, grŭi, *v.i.* 3, to grow dark
nĭhil (nīl), *n*, *indecl*, nothing
nĭhĭli, of no value
nĭhĭlōmĭnus, *adj*, nevertheless
nĭhĭlum, i, *n*, nothing
nīl, *n*, *indecl*, nothing
nimbĭfer, ĕra, ĕrum, *adj*, stormy, rainy
nimbōsus, a, um, *adj*, stormy, rainy
nimbus, i, *m*, heavy rain, rain-cloud, cloud
nīmīrum, *adv*, without doubt
nĭmis, *adv*, too much

nĭmĭum, *adv*, too much
nĭmĭum, ii, *n*, excess
nĭmĭus, a, um, *adj*, excessive
ningit, *v.i.* 3, *impers*, it is snowing
nĭsĭ, *conj*, if not, unless
nīsus, ūs, *m*, pressure, effort, labour of childbirth
nītēdŭla, ae, *f*, dormouse
nĭtens, ntis, *adj*, bright, shining, sleek, beautiful
nĭtĕo, *v.i.* 2, to shine, to look handsome, thrive
nĭtesco, tŭi, *v.i.* 3, to shine
nĭtĭdus, a, um, *adj*, shining, sleek, handsome, refined
nītor, nīsus (nixus), *v.i.* 3, *dep*, to lean, press forward, fly, make an effort, argue
nĭtor, ōris, *m*, brightness, splendour, beauty, elegance
nĭtrum, i, *n*, soda
nĭvālis, e, *adj*, snowy, cold
nĭvĕus, a, um, *adj*, snowy, white
nĭvōsus, a, um, *adj*, snowy
nix, nĭvis, *f*, snow
nixor, *v.i.* 1, *dep*, to strive
nixus, ūs, *m*, pressure, effort, labour of childbirth
no, *v.i.* 1, to swim
nōbĭlis, e, *adj*, famous, noble
nōbĭlĭtas, ātis, *f*, fame, noble birth
nōbĭlĭto, *v.t.* 1, to make famous
nōbis, *dat. or abl. of nos*
nŏcens, ntis, *adj*, wicked, bad, harmful, injurious
nŏcĕo, *v.i.* 2, *with dat*, to harm
nocte, *adv*, at night
noctĭlūca, ae, *f*, moon
noctĭvăgus, a, um, *adj*, wandering at night
noctu, *adv*, at night
noctŭa, ae, *f*, night owl
nocturnus, a, um, *adj*, nocturnal
nōdo, *v.t.* 1, to tie in a knot
nōdōsus, a, um, *adj*, knotty, difficult
nōdus, i, *m*, knot, knob, band, obligation, difficulty
nōli, nōlīte, *imper*, do not ...
nōlo, nolle, nōlŭi, *v*, *irreg*, to be unwilling
nōmen, ĭnis, *n*, name, debt, fame, repute, excuse, reason
nōmenclātor, ōris, *m*, slave who reminded his master of the names of the people he met
nōmĭnātim, *adj*, by name
nōmĭnātĭo, ōnis, *f*, nomination
nōmĭnātus, a, um, *adj*, renowned
nōmĭno, *v.t.* 1, to name, make famous
nŏmisma, ătis, *n*, a coin
nōn, *adv*, not

nōnae, ārum, *f. pl*, the Nones; 5th or 7th day of the month
nōnāgēni, ae, *adj*, ninety each
nōnāgēsĭmus, a, um, *adj*, ninetieth
nōnāgĭes, *adv*, ninety times
nōnāgintā, *indecl. adj*, ninety
nondum, *adj*, not yet
nongenti, ae, a, *adj*, nine hundred
nonnĕ, *adv*, used to introduce a question expecting the answer "yes"
nonnēmo, ĭnis, *m*, someone
nonnĭhil, *n*, something
nonnĭsi, *adv*. only
nonnullus, a, um, *adj*, several
nonnumquam, *adv*, sometimes
nōnus, a, um, *adj*, ninth
norma, ae, *f*, rule, pattern, standard
nōs, *pron*, *pl. of ĕgŏ*, we, us
noscĭto, *v.t.* 1, to know, observe
nosco, nōvi, nōtum, *v.t.* 3, to get to know, know, recognise, acknowledge
noster, tra, trum, *adj*, our, ours
nostras, ātis, *adj*, of our country
nŏta, ae, *f*, mark, sign, brand
nŏtābĭlis, e, *adj*, noteworthy
nōtātĭo, ōnis, *f*, branding, observation
nōthus, a, um, *adj*, illegitimate, counterfeit
nōtĭo, ōnis, *f*, investigation
nōtĭtĭa, ae, *f*, fame, knowledge
nŏto, *v.t.* 1, to mark, write, indicate, brand, reprimand
nōtus, a, um, *adj*, well-known
nŏtus, i, *m*, the south wind
nŏvācŭla, ae, *f*, razor
nŏvalis, is, *f*, fallow land
nŏvellus, a, um, *adj*, young, new
nŏvem, *indecl. adj*, nine
Nŏvember (mensis), November
nŏvendĭālis, e, *adj*, lasting nine days
nŏvēnus, a, um, *adj*, nine each
nŏverca, ae, *f*, stepmother
nŏvĭcĭus, a, um, *adj*, new
nŏvĭens, *adv*, nine times
nŏvĭes, *adv*, nine times
nŏvissĭmus, a, um, *adj*, last; in *m. pl*, or nŏvissĭmum agmen, rear ranks
nŏvĭtas, ātis, *f*, novelty, unusualness
nŏvo, *v.t.* 1, to renew, refresh, change
nŏvus, a, um, *adj*, new, recent, fresh; nŏvus hŏmo an upstart; nŏvae res, revolution
nox, noctis, *f*, night
noxa, ae, *f*, injury, harm, fault, crime
noxĭa, ae, *f*, injury, harm, fault, crime
noxĭus, a, um, *adj*, harmful, guilty
nūbes, is, *f*, cloud
nūbĭfer, ĕra, ĕrum, *adj*, cloud-capped, cloud-bringing

For List of Abbreviations used, turn to pages 3, 4

nūbīla, ōrum, *n.pl*, the clouds
nūbĭlis, e, *adj*, marriageable
nūbĭlus, a, um, *adj*, overcast
nūbo, psi, ptum, *v.i.t.* 3, *with dat*, to marry
nŭclĕus, i, *m*, nut, kernel
nŭdĭus, with a number (tertĭus) (three) days ago
nūdo, *v.t.* 1, to strip, expose
nūdus, a, um, *adj*, naked, destitute of, poor, simple
nūgae, ārum, *f. pl*, jokes, nonsense, trifles
nūgātor, ōris, *m*, silly person
nūgātōrĭus, a, um, *adj*, trifling
nūgor, *v.i.* 1, *dep*, to play the fool
nullus, a, um, *adj*, none, no
nullus, ĭus, *m*, no-one
num, *adv*, used to introduce a question expecting answer "no"; whether
nūmen, ĭnis, *n*, divine will, divine power, divinity
nŭmĕrābĭlis, e, *adj*, able to be counted
nŭmĕrātor, ōris, *m*, counter
nŭmĕrātum, i, *n*, ready money
nŭmĕro, *v.t.* 1, to count, pay out, number
nŭmĕrō, *adv*, in number, just
nŭmĕrōsus, a, um, *adj*, *adv*, ē, numerous, rhythmic
nŭmĕrus, i, *m*, number, band (of soldiers), class, category, sequence, rhythm, poetic-metre
nummārĭus, a, um, *adj*, of money
nummātus, a, um, *adj*, rich
nummus, i, *m*, money, a Roman silver coin, farthing
numquam, *adv*, never
numquid, *interr. adv*, is there anything . . .?
nunc, *adv*, now, at present
nuncia, nuncius . . . see nunt . . .
nuncŭpo, *v.t.* 1, to call, name
nundĭnae, ārum, *f. pl*, ninth day, market-day
nundĭnātĭo, ōnis, *f*, trading
nundĭnor, *v.i.t.* 1, *dep*, to trade; buy, sell
nunquam, *adv*, never
nuntĭātĭo, ōnis, *f*, announcement
nuntĭo, *v.t.* 1, to announce, tell
nuntĭus, i, *m*, messenger, message
nūper, *adv*, lately, recently
nupta, ae, *f*, wife, bride
nuptĭae, ārum, *f. pl*, marriage
nuptĭālis, e, *adj*, of marriage
nuptus, a, um, *adj*, married

nŭrus, ūs, *f*, daughter-in-law, young wife
nusquam, *adv*, nowhere
nūto, *v.i.* 1, to nod, waver
nūtrīcĭus, a, um, *adj*, foster-father
nūtrīco, *v.t*, 1, to nurse, rear
nūtrīcŭla, ae, *f*, nurse
nūtrīmen, ĭnis, *n*, nourishment
nūtrīmentum, i, *n*, nourishment
nūtrĭo, *v.t.* 4, to feed, bring up, support
nūtrix, īcis, *f*, nurse
nūtus, ūs, *m*, nod, command
nux, nŭcis, *f*, nut
nympha, ae, *f*, bride, nymph (demi-goddess inhabiting woods, trees, fountains, etc.)

O

ŏb, *prep. with acc*, on account of, in front of
ŏbaerātus, a, um, *adj*, involved in debt
ŏbambŭlo, *v.i.* 1, to walk about
obdo, dĭdi, dĭtum, *v.t.* 3, to shut, place, expose
obdormĭo, *v.i.* 4, to fall asleep
obdormisco, *v.i.* 3, to fall asleep
obdūco, xi, ctum, *v.t.* 3, to lead forward, bring forward, cover over, swallow
obdūresco, rŭi, *v.i.* 3, to become hardened
obdūro, *v.i.* 1, to persist
ŏbēdĭens, ntis, *adj*, obedient
ŏbēdĭentĭa, ae, *f*, obedience
ŏbēdĭo, *v.i.* 4, to obey, be subject to
ŏbēliscus, i, *m*, obelisk
ŏbĕo, *v.i.t.* 4, to go to meet, die, set (constellations); to go to, reach, travel over, visit, undertake, perform
ŏbĕquĭto, *v.i.* 1, to ride towards
ŏbēsĭtas, ātis, *f*, fatness
ŏbēsus, a, um, *adj*, fat, dull
ŏbex, ĭcis, *m, f*, bolt, barrier
obiăcĕo, *v.i.* 2, to lie opposite
ōbĭcĭo, iēci, iectum, *v.t.* 3, to throw forward, expose, oppose, taunt, reproach
obiectātĭo, ōnis, *f*, reproach
obiecto, *v.t.* 1, to place against, expose, reproach, accuse
obiectus, ūs, *m*, opposing, putting in the way
obiectus, a, um, *adj*, lying opposite
ōbĭtus, ūs, *m*, setting, downfall
obiurgātĭo, ōnis, *f*, rebuke

obiurgātor, ōris, *m*, blamer

obiurgātōrius, a, um, *adj*, reproachful

obiurgo, *v.t.* 1, to blame, rebuke

oblectāmen, ĭnis, *n*, pleasure, delight

oblectāmentum, i, *n*, pleasure, delight

oblecto, *v.t.* 1, to amuse, please

obligātio, ōnis, *f*, obligation

oblĭgo, *v.t.* 1, to bind, put under obligation, render liable

oblīmo, *v.t.* 1, to cover with mud, squander

oblĭno, lēvi, lĭtum, *v.t.* 3, to besmear, defile

oblīquo, *v.t.* 1, to bend aside

oblīquus, a, um, *adj*, *adv*, ē, slanting, sideways

oblīvio, ōnis, *f*, oblivion

oblīviōsus, a, um, *adj*, forgetful, producing forgetfulness

oblīviscor, oblītus, *v.* 3, *dep*, *with genit*, to forget

oblīvĭum, ii, *n*, oblivion

oblŏquor, lŏcūtus, *v.i.* 3, *dep*, to contradict, accompany a song

obluctor, *v.i.* 1, *dep*, to struggle against

obmūtesco, tŭi, *v.i.* 3, to become speechless

obnītor, xus, *v.i.* 3, *dep*, to push or struggle against

obnixus, a, um, *adj*, resolute

obnoxius, a, um, *adj*, liable to, submissive, indebted

obnūbo, psi, ptum, *v.t.* 3, to veil

obnuntiātio, ōnis, *f*, announcement of bad omens

obnuntio, *v.i.* 1, to announce bad omens

ŏboediens, oboedio, see obēd . . .

ŏbŏrior, ortus, *v.i.* 4, *dep*, to arise, appear

obrēpo, psi, ptum, *v.t.* 3, to creep up to, surprise

obrigesco, gŭi, *v.i.* 3, to stiffen

obrŏgo, *v.t.* 1, to invalidate

obrŭo, ŭi, ŭtum, *v.t.* 3, to overwhelm, bury, hide

obsaepio, psi, ptum, *v.t.* 4, to fence in

obscēnitas, ātis, *f*, obscenity, foulness

obscēnus, a, um, *adj*, ominous, filthy, obscene

obscūritas, ātis, *f*, uncertainty, lowness

obscūro, *v.t.* 1, to darken, hide

obscūrus, a, um, *adj*, *adv*, ē, dark, shady, indistinct, ignoble, humble, reserved

obsĕcrātio, ōnis, *f*, appeal

obsĕcro, *v.t.* 1, to implore

obsĕcundo, *v.t.* 1, to humour, obey

obsĕp . . . see obsaep . . .

obsĕquens, ntis, *adj*, amenable

obsĕquĭum, ii, *n*, compliance, obedience

obsĕquor, sĕcūtus, *v.* 3, *dep*, *with dat.* to comply with, submit to, humour

obsĕro, *v.t.* 1, to fasten

obsĕro, sēvi, sĭtum, *v.t.* 3, to sow, plant

observans, ntis, *adj*, attentive

observantia, ae, *f*, attention, respect

observātio, ōnis, *f*, care, observation

observo, *v.t.* 1, to watch, take note of, respect, comply with

obses, ĭdis, *m*, *f*, hostage

obsessio, ōnis, *f*, blockade

obsessor, ōris, *m*, besieger

obsĭdĕo, sēdi, sessum, *v.t.* 2, to besiege, hem in, frequent

obsĭdĭo, ōnis, *f*, siege

obsĭdo, *v.t.* 3, to besiege

obsignātor, ōris, *m*, witness

obsigno, *v.t.* 1, to seal up

obsisto, stĭti, stĭtum, *v.i.* 3, to resist, oppose

obsĭtus, a, um, *adj*, covered over

obsōlesco, lēvi, lētum, *v.i.* 3, to wear out, decay

obsōlētus, a, um, *adj*, worn out, low, mean

obsōnium, ii, *n*, eatables

obsōnātor, ōris, *m*, caterer

obsōno, *v.t.* 1, (obsōnor, *v.*1, *dep*), to cater

obsorbĕo, *v.t.* 2, to swallow

obstĕtrix, ĭcis, *f*, midwife

obstĭnātio, ōnis, *f*, firmness, obstinacy

obstĭnātus, a, um, *adj*, *adv*, ē, determined, resolute, stubborn

obstĭpesco, pŭi, *v.i.* 3, to be amazed

obstĭpus, a, um, *adj*, bent

obsto, stĭti, ātum, *v.i.* 1, *with dat*, to obstruct, withstand

obstrĕpo, ŭi, ĭtum, *v.i.* 3 to roar at, resound

obstringo, nxi, ctum, *v.t.* 3, to tie up, put under obligation

obstrŭo, xi, ctum, *v.t.* 3, to build up, barricade, impede

obstŭpĕfăcio, fēci, factum, *v.t.* 3, to astonish

obstŭpesco, pŭi, *v.i.* 3, to be stupified, amazed

obsum, obesse, obfŭi, *v.i.*, *irreg*, to hinder, injure

obsŭo, ŭi, ūtum, *v.t.* 3, to sew up

obsurdesco, dŭi, *v.i.* 3, to grow deaf

obtĕgo, xi, ctum, *v.t.* 3, to cover up

obtempĕro, v.t. 1, with dat, to comply with

obtendo, di, tum, v.t. 3, to spread before, hide

obtentus, ūs, m, outspreading

obtĕro, trīvi, trītum, v.t. 3, to crush to pieces

obtestātĭo, ōnis, f, appeal

obtestor, v.t. 1, dep, to call as a witness, implore

obtexo, xŭi, v.t. 3, to cover

obticesco, ticŭi, v.i. 3, to be struck dumb

obtĭnĕo, nŭi, tentum, v.i.t. 2, to prevail, continue; keep, hold, gain, obtain

obtingo, tĭgi, v.i. 3, to befall

obtorpesco, pŭi, v.i. 3, to become stiff

obtorquĕo, si, tum, v.t. 2, to twist, wrench

obtrectātĭo, ōnis, f, disparagement

obtrectātor, ōris, m, slanderer

obtrecto, v.i.t. 1, to disparage

obtrunco, v.t. 1, to trim, kill

obtundo, tŭdi, tūsum, v.t. 3, to blunt, weaken, deafen, annoy

obtūrācŭlum, i, n, stopper

obtūrāmentum, i, n, stopper

obturbo, v.t. 1, to disturb

obtūro, v.t. 1, to close

obtūsus, a, um, adj, blunt, dull

obtūtus, ūs, m, gaze, stare

ŏbumbro, v.t. 1, to overshadow

ŏbuncus, a, um, adj, hooked

ŏbustus, a, um, adj, hardened in fire

obvĕnĭo, vēni, ventum, v.i. 4, to meet, befall one, happen

obversor, v.i. 1, dep, to move to and fro, hover

obversus, a, um, adj, directed towards

obverto, ti, sum, v.t. 3, to turn towards

obvĭam, adv, with verbs of motion; towards, against

obvĭus, a, um, adj, in the way, so as to meet, courteous, exposed

obvolvo, volvi, vŏlūtum, v.t. 3, to wrap round, cover

occaeco, v.t. 1, to blind, hide

occāsĭo, ōnis, f, opportunity

occāsus, ūs, m, setting (of sun, etc.) downfall, ruin

occĭdens, ntis, m, the west

occĭdentālis, e, adj, west

occĭdĭo, ōnis, f, massacre

occīdo, cīdi, cīsum, v.t. 3, to strike down, crush, kill

occĭdo, cĭdi, cāsum, v.i. 3, to fall, perish, set (of sun, etc.)

occĭdŭus, a, um, adj, setting, western

occīsĭo, ōnis, f, slaughter

occlūdo, si, sum, v.t. 3, to close

occo, v.t. 1, to harrow

occŭbo, v.i. 1, to lie down, rest

occŭlo, lŭi, ltum, v.t. 3, to hide

occultātĭo, ōnis, f, concealment

occulto, v.t. 1, to hide

occultus, a, um, adj, adv, ē, hidden, secret

occumbo, cŭbŭi, cŭbĭtum, v.i. 3, to die

occŭpātĭo, ōnis, f, employment

occŭpātus, a, um, adj, busy

occŭpo, v.t. 1, to seize, occupy, attack, anticipate, fill

occurro, curri, cursum, v.i. 3, to meet

occursātĭo, ōnis, f, greeting

occurso, v.i. 1, to meet, attack

occursus, ūs, m, meeting

ōcĕānus, i, m, ocean

ŏcellus, i, m, small eye, darling

ōchra, ae, f, ochre

ōcĭor, ĭus, comp. adj, swifter

ōcĭus, adv, more quickly

ŏcrĕa, ae, f, leg-shield, greave

octāvus, a, um, adj, eighth

octĭens (octĭes), adv, eight times

octingenti, ae, a, pl. adj, eight hundred

octō, indecl. adj, eight

Octōber (mensis), October

octōgēsĭmus, a, um, adj, eightieth

octōginta, indecl. adj, eighty

octōgōnum, i, n, octagon

octōni, ae, a, pl. adj, eight each

octŏphŏron, i, m, sedan carried by eight men

ŏcŭlārĭus, a, um, adj, of the eyes

ŏcŭlus, i, m, eye, bud

ōdi, ōdisse, v.t. defect, to hate

ōdĭōsus, a, um, adj, adv, ē, hateful, troublesome

ōdĭum, ii, n, hatred

ŏdor, ōris, m, odour, smell

ŏdōrātĭo, ōnis, f, smell

ŏdōrātus, ūs, m, smelling

ŏdōrātus, a, um, adj, scented

ŏdōrĭfer, ĕra, ĕrum, adj, fragrant

ŏdōro, v.t. 1, to perfume

ŏdōror, v.t. 1, dep, to smell out, investigate

ŏdōrus, a, um, adj, fragrant

oestrus, i, m, gad-fly

offa, ae, f, morsel

offendo, di, sum, v.i.t. 3, to make a mistake; strike against, meet with, find, offend

offensa, ae, f, hatred, crime

offensĭo, ōnis, f, stumbling, dislike, displeasure

offensus, a, um, adj, offensive, offended

offĕro, offerre, obtŭli, oblātum, v.t,
irreg, to offer, show, cause, bring
officīna, ae, f, workshop
officio, fēci, fectum, v.i. 3, to obstruct,
hinder
officiōsus, a, um, adj, adv, ē, obliging,
courteous
officium, ii, n, kindness, duty, employment, office
offirmātus, a, um, adj, firm
offulgĕo, si, v.i, 2, to shine on, appear
offundo, fūdi, fūsum, v.t. 3, to pour
out, spread over
ŏhē, interj, ho there!
ŏlĕa, ae, f, olive
ŏlĕācĕus, a, um, adj, oily
ŏlĕārius, a, um, adj, of oil; (.. i, m),
oil-seller
ŏlĕaster, stri, m, wild olive-tree
ŏlens, ntis, adj, fragrant, rank
ŏlĕo, ŭi, v.i.t. 2, to smell of
ŏlĕum, i, n, olive-oil
olfăcio, fēci, factum, v.t. 3, to smell
ŏlĭdus, a, um, adj, stinking
ŏlim, adv, once upon a time, once,
sometime in the future
ŏlĭtor, ōris, m, market-gardener
ŏlīva, ae, f, olive tree, olive branch
ŏlīvētum, i, n, olive-grove
ŏlīvĭfer, ĕra, ĕrum, adj, olive-growing
ŏlīvum, i, n, oil
olla, ae, f, pot, jar
ŏlor, ōris, m, swan
ŏlōrīnus, a, um, adj, of swans
ŏlus, ĕris, n, vegetables
ōmāsum, i, n, tripe
ōmon, inis, n, omen, sign
ōmĭnor, v.t. 1, dep, to forbode
ōmitto, mīsi, missum, v.t. 3, to put
aside, give up, leave out
omnĭgĕnus, a, um, adj, of all kinds
omnīno, adv, altogether, entirely
omnĭpārens, ntis, adj, all-producing
omnĭpŏtens, ntis, adj, almighty
omnes, ium, c, pl, all men
omnia, ium, n.pl, all things
omnis, e, adj, all, every
omnĭvăgus, a, um, adj, wandering
everywhere
ŏnăger (grus), i, m, wild ass
ŏnĕrāria, ae, f, merchant ship
ŏnĕrārius, a, um, adj, of, or for,
freight
ŏnĕro, v.t. 1, to load, oppress
ŏnĕrōsus, a, um, adj, burdensome
ŏnŭs, ĕris, n, load, burden
ŏnustus, a, um, adj, loaded, full
ŏnyx, ychis, m, f, yellow marble
ŏpāco, v.t. 1, to cover, shade
ŏpācus, a, um, adj, shady

ŏpālus, i, m., opal
ŏpem (no nomin.), f, power, wealth,
help
ŏpĕra, ae, f, exertion, effort; in pl,
workmen
ŏpĕram do, to give careful attention
to
ŏpĕrārius, a, um, adj, of labour
ŏpĕrārius, ii, m, labourer
ŏpercŭlum, i, n, lid, cover
ŏpĕrimentum, i, n, lid, cover
ŏpĕrio, ŭi, ŏpertum, v.t. 4, to cover,
hide
ŏpĕror, v.i. 1, dep, to work, labour,
perform a sacrifice
ŏpĕrōsus, a, um, adj, adv, ē, painstaking, busy, troublesome
ŏpertus, a, um, adj, hidden
ŏpes, um, f. pl, wealth, resources
ŏpĭfer, ĕra, ĕrum, adj, helping
ŏpĭfex, icis, c, craftsman
ŏpīmus, a, um, adj, fat, rich, fertile;
spolia ŏpīma, arms won by a
general in single combat with
opposing general
ŏpīnābilis, e, adj, imaginary
ŏpīnātio, ōnis, f, supposition
ŏpīnātus, a, um, adj, imagined
ŏpīnio, ōnis, f, supposition, belief,
reputation, rumour
ŏpīnor, v.i.t. 1, dep, to suppose
ŏpīpărē, adv, sumptuously
ŏpĭtŭlor, v.t. 1, dep, to help
ŏpĭum, ii, n, opium
ŏportet, v. 2, impers, with acc. of person, it is necessary
ŏppĕrior, pertus, v.i.t. 4, dep, to wait;
wait for
oppĕto, īvi, ĭtum, v.t. 3, to encounter
(especially death)
oppĭdāni, ōrum, m. pl, townspeople
oppĭdānus, a, um, adj, provincial
oppĭdŭlum, i, n, small town
oppĭdum, i, n, town
oppignĕro, v.t. 1, to pledge
oppīlo, v.t. 1, to shut, stop
opplĕo, ēvi, ētum, v.t. 2, to fill up
oppōno, pŏsŭi, sĭtum, v.t. 3, to place
opposite, oppose, offer, expose,
object
opportūnĭtas, ātis, f, convenience,
advantage
opportūnus, a, um, adj, adv, ē, suitable,
convenient
oppŏsĭtio, ōnis, f, opposition
oppŏsĭtus, a, um, adj, opposite
opprimo, pressi, ssum, v.t. 3, to suppress, close, surprise, hide
opprŏbrium, i, n, scandal, taunt
oppugnātio, ōnis, f, attack, siege

For List of Abbreviations used, turn to pages 3, 4

oppugnātor, ōris, *m*, attacker

oppugno, *v.t.* 1, to attack

ops, ōpis, *f*, power, aid

optābilis, e, *adj*, desirable

optātio, ōnis, *f*, wish

optātum, i, *n*, wish

optātus, a, um, *adj, adv*, ō, desired, pleasant

optimas, ātis, *adj*, aristocratic

optimātes, um, *c, pl*, the aristocratic party

optimus, a, um, *adj, adv*, ē, best

optio, ōnis, *f*, choice

optio, ōnis, *m*, assistant

opto, *v.t.* 1, to choose, desire

ŏpŭlens, ntis, *adj*, rich

ŏpŭlentia, ae, *f*, wealth

ŏpŭlentus, a, um, *adj*, rich

ŏpus, ĕris, *n*, work, task; **ŏpus est,** there is need (a necessity)

ŏpuscŭlum, i, *n*, a small work

ōra, ae, *f*, border, sea-coast, region

ōrācŭlum, i, *n*, oracle

ōrātio, ōnis, *f*, speech, language, eloquence

ōrātiuncŭla, ae, *f*, brief speech

ōrātor, ōris, *m*, speaker, orator, ambassador

ōrātōrius, a, um, *adj*, oratorical

orbicŭlātus, a, um, *adj*, circular

orbis, is, *m*, circle; **orbis terrarum,** the world

orbĭta, ae, *f*, track, rut

orbĭtas, ātis, *f*, bereavement

orbo, *v.t.* 1, to bereave, deprive

orbus, a, um, *adj*, bereaved, destitute

orca, ae, *f*, large tub

orchas, ādis, *f*, olive

orchēstra, ae, *f*, a place at the front of the theatre

orchis, is, *f*, orchid

Orcus, i, *m*, death, the Lower World

ordĭnārius, a, um, *adj*, regular, usual, orderly

ordĭnātim, *adv*, in proper order

ordĭnātus, a, um, *adj*, orderly, regulated

ordĭne, *adv*, in order

ordĭno, *v.t.* 1, to arrange

ordĭor, orsus, *v.i.t.* 4, *dep*, to begin, undertake

ordo, inis, *m*, row, rank, band or company of soldiers, series, class of society

Ōrĕās, ādis, *f*, mountain-nymph

orgĭa, ōrum, *n.pl*, revels in honour of Bacchus.

ōrĭchalcum, i, *n*, copper ore

ōriens, ntis, *m*, the east

ōrigo, inis, *f*, beginning, origin, family, ancestor

ōrior, ortus, *v.i.* 4, *dep*, to arise, appear, originate

ōriundus, a, um, *adj*, descended or sprung from

ornāmentum, i, *n*, equipment, decoration

ornātus, a, um, *adj, adv*, ē, equipped, decorated

ornātus, ūs, *m*, equipment, dress, ornament

orno, *v.t.* 1, to equip, adorn, praise

ornus, i, *f*, mountain-ash

ōro, *v.t.* 1, to plead, beg, pray

orsa, ōrum, *n.pl*, undertaking, speech

orsus, ūs, *m*, undertaking

ortus, ūs, *m*, rising (of sun, etc.), beginning, source

ōrȳsa, ae, *f*, rice

ōs, ōris, *n*, mouth, face, opening

ŏs, ossis, *n*, bone

oscen, inis, *m*, singing bird from whose notes omens were taken

oscillātio, ōnis, *f*, swinging

oscillum, i, *n*, small mask

oscitātio, ōnis, *f*, yawning

oscito, *v.i.* 1, to gape, yawn

oscŭlor, *v.i.t.* 1, *dep*, to kiss

oscŭlum, i, *n*, mouth, kiss

ossĕus, a, um, *adj*, made of bone

ossifrăgus, i, *m*, sea-eagle

ostendo, di, sum, *v.t.* 3, to show, make known

ostentātio, ōnis, *f*, display

ostento, *v.t.* 1, to show, display

ostentum, i, *n*, prodigy

ostiārium, ii, *n*, door-tax

ostiātim, *adv*, from door to door

ostium, ii, *n*, door, entrance

ostrĕa, ae, *f*, oyster

ostrĕārium, ii, *n*, oyster-bed

ostrum, i, *n*, purple, purple coverings or dress

ōtior, *v.i.* 1, *dep*, to be on holiday

ōtiōsus, a, um, *adj, adv*, ē, at leisure, unemployed, quiet

ōtium, ii, *n*, leisure, peace

ŏvans, ntis, *adj*, triumphant

ōvātus, a, um, *adj*, oval

ŏvillus, a, um, *adj*, of sheep

ŏvilis, e, *adj*, of sheep

ŏvile, is, *n*, sheepfold

ŏvis, is, *f*, sheep

ŏvo, *v.i.* 1, to exult

ōvum, i, *n*, egg

P

păbo, ōnis, *m*, wheelbarrow
păbŭlātĭo, ōnis, *f*, collection of fodder
păbŭlātor, ōris, *m*, forager
păbŭlor, *v.i.* 1, *dep*, to look for fodder
păbŭlum, i, *n*, food, fodder
pācālis, e, *adj*, peaceful
pācātus, a, um, *adj*, peaceful
pācĭfer, ĕra, ĕrum, *adj*, peace-bringing
pācĭfĭcātĭo, ōnis, *f*, pacification
pācĭfĭco, *v.t.* 1, to make peace
pācĭfĭcus, a, um, *adj*, peaceable
păciscor, pactus, *v.i.t.* 3, *dep*, to make a bargain; barter
păco, *v.t.* 1, to subdue, pacify
pactĭo, ōnis, *f*, an agreement
pactum, i, *n*, an agreement
paotus, a, um, *adj*, agreed
paean, ānis, *m*, hymn to Apollo
paedăgōgus, i, *m*, slave who took children to school, and looked after them at home
paedor, ōris, *m*, filth
paelex, ĭcĭs, *f*, concubine
paenĕ, *adv*, almost, nearly
paenĭnsŭla, ae, *f*, peninsula
paenĭtens, ntis, *adj*, repentant
paenĭtentĭa, ae, *f*, penitence
paenĭtet, *v.* 2, *impers, with acc. of person, it grieves*
paenŭla, ae, *f*, cloak
paenultĭmus, a, um, *adj*, penultimate
paetus, a, um, *adj*, with a slight cast in the eye
pāgānus, a, um, *adj*, rural
pāgānus, i, *m*, country-dweller
pāgĭna, ae, *f*, page, leaf, book
pāgus, i, *m*, village, district
pāla, ae, *f*, spade
pălaestra, ae, *f*, wrestling ground or school, wrestling, rhetorical exercise
pălam, *adv*, openly; *prep. with abl*, in the presence of
pălātĭum, ii, *n*, palace
pălātum, i, *n*, palate
pălĕa, ae, *f*, chaff
pălĭūrus, i, *m*, Christ's thorn (plant)
palla, ae, *f*, stole, robe
pallens, ntis, *adj*, pale
pallĕo, *v.i.* 2, to be pale
pallesco, pallŭi, *v.i.* 3, to turn pale
palliātus, a, um, *adj*, cloaked like Greeks
pallĭdus, a, um, *adj*, pale
pallĭŏlum, i, *n*, hood

pallĭum, ii, *n*, coverlet, cloak
pallor, ōris, *m*, paleness
palma, ae, *f*, palm, hand, oar-blade, palm-tree, broom, palm-wreath, prize, glory
palmārĭs, e, *adj*, excellent, worthy of the palm
palmātus, a, um, *adj*, marked with the hand, decorated with palm
palmĕs, ĭtis, *m*, wine-shoot
palmētum, i, *n*, palm-grove
palmĭfer, ĕra, ĕrum, *adj*, palm-bearing
palmōsus, a, um, *adj*, with many palm trees
palmŭla, ae, *f*, oar-blade
palmus, i, *m*, palm of hand, span
pālor, *v.i.* 1, *dep*, to wander
palpĕbra, ae, *f*, eyelid
palpĭtātĭo, ōnis, *f*, palpitation
palpĭto, *v.i.* 1, to throb, pant
palpo, *v.t.* 1, to stroke, caress
pălūdāmentum, i, *n*, military cloak, general's cloak
pălūdātus, a, um, *adj*, dressed in general's cloak
pălūdōsus, a, um, *adj*, marshy
pălumbes, is, *m*, *f*, wood-pigeon
pālus, i, *m*, stake
pălus, ūdis, *f*, marsh
păluster, tris, tre, *adj*, marshy
pampĭnĕus, a, um, *adj*, full of vine-leaves
pampĭnus, i, *m*, *f*, vine-shoot, vine-leaf
pănăcēa, ae, *f*, a herb which healed all diseases
panchrestus, a, um, *adj*, good for anything
pando, di, nsum, *v.t.* 3, to unfold, open out, spread out, publish
pandus, a, um, *adj*, curved
pango, pĕpĭgi, pactum, *v.t.* 3, to fasten, settle, agree upon
pānis, is, *m*, bread
pannōsus, a, um, *adj*, tattered
pannus, i, *m*, garment, rags
panthēra, ae, *f*, panther
pantōmīmus, i, *m*, ballet-dancer
păpāver, ĕris, *n*, poppy
păpĭlĭo, ōnis, *m*, butterfly
păpilla, ae, *f*, breast, nipple
păpŭla, ae, *f*, pimple
păpȳrĭfer, ĕra, ĕrum, *adj*, papyrus-producing
păpȳrus, i, *m*, *f*, paper
pār, păris, *adj*, equal, suitable
pār, păris, *m*, companion
părābĭlis, e, *adj*, easily-procured
părăbŏla, ae, *f*, parable, comparison

părallēlus, a, um, *adj*, parallel
părălўsis, is, *f*, paralysis, palsy
părăsītus, i, *m*, parasite
părātus, a, um, *adj*, prepared
părātus, ūs, *m*, preparation
parco, pĕperci, parsum, *v.i.* 3, *with dat*, to spare, desist
parcus, a, um, *adj, adv,* ē, thrifty, sparing, scanty
părens, ntis, *adj*, obedient
părens, ntis, *m, f*, parent, ancestor, founder
părentālia, ium, *n.pl*, festival in honour of dead relations
părentālis, e, *adj*, parental
părento, *v.t.* 1, to honour dead relatives, avenge a relative's death by killing
pāreo, *v.i.* 2, *with dat*, to obey, to appear
părĭes, ĕtis, *m*, wall
părĭĕtinae, ārum, *f.pl*, ruins
părĭlis, e, *adj*, equal
părio, pĕpĕri, partum, *v.t.* 3, to bring forth, produce, acquire
părĭter, *adv*, equally, at the same time
parma, ae, *f*, small round shield
parmŭla, ae, *f*, small round shield
păro, *v.t.* 1, to prepare, intend, obtain
părŏchus, i, *m*, caterer
părœcia, ae, *f*, parish
parra, ae, *f*, owl
parrĭcīda, ae, *c*, murderer of a parent or relative, assassin
parrĭcīdĭum, ii, *n*, murder of a parent or relative, treason
pars, partis, *f*, part, party, faction, part in a play; *in pl*, duty, office; in utramque partem, on both sides; pro parte, to the best of one's ability
parsĭmōnĭa, ae, *f*, thrift
partĭceps, cĭpis, *adj, with genit*, sharing; *(as noun)* sharer
partĭcĭpo, *v.t.* 1, to give a share of
partĭcŭla, ae, *f*, small part
partim, *adv*, partly
partĭo, *v.t.* 4, to share, divide
partĭor, *v.t.* 4, *dep*, to share, divide
partītĭo, ōnis, *f*, division
partītus, a, um, *adj*, divided
partŭrĭo, *v.i.t.* 4, to be pregnant or in labour; produce
pārtus, ūs, *m*, birth, confinement, offspring
părum, *adv*, too little
părumper, *adv*, for a short time
parvĭtas, ātis, *f*, smallness
parvŭlus, a, um, *adj*, slight
parvus, a, um, *adj*, small, petty, short; parvi, of little value

pasco, pāvi, pastum, *v.i.t.* 3, to feed; pasture, nourish
pascor, pastus, *v.i.* 3, *dep*, to graze, feast
pascŭum, i, *n*, pasture
pascŭus, a, um, *adj*, for grazing
passer, ĕris, *m*, sparrow, turbot
passim, *adv*, in all directions
passum, i, *n*, raisin-wine
passus, a, um, *adj*, spread out, dried
passus, a, um, *partic. adj*, having suffered
passus, ūs, *m*, step, pace
pastillus, i, *m*, lozenge to dispel bad breath
pastor, ōris, *m*, shepherd
pastōrālis, e, *adj*, of shepherds, pastoral
pastōrĭcĭus, a, um, *adj*, of shepherds, pastoral
pastōrĭus, a, um, *adj*, of shepherds, pastoral
pastus, ūs, *m*, pasture, food
pătĕfăcĭo, fēci, factum, *v.t.* 3, to throw open, disclose
pătĕfactĭo, ōnis, *f*, opening up
pătella, ae, *f*, plate
pătens, ntis, *adj*, open
pătĕo, *v.i.* 2, to be open, to extend, to be evident
păter, tris, *m*, father; *in pl.* forefathers, senators
pătĕra, ae, *f*, saucer, bowl
păterfămĭlĭas, patrisfămĭlĭas, *m*, master of the house
păternus, a, um, *adj*, of a father
pătesco, pătŭi, *v.i.* 3, to be opened, to extend, be evident
pătĭbĭlis, e, *adj*, endurable
pătĭbŭlum, i, *n*, fork-shaped yoke or gibbet
pătĭens, ntis, *adj, adv,* nter, suffering, patient, hard
pătĭentĭa, ae, *f*, endurance
pătĭna, ae, *f*, pan, dish
pătĭor, passus, *v.t.* 3, *dep*, to suffer, bear, allow
pătrĭa, ae, *f*, fatherland
pătrĭarcha, ae, *m*, patriarch
pătrĭcĭus, a, um, *adj*, noble
pătrĭcĭus, i, *m*, member of the Roman nobility
pătrĭmōnĭum, ii, *n*, inherited estate
pătrĭtus, a, um, *adj*, of one's father or ancestor
pătrĭus, a, um, *adj*, of a father, hereditary, established, native
pātro, *v.t.* 1, to perform, finish
pătrōcĭnĭum, ii, *n*, defence
pătrōna, ae, *f*, patroness

pătrōnus, i, *m*, protector, patron, counsel
pătrŭēlis, is, *c*, cousin
pătrŭus, i, *m*, uncle
pătrŭus, a, um, *adj*, of an uncle
pătŭlus, a, um, *adj*, open, wide
pauci, ae, a, *pl. adj*, few
paucĭtas, ātis, *f*, small number
paucŭlus, a, um, *adj*, very few
paucus, a; um, *adj*, few, little
paulātim, *adv*, gradually
paulisper, *adv*, for a short time
paulō, *adv*, a little, somewhat
paulŭlum, *adv*, a little, somewhat
paulum, *adv*, a little, somewhat
pauper, ĕris, *adj*, poor, meagre
pauper, ĕris, *c*, a poor man
paupĕrĭes, ĕi, *f*, poverty
paupertas, ātis, *f*, poverty
paupĕro, *v.t.* 1, to impoverish
pausa, ae, *f*, stop, end
păvĕfăcio, fēci, factum, *v.t.* 3, to alarm
păvĕo, păvi, *v.i.t.* 2, to be afraid; dread
păvesco, *v.i.* 3, to become alarmed
păvĭdus, a, um, *adj*, terrified
păvīmentum, i, *n*, pavement
păvĭo, *v.t.* 4, to beat, strike
păvĭto, *v.i.t.* 1, to tremble (at)
păvo, ōnis, *m*, peacock
păvor, ōris, *m*, anxiety, dread
pax, pācis, *f*, peace, grace, favour, tranquillity; *in abl*, by permission
peccans, ntis, *c*, offender
peccātor, ōris, *m*, sinner
peccātum, i, *n*, fault, mistake
pecco, *v.i.t.* 1, to make a mistake; to miss
pecten, ĭnis, *m*, comb, reed, rake, a plectrum to strike the strings of the lyre
pecto, pexi, xum, *v.t.* 3, to comb
pectŏralis, e, *adj*, pectoral
pectus, ōris, *n*, breast, heart, soul, mind
pĕcŭārius, a, um, *adj*, of cattle
pĕcŭārius, ii, *m*, cattle-breeder
pĕcŭlātor, ōris, *m*, embezzler
pĕcŭlātus, ūs, *m*, embezzlement
pĕcŭliāris, e, *adj*, one's own, special
pĕcŭlium, ii, *n*, property, savings
pĕcūnia, ae, *f*, money
pĕcūniārius, a, um, *adj*, pecuniary
pĕcūniōsus, a, um, *adj*, rich
pĕcus, ōris, *n*, cattle, herd
pĕcus, ŭdis, *f*, an animal, beast
pĕdālis, e, *adj*, a foot in length or thickness
pĕdes, ĭtis, *m*, infantryman

pĕdes, see pes
pĕdester, tris, tre, *adj*, on foot, prosaic, plain
pĕdĕtemptim, *adv*, gradually
pĕdĭca, ae, *f*, shackle, snare
pĕdĭcŭlōsus, a, um, *adj*, lousy
pĕdĭcŭlus, i, *m*, louse
pĕdĭsĕquus, i, *m*, footman
pĕdĭtātus, ūs, *m*, infantry
pĕdum, i, *n*, shepherd's crook
pēiĕro, *v.i.* 1, to swear falsely
pēior, *comp. adj*, worse
pēius, *comp. adv*, worse
pĕlăgus, i, *n*, open sea
pellax, ācis, *adj*, seductive
pellex, ĭcis, *f*, concubine
pellĭcio, lexi, lectum, *v.t.* 3, to allure, coax
pellĭcŭla, ae, *f*, small skin
pellis, is, *f*, skin, leather, tent
pellītus, a, um, *adj*, clothed in skins
pello, pĕpŭli, pulsum, *v.t.* 3, to strike, push, drive out, rout, affect, impress
pellūcĕo, xi, *v.i.* 2, to shine through, be transparent
pellūcĭdus, a, um, *adj*, transparent
pĕlōris, ĭdis, *f*, mussel
pelta, ae, *f*, small shield
pelvis, is, *f*, basin
pĕnārius, a, um, *adj*, for provisions
pĕnātes, ĭum, *m. pl*, guardian deities of the home, home
pendĕo, pĕpendi, *v.i.* 2, to hang, float, loiter, depend upon, be interrupted, be in suspense
pendo, pĕpondi, ponsum, *v.t.* 3, to weigh or pay out, ponder
pendŭlus, a, um, *adj*, hanging, uncertain
pĕnĕs, *prep. with acc*, in the power of
pĕnĕtrābĭlis, e, *adj*, penetrable, penetrating
pĕnĕtrālia, ĭum, *n. pl*, inner places or rooms
pĕnĕtrālis, e, *adj*, inner
pĕnĕtro, *v.i.t.* 1, to enter; penetrate
pĕnĭcillum, i, *n*, painter's brush, pencil
pĕnĭcŭlāmentum, i, *n*, train of a dress
pĕnĭcŭlus, i, *m*, brush
pēnis, is, *m*, tail, penis
pĕnĭtus, *adv*, inwardly, deep within, entirely
penna, ae, *f*, feather, wing
pennātus, a, um, *adj*, winged
penniger, ĕra, ĕrum, *adj*, winged
pensĭlis, e, *adj*, hanging
pensĭo, ōnis, *f*, payment
pensĭto, *v.t.* 1, to pay, weigh, ponder

penso, *v.t.* 1, to weigh out, repay, consider

pensum, i, *n*, a task

pēnūrĭa, ae, *f*, need, want

pĕnus, ūs (*or* i), *m, f*, store of food

pĕpo, ōnis, *m*, pumpkin

per, *prep. with acc*, through, during, by means of, on account of

per . . . in compound words usually adds intensity: very. . . .

pĕractĭo, ōnis, *f*, completion

pĕrăgo, ēgi, actum, *v.t.* 3, to complete, relate, transfix

pĕrăgro, *v.t.* 1, to travel over

pĕrambŭlo, *v.t.* 1, to go through

pĕrăro, *v.t.* 1, to plough through

perbrĕvis, e, *adj*, very short

perca, ae, *f*, perch (fish)

percĕlĕbro, *v.t.* 1, to say frequently

percello, cŭli, culsum, *v.t.* 3, to upset, destroy, dishearten

percensĕo, *v.t.* 2, to reckon up

perceptĭo, ōnis, *f*, perception

percĭpĭo, cēpi, ceptum, *v.t.* 3, to gather, perceive, understand

percontātĭo, ōnis, *f*, inquiry

percontor, *v.i.t.* 1, *dep*, to investigate

percŏquo, xi, ctum, *v.t.* 3, to boil, cook, heat

percrēbesco, bŭi, *v.i.* 3, to become prevalent

percrĕpo, ŭi, ĭtum, *v.i.* 1, to resound, ring

perculsus, a, um, *adj*, upset

percurro, curri, cursum, *v.i.t.* 3, to run; pass over, mention

percussĭo, ōnis, *f*, beating

percussor, ōris, *m*, assassin

percŭtĭo, cussi, cussum, *v.t.* 3, to thrust through, kill, strike, astound

perdisco, dĭdĭci, *v.t.* 3, to learn thoroughly

perdĭtor, ōris, *m*, destroyer

perdĭtus, a, um, *adj, adv*, ē, ruined, desperate, corrupt

perdix, ĭcis, *c*, partridge

perdo, dĭdi, dĭtum, *v.t.* 3, to destroy, waste, lose

perdŏcĕo, *v.t.* 2, to teach thoroughly

perdŏmo, ŭi, ĭtum, *v.t.* 1, to subdue completely

perdūco, xi, ctum, *v.t.* 3, to conduct, bedaub, prolong, induce

perductor, ōris, *m*, pimp

perdŭellĭo, ōnis, *f*, treason

perdŭellis, is, *m*, public enemy

pĕrĕdo, ēdi, sum, *v.t.* 3, to eat up

pĕrĕgrē, *adv*, abroad

pĕrĕgrīnātĭo, ōnis, *f*, travel abroad

pĕrĕgrīnātor, ōris, *m*, traveller

pĕrĕgrīnor, *v.i.* 1, *dep*, to live or travel abroad

pĕrĕgrīnus, a, um, *adj*, foreign

pĕrĕgrīnus, i, *m*, foreigner

pĕrendĭē, *adv*, on the day after tomorrow

pĕrennis, e, *adj*, everlasting

pĕrenno, *v.i.* 1, to last, endure

pĕrĕo, ĭi, ĭtum, *v.i.* 4, *irreg*, to pass away, disappear, die, to be ruined or wasted

pĕrēquĭto, *v.i.* 1, to ride about

pĕrerro, *v.t.* 1, to wander through

perfectĭo, ōnis, *f*, completion

perfectus, a, um, *adj, adv*, ē, complete, perfect

perfĕro, ferre, tŭli, lātum, *v.t. irreg*, to bring or bear through, convey, announce, complete, suffer

perfĭcĭo, fēci, fectum, *v.t.* 3, to complete, finish

perfĭdĭa, ae, *f*, treachery

perfĭdĭōsus, a, um, *adj*, treacherous

perfĭdus, a, um, *adj*, treacherous

perflo, *v.t.* 1, to blow through

perflŭo, xi, *v.i.* 3, to flow through

perfŏdĭo, fōdi, fossum, *v.t.* 3, to dig through

perfŏro, *v.t.* 1, to bore through

perfrĭco, cŭi, cātum, *v.t.* 1, to rub all over, put on a bold front

perfringo, frēgi, fractum, *v.t.* 3, to shatter, infringe

perfrŭor, fructus, *v.* 3, *dep, with abl*, to enjoy thoroughly

perfŭga, ae, *m*, deserter

perfŭgĭo, fūgi, *v.i.* 3, to flee for refuge, desert

perfŭgĭum, ii, *n*, shelter

perfundo, fūdi, fūsum, *v.t.* 3, to pour over, besprinkle

perfungor, functus, *v.* 3, *dep, with abl*, to fulfil, discharge

perfŭro, —*v.i.* 3, to rage

pergo, perrexi, perrectum, *v.i.t.* 3, to proceed, go; continue

pĕrhĭbĕo, ŭi, ĭtum, *v.t.* 2, to extend, assert, name

pĕrhorresco, rŭi, *v.i.t.* 3, to tremble; shudder at

pĕrīclĭtor, *v.i.t.* 1, *dep*, to try, be in danger; test, endanger

pĕrīcŭlōsus, a, um, *adj, adv*, ē, dangerous

pĕrīcŭlum, i, *n*, danger, proof, attempt

pĕrĭmo, ēmi, emptum, v.t. 3, to annihilate, prevent

pĕrinde, adv, just as, equally

pĕrĭŏdus, i, f, complete sentence

pĕrītĭa, ae, f, experience, skill

pĕrītus, a, um, adj, adv, ē, with genit, skilled, expert

periūrĭum, ii, n, perjury

periūro, see pēiĕro

periūrus, a, um, adj, perjured, lying

perlābor, lapsus, v.i. 3, dep, to glide through

perlectĭo, ōnis, f, reading through

perlĕgo, lēgi, lectum, v.t. 3, to survey, examine, read through

perlūcĕo, xi, v.i. 2, to shine through, be transparent

perlŭo, ŭi, ūtum, v.t. 3, to wash

perlūcĭdus, a, um, adj, transparent

perlustro, v.t. 1, to wander through

permănĕo, nsi, nsum, v.i. 2 to last, continue

permāno, v.i. 1, to flow through, penetrate

permansĭo, ōnis, f, persisting

permĕo, v.t. 1, to cross, penetrate

permētĭor, mensus, v.t. 4, dep, to measure out, travel over

permiscŏo, scŭi, xtum, v.t. 2, to mix together

permissĭo, ōnis, f, permission, surrender

permissū, abl, by permission

permitto, misi, missum, v.t. 3, to let loose, commit, entrust; allow (with dat)

permōtĭo, ōnis, f, excitement

permŏvĕo, mōvi, mōtum, v.t. 2, to stir up, rouse

permulcĕo, mulsi, mulsum, v.t. 2, to stroke, charm, flatter

permultus, a, um, adj, adv, ō, or um, very much

permūtātĭo, ōnis, f, exchange

permūto, v.t. 1, to change

perna, ae, f, leg of pork

pernĕgo, v.t. 1, to deny flatly

pernĭcĭes, ēi, f, disaster

pernĭcĭōsus, a, um, adj, adv, ē, destructive

pernīcĭtas, ātis, f, agility

pernix, īcis, adj, agile

pernocto, v.i. 1, to stay all night

pernox, ctis, adj, night-long

pēro, ōnis, m, rawhide boot

pĕrōsus, a, um, adj, detesting, detested

pĕrōro, v.t. 1, to wind up a speech

perpendĭcŭlum, i, n, plumb-line

perpendo, pendi, pensum, v.t. 3, to ponder, consider

perpĕram, adv, untruly

perpĕtĭor, pessus, v.i.t. 3, dep, to suffer; endure

perpĕtŭĭtas, ātis, f, continuity

perpĕtŭus, a, um, adv, ō, perpetual, entire, continuous

perplexus, a, um, adj, intricate

perpŏlĭo, u.t. 4, to perfect

perprimo, pressi, ssum, v.t. 3, to press hard

perpurgo, v.t. 1, to clean up

perquam, adv, very much

perquīro, sīvi, sītum, v.t. 3, to make a careful search for

perrārō, adv, very rarely

perrumpo, rūpi, ruptum, v.i.t. 3, to break through

perscrībo, psi, ptum, v.t. 3, to write in full

perscriptĭo, ōnis, f, written entry or note

perscrūtor, v.t. 1, dep, to examine

persĕco, cui, ctum, v.t. 1, to cut up

persentĭo, si, sum, v.t. 4, to perceive plainly, feel deeply

persĕquor, secūtus, v.t. 3, dep, to pursue, overtake, revenge

persĕvērantĭa, ae, f, constancy

persĕvēro, v.i.t. 1, to persevere; persist in

persīdo, sēdi, sessum, v.i. 3, to penetrate

persisto, stiti, v.t. 3, to persist

persolvo, solvi, sōlūtum, v.t. 3, to pay out, give

persōna, ae, f, mask, character, part, person

persōnātus, a, um, adj, fictitious

persŏno, ŭi, ĭtum, v.i.t. 1, to resound; fill with sound

perspectus, a, um, adj, well-known

perspĭcācĭtas, ātis, f, perspicacity

perspĭcax, ācis, adj, astute

perspĭcĭo, spexi, spectum, v.t. 3, to look at, examine, perceive

perspĭcŭĭtas, ātis, f, clearness, perspicuity

perspĭcŭus, a, um, adj, adv, ē, clear, evident

persto, stiti, stātum, v.i. 1, to endure, continue, persist

perstringo, nxi, ctum, v.t. 3, to graze, blunt, stun, blame, allude to, slight

persuādĕo, si, sum, v.t. 2, with dat, to persuade

persuāsĭo, ōnis, f, conviction

persuāsus, a, um, adj, settled

persuāsum hăbēre, to be convinced

pertento, *v.t.* 1, to consider

pertĕrĕbro, *v.t.* 1, to bore through

perterrĕo, *v.t.* 2, to frighten thoroughly

pertĭca, ae, *f*, pole, rod

pertĭmesco, mŭi, *v.i.t.* 3, to be very afraid; to fear greatly

pertĭnācĭa, ae, *f*, obstinacy

pertĭnax, ācis, *adj*, firm, constant, stubborn

pertĭnĕo, *v.i.* 2, to extend, pertain, concern, be applicable

pertracto, *v.t.* 1, to touch

pertundo, tŭdi, tūsum, *v.t.* 3, to make a hole through

perturbātĭo, ōnis, *f*, confusion

perturbātus, a, um, *adj*, disturbed

perturbo, *v.t.* 1, to disturb

pĕrungo, nxi, nctum, *v.t.* 3, to besmear

pĕrūro, ssi, stum, *v.t.* 3, to burn up, rub sore, nip

pervādo, si, sum, *v.i.* 3, to spread through, pervade

pervăgātus, a, um, *adj*, well-known

pervăgor, *v.i.t.* 1, *dep*, to wander through; pervade

pervĕho, xi, ctum, *v.t.* 3, to carry through

pervello, velli, *v.t.* 3, to pull, disparage

pervĕnĭo, vēni, ventum, *v.i.* 4, to reach, arrive at

perversĭtas, ātis, *f*, obstinacy

perversus, a, um, *adj*, askew, perverse

perverto, ti, sum, *v.t.* 3, to overturn, destroy, corrupt

pervestĭgo, *v.t.* 1, to investigate

pervĭcācĭa, ae, *f*, obstinacy

pervĭcax, ācis, *adj*, *adv*, ĭter, stubborn, wilful

pervĭdĕo, vīdī, vīsum, *v.t.* 2, to view, survey

pervĭgĭl, is, *adj*, ever-watchful

pervĭgĭlātĭo, ōnis, *f*, vigil

pervĭgĭlo, *v.i.* 1, to remain awake all night

pervinco, vīci, victum, *v.t.* 3, to gain victory over

pervĭus, a, um, *adj*, able to be crossed or passed

pervŏlĭto, *v.i.* 1, to flit about

pervŏlo, *v.i.* 1, to fly about or through or to

pervŏlo, velle, vŏlŭi, *v.i*, *irreg*, to wish greatly

pervulgo, *v.t.* 1, to spread about

pēs, pĕdis, *m*, foot; rope attached to a sail, sheet

pessĭmē, *adv*, very badly

pessĭmus, a, um, *adj*, very bad

pessŭlus, i, *m*, latch

pessum, *adv*, to the ground; pessum ire, to go to ruin

pestĭfer, ĕra, ĕrum, *adj*, destructive, harmful

pestĭlens, ntis, *adj*, unhealthy

pestĭlentĭa, ae, *f*, infectious disease

pestis, is, *f*, disease, ruin

pĕtāsātus, a, um, *adj*, dressed for a journey

pĕtāsus, i, *m*, travelling-hat

pĕtītĭo, ōnis, *f*, blow, candidature for office

pĕtītor, ōris, *m*, candidate, plaintiff

pĕto, īvi, ītum, *v.t.* 3, to make for, seek, aim at, request

pĕtōrĭtum, i, *n*, four-wheeled carriage

pĕtŭlans, ntis, *adj*, impudent

pĕtŭlantĭa, ae, *f*, impudence

pexus, a, um, *adj*, new

phălanx, ngis, *f*, military formation

phălĕrae, ārum, *f*. *pl*, military decoration

phărĕtra, ae, *f*, quiver

phărĕtrātus, a, um, *adj*, wearing a quiver

pharmăcŏpōla, ae, *m*, quack

phărus, i, *f*, lighthouse

phăsēlus, i, *m*, *f*, kidney-bean, light boat, yacht

phengītes, ae, *m*, selenite, mica

phĭlŏlŏgĭa, ae, *f*, love of learning

phĭlŏlŏgus, i, *m*, man of learning

phĭlŏmēla, ae, *f*, nightingale

phĭlŏsŏphĭa, ae, *f*, philosophy

phĭlŏsŏphor, *v.i.* 1, *dep*, to study philosophy

phĭlŏsŏphus, i, *m*, philosopher

phĭlyra, ae, *f*, bark of the linden-tree

phīmus, i, *m*, dice-box

phōca, ae, *f*, seal, sea-dog

phoenix, īcis, *m*, bird which was said to live 500 years

phthĭsis, is, *f*, phthisis

phylarchus, i, *m*, chief, prince

phȳsĭca, ōrum, *n*. *pl*, physics

phȳsĭcus, i, *m*, naturalist

phȳsĭŏlŏgĭa, ae, *f*, physiology

pĭācŭlāris, e, *adj*, expiatory

pĭācŭlum, i, *n*, sacrificial offering of atonement, victim, sin, crime

pīca, ae, *f*, magpie

pĭcĕa, ae, *f*, pitch-pine

pĭcĕus, a, um, *adj*, pitch-black

pictor, ōris, *m*, painter

pictūra, ae, *f*, painting, picture

pictūrātus, a, um, *adj*, embroidered

pictus, a, um, *adj*, painted, decorated

pīcus, i, *m*, woodpecker

pĭĕtas, ātis, *f*, sense of duty, loyalty, mercy

pĭger, gra, grum, *adj*, lazy, sluggish

pĭget (me, te), *v*. 2, *impers*, it annoys or displeases (me, you)

pigmentum, i, *n*, paint, pigment

pignĕro, *v.t*. 1, to pledge, pawn

pignĕror, *v.t*. 1, *dep*, to take possession of

pignus, ŏris (ĕris), *n*, security, mortgage, pledge, bet

pĭgrĭtia, ae, *f*, laziness, indolence

pĭgrĭties, ĕi, *f*, laziness, indolence

pīla, ae, *f*, pillar, pier

pĭla, ae, *f*, ball

pīlātus, a, um, *adj*, armed with javelins

pīlentum, i, *n*, carriage

pĭllĕātus, a, um, *adj*, wearing a felt cap, *see below*

pĭllĕus, i, *m* (pillĕum, i, *n*), felt cap, worn by Romans at festivals, and by freed slaves

pĭlōsus, a, um, *adj*, hairy

pĭlŭla, ae, *f*, pill

pĭlum, i, *n*, the heavy javelin of the Roman infantry

pĭlus, i, *m*, a hair, the hair

pīlus, i, *m* (with prīmus), senior centurion, senior division of trĭārĭimen who fought in the 3rd rank

pīnētum, i, *n*, a wood of pines

pīnĕus, a, um, *adj*, of pinewood

pingo, nxi, ctum, *v.t*. 3, to paint, decorate

pinguesco, *v.i*. 3, to grow fat or fertile

pingue, is, *n*, fat

pinguis, e, *adj*, rich, fertile, plump, dull, stupid

pinguitūdo, ĭnis, *f*, plumpness, richness

pīnĭfer, ĕra, ĕrum, *adj*, pine-bearing

pīnĭger, ĕra, ĕrum, *adj*, pine-bearing

pinna, ae, *f*, feather, wing

pinnātus, a, um, *adj*, winged

pinnĭger, ĕra, ĕrum, *adj*, winged

pīnus, ūs (or i,) *f*, pine tree

pĭo, *v.t*. 1, to appease, atone for

pīpātus, ūs, *m*, chirping

pīper, ĕris, *n*, pepper

pīpĭlo, *v.i*. 1, to chirp

pīpĭo, *v.i*. 4, to chirp

pīrāta, ae, *m*, pirate

pīrātĭcus, a, um, *adj*, of pirates

pirum, i, *n*, pear

pirus, i, *f*, pear-tree

piscātor, ōris, *m*, fisherman

piscātōrĭus, a, um, *adj*, of fishing or fishermen

piscātus, ūs, *m*, fishing

piscīna, ae, *f*, fish-pond

piscis, is, *m*, a fish

piscor, *v.i*. 1, *dep*, to fish

piscōsus, a, um, *adj*, full of fish

pistor, ōris, *m*, miller, baker

pistrīnum, i, *n*, mill

pistris, is (pistrix, ĭcis), *f*, sea-monster

pīsum, i, *n*, pea

pītuīta, ae, *f*, phlegm

pii, ōrum, *m. pl*, the departed

pĭus, a, um, *adj*, *adv*, ē, dutiful, loyal, kind, affectionate

pix, pĭcis, *f*, pitch

plācābĭlis, e, *adj*, easily pacified, mild

plācātus, a, um, *adj*, *adv*, ē, calmed, still

plăcens, ntis, *adj*, pleasing

plăcenta, ae, *f*, cake

plăcĕo, *v.i*. 2, *with dat*, to please, to be welcome

plăcĭdus, a, um, *adj*, *adv*, ē, quiet, calm, peaceful

plăcĭtus, a, um, *adj*, agreeable

plāco, *v.t*. 1, to reconcile, soothe

plāga, ae, *f*, wound, blow

plāga, ae, *f*, region

plāga, ae, *f*, hunting-net

plāgĭārĭus, ii, *m*, oppressor

plāgōsus, a, um, *adj*, fond of flogging

plŏgŭla, ae, *f*, curtain

planctus, ūs, *m*, lamentation

plango, nxi, nctum, *v.t*. 3, to beat, strike, lament

plangor, ōris, *m*, lamentation

plānĭties, ĕi, *f*, plain

planta, ae, *f*, shoot, twig

plantāria, ium, *n. pl*, young trees

plantārĭum, ii, *n*, plantation

plānum, i, *n*, plain

plānus, a, um, *adj*, *adv*, ē, flat, level, clear

plānus, i, *m*, imposter, cheat

plătănus, i, *f*, plane-tree

plătēa, ae, *f*, street

plaudo, si, sum, *v.i.t*. 3, to applaud; strike, beat

plausĭbĭlis, e, *adj*, acceptable

plaustrum, i, *n*, cart, waggon

plausus, ūs, *m*, applause

plēbēcŭla, ae, *f*, the mob

plēbēĭus, a, um, *adj*, vulgar

plēbĭcŏla, ae, *c*, demagogue

plebs (plēbes), is, *f*, the common people

plecto, *v.t*. 3, to punish

plectrum, i, *n*, quill with which to strike a stringed instrument

plēnĭtūdo, ĭnis, *f*, fulness

plēnus, a, um, *adj*, *adv*, ē, full, laden, complete, plentiful plērīque, aeque, ăque, *adj*, most, very many

plērumque, *adv*, for the most part

pleurītis, īdis, *f*, pleurisy

plīco, *v.t.* 1, to fold up

plinthus, i, *m*, *f*, plinth

plōrātus, ūs, *m*, weeping

plōro, *v.i.t.* 1, to weep; bewail

plostellum, i, *n*, small cart

plŭit, *v. impers*, it rains

plūma, ae, *f*, feather, down

plumbĕus, a, um, *adj*, made of lead, heavy

plumbum, i, *n*, lead, bullet

plūmĕus, a, um, *adj*, downy, soft

plūrālis, e, *adj*, plural

plūres, es, a, *comp. adj*, more

plūrĭmum, *adv*, very much

plūrĭmus, a, um, *adj*, very much

plūs, plūris, *n*, more

plūs, *adv*, more

pluscŭlum, i, *n*, somewhat more

plŭtĕus, i, *m*, shed, parapet, shelf

plŭvĭa, ae, *f*, rain

plŭvĭālis, e, *adj*, rainy

plŭvĭus, a, um, *adj*, rainy

pōcŭlum, i, *n*, cup, beaker

pŏdăgra, ae, *f*, gout

pŏdĭa, ae, *f*, sail-rope

pŏdĭum, ii, *n*, height, balcony

pŏēma, ătis, *n*, poem

poena, ae, *f*, punishment, penalty

poenālis, e, *adj*, penal

pŏēsis, is, *f*, poetry

pŏēta, ae, *m*, poet

pŏētĭcus, a, um, *adj*, poetical

poi!, *interj*, indeed!

pŏlĭo, *v.t.* 4, to polish, improve

pŏlĭtĭcus, a, um, *adj*, political

pŏlĭtus, a, um, *adj*, *adv*, ē, polished, refined

pollens, ntis, *adj*, powerful

pollĕo, *v.i.* 2, to be powerful, to prevail

pollex, ĭcis, *m*, thumb

pollĭcĕor, *v.i.t.* 2, *dep*, to promise

pollĭcĭtātĭo, ōnis, *f*, promise

pollĭcĭtum, i, *n*, promise

pollinctor, ōris, *m*, undertaker

pollŭo, ŭi, ūtum, *v.t.* 3, to pollute, contaminate

pŏlus, i, *m*, pole, north-pole

pŏlўpus, i, *m*, polypus

pōmārĭum, ii, *n*, orchard

pōmārĭus, ii, *m*, fruiterer

pōmĕrīdĭānus, a, um, *adj*, in the afternoon

pōmĭfer, ĕra, ĕrum, *adj*, fruit-bearing

pōmoerĭum, ii, *n*, open space inside and outside city walls

pompa, ae, *f*, procession, retinue, pomp

pōmum, i, *n*, fruit

pōmus, i, *f*, fruit-tree

pondĕro, *v.t.* 1, to consider

pondĕrōsus, a, um, *adj*, ponderous

pondo, *adv*, by weight

pondus, ĕris, *n*, weight, mass, influence, authority

pōne, *adv. and prep. with acc*, behind, after

pōno, pŏsŭi, pŏsĭtum, *v.t.* 3, to put, place, set, plant, wager, invest, spend, lay aside, appoint, calm, allege, propose

pons, ntis, *m*, bridge

pontĭcŭlus, i, *m*, drawbridge

pontifex, ĭcis, *m*, high-priest

pontĭfĭcĭus, a, um, *adj*, of a high-priest

pontus, i, *m*, the sea

pŏpa, ae, *m*, priest's assistant

pŏpīna, ae, *f*, restaurant

poplēs, ĭtis, *m*, knee

pŏpŭlāris, e, *adj*, *adv*, ĭter, of the people, popular, democratic

pŏpŭlāris, c, fellow-countryman

pŏpŭlāres, ium, *m. pl*, the people's party

pŏpŭlātĭo, ōnis, *f*, devastation

pŏpŭlātor, ōris, *m*, plunderer

pŏpŭlĕus, a, um, *adj*, of poplars

pŏpŭlo, *v.t.* 1, to plunder, devastate

pŏpŭlor, *v.t.* 1, *dep*, to plunder, devastate

pŏpŭlus, i, *m*, the people

pŏpŭlus, i, *f*, poplar tree

porcīna, ae, *f*, pork

porcŭlus, i, *m*, young pig; (with mărīnus), porpoise

porcus, i, *m*, pig

porrectĭo, ōnis, *f*, extension

porrectus, a, um, *adj*, extended

porrĭcĭo, ēci, ctum, *v.t.* 3, to offer to the gods

porrĭgo, rexi, rectum, *v.t.* 3, to stretch out, offer

porrĭgo, ĭnis, *f*, dandruff

porro, *adv*, forwards, next, moreover

porrum, i, *n*, leek

porta, ae, *f*, gate, door

portendo, di, tum, *v.t.* 3, to foretell

portentum, i, *n*, omen, monster

portĭcus, ūs, *f*, colonnade

portĭo, *in phrase*, pro portĭōne, in proportion

portĭtor, ōris, *m*, customs-officer
portĭtor, ōris, *m*, boatman
porto, *v.t.* 1, to carry, bring
portōrĭum, ii, *n*, customs-duty
portŭōsus, a, um, *adj*, with many harbours
portus, ūs, *m*, harbour, refuge
posco, pŏposci, *v.t.* 3, to demand
pŏsĭtĭo, ōnis, *f*, placing, situation
pŏsĭtus, a, um, *adj*, situated
pŏsĭtus, ūs, *m*, arrangement, disposition
possessĭo, ōnis, *f*, seizure, occupation
possessor, ōris, *m*, possessor
possĭdĕo, sēdi, sessum, *v.t.* 2, to be master of, possess
possĭdo, sēdi, sessum, *v.t.* 3, to take possession of, occupy
possum, posse, pŏtŭi, *v.i*, *irreg*, to be able, to have power
post, *adv. and prep. with acc*, behind, backwards, after
postĕā, *adv*, afterwards
postĕāquam, *conj.* after
postĕri, ōrum, *m. pl*, posterity
postĕrĭor, ĭus, *comp. adj*, next, worse
postĕrĭtas, ātis, *f*, posterity
postĕrĭus, *adv*, later
postĕrus, a, um, *adj*, next
postgĕnĭti, ōrum, *m. pl*, posterity
posthābĕo, *v.t.* 2, to postpone, neglect
posthāc, *adv*, in future
postīcum, i, *n*, back door
postis, is, *m*, door-post
postmŏdo, *adv*, afterwards
postpōno, pŏsŭi, pŏsĭtum, *v.t.* 3, to postpone, neglect
postquam, *conj*, after, when
postrēmo, *adv*, at last
postrēmus, a, um, *adj*, the last
postrīdĭē, *adv*, on the next day
postŭlāta, ōrum, *n. pl*, demand, request
postŭlātĭo, ōnis, *f*, demands, requests
postŭlo, *v.t.* 1, to demand, prosecute, accuse
postŭmus, a, um, *adj*, last-born, posthumous
pōtātĭo, ōnis, *f*, drinking
pōtātor, ōris, *m*, drinker
pŏtens, ntis, *adj*, powerful, master of (*with genit*)
pŏtentātus, ūs, *m*, power, rule
pŏtentĭa, ae, *f*, power, authority
pŏtestas, ātis, *f*, power, dominion, control, value, force, ability, permission, opportunity
pōtĭo, ōnis, *f*, a drink
pŏtĭor, *v.* 4, *dep*, *with abl*, to obtain, hold, possess

pŏtĭor, ĭus, *comp. adj*, preferable
pŏtis, e, *adj*, possible
pŏtĭus, *adv*, preferably
pōto, *v.i.t.* 1, to drink
pōtor, ōris, *m*, drinker,
pōtus, a, um, *adj*, intoxicated, drained
pōtus, ūs, *m*, a drink
prae, *adv. and prep. with abl*, before, in comparison with
prae se ferre (gĕrere), to reveal
praeăcŭo, ŭi, ūtum, *v.t.* 3, to sharpen
praeăcūtus, a, um, *adj*, pointed
praebĕo, *v.t.* 2, to offer, give, show
praecăvĕo, cāvi, cautum, *v.i.t.* 2, to be on one's guard; prevent
praecēdo, cessi, cessum, *v.i.t.* 3, to lead the way; precede
praecellens, ntis, *adj*, excellent
praecelsus, a, um, *adj*, very high
praeceps, cĭpĭtis, *adj*, headlong
praeceps, cĭpĭtis, *n*, precipice, danger
praeceptor, ōris, *m*, teacher
praeceptum, i, *n*, rule, maxim, order, command
praecerpo, psi, ptum, *v.t.* 3, to gather before time
praecīdo, cīdi, cīsum, *v.t.* 3, to cut off, cut short
praecingo, nxi, nctum, *v.t.* 3, to encircle, gird
praecino, nŭi, centum, *v.i.t.* 3, to sing before; predict
praecĭpĭo, cēpi, ceptum, *v.t.* 3, to receive in advance, anticipate, advise, teach
praecĭpĭto, *v.i.t.* 1, to rush down; throw headlong
praecĭpŭus, a, um, *adj*, *adv*, ē, particular, especial, excellent
praeclārus, a, um, *adj*, *adv*, ē, splendid, excellent
praeclūdo, si, sum, *v.t.* 3, to close
praeco, ōnis, *m*, herald
praecōnĭum, ii, *n*, office of herald, proclamation
praecōnĭus, a, um, *adj*, of a herald
praecordĭa, ōrum, *n.pl*, midriff, heart
praecox, ōcis, *adj*, premature
praecurro, cŭcurri, cursum, *v.i.t.* 3, to run in front; excel
praecursor, ōris, *m*, scout, spy
praecŭtĭo, cussi, cussum, *v.t.* 3, to brandish in front
praeda, ae, *f*, plunder, prey
praedātor, ōris, *m*, plunderer
praedātōrĭus, a, um, *adj*, predatory
praedĭātor, ōris, *m*, estate agent
praedĭcātĭo, ōnis, *f*, proclamation, commendation

praedĭco, *v.t.* 1, to proclaim, declare, praise
praedīco, **xi**, **ctum**, *v.t.* 3, to predict, advise, command
praedictĭo, **ōnis**, *f*, prediction
praedictum, **i**, *n*, prediction
praedisco, *v.t.* 3, to learn beforehand
praedĭtus, **a**, **um**, *adj*, provided with
praedĭum, **ii**, *n*, farm, estate
praedīvĕs, **ĭtis**, *adj*, very rich
praedo, **ōnis**, *m*, robber
praedor, *v.i.t.* 1, *dep*, to plunder
praedūco, **xi**, **ctum**, *v.t.* 3, to make or put in front
praedulcis, **e**, *adj*, very sweet
praedūrus, **a**, **um**, *adj*, very hard
praeĕo, **ii**, **ĭtum**, *v.i.t.* 4, to lead the way; recite, dictate
praefātĭo, **ōnis**, *f*, preface
praefectūra, **ae**, *f*, superintendence
praefectus, **i**, *m*, director, commander, governor
praefĕro, **ferre**, **tŭli**, **lātum**, *v.t*, *irreg*, to carry in front, offer, prefer, show
praefĭcĭo, **fēci**, **fectum**, *v.t.* 3, to put in command
praefīdens, **ntis**, *adj*, over-confident
praefīgo, **xi**, **xum**, *v.t.* 3, to fix in front
praefīnĭo, *v.t.* 3, to fix, appoint
praeflŭo, *v.i.* 3, to flow past
praefŏdĭo, **fŏdi**, *v.t.* 3, to dig in front
praefor, **fātus**, *v.i.t.* 1, *dep*, to say in advance
praefringo, **frēgi**, **fractum**, *v.t.* 3, to break off
praefulgĕo, **si**, *v.i.* 2, to glitter
praegestĭo, *v.i.* 4, to desire greatly
praegnans, **ntis**, *adj*, pregnant
praegrăvis, **e**, *adj*, very heavy
praegrĕdĭor, **gressus**, *v.i.t.* 3, *dep*, to go in advance
praeiūdĭcātus, **a**, **um**, *adj*, preconceived
praeiūdĭcĭum, **ii**, *n*, precedent (at law)
praeiūdĭco, *v.t.* 1, to pre-judge
praelābor, **lapsus**, *v.i.t.* 3. *dep*, to glide or flow along or past
praelambo, *v.t.* 3, to taste in advance
praelūcĕo, **xi**, *v.i.* 2, to carry a light in front
praemandāta, **ōrum**, *n. pl*, warrant of arrest
praemĕdĭtātĭo, **ōnis**, *f*, premeditation
praemĕdĭtor, *v.t.* 1, *dep*, to premeditate
praemitto, **mīsi**, **missum**, *v.t.* 3, to send in advance
praemĭum, **ii**, *n*, booty, reward
praemŏnĕo, *v.t.* 2, to forewarn
praemūnĭo, *v.t.* 4, to fortify

praenăto, *v.i.* 1, to flow past
praenĭtĕo, *v.i.* 2, to outshine
praenōmen, **ĭnis**, *n*, first (Christian) name
praenosco, *v.t.* 3, to learn in advance
praenuntĭo, *v.t.* 1, to predict
praenuntĭus, **a**, **um**, *adj*, foreboding
praenuntĭus, **i**, *m*, foreteller
praeoccŭpo, *v.t.* 1, to seize in advance
praeopto, *v.t.* 1, to prefer
praepărātĭo, **ōnis**, *f*, preparation
praepăro, *v.t.* 1, to prepare
praepĕdĭo, *v.t.* 4, to bind, obstruct
praependĕo, *v.i.* 2, to hang down in front
praepes, **ĕtis**, *adj*, swift
praepes, **ĕtis**, *c*, bird
praepinguis, **e**, *adj*, very fat
praepōno, **pŏsŭi**, **pŏsĭtum**, *v.t.* 3, to put first, put in command, prefer
praepŏsĭtĭo, **ōnis**, *f*, preference
praepŏsĭtus, **i**, *m*, chief, head
praepostĕrus, **a**, **um**, *adj*, preposterous
praepŏtens, **ntis**, *adj*, very powerful
praeprŏpĕrus, **a**, **um**, *adj*, sudden, precipitate
praeripĭo, **rĭpŭi**, **reptum**, *v.t.* 3, to snatch away
praerōdo, **rōsum**, *v.t.* 3, to nibble
praerŏgātĭva, **ae**, *f*, the Roman tribe to which the first vote was allotted
praerumpo, **rūpi**, **ruptum**, *v.t.* 3, to break off
praeruptus, **a**, **um**, *adj*, steep
praes, **dis**, *m*, security, bail
praesaepe, **is**, *n*, stable, pen
praesaepĭo, **psi**, **ptum**, *v.t.* 4, to barricade
praesāgĭo, *v.t.* 4, to have a presentiment or premonition
praesāgĭum, **ii**, *n*, a foreboding
praesāgus, **a**, **um**, *adj*, foretelling
praescisco, *v.t.* 3, to learn in advance
praescĭus, **a**, **um**, *adj*, knowing in advance
praescrībo, **psi**, **ptum**, *v.t.* 3, to order, appoint, prescribe
praescriptĭo, **ōnis**, *f*, excuse, order, law
praescriptum, **i**, *n*, order, law
praesens, **ntis**, *adj*, present, prompt, powerful, resolute, helping
praesensĭo, **ōnis**, *f*, foreboding
praesentĭa, **ae**, *f*, presence
praesentĭa, **ium**, *n. pl*, present circumstances
praesentĭo, **si**, **sum**, *v.t.* 4, to have a premonition
praesēpe, see **praesaepe**
praesertim, *adv*, especially

praeses, ĭdis, *adj*, guarding

praeses, ĭdis, *c*, guardian, chief

praesĭdĕo, sēdi, *v.i.t.* 2, to guard, direct, superintend

praesĭdĭum, ĭi, *n*, garrison, fortification, camp

praesignis, e, *adj*, excellent, distinguished

praestābĭlis, e, *adj*, excellent, distinguished

praestans, ntis, *adj*, excellent, distinguished

praestantĭa, ae, *f*, excellence

praestat, *v.* 1, *impers*, it is preferable

praestīgĭae, ārum, *f. pl*, juggling-tricks

praestĭtŭo, ŭi, ūtum, *v.t.* 3, to appoint in advance

praesto, *adv*, ready, present

praesto, stĭti, stĭtum, *v.i.t.* 1, to be superior; surpass, vouch for, perform, fulfil, show, give, offer

praestringo, nxi, ctum, *v.t.* 3, to tie up, graze, blunt

praestrŭo, xi, ctum, *v.t.* 3, to build or block up

praesum praeesse, praefŭi, *v.i, irreg*, with *dat*, to be in command of

praesūmo, mpsi, mptum, *v.t.* 3, to anticipate, imagine in advance

praetendo, di, tum, *v.t.* 3, to hold out, pretend

praetento, *v.t.* 1, to examine in advance

praeter, *adv, and prep. with acc*, past, beyond, beside, except, unless

praetĕrĕā, *adv*, besides, henceforth

praetĕrĕo, ĭi, ĭtum, *v.i.t.* 4, to pass by; go past, omit, neglect

praeterflŭo, xi, ctum, *v.i.* 3, to flow past

praetergrĕdĭor, gressus, *v.i.t.* 3, *dep*, to pass beyond

praetĕrĭtus, a, um, *adj*, past, gone

praeterlābor, lapsus, *v.i.t.* 3, *dep*, to glide or flow past

praetermissio, ōnis, *f*, omission

praetermitto, mīsi, missum, *v.t.* 3, to let pass, omit, neglect

praeterquam, *adv*, besides, except

praetervĕhor, vectus, *v.i.t.* 3, *dep*, to sail, ride or drive past

praetervŏlo, *v.i.t.* 1, to escape; fly past

praetexo, xŭi, xtum, *v.t.* 3, to edge, border, pretend

praetexta, ae, *f*, purple-edged toga worn by Roman magistrates and children

praetexta, ae, *f*, a tragedy

praetextātus, a, um, *adj*, wearing the toga praetexta

praetextus, a, um, *adj*, wearing the toga praetexta

praetor, ōris, *m*, chief, head, Roman magistrate concerned with administration of justice

praetōrĭum, ĭi, *n*, general's tent, governor's residence

praetōrĭus, a, um, *adj*, of the praetor or general

praetūra, ae, *f*, praetorship

praeūro, ussi, ustum, *v.t.* 3, to burn at the end

praeustus, a, um, *adj*, burnt, frost-bitten

praevălĕo, *v.i.* 2, to be superior

praevălĭdus, a, um, *adj*, very strong

praevĕhor, ctus, *v.i.t.* 3, *dep*, to ride, fly or flow in front

praevĕnĭo, vēni, ventum, *v.i.t.* 4, to come before; outstrip

praeverto, ti, *v.t.* 3, to outstrip, anticipate, prevent

praevertor, sus, *v.i.t.* 3, *dep*, to concentrate one's attention (on)

praevĭdĕo, vidi, visum, *v.t.* 3, to anticipate, see in advance

praevius, a, um, *adj*, leading the way

prandĕo, di, sum, *v.i.t.* 2, to breakfast, lunch, (on)

prandĭum, ĭi, *n*, breakfast, luncheon

pransus, a, um, *adj*, having breakfasted

prātensis, e, *adj*, growing in meadows

prātĭlum, i, *n*, small meadow

prātum, i, *n*, meadow

prāvĭtas, ātis, *f*, deformity, depravity

prāvus, a, um, *adj, adv*, ē, wrong, bad, deformed

prĕcārĭus, a, um, *adj, adv*, ō, obtained by prayer

prĕcatĭo, ōnis, *f*, prayer

prĕcĭae, ārum, *f. pl*, grape-vine

prĕcor, *v.i.t.* 1, *dep*, to pray, beg

prĕhendo, di, sum, *v.t.* 3, to seize, detain, take by surprise

prĕhenso, *v.t.* 1, to grasp, detain

prēlum, i, *n*, wine-press

prĕmo, ssi, ssum, *v.t.* 3, to press, grasp, cover, close, pursue closely, load, overwhelm, plant, prune, check, repress

prendo, see prĕhendo

prensus, a, um, *adj*, grasped

presso, *v.t.* 1, to press

pressus, ūs, *m*, pressure

pressus, a, um, *adj*, subdued, compact

prĕtĭōsus, a, um, *adj, adv*, ē, valuable, costly

prĕtĭum, ii, *n*, price, value, money, wages, reward

prex, prĕcis, *f*, prayer, request

prīdem, *adv*, long ago

prīdĭē, *adv*, on the day before

prīmaevus, a, um, *adj*, youthful

prīmārius, a, um, *adj*, of the first rank, chief

prīmĭgĕnus, a, um, *adj*, primitive

prīmĭpīlus, *see* pilus

prīmĭtĭae, ārum, *f. pl*, first-fruits

prīmō, *adv*, at first

prīmordĭa, ōrum, *n. pl*, origin

prīmōris, e, *adj*, first, front end

prīmōres, um, *m. pl*, nobles

prīmum, *adv*, at first; cum prīmum, as soon as; quam prīmum, as soon as possible

prīmus, a, um, *adj*, first, chief

princeps, cĭpis, *adj*, first, chief

princeps, cĭpis, *m*, chief, originator

princĭpālis, e, *adj*, original, primitive, principal

princĭpālis, is, *m*, overseer

princĭpātus, ūs, *m*, the first place, command, rule

principĭo, *adv*, in the beginning

principĭum, ii, *n*, origin; *in pl*, principles, elements

prĭor, ĭus, *comp. adj*, previous, former

prĭōres, um, *m. pl*, ancestors

priscus, a, um, *adj*, ancient

prisma, ătis, *n*, prism

pristīnus, a, um, *adj*, primitive

prĭus, *comp. adv*, previously

prĭusquam, *conj*, before

prīvātim, *adv*, privately

prīvātĭo, ōnis, *f*, taking-away

prīvātus, a, um, *adj*, private

prīvātus, i, *m*, private citizen

prīvigna, ae, *f*, step-daughter

prīvignus, i, *m*, step-son

prīvilēgĭum, ii, *n*, bill or law concerned with an individual

prīvo, *v.t.* i, to deprive, release

prīvus, a, um, *adj*, one's own

prō, *prep. with abl*, before, in front of, on behalf of, instead of, just as, on account of, according to, in relation to

prō! (prōh!), *interj*, Ah! Alas!

prōăvus, i, *m*, great-grandfather

prōbābĭlis, e, *adj*, *adv*, iter, likely, pleasing

prōbābĭlĭtās, ātis, *f*, probability

prōbātĭo, ōnis, *f*, trial, proving

prōbātus, a, um, *adj*, tried, good

prōbĭtas, ātis, *f*, honesty

prŏbo, *v.t.* i, to try, test, approve of, recommend, prove

prŏboscis, idis, *f*, elephant's trunk

prŏbrōsus, a, um, *adj*, shameful

prŏbrum, i, *n*, disgraceful deed, lechery, disgrace, abuse

prŏbus, a, um, *adj*, *adv*, ē, good, honest, virtuous

prŏcācĭtas, ātis, *f*, impudence

prŏcax, ācis, *adj*, impudent

prŏcēdo, cessi, cessum, *v.i.* 3, to go forward, advance, turn out, prosper

prŏcella, ae, *f*, storm, violence

prŏcellōsus, a, um, *adj*, tempestuous

prŏcer, ĕris, *m*, chief, prince

prŏcērĭtas, ātis, *f*, height

prŏcērus, a, um, *adj*, tall

prŏcessus, ūs, *m*, advance

prŏcĭdo, di, *v.i.* 3, to fall flat

prŏcinctus, ūs, *m*, readiness for battle

prŏclāmo, *v.t.* i, to cry out

prŏclīno, *v.t.* i, to bend forwards

prŏclīve, is, *n*, slope, descent

prŏclīvis, e, *adj*, sloping downhill, liable, willing

prōconsul, is, *m*, provincial governor

prōcrastĭno, *v.t.* i, to defer

prōcrĕātĭo, ōnis, *f*, procreation

prōcrĕātor, ōris, *m*, creator

prōcrĕo, *v.t.* i, to produce

prōcŭbo, *v.i.* i, to lie stretched-out

prōcūdo, di, sum, *v.t.* 3, to forge

prŏcul, *adv*, in the distance

prŏculco, *v.t.* i, to trample on

prōcumbo, cŭbŭi, cŭbĭtum, *v.i.* 3, to lean or fall forwards, sink

prōcūrātĭo, ōnis, *f*, administration

prōcūrātor, ōris, *m*, manager, agent

prōcūro, *v.t.* i, to look after

prōcurro, curri, cursum, *v.i.* 3, to run forward, project

prŏcus, i, *m*, suitor

prōdĕo, ii, ĭtum, *v.i.* 3, to come forward, appear

prōdesse, *see* prōsum

prōdĭgĭōsus, a, um, *adj*, strange, marvellous

prōdĭgĭum, ii, *n*, omen, monster

prōdĭgus, a, um, *adj*, wasteful

prōdĭtĭo, ōnis, *f*, treachery

prōdĭtor, ōris, *m*, traitor

prōdo, dĭdi, dĭtum, *v.t.* 3, to bring out, relate, betray, bequeath

prōdūco, xi, ctum, *v.t.* 3, to lead forward, prolong, produce, promote

prōductus, a, um, *adj*, *adv*, ē, prolonged

proelĭor, *v.i.* i, *dep*, to join battle

proelĭum, ii, *n*, battle

prōfāno, *v.t.* 1, to desecrate

prōfānus, a, um, *adj*, wicked, common

prōfectĭo, ōnis, *f*, departure

prōfectō, *adv*, certainly

prōfectus, ūs, *m*, advance

prōfectus, a, um, *adj*, having advanced

prōfĕro, ferre, tŭli, lātum, *v.t*, *irreg*, to bring out, extend, defer, reveal, mention; with gradum, to proceed; with signa, to march forward

prōfessor, ōris, *m*, teacher, professor

prōfessĭo, ōnis, *f*, declaration

prōfessus, a, um, *adj*, avowed

prōfestus, a, um, *adj*, working (days)

prōfĭcĭo, fēci, fectum, *v.i.t.* 3, to progress; perform, help

prōfĭciscor, prōfectus, *v.i.* 3, *dep*, to set out, originate

prōfĭtĕor, fessus, *v.i.* 2, *dep*, to declare, acknowledge, promise

prōflīgātus, a, um, *adj*, wretched, dissolute

prōflīgo, *v.t.* 1, to overthrow

prōflo, *v.t.* 1, to blow out

prōflŭo, xi, xum, *v.i.* 3, to flow out, proceed

prōflŭens, ntis, *adj*, fluent

prōflŭvĭum, ii, *n*, flowing out

prōfor, *v.t.* 1, *dep*, to speak, say

prōfŭgĭo, fūgi, *v.i.t.* 3, to escape; flee from

prōfŭgus, a, um, *adj*, fugitive

prōfŭgus, i, *m*, fugitive, exile

prōfundo, fūdi, fūsum, *v.t.* 3, to pour out, utter, squander

prōfundum, i, *n*, the deep, the sea, an abyss

prōfundus, a, um, *adj*, deep

prōfūsĭo, ōnis, *f*, outpouring, prodigal use

prōfūsus, a, um, *adj*, extravagant

prōgĕnĕro, *v.t.* 1, to beget

prōgĕnĭes, ēi, *f*, family, offspring

prōgigno, gĕnŭi, gĕnĭtum, *v.t.* 3, to produce

prōgnātus, a, um, *adj*, born

prōgnātus, i, *m*, descendant

prōgrĕdĭor, gressus, *v.i.* 3, *dep*, to advance, proceed

prōgressĭo, ōnis, *f*, growth

prōgressus, ūs, *m*, advance

proh!, see prō!

prōhĭbĕo, *v.t.* 2, to prevent, prohibit, defend

prōĭectus, a, um, *adj*, projecting

prōĭcĭo, iēci, iectum, *v.t.* 3, to throw forward, extend, expel, yield, disdain

prōin or prōindē, *adv*, in the same way, equally, accordingly, therefore

prōlābor, lapsus, *v.i.* 3, *dep*, to slip or slide forward, fall

prōlātĭo, ōnis, *f*, postponement, mentioning

prōlāto, *v.t.* 1, to postpone

prōles, is, *f*, offspring, child

prōlētārĭus, ii, *m*, citizen of lowest class

prōlixus, a, um, *adj*, *adv*, ē, stretched out, fortunate

prōlŏgus, i, *m*, prologue

prōlūdo, si, sum, *v.i.* 3, to practise in advance

prōlŭo, lŭi, lūtum, *v.t.* 3, to wash away, moisten

prōlūsĭo, ōnis, *f*, prelude

prōlŭvĭes, ēi, *f*, overflow

prōmĕrĕo, *v.t.* 2, to deserve, merit

prōmĕrĕor, *v.t.* 2, *dep*, to deserve, merit

prōmĭnens, ntis, *adj*, prominent

prōmĭnĕo, *v.i.* 2, to project

prōmiscŭus, a, um, *adj*, common, indiscriminate

prōmissĭo, ōnis, *f*, promise

prōmissum, i, *n*, promise

prōmissus, a, um, *adj*, hanging

prōmitto, misi, missum, *v.t.* 3, to promise, assure

prōmo, mpsi, mptum, *v.t.* 3, to bring out, produce, tell

prōmontŭrĭum, ii, *n*, headland

prōmŏvĕo, mōvi, mōtum, *v.t.* 2, to move forward, extend

promptus, a, um, *adj*, ready, quick

promptus, ūs, *m*, only in phrase; in promptu, in public; in promptu esse, to be at hand

prōmulgo, *v.t.* 1, to publish

prōmus, i, *m*, butler

prōmūtŭus, a, um, *adj*, loaned

prōnĕpos, ōtis, *m*, great-grandson

prōnōmen, ĭnis, *n*, pronoun

prōnūba, ae, *f*, bridesmaid

prōnuntĭātĭo, ōnis, *f*, proclamation

prōnuntĭo, *v.t.* 1, to announce

prōnus, a, um, *adj*, leaning or bending forward, disposed; setting, sinking (of stars, etc.)

prōoemĭum, ii, *n*, preface

prōpāgātĭo, ōnis, *f*, extension

prōpāgo, *v.t.* 1, to generate, extend

prōpāgo, ĭnis, *f*, shoot (of plant), offspring, child

prōpālam, *adv*, openly

prōpātŭlus, a, um, *adj*, uncovered

prōpe, *adv. and prep. with acc*, near, nearly

prōpĕdĭem, *adv*, soon

prōpello, pŭli, pulsum, v.t. 3, to push or drive forward

prŏpĕmŏdum, adv, almost

prōpendĕo, di, sum, v.i. 2, to be inclined or disposed

prōpensus, a, um, adj, inclined, disposed

prŏpĕro, v.i.t. 1, to hurry

prŏpĕrus, a, um, adj, adv, ē, quick, hurrying

prŏpexus, a, um, adj, combed forward

prōpīno, v.t. 1, to drink a toast

prŏpinquĭtas, ātis, f, nearness, relationship

prŏpinquo, v.i.t. 1, to approach; hasten

prŏpinquus, a, um, adj, near

prŏpinquus, i, m, relative

prŏpior, ius, comp. adj, nearer

prŏpĭtĭus, a, um, adj, kind, favourable

prŏpius, comp. adv, nearer

prōpōno, pŏsŭi, pŏsitum, v.t. 3, to put forward, state, display, offer

prōpŏsĭtĭo, ōnis, f, representation, theme

prōpŏsitum, i, n, plan, purpose

prŏprĭĕtas, ātis, f, peculiarity

prŏprĭus, a, um, adj, adv, ē, special, particular, its (his, her) own

propter, prep. with acc, on account of, near; adv, nearby

proptĕrĕā, adv, for that reason

prōpugnācŭlum, i, n, rampart

prōpugnātĭo, ōnis, f, defence

prōpugnātor, ōris, m, defender

prōpugno, v.i.t. 1, to make sorties; defend

prōpulso, v.t. 1, to ward off

prōra, ae, f, prow, ship

prōrēpo, psi, ptum, v.i. 3, to creep out, crawl forward

prōrĭpĭo, pŭi, reptum, v.t. 3, to drag forward; with se, to rush

prōrŏgātĭo, ōnis, f, prolonging

prōrŏgo, v.t. 1, to prolong, defer

prorsus (prorsum), adv, certainly, utterly

prōrumpo, rūpi, ruptum, v.i.t. 3, to rush forward; send forward

prōrŭo, rŭi, rŭtum, v.i.t. 3, to rush forward; overthrow

proscaenĭum, ii, n, stage

prōscindo, scĭdi, scissum, v.t. 3, to tear up, plough

prōscrībo, psi, ptum, v.t. 3, to publish, confiscate, outlaw

prōscriptĭo, ōnis, f, confiscation, outlawing

prōscriptus, i, m, outlaw

prōsēmĭno, v.t. 1, to sow

prōsĕquor, sĕcūtus, v.t. 3, dep, to accompany, follow, pursue, bestow, proceed with

prōsĭlĭo, ŭi, v.i. 4, to leap up

prospecto, v.t. 1, to look at, expect, await

prospectus, ūs, m, view, sight

prospĕrus, a, um, adj, adv, ē, favourable, fortunate

prospĕrĭtas, ātis, f, prosperity

prospĕro, v.t. 1, to make (something) successful

prospĭcĭo, spexi, spectum, v.i.t. 3, to look out; discern, overlook, foresee

prōsterno, strāvi, strātum, v.t. 3, to overthrow, prostrate

prōsŭbĭgo, v.t. 3, to dig up

prōsum, prōdesse, prōfŭi, v.i, irreg. with dat, to be useful

prōtectum, i, n, eaves

prōtĕgo, xi, ctum, v.t. 3, to cover, protect

prōtēlum, i, n, team of oxen

prōtendo, di, sum (tum), v.t. 3, to stretch out, extend

prōtĕro, trīvi, trītum, v.t. 3, to trample down, crush, destroy

prōterrĕo, v.t. 2, to terrify

prōtervitas, ātis, f, impudence

prōtervus, a, um, adj, adv, ē, forward, impudent, violent

prōtĭnus, adv, straightforwards, continuously, immediately

prōtrăho, xi, ctum, v.t. 3, to drag forward, reveal

prōtrūdo, si, sum, v.t. 3, to push out

prōturbo, v.t. 1, to repel

prout, adv, just as

prōvectus, a, um, adj, advanced (of time)

prōvĕho, xi, ctum, v.t. 3, to carry forward, advance, promote

prōvĕnĭo, vēni, ventum, v.i. 4, to be born, thrive, occur, turn out (well or badly)

prōventus, ūs, m, produce, result

prōverbĭum, ii, n, proverb

prōvidens, ntis, adj, prudent

prōvidentĭa, ae, f, foresight

prōvidĕo, vīdi, visum, v.i.t. 2, to make preparations; foresee, provide for

prōvidus, a, um, adj, prudent

prōvincĭa, ae, f, province, duty, sphere of duty

prōvincĭālis, e, adj, provincial

prōvŏcātĭo, ōnis, f, appeal

prōvŏco, v.i.t. 1, to appeal; call out, challenge, rouse

prōvŏlo, v.i. 1, to fly out

prōvolvo, volvi, vŏlūtum, v.t. 3, to roll
forward
proxĭmē, adv, nearest, next
proxĭmĭtas, ātis, f, proximity
proxĭmus, a, um, adj, nearest, next,
previous
prūdens, ntis, adj, adv, nter, experienced, wise, sensible
prūdentĭa, ae, f, experience, skill,
discretion
prūīna, ae, f, frost, snow
prūīnōsus, a, um, adj, frosty
prūna, ae, f, burning coal
prūnum, i, n, plum
prūnus, i, f, plum-tree
prūrĭo, v.i. 4, to itch
prūrĭtus, ūs, m, itching
psallo, i, v.i. 3, to play on an instrument
psalmus, i, m, a psalm
psittăcus, i, m, parrot
ptĭsāna, ae, f, pearl-barley
pūbens, ntis, adj, flourishing
pūbertas, ātis, f, puberty, manhood
pūbes (pūber), ēris, adj, adult
pūbes, is, f, young men
pūbesco, bŭi, v.i. 3, to grow up, ripen
pūblĭcānus, i, m, tax-collector
pūblĭcātĭo, ōnis, f, confiscation
pūblĭco, v.t. 1, to confiscate
pūblĭcum, i, n, a public place
pūblĭcus, a, um, adj, adv, ē, of the
state, public, general
pūdendus, a, um, adj, disgraceful
pūdens, ntis, adj, adv, nter, modest
pūdet, v. 2, impers, it brings shame
pūdĭbundus, a, um, adj, modest
pūdīcĭtĭa, ae, f, modesty, virtue
pūdīcus, a, um, adj, modest, pure
pūdor, ōris, m, a sense of decency,
shyness
pŭella, ae, f, girl, sweetheart, young
wife
pŭellāris, e, adj, girlish
pŭer, ĕri, m, boy
pŭerīlis, e, adj, youthful
pŭerĭtĭa (pŭertĭa), ae, f, childhood,
youth
pŭgil, ĭlis, m, boxer
pŭgillāres, ĭum, m. pl, writing-tablets
pŭgĭo, ōnis, m, dagger
pugna, ae, f, fight, battle
pugnātor, ōris, m, fighter
pugnax, ācis, adj, warlike, quarrelsome
pugno, v.i. 1, to fight, disagree,
struggle
pugnus, i, m, fist
pulcher, chra, chrum, adj, adv, ē,
beautiful, handsome, glorious
pulchrĭtūdo, ĭnis, f, beauty

pūlex, ĭcis, m, flea
pullārĭus, ii, m, chicken-keeper
pullŭlo, v.i. 1, to sprout
pullus, i. m, young animal, chicken
pullus, a, um, adj, dark, black
pulmentārĭum, ii, n, sauce
pulmentum, i, n, sauce
pulmo, ōnis, m, lung
pulpĭtum, i, n, platform
puls, pultis, f, porridge
pulsātĭo, ōnis, f, beating
pulso, v.t. 1, to beat, push, touch,
disturb
pulsus, ūs, m, push, blow, beating
pulvĕrĕus, a, um, adj, dusty
pulvĕrŭlentus, a, um, adj, dusty
pulvīnar, āris, n, couch
pulvīnus, i, m, cushion
pulvis, ĕris, m, dust
pūmex, ĭcis, m, pumice-stone
pūmĭlĭo, ōnis, m, dwarf
punctim, adv, with the point
punctum, i, n, point, vote, moment
pungo, pŭpŭgi, punctum, v.t. 3, to
prick, sting, vex, annoy
pūnĭcĕus, a, um, adj, red
pūnĭo, v.t. (pūnĭor, v.t.dep.) 4, to
punish
pūpa, ae, f, doll
pūpilla, ae, f, orphan, ward
pūpillus, i, m, orphan, ward
puppis, is, f, ship's stern
pūpŭla, ae, f, pupil of the eye
purgāmen, ĭnis, n, refuse, filth
purgāmentum, i, n, refuse, filth
purgātĭo, ōnis, f, cleansing
purgo, v.t. 1, to clean, purify, excuse,
justify, atone for
purpŭra, ae, f, purple, purple clothes
purpŭrĕus, a, um, adj, purple, clothed
in purple, brilliant
pūrum, i, n, clear sky
pūrus, a, um, adj, adv, ē, pure, clean,
plain
pūs, pūris, n, pus
pŭsillus, a, um, adj, little, petty
pūsĭo, ōnis, m, urchin
pustŭla, ae, f, pimple
pŭtāmen, ĭnis, f, peel, shell
pŭtĕal, ālis, n, fence of a well
pŭtĕo, v.i. 2, to stink
pŭter (pŭtris), tris, tre, adj, decaying,
rotten
pŭtesco, pŭtŭi, v.i. 3, to rot
pŭtĕus, i, m, well, pit
pŭtĭdus, a, um, adj, rotten, disgusting
pŭto, v.t. 1, to think, prune
pŭtresco, v.i. 3, to decay
pŭtrĭdus, a, um, adj, rotten
pȳra, ae, f, funeral pyre

For List of Abbreviations used, turn to pages 3, 4

pȳrămis, ĭdis, f, pyramid
pȳrum, i, n, pear
pȳrus, i, f, pear-tree
pȳthon, ōnis, m, python
pyxis, ĭdis, f, box

Q

quā, adv, where, in which direction, how; qua ... qua, partly ... partly
quācumque, adv, wheresoever
quădra, ae, f, square, dining-table
quădrāgēni, ae, a, adj, forty each
quădrāgēsĭmus, a, um, adj, fortieth
quădrāgĭes, adv, forty times
quădrāgĭnta, adj, forty
quădrans, ntis, m, a quarter
quădrātum, i, n, square
quădrātus, a, um, adj, square
quădrĭdŭum, ii, n, period of four days
quădrĭfārĭam, adv, into four parts
quădrĭfĭdus, a, um, adj, split into four
quădrīgae, ārum, f. pl, four-horse team or chariot
quădrĭiŭgis, e, adj, yoked in a four-horse team
quădrĭiŭgus, a, um, adj, yoked in a four-horse team
quădrĭlătĕrus, a, um, adj, quadrilateral
quădrīmus, a, um, adj, four years old
quădringēnārĭus, a, um, adj, of four hundred each
quădringenti, ae, a, adj, four hundred
quădringentĭes, adv, four hundred times
quădro, v.i.t. 1, to be square, agree; make square, complete
quădrum, i, n, square
quădrŭpĕdans, ntis, adj, galloping
quădrŭpēs, ĕdis, adj, galloping, going on four feet
quădrŭplex, ĭcis, adj, quadruple
quădrŭplum, i, n, fourfold amount
quaero, sīvi, sītum, v.t. 3, to search for, acquire, inquire
quaesĭtĭo, ōnis, f, investigation
quaesītor, ōris, m, investigator
quaesītum, i, n, question
quaesītus, a, um, adj, far-fetched
quaeso, īvi, v.t. 3, to beseech, seek
quaestĭo, ōnis, f, investigation, trial, case, question, problem
quaestor, ōris, m, Roman magistrate in charge of public revenues
quaestōrĭus, a, um, adj, of a quaestor

quaestŭōsus, a, um, adj, profitable
quaestūra, ae, f, quaestorship
quaestus, ūs, m, gain, profit, employment
quālis, e, adj, of what kind
quāliscumque, quālĕcumque, adj, of whatever kind
quālĭtas, ātis, f, state, condition
quālum, i, n, basket, hamper
quam, adv, how; with comparatives, than
quamdĭu, adv, as long as, until
quamlĭbet, adv, as much as you wish
quămobrem, adv, why, wherefore
quamprīmum, adv, as soon as possible
quamquam, conj, although
quamvīs, conj, although; adv, very
quando, adv, when?, some time; conj, since, because
quandōcumque, adv, whenever
quandōque, adv, whenever, at some time or other
quandōquĭdem, adv, since
quanti? at what price?
quantō, adv, by as much as
quantŏpĕrē, adv, how much
quantŭlus, a, um, adj, how small
quantŭluscumque, adj, however small
quantum, adv, as much as
quantus, a, um, adj, how great
quantuscumque, adj, however big
quantusvis, quantāvis, quantumvis, adj, as big as you like
quāpropter, adv, wherefore
quārē, adv, wherefore, why
quartānus, a, um, adj, occurring on the fourth day
quartum, adv, for the fourth time
quartō, adv, for the fourth time
quartus, a, um, adj, fourth
quăsĭ, adv, as if, just as
quăsillum, i, n, small basket
quassātĭo, ōnis, f, shaking
quasso, v.t. 1, to shake, shatter
quătĕnus, adv, to what extent, how long, since
quăter, adv, four times
quăterni, ae, a, pl. adj, four each
quătĭo (no perf.), quassum, v.t. 3, to shake, shatter, excite
quattŭor, indecl. adj, four
quattŭordĕcim, adj, fourteen
quē conj, and
quĕmadmŏdum, adv, how
quĕo, ii, ĭtum, v.i. 4, to be able
quercētum, i, n, oak-forest
quercus, ūs, f, oak-tree
quĕrēla, ae, f, complaint

querĭbundus, a, um, *adj*, complaining
querĭmōnĭa, ae, *f*, complaint
quernus, a, um, *adj*, of oak
quĕror, questus, *v.i.t.* 3, *dep*, to complain
querŭlus, a, um, *adj*, full of complaints, cooing, chirping
questus, ūs, *m*, complaint
qūi, quae, quod, *rel.pron*, who, which, what
quī, *adv*, how, wherewith
quĭă, *conj*, because
quicquid, *pron*, whatever
quĭcumque, quaecumque, quodcumque, *pron*, whoever, whatever
quid, *interr. pron*, what? why?
quīdam, quaedam, quoddam, *pron*, a certain somebody or something
quĭdem, *adv*, indeed; ne ... quidem, not even ...
quidni, why not?
quĭes, ētis, *f*, rest, quiet
quĭescens, ntis, *adj*, quiescent
quĭesco, ēvi, ētum, *v.i.* 3, to rest, keep quiet, sleep
quĭētus, a, um, *adj*, calm
quīlĭbet, quaelĭbet, quodlĭbet, *pron*, anyone or anything you like
quĭn, *conj*, that not, but that, indeed, why not
quīnam, quaenam, quodnam, *pron*, who, what, which
quĭncunx, ncis, *m*, five-twelfths, trees planted in oblique lines
quindĕcĭes, *adv*, fifteen times
quindĕcĭm, *indecl. adj*, fifteen
quĭngēnī, ae, a, *pl. adj*, five hundred each
quĭngentī, ae, a, *pl. adj*, five hundred
quĭngentĭes, *adv*, five hundred times
quīnī, ae, a, *pl. adj*, five each
quinquāgēnī, ae, a, *pl. adj*, fifty each
quinquāgēsĭmus, a, um, *adj*, fiftieth
quinquāginta, *indecl. adj*, fifty
quinquātrĭa, ōrum, *n.pl*, festival of Minerva (19th-23rd March)
quinquĕ, *indecl. adj*, five
quinquennālis, e, *adj*, quinquennial
quinquennis, e, *adj*, every fifth year
quinquennĭum, ii, *n*, period of five years
quinquĕrēmis, *adj*, ship with five banks of oars
quinquĭens, *adv*, five times
Quintĭlis (mensis), July
quintus, a, um, *adj*, fifth
quippe, *adv*, certainly; *conj*, in as much as
quis, quid, *interr pron*, who? which? what? *indef.pron*, anyone, anything

quisnam, quaenam, quidnam, *interr. pron*, who? which?
quispĭam, quaepĭam, quodpĭam, *indef. pron*, anybody, anything
quisquam, quaequam, quicquam, *indef. pron*, anyone, anything
quisque, quaeque, quodque, *indef. pron*, each, every, everybody, everything
quisquĭlĭae, ārum, *f. pl*, rubbish
quisquis, quaeque, quodquod, *indef. pron*, whoever, whatever
quīvis, quaevis, quodvis, *indef. pron*, anyone or anything you please
quō, *adv. and conj*, wherefore, where to, whither, so that
quŏăd, *adv*, as long as, until, as far as
quōcircā, *conj*, wherefore
quōcumque, *adv*, to whatever place
quod, *conj*, because
quod, *neuter of* qui
quōdammŏdo, in a certain manner
quōmĭnus, *conj*, that ... not
quōmŏdō, *adv*, how
quondam, *adv*, once, at times
quŏnĭam, *adv*, since, because
quŏquam, *adv*, to any place
quŏque, *conj*, also, too
quŏquō, *adv*, to whatever place
quorsum (quorsus), *adv*, to what place, to what purpose
quŏt, *indecl. adj*, how many
quŏtannis, *adv*, every year
quōtĭdĭānus, a, um, *adj*, daily
quōtĭdĭe, *adv*, daily
quŏtĭes (quŏtĭens), *adv*, how often
quŏtĭescumquĕ, *adv*, however often
quotquŏt, *adv*, however many
quŏtus, a, um, *adj*, how many
quŏŭsquĕ, *adv*, how long
quum, see cum

R

rābĭdus, a, um, *adj*, raving, mad
rābĭes (em, e), *f*, madness, anger
rābĭōsus, a, um, *adj*, raging
rābŭla, ae, *f*, argumentative lawyer
rācēmĭfer, ĕra, ĕrum, *adj*, clustering
rācēmus, i, *m*, bunch, cluster
rādīcĭtus, *adv*, by the roots
rādĭans, ntis, *adj*, shining
rādĭātĭo, ōnis, *f*, shining
rādĭo, *v.i.* 1, to shine
rādĭus, ii, *m*, rod, spoke, radius, shuttle, ray
rādix, īcis, *f*, root, radish, source
rādo, si, sum, *v.t.* 3, to scrape, shave
raeda, ae, *f*, carriage

raedārĭus, i, *m*, coachman

raia, ae, *f*, ray (fish)

rāmālĭa, ĭum, *n.pl*, brushwood

rāmōsus, a, um, *adj*, branching

rāmus, i, *m*, branch

rāna, ae, *f*, frog

rancĭdus, a, um, *adj*, rancid

rānuncŭlus, i, *m*, tadpole

răpācĭtas, ātis, *f*, rapacity

răpax, ācis, *adj*, grasping

rāphănus, i, *m*, radish

răpĭdus, a, um, *adj*, *adv*, ē, swift, violent, tearing

răpīna, ae, *f*, robbery, plunder

răpĭo, ŭi, raptum, *v.t.* 3, to seize, snatch, drag away

raptim, *adv*, hurriedly

raptĭo, ōnis, *f*, abduction

rapto, *v.t.* 1, to snatch, drag away, plunder

raptor, ōris, *m*, robber

raptum, i, *n*, plunder

raptus, ūs, *m*, robbery, rape

rāpŭlum, i, *n*, turnip

rāpum, i, *n*, turnip

rāresco, *v.i.* 3, to grow thin, open out

rārĭtas, ātis, *f*, looseness, rarity, infrequency

rārus, a, um, *adj*, *adv*, ē, ō, loose, loose in texture, thin, scattered, straggling, few, remarkable, rare

rāsĭlis, e, *adj*, polished

rastellus, i, *m*, hoe, rake

rastrum, i, *n*, rake, hoe

rătĭo, ōnis, *f*, account, calculation, business affairs, relationship, concern for, consideration, conduct, plan, reason, motive, reckoning, order, law, theory, system, way, manner

rătĭŏcĭnor, *v.i.t.* 1, *dep*, to calculate

rătĭōnālis, e, *adj*, rational, theoretical

rătis, is, *f*, raft

rătus, a, um, *adj*, established; (*partic.*) having ·thought; pro rătā, proportionally

raucus, a, um, *adj*, hoarse

rāvus, a, um, *adj*, grey, tawny

rē, rēvērā (*adv.*), really

rēapse, *adv*, (re ipsa), in fact

rēbellĭo, ōnis, *f*, revolt

rēbellis, e, *adj*, rebellious

rēbello, *v.i.* 1, to rebel, rebuff

rēbŏo, *v.i.* 1, to re-echo

rĕcalcĭtro, *v.i.* 1, to kick back

rĕcalfăcĭo, fēci, *v.t.* 3, to warm

rĕcandesco, dŭi, *v.i.* 3, to grow white or hot

rĕcanto, (*no perf*) *v.t.* 1, to retract

rĕcēdo, cessi, cessum, *v.i.* 3, to retreat, withdraw

rĕcens, ntis, *adj*, fresh, new

rĕcens, *adv*, newly, recently

rĕcensĕo, ŭi, ītum, *v.t.* 2, to count, reckon, survey, review

rĕcensĭo, ōnis, *f*, review

rĕceptācŭlum, i, *n*, shelter

rĕcepto, *v.t.* 1, to recover

rĕceptor, ōris, *m*, receiver

rĕceptus, ūs, *m*, retreat

rĕcessus, ūs, *m*, retreat, recess

rĕcĭdīvus, a, um, *adj*, recurring

rĕcĭdo, cĭdi, cāsum, *v.i.* 3, to fall back, recoil, return

rĕcīdo, cīdi, cīsum, *v.t.* 3, to cut down, cut off, cut short

rĕcingo, (*no perf,*) cinctum, *v.t.* 3, to loosen

rĕcĭno, *v.i.* 3, to re-echo

rĕcĭpĕro (rĕcŭp-), *v.t.* 1, to regain

rĕcĭpĭo, cēpi, ceptum, *v.t.* 3, to take back, regain, receive, give an assurance; with sē, to retreat, recover oneself

rĕcĭprōco, *v.i.t.* 1, to move backwards

rĕcĭprŏcus, a, um, *adj*, receding

rĕcĭtātĭo, ōnis, *f*, reading aloud

rĕcĭtātor, ōris, *m*, reader

rĕcĭto, *v.t.* 1, to read aloud

rĕclāmātĭo, ōnis, *f*, remonstrance

rĕclāmo, *v.i.t.* 1, to resound; contradict loudly, remonstrate

rĕclīno, *v.t.* 1, to lean back

rĕclūdo, si, sum, *v.t.* 3, to reveal

rĕcognĭtĭo, ōnis, *f*, review

rĕcognosco, gnōvi, gnĭtum, *v.t.* 3, to recollect, investigate

rĕcŏlo, cŏlŭi, cultum, *v.t.* 3, to cultivate again, renew

rĕconcĭlĭātĭo, ōnis, *f*, re-establishment, reconciliation

rĕconcĭlĭo, *v.t.* 1, to restore, reconcile

rĕcondĭtus, a, um, *adj*, hidden

rĕcondo, dĭdi, dĭtum, *v.t.* 3, to put away, hide

rĕcŏquo, xi, ctum, *v.t.* 3, to cook again, forge again

rĕcordātĭo, ōnis, *f*, recollection

rĕcordor, *v.i.t.* 1, *dep*, to think over, remember

rĕcrĕātĭo, ōnis, *f*, recovery·

rĕcrĕo, *v.t.* 1, to revive, reproduce

rĕcresco, crēvi, crētum, *v.i.* 3, to grow again

rectā, *adv*, straightforwards

rector, ōris, *m*, master, leader, helmsman

rectum, i, *n*, virtue

rectus, a, um, *adj, adv,* **ē,** straight, upright, correct
rĕcŭbans, ntis, *adj,* recumbent
rĕcŭbo, *v.i.* 1, to lie back
rĕcumbo, cŭbŭi, *v.i.* 3, to lie down
rĕcŭpĕrātio, ōnis, *f,* recovery
rĕcŭpĕro, *v.t.* 1, to recover, regain
rĕcurro, curri, *v.i.* 3, to run back, return
rĕcurso, *v.i.* 1, to return
rĕcursus, ūs, *m,* return, retreat
rĕcurvo, *v.t.* 1, to bend back
rĕcurvus, a, um, *adj,* bent
rĕcūsātio, ōnis, *f,* refusal
rĕcūso, *v.t.* 1, to refuse
rĕcussus, a, um, *adj,* roused
rĕdargŭo, ŭi, *v.t.* 3, to contradict
reddo, didi, ditum, *v.t.* 3, to give back, deliver, pay, produce, render, translate, recite, repeat, resemble
rĕdemptio, ōnis, *f,* buying back
rĕdemptor, ōris, *m,* contractor
rĕdĕo, ii, itum, *v.i.* 4, to go back, return, be reduced to
rĕdigo, ēgi, actum, *v.t.* 3, to bring back, restore, collect, reduce to
rĕdimīcŭlum, i, *n,* necklace
rĕdimio, *v.t.* 4, to encircle
rĕdimo, ēmi, emptum, *v.t.* 3, to re-purchase, ransom, release, hire, obtain
rĕdintĕgro, *v.t.* 1, to restore
rĕdĭtus, ūs, *m,* return
rĕdŏlĕo, *v.i.t.* 2, to smell; smell of
rĕdōno, *v.t.* 1, to restore
rĕdūco, xi, ctum, *v.t.* 3, to bring back, restore
rĕductus, a, um, *adj,* remote
rĕdundantia, ae, *f,* redundancy
rĕdundo, *v.i.* 1, to overflow, abound in
rĕdux, dŭcis, *adj,* brought back
rĕfello, felli, *v.t.* 3, to refute
rĕfercio, si, tum, *v.t.* 4, to cram
rĕfĕro, ferre, rettŭli, rĕlātum, *v.t. irreg,* to bring back, restore, repay, report, reply, propose, record, reckon, refer, resemble; **with pedem,** to retreat
rēfert, *v, impers,* it is of importance, it matters
rĕfertus, a, um, *adj,* filled
rĕficio, fēci, fectum, *v.t.* 3, to re-make, repair, refresh
rĕfigo, xi, xum, *v.t.* 3, to unfix
rĕfingo, *v.t.* 3, to renew
rĕflecto, xi, xum, *v.i.t.* 3, to turn back; bend back
rĕflo, *v.i.* 1, to blow back
rĕflŭo, *v.i.* 3, to flow back

rĕformīdo, (*no perf,*) *v.t.* 1, to dread, avoid
rĕfrăgor, *v.i.* 1, *dep,* to resist
rĕfrēno, *v.t.* 1, to curb, check
rĕfrico, ŭi, *v.t.* 1, to scratch open
rĕfrīgĕro, *v.t.* 1, to cool
rĕfrīgesco, frixi, *v.i.* 3, to grow cool, grow stale
rĕfringo, frēgi, fractum, *v.t.* 3, to break open, break off
rĕfŭgio, fūgi, *v.i.t.* 3, to run away, escape; flee from, avoid
rĕfulgĕo, si, *v.i.* 2, to shine
rĕfundo, fūdi, fūsum, *v.t.* 3, to pour out, cause to overflow
rĕfūtandus, *gerundive,* see **rĕfŭto**
rĕfūto, *v.t.* 1, to repress, refute
rēgālis, e, *adj,* royal, splendid
rēgia, ae, *f,* palace, court
rēgĭficus, a, um, *adj,* royal
rēgigno, *v.t.* 3, to reproduce
rĕgimen, inis, *n,* guidance
rēgīna, ae, *f,* queen
rēgio, ōnis, *f,* district, region, direction, boundary; **ē rēgiōne, in a** straight line
rēgius, a, um, *adj, adv,* **ē,** royal, magnificent
regnātor, ōris, *m,* ruler
regno, *v.i.t.* 1, to reign; rule
regnum, i, *n,* kingdom, sovereignty, dominion
rĕgo, xi, ctum, *v.t.* 3, to rule, guide, direct
rĕgrĕdior, gressus, *v.i.* 3, *dep,* to return, retreat
rĕgressus, ūs, *m,* return, retreat
rēgŭla, ae, *f,* wooden-ruler, model, pattern
rēgŭlus, i, *m,* prince
rēicio, iēci, iectum, *v.t.* 3, to throw back, repel, reject, postpone
rēiectio, ōnis, *f,* rejection
rēlābor, lapsus, *v.i.* 3, *dep,* to slide or sink back
rĕlanguesco, gŭi, *v.i.* 3, to grow faint, relax
rĕlātio, ōnis, *f,* proposition
rĕlaxo, *v.t.* 1, to loosen, ease
rēlēgātio, ōnis, *f,* banishment
rēlēgo, *v.t.* 1, to send away, banish
rĕlēgo, lēgi, lectum, *v.t.* 3, to gather together, travel over again, read over again
rĕlēvo, *v.t.* 1, to lift up, lighten, comfort, refresh
rĕlictio, ōnis, *f,* abandonment
rĕlictus, a, um, *adj,* left
rĕligio, ōnis, *f,* piety, religion,

For List of Abbreviations used, turn to pages 3, 4

religious scruple, good faith, conscientiousness, sanctity

rēligiōsus, a, um, *adj*, devout, scrupulous, precise, sacred

rēlīgo, *v.t.* 1, to bind, fasten

rēlino, lēvi, *v.t.* 3, to unseal

rēlinquo, rēlīqui, lictum, *v.t.* 3, to leave, leave behind, abandon, surrender

rēlīquiae, ārum, *f. pl*, remains

rēlīquum, i, *n*, remainder

rēlīquus, a, um, *adj*, remaining

rēlūcĕo, xi, *v.i.* 2, to shine

rēluctor, *v.i.* 1, *dep*, to resist

rēmănĕo, nsi, *v.i.* 2, to stay behind, endure

rēmēdĭum, ii, *n*, cure, relief

rēmĕo, *v.i.* 1, to return

rēmētĭor, mensus, *v.t.* 4, *dep*, to remeasure

rēmex, ĭgis, *m*, oarsman

rēmĭgĭum, ii, *n*, rowing, oars, rowers

rēmĭgo, *v.i.* 1, to row

rēmĭgro, *v.i.* 1, to return

rēmĭniscor, *v.* 3, *dep, with genit*, to remember

rēmiscĕo, *no perf*, mixtum, *v.t.* 2, to mix up

rēmissĭo, ōnis, *f*, relaxation

rēmissus, a, um, *adj, adv*, ē, loose, gentle, cheerful

rēmitto, mīsi, missum, *v.i.t.* 3, to decrease; send back, send out, yield, loosen, slacken, grant, surrender, give up; *with infin*, to cease

rēmollesco, *v.i.* 3, to grow soft

rēmordĕo, *no perf*, morsum, *v.t.* 2, to torment

rēmŏror, *v.i.t.* 1, *dep*, to loiter; obstruct

rēmōtus, a, um, *adj*, distant

rēmŏvĕo, mōvi, mōtum, *v.t*, 2, to remove, withdraw, set aside

rēmūgĭo, *v.i.* 4, to resound

rēmulcum, i, *n*, tow-rope

rēmūnērātĭo, ōnis, *f*, reward

rēmūnĕror, *v.t.* 1, *dep*, to reward

rēmurmŭro, *v.i.t.* 1, to murmur back

rēmus, i, *m*, oar

rēnascor, nātus, *v.i.* 3, *dep*, to be born again, spring up again

rēnes, um, *m. pl*, kidneys

rēnīdĕo, *v.i.* 2, to glisten

rēnŏvātĭo, ōnis, *f*, renewal

rēnŏvo, *v.t.* 1, to renew, restore, refresh, repeat

rēnuntĭātĭo, ōnis, *f*, announcement

rēnuntĭo, *v.t.* 1, to report, announce, refuse, renounce

rēnŭo, ŭi, *v.i.t.* 3, to refuse

rĕor, rātus, *v.t.* 2, *dep*, to suppose, think, believe

rĕpāgŭla, ōrum, *n.pl*, bolts, bars

rĕpărābĭlis, e, *adj*, able to be repaired

rĕpăro, *v.t.* 1, to recover, repair, restore, refresh

rĕpello, pŭli, pulsum, *v.t.* 3, to drive back, reject

rĕpendo, di, sum, *v.t.* 3, to weigh out in return, repay

rĕpens, ntis, *adj, adv*, ē, sudden

rĕpentīnus, a, um, *adj, adv*, ō, sudden, unexpected

rĕpercussus, ūs, *m*, reflection

rĕpercŭtĭo, cussi, cussum, *v.t.* 3, to drive back, reflect

rĕpĕrĭo, repperi, rĕpertum, *v.t.* 4, to find, discover

rĕpertor, ōris, *m*, discoverer

rĕpĕto, ii, ītum, *v.t.* 3, to attack again, re-visit, fetch back, resume, recollect, demand back

rĕpĕtundae, ārum, *f.pl*, (*with* res), extortion

rĕplĕo, ēvi, ētum, *v.t.* 2, to fill up, complete

rĕplētus, a, um, *adj*, full

rēpo, psi, ptum, *v.i.* 3, to creep

rĕpōno, pōsŭi, pŏsĭtum, *v.t.* 3, to replace, preserve, put away

rĕporto, *v.t.* 1, to bring back, carry back, obtain

rĕposco, *v.t.* 3, to demand back

rĕpraesentātĭo, ōnis, *f*, representation

rĕpraesento, *v.t.* 1, to display, do immediately

rĕprĕhendo, di, sum, *v.t.* 3, to blame, rebuke, convict

rĕprĕhensĭo, ōnis, *f*, blame

rĕprimo, pressi, ssum, *v.t.* 3, to keep back, check, restrain

rĕpŭdĭātĭo, ōnis, *f*, refusal, renunciation

rĕpŭdĭo, *v.t.* 1, to divorce, reject, scorn

rĕpugnans, ntis, *adj*, contradictory, irreconcilable

rĕpugnantĭa, ae, *f*, opposition, inconsistency

rĕpugno, *v.i.* 1, to resist, disagree with

rĕpulsa, ae, *f*, refusal, rejection

rĕpurgo, *v.t.* 1, to clean

rĕpŭto, *v.t.* 1, to ponder, reckon

rĕquĭes, ētis, *f*, rest, relaxation

rĕquĭesco, ēvi, ētum, *v.i.* 3, to rest

rĕquīro, sīvi, sītum, *v.t.* 3, to search for, enquire, need, notice to be missing

rēs, rĕi, *f*, thing, matter, affair, reality, fact, property, profit, advantage, business, affair, lawsuit;

rēs nŏvae, rērum nŏvārum, *f. pl*, revolution, respublĭca, rĕīpublĭcae, *f*, the State, statesmanship

rēscindo, scĭdi, ssum, *v.t.* 3, to cut down, break down, abolish

rēscisco, īvi, ītum, *v.t.* 3, to learn, ascertain

rēscrībo, psi, ptum, *v.t.* 3, to write back, reply, repay

rĕsĕco, ŭi, ctum, *v.t.* 1, to cut off, curtail

rĕsĕro, *v.t.* 1, to unlock, open

rĕservo, *v.t.* 1, to save up, keep

rĕsĕs, ĭdis, *adj*, inactive

rĕsĭdĕo, sēdi, *v.i.* 2, to remain, linger, sit

rĕsīdo, sēdi, *v.i.* 3, to settle

rĕsĭdŭus, a, um, *adj*, remaining

rĕsigno, *v.t.* 1, to unseal, open

rĕsĭlĭo, ŭi, *v.i.* 4, to recoil

rēsīna, ae, *f*, resin

rĕsĭpĭo, *v.t.* 3, to taste of

rŏsĭpisoo, īvi, *v.i.* 3, to revive

rĕsisto, stĭti, *v.i.* 3, to stop, remain; *with dat*, to resist

rĕsolvo, solvi, sŏlūtum, *v.t.* 3, to untie, release, open, relax, annul, abolish

rĕsŏno, *v.i.t.* 1, to resound; re-echo with

rĕsŏnus, a, um, *adj*, resounding

rĕsorbĕo, *v.t.* 2, to re-swallow

rēspecto, *v.t.* 1, to look at, respect

rēspectus, ūs, *m*, looking back, retreat, refuge, respect

rēspergo, si, sum, *v.t.* 3, to besprinkle

rēspĭcĭo, spexi, spectum, *v.i.t.* 3, to look back, give attention; look at, regard, respect

rēspīrātĭo, ōnis, *f*, breathing

rēspīro, *v.i.t.* 1, to revive; breathe out, breathe

rēsplendĕo, *v.i.* 2, to shine

rēspondĕo, di, sum, *v.t.* 2, to reply, give advice, agree, correspond, answer one's hopes

rēsponso, *v.t.* 1, to reply, resist

rēsponsum, i, *n*, answer

respublĭca, see rēs

rēspŭo, ŭi, *v.t.* 3, to spit out, expel, reject

rēstinguo, nxi, nctum, *v.t.* 3, to quench, extinguish

restis, is, *f*, rope

rēstĭtŭo, ŭi, ūtum, *v.t.* 3, to replace, rebuild, renew, give back, restore

rēstĭtūtĭo, ōnis, *f*, restoration

rēsto, stĭti, *v.i.* 1, to remain

rēstrictus, a, um, *adj*, bound

rēstringo, nxi, ctum, *v.t.* 3, to bind, restrain

rĕsulto, *no perf*, *v.i.* 1, to jump back, resound

rĕsūmo, mpsi, mptum, *v.t.* 3, to resume, take back, recover

rĕsŭpīnus, a, um, *adj*, lying on one's back

rĕsurgo, surrexi, surrectum, *v.i.* 3, to rise, re-appear

rĕsurrectĭo, ōnis, *f*, resurrection

rĕsuscĭto, *v.t.* 1, to revive

rĕtardo, *v.i.t.* 1, to delay

rēte, is, *n*, net, snare

rĕtĕgo, xi, ctum, *v.t.* 3, to uncover, reveal

rĕtendo, di, tum, *v.t.* 3, to slacken

rĕtento, *v.t.* 1, to keep back

rĕtento, *v.t.* 1, to try again

rĕtexo, ŭi, xtum, *v.t.* 3, to unravel, cancel

rĕtĭcĕo, *v.i.t.* 2, to be silent; conceal

rĕtĭcŭlātus, a, um, *adj*, net-like

rĕtĭcŭlum, i, *n*, small net

rētĭnācŭlum, i, *n*, rope, cable

rĕtĭnens, ntis, *adj*, tenacious

rĕtĭnĕo, ŭi, tentum, *v.t.* 2, to hold back, restrain, maintain

rĕtorquĕo, si, tum, *v.t.* 2, to twist back, drive back

rĕtracto, *v.t.* 1, to handle or undertake again, reconsider, refuse

rĕtrăho, xi, ctum, *v.t.* 3, to draw back, call back, remove

rĕtrĭbŭo, ŭi, ūtum, *v.t.* 3, to repay

rĕtrō, *adv*, backwards, formerly, back, behind, on the other hand

rĕtrorsum(s), *adv*, backwards

rĕtundo, tŭdi, tūsum, *v.t.* 3, to blunt, dull, weaken

rĕtūsus, a, um, *adj*, blunt, dull

rĕus, i, *m* (rĕa, ae, *f*), defendant, criminal, culprit

rĕvălesco, lŭi, *v.i.* 3, to grow well again

rĕvĕho, xi, ctum, *v.t.* 3, to bring back; *in passive*, to return

rĕvello, velli, vulsum, *v.t.* 3, to pull out, tear away

rĕvĕnĭo, vēni, ventum, *v.i.* 4, to return

rĕvērā, *adv*, really

rĕvĕrens, ntis, *adj*, reverent

rĕvĕrentĭa, ae, *f*, respect

rĕvĕrĕor, *v.t.* 2, *dep*, to revere

rĕverto, ti, *v.i.* 3, to return

rĕvertor, versus, *v.i.* 3, *dep*, to return

rĕvincendus, *gerundive*, see **revinco**

rĕvincio, nxi, nctum, *v.t.* 4, to bind, fasten

rĕvinco, vīci, victum, *v.t.* 3, to conquer, convict

rĕvīresco, rŭi, *v.i.* 3, to grow green again

rĕviso, *v.i.t.* 3, to revisit

rĕvīvisco, vixi, *v.i.* 3, to revive

rĕvŏcābĭlis, e, *adj*, able to be recalled

rĕvŏcāmen, ĭnis, *n*, recall

rĕvŏcātĭo, ōnis, *f*, recalling

rĕvŏco, *v.t.* 1, to recall, restrain, refer

rĕvŏlo, *v.i.* 1, to fly back

rĕvolvo, volvi, vŏlūtum, *v.t.* 3, to unroll, repeat

rĕvŏmo, ŭi, *v.t.* 3, to vomit up

rex, rēgis, *m*, king

rhēda, ae, *f*, carriage

rhētor, ŏris, *m*, teacher of oratory

rhētŏrĭca, ae, *f*, rhetoric

rhētŏrĭcus, a, um, *adj*, rhetorical

rhīnŏcĕros, ōtis, *m*, rhinoceros

rhombus, i, *m*, magic circle, turbot

rhonchus, i, *m*, snore, sneer

rīca, ae, *f*, veil

rīcĭnĭum, ii, *n*, small veil

rictus, ūs, *m*, gaping mouth

rīdĕo, si, sum, *v.i.t.* 2, to laugh, smile; laugh at, ridicule

rīdĭcŭlum, i, *n*, joke

rīdĭcŭlus, a, um, *adj*, *adv*, ē, amusing, absurd

rĭgĕo, *v.i*, 2, to be stiff

rĭgesco, gŭi, *v.i.* 3, to stiffen

rĭgĭdus, a, um, *adj*, stiff, stern

rĭgo, *v.t.* 1, to wet, water

rĭgor, ōris, *m*, stiffness, hardness, chilliness, severity

rĭgŭus, a, um, *adj*, irrigating

rīma, ae, *f*, crack, chink

rīmor, *v.t.* 1, *dep*, to tear up, explore, examine

rīmōsus, a, um, *adj*, leaky

rīpa, ae, *f*, river bank

rīsus, ūs, *m*, laughter

rītē, *adv*, rightly, properly

rītus, ūs, *m*, religious ceremony, custom, way; rītu, *with genit*, in the manner of

rīvālis, is, *m*, rival

rīvŭlus, i, *m*, brook

rīvus, i, *m*, brook, stream

rixa, ae, *f*, quarrel

rixor, *v.i.* 1, *dep*, to quarrel

rōbīgĭnōsus, a, um, *adj*, rusty

rōbīgo, ĭnis, *f*, rust, mould

rōbŏro, *v.t.* 1, to strengthen

rōbur, ōris, *n*, oak, strength, power, vigour, force

rōbustus, a, um, *adj*, oaken, firm, strong, robust

rōdo, si, sum, *v.t.* 3, to gnaw, corrode, slander

rŏgātĭo, ōnis, *f*, proposed law or bill, request

rŏgātor, ōris, *m*, polling-clerk

rŏgo, *v.t.* 1, to ask; *with* legem, to propose (law), beg

rŏgus, i, *m*, funeral pile

rōro, *v.i.t.* 1, to drop, drip, trickle; wet, besprinkle

rōs, rōris, *m*, dew, moisture

rŏsa, ae, *f*, rose

rŏsārĭum, ii, *n*, rose-garden

roscĭdus, a, um, *adj*, dewy

rŏsētum, i, *n*, rose-bed

rŏsĕus, a, um, *adj*, of roses, rose-coloured

rostra, ōrum, *n.pl*, speaker's platform

rostrātus, a, um, *adj*, with beaks

rostrum, i, *n*, beak, snout

rŏta, ae, *f*, wheel, chariot

rŏto, *v.i.t.* 1, to revolve; swing round, whirl around

rŏtundĭtas, ātis, *f*, rotundity

rŏtundo, *v.t.* 1, to round off

rŏtundus, a, um, *adj*, round, polished

rŭbĕfăcĭo, fēci, factum, *v.t.* 3, to redden

rŭbens, ntis, *adj*, red

rŭbĕo, *v.i.* 2, to be red, blush

rŭber, bra, brum, *adj*, red

rŭbesco, bŭi, *v.i.* 3, to grow red

rŭbēta, ae, *f*, toad

rŭbēta, ōrum, *n.pl*, brambles

rŭbĭcundus, a, um, *adj*, red

rŭbīgo . . . see rōbīgo . . .

rŭbor, ōris, *m*, redness, blush, bashfulness

rŭbrīca, ae, *f*, red-chalk

rŭbus, i, *m*, bramble-bush

ructo, *v.i.t.* 1, to belch

ructor, *v*. 1, *dep*, to belch

ructus, ūs, *m*, belching

rŭdens, ntis, *m*, rope, rigging

rŭdīmentum, i, *n*, first try

rŭdis, e, *adj*, rough, raw, wild, awkward, inexperienced

rŭdis, is, *f*, stick, wooden sword

rŭdo, īvi, ītum, *v.i.* 3, to bellow

rŭdus, ĕris, *n*, broken stones, rubbish

rūfus, a, um, *adj*, red

rūga, ae, *f*, wrinkle

rūgo, *v.i.t.* 1, to wrinkle

rūgōsus, a, um, *adj*, shrivelled

rŭīna, ae, f, downfall, ruin
rŭīnōsus, a, um, adj, in ruins
rūmĭno, v.t. 1, to chew over
rūmor, ōris, m, rumour, general
opinion, reputation
rumpo, rūpi, ruptum, v.t. 3, to break,
burst, destroy, interrupt
runcīna, ae, f, plane
runcĭno, v.t. 1, to plane
runco, v.t. 1, to weed
rŭo, ŭi, ŭtum, v.i.t. 3, to fall, rush,
hurry; hurl down, throw up
rūpes, is, f, rock
rūrĭcŏla, ae, adj, rural
rursus (rursum), adv, again, on the
contrary, backwards
rūs, rūris, n, countryside
rustĭcānus, a, um, adj, rustic
rustĭcĭtas, ātis, f, behaviour of
country-people
rustĭcor, v.i. 1, dep, to live in the
country
rustĭcus, a, um, adj, rural
rustĭcus, i, m, countryman
rūta, ae, f, bitter herb, rue
rŭtĭlo, v.i. 1, to be red
rŭtĭlus, a, um, adj, red

S

sabbăta, ōrum, n.pl, sabbath
săbīnum, i, n, Sabine wine
săbŭlum, i, n, gravel
săburra, ae, f, sand, ballast
saccharon, i, n, sugar
saccŭlus, i, m, small bag
saccus, i, m, bag
săcellum, i, n, chapel
săcer, cra, crum, adj, sacred, venerable, accursed
săcerdos, dōtis, c, priest
săcerdōtālis, e, adj, priestly
săcerdōtium, ii, n, priesthood
săcra, ōrum, n.pl, worship, religion
săcrāmentum, i, n, oath
săcrārium, ii, n, sanctuary
săcrātus, a, um, adj, sacred
săcrĭfĭcium, ii, n, sacrifice
săcrĭfĭco, v.i.t. 1, to sacrifice
săcrĭfĭcus, a, um, adj, sacrificial
săcrĭlĕgus, a, um, adj, temple-
robbing, sacrilegious
săcro, v.t. 1, to consecrate, condemn, doom
săcrōsanctus, a, um, adj, sacred,
inviolable
săcrum, i, n, sacred thing, religious
act, religion
saecŭlum, i, n, age, generation,
century

saepe, adv, often
saepes, is, f, hedge, fence
saepīmentum, i, n, fencing
saepĭo, psi, ptum, v.t. 4, to fence in,
surround
saeptum, i, n, fence, pen
saeta, ae, f, hair, bristle
saetĭger, ĕra, ĕrum, adj, bristly
saetōsus, a, um, adj, bristly
saevĭo, v.i. 4, to rage
saevĭtĭa, ae, f, savageness
saevus, a, um, adj, savage, violent,
furious, cruel
sāga, ae, f, fortune-teller
săgācĭtas, ātis, f, shrewdness
săgax, ācis, adj, adv, ĭter, keen,
shrewd, acute
săgīno, v.t. 1, to fatten
săgitta, ae, f, arrow
săgittārius, ii, m, archer
săgŭlum, i, n, military cloak
săgum, i, n, military cloak
sal, sălis, m, salt, sea, wit, sarcasm
sălăco, ōnis, m, braggart
sălārium, ii, n, pension, salary (salt
money)
sălax, ācis, adj, lecherous
sălēbra, ae, f, roughness
sălĭāris, e, adj, splendid
sălictum, i, n, willow-grove
sălignus, a, um, adj, of willow
Sălii, ōrum, m. pl, priests of Mars
sălīnae, ārum, f. pl, salt-works
sălīnum, i, n, salt-cellar
sălĭo, ŭi, saltum, v.i. 4, to jump
sălīva, ae, f, saliva
sălix, icis, f, willow-tree
salmo, ōnis, m, salmon
salsāmentum, i, n, brine
salsus, a, um, adj, adv, ē, salted,
witty
saltātĭo, ōnis, f, dancing
saltātor, ōris, m, dancer
saltātrix, īcis, f, dancing-girl
saltātus, ūs, m, dancing
saltem, adv, at least
salto, v.i.t. 1, to dance
saltus, ūs, m, leap, bound
saltus, ūs, m, woodland, mountain-
pass
sălūbris, e, adj, adv, ĭter, health-
giving, beneficial
sălūbritas, ātis, f, wholesomeness
sălum, i, n, sea
sălūs, ūtis, f, welfare, safety
sălūtāris, e, adj, adv, ĭter, beneficial,
wholesome
sălūtātĭo, ōnis, f, greeting
sălūtātor, ōris, m, visitor
sălūtĭfer, ĕra, ĕrum, adj, healing

For List of Abbreviations used, turn to pages 3, 4

sălūto, *v.t.* 1, to greet

salvē, salvēte, salvēto, *v, imperative* how are you? welcome!

salvia, ae, *f*, sage (herb)

salvus, a, um, *adj*, safe, well; *with noun in abl*, e.g. salvā lege, without violating the law

sambūcus, i, *f*, elder-tree

sānābĭlis, e, *adj*, curable

sānātĭo, ōnis, *f*, cure

sancĭo, xi, ctum, *v.t.* 4, to appoint, establish, ratify

sanctĭfĭcātĭo, ōnis, *f*, sanctification

sanctĭo, ōnis, *f*, establishing

sanctĭtas, ātis, *f*, sacredness, purity

sanctus, a, um, *adj, adv,* ē, sacred, inviolable, good

sandix, ĭcis, *f*, scarlet

sānē, *adv*, certainly, very

sanguĭnārĭus, a, um, *adj*, bloody, blood-thirsty

sanguĭnĕus, a, um, *adj*, bloody

sanguĭnōlentus, a, um, *adj*, bloody

sanguis, ĭnis, *m*, blood, bloodshed, race, stock

sănĭes, em, e, *f*, bad blood

sānĭtas, ātis, *f*, health, good sense, discretion

sannĭo, ōnis, *m*, buffoon

sāno, *v.t.* 1, to cure, restore

sānus, a, um, *adj*, healthy, rational, discreet

săpĭdus, a, um, *adj*, tasty

săpĭens, ntis, *adj, adv,* nter, wise, sensible

săpĭens, ntis, *m*, wise man

săpĭentĭa, ae, *f*, discretion, philosophy

săpĭo, īvi, *v.i.t.* 3, to be wise, discreet; to taste of, savour of

sāpo, ōnis, *m*, soap

săpor, ōris, *m*, flavour, taste

sapphīrus, i, *f*, sapphire

sarcĭna, ae, *f*, pack, load

sarcĭo, si, tum, *v.t.* 4, to patch

sarcŏphăgus, i, *m*, sarcophagus

sarcŭlum, i, *n*, light hoe

sarda, ae, *f*, sardine

sarīsa, ae, *f*, Macedonian lance

sarmentum, i, *n*, brushwood

sarrācum, i, *n*, cart

sarrānus, a, um, *adj*, Tyrian

sarrĭo, *v.t.* 4, to hoe

sartāgo, ĭnis, *f*, frying-pan

sartus, a, um, *adj*, repaired

sāta, ōrum, *n.pl*, crops

sătelles, ĭtis, *c*, attendant; *in pl*, escort

sătĭas, ātis, *f*, abundance, disgust

sătĭĕtas, ātis, *f*, abundance, disgust

sătĭo, *v.t.* 1, to satisfy, glut

sătĭo, ōnis, *f*, sowing

sătĭrĭcus, a, um, *adj*, satirical

sătis (săt), *adv, or indecl. adj*, enough

sătisdătĭo, ōnis, *f*, giving bail

sătisfăcĭo, fēci, factum, *v.t.* 3, to satisfy, make amends

sătisfactĭo, ōnis, *f*, excuse, reparation

sătĭus, *comp. adv*, better

sător, ōris, *m*, sower, creator

sătrăpes, is, *m*, viceroy, satrap

sătur, ūra, ŭrum, *adj*, full, fertile

sătūra, ae, *f*, food made of various ingredients, satire

Sāturnālĭa, ōrum, *n.pl*, festival in honour of Saturn (Dec. 17th)

sătūro, *v.t.* 1, to fill, glut

sătus, ūs, *m*, planting

sătus, a, um, *adj*, sprung from

sătÿrus, i, *m*, forest-god

saucĭo, *v.t.* 1, to wound

saucĭus, a, um, *adj*, wounded

saxĕus, a, um, *adj*, rocky

saxĭfĭcus, a, um, *adj*, petrifying

saxōsus, a, um, *adj*, rocky

saxum, i, *n*, rock

scăbellum, i, *n*, stool

scăber, bra, brum, *adj*, rough, scabby

scăbĭes, em, e, *f*, roughness, scab, itch

scăbo, scābi, *v.t.* 3, to scratch

scaena, ae, *f*, stage, scene

scaenĭcus, a, um, *adj*, theatrical

scaenĭcus, i, *m*, actor

scāla, ae, *f*, ladder, stairs

scalmus, i, *m*, rowlock

scalpo, psi, ptum, *v.t.* 3, to carve

scalpellum, i, *n*, lancet

scalprum, i, *n*, chisel

scalptor, ōris, *m*, engraver

scalptūra, ae, *f*, engraving

scamnum, i, *n*, bench

scando, *v.i.t.* 3, to rise; climb

scăpha, ae, *f*, small boat

scăpŭlae, ārum, *f. pl*, shoulder-blades

scărăbaeus, i, *m*, beetle

scărus, i, *m*, sea-fish (scar)

scătĕbra, ae, *f*, spring water

scătĕo, *v.i.* 2, to bubble, swarm with

scaurus, a, um, *adj*, with swollen ankles

scĕlĕrātus, a, um, *adj*, wicked

scĕlĕro, *v.t.* 1, to contaminate

scĕlestus, a, um, *adj*, wicked

scĕlus, ĕris, *n*, crime, scoundrel

scēna, see scaena

scēnĭcus, see scaenĭcus

sceptrum, i, *n*, sceptre; *in pl*, dominion, authority
schĕda, ae, *f*, sheet of paper
schŏla, ae, *f*, lecture, school
sciens, ntis, *adj*, *adv*, nter, knowing, (*i.e.* purposely), expert in
scientia, ae, *f*, knowledge
scīlicet, *adv*, certainly, of course, namely
scilla, ae, *f*, sea-onion, prawn
scindo, scīdi, scissum, *v.t.* 3, to split
scintilla, ae, *f*, spark
scintillans, ntis, *adj*, sparkling
scintillo, *v.i.* 1, to sparkle
scĭo, *v.t.* 4, to know, understand
scīpĭo, ōnis, *m*, staff
scirpĕus, a, um, *adj*, of rushes
sciscitor, *v.t.* 1, *dep*, to enquire
scisco, scīvi, scītum, *v.t.* 3, to approve, appoint, decree
scissūra, ae, *f*, tearing, rending
scītor, *v.t.* 1, *dep*, to inquire
scītum, i, *n*, decree, statute
scītus, a, um, *adj*, *adv*, ē, shrewd, sensible, witty
sciūrus, i, *m*, squirrel
scŏbīna, ae, *f*, rasp, file
scŏbis, is, *f*, sawdust
scomber, bri, *m*, mackerel
scōpae, ārum, *f.pl*, broom
scŏpŭlōsus, a, um, *adj*, rocky
scŏpŭlus, i, *m*, rock, cliff
scŏpus, i, *m*, target
scorpĭo, ōnis, *m*, scorpion, missile-launcher
scortum, i, *n*, prostitute
scrība, ae, *m*, clerk
scrībo, psi, ptum, *v.t.* 3, to write, draw, compose, describe, enroll
scrīnĭum, ii, *n*, letter-case
scriptĭo, ōnis, *f*, writing
scriptor, ōris, *m*, secretary, author
scriptum, i, *n*, book, writing
scriptūra, ae, *f*, composition
scriptus, a, um, *adj*, written
scrŏbis, is, *m*, ditch
scrūpĕus, a, um, *adj*, rugged
scrūpŭlus, i, *m*, anxiety, embarrassment
scrūta, ōrum, *n.pl*, frippery
scrūtātĭo, ōnis, *f*, scrutiny
scrūtor, *v.t.* 1, *dep*, to examine
sculpo, psi, ptum, *v.t.* 3, to carve
sculpōnĕae, ārum, *f. pl*, clogs
sculptor, ōris, *m*, sculptor
sculptūra, ae, *f*, sculpture
scurra, ae, *m*, clown, dandy
scurrīlis, e, *adj*, jeering
scūtātus, a, um, *adj*, armed with oblong shields

scŭtella, ae, *f*, salver
scŭtĭca, ae, *f*, whip
scŭtŭla, ae, *f*, wooden roller
scūtum, i, *n*, oblong shield
scўphus, i, *m*, goblet
sē, *acc. or abl. of reflexive pron*, herself, itself etc.
sēbum, i, *n*, suet
sēcāle, is, *n*, rye
sēcēdo, cessi, cessum, *v.i.* 3, to go away, withdraw
sēcerno, crēvi, crētum, *v.t.* 3, to separate, part
sēcessĭo, ōnis, *f*, withdrawal
sēcessus, ūs, *m*, solitude
sēcĭus (sēquĭus), *comp. adv*, differently
sēclūdo, si, sum, *v.t.* 3, to separate, shut off
sēclūsus, a, um, *adj*, remote
sēco, ŭi, ctum, *v.t.* 1, to cut, wound, separate
sēcrētum, i, *n*, solitude
sēcrētus, a, um, *adj*, *adv*, ō, separate, remote, secret
secta, ae, *f*, way, method, sect
sectātor, ōris, *m*, follower
sectĭo, ōnis, *f*, sale by auction
sector, ōris, *m*, cutthroat, bidder at an auction
sector, *v.t.* 1, *dep*, to pursue
sectūra, ae, *f*, mine
sēcul . . . see saecul
sēcundārĭus, a, um, *adj*, secondary, second-rate
sēcundo, *v.t.* 1, to favour
sēcundum, *prep*, *with acc*, after, behind, by, next to, according to
sēcundus, a, um, *adj*, following, second, favourable
sēcūrĭger, ĕra, ĕrum, *adj*, armed with a battle-axe
sēcūris, is, *f*, axe, hatchet
sēcūrĭtas, ātis, *f*, freedom from care
sēcūrus, a, um, *adj*, carefree, tranquil
sēcus, *adv*, differently
sĕd, *conj*, but
sēdātĭo, ōnis, *f*, a calming
sēdātus, a, um, *adj*, calm
sēdĕcim, *indecl. adj*, sixteen
sĕdentārĭus, a, um, *adj*, sedentary
sĕdĕo, sēdi, sessum, *v.i.* 2, to sit, remain, settle, be settled
sēdes, is, *f*, seat, residence, temple, bottom, foundation
sĕdīle, is, *n*, seat
sēdĭtĭo, ōnis, *f*, mutiny
sēdĭtĭōsus, a, um, *adj*, *adv*, ē, mutinous, rebellious
sēdo, *v.t.* 1, to calm, check

sēdūco, xi, ctum, *v.t.* 3, to lead aside, separate
sēdūlǐtas, ātis, *f,* zeal
sēdūlō, *adv,* diligently, on purpose
sēdūlus, a, um, *adj,* industrious
sēges, ětis, *f,* cornfield, crop
segmenta, ōrum, *n.pl,* trimmings
segmentum, i, *n,* piece
segnis, e, *adj, adv,* ǐter lazy
segnǐtia, ae, *f,* inactivity, slowness
segnǐties, em, e, *f,* inactivity, slowness
sēgrěgo, *v.t.* 1, to separate
sēiungo, nxi, nctum, *v.t.* 3, to separate, divide
sēlǐgo, lēgi, lectum, *v.t.* 3, to select
sella, ae, *f,* seat, chair
sěměl, *adv,* once
sēmen, ǐnis, *n,* seed, cutting, graft, offspring, instigator
sēmentis, is, *f,* sowing
sēmestris, e, *adj,* half-yearly
sēmēsus, a, um, *adj,* half-eaten
sēmǐānǐmis, e, *adj,* half-dead
sēmǐděus, a, um, *adj,* half-divine
sēmǐfer, ěra, ěrum, *adj,* half-man, half-beast
sēmǐhǒmo, ǐnis, *m,* half-human
sēmǐhōra, ae, *f,* half-hour
sēmǐnārǐum, ii, *n,* nursery
sēmǐnātor, ōris, *m,* author
sēmǐněcis, is, *adj,* half-dead
sēmǐno, *v.t.* 1, to produce
sēmǐplēnus, a, um, *adj,* half-full
sēmǐrūtus, a, um, *adj,* half-ruined
sēmis, issis, *m,* half a farthing
sēmǐsomnus, a, um, *adj,* half-asleep
sēmǐta, ae, *f,* footpath
sēmǐustus, a, um, *adj,* half-burned
sēmǐvir, vǐri, *m,* half-man; *as adj,* effeminate
sēmǐvīvus, a, um, *adj,* half-alive
sēmōtus, a, um, *adj,* remote
sēmǒvěo, mōvi, mōtum, *v.t.* 2, to remove, separate
semper, *adv,* always
sempǐternus, a, um, *adj,* everlasting
sēmustǔlo, *v.t.* 1, to half burn
sěnātor, ōris, *m,* senator
sěnātōrius, a, um, *adj,* senatorial
sěnātus, ūs, *m,* the Senate
sěnecta, ae, *f,* old age
sěnectus, ūtis, *f,* old age
sěnesco, nǔi, *v.i.* 3, to grow old
sěnex, sěnis, *m,* old man
sēni, ae, a, *pl. adj,* six each
sěnīlis, e, *adj,* old (of people)
sěnior, ōris, *c,* elderly person
sěnǐum, ii, *n,* old age, decay, trouble
sensǐlis, e, *adj,* sensitive
sensim, *adv,* slowly, gently

sensus, ūs, *m,* perception, disposition, good taste, sense, understanding, meaning
sententia, ae, *f,* opinion, decision, meaning, sentence, axiom; *ex měā sententiā,* to my liking
sententiōsus, a, um, *adj,* sententious
sentīna, ae, *f,* bilge-water, dregs, ship's hold
sentǐo, si, sum, *v.t.* 4, to feel, perceive, endure, suppose
sentis, is, *m,* thorn, bramble
sentus, a, um, *adj,* rough
sěorsum, *adv,* separately
sēpǎrātim, *adv,* separately
sēpǎrātǐo, ōnis, *f,* separation
sēpǎrātus, a, um, *adj,* separate
sēpǎro, *v.t.* 1, to separate
sēpělǐo, līvi, pultum, *v.t.* 4, to bury, overwhelm
sēpia, ae, *f,* cuttle-fish
sēpǐo, see saepǐo
sēpōno, pǒsǔi, pǒsǐtum, *v.t.* 3, to put aside, select
septem, *indecl. adj,* seven
September (mensis), September
septemgěmǐnus, a, um, *adj,* sevenfold
septemplex, ǐcis, *adj,* seven-fold
septenděcim, *indecl. adj,* seventeen
septēni, ae, a, *pl. adj,* seven each
septentriōnālis, e, *adj,* northern
septentriōnes, um, *m. pl,* the Great Bear, the North
septǐes, *adv,* seven times
septǐmus, a, um, *adj,* seventh
septingenti, ae, a, *pl. adj,* seven hundred
septūāgēsǐmus, a, um, *adj,* seventieth
septūāginta, *indecl. adj,* seventy
septum, see saeptum
sěpulcrum, i, *n,* grave, tomb
sěpultūra, ae, *f,* burial
sěquax, ācis, *adj,* pursuing
sěquens, ntis, *adj,* following
sěquester, tris, *m,* agent
sěquor, sěcūtus, *v.i.t.* 3, *dep,* to follow, attend, pursue
sěra, ae, *f,* bolt, bar
sěrēnǐtas, ātis, *f,* fair weather
sěrēno, *v.t.* 1, to brighten
sěrēnum, i, *n,* fair weather
sěrēnus, a, um, *adj,* clear, fair, cheerful, glad
sēria, ōrum, *n.pl,* serious matters
sērǐcus, a, um, *adj,* silken
sēries, em, e, *f,* row, series
sērius, a, um, *adj,* serious
sermo, ōnis, *m,* talk, conversation, common talk

sēro, sēvi, sătum, *v.t.* 3, to sow, plant, cause

sēro, ŭi, sertum, *v.t.* 3, to plait, join, connect, compose

sērŏ, *adv,* late

serpens, ntis, *f,* snake

serpo, psi, ptum, *v.i.* 3, to crawl

serpyllum, i, *n,* thyme

serra, ae, *f,* saw

serrŭla, ae, *f,* small saw

serta, ōrum, *n.pl,* garlands

sērum, i, *n,* whey

sērus, a, um, *adj,* late

serva, ae, *f,* maid-servant

servātor, ōris, *m,* saviour

servīlis, e, *adj, adv,* **īter,** of a slave, servile

servĭo, *v.i.* 4, to be a servant, to be of use to

servĭtĭum, ii, *n,* slavery, slaves

servĭtus, ūtis, *f,* slavery, slaves

servo, *v.t.* 1, to save, protect, preserve, keep, keep watch

servus, a, um, *adj,* servile

servus, i, *m,* slave, servant

sescēni, ae, a, *pl. adj,* six hundred each

sescenti, ae, a, *pl. adj,* six hundred

sescenties, *adv,* six hundred times

sesquĭpēdālis, e, *adj,* one foot and a half long

sessĭo, ōnis, *f,* sitting, session

sestertĭum, 1,000 sestertii

sestertĭus, ii, *m,* small silver coin (worth about £1d.)

set . . . see **saet. . . .**

seu, *conj,* whether, or

sēvērĭtas, ātis, *f,* sternness

sēvērus, a, um, *adj, adv,* **ē,** stern, serious, harsh, gloomy

sēvŏco, *v.t.* 1, to call aside

sex, *indecl adj,* six

sexāgēnārĭus, i, *m,* sexagenarian

sexāgēni, ae, a, *pl. adj,* sixty each

sexāgēsĭmus, a, um, *adj,* sixtieth

sexāgĭes, *adv,* sixty times

sexāginta, *indecl. adj,* sixty

sexennĭum, ii, *n,* six years

sextans, ntis, *m,* a sixth part

sextārĭus, ii, *m,* a pint

Sextīlis, (mensis), August

sextus, a, um, *adj,* sixth

sexus, ūs, *m,* sex

sī, *conj,* if

sĭbi, *dat. of reflexive pron,* to himself, herself, itself, etc.

sībĭlo, *v.i.t.* 1, to hiss; hiss at

sībĭlus, i, *m,* hissing

sībylla, ae, *f,* prophetess

sīc, *adv,* so, in this way

sīca, ae, *f,* dagger

sīcārĭus, ii, *m,* assassin

siccĭtas, ātis, *f,* dryness, firmness

sicco, *v.t.* 1, to dry up, drain

siccum, i, *n,* dry land

siccus, a, um, *adj,* dry, firm, tough, thirsty, sober

sīcŭbĭ, *adv,* if anywhere

sīcut, (sīcŭti), *adv,* just as

sīdĕrĕus, a, um, *adj,* starry

sīdo, di, *v.i.* 3, to sit down, settle, sink

sīdus, ĕris, *n,* star, sky, constellation, season, weather

sigilla, ōrum, *n. pl,* little figures or images

sigillātus, a, um, *adj,* figured

signĭfer, ĕri, *m,* standard-bearer

significātĭo, ōnis, *f,* sign, mark

significo, *v.t.* 1, to show, notify

significans, antis, *adj,* significant

signo, *v.t.* 1, to mark out, seal, indicate

signum, i, *n,* mark, sign, military standard, watchword, statue, constellation, symptom

silens, ntis, *adj,* still, quiet

silentĭum, ii, *n,* stillness, quietness

sīlĕo, *v.i.t.* 2, to be silent; to keep quiet about

silesco, *v.i.* 3, to grow quiet

silex, icis, *m,* flint-stone

sĭlus, a, um, *adj,* snub-nosed

silva, ae, *f,* wood, forest, grove, abundance

silvestria, ium, *n. pl,* woodlands

silvestris, e, *adj,* woody, rural

silvĭcŏla, ae, *adj,* living in woods

sīmĭa, ae, *f,* ape

sĭmĭlis, e, *adj, adv,* **īter,** similar, like

sĭmĭlĭtūdo, ĭnis, *f,* resemblance

sīmĭus, ii, *m,* ape

simplex, ĭcis, *adj, adv,* **īter,** unmixed, simple, frank

simplĭcĭtas, ātis, *f,* honesty

simul, *adv,* at once, together, at the same time, as soon as

sĭmŭlac, *conj,* as soon as

sĭmŭlatque, *conj.* as soon as

sĭmŭlācrum, i, *n,* portrait, statue, phantom

sĭmŭlātĭo, ōnis, *f,* pretence

sĭmŭlātor, ōris, *m,* pretender

sĭmŭlātus, a, um, *adj,* feigned

sĭmŭlo, *v.t.* 1, to imitate, pretend

simultas, ātis, *f,* animosity

sīmus, a, um, *adj,* snub-nosed

sin, *conj,* but if

sināpi, is, *n,* mustard

sincērĭtas, ātis, *f,* cleanness, purity, entirety, sincerity

sincērus, a, um, *adj, adv,* **ē,** clean, pure, genuine, entire, sincere

For List of Abbreviations used, turn to pages 3, 4

sĭnĕ, *prep. with abl*, without
singillātim, *adv*, one by one
singŭlāris, e, *adj*, single, solitary, unique, remarkable
singŭlātim, see singillātim
singŭli, ae, a, *pl. adj*, one each
singultim, *adv*, with sobs
singultĭo, *v.i.* 4, to hiccup
singulto, *(no perf), v.i.* 1, to sob
singultus, ūs, *m*, sobbing
sĭnister, tra, trum, *adj*, left, awkward, wrong, unlucky, lucky
sĭnistra, ae, *f*, left hand
sĭnistrorsus, *adv*, to the left
sĭno, sīvi, sĭtum, *v.t.* 3, to allow
sĭnum, i, *n*, drinking-cup
sĭnŭo, *v.t.* 1, to bend, curve
sĭnŭōsus, a, um, *adj*, curved
sĭnus, ūs, *m*, curve, fold, bosom, lap, hiding-place, bay
sĭpho, ōnis, *m*, siphon, syringe
sĭquandō, *adv*, if ever
sĭquĭdem, *adv*, if indeed
sĭquis, *pron*, if any
sīrēn, ēnis, *f*, siren
sisto, stĭti, stătum, *v.i.t.* 3, to stand still, resist, hold out; put, place, bring, check, establish
sīstrum, i, *n*, rattle
sĭtiens, ntis, *adj, adv*, nter, thirsty
sĭtĭo, *v.i.t.* 4, to thirst; long for
sĭtis, is, *f*, thirst, drought
sĭtŭla, ae, *f*, bucket
sĭtus, a, um, *adj*, situated
sĭtus, ūs, *m*, position, site, rust, mould, inactivity
sīve, *conj*, whether, or
smăragdus, i, *c*, emerald
sŏbŏles, is, *f*, sprout, twig, offspring
sŏbrĭĕtas, ātis, *f*, sobriety, temperance
sōbrīnus, i, *m*, cousin
sōbrĭus, a, um, *adj, adv*, ē, sober, moderate, sensible
soccus, i, *m*, slipper
sŏcer, ĕri, *m*, father-in-law
sŏcĭālis, e, *adj*, allied
sŏcĭĕtas, ātis, *f*, fellowship, partnership, alliance
sŏcĭo, *v.t.* 1, to unite
sŏcĭus, ii, *m*, companion, ally
sŏcĭus, a, um, *adj*, allied
sōcordĭa, ae, *f*, laziness, folly
sōcors, cordis, *adj*, lazy, careless, stupid
socrus, ūs, *f*, mother-in-law
sōdālĭcĭum, ii, *n*, secret society
sŏdālis, is, *c*, companion

sŏdālĭtas, ātis, *f*, friendship
sōdes, if you wish
sōl, sōlis, *m*, sun, sunshine
sōlācĭum, ii, *n*, comfort, solace
sōlāmen, ĭnis, *n*, consolation
sōlārĭum, ii, *n*, sundial
sōlātĭum, see sōlācĭum
soldūrii, ōrum, *m. pl*, retainers of a chieftain
sŏlĕa, ae, *f*, sandal, sole (fish)
sŏlĕātus, a, um, *adj*, wearing sandals
sŏlĕo, sōlĭtus, *v.i.* 2, semi-dep, to be accustomed
sŏlĭdĭtas, ātis, *f*, solidity
sŏlĭdo, *v.t.* 1, to strengthen
sŏlĭdum, i, *n*, a solid, solidity
sŏlĭdus, a, um, *adj*, compact, complete, genuine, real
sōlĭtārĭus, a, um, *adj*, alone
sōlĭtūdo, ĭnis, *f*, loneliness, desert
sōlĭtus, a, um, *adj*, usual
sŏlĭum, ii, *n*, seat, throne
sollemnis, e, *adj*, established, appointed, usual, religious
sollemne, is, *n*, religious ceremony, sacrifice
sollers, tis, *adj*, skilled
sollertĭa, ae, *f*, skill, ingenuity
sollĭcĭtātĭo, ōnis, *f*, instigation
sollĭcĭto, *v.t.* 1, to stir up, molest, instigate
sollĭcĭtūdo, ĭnis, *f*, anxiety
sollĭcĭtus, a, um, *adj*, troubled
sōlor, *v.t.* 1, dep, to comfort, relieve
solstĭtĭālis, e, *adj*, of summer
solstĭtĭum, ii, *n*, summer-time
sŏlum, i, *n*, bottom, base, floor, sole, soil, ground, country, place
sŏlum, *adv*, only
sōlus, a, um, *adj*, alone, only, lonely, deserted
sŏlūtĭo, ōnis, *f*, unloosing, payment, explanation
sŏlūtus, a, um, *adj, adv*, ē, free, loose, independent
solvendum, see solvo
solvo, solvi, sŏlūtum, *v.t.* 3, to set free, dissolve, release, open up, pay, perform, fulfil, acquit; with ancŏram, to sail
somnĭcŭlōsus, a, um, *adj*, drowzy
somnĭfer, ĕra, ĕrum, *adj*, sleep-bringing
somnĭfĭcus, a, um, *adj*, sleep-bringing
somnĭo, *v.t.* 1, to dream
somnĭum, ii, *n*, dream
somnus, i, *m*, sleep

sŏnĭpēs, pĕdis, adj, noisy-footed
sŏnĭtus, ūs, m, noise, sound
sŏno, ŭi, ĭtum, v.i.t. 1, to resound; call out, utter
sŏnor, ōris, m, noise, sound
sŏnōrus, a, um, adj, resounding
sons, ntis, adj, guilty
sŏnus, i, m, noise, sound
sŏphistes, ae, m, philosopher
sŏpĭo, v.t. 4, to lull to sleep
sŏpor, ōris, m, sleep
sŏpōrĭfer, ĕra, ĕrum, adj, sleep-bringing
sŏpōro, v.t. 1, to heat, stupefy
sŏpōrus, a, um, adj, sleep-bringing
sorbĕo, v.t. 2, to suck in
sordĕo, v.i. 2, to be dirty, to be despised
sordes, is, f, dirt, mourning-dress, meanness
sordĭdātus, a, um, adj, shabbily dressed (in mourning)
sordĭdus, a, um, adj, adv, ē, dirty, despicable, mean
sŏror, ōris, f, sister
sŏrōrius, a, um, adj, of a sister
sors, tis, f, chance, lot, drawing of lots, prophesy, fortune, share, destiny
sortior, v.i.t. 4, dep, to draw lots; to appoint by lot, obtain by lot, choose
sortītĭo, ōnis, f, drawing of lots
sortītō, adv, by lot
sortītus, a, um, adj, drawn by lot
sospes, ĭtis, adj, safe, lucky
spadix, īcis, adj, nut-brown
spargo, si, sum, v.t. 3, to sprinkle, scatter, spread
spărus, i, m, hunting-spear
spasmus, i, m, spasm
spătior, v.i. 1, dep, to walk about
spătĭōsus, a, um, adj, spacious
spătĭum, ii, n, space, room, distance, walk, track, interval
spŏcĭes, ēi, f, sight, view, shape, appearance, pretence, display, beauty
spĕcĭmen, ĭnis, n, mark, sign, pattern
spĕcĭōsus, a, um, adj, handsome, plausible
spectābĭlis, e, adj, visible, remarkable
spectācŭlum, i, n, show, spectacle
spectātĭo, ōnis, f, sight
spectātor, ōris, m, onlooker
spectātus, a, um, adj, tested, respected
specto, v.t. 1, to watch, face, examine, consider, refer
spectrum, i, n, image

spĕcŭla, ae, f, look-out point
spĕcŭla, ae, f, slight hope
spĕcŭlātor, ōris, m, spy, scout
spĕcŭlor, v.t. 1, dep, to watch, observe, explore
spĕcŭlum, i, n, mirror
spĕcus, ūs, m,-cave, pit
spēlunca, ae, f, cave, den
sperno, sprēvi, sprētum, v.t. 3, to despise, scorn
spēro, v.t. 1, to hope, expect
spes, spēi, f, hope
sphaera, ae, f, sphere
spīca, ae, f, ear (of corn)
spīcĕus, a, um, adj, made of ears of corn
spīcŭlum, i, n, point, dart
spīna, ae, f, thorn, spine, difficulties
spīnĕtum, i, n, thorn-hedge
spīnōsus, a, um, adj, thorny
spīnus, i, f, sloe-tree
spīra, ae, f, coil, twist
spīrābĭlis, e, adj, breathable
spīrācŭlum, i, n, air-hole
spīrāmentum, i, n, air-hole
spīrĭtus, ūs, m, breath, breeze, pride, arrogance, soul
spīro, v.i.t. 1, to breathe, blow, live; exhale
spisso, v.t. 1, to condense
spissus, a, um, adj, thick, dense
splendĕo, v.i. 2, to shine
splendesco, v.i. 3, to become bright
splendĭdus, a, um, adj, adv, ō, shining, magnificent, noble
splendor, ōris, m, brilliance, excellence
spŏlĭa, see **spŏlĭum**
spŏlĭātĭo, ōnis, f, plundering
spŏlĭo, v.t. 1, to plunder, rob
spŏlĭum, ii, n, skin (of an animal); in pl, booty, spoils
sponda, ae, f, couch, sofa
spondĕo, spŏpondi, sponsum, v.t. 2, to promise, pledge, betroth, warrant
spongĭa, ae, f, sponge
spongĭōsus, a, um, adj, spongy
sponsa, ae, f, bride
sponsālĭa, ĭum, n. pl, betrothal
sponsĭo, ōnis, f, promise, guarantee, security
sponsor, ōris, m, surety
sponsum, i, n, covenant
sponsus, a, um, adj, promised
sponsus, i, m, bridegroom
spontē, (abl.) f, with mĕā, sŭā, etc., voluntarily
sportella, ae, f, fruit-basket
sportŭla, ae, f, little basket
spūma, ae, f, froth, foam

spūmĕus, a, um, *adj*, foaming
spūmĭfer, ĕra, ĕrum, *adj*, foaming
spūmĭger, ĕra, ĕrum, *adj*, foaming
spūmo, *v.i.* 1, to foam, froth
spūmōsus, a, um, *adj*, foaming
spŭo, ŭi, ūtum, *v.i.t.* 3, to spit
spūtum, i, *n*, spit
spurcus, a, um, *adj*, dirty
squālĕo, *v.i.* 2, to be stiff or rough, to be neglected, filthy
squālĭdus, a, um, *adj*, stiff, dirty, neglected
squālor, ōris, *m*, filthiness
squāma, ae, *f*, scale (of fish)
squāmĕus, a, um, *adj*, scaly
squāmĭger, ĕra, ĕrum, *adj*, scaly
squāmōsus, a, um, *adj*, scaly
stăbĭlĭo, *v.t.* 4, to fix
stăbĭlis, e, *adj*, firm, steadfast
stăbĭlĭtas, ātis, *f*, firmness
stăbŭlo, *v.i.* (stăbŭlor, *v.i. dep*,) 1, to have a home, resting-place
stăbŭlum, i, *n*, stable, hut
stădĭum, ii, *n*, stade (distance of 200 yds. approx.), racecourse
stagnans, ntis, *adj*, stagnant
stagno, *v.i.* 1, to stagnate
stagnum, i, *n*, pool, pond
stălagmĭum, i, *n*, pendant
stāmen, ĭnis, *n*, thread
stătārĭus, a, um, *adj*, firm, calm
stătim, *adv*, immediately
stătĭo, ōnis, *f*, post, station, outposts, sentries
stătīva, ōrum, *n. pl*, permanent camp
stătīvus, a, um, *adj*, stationary
stător, ōris, *m*, messenger
stătŭa, ae, *f*, statue
stătŭo, ŭi, ūtum, *v.t.* 3, to set up, place, build, establish, settle, decide
stătūra, ae, *f*, stature
stătus, ūs, *m*, posture, position, condition, state, circumstance
stătus, a, um, *adj*, fixed
stella, ae, *f*, star
stellātus, a, um, *adj*, starry
stellĭger, ĕra, ĕrum, *adj*, starry
stellĭo, ōnis, *m*, newt
stemma, ătis, *n*, garland, pedigree
stercus, ōris, *n*, manure
stĕrĭlis, e, *adj*, barren
stĕrĭlĭtas, ātis, *f*, sterility
sternax, ācis, *adj*, bucking (horse)
sterno, strāvi, strātum, *v.t.* 3, to scatter, extend, smooth, arrange, cover, overthrow, pave
sternūmentum, i, *n*, sneezing
sternŭo, ŭi, *v.i.t.* 3, to sneeze
sterto, ŭi, *v.i.* 3, to snore

stigma, ătis, *n*, brand
stillĭcĭdĭum, ii, *n*, dripping rain-water
stillo, *v.i.t.* 1, to drip; distil
stĭlus, i, *m*, pen, style
stĭmŭlo, *v.t.* 1, to torment, incite
stĭmŭlus, i, *m*, goad, sting, incentive
stĭpātor, ōris, *m*, attendant
stĭpendĭārĭus, a, um, *adj*, tribute-paying
stĭpendĭum, ii, *n*, tax, dues, pay, military service, campaign
stīpes, ĭtis, *m*, log, post
stīpo, *v.t.* 1, to compress, surround, accompany
stips, stĭpis, *f*, donation
stĭpŭla, ae, *f*, stalk, stem
stĭpŭlātĭo, ōnis, *f*, agreement
stĭpŭlor, *v.i.t.* 1, *dep*, to bargain; demand
stīria, ae, *f*, icicle
stirps, pis, *f*, root, stem, plant, race, family
stīva, ae, *f*, plough-handle
sto, stĕti, stătum, *v.i.* 1, to stand, remain, endure, persist, cost
stōĭcus, a, um, *adj*, stoic
stŏla, ae, *f*, gown, robe
stŏlĭdus, a, um, *adj*, dull, stupid
stŏmāchor, *v.i.* 1, *dep*, to be angry
stŏmāchōsus, a, um, *adj*, irritable
stŏmāchus, i, *m*, gullet, stomach, taste, distaste
stŏrĕa, ae, *f*, straw-mat
strābo, ōnis, *m*, one who squints
strāges, is, *f*, destruction, massacre, slaughter
strāgŭlum, i, *n*, rug
strāgŭlus, a, um, *adj*, covering
strāmen, ĭnis, *n*, straw
strāmentum, i, *n*, straw
strāmĭnĕus, a, um, *adj*, of straw
strangŭlo, *v.t.* 1, to strangle
strătēgēma, ătis, *n*, stratagem
strātum, i, *n*, blanket, quilt, pillow, bed
strātus, a, um, *adj*, stretched out
strēnŭus, a, um, *adj*, *adv*, ē, brisk, quick, vigorous
strēpĭto, *v.i.* 1, to rattle
strēpĭtus, ūs, *m*, din
strēpo, ŭi, *v.i.* 3, to rattle, rumble, roar
strictim, *adv*, briefly
strictūra, ae, *f*, iron bar
strictus, a, um, *adj*, tight
strīdĕo, di (strīdo, di, 3), *v.i.* 2, to creak, hiss, rattle
strīdor, ōris, *m*, creaking, hissing
strīdŭlus, a, um, *adj*, creaking, hissing
strĭgĭlis, is, *f*, scraper used by bathers for cleaning the skin

stringo, nxi, ctum, *v.t.* 3, to draw tight, graze, strip off, draw (sword)

stringor, ōris, *m,* touch, shock

strix, strigis, *f,* screech-owl

structor, ōris, *m,* builder

structūra, ae, *f,* construction

strūes, is, *f,* heap, pile

strŭo, xi, ctum, *v.t.* 3, to pile up, build, contrive

strūthiŏcămēlus, i, *m,* ostrich

stŭdĕo, *v.i.t.* 2, *with dat,* to be eager about, strive; pursue, favour

stŭdiōsus, a, um, *adj, adv,* ē, eager, anxious, friendly

stŭdium, ii, *n,* eagerness, endeavour, affection, devotion, study

stultitia, ae, *f,* foolishness

stultus, a, um, *adj, adv,* ē, foolish

stūpa, ae, *f,* flax, tow

stŭpĕfăcio, fēci, factum, *v.t.* 3, to stun, daze

stŭpĕfactus, a, um, *adj,* stunned

stŭpĕo, *v.i.t.* 2, to be stunned, amazed; be astonished at

stūpĕus, a, um, *adj,* made of tow

stŭpĭdus, a, um, *adj,* amazed

stŭpor, ōris, *m,* astonishment, stupidity

stupp . . . see **stūp. . . .**

stŭpro, *v.t.* 1, to ravish

stŭprum, i, *n,* disgrace, lewdness

sturnus, i, *m,* starling

suādĕo, si, sum, *v.i.t.* 2, *with dat,* to urge, persuade, recommend

suāsio, ōnis, *f,* recommendation

suāsor, ōris, *m,* adviser

suāvilŏquens, ntis, *adj,* pleasant speaking

suāvior, *v.t.* 1, *dep,* to kiss

suāvis, e, *adj, adv,* iter, agreeable, pleasant

suāvitas, ātis, *f,* pleasantness

suāvium, ii, *n,* kiss

sub, *prep. with acc. and abl,* under, beneath, near, during, towards, just after

sŭbactio, ōnis, *f,* preparation

sŭbausculto, *v.t.* 1, to eavesdrop

subcentŭrio, ōnis, *m,* subaltern

subditīvus, a, um, *adj,* counterfeit

subdo, dĭdi, dĭtum, *v.t.* 3, to place under, subdue

subdŏlus, a, um, *adj,* crafty

subdūco, xi, ctum, *v.t.* 3, to pull up, haul up, remove, calculate, balance (accounts)

sŭbĕo, *v.i.t.* 4, to come up to, spring up, occur; enter, submit to, suffer, incur

sūber, ĕris, *n,* cork-tree

subflāvus, a, um, *adj,* yellowish

sŭbicio, iēci, iectum, *v.t.* 3, to throw or place under or near, counterfeit, subject, affix, prompt

subiectio, ōnis, *f,* placing under, forging

subiecto, *v.t.* 1, to throw up

subiectus, a, um, *adj,* lying near, subject

sŭbigo, ēgi, actum, *v.t.* 3, to bring up, plough, conquer, subdue, compel, rub down

sŭbinde, *adv,* immediately, now and then

sŭbitō, *adv,* suddenly

sŭbitus, a, um, *adj,* sudden

subiungo, nxi, nctum, *v.t.* 3, to subordinate, subdue

sublābor, lapsus, *v.i.* 3, *dep,* to glide away

sublātus, a, um, *adj,* proud

sublēgo, lēgi, lectum, *v.t.* 3, to gather up, kidnap

sublĕvo, *v.t.* 1, to lift up, support, alleviate

sublica, ae, *f,* stake, palisade

sublĭgo, *v.t.* 1, to tie on

sublime, *adv,* aloft, on high

sublimis, e, *adj,* high, eminent

sublūcĕo, *v.i.* 2, to glimmer

sublŭo, *no perf,* lūtum, *v.t.* 3, to flow along, wash

sublustris, e, *adj,* glimmering

subm . . . see **summ. . . .**

subnecto, xŭi, xum, *v.t.* 3, to tie on underneath

subnixus, a, um, *adj,* propped up

sŭbŏles, is, *f,* offspring, race

sŭborno, *v.t.* 1, to equip, fit out, instigate

subr . . . see **surr. . . .**

subscrībo, psi, ptum, *v.t.* 3, to write underneath, note down

subscriptio, ōnis, *f,* anything written underneath

subsĕco, ŭi, ctum, *v.t.* 1, to clip

subsellium, ii, *n,* seat, law-court

subsĕquor, sĕcūtus, *v.i.t.* 3, *dep,* to follow, ensue; follow closely, imitate

subsicīvus, a, um, *adj,* remaining

subsidiārius, a, um, *adj,* reserve

subsidium, ii, *n,* reserve-ranks, assistance, aid, protection

subsido, sēdi, sessum, *v.i.t.* 3, to settle down, lie in ambush; waylay

subsisto, stĭti, *v.i.* 3, to stop, halt, remain, withstand

subsortior, *v.t.* 4, *dep,* to choose as a substitute

substerno, strāvi, strātum, *v.t.* 3, to spread underneath, cover

For List of Abbreviations used, turn to pages 3, 4

substĭtŭo, ŭi, ūtum, *v.t.* 3, to put under, substitute

substringo, nxi, ctum, *v.t.* 3, to tie; aurem prick up the ear

substructĭo, ōnis, *f,* foundation

substrŭo, xi, ctum, *v.t.* 3, to lay foundations

subsum, esse, *v, irreg,* to be under or near, to be at hand

subtēmen, ĭnis, *n,* texture, weft

subter, *adv. and prep. with abl,* beneath, below

subterfŭgĭo, fŭgi, *v.t.* 3, to avoid

subterlābens, ntis, *adj,* gliding under

subterlābor, *v.i.* 3, *dep,* to glide under

subterrānĕus, a, um, *adj,* underground

subtexo, ŭi, xtum, *v.t.* 3, to veil

subtīlis, e, *adj, adv,* **ĭter,** slender, delicate, precise

subtīlĭtas, ātis, *f,* exactness, subtlety

subtrăho, xi, ctum, *v.t.* 3, to remove stealthily, carry off

sŭbŭcŭla, ae, *f,* shirt

sŭbulcus, i, *m,* pig-keeper

sŭburbānus, a, um, *adj,* suburban

sŭburbĭum, ii, *n,* suburb

subvectĭo, ōnis, *f,* conveyance

subvecto, *v.t.* 1, to convey

subvĕho, xi, ctum, *v.t.* 3, to convey

subvĕnĭo, vēni, ventum, *v.i.* 4, *with dat,* to help, aid, occur to the mind

subverto, ti, sum, *v.t.* 3, to overthrow

subvŏlo, *v.i.* 1, to fly up

subvolvo, *v.t.* 3, to roll up

succēdo, cessi, cessum, *v.i.t.* 3, to go under, advance, enter; ascend, follow after, succeed

succendo, di, sum, *v.t.* 3, to kindle

succensĕo, ŭi, sum, *v.i.* 2, to be angry

successĭo, ōnis. *f,* succession

successor, ōris, *m,* successor

successus, ūs, *m,* advance, success

succĭdo, di, *v.i.* 3, to sink

succīdo, di, sum, *v.t.* 3, to cut down

succingo, nxi, nctum, *v.t.* 3, to surround, girdle, tuck up

succlāmo, *v.t.* 1, to shout out

succumbo, cŭbŭi, cŭbĭtum, *v.i.* 3, to surrender

succurro, curri, cursum, *v.i.* 3, *with dat,* to help, aid, occur

sūcĭnum, i, *n,* amber

sūcōsus, a, um, *adj,* juicy

suctus, ūs, *m,* sucking

sūcus, i, *m,* juice, energy, life

sūdārĭum, ii, *n,* handkerchief

sūdis, is, *f,* stake, pile

sūdo, *v.i.t.* 1, to sweat, toil; exude

sūdor, ōris, *m,* sweat, toil

sūdum, i, *n,* clear weather

sūdus, a, um, *adj,* clear, bright

sŭesco, sŭēvi, sŭētum, *v.i.t.* 3, to be accustomed

sŭētus, a, um, *adj,* accustomed

suffĕro, ferre, sustŭli, sublātum, *v, irreg,* to undergo, suffer

sufficĭo, fēci, fectum, *v.i.t.* 3, to be sufficient; impregnate, supply, substitute, elect

suffīgo, xi, xum, *v.t.* 3, to fix

suffīmentum, i, *n,* incense

suffīo, *v.t.* 4, to perfume

sufflāmen, ĭnis, *n,* drag-chain

sufflātus, a, um, *adj,* puffed up

sufflo, *v.t.* 1, to inflate

suffōco, *v.t.* 1, to strangle

suffŏdĭo, fōdi, fossum, *v.t.* 3, to pierce underneath

suffrāgātĭo, ōnis, *f,* support

suffrāgātor, ōris, *m,* supporter

suffrāgĭum, ii, *n,* vote, ballot

suffrāgor, *v.i.* 1, *dep, with dat.* to vote for, support

suffundo, fūdi, fūsum, *v.t.* 3, to spread over, tinge

suffulcĭo, fulsi, fultum, *v.t.* 4, to prop up

suffūsus, a, um, *adj,* spread over

suggĕro, gessi, gestum, *v.t.* 3, to carry up, supply

suggestum, i, *n,* platform

suggestus, ūs, *m,* platform

sūgo, xi, ctum, *v.t.* 3, to suck

sŭi, *genit. of reflexive pron,* of himself, herself, itself, etc.

sulco, *v.t.* 1, to plough

sulcus, i, *m,* furrow, ditch

sulfur, ŭris, *n,* sulphur

sulfŭrāta, ōrum, *n. pl,* matches

sulfŭrĕus, a, um, *adj,* sulphurous

sum, esse, fŭi, *v, irreg,* to be, exist, happen

summa, ae, *f,* top, chief point, perfection, amount, sum

summātim, *adv,* briefly

summē, *adv,* extremely

summergo, si, sum, *v.t.* 3, to submerge, overwhelm

summĭnistro, *v.t.* 1, to supply

summissus, a, um, *adj, adv,* **ē,** gentle, soft, low, mean

summitto, mīsi, missum, *v.t.* 3, to send up, produce, rear, raise, lower, submit, supply, send

summŏvĕo, mōvi, mōtum, *v.t.* 2, to drive away, remove

summus, a, um, *adj*, highest, topmost
sūmo, mpsi, mptum, *v.t.* 3, to take hold of, assume, inflict, choose, claim, suppose, spend, use, buy
sumptio, ōnis, *f*, assumption
sumptŭōsus, - a, um, *adj*, *adv*, ē, expensive, lavish
sumptus, ūs, *m*, expense
sŭo, sŭi, sūtum, *v.t.* 3, to sew
sŭpellex, lectilis, *f*, furniture
sŭper, *adv. and prep. with acc. and abl*, above, over, on, besides, concerning
sŭpĕrābĭlis, e, *adj*, able to be overcome
sŭperbĭa, ae, *f*, pride, arrogance
sŭperbĭo, *v.i.* 4, to be proud
sŭperbus, a, um, *adj*, *adv*, ē, proud, haughty, delicate, squeamish, magnificent
sŭpercĭlĭum, ii, *n*, eye-brow, ridge, summit, arrogance
sŭpercresco, crēvi, *v.i.* 3, to grow up
sŭpĕrēmĭnĕo, *v.t.* 2, to overtop
sŭperficies, ēi, *f*, top, surface
sŭperfundo, fūdi, fūsum, *v.l.* 3, to pour over
sŭpĕri, ōrum, *m.pl*, the gods
sŭpĕrimmĭnĕo, *v.i.* 2, to overhang
sŭpĕrimpōno, *no perf*, pŏsĭtum, *v.t.* 3, to place upon
sŭpĕrĭnĭcĭo, *no perf*, iectum, *v.t.* 3, to throw over or upon
sŭperiăcĭo, iēci, iectum, *v.t.* 3, to throw over, overflow
sŭpĕrĭor, ĭus, *comp. adj*, higher, previous, former, superior
sŭperlatĭo, ōnis, *f*, exaggeration, hyperbole
sŭpernus, a, um, *adj*, *adv*, ē, upper, on high ground
sŭpĕro, *v.i.t.* 1, to have the upper hand, remain; ascend, outstrip, conquer
sŭpersĕdĕo, sēdi, sessum, *v.i.t.* 2, *with abl*, to refrain (from)
sŭperstĕs, ĭtis, *adj*, surviving
sŭperstĭtĭo, ōnis, *f*, excessive fear of the gods
sŭperstĭtĭōsus, a, um, *adj*, superstitious
sŭpersto, *v.i.t.* 1, to stand over
sŭpersum, esse, fŭi, *v.i.*, *irreg*, to remain, survive
sŭpĕrus, a, um, *adj*, upper, higher
sŭpervācānĕus, a, um, *adj*, unnecessary
sŭpervācŭus, a, um, *adj*, unnecessary
sŭpervĕnĭo, vēni, ventum, *v.i.t.* 4, to come up, arrive; fall upon

sŭpervŏlo, *v.i.t.* 1, to fly over
sŭpīno, *v.t.* 1, to bend backwards
sŭpīnus, a, um, *adj*, lying on the back, sloping
suppĕdĭto, *v.i.t.* 1, to be enough, plenty; to supply
suppĕto, īvi, ītum, *v.i.* 3, to be at hand, to be enough
supplanto, *v.t.* 1, to trip up
supplēmentum, i, *n*, reinforcements
supplĕo, ēvi, ētum, *v.t.* 2, to complete, fill up
supplex, ĭcis, *c*, suppliant
supplex, ĭcis, *adj*, beseeching
supplĭcātĭo, ōnis, *f*, public thanksgiving
supplĭcĭum, ii, *n*, punishment
supplĭco, *v.i.* 1, to implore
supplōdo, si, *v.i.t.* 3, to stamp
suppōno, pŏsŭi, pŏsĭtum, *v.t.* 3, to put under, substitute
supporto, *v.t.* 1, to convey
supprĭmo, pressi, pressum, *v.t.* 3, to sink, suppress
suppūro, *v.i.* 1, to suppurate
sŭprā, *adv. and prep. with acc*, above, over, beyond, before
sŭprēmus, a, um, *adj*, highest, last
sūra, ae, *f*, calf of the leg
surcŭlus, i, *m*, shoot, twig
surdĭtas, ātis, *f*, deafness
surdus, a, um, *adj*, deaf
surgo, surrexi, rectum, *v.i.t.* 3, to rise, stand up; raise
surrēgŭlus, i, *m*, subordinate ruler
surrēmigo, *v.i.* 1, to row along
surrēpo, psi, ptum, *v.i.t.* 3, to creep under
surrīdĕo, si, sum, *v.i.* 2, to smile
surrīpĭo, ŭi, reptum, *v.t.* 3, to snatch away, steal
surrŏgo, *v.t.* 1, to substitute
surrŭo, ŭi, ŭtum, *v.t.* 3, to undermine, overthrow
sursum, *adv*, upwards, on high
sūs, sŭis, *c*, pig
susceptĭo, ōnis, *f*, undertaking
suscĭpĭo, cēpi, ceptum, *v.t.* 3, to undertake, acknowledge, undergo
suscĭto, *v.t.* 1, to raise, arouse
suspectus, a, um, *adj*, mistrusted
suspectus, ūs, *m*, height
suspendĭum, ii, *n*, hanging
suspendo, di, sum, *v.t.* 3, to hang up, lift up, keep in suspense, interrupt
suspensus, a, um, *adj*, raised, hesitating
suspĭcĭo, spexi, ctum, *v.i.t.* 3, to look up; admire, suspect
suspĭcĭo, ōnis, *f*, suspicion

suspĭcĭōsus, a, um, *adj*, *adv*, ē, suspicious

suspĭcor, *v.t.* 1, *dep*, to suspect, suppose

suspīritus, ūs, *m*, sigh

suspīrium, ii, *n*, sigh

suspīro, *v.i.t.* 1, to sigh; long for

sustento, *v.t.* 1, to support, maintain, endure

sustĭnĕo, ŭi, tentum, *v.t.* 2, to support, restrain, withstand, maintain

sŭsurro, *v.i.t.* 1, to hum; mutter

sŭsurrus, i, *m*, humming

sŭsurrus, a, um, *adj*, whispering

sūta, ōrum, *n. pl*, joints

sūtĭlis, e, *adj*, sewed together

sūtor, ōris, *m*, cobbler

sūtōrĭus, a, um, *adj*, of a cobbler

sūtūra, ae, *f*, seam

sŭus, a, um, *adj*, his, hers, its, their

sȳcŏmōrus, i, *f*, sycamore

sȳcŏphanta, ae, *m*, sycophant, cheat

syllăba, ae, *f*, syllable

syllăbātim, *adv*, by syllables

symphōnia, ae, *f*, harmony

symphōnĭăcus, i, *m*, chorister

sȳnăgōga, ae, *f*, synagogue

syngrăpha, ae, *f*, promissory note

syngrăphus, i, *m*, passport

syntaxis, is, *f*, syntax

T

tăbānus, i, *m*, gad-fly

tăbella, ae, *f*, small board or table, writing-tablet, letter, ballot-paper, small picture

tăbellārĭus, ii, *m*, letter-bearer

tăbĕo, *v.i.* 2, to melt away

tăberna, ae, *f*, hut, shop, inn

tăbernācŭlum, i, *n*, tent

tăbernārĭus, ii, *m*, shop-keeper

tābes, is, *f*, wasting-away, disease

tābesco, bŭi, *v.i.* 3, to melt away

tābĭdus, a, um, *adj*, decaying

tăbŭla, ae, *f*, plank, writing-tablet, letter, account-book, picture, painting, map, table

tăbŭlārĭa, ae, *f*, record-office

tăbŭlārĭum, ii, *n*, archives

tăbŭlārĭus, ii, *m*, registrar

tăbŭlātum, i, *n*, floor, storey

tābum, i, *n*, pus, matter, infectious disease

tăcĕo, *v.i.t.* 2, to be silent; to be silent about

tăcĭturnĭtas, ātis, *f*, silence

tăcĭturnus, a, um, *adj*, silent

tăcĭtus, a, um, *adj*, *adv*, ē, secret, silent

tactus, ūs, *m*, touch, feel, influence

taeda, ae, *f*, pine-tree, torch

taedet, taedŭit, *v.* 2, *impers. with acc. of person*, it offends, disgusts, wearies

taedĭum, ii, *n*, weariness, disgust

taenĭa, ae, *f*, hair-ribbon

taeter, tra, trum, *adj*, hideous

taetrĭcus, a, um, *adj*, harsh

tālāris, e, *adj*, ankle-length

tālĕa, ae, *f*, stick, stake

tălentum, i, *n*, sum of money (app. £400–£500); weight (½ cwt.)

tālĭo, ōnis, *f*, similar punishment, reprisal

tālis, e, *adj*, of such a kind

talpa, ae, *f*, mole

tālus, i, *m*, ankle-bone, heel, die (marked on four sides)

tam, *adv*, so, as, equally

tamdĭū, *adv*, so long

tămen, *adv*, nevertheless, however, still

tămetsi, *conj*, although

tamquam, *adv*, as much as, just as, as if, for example

tandem, *adv*, at length

tango, tĕtĭgi, tactum, *v.t.* 3, to touch, taste, reach, strike, affect, impress ence, mention

tanquam, see tamquam

tantisper, *adv*, so long, meanwhile

tantōpĕre, *adv*, so greatly

tantŭlus, a, um, *adj*, so little

tantum, *adv*, so much, only

tantummŏdo, *adv*, only, merely

tantundem, *adv*, just as much

tantus, a, um, *adj*, so great; tantī esse, to be worth so much; tantō, by so much

tăpēte, is, *n*, tapestry

tardĭtas, ātis, *f*, slowness

tardo, *v.i.t.* 1, to delay; hinder

tardus, a, um, *adj*, *adv*, ē, slow

tăta, ae, *m*, dad, daddy

taurĕus, a, um, *adj*, of a bull

taurīnus, a, um, *adj*, of a bull

taurus, i, *m*, bull, ox

taxus, i, *f*, yew-tree

tē, *acc. or abl. of* tū

tector, ōris, *m*, plasterer

tectōrĭum, ii, *n*, plaster

tectum, i, *n*, roof, house

tectus, a, um, *adj*, *adv*, ō, covered, hidden, secret

tĕges, ĕtis, *f*, mat

tĕgĭmen, ĭnis, *n*, cover

tĕgo, xi, ctum, *v.t.* 3, to cover, hide, protect

tĕgŭla, ae, *f*, tile

tĕgŭmen, see tĕgĭmen

tĕgŭmentum, i, n, cover

tēla, ae, f, web, warp, loom

tellūs, ūris, f, earth, globe, land, region

tēlum, i, n, weapon, javelin

tĕmĕrārius, a, um, adj, rash

tĕmĕrē, adv, by chance, rashly

tĕmĕritas, ātis, f, rashness

tĕmĕro, v.t. 1, to defile, disgrace

tēmētum, i, n, wine

temno, v.t. 3, to despise

tēmo, ōnis, m, pole, beam

tempĕrans, ntis, adj, moderate

tempĕrantĭa, ae, f, moderation

tempĕrātĭo, ōnis, f, symmetry, temperament

tempĕrātus, a, um, adj, moderate

tempĕrĭes, ēi, f, mildness

tempĕro, v.i.t. 1, to abstain, be moderate, be indulgent; mix properly, regulate, govern

tempestas, ātis, f, time, period, weather, storm

tempestīvus, a, um, adj, adv, ē, suitable, timely, early

templum, i, n, temple, open space

tempto, see tento

tempus, ŏris, n, time, opportunity; tempŏra, times, temples (of the head); ad tempus, (adv. phr.) at the right time, for the time being

tēmŭlentus, a, um, adj, drunk

tĕnācĭtas, ātis, f, tenacity

tĕnax, ācis, adj, holding tight, firm, stingy

tendo, tĕtendi, tentum, v.i.t. 3, to aim, go, march, stretch, strive, encamp; stretch, extend

tĕnĕbrae, ārum, f. pl, darkness

tĕnĕbricōsus, a, um, adj, dark, gloomy

tĕnĕbrōsus, a, um, adj, dark, gloomy

tĕnĕo, ŭi, tentum, v.i.t. 2, to hold a position, sail, continue; hold, have, keep, restrain, uphold, maintain, control, comprehend, include

tĕner, ĕra, ĕrum, adj, tender

tĕnor, ōris, m, course, career

tensa, ae, f, triumphal chariot

tentāmentum, i, n, attempt

tentātĭo, ōnis, f, trial, attempt

tentātor, ōris, m, tempter

tento (tempto), v.t. 1, to handle, attack, attempt, tempt, excite

tentōrium, ii, n, tent

tentus, a, um, adj, extended

tĕnŭis, e, adj, adv, ĭter, thin, fine, meagre, poor, subtle

tĕnŭĭtas, ātis, f, slenderness, poverty

tĕnŭo, v.t. 1, to make thin, reduce, weaken, degrade

tĕnus, prep. with abl, as far as, according to

tĕpĕfăcĭo, fēci, factum, v.t. 3, to warm

tĕpĕo, v.i. 2, to be warm

tĕpesco, pŭi, v.i. 3, to grow warm

tĕpidus, a, um, adj, warm

tĕpor, ōris, m, warmth

tĕr, adv, three times

tĕrēbinthus, i, f, terebinth tree

tĕrēbra, ae, f, tool

tĕrēbro, v.t. 1, to bore through

tĕrēs, ĕtis, adj, rounded, smooth, polished

tergĕmĭnus, a, um, adj, triple

tergĕo, si, sum, v.t. 2, to clean, polish

tergĭversātĭo, ōnis, f, backsliding

tergĭversor, v.i. 1, dep, to shuffle, refuse

tergo, si, sum, see tergĕo

tergum, i, n, back, rear, skin; a tergo, (adv. phr.) at the rear

termĭnālĭa, ĭum, n. pl, festival of Terminus (God of boundaries)

termĭnātĭo, ōnis, f, fixing

termĭno, v.t. 1, to limit, fix, define, determine, end

termĭnus, i, m, boundary, end

terni, ae, a, pl. adj, three each

tĕro, trīvi, trītum, v.t. 3, to rub, grind, smooth, polish, wear out, spend or waste time

terra, ae, f, earth, land, ground, region

terrēnus, a, um, adj, made of earth, terrestrial

terrĕo, v.t. 2, to frighten

terrestris, e, adj, of earth or land

terrĕus, a, um, adj, of earth or land

terrĭbĭlis, e, adj, dreadful

terrĭcŭla, ōrum, n. pl, scarecrow bugbear

terrĭfĭco, v.t. 1, to terrify

terrĭfĭcus, a, um, adj, frightful

terrĭgĕna, ae, c, earthborn

territo, v.t. 1, to terrify

terror, ōris, m, terror, dread

tertĭus, a, um, adj, adv, ō, third

tĕruncius, ii, m, trifling sum

tessellātus, a, um, adj, tesselated, mosaic

tessĕra, ae, f, stone or wooden cube, die, watchword, ticket

testa, ae, f, jug, broken piece of pottery, shell-fish

testāmentum, i, n, will, testament

testātor, ōris, m, testator

testātus, a, um, adj, manifest

testĭfĭcātĭo, ōnis, f, evidence

For List of Abbreviations used, turn to pages 3, 4

testĭfĭcor, *v.t.* 1, *dep*, to give evidence, demonstrate

testĭmōnĭum, ii, *n*, evidence

testis, is, *c*, witness

testor, *v.t.* 1, *dep*, to call a witness, prove, declare

testu(m), i, *n*, lid, earthen pot

testūdĭnĕus, a, um, *adj*, of a tortoise

testūdo, ĭnis, *f*, tortoise, lute, military shelter

tĕtănus, i, *m*, tetanus

tēter, tra, trum, *adj*, hideous

tĕtrarches, ae, *m*, petty princeling

tĕtrĭcus, a, um, *adj*, harsh

texo, ŭi, xtum, *v.t.* 3, to weave, build, devise

textile, is, *n*, fabric

textĭlis, e, *adj*, woven

textor, ōris, *m*, weaver

textum, i, *n*, web, fabric

textus, ūs, *m*, texture

thălămus, i, *m*, apartment, bedroom, marriage

thĕātrālis, e, *adj*, theatrical

thĕātrum, i, *n*, theatre

thēca, ae, *f*, envelope

thĕŏlŏgĭa, ae, *f*, theology

thĕŏlŏgus, i, *m*, theologian

thĕōrēma, ătis, *n*, theorem

thermae, ārum, *f. pl*, warm baths

thēsaurus, i, *m*, store, hoard, treasure, treasure-house

thĭăsus, i, *m*, dance in honour of Bacchus

thŏlus, i, *m*, dome

thōrax, ācis, *m*, breastplate

thunnus, i, *m*, tunny-fish

thūs, thūris, *n*, incense

thymbra, ae, *f*, savory (plant)

thŷmum, i, *n*, thyme

thyrsus, i, *m*, stem of plant, staff carried by Bacchus

tĭāra, ae, *f*, tiara

tībĭa, ae, *f*, flute

tībĭăle, is, *n*, stocking

tībīcen, ĭnis, *m*, flute-player

tībīcĭna, ae, *f*, flute-player

tībĭcĭnĭum, ii, *n*, flute-playing

tignum, i, *n*, timber, log

tigris, is (ĭdis), *c*, tiger

tĭlĭa, ae, *f*, linden or lime tree

tĭmĕo, *v.i.t.* 2, to fear

tĭmĭdĭtas, ātis, *f*, cowardice

tĭmĭdus, a, um, *adj*, *adv*, ē, afraid, cowardly

tĭmor, ōris, *m*, fear, alarm, object of fear

tĭnĕa, ae, *f*, moth, book-worm

tingo, nxi, nctum, *v.t.* 3, to moisten, dye

tinnĭo, *v.i.t.* 4, to ring; tinkle

tinnītus, ūs, *m*, ringing

tinnŭlus, a, um, *adj*, tinkling

tintinnābŭlum, i, *n*, bell

tīro, ōnis, *m*, recruit, novice

tīrōcĭnĭum, ii, *n*, first campaign, inexperience

tītillātĭo, ōnis, *f*, tickling

tītillo, *v.t.* 1, to tickle

tĭtŭbo, *v.i.* 1, to stagger, hesitate, be perplexed

tĭtŭlus, i, *m*, title, placard, notice, honour, glory

tōfus, i, *m*, tufa (rock)

tŏga, ae, *f*, toga: the long outer garment of the Romans

tŏgātus, a, um, *adj*, wearing the toga

tŏlĕrābĭlis, e, *adj*, endurable

tŏlĕrantĭa, ae, *f*, tolerance

tŏlĕro, *v.t.* 1, to bear, endure

tollēno, ōnis, *m*, a swing-beam

tollo, sustŭli, sublātum, *v.t.* 3, to lift, raise, remove, destroy, educate, acknowledge

tŏnans, ntis, *m*, god of thunder

tondĕo, tŏtondi, tonsum, *v.t.* 2, to shave, crop, prune, graze

tŏnĭtrus, ūs, *m*, thunder

tŏnĭtrŭum, i, *n*, thunder

tŏno, ŭi, *v.i.t.* 1, to thunder; thunder out

tonsa, ae, *f*, oar

tonsillae, ārum, *f. pl*, tonsils

tonsor, ōris, *m*, barber

tonsōrĭus, a, um, *adj*, of shaving

tonsūra, ae, *f*, shearing

tŏpĭārĭus, ii, *m*, landscape-gardener

tŏreuma, ătis, *n*, embossed work

tormentum, i, *n*, missile, rope, missile-launcher, instrument of torture, rack, pain

tormĭna, um, *n. pl*, the gripes

torno, *v.t.* 1, to round off

tornus, i, *m*, lathe

tŏrōsus, a, um, *adj*, muscular

torpĕfăcĭo, fēci, factum, *v.t.* 3, to numb

torpens, ntis, *adj*, numb

torpĕo, *v.i.* 2, to be stiff, numb, sluggish, listless

torpesco, pŭi, *v.i.* 3, to become stiff or listless

torpor, ōris, *m*, numbness

torquātus, a, um, *adj*, wearing a collar

torquĕo, torsi, sum, *v.t.* 2, to twist, bend, wield, hurl, rack, torture

torquis (torques), is, *m*, *f*, collar, necklace, wreath
torrens, ntis, *adj*, burning
torrens, ntis, *m*, torrent
torrĕo, ŭi, tostum, *v.t.* 2, to dry, bake, scorch, burn
torrĭdus, a, um, *adj*, parched
torris, is, *m*, firebrand
tortĭlis, e, *adj*, twined
tortor, ōris, *m*, torturer
tortŭōsus, a, um, *adj*, winding, complicated
tortus, a, um, *adj*, twisted
tortus, ūs, *m*, twisting
tŏrus, i, *m*, muscle, knot, cushion, sofa, bed
torvus, a, um, *adj*, wild, grim
tŏt, *indecl. adj*, so many
tŏtĭdem, *indecl. adj*, just as many
tŏtĭens (tŏtĭes), *adv*, so often
tŏtum, i, *n*, whole
tōtus, a, um, *adj*, the whole
trăbālis, e, *adj*, of a beam
trăbĕa, ae, *f*, robe of state
trabs, trăbis, *f*, beam, timber, tree, ship
tractābĭlis, e, *adj*, manageable, pliant, flexible
tractātĭo, ōnis, *f*, handling, treatment
tractātus, ūs, *m*, handling, treatment
tractim, *adv*, little by little
tracto, *v.t.* 1, to handle, manage, practise, discuss, drag
tractus, ūs, *m*, dragging, track, district, course, progress
trādĭtĭo, ōnis, *f*, surrender
trādo, dĭdi, dĭtum, *v.t.* 3, to hand over, commit, bequeath, relate
trādūco, xi, ctum, *v.t.* 3, to bring over, degrade, spend (time)
trāductĭo, ōnis, *f*, transferring
trăgĭcus, a, um, *adj*, tragic, fearful, grand
trăgoedĭa, ae, *f*, tragedy
trăgoedus, i, *m*, tragic actor
trăgŭla, ae, *f*, javelin, dart
trăhĕa, ae, *f*, sledge
trăho, xi, ctum, *v.t.* 3, to drag, extract, inhale, quaff, drag away, plunder, spin, influence, delay, protract
trāĭcĭo, iēci, iectum, *v.t.* 3, to throw across, transport, transfix
trāĭectĭo, ōnis, *f*, crossing over, passage
trāĭectus, ūs, *m*, crossing
trāmĕs, ĭtis, *m*, footpath, way
trāno, *v.t.* 1, to swim across
tranquillĭtas, ātis, *f*, calmness
tranquillo, *v.t.* 1, to calm
tranquillum, i, *n*, a calm

tranquillus, a, um, *adj*, *adv*, ē, calm, placid, serene
trans, *prep. with acc*, across, beyond, on the further side of
transābĕo, *v.t.* 4, to transfix
transādĭgo, ēgi, actum, *v.t.* 3, to thrust through
transalpīnus, a, um, *adj*, beyond the Alps
transcendo, di, sum, *v.i.t.* 3, to climb over, surmount; exceed
transcrībo, psi, ptum, *v.t.* 3, to transcribe, forge, transfer
transcurro, curri, cursum, *v.i.t.* 3, to run across; pass through
transĕo, *v.i.t.* 4, to go over or across, pass by, surpass
transfĕro, ferre, tŭli, lātum, *v.t.*, *irreg*, to bring across, carry along, transfer, translate
transfīgo, xi, xum, *v.t.* 3, to pierce through
transfŏdĭo, fōdi, fossum, *v.t.* 3, to pierce through
transformo, *v.t.* 1, to transform
transfŭga, ae, *c*, deserter
transfŭgĭo, fūgi, *v.t.* 3, to desert
transfundo, fūdi, fūsum, *v.t.* 3, to transfer
transgrĕdĭor, gressus, *v.i.t.* 3, *dep*, to pass or climb over, across
transgressĭo, ōnis, *f*, passage
transĭgo, ēgi, actum, *v.t.* 3, to complete, transact, settle (a difference)
transĭlĭo, ŭi, *v.i.t.* 4, to leap across
transĭtĭo, ōnis, *f*, going over, passage
transĭtus, ūs, *m*, going over, passage
translātĭcĭus, a, um, *adj*, handed down
translātĭo, ōnis, *f*, transferring
translātus, a, um, *adj*, transferred, copied, figurative
translūcĕo, *v.i.* 2, to shine through
transmărīnus, a, um, *adj*, across the sea
transmĭgro, *v.i.* 1, to migrate
transmissus, ūs, *m*, transferring
transmitto, mīsi, missum, *v.i.t.* 3, to go across; send across, transfer, hand over
transmūto, *v.t.* 1, to change
transnăto, *v.i.* 1, to swim over
transpădānus, a, um, *adj*, beyond the river Po
transporto, *v.t.* 1, to carry across
transtrum, i, *n*, rowing-bench
transvĕho, xi, ctum, *v.t.* 3, to carry over
transverbĕro, *v.t.* 1, to transfix
transversārĭus, a, um, *adj*, crosswise
transversus, a, um, *adj*, crosswise

transvŏlo, *v.i.t.* 1, to fly across
trēcēni, ae, a, *pl. adj*, three hundred each
trecentensĭmus, a, um, *adj*, three hundredth
trēcenti, ae, a, *pl. adj*, three hundred
trēdĕcim, *indecl. adj*, thirteen
trĕmēbundus, a, um, *adj*, trembling
trĕmēfăcĭo, fēci, factum, *v.t.* 3, to cause to tremble
trĕmendus, a, um, *adj*, dreadful
trĕmesco, *v.i.t.* 3, to tremble; tremble at
trĕmo, ŭi, *v.i.t.* 3, to tremble; tremble at
trĕmor, ōris, *m*, shuddering
trĕmŭlus, a, um, *adj*, trembling
trĕpĭdans, ntis, *adj*, trembling
trĕpĭdātĭo, ōnis, *f*, confusion
trĕpĭdo, *v.i.t.* 1, to be alarmed; tremble at
trĕpĭdus, a, um, *adj*, alarmed
trēs, tria, *adj*, three
triangŭlum, i, *n*, triangle
triangŭlus, a, um, *adj*, triangular
triārii, ōrum, *m. pl*, veteran soldiers who fought in the third rank
tribŭārĭus, a, um, *adj*, of a tribe
tribūlis, e, *adj*, of the same tribe
tribŭlum, i, *n*, threshing-platform
tribŭlus, i, *m*, thistle
tribūnal, ālis, *n*, platform, judgement-seat
tribūnātus, ūs, *m*, position of tribune
tribūnĭcĭus, a, um, *adj*, of a tribune
tribūnus, i, *m*, tribune; 1. army officer; 2. magistrate to defend the rights of the people
tribŭo, ŭi, ūtum, *v.t.* 3, to allot, give, attribute
trĭbus, ūs, *f*, tribe
trĭbus, see trēs
trĭbūtim, *adv*, by tribes
trĭbūtum, i, *n*, tribute, tax
trīcae, ārum, *f. pl*, tricks
trīcēni, ae, a, *pl. adj*, thirty each
trīceps, cĭpĭtis, *adj*, three-headed
trīcēsĭmus, a, um, *adj*, thirtieth
trīcies, *adv*, thirty times
trīclīnĭum, ii, *n*, dining-couch, dining-room
trīcorpor, ŏris, *adj*, three-bodied
trīdens, ntis, *adj*, three-pronged; *as nn*, trident
trīdŭum, i, *n*, three days
trĭennĭum, ii, *n*, three years
trĭens, ntis, *m*, a third part
trĭētērĭca, ōrum, *n. pl*, festival of Bacchus
trĭfaux, cis, *adj*, with three throats

trĭfĭdus, a, um, *adj*, three-forked
trĭfŏlĭum, ii, *n*, shamrock
trĭformis, e, *adj*, three-fold
trĭgĕmĭnus, a, um, *adj*, triple
trĭgēsĭmus, a, um, *adj*, thirtieth
trĭginta, *indecl. adj*, thirty
trĭgōn, ōnis, *m*, ball
trĭlībris, e, *adj*, weighing three pounds
trĭlinguis, e, *adj*, three-tongued
trĭlix, īcis, *adj*, with three thongs
trĭmestris, e, *adj*, of three months
trĭmus, a, um, *adj*, three years old
trīni, ae, a, *pl. adj*, three each
trĭnōdis, e, *adj*, three-knotted
trĭōnes, um, *m. pl*, constellation of the Great and Lesser Bear
trĭpartītus, a, um, *adj, adv*, ō, three-fold
trĭpēs, ĕdis, *adj*, three-footed
trĭplex, īcis, *adj*, triple
trĭplĭco, *v.t.* 1, to treble
trĭpūdĭum, ii, *n*, religious dance, favourable omen
trĭpūs, ōdis, *m*, tripod
trĭquĕtrus, a, um, *adj*, triangular
trĭrēmis, e, *adj*, with three banks of oars
tristis, e, *adj*, sad, gloomy, harsh, disagreeable
tristĭtĭa, ae, *f*, sadness, gloominess, harshness
trĭsulcus, a, um, *adj*, three-forked
trĭtĭcĕus, a, um, *adj*, of wheat
trĭtĭcum, i, *n*, wheat
trĭtūra, ae, *f*, threshing (of grain)
trītus, a, um, *adj*, beaten, common, worn, familiar
trĭumphālis, e, *adj*, triumphal
trĭumpho, *v.i.t.* 1, to celebrate a triumph; triumph over
trĭumphus, i, *m*, triumphal procession after a victory
trĭumvĭrātus, ūs, *m*, triumvirate
trĭumvĭri, ōrum, *m. pl*, board of three men
trĭvĭum, ii, *n*, cross-road
trŏchaeus, i, *m*, metrical foot
trochlĕa, ae, *f*, pulley
trŏchus, i, *m*, hoop
trŏpaeum, i, *n*, trophy, victory
trŏpĭcus, a, um, *adj*, tropical
trŭcĭdātĭo, ōnis, *f*, butchery
trŭcīdo, *v.t.* 1, to slaughter
trŭcŭlentus, a, um, *adj*, harsh
trŭdis, is, *f*, pole, pike
trūdo, si, sum, *v.t.* 3, to push, drive, put out
trulla, ae, *f*, ladle
truncātus, a, um, *adj*, maimed

trunco, *v.t.* 1, to maim, cut off
truncus, a, um, *adj*, maimed
truncus, i, *m*, trunk, stem
trūtīna, ae, *f*, pair of scales
trux, ŭcis, *adj*, harsh, stern
tū, *pron*, you (singular)
tŭba, ae, *f*, trumpet
tŭber, ĕris, *n*, swelling, tumour
tŭbĭcen, ĭnis, *m*, trumpeter
tŭbŭlātus, a, um, *adj*, tubular
tŭbŭlus, i, *m*, tube
tŭĕor, *v.t.* 2, *dep*, to look at, gaze at,
 consider, guard, maintain, support
tŭgŭrĭum, ii, *n*, cottage
tŭli, see fero
tum, *adv, and conj*, then
tŭmēfăcio, fēci, factum, *v.t.* 3, to
 cause to swell
tŭmĕo, *v.i.* 2, to swell, be puffed up
tŭmesco, mui, *v.i.* 3, to become
 swollen, be puffed up
tŭmĭdus, a, um, *adj*, swollen, excited,
 enraged
tŭmor, ōris, *m*, swelling, commotion
tŭmŭlo, *v.t.* 1, to bury
tŭmultŭārĭus, a, um, *adj*, hurried,
 hurriedly raised (troops)
tŭmultŭor, *v.i.* 1, *dep*, to be confused
tŭmultŭōsus, a, um, *adj*, *adv*, ē,
 restless, confused, turbulent
tŭmultus, ūs, *m*, uproar, tempest,
 rebellion
tŭmŭlus, i, *m*, hill, mound
tuno, *adv*, then
tundo, tŭtŭdi, tunsum (tusum), *v.t.* 3,
 to beat, strike, pound
tŭnĭca, ae, *f*, tunic, husk
tŭnĭcātus, a, um, *adj*, dressed in a
 tunic
tŭnĭcopallĭum, i, *n*, short cloak
tūrārĭus, ii, *m*, a dealer
turba, ae, *f*, hubbub, uproar, crowd,
 band, quarrel, confusion
turbātor, ōris, *m*, disturber
turbātus, a, um, *adj*, disturbed
turbĭdus, a, um, *adj*, *adv*, ē, confused,
 troubled, violent
turbo, *v.t.* 1, to confuse, disturb,
 make thick
turbo, ĭnis, *m*, hurricane, spinning-
 top, revolution
turbŭlentus, a, um, *adj*, *adv*, ē, nter,
 restless, boisterous, troublesome
turdus, i, *m*, thrush
tūrĕus, a, um, *adj*, of incense
turgĕo, rsi, *v.i.* 2, to swell
turgesco, *v.i.* 3, to swell up
turgĭdŭlus, a, um, *adj*, swollen
turgĭdus, a, um, *adj*, swollen
tūrībŭlum, i, *n*, incense-vessel

tūrĭcrĕmus, a, um, *adj*, for burning
 incense
tūrĭfer, ĕra, ĕrum, *adj*, incense-
 producing
turma, ae, *f*, cavalry-troop, crowd
turmālis, e, *adj*, of a squadron
turmātim, *adv*, by squadrons
turpis, e, *adj*, *adv*, ĭter, filthy, ugly,
 disgraceful, scandalous
turpĭtūdo, ĭnis, *f*, disgrace, baseness
turpo, *v.t.* 1, to pollute, soil
turrĭger, ĕra, ĕrum, *adj*, turreted
turris, is, *f*, tower
turrītus, a, um, *adj*, turreted
turtur, ŭris, *m*, turtle-dove
tūs, tūris, *n*, incense
tussĭo, *v.i.* 4, to cough
tussis, is, *f*, cough
tūtāmen, ĭnis, *n*, defence
tūtēla, ae, *f*, safeguard, defence,
 position of guardian, object under
 guardianship
tūtō, *adv*, safely
tūtor, ōris, *m*, guardian
tūtor, *v.t.* 1, *dep*, to guard, watch
tūtus, a, um, *adj*, safe, prudent
tŭus, a, um, *adj*, your(s)
tympănum, i, *n*, tambourine, door
 panel
tўrannĭcus, a, um, *adj*, tyrannical
tўrannis, ĭdis, *f*, despotic rule
tўrannus, i, *m*, sovereign, ruler,
 despot

U

ūber, ĕris, *n*, teat, udder, breast
ūber, ĕris, *adj*, fertile, rich
ūbertas, ātis, *f*, fertility, richness
ŭbī, *adv*, where, when, as soon as
ŭbĭcumque, *adv*, wherever
ŭbīque, *adv*, everywhere, anywhere
ŭbĭvīs, *adv*, everywhere, anywhere
ūdus, a, um, *adj*, moist, wet
ulcĕrātĭo, ōnis, *f*, ulceration
ulcĕro, *v.t.* 1, to make sore
ulcĕrōsus, a, um, *adj*, ulcerous
ulciscor, ultus, *v.t.* 3, *dep*, to avenge,
 punish, take vengeance on
ulcus, ĕris, *n*, sore, ulcer
ulex, ĭcis, *m*, furze
ūlīgĭnōsus, a, um, *adj*, moist, marshy
ūlīgo, ĭnis, *f*, moisture
ullus, a, um, *adj*, (*genit*, ullīus, *dat*,
 ulli), any
ulmĕus, a, um, *adj*, of elm
ulmus, i, *f*, elm, elm-tree
ulna, ae, *f*, elbow, arm, ell
ultĕrĭor, ĭus, *comp. adj*, beyond, on
 the farther side

For List of Abbreviations used, turn to pages 3, 4

ultĕrĭus, *comp. adv*, beyond, farther

ultĭmus, a, um, *sup. adj*, farthest, extreme, last

ultĭo, ōnis, *f*, revenge

ultor, ōris, *m*, avenger

ultrā, *adv. and prep. with acc*, beyond, past, farther, besides

ultrix, īcis, *adj*, avenging

ultrō, *adv*, on the other side, moreover, spontaneously

ŭlŭla, ae, *f*, screech-owl

ŭlŭlātus, ūs, *m*, wailing

ŭlŭlo, *v.i.t.* 1, to howl; cry out to

ulva, ae, *f*, sedge

umbella, ae, *f*, parasol

umbilĭcus, i, *m*, navel, centre, end of rod on which Roman books were rolled

umbo, ōnis, *m*, shield, knob

umbra, ae, *f*, shadow, shade, ghost, trace, shelter

umbrācŭlum, i, *n*, shady spot, school

umbrātĭlis, e, *adj*, private, retired

umbrĭfer, ĕra, ĕrum, *adj*, shady

umbro, *v.t.* 1, to shade, cover

umbrōsus, a, um, *adj*, shady

ūmecto, *v.t.* 1, to moisten

ūmĕo, *v.i.* 2, to be damp

ūmĕrus, i, *m*, shoulder, arm

ūmesco, *v.i.* 3, to grow wet

ūmĭdus, a, um, *adj*, wet, damp

ūmor, ōris, *m*, moisture, liquid

umquam, *adv*, ever

ūnā, *adv*, at the same time, in the same place, together

ūnănĭmus, a, um, *adj*, of one mind

ūnănĭmĭtas, ātis, *f*, unanimity

uncĭa, ae, *f*, a twelfth, ounce

unctĭo, ōnis, *f*, anointing

unctus, a, um, *adj*, oiled, rich, luxurious

uncus, i, *m*, hook

uncus, a, um, *adj*, hooked

unda, ae, *f*, wave, tide

undĕ, *adv*, from where, whence

undĕ . . . (with number) one from. . . . e.g. undēvĭginti (one from 20) 19

undĕcĭes, *adv*, eleven times

undĕcĭm, *indecl. adj*, eleven

undĕcĭmus, a, um, *adj*, eleventh

undēni, ae, a, *pl. adj*, eleven each

undĭquĕ, *adv*, from all sides, everywhere

undo, *v.i.* 1, to surge, undulate

undōsus, a, um, *adj*, billowy

ungo (unguo), unxi, unctum, *v.t.* 3, to besmear, oil

unguen, ĭnis, *n*, ointment

unguentārĭus, ii, *m*, perfume-seller

unguentum, i, *n*, ointment, perfume

unguis, is, *m*, finger or toe nail

ungŭla, ae, *f*, hoof, claw

unguo (3), see ungo

ūnĭcŏlor, ōris, *adj*, of one colour

ūnĭcus, a, um, *adj, adv*, ē, only, single, singular, unique

ūnĭo, ōnis, *m, f*, unity

ūnĭversĭtas, ātis, *f*, universe

ūnĭversum, i, *n*, whole world

ūnĭversus, a, um, *adj, adv*, ē, entire, all together

unquam, *adv*, ever

ūnus, a, um, *adj*, one, only

ūnusquisque, *pron*, each

ūpĭlĭo, ōnis, *m*, shepherd

urbānĭtas, ātis, *f*, city-life, elegance, courtesy, refinement

urbānus, a, um, *adj, adv*, ē, of the city, refined, elegant, courteous, humorous

urbs, urbis, *f*, city

urcĕus, i, *m*, water-jug

urgĕo, ursi, *v.t.* 2, to press, push, oppress, urge, crowd

ūrīna, ae, *f*, urine

ūrīnātor, ōris, *m*, diver

urna, ae, *f*, water-jar, urn (for voting-tablets or ashes of the dead)

ūro, ussi, ustum, *v.t.* 3, to burn, destroy by fire, scorch, nip with cold

ursa, ae, *f*, she-bear

ursus, i, *m*, bear

urtĭca, ae, *f*, nettle

ūrus, i, *m*, wild-ox

ūsĭtātus, a, um, *adj*, usual

uspĭam, *adv*, anywhere, somewhere

usquam, *adv*, anywhere

usquĕ, *adv*, all the way, all the time, as far as, until

ustor, ōris, *m*, corpse-burner

ūsūra, ae, *f*, money-lending, interest

ūsurpātĭo, ōnis, *f*, using, use

ūsurpo, *v.t.* 1, to use, practise, exercise, acquire

ūsus, ūs, *m*, using, use, practice, custom, habit, familiarity, advantage

ut (ūti), *conj,* so that, that, in order to, to; *adv*, now, as, when, as soon as, where

utcumquĕ (utcunquĕ), *adv*, in whatever way, however, whenever

ūter, tris, *m*, bottle, bag

ūter, tra, trum, *interr. pron*, which of the two

ŭtercumquĕ, utrăcumque, utrumcumque, *pron,* whichever of the two
ŭterlĭbet, utrălĭbet, utrumlĭbet, *pron,* which of the two you please
ŭterque, utrăque, utrumque, *pron,* each of the two, both
ŭtĕrus, i, *m,* womb, belly
ŭtervīs, utrăvīs, utrumvīs, *pron,* which of the two you please
ŭti, see ut
ŭti, see ūtor
ŭtĭlis, e, *adj, adv,* ĭter, useful, suitable, advantageous
ŭtĭlĭtas, ātis, *f,* usefulness, advantage
ŭtĭnam, *adv,* if only! would that!
ŭtĭquĕ, *adv,* at any rate, at least, certainly
ūtor, ūsus, *v.* 3, *dep, with abl,* to use, practise, be familiar with
utpŏtĕ, *adv,* namely, as, since
ŭtrimquĕ, *adv,* on both sides
ŭtrŏbīquĕ (ŭtrŭbīquĕ), *adv,* on both sides
ŭtrŏquĕ, *adv,* in both directions
ŭtrum, *adv, used to form an alternative question,* is it this . . . or that?
ūva, ae, *f,* grape, cluster
ūvĭdus, a, um, *adj,* moist, damp
uxor, ōris, *f,* wife
uxŏrĭus, a, um, *adj,* of a wife

V

văcans, ntis, *adj,* unoccupied
văcātio, ōnis, *f,* exemption
vacca, ae, *f,* cow
vaccĭnĭum, ii, *n,* whortleberry
văcillātio, ōnis, *f,* vacillation
văcillo, *v.i.* 1, to stagger, sway, hesitate
văco, *v.i.* 1, to be empty, free from, have leisure (for)
văcŭĕfăcĭo, fēci, factum, *v.t.* 3, to empty, clear
văcŭĭtas, ātis, *f,* exemption
văcŭus, a, um, *adj,* empty, free, without, unoccupied, worthless
vădĭmōnĭum, ii, *n,* bail, security
vādo, *v.i.* 3, to go, walk, rush
vădor, *v.t.* 1, *dep,* to bind over by bail
vădōsus, a, um, *adj,* shallow
vădum, i, *n,* a shallow, ford (*often in pl.*)
vae, *interj,* ah! alas!
văfer, fra, frum, *adj,* sly
văgātio, ōnis, *f,* wandering
vāgīna, ae, *f,* sheath; scabbard
văgĭo, *v.i.* 4, to cry, bawl
vāgītus, ūs, *m,* crying, bawling
văgor, *v.i.* 1, *dep,* to wander, roam

văgus, a, um, *adj,* wandering, roaming, uncertain, vague
valdĕ, *adv,* energetically, very much, very
văle, *imperative,* (*pl,* vălēte), farewell!
vălens, ntis, *adj,* powerful, strong, healthy
vălĕo, *v.i.* 2, to be strong, vigorous or healthy, to have power or influence, to be capable or effective, be worth
vălesco, *v.i.* 3, to grow strong
vălētūdĭnārĭum, ii, *n,* hospital
vălētūdĭnārĭus, i, *m,* invalid
vălētūdo, ĭnis, *f,* health (good or bad)
vălĭdus, a, um, *adj,* strong, powerful, healthy
valles (vallis), is, *f,* valley
vallo, *v.t.* 1, to fortify with a rampart, protect
vallum, i, *n,* rampart, palisade
vallus, i, *m,* stake, palisade
valvae, ārum, *f. pl,* folding-doors
vānesco, *v.i.* 3, to disappear
vānĭtas, ātis, *f,* emptiness, uselessness, vanity
vannus, i, *f,* fan
vānus, a, um, *adj,* empty, groundless, false, deceptive
văpĭdus, a, um, *adj,* spoiled, flat
văpor, ōris, *m,* steam, vapour
văpōro, *v.t.* 1, to fumigate, warm
vappa, ae, *f,* flat wine; *m,* a good-for-nothing
văpŭlo, *v.i.* 1, to be flogged
vārĭco, *v.i.* 1, to straddle
vārĭcōsus, a, um, *adj,* varicose
vărĭĕtas, ātis, *f,* variety
vărĭo, *v.i.t.* 1, to vary; diversify, change
vărĭus, a, um, *adj, adv,* ē, variegated, changing, varying
vărix, ĭcis, *m, f,* varicose vein
vārus, a, um, *adj,* knock-kneed
văs, vădis, *m,* bail, security
văs, vāsis, *n,* dish, utensil, military equipment
vāsārĭum, ii, *n,* expense-account
vascŭlārĭus, ii, *m,* metal-worker
vastātio, ōnis, *f,* devastation
vastātor, ōris, *m,* destroyer
vastĭtas, ātis, *f,* desert, destruction, ruin
vasto, *v.t.* 1, to devastate, destroy, leave vacant
vastus, a, um, *adj,* deserted, desolate, rough, devastated, enormous, vast
vātes, is, *c,* forecaster, poet
vātĭcĭnātĭo, ōnis, *f,* prediction
vātĭcĭnātor, ōris, *m,* prophet

vāticĭnor, *v.i.t.* 1, *dep*, to predict
vātĭus, a, um, *adj*, bow-legged
vě, *conj*, or
vēcordĭa, ae, *f*, folly, madness
vēcors, dis, *adj*, foolish, mad
vectĭgal, ālis, *n*, tax, income
vectĭgālis, e, *adj*, tax-paying
vectis, is, *m*, pole, bar, lever
vecto, *v.t.* 1, to convey
vector, ōris, *m*, carrier, traveller, passenger
vectōrĭus, a, um, *adj*, for carrying
vectūra, ae, *f*, transportation, fare
vectus, a, um, *adj*, conveyed, carried
vĕgĕtus, a, um, *adj*, lively
vēgrandis, e, *adj*, small
vĕhĕmens, ntis, *adj*, *adv*, nter, violent, powerful, strong
vĕhĭcŭlum, i, *n*, vehicle
vĕho, xi, ctum, *v.t.* 3, to convey; *in passive, or with reflexive pron,* to ride, sail, go
vĕl, *conj*, either, or, indeed
vēlāmen, ĭnis, *n*, cover, garment
vēlāmentum, i, *n*, olive-branch
vēles, ĭtis, *m*, light-armed soldier
vēlĭfer, ĕra, ĕrum, *adj*, carrying sails
vēlĭfĭcātĭo, ōnis, *f*, sailing
vēlĭfĭcor, *v.i.* 1, *dep*, to sail, gain, procure
vēlĭvŏlus, a, um, *adj*, sail-winged; (mare) dotted with ships
vellĭco, *v.t.* 1, to nip, taunt
vello, vulsi, vulsum, *v.t.* 3, to tear out, pluck off
vellus, ĕris, *n*, fleece, hide
vēlo, *v.t.* 1, to cover, wrap up
vēlōcĭtas, ātis, *f*, speed
vēlox, ōcis, *adj*, *adv*, iter, swift, fast, fleet
vēlum, i, *n*, sail, covering
vēlut, *adv*, just as, like
vēna, ae, *f*, vein, disposition
vēnābŭlum, i, *n*, hunting-spear
vēnālĭcĭum, ii, *n*, slave-dealing
vēnālĭcĭus, ii, *m*, slave-dealer
vēnālis, e, *adj*, for sale, able to be bribed, corrupt
vēnālis, is, *m*, slave for sale
vēnātĭcus, a, um, *adj*, of hunting
vēnātĭo, ōnis, *f*, hunting, a hunt, combat of wild beasts
vēnātor, ōris, *m*, hunter
vēnātrix, īcis, *f*, huntress
vēnātus, ūs, *m*, hunting
vendĭbĭlis, e, *adj*, saleable
vendĭtātĭo, ōnis, *f*, boasting
vendĭtĭo, ōnis, *f*, sale
vendĭto, *v.t.* 1, to try to sell
vendĭtor, ōris, *m*, salesman

vendo, dĭdi, dĭtum, *v.t.* 3, to sell, betray, praise
vēnēfĭca, ae, *f*, witch
vēnēfĭcĭum, ii, *n*, poisoning, magic
vēnēfĭcus, a, um, *adj*, poisonous, magic
vēnēfĭcus, i, *m*, poisoner, sorcerer
vēnēnātus, a, um, *adj*, poisonous
vēnēnĭfer, ĕra, ĕrum, *adj*, poisonous
vēnēno, *v.t.* 1, to poison, dye
vēnēnum, i, *n*, poison, magic charm, drug
vēnĕo, ii, ītum, *v.i.* 4, to be sold
vĕnĕrābĭlis, e, *adj*, worthy of respect
vĕnĕrābundus, a, um, *adj*, devout
vĕnĕrātĭo, ōnis, *f*, great respect
vĕnĕrĕus, a, um, *adj*, venereal
vĕnĕror, *v.t.* 1, *dep*, to worship, revere, honour, entreat
vĕnĭa, ae, *f*, indulgence, mercy, permission, pardon
vĕnĭo, vēni, ventum, *v.i.* 4, to come
vēnor, *v.i.t.* 1, *dep*, to hunt
venter, tris, *m*, belly
ventĭlo, *v.t.* 1, to wave, fan
ventĭto, *v.i.* 1, to keep coming
ventōsus, a, um, *adj*, windy, swift, light, changeable, vain
ventrĭcŭlus, i, *m*, ventricle
ventūrus, *fut. partic.* from **vĕnĭo**
ventus, i, *m*, wind
vēnŭcŭla (uva), a preserving grape
vēnundo, dĕdi, dătum, *v.t.* 1, to sell
vĕnus, ĕris, *f*, love, beauty, highest throw of the dice
vēnus, ūs, *m*, (**vēnum, i,** *n*), sale
vĕnustas, ātis, *f*, charm, beauty
vĕnustus, a, um, *adj*, *adv*, ē, charming, graceful, beautiful
vĕprēcŭla, ae, *f*, small thorn-bush
vĕpres, is, *m*, thorn-bush
vēr, vēris, *n*, spring
vēra, see **vērus**
vērācĭtas, ātis, *f*, veracity
vērax, ācis, *adj*, true
verbēna, ae, *f*, foliage, branches
verber, ĕris, *n*, lash, whip, flogging, blow
verbĕrātĭo, ōnis, *f*, punishment
verbĕro, *v.t.* 1, to whip, strike
verbōsus, a, um, *adj*, effusive
verbum, i, *n*, word, language, conversation; **verba dare** to deceive
vērē, *adv*, really, truly
vĕrēcundĭa, ae, *f*, shyness
vĕrēcundor, *v.i.* 1, *dep*, to be shy
vĕrēcundus, a, um, *adj*, *adv*, ē, shy, modest
vĕrendus, a, um, *adj*, venerable, terrible

vĕrĕor, *v.i.t.* 2, *dep*, to fear, respect
vergo, *v.i.* 3, to turn, bend, lie, be situated
vĕridĭcus, **a**, **um**, *adj*, truthful
vĕrisimilis, **e**, *adj*, probable
vĕritas, **ātis**, *f*, truth, reality
vermĭcŭlus, **i**, *m*, worm, grub
verminōsus, **a**, **um**, *adj*, worm-eaten
vermis, **is**, *m*, worm
verna, **ae**, *c*, slave born in his master's house
vernācŭlus, **a**, **um**, *adj*, domestic
vernĭliter, *adv*, slavishly
verno, *v.i.* 1, to flourish, bloom
vernus, **a**, **um**, *adj*, of spring
vĕrō, *adv*, in fact, certainly, but indeed, however
verres, **is**, *m*, pig
verro, **verri**, **versum**, *v.t.* 3, to sweep, brush, impel, take away
verrūca, **ae**, *f*, wart, blemish
vorsūtilis, **e**, *adj*, movable
versĭcŏlor, **ōris**, *adj*, of different colours
versĭcŭlus, **i**, *m*, single line of verse (or prose)
verso, *v.t.* 1, to turn, twist, whirl, consider
versor, *v.i.* 1, *dep*, to live, stay, be situated, be engaged on
versūra, **ae**, *f*, borrowing, loan
versus, *adv*, towards
versus, **ūs**, *m*, row, line, verse
versūtus, **a**, **um**, *adj*, *adv*, **ē**, clever, shrewd, cunning, sly
vertĕbra, **ae**, *f*, vertebra
vertex, **ĭcis**, *m*, whirlpool, whirlwind, flame, crown of the head, summit, peak
vertĭcōsus, **a**, **um**, *adj*, eddying
vertĭgĭnōsus, **a**, **um**, *adj*, suffering from giddiness
vertĭgo, **ĭnis**, *f*, dizziness
vĕro, see **vĕrus**
verto, **ti**, **sum**, *v.i.t.* 3, to turn, change; turn, change, alter, overthrow, translate
vĕru, **ūs**, *n*, roasting-spit, javelin
vĕrūcŭlum, **i**, *n*, skewer, small javelin
vĕrum, *adv*, but, yet, still
vērum, **i**, *n*, truth, reality, fact
vērumtămen, *conj*, nevertheless
vērus, **a**, **um**, *adj*, *adv*, **ō**, **ē**, true, real, proper, right
vĕrūtum, **i**, *n*, javelin
vĕrūtus, **a**, **um**, *adj*, armed with a javelin
vervex, **ēcis**, *m*, wether, sheep
vēsānĭa, **ae**, *f*, insanity

vēsānus, **a**, **um**, *adj*, mad, fierce
vescor, *v.i.t.* 3, *dep. with abl*, to feed on
vescus, **a**, **um**, *adj*, thin, weak
vēsīca, **ae**, *f*, bladder
vespa, **ae**, *f*, wasp
vesper, **ĕris** (**ĕri**), *m*, evening, the West
vespĕra, **ae**, *f*, evening, the West
vespĕrasco, **āvi**, *v.i.* 3, to draw towards evening
vespertīnus, **a**, **um**, *adj*, of evening, western
vespillo, **ōnis**, *m*, undertaker
vesta, **ae**, *f*, fire
vestālis, **e**, *adj*, of Vesta, the Goddess of Fire, Hearth, Home
vestālis, **is**, *f*, priestess of Vesta
vester, **tra**, **trum**, *adj*, your
vestĭārĭum, **ii**, *n*, wardrobe
vestĭbŭlum, **i**, *n*, entrance-hall
vestīgĭum, **ii**, *n*, footstep, track, sole of foot, mark, moment, instant; **ē** **vestigĭo**, instantly
vestīgo, *v.t.* 1, to search out, investigate
vestĭmentum, **i**, *n*, clothing
vestĭo, *v.t.* 4, to clothe, cover
vestis, **is**, *f*, clothing, clothes, carpet, curtain
vestītus, **ūs**, *m*, clothes, dress
vĕtĕrānus, **a**, **um**, *adj*, old, veteran
vĕtĕrānus, **i**, *m*, veteran soldier
vĕtĕrātor, **ōris**, *m*, crafty, wily or sly person
vĕtĕrātōrĭus, **a**, **um**, *adj*, sly
vĕtĕres, **um**, *m. pl*, ancestors
vĕtĕrīnārĭus, **a**, **um**, *adj*, veterinary
vĕternus, **i**, *m*, sluggishness
vĕtĭtum, **i**, *n*, something forbidden, prohibition
vĕtĭtus, **a**, **um**, *adj*, forbidden
vĕto, **ŭi**, **ĭtum**, *v.t.* 1, to forbid
vŏtŭlus, **a**, **um**, *adj*, old
vĕtus, **ĕris**, *adj*, old, former
vĕtustas, **ātis**, *f*, old age, antiquity, posterity
vĕtustus, **a**, **um**, *adj*, old
vexātĭo, **ōnis**, *f*, distress
vexillārĭus, **ii**, *m*, standard-bearer
vexillum, **ii**, *n*, standard, ensign
vexo, *v.t.* 1, to shake, injure, molest, harass, torment
vĭa, **ae**, *f*, road, street, way, method
vĭātĭcum, **i**, *n*, travelling-expenses, soldier's savings
vĭātor, **ōris**, *m*, traveller
vĭbex, **ĭcis**, *f*, weal
vĭbro, *v.i.t.* 1, to quiver; brandish, shake
vĭcārĭus, **ii**, *m*, deputy

For List of Abbreviations used, turn to pages 3, 4

vīcēni, ae, a, *pl. adj,* twenty each
vīcēsĭmus (vĭcensĭmus), a, um, *adj,* twentieth
vicia, ae, *f,* vetch
vĭcies (vĭciens), *adv,* twenty times
vīcīnia, ae, *f,* neighbourhood
vīcīnĭtas, ātis, *f,* proximity, neighbourhood
vīcīnus, a, um, *adj,* neighbouring, similar
vīcīnus, i, *m,* neighbour
vĭcis (*genitive*), **vĭcem, vĭce,** change, alternation, recompense, lot, misfortune, position, duty; **in vĭcem, per vĭces,** alternately; **vĭcem, vĭce,** instead of
vĭcissim, *adv,* in turn
vĭcissĭtūdo, ĭnis, *f,* change
victĭma, ae, *f,* victim for sacrifice
victor, ōris, *m,* conqueror
victōria, ae, *f,* victory
victrix, īcis, *f,* female conqueror
victrix, īcis, *adj,* victorious
victus, ūs, *m,* nutriment, diet
vīcus, i, *m,* street, village
vidēlicet, *adv,* obviously
vĭdĕo, vĭdi, vīsum, *v.t.* 2, to see, perceive, understand, consider, take care, see to it
vĭdĕor, vīsus, *v.* 2, *dep,* to seem; *impers,* it seems right or good
vĭdŭa, ae, *f,* widow
vĭdŭĭtas, ātis, *f,* bereavement
vĭdŭlus, i, *m,* valise
vĭdŭo, *v.t.* 1, to deprive
vĭdŭus, a, um, *adj,* robbed, widowed
vĭētus, a, um, *adj,* withered
vĭgĕo, *v.i.* 2, to flourish, thrive
vĭgesco, gŭi, *v.i.* 3, to flourish, thrive
vĭgil, ĭlis, *adj,* alert, watching
vĭgil, ĭlis, *m,* watchman
vĭgĭlans, ntis, *adj, adv,* **nter,** watchful, careful
vĭgĭlantĭa, ae, *f,* watchfulness
vĭgĭlĭa, ae, *f,* wakefulness, vigilance, guard, watch
vĭgĭlo, *v.i.t.* 1, to keep awake, be vigilant; spend (time) in watching
vīgintī, *indecl. adj,* twenty
vĭgor, ōris, *m,* liveliness
vīlĭco, *v.i.t.* 1, to superintend
vīlĭcus (villĭcus), i, *m,* superintendent
vīlis, e, *adj,* cheap, mean
vīlĭtas, ātis, *f,* cheapness
villa, ae, *f,* country-house
villātĭcus, a, um, *adj,* of a villa
villĭcus see vīlĭcus
villōsus, a, um, *adj,* hairy, shaggy

villŭla, ae, *f,* small villa
villus, i, *m,* tuft of hair
vīmen, ĭnis, *n,* pliant branch
Vīmĭnālis (collis), the Viminal, one of the seven hills of Rome
vīmĭnĕus, a, um, *adj,* of wickerwork
vīnārĭum, ii, *n,* wine-bottle
vīnārĭus, a, um, *adj,* of wine
vīnārĭus, i, *m,* vintner
vincĭo, nxi, nctum, *v.t.* 4, to bind, tie, surround
vinco, vīci, victum, *v.i.t.* 3, to prevail; conquer, overcome, prove conclusively
vincŭlum (vinclum), i, n, cord, bond, fetter; *pl,* prison
vindēmĭa, ae, *f,* grape-gathering, wine
vindēmĭātor, ōris, *m,* grape-gatherer
vindex, ĭcis, c, claimant, defender, liberator, avenger
vindĭcĭae, ārum, f. pl, legal claim
vindĭco, *v.t.* 1, to claim, appropriate, set free, protect, avenge
vindicta, ae, *f,* rod used to set free a slave
vīnĕa, ae, *f,* vineyard, protective shed for soldiers
vīnētum, i, *n,* vineyard
vīnĭtor, ōris, *m,* vine-pruner
vīnŏlentĭa, ae, *f,* wine-drinking
vīnŏlentus, a, um, *adj,* drunk
vīnōsus, a, um, *adj,* drunken
vīnum, i, *n,* wine
vĭŏla, ae, *f,* violet
vĭŏlābĭlis, e, *adj,* able to be injured or harmed
vĭŏlārĭum, ii, *n,* bed of violets
vĭŏlātĭo, ōnis, *f,* violation, profanation
vĭŏlātor, ōris, *m,* injurer
vĭŏlens, ntis, *adj, adv,* **nter,** impetuous, furious
vĭŏlentĭa, ae, *f,* ferocity
vĭŏlentus, a, um, *adj,* violent, impetuous
vĭŏlo, *v.t.* 1, to injure, outrage, break
vīpĕra, ae, *f,* viper
vīpĕrĕus, a, um, *adj,* of a viper or snake
vīpĕrīnus, a, um, *adj,* of a viper or snake
vir, vĭri, *m,* man, husband
vĭrāgo, ĭnis, *f,* female soldier, heroine
vĭrectum, i, *n,* glade, turf
vĭrĕo, *v.i.* 2, to be green, flourish
vīres, see vis
vĭresco, *v.i.* 3, to become green, flourish
vĭrētum, i, *n,* glade, turf

virga, ae, f, twig, rod
virgātus, a, um, adj, striped
virgĕus, a, um, adj, made of rods
virginālis, e, adj, girl-like
virginĕus, a, um, adj, of a virgin
virginĭtas, ātis, f, virginity
virgo, ĭnis, f, virgin, girl
virgŭla, ae, f, small twig
virgultum, i, n, shrubbery
virgultus, a, um, adj, bushy
virĭdārĭum, ii, n, park
virĭdis, e, adj, green, fresh, young, blooming
virĭdĭtas, ātis, f, greenness, freshness
virĭdo, v.i.t. 1, to be green; make green
virīlis, e, adj, male, manly, full-grown, vigorous
virĭtim, adv, individually
virōsus, a, um, adj, stinking
virtūs, ūtis, f, courage, manhood, military skill, goodness, moral perfection
vīrus, i, n, slime, poison, virus
vīs, (no genit), vim, vi, f, force, power, violence, quantity, meaning; vires, ĭum, pl, strength, power
viscātus, a, um, adj, sprinkled with lime
viscĕra, um, n, pl, inwards, flesh, bowels
viscum, i, n, mistletoe, birdlime
vīsĭo, ōnis, f, idea, notion
vīsĭto, v.t. 1, to visit
vīso, si, sum, v.t. 3, to survey, visit
vīsum, i, n, appearance, sight
vīsus, ūs, m, look, sight, appearance
vīta, ae, f, life
vītābĭlis, e, adj, to be avoided
vītālis, e, adj, of life, vital
vītātĭo, ōnis, f, avoidance
vītellus, i, m, small calf, egg-yolk
vītĕus, a, um, adj, of the vine
vĭtĭo, v.t. 1, to spoil, mar, infect
vĭtĭōsĭtas, ātis, f, vice
vĭtĭōsus, a, um, adj, adv, ē, faulty, defective, wicked
vītis, is, f, vine, vine-branch
vītĭsātor, ōris, m, vine-planter
vĭtĭum, ii, n, fault, defect, blemish, error, crime
vīto, v.t. 1, to avoid
vĭtrĕus, a, um, adj, made of glass, transparent, shining
vĭtrĭcus, i, m, step-father
vĭtrum, i, n, glass, woad
vitta, ae, f, hair-ribbon
vittātus, a, um, adj, bound with a hair-ribbon
vĭtŭlīnus, a, um, adj, of a calf

vĭtŭlus, i, m (vĭtŭla, ae, f), calf
vĭtŭpĕrātĭo, ōnis, f, blame, censure
vĭtŭpĕro, v.t. 1, to blame, censure
vīvārĭum, ii, n, fish-pond, game-reserve
vīvācĭtas, ātis, f, vigour or length of life
vīvax, ācis, adj, long-lived
vīvidus, a, um, adj, lively, animated
vīvo, xi, ctum, v.i. 3, to live
vīvus, a, um, adj, alive, fresh, natural, life-like
vix, adv, scarcely, barely
vixdum, adv, scarcely then
vŏcābŭlum, i, n, name
vōcālis, e, adj, vocal
vŏcātu, abl, at the bidding
vōcĭfĕrātĭo, ōnis, f, outcry
vōcĭfĕror, v.i.t. 1, dep, to cry out
vŏcĭto, v.i.t. 1, to call out; name
vŏco, v.i.t. 1, to call; summon, urge, challenge, arouse, name
vōcŭla, ae, f, feeble voice
vŏlantes, ĭum, c, pl, birds
vŏlātĭcus, a, um, adj, flighty, fleeting
vŏlătĭlis, e, adj, flying, swift
vŏlātus, ūs, m, flight
vŏlens, ntis, adj, willing, favourable
volg . . . see vulg. . . .
vŏlĭto, v.i. 1, to fly about, flit, flutter
vŏlo, velle, vŏlŭi, v.i.t. (irreg), to wish, mean
vŏlo, v.i. 1, to fly
volp . . . see vulp. . . .
volsella, ae, f, tweezers
volt, see vult. . . .
vŏlūbĭlis, e, adj, turning, spinning, changeable
vŏlūbĭlĭtas, ātis, f, whirling motion, fluency
vŏlŭcer, cris, cre, adj, flying, swift, transient
vŏlūmen, ĭnis, n, book, roll, fold
vŏluntārĭus, a, um, adj, voluntary; (of soldiers) volunteers
vŏluntas, ātis, f, wish, choice, will, affection, good-will
vŏluptārĭus, a, um, adj, sensual
vŏluptas, ātis, f, pleasure, delight
vŏlūto, v.i.t. 1, to roll, twist, writhe about; ponder, consider
volva (vulva), ae, f, womb
volvo, volvi, vŏlūtum, v.t. 3, to roll, unroll, turn, ponder, consider
vōmer, ĕris, m, ploughshare
vŏmĭca, ae, f, abscess, boil
vŏmĭtĭo, ōnis, f, vomiting
vŏmo, ŭi, ĭtum, v.i.t. 3, to vomit; throw up, pour out
vŏrāgo, ĭnis, f, abyss, whirlpool

vŏrax, ācis, *adj*, greedy, destructive
vŏro, *v.t.* 1, to devour, destroy
vortex, see vertex
vos, *pron*, you (*plural*)
vōtīvus, a, um, *adj*, concerning a promise or vow
vōtum, i, *n*, promise, vow, offering, wish, longing
vŏvĕo, vōvi, vōtum, *v.t.* 2, to promise, vow, dedicate
vox, vōcis, *f*, voice, sound, speech, saying, proverb
vulgāris, e, *adj*, general, ordinary, common
vulgātor, ōris, *m*, a gossip
vulgātus, a, um, *adj*, ordinary, notorious
vulgo, *v.t.* 1, to divulge, spread about
vulgō, *adv*, everywhere, openly
vulgus, i, *n*, the public, crowd, rabble
vulnĕrātus, a, um, *adj*, wounded

vulhĕro, *v.t.* 1, to wound, hurt
vulnīfĭcus, a, um, *adj*, wounding
vulnus, ĕris, *n*, wound, blow
vulpēcŭla, ae, *f*, small fox
vulpes, is, *f*, fox
vulsus, a, um, *adj*, hairless, effeminate
vultur, ŭris, *m*, vulture
vultŭrius, ii, *m*, vulture
vultus, ūs, *m*, expression, look, features, aspect, face

X

xĭphĭas, ae, *m*, sword-fish
xystus, i, *m* (xystum, i, *n*), open colonnade

Z

zĕphy̆rus, i, *m*, west wind
zōdĭăcus, i, *m*, zodiac
zōna, ae, *f*, belt, girdle, zone

PROPER NAMES

For List of Abbreviations used, turn to pages 3, 4

A

Acădēmĭa, ae, *f,* the Academy, a gymnasium near Athens where Plato taught

Acādēmus, i, *m,* a Greek hero

Acestes, ae, *m,* a king of Sicily

Achaemĕnes, is, *m,* a king of Persia

Achāĭa, ae, *f,* a Roman province in the northern part of the Peloponessus

Achātes, ae, *m,* 1, a river in Sicily; 2, a friend of Aeneas

Achĕron, ntis, *m,* 1, a river in Epirus; 2, a river in the Lower World

Achilles, is, *m,* the Greek hero, son of Peleus and Thetis

Achīvus, a, um, *adj,* Achaean, Greek

Acrŏcĕraunia, ōrum, *n.pl,* a rocky headland in Epirus

Actē, es, *f,* an old name of Attica

Actĭum, ĭi, *n,* a town in Epirus

Adherbal, ălis, *m,* a Numidian prince

Adōnis, is, *m,* a beautiful youth, beloved of Venus

Aduātūci, ōrum, *m, pl,* a Gallic tribe

Aeācus, i, *m,* a king of Aegina who became a judge in the Lower World

Aedŭi, ōrum, *m. pl,* a Gallic tribe

Aeētēs, ae, *m,* a king of Colchis, father of Medea

Aegaeum mare, *n,* the Aegean Sea

Aegātes, um, *f. pl,* three islands off the west coast of Sicily

Aegeus, i, *m,* a king of Athens, father of Theseus

Aegīna, ae, *f,* an island near Athens

Aegyptus, i, *f,* Egypt

Aemilius, a, um, *adj,* the name of a Roman patrician "gens"

Aenēas, ae, *m,* the hero of Vergil's Aeneid, son of Venus and Anchises

Aeŏlus, i, *m,* the god of the winds

Aequi, ōrum, *m.pl,* an Italian people

Aeschўlus, i, *m,* the Athenian tragic poet

Aesōpus, i, *m,* the Greek writer of fables (sixth century B.C.)

Aethĭŏpia, ae, *f,* Ethiopia

Aethĭŏpissa, ae, *f,* Ethiopian, negress

Aethiops, ŏpis, *m,* Ethiopian, negro

Aetna, ae, *f,* Etna, the volcano in Sicily

Afer, fra, frum, *adj,* African

Africa, ae, *f,* Africa

Africus, i, *m,* the south-west wind

Agămemnon, ŏnis, *m,* a king of Mycenae

Agāthoclēs, is, *m,* a king of Sicily

Agēnor, ŏris, *m,* king of Phoenicia

Agēsilāus, i, *m,* a king of Sparta

Aglāia, ae, *f,* one of the Graces

Agricŏla, ae, *m,* (A.D. 37–93) governor of Britain, father-in-law of Tacitus

Agrĭgentum, i, *n,* a city on the south coast of Sicily

Agrippa, ae, *m,* a Roman family name; Marcus Vipsanius A., the friend of Augustus

Agrippīna, ae, *f,* mother of Nero

Ahēnōbarbus, i, *m,* the name of a Roman family ("red-beard")

Ajax, ācis, *m,* the name of a Greek hero

Alba Longa, *f,* the founder city of Rome

Alcaeus, i, *m,* the Greek lyric poet (c. 600 B.C.)

Alcestis, is, *f,* the wife of Admetus, whose life she saved by her own death

Alceus, ĕi, *m,* grandfather of Hercules

Alcibiădes, is, *m,* an Athenian general

Alcmēne, es, *f,* the mother of Hercules by Juppiter

Alecto (Allecto),us, *f,* one of the three Furies

Alēmanni, ōrum, *m. pl,* a German tribe

Alexander, dri, *m* (the Great: 356–323 B.C.), king of Macedonia

Alexandria, ae, *f,* a city on the coast of Egypt

Allia, ae, *f,* a small river north of Rome

Allōbrŏges, um, *m. pl,* a Gallic tribe

Alpēs, ium, *f. pl,* the Alps

Amăryllis, ĭdis, *f,* a shepherdess

Amastris, is, *f,* a town in Paphlagonia

Amāzon, ŏnis, *f,* an Amazon; (pl.) a race of warlike women

Ambiŏrix, rīgis, *m,* a chief of the Eburones

131

Ammōn, ōnis, *m*, a name of Juppiter

Amphiārāus, i, *m*, a famous Greek prophet

Amphīōn, ōnis, *m*, a king of Thebes

Amphītrŭo, ōnis, *m*, a king of Thebes

Amūlius, i, *m*, a king of Alba Longa

Ănăcrĕōn, ontis, *m*, a Greek lyric poet

Anchīses, ae, *m*, the father of Aeneas

Ancus Martius, i, *m*, the fourth king of Rome (640–616 B.C.)

Andrŏmăchē, es, *f*, wife of Hector

Andrŏmĕda, ae, *f*, daughter of Cepheus, rescued from a sea-monster by Perseus became a star

Andrŏnicus, i, *m*, L. Livius A., the first Roman poet

Andros, i, *f*, one of the Cyclades Islands

Angli, ōrum, *m. pl*, a German tribe

Antĭgŏnē, es, *f*, daughter of Oedipus

Antiŏchīa, ae, *f*, Antioch

Antiŏchus, i, *m*, a king of Syria

Antīpăter, tri, *m*, 1, one of Alexander's generals; 2, L. Caelius A. a Roman annalist

Antōnīnus, i, *m*, the name of two Roman emperors

Antōnius, a, um, *adj*, the name of a Roman "gens": Marcus Antonius, the triumvir, opponent of Octavianus

Ănūbis, bis, *m*, an Egyptian god

Anxur, ŭris, *n*, an ancient Volscian town

Äornos, i, *m*, ("birdless"), Lake Avernus

Ăpennīnus, i, *m*, the Apennine Mts.

Apis, is, *m*, the ox worshipped as a god by the Egyptians

Ăpollo, ĭnis, *m*, Apollo, the sun god, also the god of archery, music and poetry

Ăpollōnius Rhŏdius, ii, *m*, a Greek poet

Appius, ii, *m*, a Roman praenomen; Appia Via, *f*, the Appian Way from Rome to Capua, begun by Appius Claudius, the censor (312 B.C.)

Apūlia, ae, *f*, a region of south Italy

Ăquilēia, ae, *f*, a town of north Italy

Ăquilo, ōnis, *m*, the north wind

Ăquinum, i, *n*, a town in Latium

Ăquitānia, ae, *f*, a province in south-west Gaul

Ărăbia, ae, *f*, Arabia

Ărabs, ăbis, *adj*, Arabian

Ărar, ăris, *m*, a river in Gaul

Arcădia, ae, *f*, a region of the Peloponnesus

Arcas, ădis, *m*, an Arcadian

Archilŏchus, i, *m*, a Greek poet

Archimēdēs, is, *m*, a famous mathematician -

Ardĕa, ae, *f*, a town in Latium

Ardŭenna, ae, *f*, the Ardennes

Ărĕŏpăgus, i, *m*, Ares' hill at Athens, seat of the supreme court

Ărēs, is, *m*, the Greek war god

Argīlētum, i, *n*, a district of Rome

Argō, us, *f*, the ship in which Jason sailed to recover the Golden Fleece

Argōlis, ĭdis, *f*, a district of the Peloponnesus

Argos, *n*, the capital of Argolis

Ăriadne, es, *f*, daughter of Minos, king of Crete, who helped Theseus to kill the Minotaur

Ărīcia, ae, *f*, an old town in Latium

Ărīminum, i, *n*, a town in Umbria

Ărīon, ŏnis, *m*, a famous poet who was saved from drowning by a dolphin

Ăriŏvistus, i, *m*, a German chieftain

Ăristŏphănēs, is, *m*, a Greek comic poet

Ăristŏtĕles, is, *m*, the famous Greek philosopher

Armĕnia, ae, *f*, a country in Asia

Armīnius, i, *m*, a German prince

Armŏricae, ārum, *f. pl*, states in north-west Gaul

Arnus, i, *m*, a river of Etruria

Arpīnum, i, *n*, a town in Latium

Artaxăta, ōrum, *n.pl*, capital of Armenia

Artaxerxēs, is, *m*, name of four Persian kings

Arverni, ōrum, *m. pl*, a Gallic tribe

Ascănius, i, *m*, the son of Aeneas

Ăsia, ae, *f*, Asia

Assărăcus, i, *m*, a king of Troy

Assўria, ae, *f*, a country of Asia

Ătălanta, ae, *f*, a Boeotian girl famous for the speed of her running

Ăthēnae, ārum, *f. pl*, Athens

Ăthos, *m*, a mountain in Macedonia

Ătīlius, a, um, *adj*, the name of a Roman "gens"

Atlas, antis, *m*, a mountain in Africa

Ătrĕbătes, um, *m. pl*, a Gallic tribe

Ătreus, ei, *m*. the son of Pelops

Attălus, i, *m*. the name of several kings of Pergamum

Attica, ae, *f*, the region around Athens

Atticus, a, um, *adj*, Athenian, Attic

Atўs, yos, *m*, the son of Hercules

Augustus, i, *m*, surname of Octavius, and all Roman emperors

Aulis, ĭdis, *f*, a port in Boeotia

Avārĭcum, i, *n,* a Gallic town
Āventīnus, i, *m,* one of the seven hills of Rome
Āvernus lacus, i, *m,* a lake near Cumae
Axĭus, ii, *m,* a river in Macedonia

B

Băbўlŏn, ōnis, *f,* Babylon
Baccha, ae, *f,* a female worshipper of Bacchus
Bacchus, i, *m,* the god of wine
Bāiae, ārum, *f. pl,* a town and Roman holiday-resort on the Campanian coast
Bălĕāres insulae, *f. pl,* the Balearic Islands (Majorca)
Barcas, ae, *m,* the founder of the famous Carthaginian family to which Hannibal belonged
Bătāvi, ōrum, *m. pl,* a tribe inhabiting what is now Holland
Belgae, ārum, *m. pl,* a tribe inhabiting northern Gaul
Bellĕrŏphon, ontis, *m,* the rider of Pegasus who went to kill the Chimaera
Bellōna, ae, *f,* the goddess of War
Bĕnĕventum, i, *n,* a town in Samnium
Bibractĕ, is, *n,* capital of the Gallic tribe, the Aedui
Bīthȳnĭa, ae, *f,* a country in Asia Minor
Bitŭrĭges, um, *m. pl,* a tribe of Aquitania
Boadĭcēa (or Boudicca), ae, *f,* a queen of the Iceni
Bocchus, i, *m,* a king of Mauritania
Boeōtĭa, ae, *f,* a district in northern Greece
Bōii, ōrum, *m, pl,* a Celtic people
Bōla, ae, *f,* a town of the Aequi
Bŏmilcar, ăris, *m,* a Carthaginian general
Bŏnōnĭa, ae, *f,* a town in Cisalpine Gaul
Bŏōtes, ae, *m,* a constellation (from "bos", an ox)
Bŏrēās, ae, *m,* the north wind
Bosphŏrus, i, *m,* the Straits between Thrace and Asia Minor
Brennus, i, *m,* a Gallic leader who defeated the Romans at the river Allia, 390 B.C.
Briāreus, i, *m,* a hundred-armed giant
Brĭgantes, um, *m. pl,* a British tribe
Brīsēis, ĭdis, *f,* Hippodamia, the slave of Achilles
Britanni, ōrum, *m.pl,* the Britons
Brĭtannus, Brĭtannĭcus, a, um, British

Brundĭsĭum, ii, *n,* a town in Calabria and a Roman port
Brutii, ōrum, *m. pl,* a tribe in the southern tip of Italy
Brūtus, i, *m,* a Roman surname; 1, L. Junius B. the first Roman consul; 2, M. Junius B. the murderer of Caesar
Bȳzantĭum,·ii, *n,* a Greek city in Thrace

C

Cācus, i, *m,* a giant, son of Vulcan, ·slain by Hercules
Cadmus, i, *m,* the son of Agenor
Caelĭus mons, one of the seven hills of Rome
Caerĕ, itis, *n,* an Etruscan city
Caesar, ăris, *m,* a Roman family name; Caius Julius C. general, statesman author and dictator
Caesārēa, ae, *f,* a town in Palestine
Caius, i, *m,* a Roman "praenomen"
Călābrĭa, ae, *f,* the south-eastern part of Italy
Călēdŏnĭa, ae, *f,* the Highlands of Scotland
Călĭgŭla, ae, *m,* the nickname of Gaius, the third Roman emperor, ("little-boots")
Callĭmachus, i, *m,* a Greek poet
Callĭŏpē, ēs, *f,* the Muse of poetry
Cămillus, i, *m,* M. Furius C. a Roman statesman and general
Campānĭa, ae, *f,* a district of Central Italy, famous for its fertility
Cămŭlōdūnum, i, *n,* a town in Britain (now Colchester)
Cannae, ārum, *f. pl,* a village in Apulia, scene of a great defeat of the Romans by Hannibal
Cantābrĭa, ae, *f,* a region in north-west Spain
Cantĭum, ii, *n,* a district in Britain (now Kent)
Cănŭsĭum, ii, *n,* a town in Apulia
Căpĭtōlĭum, ii, *n,* the Capitol and the Capitol Hill at Rome
Cappădŏcĭa, ae, *f,* a district of Asia Minor
Căprĕae, ārum, *f. pl,* an island off the Campanian coast (now Capri)
Căpŭa, ae, *f,* a city of Campania
Cărăcalla, ae, *m,* a Roman emperor
Cărătācus, i, *m,* a British king
Cārĭa, ae, *f,* a province of Asia Minor
Carnūtes, um, *m. pl,* a Gallic tribe
Carrhae, ārum, *f. pl,* a town in Mesopotamia

For List of Abbreviations used, turn to pages 3, 4

Carthāgo, īnis, *f,* Carthage, a city in North Africa

Cassander, dri, *m,* a king of Macedonia

Cassandra, ae, *f,* the daughter of Priam, gifted with prophecy

Cassius, a, um, *adj,* the name of a Roman "gens": C. Cassius Longinus, one of Caesar's murderers

Cassivellaunus, i, *m,* a British chief

Castor, ŏris, *m,* twin-brother of Pollux; a twin-star and a guide to sailors

Cătilīna, ae, *m,* L. Sergius C., an impoverished patrician who led a conspiracy against the state

Căto, ōnis, *m,* a Roman family name; M. Porcius C., famous for his attacks on Roman luxury and indulgence

Cătullus, i, *m,* a Roman lyric poet

Cătŭlus, i, *m,* a Roman family name

Caucăsus, i, *m,* the Caucasus Mts.

Caudĭum, ii, *n,* a city in Samnium

Caurus, i, *m,* the north-west wind

Cēbenna, ae, *f,* a mountain range in Gaul (now the Cevennes)

Cēcrops, ŏpis, *m,* the first king of Athens

Celtae, ārum, *m. pl,* the Celts

Celtĭbēri, ōrum, *m. pl,* a people of central Spain, originally Celts

Cēphīsus, i, *m,* a river(god)

Cerbĕrus, i, *m,* the three-headed dog guarding the entrance to Hades

Cērēs, ĕris, *f,* the goddess of agriculture

Chaerōnēa, ae, *f,* a town in Boeotia

Chalcēdon, ŏnis, *f,* a town in Bithynia

Chalcis, ĭdis, *f,* a town of Euboea

Chaldaei, ōrum, *m. pl,* an Assyrian people

Chāōs, i, *n,* the Lower World

Chāron, ontis, *m,* the ferryman who took the dead across the Styx

Chărybdis, is, *f,* a whirlpool off Sicily

Chatti, ōrum, *m. pl,* German tribe

Chauci, ōrum, *m. pl,* German tribe

Cherusci, ōrum, *m. pl,* German tribe

Chimaera, ae, *f,* a fire-breathing monster

Chios, ii, *f,* an island in the Aegean Sea

Chrȳsippus, i, *m,* a Stoic philosopher

Cicĕro, ŏnis, *m,* M. Tullius C., the great Roman statesman and orator

Cilicia, ae, *f,* a province in Asia Minor

Cimbri, ōrum. *m. pl,* a German tribe who invaded Italy

Cīmon, ōnis, *m,* an Athenian statesman and general

Cincinnātus, i, *m,* a Roman family name: L. Quinctius C. dictator in 458 B.C.

Cīnĕas, ae, *m,* the friend of Pyrrhus

Cingĕtŏrix, ĭgis, *m,* a chief of the Treveri

Cinna, ae, *m,* a Roman family name: L. Cornelius C., one of Marius' lieutenants

Circē, es, *f,* an enchantress, daughter of the sun

Cirta, ae, *f,* a Numidian city

Claudius, a, um, *adj,* the name of two Roman "gentes": the fourth Roman emperor

Clĕon, ŏnis, *m,* an Athenian demagogue

Clĕŏpătra, ae, *f,* Queen of Egypt

Clisthĕnes, is, *m,* an Athenian statesman

Clītumnus, i, *m,* a river in Umbria

Clōdius, i, *m,* P. Clodius Pulcher, tribune of the People, killed by Milo

Clūsium, ii, *n,* an Etruscan town

Clȳtaemnēstra, ae, *f,* the wife of Agamemnon

Cōcȳtus, i, *m,* a river in the Lower World

Cōdrus, i, *m,* an Athenian king

Colchis, ĭdis, *f,* a country on the Black Sea

Collātia, ae, *f,* a town in Latium

Collīna porta, *f,* a gate of Rome

Commŏdus, i, *m,* a Roman emperor

Cōmum, i, *n,* a town of Cisalpine Gaul

Concordia, ae, *f,* the goddess of Concord

Cŏnōn, ōnis, *m,* an Athenian general

Constantīnus, i, *m,* a Roman emperor

Constantĭus, i, *m,* the name of three Roman emperors

Corbŭlo, ōnis, *m,* a Roman general

Corcȳra, ae, *f,* an island in the Ionian Sea (now Corfu)

Corfīnĭum, ii, *n,* capital of the Paeligni

Coriŏtanus, i, *m,* an early Roman hero

Cornēlia, ae, *f,* the daughter of P. Scipio Africanus, and mother of the Gracchi

Cornēlius, ii, *m,* the name of a Roman "gens", to which belonged the Scipios, and Sulla

Corsica, ae, *f,* Corsica

Côs, Cõi, *f,* an island in the Aegean

Cotta, ae, *m,* a Roman family name

Crassus, i, *m,* a Roman family name; 1, L. Licinius C., the orator; 2, M. Licinius C., the triumvir

Crĕmōna, ae, *f,* a town in Cisalpine Gaul

Crĕon, ontis, *m,* a king of Corinth

Crēta, ae, *f,* Crete

Crĕūsa, ae, *f,* the wife of Aeneas

Croesus, i, *m,* a king of Lydia, famous for his riches

Crŏtōn, ōnis, *c,* (**Crotona, ae,** *f*), a Greek settlement in Bruttium

Cūmae, ārum, *f. pl,* an ancient city of Campania, the home of the Sibyl

Cŭpīdo, ĭnis, *m,* the god of love

Cŭres, ium, *f. pl,* an ancient town of the Sabines

Cŭriātii, ōrum, *m. pl,* an Alban family, from which came the three brothers who fought with the Roman Horatii

Cŭrius, a, um, *adj,* the name of a Roman "gens"

Curtius, a, um, *adj,* the name of a Roman "gens"

Cўbĕlē, es, *f,* a Phrygian goddess, worshipped in Rome

Cўclădes, um, *f. pl,* a group of islands in the Aegean Sea

Cўclōpes, um, *m. pl,* a race of one eyed giants

Cydnus, i, *m,* a river in Cilicia

Cynthia, ae, *f,* Diana

Cўprus, i, *f,* Cyprus

Cўrēnē, es, *f,* a Greek city of north Africa

Cўrus, i, *m,* the founder of the Persian Empire

Cўthĕrēia, ae, *f,* Venus

Cўtōrus, i, *m,* a mountain-range of Paphlagonia

D

Dāci, ōrum, *m. pl,* the Dacians, a tribe of Thracian origin

Daedălus, i, *m,* an Athenian craftsman and architect

Dalmātae, ārum, *m. pl,* the Dalmatians, a tribe on the east coast of the Adriatic

Dămascus, i, *f,* Damascus

Dămŏclēs, is, *m,* a courtier of Dionysius

Dāmōn, ōnis, *m,* a Pythagorean

Dănăi, ōrum, *m. pl,* the Greeks

Dānŭbius, i, *m,* the Danube

Daphne, as, *f,* the daughter of the river-god Peneus

Dardănus, i, *m,* the ancestor of the Trojans

Dārēus (or **Darius**), **i,** *m,* a king of Persia

Dĕcius, a, um, *adj,* the name of a Roman "gens"

Dēiŏtărus, i, *m,* a king of Galatia

Dēïphŏbus, i, *m,* the son of Priam and husband of Helen

Dēlos, i, *f,* an island in the Aegean, birthplace of Apollo and Diana

Delphi, ōrum, *m. pl,* a town in Phocis, famous for its oracle

Dēmosthĕnēs, is, *m,* 1. a famous Athenian orator; 2. an Athenian general

Deucăliōn, ōnis, *m,* he was saved from the Flood with his wife Pyrrha

Diăna, ae, *f,* the goddess of the moon and of hunting

Dictē, es, *f,* a mountain in Crete

Dīdō, ūs, *f,* the founder-queen of Carthage

Dioclētiānus, i, *m,* a Roman emperor

Diŏgĕnes, is, *m,* a Greek philosopher of the fourth century B.C.

Diŏmēdes, is, *m,* a Greek hero of the siege of Troy

Diŏnỹsius, ii, *m,* a tyrant of Syracuse

Diŏnỹsus, i, *m,* the god of wine

Dīs, Dītis, *m,* Pluto, king of the Lower World

Dōdōna, ae, *f,* a city of Epirus

Dŭlābella, ae, *m,* a Roman family name

Dŏlōpes, um, *m. pl,* a people of Thessaly

Dŏmītiānus, i, *m,* a Roman emperor

Dŏmītius, a, um, *adj,* the name of a Roman "gens"

Dōres, um, *m. pl,* the Dorians, a Greek people

Drāco, ōnis, *m,* an Athenian lawgiver

Drĕpăna, ōrum, *n.pl,* a town in Sicily

Drŭides, um, *m. pl,* the Druids

Drūsus, i, *m,* a Roman surname

Drўas, ădis, *f,* a wood-nymph

Dŭillius, ii, *m,* a Roman consul who won a naval victory over the Carthaginians in 260 B.C.

Dyrrăchium, ii, *n,* a town in Illyria

E

Eborācum, i, *n,* York

Ebŭrōnes, um, *m. pl,* a German tribe

Ědessa, ae, f, a town in Macedonia

Ědōni, ōrum, m. pl, a Thracian people

Ēlectra, ae, f, daughter of Agamemnon

Ēleusis, ĭnis, f, a city of Attica where the mysteries of Ceres were held

Ēlis, ĭdis, f, a country in the Peloponnesus

Ēlўsĭum, ĭ, n, the dwelling-place of the Blessed in the Lower World

Ēmāthĭa, ae, f, a district of Macedonia

Encēlădus, ĭ, m, a giant slain by Iuppiter and buried under Etna

Ennĭus, ĭ, m, the father of Roman poetry

Ēōs, f, the dawn

Ēphĕsus, ĭ, f, an Ionian city of Asia Minor

Ēpĭcūrus, ĭ, m, an Athenian philosopher (342–270 B.C.)

Ēpīrus, ĭ, f, a region of northern Greece

Ērĕbus, ĭ, m, a god of the Lower World

Ērectheus, ĕĭ, m, a king of Athens

Ērětrĭa, ae, f, a town of Euboea

Ērĭdānus, ĭ, m, one of the names of the river Po

Ērīnys, ўos, f, one of the Furies

Ērўmanthus, ĭ, m, a chain of mountains in Arcadia

Ērўthēa, ae, f, an island near Gades

Ēryx, ўcis, m, a mountain on the N.W. coast of Sicily

Esquilĭae, ārum, f. pl, the Esquiline, the largest of the hills of Rome

Ētrūrĭa, ae, f, a district of western Italy

Euboea, ae, f, an island in the Aegean

Euclīdēs, is, m, the famous mathematician of Alexandria

Eumĕnĭdes, um, f.pl, a name of the Furies

Euphrātēs, is, m, the Euphrates

Eurīpĭdes, is, m, the famous Athenian poet (480–406 B.C.)

Eurīpus, ĭ, m, the strait between Boeotia and Euboea

Eurōpa, ae, f, 1. the daughter of king Agenor; 2. the continent of Europe

Eurўălus, ĭ, m, friend of Nisus (in Vergil's Aeneid)

Eurўdĭce, es, f, the wife of Orpheus

Eurystheus, eĭ, m, a king of Mycenae, who imposed on Hercules his Twelve Labours

Euxīnus Pontus, ĭ, m, the Black Sea

Ēvander, dri, m, the son of Mercury, who founded a colony on the Tiber

F

Fābĭus, a, um, adj, the name of a Roman "gens"; Q. Fabius Maximus Cunctator, the famous Roman general of the second Punic War

Fābrĭcĭus, a, um, adj, the name of a Roman "gens"

Faesŭlae, ārum, f.pl, an Etruscan town

Fălernus ager, m, the territory of Falernus in Campania, famous for its wine

Faunus, i, m, a forest god

Faustŭlus, i, m, the shepherd who found Romulus and Remus

Faustus, i, m, a Roman surname

Făvōnĭus, i, m, the west wind

Flaccus, i, m, a Roman surname

Flāmĭnĭus, a, um, adj, the name of a Roman "gens"

Flāvĭus, a, um, adj, the name of a Roman "gens"

Flōra, ae, f, the goddess of Flowers

Flōrentĭa, ae, f, an Etruscan town (now Florence)

Fŏrentum, i, n, a town in Apulia

Formĭae, ārum, f. pl, a town in Latium

Frěgellae, ārum, f. pl, a town in Latium

Frisĭi, ōrum, m. pl, the Frisians, a north German tribe

Fulvĭa ae, f, 1. mistress of Curius 2. wife of M. Antony.

G

Găbăli, ōrum, m. pl, a Gallic tribe

Găbĭi, ōrum, m. pl, a city of Latium

Găbĭnĭus, a, um, adj, the name of a Roman "gens"

Gādēs, ium, f. pl, a town in Spain

Gaetūli, ōrum, m. pl, a people of north-west Africa

Gāĭus (Caius), i, m, a Roman "praenomen"

Galba, ae, m, a Roman family name; Servius Sulpicius G. a Roman emperor

Galli, ōrum, m, pl, the Gauls

Gallĭa, ae, f, Gaul; Gallia Cisalpina, Gaul on the Roman side of the Alps; Gallia Transalpina, Gaul on the further side of the Alps

Gallĭcus, Gallus, a, um, adj, Gallic

Gangēs, is, m, the river Ganges

Gănўmēdes, is, m, a youth who was carried off to be Juppiter's cup-bearer

Gărămantes, um, *m.* *pl*, a people of Africa

Gărumna, ae, *m*, a river of Gaul

Gĕla, ae, *f*, a town of Sicily

Gĕlon, ōnis, *m*, a king of Syracuse

Gĕnēva, ae, *f*, Geneva

Gĕnŭa, ae, *f*, a town in Liguria (now Genoa)

Gergŏvia, ae, *f*, a town of the Arverni in Aquitania

Germāni, ōrum, *m. pl*, the Germans

Germānia, ae, *f*, Germany

Germānus, a, um, *adj*, German

Gēryon, ōnis, *m*, a king of Spain slain by Hercules

Gĭgantes, um, *m. pl*, the Giants, who attacked Olympus and were killed by the thunder-bolts of Juppiter

Glaucus, i, *m*, 1. the son of Sisyphus; 2, the leader of the Lycians in the Trojan War

Gnossos, i, *f*, an ancient city of Crete

Gordĭum, ii, *n*, a city of Phyrgia

Gorgĭas, ae, *m*, a Greek sophist

Gorgo, ōnis, *f*, a daughter of Phorcus whose look turned people to stone

Gŏthi, ōrum, *m. pl*, the Goths

Gracchus, i, *m*, a Roman family name

Graeci, ōrum, *m. pl*, the Greeks

Grāii, ōrum, *m. pl*, the Greeks

Grampius mons, *m*, the Grampian mountains

Grātiae, ārum, *f. pl*, the Graces

Gȳās, ae, *m*, a hundred-armed giant

Gȳgēs, is, *m*, a wealthy king of Lydia

H

Hădria, ae, *f*, the Adriatic Sea

Hadriānus, i, *m*, a Roman emperor

Hălicarnassus, i, *f*, a town in Caria

Hămilcar, ăris, *m*, a famous Carthaginian general of the first Punic War, father of Hannibal

Hannibal, ălis, *m*, a famous Carthaginian general of the second Punic War, son of Hamilcar

Harpȳiae, ārum, *f. pl*, the Harpies, monsters half-vulture, half-woman

Hasdrŭbal, ălis, *m*, a Carthaginian general, brother of Hannibal

Hĕbē, is, *f*, the daughter of Iuppiter, and wife of Hercules

Hĕbrus, i, *m*, a river in Thrace

Hĕcăte, es, *f*, the goddess of magic

Hector, ŏris, *m*, the son of Priam, hero of the Trojans

Hĕcŭba, ae, *f*, the wife of Priam

Hĕlĕna, ae, *f*, the wife of Menelaus; she was carried off to Troy by Paris, thus causing the Trojan War

Hĕlice, es, *f*, the Great Bear

Hĕlicon, ōnis, *m*, a mountain in Boeotia

Hellas, ădis, *f*, Greece

Hellespontus, i, *m*, the Hellespont (now the Dardanelles)

Hĕlōtes, um, *m. pl*, the slaves of the Spartans

Helvētii, ōrum, *m. pl*, a Celtic people inhabiting the region of Switzerland

Helvii, ōrum, *m. pl*, a Gallic tribe

Henna, ae, *f*, a city in Sicily

Hēra, ae, *f*, a Greek goddess

Hēraclēa, ae, *f*, the name of several Greek towns

Hērāclēum, i, *n*, a town in Macedonia

Hercŭlānĕum, i, *n*, a town of Campania, buried in A.D. 79 by an eruption of Vesuvius

Hercŭles, is, *m*, Hercules

Hercȳnia silva, *f*, the Hercynian forest in Germany

Hermes, ae, *m*, a Greek god identified with the Roman Mercury

Hermiŏne, es, *f*, the daughter of Menelaus and Helen

Hernici, ōrum, *m. pl*, a people of Latium, Sabine in origin

Hēro, us, *f*, a priestess of Aphrodite

Hĕrŏdŏtus, i, *m*, the first Greek historian

Hēsiŏdus, i, *m*, a Greek poet

Hespĕrus, i, *m*, the Evening Star

Hibēri, ōrum, *m. pl*, the Spaniards

Hibēria, ae, *f*, Spain

Hibērus, a, um, *adj*, Spanish

Hibērus, i, *m*, the Ebro

Hiempsal, ălis, *m*, son of Micipsa, king of Numidia

Hiĕro, ōnis, *m*, king of Syracuse

Hippocrātes, is, *m*, a Greek physician

Hippŏdămus, i, *m*, the horse-tamer, i.e. Castor

Hippŏlȳte, es, *f*, the Queen of the Amazons, taken captive by Theseus

Hippŏlȳtus, i, *m*, the son of Theseus

Hirpīni, ōrum, *m. pl*, a people of Central Italy

Hispāni, ōrum, *m. pl*, the Spaniards

Hispānia, ae, *f*, Spain

Hispānus, a, um, *adj*, Spanish

Hŏmērus, i, *m*, Homer

Hōrae, ārum, *f. pl*, the Hours

Hōrātius, a, um, *adj*, the name of a Roman "gens"

Hortensius, a, um, *adj*, the name of a Roman "gens"

Hostīlius, a, um, *adj*, the name of a Roman "gens"

Hўădes, um, *f. pl*, a group of seven stars

Hўdra, ae, *f*, a many-headed water snake

Hўmen, ĕnis, *m*, the god of Marriage

Hўpĕrīon, ŏnis, *m*, 1, the father of the sun; 2. the sun god

Hўpermnestra, ae, *f*, the only daughter of Danaus who did not kill her husband

I

Ĭacchus, i, *m*, a name of Bacchus

Ĭăpĕtus, i, *m*, a Titan, father of Prometheus

Ĭāpix, -pygis, *m*, 1. son of Daedalus; 2. a west wind

Ĭcărus, i, *m*, son of Daedalus

Ĭcēni, ōrum, *m. pl*, a British tribe in East Anglia

Ĭda, ae, *f*, a mountain in Crete

Ĭdŏmĕneus, i, *m*, a king of Crete

Ĭdūmaea, ae, *f*, a region of Palestine

Ĭlerda, ae, *f*, a town in Spain

Ĭlia, ae, *f*, a name of Rhea Silvia

Ĭlĭum (or Ĭlion), ii, *n*, a name of Troy

Illўrĭa, ae, *f*, a region on the Adriatic Sea

Illўrii, ōrum, *m. pl*, a people on the Adriatic Sea

Ĭnăchus, i, *m*, the first king of Argos

Indus, i, *m*, a river in India

Insŭbres, ĭum, *m. pl*, a people of Cisalpine Gaul

Ĭo, see Ĭon

Ĭolcus, i, *m*, a town in Thessaly

Ĭon, ōnus, *f*, daughter of Inachus, beloved by Juppiter

Ĭōnĭa, ae, *f*, a country of Asia Minor, on the W. Coast

Ĭphĭgĕnĭa, ae, *f*, the daughter of Agamemnon

Ĭris, ĭdis, *f*, the messenger of the gods

Ĭsis, ĭdis, *f*, an Egyptian goddess

Ĭsŏcrătes, is, *m*, an Athenian orator

Isthmus, i, *m*, the Isthmus of Corinth

Ĭtălĭa, ae, *f*, Italy

Ĭtăli, ōrum, *m. pl*, the Italians

Ĭtălĭcus, a, um, *adj*, Italian

Ĭtălus, a, um, *adj*, Italian

Ĭthăca, ae, *f*, an island in the Ionian Sea

Itius Portus, ūs, *m*, a port in Belgic Gaul

Ĭtўs, ўos, *m*, son of Tereus and Procne

Ixīōn, ŏnis, *m*, a king of the Lapithae

J

Ĭăcĕtāni, ōrum, *m. pl*, a people of Spain

Iānĭcŭlum, i, *n*, one of the seven hills of Rome

Iānus, i, *m*, an Italian god

Iāsōn, ŏnis, *m*, leader of the Argonauts

Iūdaea, ae, *f*, the country of the Jews, Palestine

Iūdaei, ōrum, *m. pl*, the Jews

Iŭgurtha, ae, *m*, a king of Numidia

Iūlĭānus, a, um, *adj*, of Julius Caesar

Iūlĭus, a, um, *adj*, the name of a famous Roman "gens"; C. Julius Caesar, statesman, soldier, author

Iūnĭus, a, um, *adj*, the name of a Roman "gens"

Iūno, ōnis, *f*, a goddess, daughter of Saturn, wife of Juppiter

Iūppiter, Iovis, *m*, the chief god of the Romans

Iūra, ae, *m*, Mt. Jura, in Gaul

Iustīnĭānus, i, *m*, a Roman emperor

Iūturna, ae, *f*, sister of Turnus

Iŭvĕnālis, is, *m*, D. Junius J., a Roman satirist

K

Karthāgo, ĭnis, *f*, see **Carthago**

L

Lăbĭēnus, i, *m*, a lieutenant of Julius Caesar

Lăcaena, ae, *adj*, Spartan

Lăcĕdaemon, ŏnis, *f*, Sparta

Lăcĕdaemŏnĭus, a, um, *adj*, Spartan

Lacĕtāni, ōrum, *m. pl*, a people of Spain

Lăco, ōnis, *m*, a Spartan

Laelĭus, a, um, *adj*, the name of a Roman "gens"

Lāertes, ae, *m*, the father of Ulysses

Laestrȳgŏnes, um, *m. pl*, a race of giants in Sicily

Lampsăcus, i, *f*, a city on the Hellespont

Lāŏcŏōn, ontis, *m*, a Trojan priest

Lāŏmĕdōn, ontis, *m*, the father of Priam, king of Troy

Lăpĭthae, ārum, *m. pl*, a people of Thessaly

Lăres, um, *m. pl*, household gods

Largus, i, *m,* a Roman surname

Lārissa, ae, *f,* a city in Thessaly

Lātīnus, i, *m,* a king of the Laurentines

Lātīnus, a, um, *adj,* Latin

Lātium, ii, *n,* Latium, the country of Italy in which Rome was situated

Lātōna, ae, *f,* the mother of Apollo and Diana

Laurentum, i, *n,* a town in Latium

Lāvīnia, ae, *f,* daughter of Latinus, wife of Aeneas

Lāvīnium, ii, *n,* a city of Latium

Lēander, dri, *m,* a youth who swam the Hellespont every night to visit Hero in Sestos

Lēda, ae, *f,* mother of Castor, Pollux, Helen and Clytemnestra

Lēmannus, i, *m,* Lake Geneva

Lemnos, i, *f,* an island in the Aegean

Leōnidās, ae, *m,* a king of Sparta

Lēpidus, i, *m,* a Roman family name; 1, M. Aemilius L. enemy of Sulla, consul 79 B.C.; 2. M. Aemilius L. triumvir 43 B.C.

Lerna, ae, *f,* a river and marsh near Argos

Lesbos, i, *f,* an island in the Aegean

Lēthē, ēs, *f,* a river in the Lower World, where departed souls drank "forgetfulness" of their past lives

Lexovii, ōrum, *m. pl,* a Gallic tribe

Līber, ĕri, *m,* an Italian god, identified with Bacchus

Lībĕra, ae, *f,* Proserpina, sister of Liber, daughter of Ceres

Liburni, ōrum, *m. pl,* a people of N. Illyria

Libÿa, ae, *f,* Libya

Licīnius, a, um, *adj,* the name of a Roman "gens"

Liger, ĕris, *m,* a river in Gaul (now the Loire)

Ligŭres, um, *m. pl,* a people of northwest Italy

Lingŏnes, um, *m. pl,* a Gallic tribe

Lipăra, ae, *f,* an island north of Sicily

Līvius, a, um, *adj,* the name of a Roman "gens"; T. Livius Patavinus, the Roman historian

Lōcusta, ae, *f,* a Roman woman skilled in poisoning

Lollius, a, um, *adj,* the name of a Roman "gens"

Londīnium, ii, *n,* London

Lūcāni, ōrum, *m. pl,* a people of South Italy

Lūcānia, ae, *f,* a region of South Italy

Lūcānus, i, *m,* a Roman poet

Lūcrētius, a, um, *adj,* the name of a Roman "gens"; T. Lucretius Carus, a Roman poet

Lūcrīnus, i, *m,* a lake of Campania

Lūcullus, i, *m,* a Roman family name; Lucius Licinius L., conqueror of Mithridates

Lugdūnum, i, *n,* a city of Gaul (now Lyons)

Lūna, ae, *f,* the moon-goddess

Lūpercālia, ōrum, *n. pl,* a Roman festival celebrated in February

Lūpercus, i, *m,* a pastoral god who protected flocks from wolves

Lūsītānia, ae, *f,* the western part of Spain (now Portugal)

Lȳcēum, i, *n,* a gymnasium at Athens where Aristotle taught

Lȳcia, ae, *f,* a country of Asia Minor

Lȳcurgus, i, *m,* a Spartan lawgiver

Lȳdia, ae, *f,* a country of Asia Minor

Lynceus, i, *m,* 1. one of the Argonauts; 2. son of Aegyptus and husband of Hypermnestra

Lȳsander, dri, *m,* a Spartan general

Lȳsias, ae, *m,* a Greek orator

Lȳsimăchus, i, *m,* one of Alexander's generals

M

Măcĕdōnes, um, *m. pl,* the Macedonians

Măcĕdōnia, ae, *f,* Macedonia

Maecēnas, ātis, *m,* the friend of Augustus and patron of Horace and Vergil

Magnēsia, ae, *f,* a district in Thessaly

Māgo, ōnis, *m,* brother of Hannibal

Maharbal, ălis, *m,* a Carthaginian general

Māia, ae, *f,* daughter of Atlas and mother of Mercury

Māmers, ertis, *m,* a name of Mars

Māmertīni, ōrum, *m. pl* (sons of Mars), the name adopted by the mercenary troops who seized Messana in Sicily in 289 B.C.

Mandūbii, ōrum, *m. pl,* a Gallic tribe

Mānīlius, a, um, *adj,* the name of a Roman "gens"

Mantŭa, ae, *f,* a city in north Italy

Mărăthōn, ōnis, *f,* a village in Attica, where the Athenians defeated the Persian army in 490 B.C.

Marcellus, i, *m,* a Roman family name: Marcus Claudius M. conqueror of Syracuse, Roman general against Hannibal

Marcĭus, a, um, *adj,* the name of a Roman "gens"; Ancus M. the fourth king of Rome

Marcus, i, *m,* a Roman praenomen

Marĭus, a, um, *adj,* the name of a Roman "gens"; C. Marius, conqueror of Jugurtha and the Cimbri, leader of the Popular Party against Sulla

Măro, ōnis, *m,* the surname of Vergil

Mars, tis, *m,* the god of War

Marsi, ōrum, *m. pl,* a people of Latium

Martĭālis, is, *m,* Marcus Valerius M., a Roman epigrammatic poet

Martĭus, a, um, *adj,* from Mars

Măsĭnissa, ae, *m,* a king of Numidia

Massilĭa, ae, *f,* seaport of Gaul (now Marseilles)

Mātūta, ae, *f,* the goddess of morning

Mauri, ōrum, *m. pl,* the Moors

Maurītānĭa, ae, *f,* a country in northwest Africa

Mausōlus, i, *m,* a king of Caria

Māvors, ortis, m, Mars

Mēdēa, ae, *f,* daughter of king Aeetes

Mēdi, ōrum, *m. pl,* the Medes, a people of Asia

Mĕdullĭa, ae, *f,* a town in Latium

Mĕdūsa, ae, *f,* one of the Gorgons; everything she looked at turned to stone

Mĕgălŏpŏlis, is, *f,* a town in Arcadia

Mĕgăra,·ae, *f* (or **ōrum,** *n.pl*), a city of Megaris

Mĕgăris, idis, *f,* a country of Greece

Mĕlĭta, ae, *f,* Malta

Mēlos, i, *f,* an island in the Aegean

Melpŏmĕnē, es, *f,* the muse of tragic poetry

Memmĭus, a, um, *adj,* the name of a Roman "gens"

Memnon, ŏnis, *m,* a king of Ethiopia, killed by Achilles in the Trojan War

Memphis, is, *f,* a city of Egypt

Mĕnander, dri, *m,* a Greek poet

Mĕnăpĭi, ōrum, *m. pl,* a Gallic tribe

Mĕnēlāus, i, *m,* brother of Agamemnon and husband of Helen

Mentor, ŏris, *m,* a friend of Ulysses

Mercŭrĭus, ii, m, Mercury, the messenger of the gods

Mĕsŏpŏtămĭa, ae, *f,* a country of Asia

Messālīna, ae, *f,* the wife of the emperor Claudius

Messalla, ae, *m,* a Roman family name

Messāna, ae, *f,* a Sicilian city (now Messina)

Mĕtaurus, i, *m,* a river in Umbria where Hasdrubal was defeated

Mĕtellus, i, *m,* a Roman family name; 1. Q. Metellus Macedonicus, who made Macedonia a Roman province; 2. Q. Caecilius Metellus Numidicus, who defeated Jugurtha

Mĕthymna, ae, *f,* a city of Lesbos

Mĕtiscus, i, *m,* the charioteer of Turnus

Mezentĭus, ii, *m,* a tyrant of Caere

Mĭcipsa, ae, *m,* a king of Numidia

Mĭdās, ae, *m,* a king of Phrygia who received from Bacchus the gift of turning everything he touched to gold

Mīlētus, i, *f,* a town in Asia Minor

Milo, ōnis, *m,* 1. famous athlete of Crotona; 2, T. Annius M. the enemy of Clodius

Miltĭădes, is, *m,* the famous general of the Athenians at Marathon

Mincĭus, ii, *m,* a river in Gaul

Minerva, ae, *f,* the Roman goddess of wisdom, the arts and sciences

Mīnos, ōis, *m,* a king of Crete

Mĭnōtaurus, i, *m,* a monster with a bull's head and a man's body, slain by Theseus with the help of Ariadne

Mĭsēnum, i, *n,* a promontory and town in Campania

Mĭsēnus, i, *m,* the trumpeter of Aeneas

Mĭthras, ae, *m,* the Persian sun-god

Mĭthrĭdātes, is, *m,* a king of Pontus who fought the Romans and was finally defeated by Pompey

Mĭtўlēnē, es, *f,* the capital of Lesbos

Mŏlossi, ōrum, *m. pl,* a people of Epirus

Mŏlossus, i, *m,* a Molossian hound (famous for hunting)

Mŏna, ae, *f,* the Isle of Man

Mŏnēta, ae, *f,* a surname of Juno in whose temple money was minted

Mŏrini, ōrum, *m. pl,* a Gallic tribe

Mōsa, ae, *m,* a river in Gaul (now the Meuse)

Mŏsella, ae, *m,* a river in Gaul (now the Moselle)

Mōses, is, *m,* Moses

Mūcĭus, a, um, *adj,* the name of a Roman "gens"; C. Mucius Scae-·vola, who tried to assassinate Porsenna

Mulcĭber, bĕri, *m,* a surname of Vulcan

Mulvĭus pons, *m,* a bridge across the Tiber

Mummius, a, um, *adj,* the name of a Roman "gens"

Munda, ae, *f,* a city in Spain where Julius Caesar defeated Pompey's son

Mūsa, ae, *f,* a goddess of the Arts

Mūsaeus, i, *m,* a Greek poet

Mўcēnae, ārum, *f. pl,* a famous city of Argolis where Agamemnon was king

Mўlae, ārum, *f. pl,* a city in Sicily

Myrmidōnes, um, *m. pl,* a people of Thessaly, under the rule of Achilles

Mўsia, ae, *f,* a country of Asia Minor

N

Naevius, a, um, *adj,* the name of a Roman "gens"

Nāiās, ādis, *f,* a water-nymph

Namnētes, um, *m. pl,* a Gallic tribe

Nantūātes, um, *m. pl,* a Gallic tribe

Narbo, ōnis, *m,* a city of southern Gaul

Narcissus, i, *m,* son of Cephisus, who fell in love with his own reflection and was changed into a flower

Nāsica, ae, *m,* a Roman family name

Naxos, i, *f,* an island in the Aegean Sea

Neāpölis, is, *f,* a sea-port of Campania (now Naples)

Nemea, ae, *f,* a city in Argolis

Nĕmĕsis, is, *f,* the goddess of justice

Nĕpos, ōtis, *m,* C. Cornelius N., a Roman historian

Neptūnus, i, *m,* Neptune, god of the sea

Nēreus, ei, *m,* a sea-god

Nēro, ōnis, *m,* a Roman family name; C. Claudius N., the fifth Roman emperor

Nerva, ae, *m,* a Roman family name; M. Cocceius N., a Roman emperor

Nervii, ōrum, *m. pl,* a Gallic tribe

Nestōr, ŏris, *m,* a king of Pylos who fought with the Greeks at Troy

Nicōmēdēs, is, *m,* a king of Bithynia

Nīlus, i, *m,* the river Nile

Niŏbē, es, *f,* daughter of Tantalus, wife of Amphion

Nīsus, i, *m,* 1. king of Megara; 2, a friend of Euryalus (in Vergil's Aeneid)

Nōla, ae, *f,* a town in Campania

Nōrĭcum, i, *n,* a country between the Danube and the Alps

Nŏtus, i, *m,* the south wind

Nŏviŏdūnum, i, *n,* 1, a town of the Aedui; 2. a town of the Bituriges; 3. a town of the Sessiones

Nŭma, ae, *m,* N. Pompilius, the second king of Rome

Nŭmantia, ae, *f,* a city in northern Spain

Nŭmĭdae, ārum, *m. pl,* the Numidians, a people of N. Africa

Nŭmĭdĭa, ae, *f,* Numidia

Nŭmĭtor, ōris, *m,* king of Alba Longa, grandfather of Romulus and Remus

Nўsa, ae, *f,* a city in India, where Bacchus was born

O

Ocrĭcŭlum, i, *n,* a town in Umbria

Octāviānus, i, *m,* the surname of the Emperor Augustus

Octāvius, a, um, *adj,* the name of a Roman "gens"; C. Octavius, the father of the emperor Augustus

Oebălus, i, *m,* a king of Sparta

Oedĭpus, i, *m,* a king of Thebes, who killed his father and married his mother

Oenōnē, es, *f,* a Phrygian nymph, loved and then deserted by Paris

Ölympĭa, ae, *f,* a sacred plain in Elis where the Olympic Games were held

Ölympĭa, ōrum, *n. pl,* the Olympic Games

Ölympĭas, ădis, *f,* 1, an Olympiad, a four-year period which elapsed between Olympic Games; 2. wife of Philip of Macedon, and mother of Alexander the Great

Ölympĭcus, a, um, *adj,* Olympic

Ölympus, i, *m,* a mountain on the borders of Macedonia and Thessaly, the abode of the gods

Orbīlius, i, *m,* a famous Roman grammarian and schoolmaster

Orcădes, um, *f. pl,* the Orkney Islands

Orchŏmĕnus, i, *m,* the name of two cities, one in Boeotia, one in Thessaly

Orcus, i, *m,* the Lower World

Ordŏvices, um, *m. pl,* a British tribe

Ŏrēăs, ădis, *f,* a mountain-nymph

Ŏrestēs, is, *m,* the son of Agamemnon

Ŏrĭcum, i, *n,* a seaport in Illyria

Ŏrion, ōnis, *m,* a hunter who was changed into a constellation

Ŏrŏdēs, is, *m,* a king of Parthia

Ŏrontēs, is, *m,* a river in Syria

Orpheus, i, *m,* a famous Thracian singer

For List of Abbreviations used, turn to pages 3, 4

Osci, ōrum, *m. pl*, an ancient Italian tribe of Campania

Ŏsīris, is, *m*, an Egyptian god

Ossa, ae, *f*, a mountain range in Thessaly

Ostĭa, ae, *f*, a seaport at the mouth of the Tiber

Ostŏrĭus, i, *m*, P. Ostorius Scapula, governor of Britain

Ŏtho, ōnis, *m*, a Roman surname; M. Salvius O., a Roman emperor

Othrys, ўos, *m*, a mountain in Thessaly

Ŏvĭdĭus, a, um, *adj*, the name of a Roman "gens" P. Ovidius Naso, the Roman poet

Oxos, i, *m*, a river in Asia

P

Păcŏrus, i, *m*, a king of Parthia

Păcŭvĭus, i, *m*, a Roman poet

Pădus, i, *m*, the river Po

Paeligni, ōrum, *m. pl*, an Italian tribe

Pălaestīna, ae, *f*, Palestine

Pălātĭum, ii, *n*, the Palatine, one of the seven hills of Rome

Pălĭnūrus, i, *m*, Aeneas' pilot who fell into the sea off the coast of Lucania

Pallăs, ădis, *f*, a surname of Athene, the Greek goddess of Wisdom

Pallăs, antis, *m*, son of Pandion

Pamphylĭa, ae, *f*, a district of Asia Minor

Pān, Pānos, *m*, the god of woods and flocks

Panchāĭa, ae, *f*, a region of Arabia

Pandīōn, ōnis, *m*, a king of Athens

Pandōra, ae, *f*, the first woman

Pannŏnĭa, ae, *f*, a country on the Danube

Pănŏpēa, ae, *f*, a sea-nymph

Pănormus, i, *f*, a city in Sicily

Paphlăgŏnĭa, ae, *f*, a district in Asia Minor

Păpīrĭus, a, um, *adj*, the name of a Roman "gens"

Parca, ae, *f*, the goddess of fate

Păris, ĭdis, *m*, the son of Priam and Hecuba who carried away Helen from her husband Menelaus and thus caused the Trojan War

Părīsĭi, ōrum, *m. pl*, a Gallic tribe

Parma, ae, *f*, a town in Gaul

Parmĕnĭo, ōnis, *m*, one of Alexander's generals

Parnāsus, i, *m*, a mountain in Phocis, sacred to Apollo

Păros, i, *f*, an island in the Aegean

Parrhāsĭus, i, *m*, a Greek painter

Parthĕnon, ōnis, *m*, the temple of Athene at Athens

Parthĕnŏpē, es, *f*, a Siren who gave her name to Neapolis (Naples)

Parthi, ōrum, *m. pl*, the Parthians, a Scythian people, famous archers

Pāsĭphae, es, *f*, daughter of Helios, mother of the Minotaur

Pāsĭthĕa, ae, *f*, one of the three Graces

Pătăvĭum, i, *n*, a town in North Italy, birthplace of Livy

Pătrŏclus, i, *m*, friend of Achilles

Paulus, i, *m*, a Roman surname

Pausănĭas, ae, *m*, the leader of the Spartans in the battle of Plataea

Pēgăsus, i, *m*, the winged horse of the Muses

Pĕlasgi, ōrum, *m. pl*, the oldest inhabitants of Greece

Pēleus, i, *m*, a king of Thessaly

Pēligni, ōrum, *m. pl*, a people of Central Italy

Pēlĭon, ii, *n*, a mountain in Thessaly

Pella, ae, *f*, a city in Macedonia

Pĕlŏponnēsus, i, *f*, the southern part of Greece

Pĕlops, ŏpis, *m*, son of Tantalus, king of Phrygia

Pēlūsĭum, i, *n*, a town in Egypt

Pĕnātes, ĭum, *m. pl*, Roman guardian deities of the household

Pēnĕlŏpē, es, *f*, the wife of Ulysses

Pentheus, ĕi, *m*, a king of Thebes

Pergămum, i, *n*, a city of Asia

Pĕrĭcles, is, *m*, an Athenian statesman of the fifth century B.C.

Persae, ārum, *m. pl*, the Persians

Persĭa, ae (or Persĭs, ĭdis), *f*, Persia

Persĕphŏnē, es, *f*, Proserpine, daughter of Ceres

Persēs, ae, *m*, the last king of Macedonia

Perseus, ĕi, *m*, son of Iuppiter and Danae who killed Medusa

Phaedo, ōnis, *m*, a pupil of Socrates and friend of Plato

Phaedra, ae, *f*, daughter of Minos and wife of Theseus

Phaedrus, i, *m*, a pupil of Socrates

Phaethōn, ontis, *m*, son of Helios (the sun-god)

Phălērum, i, *n*, the oldest part of Athens

Pharsālus, i, *f*, a town of Thessaly where Pompey was defeated by Caesar

Phăros, i, *f,* an island near Alexandria with a famous light-house

Phīdias, ae, *m,* a famous Athenian sculptor

Philippi, ōrum, *m. pl,* a city in Macedonia

Phīlippus, i, *m,* the name of four kings of Macedonia

Philoctētēs, ae, *m,* a famous archer, and a friend of Hercules

Philōmēla, ae, *f,* daughter of Pandion, she was changed into a nightingale

Philŏpoemen, ĕnis, *m,* a famous Greek general

Phlĕgĕthon, ontis, *m,* a river in the Lower World

Phōcaea, ae, *f,* a sea-port of Ionia

Phōcis, idis, *f,* a country of northern Greece

Phoēbē, es, *f,* the moon-goddess

Phoebus, i, *m,* the name of Apollo

Phoenīcē, es, *f,* Phoenicia, a country of Syria

Phorcus, i, *m,* a sea-god

Phrȳges, um, *m. pl,* the Phrygians, a people of Asia Minor

Phthīa, ae, *f,* a region of Thessaly

Phȳlăcē, ēs, *f,* a city of Thessaly

Picēnum, i, *n,* a district on the eastern side of Italy

Picti, ōrum, *m. pl,* a British tribe

Pictōnes, um, *m. pl,* a Gallic tribe

Pleus, i, *m,* son of Saturn

Pilumnus, i, *m,* ancestor of Turnus

Pindărus, i, *m,* Pindar, the lyric poet of Thebes

Piraeus, i, *m,* the port of Athens

Pirithŏus, i, *m,* son of Ixion, friend of Theseus

Pīsa, ae, *f.* a town in Elis

Pīsae, ārum, *f. pl,* an Etruscan city

Pīsistrătus, i, *m,* a tyrant of Athens

Plăcentia, ae, *f,* a city on the river Po

Plancus, i, *m,* a Roman surname

Plătaeae, ārum, *f. pl,* a town in Boeotia, where the Greeks defeated the Persians in 479 B.C.

Plăto, ōnis, *m,* the famous Greek philosopher, pupil of Socrates

Plautus, i, *m,* T. Maccius P. the famous Roman comic poet

Plīnius, a, um, *adj,* the name of a Roman "gens", 1. C. Plinius Secundus (the "Elder"), author of a work on Natural History; 2. C. Plinius Caecilius (the "Younger"), author of letters

Plūto, ōnis, *m,* the king of the Lower World

Poeni, ōrum, *m. pl,* the Carthaginians

Pollĭo, ōnis, *m,* a Roman surname; C. Asinius P., a Roman orator

Pollux, ūcis, *m,* twin brother of Castor

Pŏlȳbius, ii, *m,* a famous Greek historian

Pŏlȳclitus, i, *m,* a famous Greek sculptor

Pŏlyxĕna, ae, *f,* daughter of Priam

Pompēii, ōrum, *m. pl,* a city in the south of Campania

Pompēius, a, um, *adj,* the name of a Roman "gens"; Cn. P. Magnus, the triumvir, opponent of Julius Caesar

Pompīlius, a, um, *adj,* Numa Pompilius, the second king of Rome

Pomptīnus, a, um, *adj* (**paludes**), the Pomptine Marshes, in Latium

Pontius, a, um, *adj,* the name of a Roman "gens"; Pontius Pilatus governor of Judaea at the time of Christ's crucifixion

Pontus, i, *m,* the Black Sea

Porcius, a, um, *adj,* the name of a Roman "gens"; M. Porcius Cato, the Censor

Porsenna, ae, *m,* an Etruscan king

Portūnus, i, *m,* god of harbours

Pōrus, i, *m,* a king of India

Praeneste, is, *n,* a town in Latium

Praxitĕlēs, is, *m,* an Athenian sculptor

Priāmus, i, *m,* the last king of Troy

Prōcas, ae, *m,* a king of Alba

Procnē, es, *f,* a daughter of Pandion who was changed into a swallow

Prōmēthous, ei, *m,* son of Iapetus, father of Deucalion; he brought fire from heaven for mankind

Prŏpertius, i, *m,* Sextus Aurelius P. a Roman elegiac poet

Prŏpontis, idis, *f,* the Sea of Marmora

Prŏserpina, ae, *f,* daughter of Ceres

Prōtăgŏras, ae, *m,* a Greek sophist

Prōteus, ei, *m,* a sea-god

Prūsias, ae, *m,* a king of Bithynia

Ptŏlēmaeus, i, *m,* Ptolemy, the name of a dynasty of Egyptian kings

Publius, ii, *m,* a Roman praenomen

Pŭtĕŏli, ōrum, *m. pl,* a city on the coast of Campania

Pydna, ae, *f,* a town in Macedonia

Pygmaei, ōrum, *m. pl,* a race of dwarfs

Pygmălion, ōnis, *m,* grandson of Agenor, who fell in love with a statue, to which Venus later gave life

Pȳlos, i, *f,* the name of three towns of the Peloponnesus

Pȳrēnē, es, *f,* the Pyrenees

Pyrŏis, entis, *m,* the planet Mars

Pyrrha, ae, *f,* the wife of Deucalion

Pyrrhus, i, *m,* 1. son of Achilles and founder of a kingdom in Epirus; 2. a king of Epirus who invaded Italy and fought the Romans

Pȳthăgŏras, ae, *m,* the famous Greek philosopher (550 B.C.)

Pȳtho, us, *f,* the old name of Delphi

Q

Quinctĭus, a, um, *adj,* the name of a Roman "gens"; L. Quinctius Cincinnatus, who came from the plough to be dictator of Rome

Quintĭlĭānus, i, *m,* a Roman surname; L. Fabius Q., teacher and rhetorician

Quirīnus, i, *m,* a name of Romulus after he became a god

R

Raetĭa, ae, *f,* a country between the Alps and the Danube

Răvenna, ae, *f,* a Gallic town on the Adriatic

Rēgillus, i, *m,* a lake in Latium

Rēgĭum, i, *n,* a town of south Calabria

Rēgŭlus, i, *m,* a Roman family name; M. Atilius R. a famous Roman general of the first Punic War

Rēmi, ōrum, *m. pl,* a Gallic tribe

Rēmus, i, *m,* the brother of Romulus

Rhădămanthus, i, *m,* son of Juppiter, a judge in the Lower World

Rhĕa Silvia, she became, by Mars, mother of Romulus and Remus

Rhēnus, i, *m,* the Rhine

Rhŏdănus, i, *m,* the Rhone

Rhŏdos, i, *f,* the island of Rhodes

Rhoetēum, i, *n,* a promontory in the Hellespont

Rōma, ae, *f,* Rome

Rōmŭlus, i, *m.* son of Mars, founder and first king of Rome

Roscĭus, a, um, *adj,* the name of a Roman "gens"

Rŭbi, ōrum, *m. pl,* a town in Apulia

Rŭbĭco, ōnis, *m,* a river which marked the boundary between Italy and Gaul

Rŭdiae, ārum, *f. pl,* a town in Apulia

Rŭtĭlĭus, a, um, *adj,* the name of a Roman "gens"

Rŭtŭli, ōrum, *m. pl,* a people of Latium

S

Săbelli, ōrum, *m. pl,* a name of the Sabines

Săbīni, ōrum, *m. pl,* a people of Central Italy, the Sabines

Săgittārĭus, i, *m,* a constellation

Săguntum, i, *n,* a town on the coast of Spain

Sălămis, mĭnis, *f,* an island near Eleusis

Sălentīni, ōrum, *m. pl,* a people of southern Italy

Sălernum, i, *n,* a town of Campania (now Salerno)

Sălii, ōrum, *m. pl,* a Roman college of priests

Sallustĭus, a, um, *adj,* the name of a Roman "gens"; C. Sallustius Crispus, the famous Roman historian

Sămărŏbrīva, ae, *f,* a town in Gaul

Samnĭum, ii, *n,* a region of Central Italy

Sămos, i, *f,* an island in the Aegean

Santōnes, um, *m. pl,* a Gallic tribe

Sappho, ūs, *f,* the famous Greek lyric poetess

Sardes, ĭum, *f. pl,* the capital of Lydia

Sardi, ōrum, *m. pl,* the inhabitants of Sardinia

Sarmătĭa, ae, *f,* a country in South Russia

Sāturnālĭa, ōrum, *n. pl,* the festival of Saturn, held in December

Sāturnīnus, i, *m,* a Roman surname

Sāturnus, i, *m,* father of Juppiter

Scaevŏla, ae, *m,* a Roman family name; C. Mucius Sc., opponent of Porsenna

Scămander, dri, *m,* a river at Troy

Scăpŭla, ae, *m,* a Roman family name

Scīpĭo, ōnis, *m,* a Roman family name; 1. P. Cornelius Scipio Africanus; 2. P. Cornelius Scipio Aemilienus Africanus, two conquerors of the Carthaginians

Scŏpas, ae, *m,* a famous Greek sculptor

Scylla, ae, *f,* a rock in the straits between Italy and Sicily

Scythae, ārum, *m. pl,* the Scythians

Scythĭa, ae, *f,* a region to the north of the Black Sea

Sĕgesta, ae, *f,* a city of Sicily

Sējānus, i, *m,* the prefect of the Praetorian Guard under Tiberius

Sĕleucus, i, *m,* the name of several kings of Syria

Sĕlīnus, untis, *f,* a port in Sicily

Sĕmĕlĕ, es, *f,* daughter of Cadmus, mother of Bacchus

Semprōnĭus, a, um, *adj,* the name of a Roman "gens", to which belonged the brothers Tiberius and Gaius Sempronius Gracchus

Sĕnĕca, ae, *m,* a Roman family name; 1. M. Annaeus S., a famous rhetorician from Spain; 2. L. Annaeus S., his son, Stoic philosopher and tutor of Nero

Sĕnŏnes, um, *m. pl,* a Gallic tribe

Sēquăna, ae, *f,* the river Seine

Sēquāni, ōrum, *m. pl,* a Gallic tribe

Sertōrĭus, i, *m,* a general of Marius

Servīlĭus, a, um, *adj,* the name of a Roman "gens"

Servĭus Tullĭus, *m,* the sixth king of Rome

Sestos, i, *f,* a city in Thrace

Sĕvērus, i, *m,* a Roman family name

Sextīlis (mensis), another name for the month of August

Sĭbylla, ae, *f,* a priestess of Apollo

Sĭcāni, ōrum, *m. pl,* a people of Italy

Sĭchaeus, i, *m,* the husband of Dido

Sĭcŭli, ōrum, *m. pl,* the Sicilians

Sīdon, ōnis, *f,* a Phoenician city

Sĭgēum, i, *n,* a promontory in Troas

Sĭlēnus, i, *m,* the attendant of Bacchus

Sĭlĭus, a um, *adj,* the name of a Roman "gens"

Sĭlūres, um, *m. pl,* a British tribe

Silvānus, i, *m,* the god of woods

Sĭmōnĭdes, is, *m,* a famous lyric poet of Ceos

Sĭnōpē, es, *f,* a town on the Black Sea

Sīrēnes, um, *f. pl,* nymphs who lived off the coast of south Italy and lured sailors to their death

Sĭsyphus, i, *m,* son of Aeolus, king of Corinth, a robber

Smyrna, ae, *f,* a trading city of Iona

Sōcrătes, is, *m,* the famous Athenian philosopher

Sŏlon, ōnis, *m,* one of the seven wise men of Greece (*c.* 600 B.C.)

Sontĭātes, um, *m. pl,* a Gallic tribe

Sŏphŏcles, is, *m,* the famous Greek tragic poet

Sŏphŏnisba, ae, *f,* daughter of Hasdrubal

Sōracte, is, *n,* a mountain in Etruria

Sparta, ae, *f,* the capital of Laconia

Spartăcus, i, *m,* leader of the gladiators against Rome

Stŏĭcus, i, *m,* a Stoic philosopher

Styx, ўgis, *f,* a river of the Lower World

Sŭessĭōnes, um, *m. pl,* a Gallic tribe

Sŭĕtōnĭus, Gaius S. Tranquillus, the biographer of the Caesars

Suēvi, ōrum, *m. pl,* a German tribe

Sŭgambri, ōrum, *m. pl,* a German tribe

Sullc, ae, *m,* a Roman family name; L. Cornelius S., dictator, opponent of Marius

Sulmo, ōnis, *m,* a town of the Paeligni

Sulpĭcĭus, a, um, *adj,* the name of a Roman "gens"

Sūnĭum, i, *n,* a town of Attica

Sўbăris, is, *f,* a town of Lucania

Sychaeus, see **Sĭchaeus**

Sўphax, ācis, *m,* a king of Numidia

Sўrācūsac, ārum, *f. pl,* Syracuse

Sўrĭa, ae, *f,* Syria

Syrtes, ĭum, *f. pl,* two sandbanks on the north coast of Africa

T

Tăburnus, i, *m,* a range of mountains between Samnium and Campania

Tăcĭtus, i, *m,* Cornelius T. the famous Roman historian

Taenăros, i, *c,* a town in Laconia, near which was thought to be an entrance to the Lower World

Tāges, is, *m,* an Etruscan god

Tăgus, i, *m,* a river in Lusitania

Tămŏsĭs, is, m, the river Thames

Tănăis, is, m, the river Don

Tănăquil, īlis, *f,* the wife of Tarquinius Priscus

Tantălus, i, *m,* a son of Juppiter

Tarbelli, ōrum, *m. pl,* a tribe of Aquitania

Tărentum, i, *n,* a Greek city on the south coast of Italy

Tarpēĭus, a, um, *adj,* 1. the name of a Roman "gens"; Tarpeia, who betrayed the citadel to the Sabines; 2. The Tarpeian Rock at Rome from which criminals were thrown

Tarquĭnĭi, ōrum, *m. pl,* an Etruscan town

Tarquĭnĭus, ii, *m,* the name of two Etruscan kings of Rome

Tarsus, i, *f.* the capital of Cilicia

Tartărus, i, *m.* the Lower World

Tātĭus, i, *m,* Titus T., a king of the Sabines

Taurus, i, *m,* a mountain range in Asia Minor

Tĕgĕa, ae, *f,* a town in Arcadia

Tĕlămon, ōnis, *m,* an Argonaut

Tĕlĕmăchus, i, *m,* son of Ulysses and Penelope

For List of Abbreviations used, turn to pages 3, 4

Tempē, *n. pl*, a valley in Thessaly
Tenctēri, ōrum, *m. pl*, a German tribe
Tĕnĕdos, i, *f*, an island in the Aegean
Tĕrentius, a, um, *adj*, the name of a Roman "gens"; M. Terentius Afer a "freed man" and famous dramatist
Tēreus, i, *m*, a king of Thrace
Teucer, cri, *m*, the first king of Troy
Teutŏnes, um, *m. pl*, a German people
Thapsus, i, *f*, 1. a city in Africa; 2. a city in Sicily
Thēbae, ārum, *f. pl*, the capital of Boeotia
Thĕmistŏcles, is, *m*, a famous Athenian general and statesman
Thĕŏcrĭtus, i, *m*, the famous Greek pastoral poet
Thĕophrastus, i, *m*, a Greek philosopher
Thermŏpўlae, ārum, *f. pl*, a famous mountain-pass on the borders of Thessaly
Thēseus, ei, *m*, king of Athens and slayer of the Minotaur
Thessālĭa, ae, *f*, Thessaly, a region of north Greece
Thessălŏnīca, ae, *f*, a town of Macedonia
Thētis, ĭdis, *f*, a sea-nymph
Thisbē, es, *f*, a Babylonian maiden
Thrācĭa, ae, *f*, Thrace, a country to the north of the Propontis
Thūcўdĭdes, is, *m*, the famous Athenian historian
Thūlē, es, *f*, an island of northern Europe (perh. Iceland)
Thūrii, ōrum, *m. pl*, a city of Lucania
Thўăs, ădis, *f*, a female attendant of Bacchus
Thўestes, ae, *m*, son of Pelops and brother of Atreus
Thўni, ōrum, *m. pl*, a Thracian people who emigrated to Bithynia
Tĭbĕris, is, *m*, the river Tiber
Tĭbĕrius, i, *m*, a Roman praenomen; Ti. Claudius Nero Caesar, the second Roman emperor
Tĭbullus, i, *m*, a Roman poet
Tĭbur, ŭris, *n*, a town in Latium
Tīcīnus, i, *m*, a river in Cisalpine Gaul
Tĭgrānes, is, *m*, a king of Armenia
Tĭgris, ĭdis, *m*, a river of Asia
Tīrĭdātes, is, *m*, the name of several Armenian kings
Tīryns, ntis, *f*, a town of Argolis
Tīsĭphŏnē, es, *f*, one of the Furies
Tītan, ānis, *m*, ancestor of the Titans

Tīthōnus, i, *m*, the wife of Aurora who received the gift of immortality
Tītus, i, *m*, a Roman praenomen
Tītўos, i, *m*, giant son of Juppiter, slain by Apollo
Tŏlōsa, ae, *f*, a city of southern Gaul
Tŏlumnius, i, *m*, a Rutulian soothsayer
Tŏmi, ōrum, *m. pl*, a town on the Black Sea
Torquātus, i, *m*, surname gained by T. Manlius who slew a Gaul and took his neck-chain
Trāiānus, i, *m*, a Roman emperor
Tralles, ium, *f. pl*, a town in Western Asia
Trăsĭmēnus, i, *m*, Lake Trasimene, where Hannibal gained a victory over the Romans (217 B.C.)
Trĕbĭa, ae, *m*, a river of Cisalpine Gaul, where Hannibal defeated the Romans (218 B.C.)
Trĕvĕri, ōrum, *m. pl*, a Belgian tribe
Trinŏbantes, um, *m. pl*, a British tribe
Triptŏlĕmus, i, *m*, the inventor of agriculture
Triton, ōnis, *m*, a sea-god son of Neptune
Troezēn, ēnis, *f*, a town of Argolis
Trōia, ae, *f*, Troy
Trōiānus, a, um, Trojan
Trōicus, a, um, Trojan
Trōius, a, um, Trojan
Trōs, ōis, *m*, a king of Phrygia, after whom Troy was named
Tullius, a, um, *adj*, the name of a Roman "gens"; 1. Servius T., sixth king of Rome; 2. Marcus T. Cicero, famous orator and statesman
Turnus, i, *m*, a Rutulian prince killed by Aeneas
Tusci, ōrum, *m. pl*, the Etruscans
Tuscŭlum, i, *n*, a town of Latium
Tyndăreus, ĕi, *m*, a king of Sparta
Tўphōeus, ĕos, *m*, a giant buried beneath Mount Etna
Tўphōn, ōnis, *m*, another name for Typhoeus
Tyrrhēni, ōrum, *m. pl*, a Pelasgian colony which came to Italy
Tўrus, i, *f*, Tyre, a famous Phoenician city

U

Ubii, ōrum, *m. pl*, a German tribe

Ŭcălēgōn, ontis, *m*, a Trojan, mentioned in Vergil's Aeneid

Ŭfens, ntis, *m*, a river of Latium

Ŭlysses (Ŭlixes), is, *m*, Ulysses (or Odysseus) king of Ithaca and husband of Penelope

Umbri, ōrum, *m. pl*, a people of Italy

Ŭsīpētes, um, *m. pl*, a German tribe

Ŭtĭca, ae, *f*, a city of North Africa

V

Vălĕrĭus, a, um, *adj*, the name of a Roman "gens"

Varro, ōnis, *m*, a Roman surname; M. Terentius V., a Roman writer

Vātĭcānus mons, the Vatican hill at Rome

Vectis, is, *f*, the Isle of Wight

Vēii, ōrum, *m. pl*, an Etruscan city

Vellēius, a, um, *adj*, the name of a Roman "gens"

Vĕnĕti, ōrum, *m. pl*, 1. a people of north-east Italy; 2. a people of north-west Gaul

Vēnus, ĕris, *f*, the goddess of love

Vĕnŭsia, ae, *f*, a town on the border of Apulia

Vercellae, ārum, *f. pl*, a town of Cisalpine Gaul

Vercingĕtŏrix, igis, *m*, a Gallic chieftain

Vergĭlĭus, i, *m*, P. Vergilius Maro, the Roman poet, author of the Aeneid and the Georgics

Verginĭus, a, um, *adj*, the name of a Roman "gens"

Vērōna, ae, *f*, a town of north Italy

Verres, is, *m*, C. Cornelius V., the notorious praetor of Sicily

Vertumnus, i, *m*, the god of the changing seasons

Vĕrŭlāmĭum, ii, *n*, St Albans

Vespāsĭānus, i, *m*, Ti. Flavius V., a Roman emperor

Vesta, ae, *f*, the goddess of the hearth

Virgĭlĭus, see Vergilius

Volcae, ārum, *m. pl*, a Gallic tribe

Volcānus, i, *m*, son of Iuppiter and Juno, god of fire

Volsci, ōrum, *m. pl*, a people of Latium

Vulcānus, see Volcanus

Vulturnus, i, *m*, a river in Campania

X

Xantho, ūs, *f*, a sea-nymph

Xanthus, i, *m*, a river in Lycia

Xĕno, ōnis, *m*, an Epicurean philosopher

Xĕnŏphon, ontis, *m*, the famous Athenian historian, philosopher and general

Xerxes, is, *m*, a Persian king

Z

Zăma, ae, *f*, a town in Numidia where Scipio defeated Hannibal

Zanclē, ēs, *f*, another name of Messana in Sicily

Zēno, ōnis, *m*, a Greek philosopher

Zĕphyrus, i, *m*, the west wind

ENGLISH–LATIN

For List of Abbreviations used, turn to pages 3, 4

A

a, an, (*indefinite article*), no equivalent in Latin
abandon, *v.t*, rĕlinquo (3), dēsĕro (3)
abandoned, dērĕlictus, dēsertus; **(person),** perdĭtus
abandonment, rĕlictĭo, *f*
abase, *v.t*, dēprĭmo (3)
abasement, hŭmĭlĭtas, *f*, dēmĭssĭo, *f*
abash, *v.t*, confundo (3), perturbo (1)
abashed, pŭdōre confūsus **(perplexed with shame)**
abate, *v.t*, immĭnŭo (3), rĕmitto (3)
abatement, dēcessus, *m*, dōoossĭo, *f*, dēmĭnūtĭo, *f*
abbot, pontĭfex, *m*, **(high-priest),** săcerdos, *o*
abbreviate, *v.t*, immĭnŭo (3), contrăho (3)
abbreviation, compendĭum, *n*, contractĭo, *f*
abdicate, *v.i*, se abdĭcare (1. *reflex*)
abdication, abdĭcātĭo, *f*
abdomen, venter, *m*, abdōmen, *n*
abduction, raptus, *m*, raptĭo, *f*
abet, *v.i*, adsum (*irreg. with dat. of person*), adiŭvo (1)
abettor, mĭnister, *m*, adiūtor, *m*
abeyance (to be in —), *v.i*, iăcĕo (2)
abhor, ăbhorrĕo (2) (*with acc. or* ab *and* abl), ōdi. (*v. defect*)
abhorrence, ōdĭum, *n*
abide, *v.i*, mănĕo (2), hăbĭto (1)
abide, *v.t*, **(wait for),** exspecto (1)
abiding, *adj*, **(lasting),** mansūrus
ability (mental —), ingĕnĭum, *n*; **(power),** pŏtestas, *f*
abject, abiectus, hŭmĭlis
abjectness, hŭmĭlĭtas, *f*
abjure, *v.t*, abiūro (1), ēiūro (1)
ablaze, *adj*, flăgrans
able, *use* possum **(be able),** pŏtens
able (to be —), *v.i*, possum (*irreg*)
able-bodied, vălĭdus
ablution, lăvātĭo, *f*, ablūtĭo, *f*
ably, *adv*, ingĕnĭōse
abnegation, nĕgātĭo, *f*, mŏdĕrātĭo, *f*

abnormal, abnormis, ĭnūsĭtātus
aboard, in năve; **(to go —),** *v.i*, năvem conscendo (3); **(to put —),** *v.t*, in năvem impōno (3)
abode, dŏmus, *f*, dŏmĭcĭlĭum, *n*, sēdes, *f*, hăbĭtātĭo, *f*
abolish, *v.t*, tollo (3), ăbŏlĕo (2), dissolvo (3)
abolition, dissŏlūtĭo, *f*, ăbŏlĭtĭo, *f*
abominable, infandus, dētestābĭlis
abominate, *v.t*, ōdī (*defect*), ăbhorrĕo (2)
abomination (hatred), ōdĭum, *n*; **(crime),** flāgĭtĭum, *n*
aborigines, indĭgĕnae, *m. pl*
abortion, ăbortus, *m*, ăbortĭo, *f*
abortive (unsuccessful), irrĭtus
abound (in), *v.i*, ăbundo (1), sŭpĕro (1), circumflŭo (3), suppĕdĭto (1)
abounding, ăbundans, afflŭens, fēcundus
about, *prep*, circā, circum, ăd, sŭb (*with acc*), dē (*with abl*); **(of time),** circĭter (*with acc*)
about, *adv*, **(nearly),** circĭter, fermē, fĕrē
above, *prep*, sŭper, sŭprā (*with acc*); **(more than),** amplĭus
above, *adv*, sŭprā, insŭper; **(from above),** dēsŭper, sŭpernē
abrasion, attrītus, *m*
abreast, *adv*, părĭter
abridge, *v.t*, contrăho (3)
abridgement, ĕpĭtŏmē, *f*, ĕpĭtŏma, *f*
abroad, *adv*, **(in a foreign country),** pĕrĕgrē
abroad (to be —), *v.i*, pĕrĕgrīnor (1. *dep*)
abrogate, *v.t*, abrŏgo (1); rescindo (3)
abrogation, abrŏgātĭo, *f*
abrupt (sudden), sŭbĭtus; **(steep),** praeruptus
abruptly, *adv*, sŭbĭto, praerupte
abscess, vŏmĭca, *f*
abscond, *v.i*, lătĕo (2)
abscence, absentĭa, *f*
absent, absens
absent (to be —), *v.i*, absum (*irreg*)

absinth, absinthĭum, *n*
absolute, absŏlūtus
absolute power, tўrannis, *f*, impĕrĭum, *n*, dŏmĭnātĭo, *f*
absolutely (completely), *adv*, prorsum, prorsus
absolve, *v.t*, absolvo (3), lībĕro (1)
absorb, *v.t*, bĭbo (3), haurĭo (4), absorbĕo (2)
absorbent, *adj*, bĭbŭlus
abstain, *v.i*, abstĭnĕo (2)
abstemious, tempĕrātus
abstinence, abstĭnentĭa, *f*
abstinent, abstĭnens, mŏdĕrātus
abstract, *nn*, ĕpĭtŏme, *f*
abstract, *adj*, abstractus
abstract, *v.t*, abstrăho (3)
abstruse, rĕcondĭtus, obscūrus
absurd, ĭneptus, absurdus
absurdity, ĭneptĭa, *f*, insulsĭtas, *f*
absurdly, *adv*, ĭneptē, absurdē
abundance, cōpĭa, *f*, ăbundantĭa, *f*
abundant, largus, fēcundus
abuse, *nn*, (insult), contŭmēlĭa
abuse, *v.t*, (revile), mălĕdīco (3); (misuse), ăbūtor (3 *dep*)
abusive, contŭmēlĭōsus
abut, *v.i*, adiăcĕo (2)
abutting, adiunctus
abyss, gurges, *m*, vŏrāgo, *f*
acacia, ăcācĭa, *f*
academic, ăcădēmĭcus
academy, ăcădēmĭa, *f*
accede, *v.i*, consentĭo (4)
accelerate, *v.t*, accĕlĕro (1)
accent, vox, *f*
accentuate, *v.t*, ăcŭo (3)
accentuation, accentus, *m*
accept, *v.t*, accĭpĭo (3), rĕcĭpĭo (3)
acceptability, suāvĭtas, *f*, făcĭlĭtas, *f*
acceptable, grātus
acceptance, acceptĭo, *f*
access (approach), ădĭtus, *m*, accessus, *m*
accessible, făcĭlis; (to be ─), *v.i*, pătĕo (3)
accession (─ to the throne), ĭnĭtĭum (*n*) regni (beginning of reign); *or use phr. with* incipio (to begin) *and* regno (to reign)
accessory (of crime), *adj*, conscĭus; (helper), auctor, *m*
accident, cāsus, *m*
accidental, fortŭĭtus
accidentally, *adv*, cāsū, fortē
acclaim, *v.t*, clāmo (1)
acclamation, clāmor, *m*
acclimatized, assŭētus
accommodate, *v.t*, accommŏdo (1)
accommodating, obsĕquens

accommodation (lodging), hospĭtĭum, *n*; (loan), commŏdum, *n*
accompaniment (musical), cantus, *m*
accompany, *v.t*, prōsĕquor (3 *dep*), cŏmĭtor (1 *dep*); (─ in singing), oblŏquor (3 *dep*)
accomplice, *adj*, conscĭus, partĭceps
accomplish, *v.t*, confĭcĭo (3)
accomplished (learned), ērŭdītus
accomplishment (completion), confectĭo, *f*
accord (of my (your) own ─), mĕā (tŭā) spontē, ultrō
accord, *v.t*, concēdo (3); *v.i*, consentĭo (4)
accordance (in ─ with), *prep*, ex, dē, prō (*with abl*)
according to, *as above*
accordingly, *adv*, ĭtăque
accost, *v.t*, compello (1); allŏquor (3 *dep*)
account, *nn*, rătĭo, *f*; (statement), mĕmŏrĭa, *f*
on account of, *prep*, propter, ŏb (*with acc*)
to render account for, rătĭonem reddo (3)
accountant, calcŭlātor, *m*, scrība, *m*
account-book, tăbŭlae, *f. pl*
accoutre, *v.t*, orno (1); armo (1)
accoutrements, arma, *n. pl*
accredit, *v.t*, (establish), confirmo (1)
accrue, *v.i*, accēdo (3)
accumulate, *v.t*, cŭmŭlo (1), cŏăcervo (1); *v.i*, cresco (3)
accumulation (bringing together), collātĭo, *f*
accuracy (exactness), subtīlĭtas, *f*; (carefulness), cūra, *f*
accurate (exact), subtīlĭs, vērus; (careful), dīlĭgens
accursed, exsēcrābĭlĭs
accusation, crīmen, *n*, accūsātĭo, *f*
accuse, *v.t*, accūso (1); arcesso (3), nōmen dēfĕro (*v. irreg*)
accused person, rĕus, *m*
accuser, accūsātor, *m*, dēlātor, *m*
accustom, *v.t*, assŭēfăcĭo (3)
to be accustomed, *v.i*, sŏlĕo (2)
to become accustomed, *v.i*, assŭesco (3)
accustomed, assŭētus, sŏlĭtus
ache, *v.i*, dŏlĕo (2)
ache, *nn*, dŏlor, *m*
achieve, *v.t*, confĭcĭo (3), perfĭcĭo (3)
achievement, res gesta, *f*, făcĭnus, *n*
acid, *adj*, ăcerbus, ăcĭdus
acknowledge, *v.t*. (confess), confĭtĕor (2 *dep*), agnosco (3); (accept), tollo (3)

acknowledgement, confessĭo, *f*
acme, summa, *f*
aconite, ăcŏnītum, *n*
acorn, glans, *f*
acquaint, *v.t*, certĭōrem făcĭo (3) (*with acc. of person, and* dē *with abl*)
to become acquainted with, *v.t*, nosco (3), cognosco (3)
acquaintance (knowledge of), scĭentĭa, *f*; (with a person), consŭētūdo, *f*; (a person), nōtus, *m*
acquiesce, *v.i*, acquĭesco (3)
acquire, *v.t*, acquīro (3)
acquirement (obtaining), ădeptĭo, *f*
acquit, *v.t*, absŏlvo (3), lībĕro (1)
acquittal, absŏlūtĭo, *f*, lībĕrātĭo, *f*
acre, iūgĕrum, *n*
acrid, asper, ācer
acrimonious, ăcerbus, asper, ămārus
acrimony, ăcerbĭtas, *f*
across, *prep*, trans (*with acc*)
act, *v.i*, ăgo (3), ğero (3)
act, *v.t*. (a part in a play), ăgo (3)
act, *nn*, factum, *n*; (law) lex, *f*
action (carrying out), actĭo, *f*, actus, *m*; (at law) līs, *f*, (battle), proelĭum, *n*
active, impĭger, ălăcer
actively, impĭgrē
activity (energy), industrĭa, *f*; (agility, mobility) ăgĭlĭtas, *f*
actor, actor, *m*
actual, vērus
actually, *adv*, rē vērā
actuary, actŭārĭus, *m*
actuate, *v.t*, mŏvĕo (2), impello (3)
acumen, ăcūmen, *n*
acute, ācer, ăcūtus
acuteness, ăcĭes, *f*, ăcūmen,, *n*
adage, dictum, *n*
adapt, *v.t*, accommŏdo (1), compōno (3)
adapted, accommŏdātus, aptus
add, *v.t*, addo (3), adĭcĭo (3)
adder, vīpĕra, *f*
addict, *v.t*, dēdo (3) (*with dat*)
addicted, dēdĭtus
addition (numerical), *use verb* addo (3); (increase) accessĭo, *f*
additional (more, new, fresh), nŏvus
address, *v.t*. (a letter), inscrībo (3); (person) allŏquor (3 *dep*)
address, *nn*, (letter), inscriptĭo, *f*; (speaking) allŏquĭum, *n*
adduce, *v.t*, prōdūco (3), prōfĕro (*v. irreg*)
adept, pĕrītus
adequacy, *use* sătis (enough) (*with nn. in genit*)
adequate, sătis (*with genit*)

adhere, *v.i*, (cling) haerĕo (2)
adherent, clĭens, *m*, sectātor, *m*
adhesive, tĕnax
adjacency, vīcīnĭtas, *f*
adjacent, fīnĭtĭmus, vīcīnus, contermĭnus
adjoin, *v.i*, adĭăcĕo (2)
adjoin, *v.t*, adiungo (3)
adjoining, coniunctus, contĭgŭus
adjourn, *v.t*, diffĕro (*v. irreg*)
adjournment, dīlātĭo, *f*
adjudge (adjudicate), *v.t*, adiūdĭco
adjudication, addictĭo, *f*
adjure, *v.t*, obtestor (1 *dep*), obsĕcro (1)
adjust, *v.t*, apto (1), compōno (3)
adjustment, compŏsĭtĭo, *f*
adjutant, optĭo, *m*
administer, *v.t*, admĭnistro (1)
administration, admĭnistrātĭo, *f*, prōcūrātĭo, *f*
administrator, prōcūrātor, *m*
admirable, mīrābĭlis
admirably, *adv*, praeclārē
admiral, praefectus, (*m*) classis
admiration, admīrātĭo, *f*
admire, *v.t*, admīror (1 *dep*), mīror (1 *dep*)
admirer, laudātor, *m*
admissible, accĭpĭendus, a, um
admission, (letting in), ădĭtus, *m*; (acknowledgement) confessĭo, *f*
admit, *v.t*. (let in) admĭtto (3); (grant) dō (1), concēdo (3); (confess) confĭtĕor (2 *dep*)
admonish, *v.t*, mŏnĕo (2)
admonition, admŏnĭtĭo, *f*
adolescence, ădŏlescentĭa, *f*
adolescent, ădŏlescens, *c*
adopt, *v.t*, (person), ădopto (1); (custom) ascisco (3)
adoption, ădoptĭo, *f*
adorable, cŏlendus
adoration, cultus, *m*, ădōrātĭo, *f*
adore, *v.t*, cŏlo (3), ădōro (1)
adorn, *v.t*, orno (1)
adorned, ornātus
adornment (as an act), exornātĭo, *f*; (a decoration) ornāmentum, *n*
adrift, *adj*, in mări iactātus (driven about on the sea)
adroit, callĭdus, sollers
adroitness, dextĕrĭtas, *f*
adulation, ădūlātĭo, *f*
adult, *adj*, ădultus
adulterate, *v.t*, vĭtĭo (1)
adulteration, adultĕrātĭo, *f*
adulterer(-ess), ădulter, *m*, (-era, *f*)
adultery, ădultĕrĭum, *n*
advance, *nn*, prōgressus, *m*

For List of Abbreviations used, turn to pages 3, 4

advance, *v.i*, prōcēdo (3), prōgrĕdĭor (3 *dep*), incēdo (3), pĕdem infĕro (*irreg*)
advance, *v.t*, infĕro (*irreg*), prōmŏvĕo (2)
in advance, *adv*, prae, *compounded with vb: e.g.* **send in advance**, praemitto (3)
advance-guard, prīmum agmen, *n*
advantage, commŏdum, *n*
to be advantageous, *v.i*, prōsum (*irreg*), ūsui esse (*irreg*) (*with dat*)
advantageous, ūtĭlis
advantageously, *adv*, ūtĭlĭter
advent, adventus, *m*
adventure, făcĭnus, *n*
adventurous, audax
adventurously, *adv*, audacter
adversary, hostis, *c*
adverse, adversus
adversity, res adversae, *f. pl*
advert to, *v.t*, attingo (3)
advertise, *v.t*, prōscrībo (3), prōnuntĭo (1)
advertisement, prōscriptĭo, *f*
advice, consĭlĭum, *n*
advisable (advantageous), ūtĭlis
advise, *v.t*, mŏnĕo (2), suādĕo (2), censĕo (2)
advisedly, *adv*, consultō
adviser, suāsor, *m*, auctor, *m*
advocate, *nn*, patrōnus, *m*
advocate, *v.t*, suādĕo (2)
adze, ascĭa, *f*
aedile, aedĭlis, *m*
aedileship, aedilĭtas, *f*
aerial, *adj*, (**of the air**), āĕrĭus
afar, *adv*, prŏcŭl
affability, cōmĭtas, *f*
affable, cōmis
affably, *adv*, cōmĭter
affair, rēs, *f*, nĕgōtĭum, *n*
affect, *v.t*, affĭcĭo (3); (**the feelings**) mŏvĕo (2)
affectation (show), sĭmŭlātĭo, *f*
affected, pūtĭdus
affection (love), ămor, *m*
affectionate, ămans
affiance, *v.t*, spondĕo (2)
affianced, sponsus
affidavit, testĭmōnĭum, *n*
affiliate, *v.t*, cŏ-opto (1)
affinity, cognātĭo, *f*
affirm, *v.t*, affirmo (1)
affix, *v.t*, affīgo (3)
afflict, *v.t*, affĭcĭo (3)
afflicted (with grief), mĭser
affliction (with grief etc), mĭsĕrĭa, *f*; (**a bad thing**), mălum, *n*

affluence, dīvĭtĭae, *f. pl*
affluent, dīves
afford, *v.t*. (**give**), praebĕo (2); *otherwise use phr. with* satis pecuniae habere ut . . . (**to have enough money to. . . .**)
affright, *v.t*, terrĕo (2)
affront, contŭmēlĭa, *f*
affront, *v.t*, contŭmēlĭam facio (3) (*with dat*)
afire, *adj*, flăgrans
afloat, (*use phr. with* in aquā (**on the water**))
afoot, *adv*, pĕdĭbus
afore, *adv*, sŭprā
aforementioned, sŭprā scriptus
aforesaid, sŭprā scriptus
afraid, tĭmĭdus
afraid (to be —), *v.i. and v.t*, tĭmĕo (2), vĕrĕor (2 *dep*), mĕtŭo (3)
afresh, *adv*, rursus
aft, *nn*, puppis, *f*
after, *prep*, post (*with acc*)
after, *conj*, postquam
after, *adv*, post, postĕa
after all (nevertheless), *adv*, tămen
afternoon, *adv*, post mĕrīdĭem
afternoon, *adj*, pōmĕrīdĭānus
afterwards, *adv*, post, postĕa
again, *adv*, ĭtĕrum, rursus
again and again, *adv*, ĭdentĭdem
against, *prep*, contra, in (*with acc*)
agape, *adj*, hĭans
age, aetas, *f*, aevum, *n*, (**old —**) sĕnectus, *f*
aged (old), sĕnex
aged (three) years, nātus (tres) annos
agency (doing, action), ŏpĕra, *f*
agent, actor, *m*
aggrandize, *v.t*, amplĭfĭco (1)
aggrandizement, amplĭfĭcātĭo, *f*
aggravate, *v.t*, grăvo (1); (**annoy**) aspĕro (1); (**increase**) augĕo (2)
aggregate, *nn*, summa, *f*
aggression, incursĭo, *f*
aggressive, hostīlis
aggressor, *use phr.* suā sponte bellum inferre *irreg*, (**inflict war of one's own accord**)
aggrieve, *v.t*, *use* affĭcĭo (3) (**affect**)
aghast, stŭpĕfactus
agile, ăgĭlis
agility, ăgĭlĭtas, *f*
agitate, *v.t*, ăgĭto (1), commŏvĕo (2)
agitated, sollĭcĭtus
agitation (violent movement), ăgĭtātĭo, *f*; (**of the mind**), commōtĭo, *f*
agitator (political), turbātor, *m*

ago, *adv,* ăbhinc (*with acc*) e.g. **two years** —, ăbhinc duos annos
agonize, *v.t,* crŭcĭo (1)
agony, dŏlor, *m*
agrarian, ăgrārĭus
agree with, *v.i,* consentĭo (4) (*with cum and abl*); *v.t* compōno (3); (**it is — by all**) constat inter omnes
agreeable, grātus
agreeableness, dulcēdo, *f*
agreed upon (it is —), constat, convĕnit, *v. impers*
agreeing, congrŭens, convĕnĭens
agreement (the — itself), pactum, *n;* (**of opinions,** etc) consensĭo, *f*
agricultural, rustĭcus
agriculture, agrĭcultūra, *f*
agriculturist, agrĭcŏla, *m*
aground (to run —) *use phr.* in vădo haerĕo (2) (**stick fast in a shallow place**)
ague, horror, *m*
ah! (alas!), eheu!
ahead, *adv, use* prae, pro, *compounded with verbs,* e.g. **send ahead,** praemitto (3)
aid, auxĭlĭum, *n,* subsĭdĭum, *n*
aid, *v.t,* adĭŭvo (1), subvĕnĭo (4) (*with dat*)
ail, *v.i,* aegresco (3)
ailing, aeger, aegrōtus
aim, *v.t.* (**point a weapon,** etc.) dīrĭgo (3); (**to aim at**) pĕto (3)
aim, *nn,* (**purpose**) finis, *m,* (**throwing**) conĭectus, *m*
air, āĕr, *m*; (**manner**) spĕcĭes, *f*
air, *v.t,* ventĭlo (1)
air-hole, spīrācŭlum, *n*
airy, āĕrĭus
akin, *adj,* (**similar**) fīnĭtĭmus
alabaster, ălăbastrītes ae, *m*
alacrity, ălăcrĭtas, *f*
alarm (fear), păvor, *m,* trĕpĭdātĭo, *f*; (**confusion**) tŭmultus, *m*
alarm, *v.t,* perturbo (1), terrĕo (2)
alarmed, trĕpĭdus
alas!, heu!
alcove, angŭlus, *m* (**corner**)
alder, alnus, *f*
alderman, măgistrātus, *m*
ale, cerevisia, *f*
ale-house, caupona, *f*
alert, ălăcer
alertness, ălăcrĭtas, *f*
alien (*adj and nn*) (**foreign**), pĕrĕgrīnus
alienate, *v.t,* ălĭēno (1)
alienation, ălĭēnātĭo, *f*
alight, *v.i,* dēsĭlĭo (4)
alike, *adj,* sĭmĭlis
alike, *adv,* sĭmĭlĭter

alive, vīvus
alive (to be —), vīvo (3)
all, *adj,* (**every**) omnis; (**the whole**) tōtus; (*with superlative,* e.g. **all the best people**) optĭmus quisque; (**at all, in all**), *adv,* omnīno
all-powerful, omnĭpŏtens
allay, *v.t,* sēdo (1)
allegation, affirmātĭo, *f*
allege, *v.t.* (**assert**), argŭo (3), affĕro (*irreg*)
allegiance fĭdes, *f,* offĭcĭum, *n*
allegory, allēgŏrĭa, *f*
alleviate, *v.t,* lĕvo (1)
alleviation, (as an act), lĕvātĭo, *f*; (**something which brings —**) lĕvāmen, *n*
alley, angĭportus, *m*
alliance, sŏcĭĕtas, *f,* foedus, *n*; (**to make an —**) foedus făcĭo (3)
allied (states), foedĕrātus
allot, *v.t,* distrĭbŭo (3), assigno (1)
allotment (of land), ăger assignātus, *m*
allow, *v.t.* (**permit**), pătĭor (3 *dep*), sĭno (3), concēdo (3); *or use impers. vb.* lĭcet (*with dat. of person allowed*)
allowable, *use* făs, (*indecl. nn*) (**right**)
allowance (to make —), ignosco (3), rĕmitto (3)
allude to, *v.t,* signĭfĭco (1)
allure, *v.t,* allĭcĭo (3)
allurement, blandĭtĭa, *f,* illĕcĕbra, *f*
alluring, blandus
allusion, signĭfĭcātĭo, *f*
alluvium, allŭvĭo, *f*
ally, *nn,* sŏcĭus, *m*
ally, *v.t,* (**unite**), iungo (3); (**— oneself**) se conĭungere (*with dat*)
almanack, fasti, *m. pl*
almighty, omnĭpŏtens
almond, ămygdălum, *n;* (**tree**) ămygdăla, *f*
almost, *adv,* paenĕ, prŏpĕ, fĕrē, fermē
alms, stips, *f*
aloe, ălŏē, *f*
aloft, *adv,* sublĭmē; *adj,* sublīmis
alone, *adj,* sōlus
alone, *adv,* sōlum
along, *prep,* sĕcundum, praeter (*with acc*)
aloof, *adv,* prŏcŭl; (**to stand — from**), discēdo (3)
aloud, *adv,* magnā vōcē
alphabet, *use* litterae *f. pl* (**letters**)
already, *adv,* iam
also, *adv,* ĕtiam, quŏque, ĭtem; (**likewise**), necnōn
altar, āra, *f*

alter, *v.t*, mūto (1), verto (3), corrĭgo (3)
alter, *v.i*, mūtor (1 *dep*)
alteration, mūtātĭo, *f*
altercation, rixa, *f*
alternate, *v.t*, alterno (1)
alternate, *adj*, alternus
alternately, *adv*, invĭcem
alternation, vĭcissĭtūdo, *f*
alternative, *use phr. with* ălĭus mŏdus (other way)
although, *conj*, quamquam (*indicating fact*); quamvis (*indicating a supposition*); etsi, tămetsi
altitude, altĭtūdo, *f*
altogether, *adv*, omnīno
always, *adv*, semper
amalgamate, *v.t*, iungo (3), miscĕo (2)
amalgamation, coniunctĭo, *f*
amass, *v.t*, cŏăcervo (1), cŭmŭlo (1)
amatory, ămātōrĭus
amaze, *v.t*, obstŭpĕfăcĭo (3)
amazed, stŭpĭdus, stŭpĕfactus
amazement, stŭpor, *m*
amazing, mīrus
amazingly, *adv*, mīris mŏdis
amazon, vĭrāgo, *f*
ambassador, lēgātus, *m*
amber, sūcĭnum, *n*
ambiguity, ambāges, *f. pl*
ambiguous, ambĭgŭus, anceps
ambiguously, *adv*, per ambāges
ambition, glōrĭa, *f*, ambĭtĭo, *f*
ambitious, *use phr*. cŭpĭdus glōrĭae (keen on glory)
amble, *v.i*, lēnĭter ambŭlo (1) (walk quietly)
ambrosia, ambrŏsĭa, *f*
ambrosial, ambrŏsĭus
ambush, insĭdĭae, (*f. pl*); (to ambush) insĭdĭor (1 *dep*)
ameliorate, *v.t*, mēlĭōrem făcĭo (3)
amen! fīat! (let it be)
amenable, ŏbēdĭens
amend, *v.t*, ēmendo (1), corrĭgo (3)
amendment (correction), ēmendātĭo, *f*
amends, *use* expĭo (1) (to make —s)
amenity, ămoenĭtas, *f*
amethyst, ămĕthystus, *f*
amiability, suāvĭtas, *f*
amiable, suāvis
amiably, *adv*, suāvĭter
amicable, ămīcus
amid(st), *prep*, inter (*with acc*)
amiss, *adv*, māle; (to take —) aegre fĕro (*irreg*)
amity, ămīcĭtĭa, *f*
ammunition, arma, *n. pl*
amnesty, vĕnĭa, *f*
among, *prep*, inter, ăpud (*with acc*)

amorous, ămans
amount, summa, *f*, fīnis, *m*
amount to, *v.t*, *use* esse (to be)
amphitheatre, amphĭthĕātrum, *n*
ample, amplus, cōpĭōsus
amplify, *v.t*, amplĭfīco (1), dīlāto (1)
amplitude, amplĭtūdo, *f*
amply, *adv*, amplē
amputate, *v.t*, sĕco (1), ampŭto (1)
amputation, ampŭtātĭo, *f*
amuse, *v.t*, dēlecto (1)
amusement, dēlectātĭo, *f*
amusing, făcētus
anaesthetic, *adj*, sŏpōrĭfer
analogy (comparison), compărātĭo, *f*
analyse, *v.t*, discerpo (3), explĭco (1)
analysis, explĭcātĭo, *f*
anarchical, turbŭlentus
anarchy, lĭcentĭa, *f*
anathema, exsecrātĭo, *f* (curse)
anatomy, incīsĭo (*f*) corporis (incision of the body)
ancestor, auctor, *m*; (*in pl*), māiōres, *m. pl*
ancestral, proăvītus
ancestry (descent, origin), gĕnus, *n*
anchor, ancŏra, *f*
anchor, *v.i*, *use phr*. nāvem ad ancŏras dēlĭgo (1) (fasten a ship to the anchors)
anchorage, stătĭo, *f*
ancient, antīquus, vĕtus
and, et, atque, ac; quĕ (*joined to the second of two words*, e.g. I and you: ego tuque); (and . . . not) nĕque
anecdote, fābella, *f*
anew, *adv*, dēnŭo, dē intĕgro
anger, īra, *f*, īrācundĭa, *f*
anger, *v.t*, irrīto (1), lăcesso (3)
angle, angŭlus, *m*
angle, *v.i* (fish), piscor (1 *dep*)
angler, piscātor, *m*
angrily, *adv*, īrācundē, īrātē
angry, īrātus; (irascible) īrācundus
anguish, angor, *m*, dŏlor, *m*, ăcerbĭtas, *f*
angular, angŭlātus, angŭlāris
animal, ănĭmal, *n*, pĕcus, *f*
animal, *adj*, ănĭmālis
animate, *v.t*, ănĭmo, excĭto (1)
animated, ănĭmans; (lively) vĕgĕtus, ălăcer, vĕhĕmens
animation (liveliness), vĭgor, *m*
animosity, sĭmultas, *f*
ankle, tālus, *m*
annalist, annālĭum scriptor, *m*
annals, annāles, *m. pl*
annex, *v.t*, addo (3), iungo (3)
annihilate, *v.t*, dēlĕo (2)
annihilation, exĭtĭum, *n*, exstinctĭo, *f*

anniversary, *adj,* anniversārĭus
anniversary, *nn,* dĭes anniversārĭus, *m*
annotate, *v.t,* annŏto (1)
annotation, annŏtātĭo, *f*
announce, *v.t,* nuntĭo (1)
announcement, prōnuntĭātĭo, *f*
announcer, nuntĭus, *m,* praeco, *m*
annoy, *v.t,* irrīto (1), lācesso (3)
annoyance, mŏlestĭa, *f,* vexātĭo, *f*
annual, anniversārĭus
annually, *adv,* quŏtannis
annuity, annŭa, *n. pl*
annul, *v.t,* abrŏgo (1), tollo (3)
annulment, ăbŏlĭtĭo, *f*
anoint, *v.t,* unguo (3)
anointing, *nn,* unctĭo, *f*
anomaly, ănōmălĭa, *f*
anon, *adv* **(immediately),** stătim; **(in a short time)** brĕvi tempŏre
anonymously, *(adv. phr),* sĭne. nōmĭne
another, ălĭus; **(the other of two),** alter; **(another's),** *adj,* ălĭēnus
answer, *nn,* responsum, *n*
answer, *v.t,* respondĕo (2); **(in writing)** rescrĭbo (3); **(to — for, be surety for),** praesto (1)
answerable, *use phr,* rătĭōnem reddo (3) **(to render an account)**
ant, formĭca, *f*
antagonism, ĭnĭmīcĭtĭa, *f*
antagonist, adversārĭus, *m*
antagonistic, contrārĭus
antecedent, *adj,* antĕcēdens
antechamber, ātrĭŏlum, *n*
anterior, prior
ante-room, ātrĭŏlum, *n*
anticipate, *v.t,* occŭpo (1), antĕverto (3), praecĭpĭo (3); **(expect),** exspecto (1)
anticipation (expectation), exspectātĭo, *f*
antics, lūdi, *m, pl*
antidote, rĕmĕdĭum, *n,* antĭdŏtum, *n*
antipathy rĕpugnantĭa, *f;* **(of people)** ŏdĭum, *n*
antipodes, antĭpŏdes, *m. pl*
antiquarian, *adj,* antīquĭtatis stŭdĭōsus **(keen on antiquity)**
antiquated, priscus
antique, *adj,* vĕtus, antīquus
antiquity, antīquĭtas, *f,* vĕtustas, *f*
antithesis (opposite), contrārĭum, *n;* **(in argument),** contentĭo, *f*
antler, rāmus, *m,* cornu, *n*
anvil, incūs, *f*
anxiety, anxĭĕtas, *f,* sollĭcĭtūdo, *f,* cūra, *f;* **(alarm)** păvor, *m*
anxious, anxĭus, sollĭcĭtus; **(alarmed)** trĕpĭdus
anxiously, *adv,* anxĭē

any, *adj,* ullus *(after negatives, and in questions, and comparisons)*; quisquam *(pron. used like ullus)*; qui, quae, quod *(after si, nisi, ne num)*
anyone, anybody, *pron,* quis *(after si, nisi, ne, num)*; quisquam *(after a negative)*
anything, *use neuter of prons. given above)*
anywhere, *adv,* **(in any place),** usquam; **(to any place),** quŏ, quōquam; **(in any place),** ŭbīquĕ
apace, *adv,* **(quickly),** cĕlĕrĭtĕr
apart, *adv,* sēorsum; *(adj)* dīversus
apartment, conclāve, *n*
apathetic, lentus, pĭger
apathy, ignāvĭa, *f,* lentĭtūdo, *f*
ape, sĭmĭa, *f*
aperture, fŏrāmen, *n*
apex, căcūmen, *n,* ăpex, *m*
aphorism, sententĭa, *f*
apiary, alvĕārĭum, *n*
apiece, *use distributive numeral, e.g.* two each, bīni
apologize, *v.i,* excūso (1), dēfendo (3)
apology, excusātĭo, *f*
appal, *v.t,* perterrĕo (2)
apparatus, appărātus, *m*
apparel, vestis, *f,* vestimentum, *n*
apparent. mănĭfestus, ăpertus
apparently, *adv,* per spĕcĭem
apparition (ghost), spĕcĭes, *f,* ĭmāgo *f*
appeal, *v.i,* appello (1), prŏvŏco (1), **(to — to)** *v.t,* obtestor (1 *dep)*
appeal, *nn,* appellātĭo, *f,* obsecrātĭo, *f*
appear, *v.i,* appārĕo (2), conspĭcĭor (3 *pass)*; **(to seem)** vĭdĕor (2 *pass)*; **(to come forward)** prōdĕo (4)
appearance (looks), spĕcĭes, *f,* aspectus, *m;* **(show),** spĕcĭes, *f;* **(image),** sĭmŭlācrum, *n*
appeasable, plācābĭlis
appease, *v.t,* **(people),** plāco (1); **(feelings),** sēdo (1)
appeasement, plācātĭo, *f*
appellant, appellātor, *m*
append, *v.t.* **(attach),** addo (3)
appendage, appendix, *f*
appertain, *v.i,* pertĭnĕo (2)
appetite, appĕtītus, *m;* **(hunger),** fămes, *f*
applaud, *v.t,* plaudo (3), laudo (1)
applause (clapping), plausus, *m;* **(cheers),** clāmor, *m*
apple, mālum, *n;* **(— tree),** mālus, *f*
appliance (apparatus), appărātus, *m*
applicable to, commŏdus *(with dat)*
applicant, pĕtītor, *m*
application (asking), pĕtītĭo, *f;* **(mental),** stŭdĭum, *n,* dĭlĭgentĭa, *f*

For List of Abbreviations used, turn to pages 3, 4

apply, *v.t*, adhǐběo (2), admǒvěo (2); (to — oneself to) se, dēděre (3 *with dat*); *v.i*, (refer to), pertǐněo (2); (— for), flāgǐto (1)

appoint, *v.t*, constǐtŭo (3) (people in office, etc.), crěo (1); (to appoint to a command) praefǐcǐo (3) (*acc. of person appointed, dat. of person or thing commanded*)

appointment (office), mūnus, *n*; (creation), crěātǐo, *f*; (agreed meeting), constǐtūtum, *n*

apportion, *v.t*, dīvǐdo (3), distrǐbǔo (3)

apposite, aptus

appraise, *v.t*, (evaluate), aestǐmo (1)

appraisement, aestǐmātǐo, *f*

appreciate, *v.t*, (value), aestǐmo (1) magni

appreciation, aestǐmātǐo, *f*

apprehend, *v.t*, (arrest), comprěhendo (3); (understand), intellěgo (3), percǐpǐo (3)

apprehension (fear), formǐdo, *f*; (arrest) comprěhensǐo, *f*; (understanding), intellěgentǐa, *f*

apprehensive (fearful), tǐmǐdus

apprentice, tǐro, *m*

approach, *v.i*, apprǒpinquo (1) (*with* ad *and acc. or dat*), accēdo (3)

approach, *nn*, ădǐtus, *m*, adventus, *m*, accessus, *m*

approbation, apprǒbātǐo, *f*, laus, *f*

appropriate, *adj*, aptus, accommǒdātus (*with dat*)

appropriate, *v.t*, sūmo (3)

appropriately, *adv*, aptē

approval, apprǒbātǐo, *f*

approve (of), *v.t*, apprǒbo (1)

approved, spectātus, prǒbātus

approximate, proxǐmus

approximate, *v.i*, accēdo (3)

April, Aprǐlis (mensis)

apron, ǒpěrīmentum, *n*

apt, aptus, ǐdōněus; (inclined), prōnus, prǒpensus

aptitude (ability), ingěnǐum, *n*

aptly, *adv*, aptē

aptness, *use adj*, aptus (suitable)

aquatic, ăquātǐlis

aqueduct, ăquae ductus, *m*

aquiline, ăquǐlīnus, ăduncus

arable land, arvum, *n*

arbiter, arbǐter, *m*

arbitrarily, *adv*, (according to whim), ad lǐbǐdǐnem

arbitrary (capricious), lǐbǐdǐnōsus

arbitrate, *v.t*, discepto (1)

arbitration, arbǐtrǐum, *n*

arbitrator, arbǐter, *m*

arbour, umbrācǔlum, *n*

arc, arcus, *m*

arcade, portǐcus, *f*

arch, fornix, *m*, arcus, *m*

arch, *adj*, (playful), lascīvus

archaeology, investǐgātǐo, (*f*) rērum antīquārum (search for ancient things)

archaism, verbum obsǒlētum, *n*

archer, săgittārǐus, *m*

archipelago, *use phr*, măre, (*n*) insǔlis consǐtum (sea set with islands)

architect, archǐtectus, *m*, ǒpǐfex, *c*

architecture, archǐtectūra, *f*

archives, tăbǔlae, *f. pl*

arctic, septentrǐōnālis

ardent, ardens, fervǐdus

ardently, *adv*, ardenter, věhěmenter

ardour, ardor, *m*, călor, *m*, fervor, *m*

arduous, ardǔus

area, spătǐum, *n*

arena, hărēna, *f*, ărēna, *f*

argue, *v.i*, discepto (1), dissěro (3)

argument (quarrel), rixa, *f*, argūmentum, *n*; (discussion), dispǔtātǐo, *f*

arid, ārǐdus, siccus

aridity, ārǐdǐtas, *f*, siccǐtas, *f*

aright, *adv*, rectē

arise, *v.i*, surgo (3); (heavenly bodies), ǒrǐor (4 *dep*)

aristocracy (aristocratic party), optǐmātes, *c. pl*; (govt.) optimātǐum dǒmǐnātus, *m*

aristocratic, patrǐcǐus

arithmetic, ărǐthmētǐca, *n. pl*

ark, arca, *f*

arm (fore —), brācchǐum, *n*; (upper —), lăcertus, *m*; (weapon), telum, *n*

arms (weapons), arma, *n. pl*, tēla, *n. pl*; (call to —s), ad arma vǒco (1); (to take —s), arma căpǐo (3); (to lay down —s), arma dēdo (3)

arm, *v.t*, armo (1); (to take —s), arma căpǐo (3)

armament (forces), cōpǐae, *f*, *pl*; (weapon), tēlum, *n*

armed, armātus

armistice, indūtǐae, *f. pl*

armour, arma, *n. pl*

armourer, făber, *m*

armour-bearer, armǐger, *m*

armoury, armāmentārǐum, *n*

army, exercǐtus, *m*; (marching —), agmen, *n*; (drawn up for battle), ăcǐes, *f*

around, *adv. and prep. with acc*, circā, circum
arouse, *v.t*, suscĭto (1), excĭto (1)
arraign, *v.t*, accūso (1)
arrange, *v.t*, compōno (3), constĭtŭo (3), collŏco (1), instrŭo (3)
arrangement (as an act), collŏcātĭo, *f* (order), ordo, *m*
array, *nn*, (clothing), vestis, *f*, vestĭmenta, *n. pl*; (battle —), ăcĭes, *f*
array, *v.t*, compōno (3)
arrears, rĕlĭquae pĕcūnĭae, *f. pl* (money remaining)
arrest, *v.t*, comprĕhendo (3)
arrest, *nn*, comprĕhensĭo, *f*
arrival, adventus, *m*
arrive, *v.i*, advĕnĭo (4), pervĕnĭo (4)
arrogance, arrŏgantĭa, *f*
arrogant, arrŏgans
arrogate, *v.t*, arrŏgo (1) (*with dat*)
arrow, săgĭtta, *f*
arsenal, armāmentārĭum, *n*
art, ars, *f*
artery, vēna, *f*
artful, callĭdus, văfer
artfully, *adv*, callĭde
artfulness, callĭdĭtas, *f*
article (thing), rēs, *f*; (term of a treaty, etc.), condĭcĭo, *f*
articulate, *adj*, clārus, distinctus
articulate, *v.i*, exprĭmo (3)
articulation, explānātĭo, *f*
artifice, ars, *f*
artificer (craftsman), artĭfex, *m*, ŏpĭfex, *c*
artificial, artĭfĭcĭōsus
artificially, *adv*, mănu, artē
artillery, tormenta, *n. pl*
artisan, făber, *m*, ŏpĭfex, *c*
artist, artĭfex, *m*; (painter), pictor, *m*
artistic, artĭfĭcĭōsus
artless (person), simplex; (work), incomptus
artlessness, simplĭcĭtas, *f*
as, *conj*, (because), quod, cum, quĭa; (*in a comparative phr, e.g.* as strong as) tam fortis quam; (the same as) īdem atque; (as . . . as possible) quam *with the superlative*, *e.g.* as quickly as possible; quam cĕlerrime; (as if) tamquam, quăsĭ, vĕlut
ascend, *v.t*, ascendo (3)
ascendant (to be in the —), *v.i*, praesto (1)
ascendancy, praestantĭa, *f*
ascent, ascensus, *m*
ascertain, *v.t*, (find out), cognosco (3), compĕrĭo (4)
ascetic, *adj*, abstĭnens

ascribe, *v.t*, ascrībo (3), assigno (1), attrĭbŭo (3)
ash (tree), fraxĭnus, *f*, (*adj*), fraxĭnĕus
ashamed (to be —), pŭdet; *impers. with acc. and genit*, (*e.g.* I am ashamed of my brother), pŭdet me frātris
ashes, cĭnis, *m*
ashore, *adv*, (on shore), in lītŏre; (to shore), in lītus
aside, *use* se, *compounded with verb*, *e.g.* to put aside, sēcerno (3)
ask, *v.t*, rŏgo (1) (*with 2 accs*) *e.g.* I ask you for a sword, tē glădĭum rŏgo
askance (to look — at), līmis ŏcŭlis aspĭcĭo (3) (look with a sidelong glance)
aslant, *adv*, oblīque
asleep (to be —), *v.i*, dormĭo (4); (to fall —) obdormĭo (4)
asp, aspis, *f*
aspect (appearance), aspectus, *m*, făcĭes, *f*
asperity, ăcerbĭtas, *f*
asperse, *v.t*, aspergo (3)
aspersion, călumnĭa, *f*
asphalt, bĭtūmen, *n*
aspirate, *nn*, aspīrātĭo, *f*
aspiration (desire), affectătĭo, *f*; (hope) spes, *f*
aspire to, affecto (1)
ass, ăsĭnus, *m*
assail, *v.t*, appĕto (3), oppugno (1)
assailant, oppugnātor, *m*
assassin, percussor, *m*, sĭcārĭus, *m*
assassinate, *v.t*, trŭcīdo (1)
assassination, caedes, *f*
assault, *nn*, impĕtus, *m*, oppugnātĭo, *f*
assault, *v.t*, oppugno (1), ădŏrĭor (4 *dep*)
assemble, *v.i*, convĕnĭo (4); *v.t*, cōgo (3)
assembly, coetus, *m*, conventus, *m*; (— of the Roman people), cŏmĭtĭa, *n. pl*
assent, *nn*, assensĭo, *f*
assent to, *v.i*, assentĭor (4 *dep*) (*with dat*)
assert, *v.t*, affirmo (1), confirmo (1)
assertion, affirmātĭo, *f*, dēfensĭo, *f*
assess, *v.t* (evaluate), aestĭmo (1)
assessment (valuation), aestĭmātĭo, *f*
assessor, censor, *m*
assets, bŏna, *n. pl*
assiduity, assĭdŭĭtas, *f*, sēdŭlĭtas, *f*
assiduous, assĭdŭus, sēdŭlus
assiduously, *adv*, assĭdŭe, sēdŭlō
assign, *v.t*, assigno (1), trĭbŭo (3)
assignation, constĭtūtum, *n*

assimilate, v.t, sĭmĭlem fācĭo (3)
assist, v.t, iŭvo (1), auxĭlĭor (1 dep), subvĕnĭo (4) (with dat)
assistance, auxĭlĭum, n, ŏpem (no nomin), f
assistant, adiūtor, m
assize (provincial law-court), conventus, m
associate, nn, sŏcĭus, m
associate, v.t (join), coniungo (3); v.i, ūtor (3 dep. with abl)
association, sŏcĭĕtas, f, consortĭo, f
assort, v.t. (arrange), dīgĕro (irreg)
assortment (heap), ăcervus m.
assuage, v.t, lēvo (1), mītĭgo (1)
assume, v.t, pōno (3), sūmo (3); (take on) suscĭpĭo (3)
assumption (hypothesis), sumptĭo, f
assurance (promise), fĭdes, f; (confidence) fīdūcĭa, f
assure, v.t, confirmo (1)
assured (certain), explōrātus
assuredly, adv, (certainly), prōfecto
astern, adv, ā puppi
asthma, dyspnoea, f
astonish, v.t, obstŭpĕfācĭo (3)
astonished, stŭpĕfactus; (to be —), v.i, obstŭpesco (3)
astonishing, mīrĭfĭcus, admīrābĭlis
astonishingly, adv. phr, mīrum in mŏdum
astonishment, stŭpor, m
astound, v.t, obstŭpĕfācĭo (3)
astray (to go —), v.i, erro (1); (to lead —), v.t, indūco (3)
astrologer, măthēmătĭcus, m
astrology, astrŏlŏgĭa, f
astronomy, astrŏlŏgĭa, f
astute, callĭdus
astuteness, callĭdĭtas, f
asylum (refuge), perfŭgĭum, n
at, (of place) in (with abl), ad, ăpŭd (with acc); with proper names and dŏmus use locative case, e.g. at Rome, Rōmae, at home, dŏmi; (of time) use abl. case, e.g. at the third hour, tertĭa hōra; or sometimes ăd with the acc. case
atheist, ăthĕŏs, m
athlete, āthlēta, c
athletic (strong), fortis
athwart, prep (across), trans (with acc)
Atlantic, Ocĕānus, m
atmosphere, āēr, m
atom, ătŏmus, f, sēmĭna (n.pl) rērum (seeds of things)
atone for, v.t, expĭo (1)
atonement, expĭātĭo, f
atrocious, nĕfārĭus

atrociousness, fĕrĭtas, f
atrocity, nĕfas, n
atrophy, tābes, f
atrophy, v.i, tābesco (3)
attach, v.t. (fasten), affĭgo (3), applĭco (1); (connect) adiungo (3)
attached (fastened), fĭxus, aptus; (fond) dēvinctus, āmans
attachment (affection), stŭdĭum, n, ămor, m
attack, nn, impĕtus, m, oppugnātĭo, f
attack, v.t, oppugno (1), aggrĕdĭor (3 dep), ădŏrĭor (4 dep), invādo (3), pĕto (3)
attacker, oppugnātor, m
attain, v.i. (reach), pervĕnĭo (4) (with ad and acc); v.t. (obtain), consĕquor (3 dep)
attainable, impĕtrābĭlis
attainment (obtaining), ădeptĭo, f; (learning) ērŭdītĭo, f
attempt nn, inceptum, n, cōnātum, n
attempt, v.i, cōnor (1 dep)
attend, v.i. (be present at), intersum (irreg. with dat); v.t. (accompany), cŏmĭtor (1 dep), prōsĕquor, (3 dep); (pay attention) ŏpĕram do (1), ănĭmadverto (3)
attendance (being present), use vb. adsum (irreg) (to be present); (of crowds), frĕquentĭa, f; (service), appārĭtĭo, f
attendant, nn, (servant) mĭnister, m; (of a nobleman) sectātor, m, sătellĕs, c
attention (concentration), attentĭo (f) ănĭmi; (to pay —); ŏpĕram, (f) do (1)
attentive (alert), intentus, attentus; (respectful), observans
attentively, adv, sēdŭlo
attenuate, v.t, attĕnŭo (1)
attest, v.t, testor (1 dep)
attestation, testĭfĭcātĭo, f
attire, nn, vestis, f
attire, v.t, vestĭo (4)
attitude (of mind), ănĭmus, m; (of body), gestus m, hăbĭtus, m
attract, v.t, attrăho (3), allĭcĭo (3)
attraction (charms), illĕcĕbrae (f. pl)
attractive, blandus, iūcundus
attribute, v.t, attrĭbŭo (3), assigno (1)
attune, v.t, (adjust), consŏnum (aptum) reddo (3) (make harmonious (suitable))
auburn, flāvus
auction, auctĭo, f; (to sell by public—), sub hastā vendo (3) (sell under the spear)

auctioneer, praeco, *m*
audacious, audax
audacity, audācĭa, *f*, confīdentĭa, *f*
audibly, *use phr.* quod audīri pŏtest (that can be heard)
audience (of people), audītōres, *m,pl* (hearing), ădītus, *m*
audit, *v.t*, inspĭcĭo (3)
auditorium, auditorĭum, *n*
augment, *v.t*, augĕo (2)
augur, *nn*, augur, *c*
augur, *v.t*, vātĭcĭnor (1 *dep*)
augury, augŭrĭum, *n*, auspĭcĭum, *n*
August, Sextīlis or Augustus (mensis)
august, *adj*, augustus
aunt (paternal), ămĭta, *f*; (maternal), mātertĕra, *f*
auspices, auspĭcĭum, *n*
auspicious, faustus, sĕcundus
auspiciously, *adv*, fēlīcĭter
austere (severe), sĕvērus
austerity, sĕvērĭtas, *f*
authentic, vērus, certus
authentically, *adv*, certō
authenticate, *v.t*, rĕcognosco (3)
authenticity, auctōrĭtas, *f*
author (writer), scrīptor, *m*; (instigator), auctor, *m*
authoritative, grăvis, impērĭosus
authority, auctōrĭtas, *f*, pŏtestas, *f*, impērĭum, *n*
authorize (give permission to), *v.t*, pŏtestātem (auctōrĭtātem) făcĭo (3) (*with dat*)
autocracy, tȳrannis, *f*
autocrat, dŏmĭnus, *m*,
autograph, mănus, *f*
autumn, auctumnus, *m*
autumnal, auctumnālis
auxiliary, *adj*, auxĭlĭāris, auxĭlĭārĭus; *nn* adiūtor, *m*; (—forces) auxilĭa, *n.pl*
avail, *v.t* (assist), prōsum (*irreg*) (*with dat*.); (make use of), ūtor (3 *dep. with abl*)
available (ready), expĕdītus, părātus
avarice, ăvārĭtĭa, *f*
avaricious, ăvārus
avenge, *v.t*, ulciscor (3 *dep*)
avenger, ultor, *m*
avenging, *adj*, ultrix
avenue, xystus, *m*
aver, *v.t* (affirm), affirmo (1)
average, *adj*, mĕdĭus (middle)
averse, āversus
aversion, ŏdĭum, *n*,
avert, *v.t*, āverto (3), dēpello (3)
aviary, ăvĭārĭum, *n*
avid, ăvĭdus
avidity, ăvĭdĭtas, *f*

avoid, *v.t*, vīto (1), fŭgĭo (3)
avoidance, vītātĭo, *f*, fŭga, *f*
avow, *v.t*, fătĕor (2 *dep*)
avowal, confessĭo, *f*
avowed, prŏfessus, ăpertus
await, *v.t*, exspecto (1)
awake, *adj*, vĭgĭlans; (to be —), *v.t*, vĭgĭlo (1); (to awake), *v.t*, excĭto (1)
award, *nn*, (judicial decision); arbĭtrĭum, *n* (prize), palma, *f*
award, *v.t*, trĭbŭo (3), adiūdĭco (1)
aware, gnārus; (to be —), sentĭo (4); (know), scĭo (4)
away, *use* a, ab *compounded with a verb, e.g.* (ăbĕo) go away (4)
awe, formīdo, *f*, mĕtus, *m*, rĕvĕrentĭa, *f*
awe (be in —) vĕrĕor, (2 *dep*.)
awful, vĕrendus
awestruck, păvĭdus
awhile, *adv*, paulisper, părumper
awkward, rŭdis, impērītus
awkwardness, inscĭtĭa, *f*
awning, vēlum, *n*
awry, *adj*, perversus; *adv*, perversē
axe, sĕcūris, *f*
axiom, sententĭa, *f*
axis, axle, axis, *m*
ay, aye, *adv*, ĭta, vērō; (forever) in perpĕtŭum
azure, *adj*, caerŭlĕus

B

babble, *v.i*, garrĭo (4), blătĕro (1)
babbler, babbling, *adj*, garrŭlus
baby, infans, *c*
babyhood, infantĭa, *f*
bacchanalian, bacchānālis
bachelor, *adj*, caelebs
back, *nn*, tergum, *n*, dorsum, *n*; (at the —) a tergo; (to move something —), rĕtro mŏvĕo (2), rēĭcĭo (3); (to go —) se rĕcĭpĕre (3 *reflex*)
backbite, *v.t*, obtrecto (1)
backwards, *adj*, (dull) pĭger
backwards, *adv*, rĕtro
bacon, lārīdum, *n*
bad, mălus; (of health), aeger; (of weather), ădversus
badge, insigne, *n*
badger, mēles, *f*
badly, *adv*, mălē, prāvē, imprŏbē
badness (worthlessness), nēquĭtĭa, *f*
baffle, *v.t*, ēlūdo (3)
bag, saccus, *m*
baggage (military), impĕdīmenta, *n.pl*; (individual packs), sarcĭnae, *f. pl*
bail, *nn*, (person), văs, *m*; (security) vădĭmōnĭum, *n*

bail (to give — for), *v.t*, spondĕo (2) prō (*with abl*)

bailiff (estate manager), villĭcus, *m*; (official), appārĭtor, *m*

bait, *nn*, esca, *f*

bait, *v.t*, (tease), lăcesso (3), illūdo (3)

bake, *v.t*, torrĕo (2), cŏquo (3)

baker, pistor, *m*

bakery, pistrīnum, *n*

balance, *nn*, (scales), lībra, *f*; (equilibrium), lībrāmentum, *n*

balance, *v.t*, lībro (1), compenso (1)

balcony, maenĭāna, *n.pl*

bald, calvus, glăber; (unadorned), ārĭdus

baldness, calvĭtĭum, *n*

bale out, *v.t*, (discharge), ēgĕro (3)

bale (bundle), fascis, *m*

baleful, pernĭcĭōsus

balk (beam), trabs, *f*

balk, *v.t*, frustror (1 *dep*)

ball (for play), pīla, *f*; (globe, sphere), glŏbus, *m*

ballad, carmen. *n*

ballad-singer, cantātor, *m*

ballast, săbura, *f*

ballet, *use vb*. salto (1) (dance)

ballista, ballista, *f*

ballot, suffrāgĭum, *n*

ballot-box, cista, *f*, urna, *f*

balm, balsāmum, *n*, unguentum, *n*

balmy (soothing), mollis, lēnis

balustrade (railings), cancelli, *m. pl*

bamboo, hărundo, *f* (reed)

ban, *v.t*, vēto (1)

band (bond), vincŭlum, *n*; (of people), mănus, *f*, grex, *m*

band together, *v.i*, coniūro (1)

bandage, fascĭa, *f*

bandage, *v.t*, lĭgo (1)

bandit, lătro, *m*

bandy (to — words), *v.i*, altercor (1 *dep*)

bandy-legged, lōrĭpes

bane (injury), pernĭcĭes, *f*; (poison), vĕnēnum, *n*

baneful, pernĭcĭōsus

bang, crĕpĭtus, *m*

bang, *v.t*. (beat), tundo (3)

banish, *v.t, use phr*. ăquā et ĭgni interdīco (3) (*with dat*) (forbid one the use of fire and water), expello (3)

banishment, rĕlēgātĭo, *f*, exsĭlĭum, *n*

bank, *nn*, (of earth), tŏrus, *m*; (of a river), rīpa, *f*; (for money), argentārĭa tăberna (money shop)

banker, argentārĭus, mensārĭus, *m*

bankrupt, *nn*, dēcoctor, *m*, (to be —), *v.i*, solvendo non esse

bankruptcy (personal), rŭīna, *f* (downfall)

banner, vexillum, *n*

banquet, convīvĭum, *n*, ĕpŭlae, *f. pl*

banter, *nn*, căvillātĭo, *f*

banter, *v.i*, căvillor (1 *dep*)

bar (wooden), asser, *m*; (lock), claustra, *n. pl*; (bolt), sĕra, *f*; (barrier), rĕpāgŭla, *n. pl*

bar, *v.t* (fasten), obsĕro (1); (— the way), obsto (1) (*with dat*)

barb (hook), uncus, *m*

barbarian, barbărus, *m*

barbaric (barbarous), barbărus, crūdēlis, immānis

barbarity, barbărĭa, *f*

barbarously, *adv*, (cruelly), crūdēlĭter

barbed, hāmātus

barber, tonsor, *m*

bard (poet, etc.), poēta, *m*

bare, nūdus; (to make —), *v.t*, ăpĕrĭo (4), nūdo (1)

barefaced, (shameless), impŭdens

barefoot, *adv*, nūdo pĕde

barely, *adv*, vix

bargain, *nn*, pactum, *n*

bargain, *v.i*, (make a — with), pacīscor (3 *dep*) (*with* cum *and abl.* of *person*)

barge, linter, *f*; (— man), nauta, *m*

bark, *nn*, (of trees), cortex, *m*; (of dogs), lātrātus, *m*; (boat), rătis, *f*

bark, *v.i*, lātro (1)

barley, hordĕum, *n*

barley-water, ptīsăna, *f*

barn, horrĕum, *n*

baron, princeps, *m*

barque, rătis, *f*

barracks, castra, *n. pl*

barrel, dōlĭum, *n*

barren, stĕrĭlis

barrenness, stĕrĭlĭtas, *f*

barricade, *nn*, agger, *m*

barricade, *v.t*, obsaepĭo (4)

barrier, impĕdĭmentum, *n*, claustra, *n. pl*

barrister, pătrōnus, *m*

barrow, fercŭlum, *n*

barter, *v.t*, (exchange), mūto (1);

barter, *nn*, permūtātĭo, (*f*,) mercĭum (exchange of goods)

base, *nn*, băsis, *f*, fundāmentum, *n*

base, *adj*, (worthless), turpis; (lowborn), hŭmĭlis

baseless, *adj*, falsus

basely, *adv*, turpĭter

basement, băsis, *f*

baseness, turpĭtūdo, *f*

bashful, vĕrēcundus

bashfulness, vĕrēcundĭa, *f*

basin, pelvis, *f*

basis, băsis, *f*, fundāmentum, *n*

bask, *v.i*, āprĭcor (1 *dep*)

basket, călăthus, *m*, corbis, *f*, quālum, *n*

bass, *adj*, grăvis

bastard, *adj*, nŏthus

bastion, turris, *f*

bat (animal), vespertīlĭo, *m*; (club, stick), clāva, *f*

bath, *nn*, balnĕum, *n*; (public —) balnĕae, *f. pl*

bath, bathe *v.i*, lăvor (1 *pass*); v.t, lăvo (1)

bathing, *nn*, lăvātĭo, *f*

baton, scīpĭo, *m*

battalion, cŏhors, *f*

batter, v.t, pulso (1), verbĕro (1)

battering-ram, ărĭes, *m*

battery (assault), vīs, *f*; (cannon), tormenta, *n. pl*

battle, proelĭum, *n*; (—line), ăcĭes, *f*; (—ory), clāmor, *m*; (—field), lŏcus (*m*) pugnae

battlement, pinna, *f*, mūnītĭōnes, *f. pl*

bawd, lēna, *f*

bawl, *v.i*, clāmĭto (1)

bawling, *nn*, clāmor, *m*

bay (of the sea), sĭnus, *m*; (tree) laurus, *f*; (at bay) (*adj*) părātus ad pugnam (ready for a fight)

bay, *v.i*, lātro (1)

bayonet, pūgĭo, *m*

be, *v.i*, sum (*irreg*)

beach, lītus, *n*

beacon (fire), ignis, *m*

bead, băca, *f*

beak, rōstrum, *n*

beaker, pōcŭlum, *n*

beam (of timber), tignum, *n*, trabs, *f*; (cross —), transtrum, *n*; (ray) rădĭus, *m*

bean, făba, *f*

bear, *nn*, ursus, *m*, ursa, *f*; (constellation), septentrĭōnes, *m. pl*; (The Great —), ursa maior; (The Little —) septentrio minor

bear, *v.t*, fĕro (*irreg*), gĕro (3); (carry), porto (1); (produce), părĭo (3); (— away) aufĕro (*irreg*)

bearable, *adj*, tŏlĕrābĭlis

beard, barba, *f*; (bearded), barbātus

bearer (carrier), băiŭlus, *m*, portĭtor, *m*

bearing (posture), gestus, *m*

beast (wild), bestĭa, *f*, fĕra, *f*; (domestic), pĕcus, *f*

beastly (filthy), obscēnus

beat (in music, poetry), ictus, *m*

beat, *v.t*, caedo (3), fĕrĭo (4), verbĕro (1); (conquer), sŭpĕro (1), vinco (3); (— back), rĕpello (3); (— down) sterno (3); (be beaten), *v.i*, vāpŭlo (1)

beating, *nn*, verbĕra, *n. pl*

beautiful, pulcher

beautifully, *adv*, pulchre

beautify, *v.t*, orno (1)

beauty, pulchrĭtūdo, *f*, forma, *f*

beaver, castor, *m*

becalmed, vento dēstĭtūtus (deserted by the wind)

because, *conj*, quod, quĭa, cum; (because of) *prep*, propter, ŏb (*with acc*)

beckon, *v.t*, innŭo (3) (*with dat*)

become, *v.i*, fīo (*irreg*); *v.t* (to suit, adorn), dĕcet (2 *impers. with acc. of person*)

becoming, *adj*, dĕcōrus

bed, lectus, *m*; (go to —), cŭbĭtum ēo (4)

bedroom, cŭbĭcŭlum, *n*

bedaub, *v.t*, lĭno (3)

bedeck, *v.t*, orno (1); (bedecked), ornātus

bedew, *v.t*, irrōro (1)

bee, ăpis, *f*

bee-hive, alvĕārĭum, *n*

beech-tree, făgus, *f*

beef, căro būbŭla, *f*, (ox flesh)

beer, cerevisia, *f*

beetle, scarabaeus, *m*

befall, *v.i*, accĭdo (3)

befit, *v.i* (suit), convĕnĭo (4)

before, *prep*, (time and place), antĕ (*with acc*); (place), prae, prō (*with abl*); (in the presence of), cōram (*with abl*); before, *adv*, (time), antĕ, prĭus; (space) prae; before, *conj*, antĕquam, prĭusquam

befoul, *v.t*, inquĭno (1)

befriend, *v.t*, adiŭvo (1)

beg, *v.t* (request), pĕto (3), ōro (1); (be a beggar), *v.i*, mendīco (1)

beget, *v.t*, gigno (3)

begetter, gĕnĭtor, *m*

beggar, mendīcus, *m*

begin, *v.i*, incĭpĭo (3), coepī (3 *defect*)

beginner (originator), auctor, *m*; (learner), tīro, *m*

beginning, *nn*, inĭtĭum, *n*, princĭpĭum, *n*, inceptum, *n*

begone! ăpăgĕ!

begrudge, *v.t* (envy), invĭdĕo (2) (*with dat*)

beguile, v.t, fallo (3), dēcĭpĭo (3)
behalf (on — of), (prep), prō (with abl)
behave oneself, v. reflex, se gĕrĕre (3)
behaviour (manners), mōres, m. pl
behead, v.t, sĕcūri fĕrĭo (4) (strike with an axe)
behest (command), iussum, n
behind (prep), post (with acc)
behind, adv, post, ā tergo
behold, v.t, conspĭcĭo (3)
behold! (exclamation), eccĕ!
being (human —), hŏmo, c
belabour, v.t, verbĕro (1)
belated, sērus
belch, v.i, and v.t, ructo (1)
belch, nn, ructus, m
beleaguer, v.t, obsĭdĕo (2)
belfry, turris, f
belie, v.t, (conceal), dissĭmŭlo (1)
belief, fĭdes, f; (impression), ŏpīnĭo, f, persuāsĭo, f
believe, v.t, crēdo (3) (with dat. of person), pŭto (1), arbĭtror (1 dep), censĕo (2)
believer, crēdens, c
bell, tintinnābŭlum, n
belligerent, bellans, belli cŭpĭdus (keen on war)
bellow, v.i, mūgĭo (4)
bellowing, nn, mūgītus, m
bellows (pair of —), follis, m
belly, venter, m, abdōmen, n
belong to, v.i, use esse (irreg) (to be) with genit. of person
beloved, cārus, dīlectus
below, prep, infrā, subter (with acc) sub (with abl. or acc)
below, adv, infrā, subter
belt, baltĕus, m
bemoan, v.t, gĕmo (3)
bench, scamnum, n; (for rowers) transtrum, n
bend, v.t, flecto (3), curvo (1); v.i, se flectĕre (3 pass)
bend, bending, nn, flexus, m
beneath, see below
benefactor, phr, qui bĕnĕfĭcĭa confert (who confers favours)
beneficence, bĕnĕfĭcentĭa, f
beneficent, bĕnĕfĭcus
beneficial, sălūtāris, ūtĭlis; (to be —) v.i, prōsum (irreg) (with dat)
benefit, v.i, prōsum (irreg) (with dat), adiŭvo (1)
benefit, nn, bĕnĕfĭcĭum, n
benevolence, bĕnĕfĭcentĭa, f, bĕnĕvŏlentĭa, f
benevolent, bĕnĕfĭcus, bĕnĕvŏlus
benign, bĕnignus

benignity, bĕnignĭtas, f
bent, adj, curvus; (— on) attentus; (— back) rĕsŭpīnus; (— forward) prōnus
benumb, v.t, phr torpōre affĭcĭo (3) (affect with numbness)
bequeath, v.t, lēgo (1)
bequest, lēgātum, n
bereave, v.t, orbo (1)
bereaved, orbus
bereavement, orbĭtas, f, damnum, n
berry, bāca, f
berth (for a ship), stătĭo, f
beseech, ōro (1), obsecro (1), quaeso (3)
beseem (become), dĕcet (2 impers. with acc. of person)
beset, v.t, obsĭdĕo (2), circumvĕnĭo (4)
beside, prep, (near), prŏpĕ (with acc); (except), praeter (with acc)
besides, prep, praeter (with acc)
besides, adv or conj, praeterquam
besides, adv, (further), praetĕrĕā, insŭper
besiege, v.t, obsĭdĕo (2), circum sĕdĕo (2)
besieger, obsessor, m
besmear, v.t, illĭno (3)
bespatter, v.t, aspergo (3)
bespeak, v.t, (hire) condūco (3)
besprinkle, v.t, aspergo (3)
best, adj, optĭmus; (to the best of (one's) ability) prō (vīrili) parte; best, adv, optĭmē
bestial, use phr, bestĭārum mōre (after the manner of beasts)
bestir (to — oneself), v.i, expergiscor (3 dep)
bestow, v.t, do (1), trĭbŭo (3), confĕro (irreg)
bestowal, largītĭo, f
bet, nn, pignus, n
bet, v.t, pignŏre contendo (3)
betake, v.t, conferre (irreg)
betimes, adv, mātūrē
betray, v.t, prōdo (3)
betrayal, prōdĭtĭo, f
betrayer, prōdĭtor, m
betroth, v.t, spondĕo (2)
betrothal, sponsālĭa, n. pl
better, adj, mēlĭor; (of health), sānus; **better,** adv, mēlĭus
better, v.t, (improve), corrĭgo (3); ēmendo (1)
between, prep, inter (with acc)
beverage, pōtĭo, f, pōtus, m
bevy, căterva, f
bewail, v.t, dēplōro (1), lūgeo (2)
beware, v.i and v.t, căvĕo (2)
bewilder, v.t, perturbo (1), distrăho (3)

bewildered, turbātus, distractus
bewitch, *v.t*, fascīno (1); (charm), căpĭo (3)
beyond, *prep*, ultrā, trans, sŭprā, extrā (*with acc*)
beyond, *adv*, ultrā, sŭprā
bias, inclīnātĭo, *f*
bias, *v.t*, inclīno (1)
Bible, *use phr.* scripta săcra, *n. pl* (sacred writings)
bicker, *v.i*, altercor (1 *dep*)
bid, *nn*, (of a price) lĭcĭtātĭo, *f*
bid, *v.t* (tell, order), iŭbĕo (2)
bide, *v.i* (stay), mănĕo (2)
bier, fĕrĕtrum, *n*, fercŭlum, *n*
big, magnus, vastus, ingens
bigotry, obstĭnātĭo, *f*
bile, bīlis, *f*
bilge-water, sentīna, *f*
bilious, bīliōsus
bill (written, financial), lĭbellus, *m*, rātĭo, *f*, syngrăpha, *f*; (proposal in Parliament), rŏgātĭo, *f*; (a law), lex, *f*; (of a bird), rōstrum, *n*
billet (of wood), lignum, *n*; (lodging of soldiers), hospĭtĭum, (*n*) mīlĭtum
billet, *v.t* (soldiers), per hospĭtĭa dispōno (3) (distribute through lodgings)
billow, fluctus, *m*
billowy, fluctŭosus
bind, *v.t*, lĭgo (1), vincĭo (4); (oblige), oblĭgo (1); (— together), collĭgo (1)
biographer, scriptor rērum gestārum (writer of exploits)
biography, vĭta, *f*
birch (tree), bĕtŭla, *f*
bird, ăvis, *f*; (— cage), căvĕa, *f*; (— nest), nīdus, *m*
birth, ortus, *m*, gĕnus, *n*
birthday, (dĭes) nātālis
birth-place, sōlum, *n*, (*n*) nātāle
bishop, pontĭfex, *m*
bit (bite), offa, *f*; (small piece of food), frustrum, *n*; (for a horse), frēnum, *n*
bitch, cănis, *f*
bite, *nn*, morsus, *m*
bite, *v.t*, mordĕo (2)
biting, *adj*, mordax, asper
bitter, ămārus, ăcerbus, asper
bitterness, ăcerbĭtas, *f*
bitumen, bĭtūmen, *n*
bivouac, *nn*, excŭbĭae, *f. pl*
bivouac, *v.i*, excŭbo (1)
blab, *v.i*, blătĕro (1)
black, nĭger; (— art), măgĭce, *f*
blackberry, mōrum, *n*, rŭbus, *m*
blackbird, mĕrŭla, *f*
blacken, *v.t*, nigrum reddo (3)

blackguard, nēbŭlo, *m*
Black Sea, Pontus Euxīnus, *m*
blacksmith, făber, *m*
bladder, vēsīca, *f*
blade (of grass), herba, *f*; (of sword, knife), lămĭna, *f*
blame, *nn*, culpa, *f*
blame, *v.t*, culpo (1)
blameable, culpandus
blameless, innŏcens, intĕger
blamelessness, innocentĭa, *f*
bland, blandus
blandishment, blandītĭa, *f*, blandīmentum, *n*
blank, *adj*, (empty), văcŭus; (paper), pūrus
blank, *nn*, ĭnāne, *n*
blanket, lōdix, *f*
blaspheme, *v.t*, blasphēmo (1)
blast, *nn*, flāmen, *n*, flātus, *m*
blast, *v.t*, ūro (3)
blatant, *adj*, (manifest), ăpertus
blaze, *nn*, flamma, *f*
blaze, *v.i*, ardĕo (2), flăgro (1)
bleach, candĭdum reddo (3)
bleak, algĭdus, frīgĭdus
blear-eyed, lippus
bleat, bleating, bālātus, *m*
bleat, *v.i*, bālo (1)
bleed, *v.i*, sanguĭnem effundo (3); *v.t*, sanguĭnem mitto (3)
bleeding, *adj*, (wound), crūdus
bleeding, *nn*, *use phr* effūsĭo, (*f*), sanguĭnis (shedding of blood)
blemish, *nn*, (physical), vĭtĭum, *n*, (moral), măcŭla, *f*
blemish, *v.t*, măcŭlo (1)
blend, *v.t*, miscĕo (2)
bless, *v.t*, (favour, make successful), sĕcundo (1), bĕnĕdīco (3)
blessed, beātus; (of the dead), pĭus
blessedness, bĕātĭtūdo, *f*, fēlĭcĭtas, *f*
blessing, *nn*, bĕnĕdictĭo, *f*, bŏnum, *n*
blight, *nn*, rōbīgo, *f*
blight, *v.t*, ūro (3); (— of hopes) frustror (1 *dep*)
blind, *adj*, caecus
blind, *v.t*, caeco (1)
blindly (rashly), *adv*, tĕmĕre
blindness, caecĭtas, *f*
blink, *v.i*, connīvĕo (2)
bliss, fēlĭcĭtas, *f*
blissful, *adj*, fēlix
blister, pustŭla, *f*
blithe, hĭlăris
blizzard, imber, *m*
bloated, sufflātus
block, *nn*, (of wood), stīpes, *m*, massa, *f*
block, *v.t*, obstrŭo (3), obsaepĭo (4)

blockade, *nn*, obsĭdĭo, *f*
blockade, *v.t*, obsĭdĕo (2)
blockhead, caudex, *m*
blood, sanguis, *m*; (gore), crŭor, *m*
blood-letting, *nn*, missĭo, (*f*) sanguĭnis
bloodshed, caedes, *f*
bloodshot, crŭōre suffusus (spread over with blood)
blood-stained, crŭentus
blood-thirsty, sanguĭnārĭus
bloody, crŭentus, sanguĭnĕus
bloom, *nn*, flōs, *m*
bloom, *v.i*, flōrĕo (2)
blooming, flōrens
blossom, etc.; *see* bloom
blot, *v.t*, măcŭlo (1); (— out, obliterate), dēlĕo (2)
blot, *nn*, măcŭla, *f*
blow, *nn*, (stroke), plāga, *f*, ictus, *m*
blow, *v.i and v.t*, flo (1)
blowing, *nn*, flātus, *m*
bludgeon, fustis, *m*
blue, *adj*, caerŭlĕus
bluff, *v.t*, illūdo (3)
blunder, *nn*, mendum, *n*, error, *m*
blunder, *v.i*, offendo (3), erro (1)
blunt, *adj*, hĕbes; (frank), lĭber
blunt, *v.t*, hĕbĕto (1), obtundo (3)
bluntly, *adv*, lĭbĕrē, plāne
blush, *nn*, rŭbor, *m*
blush, *v.i*, ērŭbesco (3)
bluster, *v.i*, dēclāmo (1)
bluster, *nn*, dēclāmātĭo, *f*
blusterer, iactātor, *m*
boar, verres, *m*, ăper, *m*
board, *nn*, tăbŭla, *f*; (council), concĭlĭum, *n*
board, *v.t* (ship), conscendo (3); (to — up), contăbŭlo (1); (provide food), victum praebĕo (2)
boast, *v.i*, glōrĭor (1 *dep*.), se iactare (1 *reflex*)
boasting, *nn*, glōrĭātĭo, *f*, iactātĭo, *f*
boat, scăpha, *f*, linter, *f*
boatman, nauta, *m*
bode, *v.t* (predict), praesāgĭo (4)
bodily, *adj*, corpŏrĕus
bodkin, ăcus, *f*
body, corpus, *n*; (— of soldiers, etc.), mănus, *f*, nŭmĕrus, *m*, multĭtūdo, *f*
body-guard, stĭpātōres, *m. pl*
bog, pălus, *f*
boggy, păluster
boil, *nn*, vŏmĭca, *f*
boil, *v.t*, cŏquo (3); *v.i*, fervĕo (2)
boiled, *adj*, ēlixus
boiler, caldarĭum, *n*
boisterous, prŏcellōsus, turbĭdus

bold, audax, ănĭmōsus, fortis
boldly, *adv*, audacter, anĭmōse, fortĭter
boldness, audācĭa, *f*, fĭdentĭa, *f*
bolster, cervical, *n*, pulvīnus, *m*
bolt, *nn* (door, etc.), ŏbex, *m*, rĕpāgŭla, *n.pl*
bolt, *v.t* (door, etc.), obsĕro (1), claudo (3); (food), obsorbĕo (2)
bombastic, inflātus
bond, vincŭlum, *n*, cătēna, *f*; (legal), syngrăpha, *f*
bondage, servĭtus, *f*
bone, ŏs, *n*
book, lĭber, *m*, lĭbellus, *m*
bookbinder, glūtĭnātor, *m*
bookcase, armārĭum, *n*
book-keeper, actŭārĭus, *m*
bookseller, bibliŏpōla, *m*
boom, *v.i*, sŏno (1)
boon (good thing), bŏnum, *n*
boor, hŏmo ăgrestis
boorish, agrestis
boot, calcĕus, *m*; (heavy —), călĭga, *f*
bootless (unsuccessful), *adj*, irrĭtus
booth, tăberna, *f*
booty, praeda, *f*, spŏlĭa, *n.pl*
booze, *v.i. and v.t*, pōto (1)
border, margo, *m*, *f*; (of a country), fĭnis, *m*
border, *v.i*, attingo (3)
bordering, *adj*, fĭnītĭmus
bore (person) use, *adj*, importūnus (rude)
bore, *v.t*, perfŏro (1), tĕrĕbro (1); (— someone), fătīgo (1)
boredom, taedĭum, *n*
born, *adj*, nātus; (to be —), *v.i*, nascor (3 *dep*.)
borough, mūnĭcĭpĭum, *n*
borrow, mūtŭor (1 *dep*.)
bosom, sĭnus, *m*, pectus, *n*
boss (of a shield), umbo, *m*
botany, ars herbārĭa, *f*
botch, *v.t*, măle sarcĭo (4), (patch badly)
both, ambo; (each ∙of two), ŭterquĕ; (both . . . and), et . . . et
bother, *nn*, use *adj*, mŏlestus (troublesome)
bother, *v.t*, lăcesso (3), vexo (1)
bottle, ampulla, *f*, lăgēna, *f*
bottom, fundus, *m*, or use *adj*. īmus *in agreement with noun, e.g.* at the bottom of the tree, ad īmam arbŏrem
bottomless (very deep), prŏfundus
bough, rāmus, *m*
boulder, saxum, *n*

bounce, *v.i*, rĕsĭlĭo (4)
bound (limit), fīnis, *m*, mŏdus, *m*; (leap), saltus, *m*
bound, *v.i*, (leap), sălĭo (4); *v.t*, (limit), contĭnĕo (2)
boundary, fīnis, *m*
boundless, infīnītus
bountiful, largus, bĕnignus
bounty, largĭtas, *f*, bĕnignĭtas, *f*
bouquet, serta, *n.pl*
bout (contest), certāmen, *n*
bow (archery), arcus, *m*; (of a ship), prōra, *f*; (of salutation), sălūtātĭo, *f*
bow, *v.t*, inclīno (1), dēmitto (3); *v.i*, se dēmittĕre (3 *reflex*)
bow-legged, vătĭus
bowman, săgittārĭus, *m*
bowels, viscĕra, *n.pl*
bower, umbrācŭlum, *n*
bowl, crātēra, *f*
box, arca, *f*, cista, *f*; (tree), buxus, *f*; (slap), cŏlăphus, *m*
box, *v.i*, pugnis certo (1), (fight with the fists)
boxer, pŭgil, *m*
boxing, *nn*, pŭgĭlātĭo, *f*
boy, pŭer, *m*
boyhood, pŭerĭtĭa, *f*
boyish, pŭerīlis
brace (support), fascĭa, *f*; (in architecture), fībŭla, *f*
brace, *v.t*, lĭgo (1), firmo (1)
bracelet, armilla, *f*
bracket, mūtŭlus, *m*
brackish, ămārus
brag, *v.i*, glōrĭor (1 *dep*.)
braggart, iactator, *m*
braid, *nn*, (of hair), grădus, *m*
braid, *v.t*, necto (3)
brain, cĕrĕbrum, *n*
brainless (stupid), sōcors
bramble, dūmus, *m*
bran, furfur, *m*
branch, rāmus, *m*
branch, *v.i*, (separate), dīvĭdor (3 *pass*)
branching, *adj*, rāmōsus
brand (fire —), fax, *f*, torris, *m*; (burn-mark), nŏta, *f*; (stigma), stigma, *n*
brand, *v.t*, ĭnūro (3), nŏto (1)
brandish, *v.t*, vibro (1)
brass, ŏrĭchalcum, *n*
brave, fortis, ănĭmōsus, ăcer
bravely, *adv*, fortĭter, ănĭmōsē
bravery, fortĭtūdo, *f*
brawl, *v.i*, rixor (1 *dep*.)
brawl, *nn*, rixa, *f*
brawny, lăcertōsus
bray, *v.i*, rŭdo (3)

brazen (made of brass), aēnĕus, aerĕus; (impudent), impŭdens
breach, rŭīna, *f*, *or use vb.* rumpo (3) (to burst); (— in a treaty, etc.) *use* vĭŏlo (1) (to violate)
bread, pānis, *m*
breadth, lātĭtūdo, *f*
break, *v.t*, frango (3); (treaty, etc.) vĭŏlo (1); (— promise), fĭdem fallo (3); (— down), *v.t*, rēscindo (3); (— in), *v.t*, (horses), dŏmo (1); (— into), *v.t*, irrumpo (3); (— loose) ērumpo (3)
break (of day), prīma lux, *f*, (first light); (fracture), fractūra, *f*
breakfast, ientācŭlum, *n*
breakfast, *v.i*, iento (1)
breakwater, mōles, *f*
breast, pectus, *n*, mamma, *f*
breast-plate, lōrīca, *f*
breath, spīrĭtus, *m*, ănĭma, *f*; (out of —), exănĭmātus; (to hold one's —), ănĭmam comprĭmo (3)
breathe, *v.i*, spīro (1); (— out), exspīro (1)
breathing, *nn*, aspīrātĭo, *f*
breathless, cxănĭmātus
breed, *v.t*, gĕnĕro (1); *v.i*, nascor (3 *dep*.) (to be born)
breed, *nn*, gĕnus, *n*
breeding, *nn*, (giving birth) partus, *m*; (manners), hūmānĭtas, *f*
breeze, aura, *f*
breezy, ventōsus
brevity, brĕvĭtas, *f*
brew, *v.t*, cŏquo (3); *v.i* (overhang) impendĕo (2)
bribe, *nn*, praemĭum, *n*
bribe, *v.t*, corrumpo (3)
bribery, ambĭtus, *m*
brick, lăter, *m*; (made of —), *adj*, lătĕrīcĭus
bricklayer, structor, *m*
bridal, nuptĭālis
bride (before marriage), sponsa, *f* (after marriage), nupta, *f*
bridegroom (before marriage), sponsus, *m*; (after marriage), nuptus, *m*, mărītus, *m*
bridge, pons, *m*
bridle, frēnum, *n*
brief, *adj*, brĕvis
briefly, *adv*, brĕvĭter
briar, dūmus, *m*
brigade, lĕgĭo, *f*
bright, clārus
brighten, *v.t*, illustro (1); *v.i*, clāresco (3)
brightly, *adv*, clāre
brilliance, splendor, *m*, nĭtor, *m*

brilliant, splendĭdus; (famous), praeclārus

brim, margo, *m, f,* labrum, *n*

brimstone, sulfur, *n*

brine, salsāmentum, *n*

bring, *v.t,* fĕro, affĕro (*irreg*), addūco
(3) apporto (1); (— about), confĭcĭo
(3); (— back, — before), rĕfĕro
(*irreg*); (— down), dēfĕro (*irreg*);
(— forward), prōfĕro (*irreg*); (—
in), infĕro (*irreg*); (— out), ēffĕro
(*irreg*); (— over), perdūco (3);
(— together), cōgo (3); (— up)
(children), ēdūco (1)

brink (river, etc.), rīpa, *f;* (of cliff,
etc.) *use adj,* summus (highest)

brisk, ălăcer

briskness, ălacrĭtas, *f*

bristle, saeta, *f*

bristle, *v.i,* horrĕo (2)

brittle, frăgĭlis

broach, *v.t,* ăpĕrĭo (4), prōfĕro (*irreg*)

broad, lātus

broadly (widely), *adv,* lātē

broil (quarrel), rixa, *f*

broil, *v.t,* torrĕo (2)

broken, fractus; (disabled), confectus

broker, interpres, *c* (agent)

bronze, aes, *n;* (*adj*), aēnĕus, aerĕus

brooch, fĭbŭla, *f*

brood, *v.i,* incŭbo (1)

brood (of young, etc.), fētus, *m*

brook, rīvus, *m*

brook (no interference etc), pătĭor (3
dep)

broom, scōpae, *f. pl*

broth, ius, *n*

brothel, gănĕa, *f*

brother, frāter, *m*

brotherhood sŏcĭĕtas, *f*

brow (forehead), frons, *f;* (eye-brow),
sŭpercĭlĭum, *n;* (of hill), căcūmen, *n*

brown, fuscus

browse, *v.t* (read), perlĕgo (3)

bruise, *nn,* contūsum, *n*

bruise, *v.t,* contundo (3)

brunt (bear the — of), *use* sustĭnĕo (2)
(to bear)

brush, *nn,* pēnĭcŭlus, *m*

brush, *v.t,* dētergĕo (2)

brushwood, sarmenta, *n.pl*

brutal, fĕrus, ătrox

brutality, immānĭtas, *f*

brutally, *adv,* immānĭter

brute, bestĭa, *f,* fĕra, *f*

bubble, bulla, *f*

bubble, *v.i,* bullo (1)

buccaneer, pīrāta, *m*

buck (male stag), cervus, *m*

bucket, sĭtŭla, *f*

buckle, fībŭla, *f*

buckle, *v.t,* fĭbŭlā necto (3) (fasten
with a buckle)

buckler (shield), scūtum, *n*

bud, *nn,* gemma, *f*

bud, *v.i,* gemmo (1), germĭno (1)

budge, *v.i,* cēdo (3); *v.t,* mŏvĕo (2)

budget, rătĭo, *f* (reckoning, account)

buff, lūtĕus

buffet (blow), cŏlăphus, *m*

buffoon, scurra, *m*

bug, cīmex, *m*

bugbear, terrĭcŭla, *n.pl*

bugle, būcĭna, *f*

build, *v.t,* aedĭfĭco (1)

builder, aedĭfĭcātor, *m*

building (act of —), aedĭfĭcātĭo, *f,*
(structure itself), aedĭfĭcĭum, *n*

bulb, bulbus, *m*

bulk, magnĭtūdo, *f,* mōles, *f*

bulky, ingens, grandis

bull, taurus, *m*

bullet, glans, *f*

bullion, aurum, *n*

bullock, iŭvencus, *m*

bulrush, iuncus, *m*

bulwark, mūnīmentum, *n*

bump, *nn,* tūber, *n,* tŭmor, *m*

bump, *v.i,* offendo (3)

bumpkin, rustĭcus, *m*

bunch, ūva, *f,* răcēmus, *m*

bundle, fascis, *m*

bung (stopper), obtūrāmentum, *n*

bungle, *v.i,* inscītē ăgo (3) (do unskilfully)

bungler, *adj,* impĕrītus

buoyancy, lĕvĭtas, *f*

buoyant, lĕvis

burden, ŏnus, *n*

burden, *v.t,* ŏnĕro (1)

burdensome, grăvis

bureau, scrīnĭum, *n,* armārĭum, *n*

burgess, cīvis, *c*

burglar, fūr, *m*

burglary, furtum, *n*

burgle, *v.t,* fūror (1 *dep.*) (steal)

burial, fūnus, *n,* sĕpultūra, *f*

burial-place, lŏcus, (*m*) sĕpultūrae

burly, lăcertōsus

burn, *v.t,* ūro (3), incendo (3); *v.i,*
ardĕo (2), flagro (1)

burn, *nn,* ambustum, *n*

burning, *adj,* ardens

burnish, *v.t,* pŏlĭo (4)

burrow, cŭnĭcŭlum, *n*

burst, *v.t,* rumpo (3); *v.i,* rumpor (3
pass)

burst out, *v.i,* ērumpo (3)

bursting out, *nn,* ēruptĭo, *f*

bury, *v.t,* sĕpĕlĭo (4), abdo (3)

bush, dūmus
bushel, mĕdimnum, *n*
bushy, frŭtĭcōsus
busily, *adv*, sēdŭlō
business, nĕgōtĭum, *n*, res, *f*
bust (statue), ĭmāgo, *f*
bustle, *nn*, festīnātĭo, *f*
bustle, *v.i*, festīno (1)
busy, occŭpātus
but, *conj*, sed, vērum, at (*first word in clause*): autem, vēro (*second word in clause*); (except), praeter (*with acc*)
butcher, lănĭus, *m*
butcher, *v.t* (murder), trŭcīdo (1)
butchery, trŭcīdātĭo, *f*
butler, prōmus, *m*
butt (laughing stock), lūdĭbrĭum, *n*
butt, *v.t*, cornū fērĭo (4) (strike with the horn)
butter, būtȳrum, *n*
butterfly, pāpĭlĭo, *m*
buttock, clūnis, *m*, *f*
buttress, antēris, *f*
buxom, vĕnustus
buy, *v.t*, ĕmo (3)
buyer, emptor, *m*
buying, *nn*, emptĭo, *f*
by, *prep*, (of place, near), ad, prŏpe (*with acc*); (of time) *often expressed by abl. of noun, e.g.* by night, nocte; (— means of), per (*with acc*) (by an agent, *e.g.* by a man), ab (*with abl*), ab hōmĭne; (by an instrument, *e.g.* by a spear, *abl. case alone*), hastā; (— chance), *adv*, fortĕ
by-gone, *adj*, praetĕrĭtus
by-stander, spectātor, *m*
by-way, trāmes, *m*

C

cab, raeda, *f*, cīsĭum, *n*
cabal (faction), factĭo, *f*
cabbage, brassĭca, *f*
cabin (hut), căsa, *f*
cabinet (furniture), armārĭum, *n*; (council), summum consĭlĭum, *n*
cable (anchor —), ancŏrāle, *n*
cackle, cackling, *nn*, strĕpĭtus, *m*
cackle, *v.i*, strĕpo (3)
cadaverous, cădāvĕrōsus
cadence, cursus, *m*
cadet, discĭpŭlus, *m*, tīro, *m*
cage, căvĕa, *f*
cajole, *v.t*, blandĭor (4 *dep. with dat*)
cajolery, blandĭtĭae, *f. pl*
cake, *nn*, plăcenta, *f*, lībum, *n*
calamitous, exĭtĭōsus
calamity, clādes, *f*, mălum, *n*

calculate, *v.t*, compŭto (1), aestĭmo (1)
calculation, rătĭo, *f*
calendar, fasti, *m. pl*
calf, vĭtŭlus, *m*; (of the leg), sūra, *f*
call, *v.t*, (name), vŏco (1), appello (1); dico (3); (— back), rĕvŏco (1); (— to, summon), advŏco (1); (— together), convŏco (1); (— up or out), suscĭto (1)
call, *nn* (cry), clāmor, *m*; (visit) sălūtātĭo, *f*
caller, sălūtātor, *m*
calling, *nn* (vocation), ars, *f*, artĭfĭcĭum, *n*
callous, callōsus
callow, implūmis
calm, *adj*, plăcĭdus, tranquillus
calm, *nn*, tranquillĭtas, *f*, mălăcĭa, *f*
calm, *v.t*, sēdo (1), plāco (1)
calmly, *adv*, tranquille, plăcĭde
calumniate, *v.t*, crīmĭnor (1 *dep.*)
calumnious, crīmĭnōsus
calumny, crīmĭnātĭo, *f*
camel, cămēlus, *m*
camp, castra, *n.pl*; (to pitch —), castra pōno (3); (to move —), castra mŏvĕo (2); (a winter —), hīberna, *n.pl*
campaign, stĭpendĭum, *n*
campaign, *v.i*, stĭpendĭum mĕrĕor (2 *dep.*)
can, *nn*, urcĕus, *m*
can, *v.i* (to be able), possum (*irreg*)
canal, fossa, *f*
cancel, *v.t*, dēlĕo (2), abrŏgo (1)
cancer (sign of Zodiac), cancer, *m*
candid, ăpertus, līber
candidate, candĭdātus, *m*
candle, candēla, *f*
candlestick, candēlābrum, *n*
candour, lībertas, *f*
cane, hărundo, *f*, băcŭlum, *n*, virga, *f*
cane, *v.t*, verbĕro (1)
canister, arca, *f*, pyxis, *f*
canker, rōbīgo, *f*
canker, *v.t*, corrumpo (3)
cannibal, anthrōpŏphăgus, *m*
cannon, tormentum, *n*
canoe, scăpha, *f*
canon (rule), rēgŭla, *f*
canopy, vēla, *n.pl*
cant, ostentātĭo, *f*
canter, *v.i*, lēnĭter curro (3) (run smoothly)
canton, păgus, *m*
canvas, vēla, *n.pl*, carbăsus, *f*
canvass, *v.i*, ambĭo (4)
canvass, *nn*, ambĭtĭo, *f*; (illegal), ambĭtus, *m*
cap, pillĕus, *m*

For List of Abbreviations used, turn to pages 3, 4

capability, făcultas, *f*
capable, căpax
capacious, căpax
capacity, căpācĭtas, *f*; (mental —),
  ingĕnĭum, *n*
cape, prōmontŭrĭum, *n*
caper, *v.i,* exsulto (1), salĭo (4)
capital, *nn,* (city), căput, *n*
capital, *adj* (crime, etc.), căpĭtālis;
  (chief), princeps
capitulate, *v.t,* dēdo (3); *v.i,* se
  dēdĕre (3 *reflex*)
caprice, lĭbīdo, *f*
capricious, lĕvis
captain, dux, *m,* princeps, *m*; (of a
  ship), măgister, *m,* nauarchus, *m*
captivate, *v.t,* căpĭo (3), dēlēnĭo (4)
captive, *adj. and nn,* captīvus, *m.*
captivity, captīvĭtas, *f*
capture, *nn,* (of city, camp, etc.),
  expugnātĭo, *f*; (of persons), *use vb,*
  căpĭo (3) (to capture)
capture, *v.t,* căpĭo (3)
car, currus, *m,* plaustrum, *n*
caravan (convoy), commĕātus, *m,*
  (vehicle), raeda, *f*
carbuncle, fūruncŭlus, *m*
carcass, cădāver, *n,* corpus, *n*
card, charta, *f*
cardinal, *adj,* prīmus, princeps
care, cūra, *f,* sollĭcĭtūdo, *f*
care, *v.t* (to — about or for), cūro (1)
career, currĭcŭlum, *n*
careful, dīlĭgens; (carefully prepared) accūrātus; (cautious)
  cautus
carefully, *adv,* dīlĭgenter
careless, neglĕgens, indīlĭgens
carelessly, *adv,* neglegenter
carelessness, neglĕgentĭa, *f*
caress, blandĭmenta, *n.pl,* complexus,
  m
caress, *v.t,* blandĭor (4 *dep.*) *(with dat.)*
caressing, *adj,* blandus
cargo, ŏnus, *n*
caricature, ĭmāgo, *f*
caricature, *v.t, use phr.* vultum
  dētorquĕo (2) (distort the features)
carnage, caedes, *f,* strāges, *f*
carnal, corpŏrĕus
carnival, fērĭae, *f.pl*
carnivorous, carnĭvŏrus
carol, cantus, *m*
carousal, cōmissātĭo, *f*
carouse, *v.i,* cōmissor (1 *dep.*)
carp at, *v.t,* carpo (3), mordĕo (2)
carpenter, făber, *m*
carpet, strāgŭlum, *n*

carriage (vehicle), raeda, *f,* carpentum, *n*; (transportation), vectūra,*f*;
  (poise), incessus, *m*
carrier, vector, *m*
carrion, căro, *f,* cădāver, *n*
carrot, pastĭnāca, *f*
carry, *v.t,* porto (1), fĕro (*irreg.*), vĕho
  (3), gĕro (3); (— away or off),
  aufĕro (*irreg.*); (— back) rēfĕro
  (*irreg.*); (— in) infĕro (*irreg.*);
  (— on) gĕro (3); (— over) transporto (1); (— out, perform) exsĕquor (3 *dep.*); (— through a law,
  etc.), perfĕro (*irreg.*)
cart, plaustrum, *n*
cart, *v.t,* vĕho (3)
cart-horse, iūmentum, *n*
cartilage, cartĭlāgo, *f*
carve, *v.t,* caelo (1), sĕco (1), sculpo
  (3)
carver, sculptor, *m*
carving, *nn,* caelātūra, *f*
case (in law), causa, *f* (circumstances),
  cāsus, *m* (cover), thēca,*f*
casement, fĕnestra, *f*
cash, nummus, *m,* pĕcūnĭa nŭ-
  mērāta, *f*
cashier, *nn, use phr.* qui nummos
  dispensat (who dispenses the cash)
cashier, *v.t,* (from the army), ex-
  auctoro (1)
cask, cūpa, *f*
casket, arcŭla, *f*
cast, *nn,* (throw), iactus, *m*
cast, *v.t,* iăcĭo (3), mitto (3); (—
  down) dēĭcĭo (3); (— off) dēpōno
  (3); (— out) expello (3)
castaway, perdĭtus, *m*
caste, ordo, *m*
castigate, *v.t,* castīgo (1)
castle, castellum, *n*
castor-oil, cĭcĭnum ŏlĕum, *n*
castrate, *v.t,* castro (1)
casual, fortŭĭtus
casually, *adv,* neglĕgenter
casualty (accident), cāsus, *m*; (killed)
  adj, interfectus
cat, fēles, *f*
catalogue, index *c*
catapult, cătăpulta, *f,*
cataract (waterfall), cătăracta, *f*
catarrh, grăvēdo, *f*
catastrophe, rŭīna, *f*
catch, căpĭo (3), comprĕhendo (з);
  (a disease), contrăho (3)
categorical (absolute), simplex,
  plānus
category, nŭmĕrus, *m*

cater, *v.t*, obsōno (1)
caterpillar, ērūca, *f*
catgut, chorda, *f*
cattle, pĕcus, *n*
cauldron, cortīna, *f*
cause, *nn*, causa, *f*
cause, *v.t*, făcĭo (3), effĭcĭo (3)
causeway, agger, *m*
caustic, *adj*, mordax (biting)
caution, cautĭo, *f*
caution, *v.t*, mŏnĕo (2)
cautious, cautus,
cavalry, ĕquĭtātus, *m*, ĕquĭtes, *m. pl*
cave, spēlunca, *f*, căverna, *f*, antrum, *n*
caw, *v.i*, crōcĭo (4)
cease, *v.i*, dēsĭno (3) (*with infin*)
ceaseless, perpĕtŭus
cedar, cedrus, *f*
ceiling, tectum, *n*
celebrate, *v.t*, căno (3), cĕlĕbro (1)
celebrated, clārus, illustris
celebration, cĕlĕbrātĭo, *f*
celebrity, fāma, *f*, glōrĭa, *f*; (person), vir praeclārus
celerity, cĕlĕrĭtas, *f*
celestial, caelestis
celibacy, caelĭbātus, *m*
cell, cellar, cella, *f*
cement, ferrūmen, *n*
cement, *v.t*, glūtĭno (1), ferrūmĭno (1)
cemetery, sĕpulcrētum, *n*
censor, censor, *m*
censure, vĭtŭpĕrātĭo, *f*
censure, *v.t*, vĭtŭpĕro (1) reprĕhendo (3)
conduct, consuo, *m*
per cent, *use nn*, centēsĭma, *f* (one hundredth part)
centaur, centaurus, *m*
central, mĕdĭus
centre (of) mĕdĭus, *in agreement with noun, e.g.* in the centre of the line, in mĕdĭā ăcĭe
centre on, *v.i* (depend on), pendĕo (2) (*with* ab *and* abl)
centurion, centŭrĭo, *m*
century, saecŭlum, *n*
ceremonial, rītus, *m*, caerĭmōnĭa, *f*
ceremonious, sollemnis
certain, certus, explōrātus; (a — person), *use pron*, quīdam
certainly, *adv*, certo, certē, prŏfecto
certainty, res certa; *or use adj*, certus (certain)
certificate, scriptum testĭmōnĭum (written proof)
certify, *v.i*, rĕcognosco (3), confirmo (1)
cessation, intermissĭo, *f*

chafe, *v.t*, fŏvĕo (2), cālĕfăcĭo (3); *v.i*, stŏmăchor (1 *dep*.) (be irritated)
chaff, pălĕa, *f*
chaffinch, fringilla,
chagrin, stŏmăchus, *m*
chain, cătēna, *f*, vincŭlum, *n*
chain, *v.t*, cătēnas inĭcĭo (3) (*with dat*)
chair, sella, *f*
chairman, măgister, *m*
chalk, crēta, *f*
chalk out (mark out), *v.t*, dēsigno (1)
challenge, *nn*, prōvŏcātĭo, *f*
challenge, *v.t*, prōvŏco (1)
chamber, conclāve, *n*; (bed —), cŭbĭcŭlum, *n*
chamberlain, cŭbĭcŭlārĭus, *m*
chamois, căprĕŏlus, *m*
champ, *v.t*, mando (3)
champion victor *m;* (defender), prōpugnātor, *m*
chance, *nn*, cāsus, *m*, fors, *f*, fortūna, *f*
by chance, *adv*, (happen), forte, cāsu
chance, *v.i*, accĭdo (3)
chandelier, candēlābrum, *n*
change, changing, *nn*, mūtātĭo, *f*, permūtātĭo, *f*
change, *v.t*, mūto (1), converto (3); *v.i*, mūtor (1 *pass*)
changeable, mūtābĭlis
channel, cănālis, *m*, alvĕus, *m*
chant, *v.i and v.t*, canto (1)
chaos, perturbātĭo, *f*
chaotic, perturbātus
chapel, săcellum, *n*
chapter, căpŭt, *n*
char, *v.t*, ambūro (3)
character, mōres, *m. pl*, ĭngĕnĭum, *n*; (reputation), existĭmātĭo, *f*, ŏpīnĭo, *f*; (in a play), persōna, *f*
characteristic, *adj*, prŏprĭus
charcoal, carbo, *m*
charge, *nn*, (attack), impĕtus, *m;* (accusation), crīmen, *n*; (price), prĕtĭum, *n*; (care of), cūra, *f*
charge, *v.t*, (attack), impĕtum făcĭo (3); signa infero (*irreg*); (accuse), accūso (1); (of price), vendo (3) (sell) (3); (put in—) praefĭcĭo (3) (*with dat*); (be in—) praesum (*irreg*.) (*with dat*)
chariot, currus, *m*, essĕdum, *n*
charioteer, aurīga, *c*
charitable, bĕnignus, mītis
charity, ămor *m*, bĕnĕfĭcentĭa, *f*
charm, blandĭmentum, *n*, grātĭa, *f* (trinket), bulla, *f*
charm, *v.t*, fascĭno (1), dēlēnĭo (4), dēlecto (1)
charming, vĕnustus, lĕpĭdus

chart, tăbŭla, f
charter, v.t, (hire), condūco (3)
chase, nn, (hunt), vēnātĭo, f, vēnātus, m
chase, v.t, sector (1 dep.), vēnor (1 dep.)
chasm, hĭātus, m
chaste, castus
chastise, v.t, castīgo (1), pūnĭo (4)
chastisement, castīgātĭo, f
chastity, castĭtas, f
chat, v.i, fābŭlor (1 dep.)
chat, nn, sermo, m
chatter, v.i, garrĭo (4); (of teeth), crĕpĭto (1)
chatter, nn, garrŭlĭtas, f
chattering, adj, garrŭlus
cheap, vīlis
cheapness, vīlĭtas, f
cheat, nn, (person), fraudātor, m
cheat, v.t, fraudo (1)
cheating, nn, fraudātĭo, f
check, nn, (hindrance), impedīmentum, n, incommŏdum, n; (set back), incommŏdum, n
check, v.t, cŏhĭbĕo (2), contĭnĕo (2), comprĭmo (3), cŏercĕo(2)
cheek, gĕna, f
cheer, nn, (shout), clāmor, m
cheer, v.i, (applaud), plaudo (3), clāmo (1)
cheerful, hĭlăris
cheerfulness, hĭlărĭtas, f
cheerless, tristis
cheese, cāsĕus, m
cheque, perscriptĭo, f, (written entry)
chequered, vărĭus
cherish, v.t, fŏvĕo (2), cŏlo (3)
cherry, cherry-tree, cĕrăsus, f
chess, latruncŭli, m. pl
chest (box), amārĭum, n, cista, f; (body), pectus, n, thorax, m
chestnut, glans, f; (— tree), castănĕa, f
chew, mando (3)
chicken, pullus, m
chide, v.t, obiurgo (1), incrĕpĭto (1), rĕprĕhendo (3)
chiding, rĕprĕhensĭo, f
chief, nn, princeps, m, prōcer, m
chief, adj, prīmus, princeps
chieftain, see chief
child, pŭer, m, infans, c; (pl.) lībĕri, m. pl
childbirth, partus, m
childhood, pŭĕrītĭa, f
childish, pŭĕrīlis
childless, orbus
chill, chilly, adj, frīgĭdus
chill, v.t, rĕfrīgĕro (1)

chime, nn, concentus, m
chime, v.i, (sound), căno (3)
chimney, cămīnus, m
chin, mentum, n
chine, tergum, n
chink, rīma, f
chip, assŭla, f
chirp, chirping, nn, pīpātus, m
chirp, v.i, pīpĭo (4)
chisel, scalprum, n
chisel, v.t, sculpo (3)
chivalrous, magnănĭmus
chivalry, magnănĭmĭtas, f
choice, nn, dēlectus, m; (— between), optĭo, f
choice, adj, ēlectus
choir, chŏrus, m
choke, v.t, suffōco (1); v.i, suffōcor (1 pass)
choose, v.t, lĕgo (3), ēlĭgo (3)
chop, v.t, caedo (3); (cut off), abscīdo (3)
chord, use nervus, m, (string)
chorus, chŏrus, m
Christ, Christus, m
Christian, Christĭānus
chronic (long-lasting), dĭūturnus
chronicle, annāles, m. pl
chuckle, v.i, căchinno (1)
church, templum, n
church-yard, ārĕa, f
churl, hŏmo rustĭcus
churlish, rustĭcus
churn, v.t, (stir), ăgĭto (1)
cinder, cĭnis, m, făvilla, f
cipher (a nonentity), nŭmĕrus, m; (secret writing), nŏta, f
circle, orbis, m
circuit, circŭĭtus, m
circuitous (route, etc.), flexŭōsus
circular, rŏtundus
circulate, v.t, spargo (3), dīvulgo (1); v.i, diffundor (3 pass), percrēbresco (3)
circulation, (to be in —) (of books etc.) in mănĭbus esse (irreg)
circumcise, v.t, circumcīdo (3)
circumference, ambĭtus, m
circumscribe, v.t, circumscrībo (3)
circumstance, res, f; or use neuter of an adj, e.g. adversa (adverse circumstances)
circumstantial evidence, coniectūra, f
circumvent, v.t, circumvĕnĭo (4)
circus, circus, m
cistern, cisterna, f
citadel, arx, f
cite, v.t, (quote), prōfĕro (irreg)
citizen, cīvis, c
citizenship, cīvĭtas, f

city, urbs, *f*
civic, cīvīlis
civil (polite), urbānus; **(civic)** cīvīlis;
(— **war**), bellum dŏmestĭcum
civilian (opp. military), tŏgātus, *m*
civilization, cultus, *m*, hūmānĭtas, *f*
civilize, *v.t,* excŏlo (3), expŏlio (4)
civilized, hūmānus, cultus
claim, *v.t,* postŭlo (1), rĕposco (3)
claim, *nn,* postŭlātĭo, *f*
claimant, pĕtītor, *m*
clammy, lentus
clamorous, clāmans
clamour, *nn,* clāmor, *m,* strĕpĭtus, *m*
clamour, *v.i,* vōcĭfĕror (1 *dep*)
clandestine, clandestīnus
clang, *nn,* clangor, *m*
clang, *v.i. and v.t,* strĕpo (3)
clank, crĕpĭtus, *m*
clank, *v.i,* crĕpo (1)
clap, *nn,* **(hands),** plausus, *m*;
(thunder), frăgor, *m*
clap, *v.i. and v.t,* plaudo (3)
clash, *v.i.,* concrĕpo (1), crĕpĭto (1);
(opinions) rĕpugno (1); **(fight),**
conflīgo (3)
clash, *nn,* **(noise),** crĕpĭtus, *m;* **(collision),** concursus, *m*
clasp, *nn,* **(embrace),** complexus, *m;*
(fastener), fĭbŭla, *f*
clasp, *v.t.* **(fasten),** fĭbŭlo (1); **(embrace),** complector (3 *dep.*)
class, classis, *f,* gĕnus, *n*
classic, classical (well-established),
prŏbus
classify, *v.t,* dēscrībo (3) ordĭne
clatter, *nn,* strĕpĭtus, *m*
clatter, *v.i,* increpo (1)
clause, membrum, *n,* căpŭt, *n*
claw, unguis, *m*
clay, argilla, *f,* lŭtum, *n*
clean, *adj,* mundus, pūrus
clean, *v.t,* purgo (1), mundo (1)
cleanliness, mundĭtĭa, *f*
cleanse, *v.t,* purgo (1)
clear, clārus; **(weather),** sĕrēnus;
(matter), mănĭfestus
clear, *v.t,* **(open up),** expĕdĭo (4);
(— **oneself),** sē purgāre (1 *reflex*);
v.i, **(of the weather),** dissĕrēnat
(1 *impers*)
clearing, *nn,* **(open space),** lŏcus
ăpertus
clearly, *adv,* clārē, ăpertĕ, plānē
clearness, clārĭtas, *f*
cleave, *v.t,* **(split),** findo (3); *v.i* **(stick
to),** adhaerĕo (2)
cleft, hĭātus, *m,* rīma, *f*
clemency, clēmentĭa, *f*
clement, clēmens, lēnis

clench (the fist), *v.t,* comprĭmo (3)
clerk, scrība, *m*
clever, callĭdus, astūtus
cleverness, *f,* callĭdĭtas, *f*
client, clĭens, *m,* consultor, *m*
cliff, cautes, *f,* scŏpŭlus, *m,* rūpes,
climate, caelum, *n*
climax, grădātĭo, *f*
climb, *v.i. and v.t,* ascendo (3), scando
(3)
climb, *nn,* ascensus, *m*
cling to, *v.i,* ădhaerĕo (2) *(with dat)*
clip, *v.t,* tondĕo (2)
cloak, pallĭum, *n,* lăcerna, *f*
cloak, *v.t,* **(hide),** dissĭmŭlo (1)
clock, hŏrŏlŏgĭum, *n*
clod, glaeba, *f*
clog (hindrance), impĕdīmentum, *n;*
(shoe), sculpŏnĕa, *f*
clog, *v.t,* **(impede),** impĕdĭo (4)
close, *adj,* **(near),** vīcīnus; **(packed together)** confertus, densus; **(at close
quarters),** commĭnus, *adv*
close, *nn,* **(end),** fīnis, *m,* termĭnus, *m*
close, *adv,* prŏpe, iuxta
close, *v.t,* claudo (3); *v.i,* claudor (3
pass)
close in on, *v.t,* prĕmo (3) **(press)**
closely, *adv,* prŏpe; **(accurately),**
exacte
closeness, prŏpinquĭtas, *f,*
closet, cella, *f*
clot (of blood), crŭor, *m*
cloth, textum, *n*
clothe, *v.t,* vestĭo (4), indŭo (3)
clothes, vestis, *f,* vestīmenta, *n.pl*
cloud, nūbes, *f*
cloudy, nūbĭlus
cloven, bīsulcus
clown, scurra, *m*
club (cudgel), clāva, *f;* **(association),**
' sŏdālĭtas, *f*
cluck, *v.i,* singultĭo (4)
clump, massa, *f*
clumsy, inhăbĭlis, rustĭcus
cluster, *nn,* răcēmus, *m;* **(people),**
glŏbus, *m*
clutch, *v.t,* arrĭpĭo (3)
coach, carpentum, *n,* raeda, *f*
coachman, raedārĭus, *m*
coagulate, *v.i,* concresco (3)
coal, carbo, *m*
coalition, coniunctĭo, *f,* conspīrātĭo, *f*
coarse, crassus; **(manners),** incultus
coarseness, crassĭtūdo, *f,* inhūmānĭtas,
f
coast, ōra, *f,* lītus, *n*
coast, *v.i,* praetervĕhor (3 *pass*)
coat, tŭnĭca, *f,* ămictus, *m;* **(animal's),**
pellis, *f*

For List of Abbreviations used, turn to pages 3, 4

coat, *v.t*, illĭno (3)
coax, *v.t*, mulcĕo (2), blandĭor (4 *dep*)
cobble, *v.t*, sarcĭo (4)
cobbler, sūtor, *m*
cock, gallus, *m*
code, (method, system), rătĭo, *f*
coerce, *v.t*, cōgo (3), cŏercĕo (2)
coercion, cŏercĭtĭo, *f*
coffin, arca, *f*
cog, dens, *m*
cogent, vălĭdus
cogitate, *v.i*, cōgĭto (1)
cognizance, cognĭtĭo, *f*
cohabit, *v.i*, consŭesco (3)
cohere, *v.i*, cŏhaerĕo (2)
coherent, cŏhaerens
cohesion, cŏhaerentĭa, *f*
cohort, cŏhors, *f*
coil, *nn*, spīra, *f*
coil, *v.t*, glŏmĕro (1)
coin, *nn*, nummus, *m*
coin, *v.t*, cūdo (3)
coinage, nummi, *m. pl*
coincide, *v.i*, compĕto (3), concurro (3)
coincidence, concursātĭo, *f*, concursus, *m*
cold, *adj*, frīgĭdus, gĕlĭdus
cold (to be —), *v.i*, algĕo (2)
coldness, frīgus, *n*
collapse, *v.i*, collābor (3 *dep*.)
collar, torques, *m and f*
collation (comparison), collātĭo, *f*
colleague, collēga, *m*
collect, *v.t*, collĭgo (3), cōgo (3)
collection (act of —), collātĭo, *f*; (heap, etc.), congĕrĭes, *f*
collector (of taxes, etc.), exactor, *m*
college, collēgĭum, *n*
collide, *v.i*, conflīgo (3), concurro (3)
collision, concursus, *m*
colloquial (speech), *use* sermo, *m*
collusion, collūsĭo, *f*
colon, cōlon, *n*
colonel, praefectus, *m*
colonist, cŏlōnus, *m*
colony, cŏlōnĭa, *f*
colonnade, portĭcus, *f*
colossal, ingens
colour, cŏlor, *m*; (flag), vexillum, *n*; (— bearer), signĭfer, *m*
colour, *v.t*, cŏlōro (1)
coloured, pictus
colourful, fūcātus
colt, equŭlĕus, *m*
column (pillar), columna, *f*; (military), agmen, *n*

comb, *nn*, pecten, *m*
comb, *v.t*, pecto (3)
combat, *nn*, proelĭum, *n*
combat, *v.i*, pugno (1), luctor (1 *dep*)
combat, *v.t*, (oppose), obsto (1)
combatant, pugnātor, *m*
combination, coniunctĭo, *f*
combine, *v.t*, coniungo (3)
come, *v.i*, vĕnĭo (4); (— about, happen), ēvĕnĭo (4); (— across, find), *v.t*, invĕnĭo (4); (— back), *v.i*, rĕvĕnĭo (4); (— by, obtain), *v.t*, ădĭpiscor (3 *dep*); (— down), *v.i*, dēscendo (3); (— in) incēdo (3); (— near) apprŏpinquo (1); (— on, advance), prōgrĕdĭor (3 *dep*); (— out) exĕo (4); (— to) advĕnĭo (4) (regain consciousness) ad se rĕdire (4); (— together) convĕnĭo (4); (— upon), *v.t*, sŭpervĕnĭo (4) (attack) incĭdo (3)
comedian, cōmoedus, *m*
comedy, cōmoedĭa, *f*
comely, pulcher
comet, cŏmētes, *m*
comfort, sōlācĭum, *n*, consōlātĭo, *f*
comfort, *v.t*, consōlor (1 *dep*.)
comfortable, commŏdus
comforter, consōlātor, *m*
comic, comical, cōmĭcus
coming, *adj*, ventūrus
coming, *nn*, adventus, *m*
command, *nn*, (power), impĕrĭum, *n*; (an order), iussum, *n*, mandātus, *m*; (to be in —) *v.i*, praesum (*with dat*)
command, *v.t.* impĕro (1) (*with dat.*), iŭbĕo (2)
commander, dux, *m*, impĕrātor, *m*
commemorate, *v.t*, cĕlĕbro (1)
commemoration, cĕlĕbrātĭo, *f*
commence, *v.i*, incĭpĭo (3)
commencement, ĭnĭtĭum, *n*
commend, *v.t*, commendo (1); (praise), laudo (1)
commendable, laudābĭlis
comment, *v.i*, dīco (3), sententĭas dīco (3) (declare one's opinion)
comment, *nn*, dicta, *n.pl*
commentary, commentārĭi, *m. pl*
commerce, commercĭum, *n*
commercial traveller, instĭtor, *m*
commiserate, *v.i. and v.t*, mĭsĕror (1 *dep*.)
commisariat, praefecti (*m. pl.*) rĕi frūmentārĭae (superintendents of corn supply); (provisions), commĕātus, *m*

commissary, prōcūrător, *m*, lēgātus, *m*
commission (task), mandātum, *n*
commission, *v.t*, (give a task to), mando (1) (*dat. of person*)
commit, *v.t*, (crime, etc.), admitto (3); (entrust), committo (3), mando (1)
committee, dēlecti, *m. pl*, (selected ones)
commodious (opportune), commŏdus; (capacious), amplus
commodity (thing), res, *f*
common, *adj*, commūnis; (belonging to the public), pūblĭcus; (ordinary), vulgāris; (common land), ăger pūblĭcus, *m*, (usual), ūsĭtātus
commonplace, *adj*, vulgāris, trītus
commonly, *adv*, (mostly), plērumque
commonwealth, respublĭca, *f*
commotion, mōtus, *m*, tŭmultus, *m*, commōtĭo, *f*
communicate, *v.t*, commūnĭco (1); (report), dēfĕro (*irreg*)
communication, commūnĭcātĭo, *f*; (reporting), nuntĭus, *m*
communicative, lĭber, lŏquax
communion, sŏcĭĕtas, *f*
community, cīvĭtas, *f*, sŏcĭĕtas, *f*
commute, *v.t*, mūto (1)
compact, *adj*, confertus, pressus
compact, *nn*, pactum, *n*, foedus, *n*
companion, sŏcĭus, *m*, cŏmes, *c*
companionable, făcĭlis
companionship, sŏdālĭtas, *f*
company, coetus, *m*, sŏcĭĕtas, *f*; (military body), mănĭpŭlus, *m*
comparable, conferendus
comparative, compărātīvus
compare, *v.t*, compăro (1), confĕro (*irreg*)
comparison, compărātĭo, *f*
compartment, lŏcŭlus, *m*
compass (range), fīnes, *m. pl*; (pair of compasses), circĭnus, *m*
compass, *v.t*, complector (3 *dep*)
compassion, mĭsĕrĭcordĭa, *f*
compassionate, mĭsĕrĭcors
compatability, congrŭentĭa, *f*
compatible, congrŭens
compatriot, cīvis, *c*
compel, *v.t*, cōgo (3), compello (3)
compensate for, *v.t*, compenso (1)
compensation, compensātĭo, *f*
compete, *v.i*, certo (1) (struggle)
competent, căpax; (to be — to), *v.i*, sufficĭo (3)
competition, certāmen, *n*
competitor, compĕtītor, *m*
complacent, sĭbi plăcens (pleasing to oneself)

complain, *v.i*, gĕmo (3); *v.t*, quĕror (3 *dep*.)
complaint, questus, *m*, quĕrēla, *f*; (disease), morbus, *m*
complement, complēmentum, *n*
complete, plēnus, perfectus
complete, *v.t*, complĕo (2), confĭcĭo (3)
completely, *adv*, omnīno
completion, perfectĭo, *f*, confectĭo, *f*
complex, multĭplex
complexion, cŏlor, *m*
compliance, obsĕquĭum, *n*
compliant, obsĕquens
complicated, invŏlūtus
complication, implĭcātĭo, *f*
compliment, *nn*, (esteem), hŏnor, *m*; (praise) laus, *f*; (greeting), sălūtātĭo, *f*
compliment, *v.t*, (praise), laudo (1)
complimentary, hŏnōrĭfĭcus
comply with, *v.i*, concēdo (3) (*with dat*)
component, *nn*, (part), ĕlĕmentum, *n*
compose, *v.t*, compōno (3)
composed (calm), sēdātus
composer, scriptor, *m*
composition (act of —), compŏsĭtĭo, *f*; (a literary —), ŏpus scriptum, *n*
composure, tranquillĭtas, *f*
compound, *adj*, compŏsĭtus
compound, *v.t*. compōno (3), miscĕo (2)
comprehend, *v.t*, (understand), intellēgo (3)
comprehension, comprĕhensĭo, *f*
comprehensive, *use phr*, ad omnĭa pertĭnens (extending to everything)
compress, *v.t*, comprĭmo (3)
comprise, *v.t*, contĭnĕo (2)
compromise, *nn*, (agreement), compŏsĭtĭo, *f*
compromise, *v.t*, compōno (3); (implicate), implĭco (1)
compulsion, nĕcessĭtas, *f*
compunction, paenĭtentĭa, *f*
compute, *v.t*, compŭto (1)
comrade, sŏcĭus, *m*, cŏmes, *c*
concave, căvus
conceal, *v.t*, cēlo (1), abdo (3)
concede, *v.t*, cēdo (3)
conceit, arrŏgantĭa, *f*
conceited, arrŏgans
conceive, *v.t*, concĭpĭo (3)
concentrate (mentally), *v.i*, ănĭmum intendo (3); (bring together), *v.t*, contrăho (3), cōgo (3)
conception (mental), nōtĭo, *f*; (physical), conceptĭo, *f*

concern, *nn*, (affair, circumstance), rēs, *f*; (worry), sollĭcĭtūdo, *f*

concern, *v.t*, pertĭneo (2); (it concerns), rēfert (*irreg. impers*)

concerned (to be —), *v.i*, sollĭcĭtus esse

concerning, *prep*, dē (*with abl. of nn. etc*)

concert, *v.t*, (plans, etc.), confĕro (*irreg*), compōno (3)

concession, concessĭo, *f*

conciliate, *v.t*, concĭlĭo (1)

conciliation, concĭlĭātĭo, *f*

conciliatory, pācĭfĭcus

concise, brĕvis

conciseness, brĕvĭtas, *f*

conclude, *v.t*, (decide), stătŭo (3); (end), perfĭcĭo (3)

conclusion (end), exĭtus, *m*, fīnis, *m*; (decision), decrētum, *n*

conclusive, certus

concord, concordĭa, *f*

concourse, concursus, *m*

concubine, pellex, *f*

concupiscence, lĭbīdo, *f*

concur, *v.i*, consentĭo (4)

concurrence, consensus, *m*

concurrent, *use adv*, sĭmŭl (at the same time)

concurrently, *adv*, sĭmŭl

condemn, *v.t*, damno (1) (*with acc. of person and genit. of crime or punishment*)

condemnation, damnātĭo, *f*

condense, *v.t*, denso (1), comprĭmo (3)

condensed, densus

condescend, *v.i*, dēscendo (3)

condescension, cōmĭtas, *f*, (friendliness)

condition, condĭcĭo, *f*, stătus, *m*

condole, *v.i*, dŏleo (2) cum (*with abl*)

condone, *v.t*, condōno (1)

conduce, *v.t*, condūco (3)

conducive, ūtĭlis (advantageous)

conduct, *nn*, (personal, etc.), mōres, *m. pl*; (administration), admĭnistrātĭo, *f*

conduct, *v.t* (lead), dūco (3); (administer), admĭnistro (1); (— oneself), sē gĕrĕre (3 *reflex*)

conductor, dux, *m*

conduit, cănālis, *m*

cone, cōnus, *m*

confectionery, crustum, *n*

confederacy, sŏcĭĕtas, *f*

confederate, foedĕrātus

confer, *v.t*, confĕro (*irreg*); (— with), collŏquor (3 *dep*); (— about), ăgo (3) dē

conference, collŏquĭum, *n*

confess, *v.t*, confĭtĕor (2 *dep*)

confession, confessĭo, *f*

confide, *v.t*, confīdo (3), fīdo (3) (*with dat*)

confidence, fĭdes, *f*, fĭdūcĭa, *f*

confident, fīdens

confidential (trusty), fīdus; (one's own, special), prŏprĭus; (secret), arcānus

confine, *v.t*, inclūdo (3), contĭneo (2)

confinement, inclūsĭo, *f*, custōdĭa, *f*; (childbirth), partus, *m*; pŭerpĕrĭum, *n*

confirm, *v.t*, confirmo (1)

confiscate, *v.t*, pūblĭco (1), ădĭmo (3)

confiscation, pūblĭcātĭo, *f*

conflagration, incendĭum, *n*

conflict, *nn*, certāmen, *n*

conflict, *v.i*, certo (1); dissentĭo (4)

confluence, conflŭens, *m*

conform to, *v.i*, obtempĕro (1) (*with dat*); *v.t*, accommŏdo (1)

conformity, convĕnĭentĭa, *f*

confound, *v.t*, (disturb), turbo (1); (amaze), obstŭpĕfăcĭo (3); (bring to nothing, thwart), frustor (1 *dep*.)

confront, *v.i*, obvĭam ĕo (*irreg*.) (*with dat*)

confuse, *v.t*, turbo (1)

confused, perturbātus

confusion, perturbātĭo, *f*

congeal, *v.i, and v.t*, congĕlo (1)

congenial, concors

congested, frĕquens

congratulate, *v.t*, grātŭlor (1 *dep*)

congratulation, grātŭlātĭo, *f*

congregate, *v.i*, sē congrĕgare (1 *reflex*.)

congress, concĭlĭum, *n*, conventus, *m*

congruous, congrŭens

conjecture, *nn*, conĭectūra, *f*

conjecture, *v.i*, cōnĭcĭo (3)

conjugate, *v.t*, dēclīno (1)

conjunction (grammar), conĭunctĭo, *f*

conjure, *v.i* (perform tricks), praestigĭis ūtor (3 *dep*.); (image) cōgĭto (1)

conjurer, măgus, *m*

connect, *v.t*, conĭungo (3)

connected, conĭunctus

connection, conĭunctĭo, *f*; (by marriage), affīnĭtas, *f*

connive at, *v.i*, connīveo (2) in (*with abl*)

connoisseur, *use vb*, stŭdeo (2) (to be keen on)

conquer, *v.t*, vinco (3), sŭpĕro (1)

conqueror, victor, *m*

conquest, victōrĭa, *f*

conscience, conscĭentĭa, *f*

conscientious, rēlĭgĭōsus

conscientiousness, fĭdes, *f*

conscious, conscĭus

consciously, *adv,* *use adj,* scĭens (knowing)

consciousness, conscĭentĭa, *f,* sensus, *m*

conscript (recruit), tĭro, *m*

consecrate, *v.t,* conscĕro (1)

consecrated, săcer

consecutive, contĭnŭus

consent, *nn,* consensus, *m;* (by the — of), consensu;

consent to, *v.i,* assentĭo (4)

consequence (result), exĭtus, *m;* (importance), mōmentum, *n;* (in — of), *prep,* propter (*with acc*)

consequent, sĕquens

consequently, *adv,* ĭgĭtur, ĭtăque

conserve, *v.t,* conservo (1)

consider, *v.t,* cōgĭto (1), dēlībĕro (1), existĭmo (1);(— with respect), respĭcĭo (3)

considerable, ălĭquantus

considerate, hūmānus

considerateness, hūmānĭtas, *f*

consideration, consīdĕrātĭo,*f;* (regard), rătĭo, *f*

considering, *conj,* ut

consign, *v.t,* mando (1), committo (3)

consignment (of goods), merces, *f.pl*

consist of, *v.i,* consisto (3) in (*with abl*)

consistency, constantĭa, *f*

consistent (constant), constans; (consistent with), consentănĕus

console, *v.t,* consōlor (1 *dep.*)

consolidate, *v.t,* firmo (1), sōlĭdo (1)

consonant, consŏnans littĕra

consort (husband), mărītus, *m;* (wife), mărīta, *f*

consort with, *v.i,* ūtor (3 *dep*) (*with abl*)

conspicuous, mănĭfestus, insignis

conspiracy, conĭŭrātĭo, *f*

conspirator, conĭŭrātus, *m*

conspire, *v.i,* conĭŭro (1)

constable, dĕcŭrĭo, *m,* lictor, *m*

constancy, fĭdes, *f;* (steadiness), constantĭa, *f,* fĭdēlĭtas, *f*

constant, fĭdēlis, constans

constellation, sīdus, *n*

consternation, păvor, *m*

constituent parts, ĕlĕmenta, *n.pl*

constitute, *v.t,* constĭtŭo (3), compōno (3), crĕo (1)

constitution (of a state), respūblĭca, *f;* (of a body), hăbĭtus, *m*

constitutional, lēgĭtĭmus

constrain, *v.t,* cōgo 3), compello (3)

construct, *v.t,* făbrĭcor (1 *dep.*), exstrŭo (3)

construction (act of —), făbrĭcātĭo, *f;* (method), fĭgūra, *f,* structūra, *f*

construe, *v.t,* interprĕtor (1 *dep*)

consul, consul, *m*

consulship, consŭlātus, *m*

consult, *v.t,* consŭlo (3); *v.i,* dēlībĕro (1); (— someone's interests), consŭlo (3) (*with dat*)

consultation, collŏquĭum, *n*

consume, *v.t,* consumo (3), confĭcĭo (3)

consummate, *v.t,* consummo (1), perfĭcĭo (3)

consummate, *adj,* summus

consummation, consummātĭo, *f*

consumption, consumptĭo, *f*

contact, tactus, *m*

contagion, contāgĭo, *f*

contain, *v.t,* contĭnĕo (2)

contaminate, *v.t,* contămĭno (1)

contamination, contāgĭo, *f,* măcŭla, *f*

contemplate, *v.t,* contemplor (1 *dep.*)

contemplation (study), mĕdĭtātĭo, *f*

contempory, aequālis

contempt, contemptus, *m*

contemptible, contemnendus

contend, *v.i,* contendo (3), certo (1), pugno (1); (argue), *v.t,* affirmo (1)

content, contentus

content, *v.t,* sătisfăcĭo (3) (*with dat.*); *v.i,* (be content), sătis hăbĕo (2)

contentment, aequus ănĭmus, *m*

contest, *nn,* certāmen, *n,* pugna, *f*

contest, *v.t,* certo (1), contendo (3)

contestant, pugnātor, *m,* pĕtītor, *m*

contiguous, contĭgŭus, confīnis

continent, *adj,* contĭnens

continent, *nn,* contĭnens, *f*

contingency, cāsus, *m*

continual, perpĕtŭus, contĭnens

continually, *adv,* perpĕtuo, contĭnenter

continuation, perpĕtŭĭtas, *f*

continue, *v.t,* prōdūco (3), prōrŏgo (1); *v.i,* mănĕo (2)

continuity, perpĕtŭĭtas, *f*

continuous, contĭnens

contort, *v.t,* torquĕo (2)

contour, fĭgūra, *f*

contraband, *adj,* vĕtĭtus

contract, *nn,* pactum, *n*

contract, *v.i,* (grow smaller), sē contrăhĕre (3 *reflex*); *v.t,* contrăho (3)

contraction, contractĭo, *f*

contractor, conductor, *m*

contradict, *v.t,* contrādīco (3) (*with dat*)

For List of Abbreviations used, turn to pages 3, 4

contradiction, contrādictĭo, *f*; (inconsistency), rĕpugnantĭa, *f*
contradictory, rĕpugnans
contrary, *adj*, adversus, contrārĭus; (— to), *prep*, contrā (*with acc*); **the contrary,** *nn*, contrārĭum, *n*; (on the —), *adv*, contrā
contrast, *v.t*, confĕro (*irreg*); *v.i*, discrĕpo (1)
contravene, *v.t*, vĭŏlo (1)
contribute, *v.t*, confĕro (*irreg*)
contribution, collātĭo, *f*, trĭbūtum, *n*
contrivance (gadget), māchĭna, *f*
contrive, *v.t*, (think out), excōgĭto (1)
control, *v.t*, mŏdĕror (1 *dep*) (*with dat*); (guide), rĕgo (3)
control, *nn*, pŏtestas, *f*, tempĕrantĭa, *f*
controversy, contrōversĭa, *f*
contumacious, pertĭnax
contumacy, pertĭnācĭa, *f*
contumely, contŭmēlĭa, *f*
convalescent, convălescens
convenience, commŏdĭtas, *f*, opportūnĭtas, *f*
convenient, commŏdus, opportūnus
convention (meeting), conventus, *m*; (agreement), conventĭo, *f*
converge, *v.i*, ĕōdem vergo (3)
conversation, sermo, *m*, collŏquĭum, *n*
converse, *v.i*, collŏquor (3 *dep*)
conversion, commūtātĭo, *f*
convert, *v.t*, mūto (1), converto (3)
convex, convexus
convey, *v.t*, vĕho (3), porto (1)
conveyance (act of —), vectūra, *f*; (vehicle), vĕhĭcŭlum, *n*
convict, *v.t*, damno (1)
conviction (belief), *use phr*, persuāsum est (*with dat. of person*), e.g. persuāsum est mĭhi (**it is my conviction**); (convicting), damnātĭo, *f*
convince, *v.t*, persuādĕo (2) (*with dat.*)
conviviality, hĭlărĭtas, *f*
convoke, *v.t*, convŏco (1)
convoy, *nn*, commĕātus, *m*; (escort), praesĭdĭum, *n*
convulse, *v.t*, concŭtĭo (3), ăgĭto (1)
convulsion, tŭmultus, *m*, mōtus, *m*; (medical), convulsĭo, *f*
cook, *nn*, cŏquus, *m*
cook, *v.t*, cŏquo (3)
cool, frīgĭdus; (of mind), lentus
cool, *v.t*, rĕfrīgĕro (1); *v.i*, rĕfrīgĕror (1 *pass*)
coolly, *adv*, frīgĭde, lentē
coolness, frīgus, *n*

co-operate with, *v.t*, adiŭvo (1)
co-operation, auxĭlĭum, *n*, (help)
cope with, *v.i*, congrĕdĭor (3 *dep.*)
copious, largus, cōpĭōsus
copper, aes, *n*
copper, *adj*, aēnĕus
coppice, dūmētum, *n*
copy, exemplum, *n*
copy, *v.t*, ĭmĭtor (1 *dep*), dēscrībo (3)
coral, cŏrālĭum, *n*
cord, fūnis, *m*
cordial, *adj*, bĕnignus
cordiality, bĕnignĭtas, *f*
cordon, cŏrōna, *f*
core, nuclĕus, *m*
cork, *nn*, cortex, *m*, *f*
corn, frūmentum, *n*; (-crop), sĕges, *f*; (on the foot), clāvus, *m*
corner, angŭlus, *m*
cornice, cŏrōna, *f*
coronation, *use* crĕo (1) (**elect to office**)
coroner, quaesĭtor, *m*
corporal, *adj*, corpŏrĕus
corporal, *nn*, dĕcŭrĭo, *m*
corps (company), mănus, *f*
corpse, cădāver, *n*, corpus, *n*
corpulence, ŏbēsĭtas, *f*
corpulent, ŏbēsus
correct, rectus, pūrus
correct, *v.t*, corrĭgo (3), ēmendo (1)
correction, ēmendātĭo, *f*; (chastisement), castīgātĭo, *f*
correctly, *adv*, rectē
correctness, vērĭtas, *f*
correspond, *v.i*, (agree with), convĕnĭo (4) (*with dat*); (write), littĕras mitto (3) et accĭpĭo (3) (**send and receive letters**)
correspondence, missĭo et acceptĭo ĕpistŏlārum (**sending and receiving of letters**)
corresponding, par, gĕmellus
corroborate, *v.t*, confirmo (1)
corrode, *v.t*, rōdo (3), ĕdo (3)
corrosive, mordax
corrupt, *v.t*, corrumpo (3)
corrupt, *adj*, corruptus
corruption, dēprāvātĭo, *f*
corselet, lōrĭca, *f*
cost, *nn*, prĕtĭum, *n*, sumptus, *m*
cost, *v.i*, sto (1) (*with dat. of person and abl. or genit. of price*) *e.g.* **the victory cost the Carthaginians much bloodshed:** victōrĭa stĕtit Poenis multo sanguĭne
costly, *adj*, prĕtĭōsus
costume, hăbĭtus, *m*

cot, lectŭlus, *m*

cottage, cāsa, *f*

cotton, gossypĭum, *n*

couch, lectus, *m*

couch, *v.i*, subsīdo (3); *v.t* (— a weapon), intendo (3)

cough, *nn*, tussis, *f*

cough, *v.i*, tussĭo (4)

council, concĭlĭum, *n*

counsel (advice), consĭlĭum, *n*; (lawyer), pătrōnus, *m*

count, *v.t*, nŭmĕro (1); (— upon, trust), confīdo (3) (*with dat*)

countenance, *nn*, vultus, *m*

countenance, *v.t*, permitto (3), făvĕo (2), indulgĕo (2)

counter (in shop), mensa, *f*; (for counting), calcŭlus, *m*

counter, *adv*, contra

counteract, *v.t*, obsisto (3) (*with dat.*)

counter-balance, *v.t*, exaequo (1)

counterfeit, *adj*, ădultĕrīnus, fictus

counterfeit, *v.t*, sĭmŭlo (1), fingo (3)

counterpart, res gĕmella (paired, twin thing)

countless, innŭmĕrābĭlis

country (fatherland), pătrĭă, *f*; (countryside), rūs, *n*; (region), rēgĭo, *f*

country-house, villa, *f*

countryman (of the same country), cīvis, *c*; (living in the countryside), rusticus, *m*

couple, *nn*, (pair), pār *n*

couple, *v.t*, conĭungo (3)

courage, virtus, *f*, ănĭmus, *m*

courageous, fortis, ācer, fĕrox

courier (messenger), nuntĭus, *m*

course (motion), cursus, *m*; (route), vĭa, *f*, ĭter *n*; (plan), rătĭo, *f*; (race —), circus, *m*; (of —), *adv*, nĭmīrum, certē

court (— of justice), iūdĭcĭum, *n*; (judges themselves), iūdĭces, *m. pl*; (palace), aula, *f*, dŏmus, (f) rēgis (the house of the king); (courtyard), ārĕa, *f*

court, *v.t*, cŏlo (3)

court-martial, *use phr.* in castris iudĭcare (1) (to try in camp)

courteous, cōmis, hūmānus

courtesy, cōmĭtas, *f*, hūmānĭtas, *f*

courtier, aulĭcus, *m*

courtship, ămor, *m*

cousin, consōrbrīnus, *m* (. . . a), *f*

covenant, pactum, *n*

cover, *v.t*, tĕgo (3); (conceal) occulto (1)

cover, covering, *nn*, tĕgŭmen, *n*; (lid), ŏpĕrimentum, *n*

coverlet, strāgŭlum, *n*

covert, *nn*, dūmētum, *n*

covet, *v.t*, cŭpĭo (3)

covetous, ăvārus, ăvĭdus, cŭpĭdus

covetousness, ăvārĭtĭa, *f*, cŭpĭdĭtas, *f*

cow, vacca, *f*

cow, *v.t*, terrĕo (2), dŏmo (1) (tame)

coward, ignāvus, *m*

cowardice, ignāvĭa, *f*

cowardly, *adj*, ignāvus

cowl, cŭcullus, *m*

coy (bashful), vĕrēcundus

crab, cancer, *m*

crabbed, mōrōsus

crack, *nn*, (noise), crĕpĭtus, *m*; (chink), rīma, *f*

crack, *v.t*, findo (3), frango (3); *v.i*, (open up), dēhisco (3); (sound), crĕpo (1)

cradle, cūnae, *f. pl.*

craft (deceit), dŏlus, *m*; (skill), artĭfĭcĭum, *n*; (boat), rătis, *f*, nāvis, *f*

craftsman, ŏpĭfex, *m*

crafty, callĭdus

crag, scŏpŭlus, *m*

cram, *v.t*, confercĭo (4)

cramp, *v.t*, comprĭmo (3)

crane (bird), grus, *m*, *f*; (machine), tollēno, *f*

crank, uncus, *m*

cranny, rīma, *f*

crash, *nn*, frăgor, *m*

crash, *v.i*, (noise), strĕpo (3); (bring into collision), *v.t*, collīdo (3)

crate, corbis, *m*

crater, crāter, *m*

crave for, *v.t*, ōro (1), appĕto (3)

craving, *nn*, dēsīdĕrĭum, *n*

crawl, *v.i*, rēpo (3)

crayon, crēta, *f*

crazy, cerrītus, dēmens

creak, *v.i*, crēpo (1)

creaking, *nn*, strīdor, *m*, crĕpĭtus, *m*

crease, *nn*, rūga, *f*

crease, *v.t*, rūgo (1)

create, *v.t*, crĕo (1)

creation (act of —), crĕātĭo, *f*; (making), făbrĭcātĭo, *f*; (universe), mundus, *m*

creator, auctor, *m*, crĕātor, *m*

creature, ănĭmal, *n*

credence (belief), fĭdes, *f*

credible, crēdĭbĭlis

credit (belief or commercial credit), fĭdes, *f*; (reputation), existĭmātĭo, *f*

credit, *v.t*, (believe), crēdo (3); (— an account, person, etc.), acceptum rĕfĕro (*irreg*) (*with dat. of person*)

creditable (honourable), hŏnestus

creditor, crēdĭtor, *m*
credulous, crēdŭlus, *m*
creek, sĭnus, *m*
creep, *v.i*, serpo (3), rēpo (3)
crescent, lūna, *f*, (crescent moon)
crescent-shaped, lūnātus
crest, crista, *f*
crested, cristātus
crest-fallen, dēmissus
crevice, rīma, *f*
crew, nautae, *m*, *pl*, rēmĭges, *m*, *pl*
crib (child's bed), lectŭlus, *m*
cricket (insect), cĭcāda, *f*
crime, făcĭnus, *n*, scĕlus, *n*
criminal, *nn*, hŏmo sons, hŏmo nŏcens
criminal, *adj*, nēfārĭus, scĕlestus
crimson, *adj*, coccĭnĕus
cringe to, *v.i*, ădūlor (1 *dep*)
cripple, *nn*, hŏmo claudus
cripple, *v.t*, dēbĭlĭto (1); (— a person), claudum reddo (3)
crippled, dēbĭlis, claudus
crisis, discrīmen, *n*
crisp, frăgĭlis
critic, existĭmātor, *m*, censor, *m*
critical, ēlĕgans; (of a crisis, etc.), *use* discrīmen, *n* (crisis)
criticise, *v.t*, (find fault) rĕprĕhendo (3), iūdĭco (1)
croak, *nn*, quĕrēla, *f*, clāmor, *m*
croak, *v.i*, căno (3), crōcĭo (4)
crockery, fictĭlia, *n.pl*
crocodile, crŏcŏdīlus, *m*
crocus, crŏcus, *m*
crook (shepherd's —), pĕdum, *n*
crooked, curvus; (bad, etc.), prāvus
crop (of corn), sĕges, *f*, frūges, *f*, *pl*; (of a bird), inglŭvĭes, *f*
crop, *v.t*, tondĕo (2)
cross, *nn*, crux, *f*
cross, *adj*, transversus; (annoyed), īrātus
cross, *v.i. and v.t*, transĕo (4 *irreg*)
cross-examine, *v.t*, interrŏgo (1)
crossing (act of —), transĭtus, *m*; (cross-road), compĭtum, *n*
crouch, *v.i*, sē dēmittĕre (3 *reflex*)
crow (bird), cornix, *f*
crow, *v.i*, (of a cock), căno (3); (boast), sē iactare (1 *reflex*)
crowd, turba, *f*
crowd together, *v.i*, congrĕgor (1 *dep*); *v.t*, stīpo (1), frĕquento (1)
crowded, confertus, cĕlĕber
crown, cŏrōna, *f*; (royal), dĭădēma, *n*; (of head, etc.), vertex, *m*
crown, *v.t*, cŏrōno (1)
crucifixion, *use phr. with* crux, *f*, (cross)

crucify, *v.t*, crŭce affĭcĭo (3)
crude, rŭdis
cruel, crūdēlis, atrox
cruelty, crūdēlĭtas, *f*
cruet, gutus, *m*
cruise, *nn*, nāvĭgātĭo, *f*
cruise, *v.i*, nāvĭgo (1)
crumb, mīca, *f*
crumble, *v.t*, tĕro (3); *v.i*, corrŭo (3)
crumple, *v.t*, rūgo (1)
crush, *v.t*, contundo (3), opprĭmo (3)
crust, crusta, *f*
crutch, băcŭlum, *n*
cry, *nn*, clāmor, *m*, vox, *f*
cry, *v.i*, clāmo (1); (weep), lacrĭmo (1)
crystal, *nn*, crystallum, *n*
cub, cătŭlus, *m*
cube, tessĕra, *f*
cubic, cūbĭcus
cuckoo, cŭcūlus, *m*, coccyx, *m*
cucumber, cŭcŭmis, *m*
cudgel, fustis, *m*
cudgel, *v.t*, verbĕro (1), mulco (1)
cue, signum, *n*
cuff, *nn*, (blow), cŏlăphus, *m*, ălăpa, *f*
cuff, *v.t*, incŭtĭo (3)
cuirass, lōrīca, *f*, thōrax, *m*
culminate, *use adj*, summus (topmost)
culpable, culpandus, nŏcens
culprit, hŏmo nŏcens
cultivate, *v.t*, cŏlo (3)
cultivation, cultus, *m*, cultūra, *f*
cultivator, cultor, *m*
culture, cultus, *m*, cultūra, *f*
cumbersome, inhăbĭlis
cunning, *adj*, callĭdus, dŏlōsus
cunning, *nn*, callĭdĭtas, *f*, dŏlus, *m*
cup, pōcŭlum, *n*
cupboard, armārĭum, *n*
cupidity, cŭpĭdĭtas, *f*
cupola, thŏlus, *m*
curate, săcerdos, *c*, (priest)
curator, cūrātor, *m*
curb, *v.t*, frēno (1), cŏhĭbĕo (2)
curdle, *v.t*, cōgo (3), cŏăgŭlo (1); *v.i*, concresco (3)
cure, *nn*, sānātĭo, *f*
cure, *v.t*, mĕdĕor (2 *dep*) (*with dat.*)
curiosity, stŭdĭum, *n*
curious (inquisitive), cūrĭōsus; (rare), rārus
curl, *v.t*, crispo (1)
curl, *nn*, cincinnus, *m*
curly, cincinnātus
currant, ăcĭnus, *m*
currency, mŏnēta, *f*, nummi, *m. pl*
current, *nn*, (of river), flūmen, *n*
current, *adj*, (present), hic; (general), ūsĭtātus

curse, *nn*, imprĕcātĭo, *f*, dīrae, *f. pl*
curse, *v.t*, exsĕcror (1 *dep.*)
cursed, exsĕcrābĭlis
cursorily, *adv*, summātim, brĕvĭter
curt, brĕvis
curtail, *v.t*, arto (1)
curtain, aulaeum, *n*
curve, *nn*, flexus, *m*
curve, *v.t*, flecto (3), curvo (1)
curved, curvātus
cushion, pulvīnar, *n*
custodian, cūrātor, *m*
custody (keeping), custōdĭa, *f*; (imprisonment), vincŭla, *n.pl*
custom, mos, *m*, consŭētūdo, *f*; (— duty), portōrĭum, *n*
customary, ūsĭtātus, sŏlĭtus
customer, emptor, *m*
cut, *nn*, (incision), incīsĭo, *f*; (blow), ictus, *m*, plāga, *f*
cut, *v.t*, sĕco (1), caedo (3); (— away), abscīdo (3); (— down), succīdo (3); (— off), praecīdo (3); (— off from communications, supplies, etc.) interclūdo (3); (— out), excīdo (3); (— short), praecīdo (3); (— to pieces), concīdo (3), trŭcīdo (1)
cutaneous, *use genit. of* cŭtis (skin)
cutlass, glădĭus, *m*
cutlery, cultri, *m. pl* (knives)
cutter (boat), phăsēlus, *m*, cĕlox, *f*
cutting, *adj*, (biting), mordax
cuttle-fish, sepĭa, *f*
cycle (circle), orbis, *m*
cygnet, pullus, *m*
cylinder, cȳlindrus, *m*
cymbal, cymbălum, *n*
cynic, cȳnĭcus, *m*
cynical, mordax, difficĭlis
cynicism, dūrĭtĭa, *f*
cypress, cupressus, *f*

D

dab, *v.t*, illīdo (3)
dabble in, *v.t*, attingo (3)
daffodil, narcissus, *m*
dagger, pūgĭo, *m*
daily *adj*, quŏtīdĭānus
daily, *adv*, quŏtīdĭē
daintiness (of manners), fastīdĭum, *n*
dainty (things), dēlĭcātus; (people), fastīdĭōsus
daisy, bellis, *f*
dale, valles, *f*
dalliance, lūsus, *m*
dally, *v.i*, (delay), mŏror (1 *dep*)
dam (breakwater), mōles, *f*
dam, *v.t*, obstrŭo (3)

damage, *nn*, dētrīmentum, *n*, damnum, *n*
damage, *v.t*, laedo (3), affīgo (3)
dame, dŏmĭna, *f*, mātrōna, *f*
damn, *v.t*, damno (1)
damp, *adj*, hūmĭdus
damp, *v.t*, hūmecto (1); (enthusiasm, etc.), immĭnŭo (3) (lessen)
damp, *nn*, hūmor, *m*
dance, *v.i*, salto (1)
dance, *nn*, saltātus, *m*
dancer, saltātor, *m* (... trix, *f*)
dandy, hŏmo lĕpĭdus, ēlĕgans, bellus
danger, pĕrīcŭlum, *n*
dangerous, pĕrĭcŭlōsus
dangle, *v.i*, pendĕo (2)
dank, hūmĭdus, ūvĭdus
dapper (spruce), nĭtĭdus
dappled, măcŭlōsus
dare, *v.i*, audĕo (2 *semi-dep*) mōlĭor (4 *dep*)
daring, *adj*, audax
daring, *nn*, audācĭa, *f*
dark, *adj*, obscūrus tĕnĕbrōsus; (in colour), fuscus
dark, darkness, *nn*, tĕnĕbrae, *f. pl*
darken, *v.t*, obscūro (1), occaeco (1)
darling, *nn*, dēlĭcĭae, *f. pl*; *adj*, mollītus
darn, *v.t*, sarcĭo (4)
dart, *nn*, tēlum, *n*, iăcŭlum, *n*
dart, *v.i*, (rush), *use compound of* vŏlo (1) (to fly)
dash, *nn*, (rush), *use vb*, vŏlo (1) (to fly)
dash, *v.t*, prōvŏlo (1), rŭo (3); *v.i*, affīgo (3), impingo (3)
dashing, *adj*, ălăcer
dastardly, *adj*, ignāvus
date (fruit), palmŭla, *f*; (time), dĭes, *f*
date, *v.t*, (something), dĭem ascrībo (3) in (*with abl.*)
daub, *v.t*, oblĭno (3)
daughter, fīlĭa, *f*; (— in-law), nŭrus, *f*
daunt, *v.t*, percello (3)
dauntless, impăvĭdus
dawdle, *v.i*, cesso (1)
dawn, prīma lux, aurōra, *f*
dawn, *v.i*, dīlūcesco (3)
day, dĭes, *m*, *f*; (at — break), *adv. phr*, prīmā lūce; (by —), *adv*, interdĭu; (every —), *adv*, quŏtīdĭē; (late in the —), multo dĭe; (on the — before), prīdĭe; (on the next —), postrīdĭe; (— time), tempus dĭurnum, *n*
daze, *v.t*, stŭpĕfăcĭo (3)
dazzle, *v.t*, perstringo (3)

For List of Abbreviations used, turn to pages 3, 4

dazzling, splendĭdus

dead, *adj*, mortŭus; (the dead or departed), mānes, *m. pl*; (a — body), corpus, *n*

deaden, *v.t*, (senses, etc.), hēbĕto (1)

deadly, *adj*, mortĭfer, pernĭcĭōsus, fūnestus

deaf, surdus

deafen, *v.t*, exsurdo (1), obtundo (3)

deafness, surdĭtas, *f*

deal (a good-,), ălĭquantum, (business) nĕgōtĭum, *n*

deal, *v.t*, (distribute), distrĭbŭo (3); mētĭor (4 *dep*.); *v.i*, (deal with), ăgo (3) cum (*with abl*)

dealer, mercātor, *m*

dealings, *nn*, ūsus, *m*, commercĭum, *n*

dear, cārus; (of price), prĕtĭōsus

dearly, *adv*, (at a high price), magni

death, mors, *f*

death-bed (on his —), *use adj*, mŏrĭens (dying)

deathless, immortālis

debar, *v.t*, exclūdo (3)

debase, *v.t*, dēmitto (3), vĭtĭo (1)

debate, contrōversĭa, *f*

debate, *v.t*, dispŭto (1), discepto (1)

debater, dispŭtātor, *m*

debauch, *v.t*, corrumpo (3)

debauchery, stŭprum, *n*

debit, *nn*, expensum, *n*

debit, *v.t*, expensum fĕro (*irreg*) (*with dat*)

debt, aes ălĭēnum, *n*

debtor, dēbĭtor, *m*

debut, ĭnĭtĭum, *n*

decamp, *v.i*, castra mŏvĕo (2); discēdo (3)

decant, *v.t*, diffundo (3)

decanter, lăgēna, *f*

decapitate, *v.t*, sĕcūri fĕrĭo (4)

decay, *nn*, tābes, *f*, dēmĭnūtĭo, *f*

decay, *v.i*, dīlābor (3 *dep*), tābesco (3)

decease, dēcessus, *m*

deceased, *adj*, mortŭus

deceit, fraus, *f*, dŏlus, *m*

deceitful, fallax

deceive, *v.t*, dēcĭpĭo (3), fallo (3)

December, Dĕcember (mensis)

decency, dĕcōrum, *n*, hŏnestas, *f*

decent, dĕcōrus, hŏnestus

deception, fraus, *f*, dŏlus, *m*

deceptive, fallax

decide, *v.t*, constĭtŭo (3), stătŭo (3), dēcerno (3)

decided (persons), firmus; (things), .certus

decidedly, *adv*, (assuredly), plānē, vēro

decimate, *v.t*, dĕcĭmo (1)

decision, arbitrĭum, *n*, dēcrētum *n*

deck, pons, *m*

deck, *v.t*, orno (1)

declaim, *v.t*, dēclāmo (1)

declaration, prŏfessĭo, *f* (— of war), dēnuntĭātĭo, *f* (belli)

declare, *v.i*, prŏfĭtĕor (2 *dep*), affirmo (1); *v.t*, dēclāro (1); (— war), dēnuntĭo (1) (bellum)

decline, *nn*, dēmĭnūtĭo, *f* (diminution)

decline, *v.t*, (refuse), rĕcūso (1); *v.i*, inclīno (1), dēcresco (3)

declivity, clīvus, *m*

decompose, *v.t*, solvo (3); *v.i*, solvor (3 *pass*)

decomposition, sŏlūtĭo, *f*

decorate, *v.t*, orno (1), dĕcŏro (1)

decoration (ornament), ornāmentum, *n*, dĕcus, *n*; (badge), insigne, *n*

decorous, dĕcōrus

decorum, dĕcōrum, *n*, pŭdor, *m*

decoy, illex, *m*; (bait), esca, *f*

decrease, *nn*, dēmĭnūtĭo, *f*

decrease, *v.i*, dēcresco (3); *v.t*, mĭnŭo (3)

decree, *nn*, dēcrētum, *n*; (— of the Senate), consultum, *n*

decree, *v.t*, dēcerno (3), censĕo (2)

decrepit, dēcrĕpĭtus, dēbĭlis

decry, *v.t*, vĭtŭpĕro (1), obtrecto (1)

dedicate, *v.t*, consĕcro (1)

deduce, *v.t*, conclūdo (3)

deduct, *v.t*, dēdūco (3)

deduction (taking away), dēductĭo, *f*

deed, factum, *n*, făcĭnus, *n*; (legal), tābŭla, *f*

deem, *v.t*, pŭto (1)

deep, *nn*, (the sea), altum, *n*

deep, altus; (of sound), grăvis

deepen, *v.t*, altĭōrem reddo (3)

deeply, *adv*, altē, pĕnĭtus (deep within)

deer, cervus, *m* cerva, *f*

deface, *v.t*, dēformo (1)

defame, *v.t*, mălĕdīco (3) (*with dat*)

default, *v.i*, dēfĭcĭo (3) (fail to answer bail), vădĭmōnĭum dēsĕro (3)

defeat, *nn*, clādes, *f*

defeat, *v.t*, vinco (3), sŭpĕro (1)

defect, vĭtĭum, *n*

defective, vĭtĭōsus

defence (protection), praesĭdĭum, *n*; (legal), dēfensĭo, *f*

defenceless, ĭnermis

defend, *v.t,* dēfendo (3)
defendant (in a trial), rĕus, *m*
defender, dēfensor, *m*; **(in court),** pătrōnus, *m*
defer, *v.t,* **(put off),** differo (*irreg*); *v.i,* **(show deference to),** cēdo (3)
deference, observantĭa, *f*
defiance, prōvŏcātĭo, *f*
defiant, fĕrox
deficiency, dēfectĭo, *f*
deficient, inops, mancus
deficit, lăcūna, *f*
defile, *v.t,* contămĭno (1)
defile, *nn,* angustĭae, *f, pl*
define, *v.t,* circumscrībo (3)
definite, constĭtūtus, certus
definition, dēfīnītĭo, *f*
deflect, *v.t,* dēflecto (3)
deform, *v.t,* dēformo (1)
deformity, dēformĭtas, *f*
defraud, *v.t,* fraudo (1)
defray, *v.t,* suppĕdĭto (1) **(supply)**
deft, doctus **(skilled)**
defy, *v.t* obsto (1), prōvŏco (1)
degenerate, *v.i,* dēgĕnĕro (1)
degenerate, *adj,* dēgĕner
degradation, ignōmĭnĭa, *f*
degrade, *v.t,* mŏvĕo (2), dē *or* ex (*with abl*), **(move down from); dēhŏnesto** (1)
degree (interval, stage, rank), grădus, *m*; **(to such a degree),** *adv,* ădĕo; **(by degrees),** *adv,* **(gradually), grădātim**
deify, *v.t,* consĕcro (1)
deign, *v.t,* dignor (1 *dep*)
deity, dĕus, *m*
deject, *v.t,* afflīgo (3)
dejected, dēmissus, afflictus
dejection, maestĭtĭa, *f*
delay, *nn,* mŏra, *f*
delay, *v.i,* mŏror (1 *dep*), cunctor (1 *dep*); *v.t,* mŏror (1 *dep*), tardo (1)
delegate, *nn,* lēgātus, *m*
delegate, *v.t* **(depute),** lēgo (1), mando (1) **(*with acc. of thing and dat. of person*)**
delegation, lēgātĭo, *f*
deliberate, *adj,* consĭdĕrātus
deliberate, *v.t,* consŭlo (3), dēlībĕro (1)
deliberately, *adv,* consultō
deliberation, dēlībĕrātĭo, *f*
delicacy, subtīlĭtas, *f,* suāvĭtas, *f*; **(food),** cūpēdĭa, *n.pl*
delicate, subtīlis, tĕner; **(of health),** infirmus
delicious, suāvis
delight, *nn,* **(pleasure),** vŏluptas, *f*
delight, *v.t,* dēlecto (1); *v.i,* gaudĕo (2)
delightful, iūcundus, ămoenus
delineate, *v.t,* dēscrībo (3)

delinquency, dēlictum, *n*
delinquent, *nn,* peccātor, *m*
delirious, dēlīrus
delirium, dēlīrĭum, *n*
deliver, *v.t,* **(set free),** lībĕro (1); **(hand over),** do (1), trādo (3), dēdo (3); **(— a speech),** hăbĕo (2), ōrātĭonem
deliverance (freeing), lībĕrātĭo, *f*
deliverer, lībĕrātor, *m*
delivery (freeing), lībĕrātĭo, *f*; **(childbirth),** partus, *m*; **(of a speech),** ēlŏcūtĭo, *f*
delude, *v.t,* dēcĭpĭo (3)
deluge, dīlŭvĭum, *n,* inundātĭo, *f*
delusion, error, *m*; **(trick),** fallācĭa, *f,* fraus, *f*
delusive (deceitful), fallax; **(empty),** vānus
demagogue, plēbĭcŏla, *c*
demand, *nn,* postŭlātĭo, *f*
demand, *v.t,* posco (3), postŭlo (1)
demean oneself, dēmittor (3 pass), sē dēmittĕre (3 *reflex*)
demeanour, mōres, *m. pl,* hăbĭtus, *m*
demented, dēmens
demise, *nn,* **(death),** dēcessus, *m,* mors, *f*
democracy, cīvĭtas pŏpŭlāris, *f*
democrat, plēbĭcŏla, *c*
demolish, *v.t,* dīrŭo (3), dēlĭco (2), dēmōlĭor (4 *dep.*)
demolition, ēversĭo, *f,* rŭīna, *f*
demon, daemōnĭum, *n*
demonstrate, *v.t,* dēmonstro (1)
demonstration, dēmonstrātĭo, *f*
demur, *v.i,* haesĭto (1)
demure, *adj,* vērēcundus
den, lătĭbŭlum, *n*
denial, nĕgātĭo, *f*
denominate, *v.t,* nōmĭno (1)
denote, *v.t,* indĭco (1), signĭfĭco (1), nŏto (1)
denounce, *v.t,* **(nomen)** dēfĕro (*irreg*)
dense, densus, confertus
density, crassĭtūdo, *f*
dent, nŏta, *f*
dentist, dentĭum mĕdĭcus, *m*
denude, *v.t,* nūdo (1)
deny, *v.t,* nĕgo (1), abnŭo (3)
depart, *v.i,* ăbĕo (4), discēdo (3)
departed (dead), mortŭus
department (of administration, etc.), prōvincĭa, *f,* **(part),** pars, *f*
departure, discessus, *m*
depend on, *v.i,* pendĕo (2) ex *or* in (*with abl*); **(rely on),** confīdo (3 *semi-dep*) (*with dat*)
dependant, *nn,* clĭens, *c*
dependence on, clĭentēla, *f*; **(reliance),** fĭdes, *f*

dependency (subject state), prōvincĭa, *f*

depict, *v.t*, dēscrībo (3), effingo (3)

deplorable, mĭsĕrābĭlis

deplore, *v.t*, dēplōro (1)

deploy, *v.t*, explĭco (1)

depopulate, *v.t*, pŏpŭlor (1 *dep*); vasto (1)

deport, *v.t*, dēporto (1); (behave oneself), se gĕrĕre (3 *reflex*)

deportment, hăbĭtus, *m*

depose, *v.t*, mŏvĕo (2) (*with abl*)

deposit, *v.t*, dēpōno (3)

deposit, *nn*, dēpŏsĭtum, *n*

deprave, *v.t*, dēprāvo (1), corrumpo (3)

depravity, prāvĭtas, *f*

deprecate, *v.t*, dēprĕcor (1 *dep*)

depreciate, *v.t*, dētrăho (3); *v.i*, mĭnŭor (3 *pass*) (grow less)

depreciation (decrease), dēmĭnūtĭo, *f*; (disparagement), obtrectātĭo, *f*

depredation, expīlātĭo, *f*, praedātĭo, *f*

depress, *v.t*, dēprĭmo (3); (spirits, etc.), infringo (3)

depression (sadness), tristĭtĭa, *f*

deprive, *v.t*, prīvo (1) (*with acc. of person deprived, and abl. of thing*)

depth, altĭtūdo, *f*

deputation, lēgātĭo, *f*

depute, *v.t*, lēgo (1), mando (1) (*with dat*)

deputy, lēgātus, *m*

deputy-governor, prōcūrātor, *m*

derange, *v.t*, perturbo (1)

deride, *v.t*, dērīdĕo (2)

derision, irrīsĭo, *f*, rīsus, *m*

derive (from), *v.t*, (deduce), dūco (3), ab (*and abl*)

derogate from, *v.i*, dērŏgo (1) dē (*with abl*)

derogatory (remark), noxĭus

descend, *v.i*, dēscendo (3)

descendant, prōgĕnĭes, *f*

descent (lineage), prōgĕnĭes, *f*; (movement), dēscensus, *m*; (slope), dēclīve, *n*

describe, *v.t*, dēscrībo (3), expōno (3)

description, dēscriptĭo, *f*, narrātĭo, *f*

descry, *v.t*, conspĭcor (1 *dep*)

desecrate, *v.t*, prŏfāno (1)

desert (wilderness), sōlĭtūdo, *f*

desert, *v.t*, dēsĕro (3), rĕlinquo (3)

deserted, dēsertus

deserter, perfŭga, *m*, transfŭga, *m*

deserve, *v.t*, mĕrĕor (2 *dep*); dignus esse (*irreg*) (*with abl*)

deservedly, *adv*, mĕrĭto

design, dēscriptĭo, *f*; (plan), consĭlĭum, *n*

design, *v.t*, dēscrībo (3); (intend), in ănĭmo hăbĕo (2)

designate, *v.t*, dēsigno (1)

designing, *adj*, callĭdus, dŏlōsus

desirable, optābĭlis

desire, *nn*, dēsĭdĕrĭum, *n*, cŭpĭditas,

desire, *v.t*, cŭpĭo (3), opto (1)

desirous, cŭpĭdus

desist, *v.i*, dēsisto (3), dēsĭno (3)

desk, scrīnĭum, *n*

desolate, dēsertus, sōlus

despair, *nn*, dēspērātĭo, *f*

despair, *v.i*, dēspēro (1)

despatch, *v.t* mitto (3); (kill), interfĭcĭo (3)

despatch, *nn*, (sending), dīmissĭo, *f*; (letter), littĕrae, *f. pl*; (speed), cĕlĕrĭtas, *f*

desperate, dēspērātus; (situation), extrēmus

desperation, dēspērātĭo, *f*

despicable, contemptus

despise, *v.t*, dēspĭcĭo (3), sperno (3)

despite, *prep*, contrā (*with acc*)

despoil, *v.t*, spŏlĭo (1)

despond, *v.i*, ănĭmum dēmitto (3)

despondent, *use adv. phr*, ănĭmo dēmisso

despot, dŏmĭnus, *m*

despotic, ty̆rannĭcus, *m*

despotism, dŏmĭnātus, *m*

dessert, mensa sĕcunda (second table)

destination, *often* quo? (whither), *or* ĕo (to that place)

destine, *v.t*, dēstĭno (1), dēsigno (1)

destiny, fātum, *n*

destitute, ĭnops

destroy, *v.t*, perdo (3), dēlĕo (2), ēverto (3)

destroyer, vastātor, *m*

destruction, pernĭcĭes, *f*, ēversĭo, *f*, exĭtĭum, *n*

destructive, pernĭcĭōsus

desultory, inconstans

detach, *v.t*, sēiungo (3), sēpăro (1)

detached, sēpărātus

detachment (of troops, etc.), mănus,

details, singŭla, *n.pl*

detail, *v.t*, explĭco (1)

detain, *v.t*, rĕtĭnĕo (2)

detect, *v.t*, dēprĕhendo (3), compĕrĭo (4)

deter, *v.t*, dēterrĕo (2), dēpello (3)

deteriorate, *v.i*, corrumpor (3 *pass*)

determinate, *adj*, certus

determination (resolution), constantĭa, *f*; (intention), consĭlĭum, *n*

determine, *v.i and v.t*, constĭtŭo (3)

determined (resolute), firmus; (fixed), certus

detest, *v.t,* ōdi (*v. defect*)

detestable, ōdǐōsus

dethrone, *v.t,* regno pello (3) **(expel from sovereignty)**

detour, circŭǐtus, *m*

detract from, *v.t,* dētrăho (3) dē (*with abl*)

detriment, dētrĭmentum, *n*

detrimental (to be —), *v.i,* esse (*irreg*) dētrĭmento (*with dat*)

devastate, *v.t,* vasto (1)

devastation, vastātĭo, *f*

develop, *v.t,* explĭco (1), ēdŭco (1); *v.i,* cresco (3) **(grow)**

development, prōlātĭo, *f*; **(unfolding),** explĭcātĭo, *f*

deviate, *v.i,* dēclīno (1), discēdo (3)

deviation, dēclīnātĭo, *f*

device (contrivance), artĭfĭcĭum, *n*; **(emblem),** insigne, *n*; **(plan),** dŏlus, *m*

devil, daemŏnĭum, *n*

devilish, nēfandus

devious, dēvĭus

devise, *v.t,* excōgĭto (1), fingo (3)

devoid, expers, văcŭus

devolve, *v.i,* obvĕnĭo (4); *v.t,* dēfĕro (*irreg*)

devote, *v.t,* dēdĭco (1), dēdo (3); **(consecrate),** dēvŏvĕo (2)

devoted, dedĭtus, devotus

devotion, stŭdĭum, *n*; **(love),** ămor, *m*

devour, *v.t,* dēvŏro (1), consūmo (3)

devouring, ēdax

devout, pĭus, vĕnĕrābundus, rēlĭgĭōsus

dew, rōs, *m*

dexterity, sollertĭa, *f,* callĭdĭtas, *f*

dexterous, sollers, callĭdus

diadem, dĭădēma, *n*

diagonal, *adj,* dĭăgōnālis

diagram, forma, *f*

dial, sōlārĭum, *n*

dialect, dĭălectus, *f*

dialectics, dĭălectĭca, *n.pl*

dialogue, sermo, *m*; **(written),** dĭălŏgus, *m*

diameter, crassĭtūdo, *f*

diamond, ădămas, *m*

diaphragm, praecordĭa, *n.pl*

diarrhoea, prōflŭvĭum, *n*

diary, commentārĭi dĭurni, *m. pl*

dice, tāli, *m. pl*; **(the game),** ălĕa, *f*

dictate, *v.t,* dicto (1); *v.i,* impĕro (1) (*with dat*)

dictation, dictātĭo, *f*

dictator, dictātor, *m*

dictatorial, impĕrĭōsus

dictatorship, dictātūra, *f*

dictionary, glossārĭum, *n*

die, *v.i,* mŏrĭor (3 *dep*), cădo (3)

diet, victus, *m*

differ, *v.i,* discrĕpo (1), diffĕro (*irreg*)

difference, discrīmen, *n,* dīversĭtas, *f*; **(— of opinion),** discrĕpantĭa, *f*

different, ălĭus, dīversus

difficult, diffĭcĭlis

difficulty, diffĭcultas, *f*; **(to be in —),** lăbōro (1); **(with —),** *adv,* aegrē

diffidence, diffīdentĭa, *f*

diffident, diffīdens

diffuse, *v.t,* diffundo (3)

dig, *v.t,* fŏdĭo (3)

digest, *v.t,* concŏquo (3)

digestion, concoctĭo, *f*

dignified, grăvis

dignify, *v.t,* hŏnesto (1)

dignity (of character), grăvĭtas, *f,* dignĭtas, *f*

digress, *v.i,* dīgrĕdĭor (3 *dep*)

digression, dīgressĭo, *f*

dike (ditch), fossa, *f*; **(mound),** agger, *m*

dilapidated, ruīnōsus

dilate, *v.i,* sē dīlātāre (1 *reflex*); *v.t* **(— upon),** dīlāto (1)

dilatory, ignāvus, lentus

dilemma (difficulty), angustĭae, *f. pl*

diligence, dīlĭgentĭa, *f*

diligent, dīlĭgens, industrĭus

dilute, *v.t,* dīlŭo (3), miscĕo (2)

dim, *adj,* **(light, etc.),** obscūrus; **(dull, stupid),** hĕbes

dim, *v.t,* obscūro (1)

dimension, mŏdus, *m*

diminish, *v.t,* mĭnŭo (3); *v.i,* mĭnŭor (3 *pass*)

diminution, dēmĭnūtĭo, *f*

diminutive, parvus, exĭgŭus

dimness, obscūrĭtas, *f*

dimple, lăcūna, *f*

din, strĕpĭtus, *m*

dine, *v.i,* cēno (1)

dingy, sordĭdus

dining-room, trīclīnĭum, *n,* cēnātĭo, *f*

dinner, cēna, *f*

by dint of, *prep,* per (*with acc*)

dip, *v.t,* mergo (3); *v.i,* mergor (3 *pass*)

diploma, dĭplōma, *n*

diplomacy (by —), per lēgātos **(by means of diplomats)**

diplomat(ist), lēgātus, *m*

direct, *adj,* rectus

direct, *v.t,* dīrĭgo (3); **(order),** praecĭpĭo (3) (*with dat. of person*); **(show),** monstro (1)

direction (of motion), cursus, *m*; **(pointing out),** monstrātĭo, *f*; **(affairs),** admĭnistrātĭo, *f*; **(in different —s),** (*pl. adj*), dīversi

director, cūrātor, *m*

dirt, sordes, *f*

For List of Abbreviations used, turn to pages 3, 4

dirty, sordĭdus, spurcus
dirty, *v.t*, inquĭno (1), foedo (1)
disable, *v.t*, dēbĭlĭto (1)
disabled, inhăbĭlis, confectus
disadvantage, incommŏdum, *n*
disadvantageous, incommŏdus
disaffected, ălĭēnātus
disaffection, ănĭmus āversus, *m*
disagree, *v.i*, discrĕpo (1), dissentĭo (4)
disagreeable (unpleasant), iniūcundus
disagreement, discrĕpantĭa, *f*, dissensĭo, *f*
disappear, *v.i*, ēvānesco (3), diffŭgĭo (3)
disappearance, exĭtus, *m*
disappoint, *v.t*, frustror (1 *dep*)
disappointment, incommŏdum, *n*
disapproval, rĕprĕhensĭo, *f*
disapprove, *v.t*, imprŏbo (1)
disarm, *v.t*, armis exŭo (3) (strip of arms)
disaster, clādes, *f*
disastrous, pernĭcĭōsus
disavow, *v.t*, diffĭtĕor (2 *dep*)
disavowal, infĭtĭātĭo, *f*
disband, *v.t*, dīmitto (3)
disbelieve, *v.t*, non crēdo (3), diffīdo (3) (*with dat*)
disburse, *v.t*, expendo (3)
disc, orbis, *m*
discard, *v.t*, rĕpŭdĭo (1)
discern, *v.t*, cerno (3)
discerning, *adj*, perspĭcax
discernment, intellĕgentĭa, *f*
discharge, *v.t*, (missiles, etc.), ēmitto (3), iăcŭlor (1 *dep*); (soldiers, etc.), dīmitto (3); (duties, etc.), fungor (3 *dep*) (*with abl*)
discharge, *nn*, ēmissĭo, *f*, dīmissĭo, *f*
disciple, discĭpŭlus, *m*
discipline, disciplīna, *f*
discipline, *v.t*, instĭtŭo (3)
disclaim, *v.t*, nĕgo (1), rĕpŭdĭo (1)
disclose, *v.t*, ăpĕrĭo (4)
disclosure, indĭcĭum, *n*
discolour, *v.t*, dēcŏlōro (1)
discomfiture, clādes, *f*
discomfort, incommŏdum, *n*
disconcert, *v.t*, perturbo (1)
disconnect, *v.t*, sēiungo (3)
disconsolate, maestus
discontented, măle contentus
discontinue, *v.t*, intermitto (3)
discord (strife), discordĭa, *f*, dissensĭo, *f*
discount, *nn*, dēcessĭo, *f* (decrease)
discourage, *v.t*, ănĭmum dēmitto (3)

discouragement, ănĭmi infractĭo, *f*, *or* dēmissĭo, *f*
discourse, *v.i*, dissĕro (3)
discourse, *nn*, sermo, *m*, contĭo, *f*
discover, *v.t*, invĕnĭo (4), rĕpĕrio (4), cognosco (3)
discovery inventĭo, *f*; (thing discovered), inventum, *n*
discredit, *v.t*, fĭdem abrŏgo (1)
discreditable, ĭnhŏnestus
discreet, consīdĕrātus, prūdens
discretion, prūdentĭa, *f*
discriminate, *v.t*, discerno (3)
discuss, *v.t*, discepto (1), dispŭto (1)
discussion, dispŭtātĭo, *f*
disdain, *v.t*, sperno (3), dēspĭcĭo (3)
disdain, *nn*, fastīdĭum, *n*
disdainful, fastīdĭōsus
disease, morbus, *m*
diseased, aeger
disembark, *v.t*, expōno (3); *v.i*, ēgrĕdĭor (3 *dep*)
disengage, *v.t*, (release), solvo (3)
disengaged (at leisure), ōtĭōsus; (free, loose), sŏlūtus
disentangle, *v.t*, explĭco (1)
disfigure, *v.t*, dēformo (1)
disgrace, *nn*, dēdĕcus, *n*, ignōmĭnĭa, *f*
disgrace, *v.t*, dēdĕcŏro (1)
disgraceful, turpis, flāgĭtĭōsus
disguise, *nn*, persōna, *f*, intĕgŭmentum, *n*
disguise, *v.t*, vestem mūto (1) (change the clothes); dissĭmŭlo (1) (pretend, hide)
disgust, *nn*, fastīdĭum, *n*, taedĭum, *n*
disgust, *v.t*, taedĭum mŏvĕo (2) (*with dat*)
disgusted (to be —), *use impersonal vb*, pĭget (2) (it disgusts)
disgusting, foedus
dish, *nn*, pătĭna, *f*
dishearten, *v.t*, exănĭmo (1), percello (3)
dishonest, imprŏbus, perfĭdus
dishonesty, *f*, imprŏbĭtas, *f*
dishonour, *nn*, dēdĕcus, *n*
dishonour, *v.t*, dēdĕcŏro (1)
dishonourable, ĭnhŏnestus
disinclination, dēclīnātĭo, *f*
disinherit, *v.t*, exhērēdo (1)
disintegrate, *v.t*, solvo (3); *v.i*, solvor (3 *pass*)
disinterested, neutri făvens (favouring neither side)
disjointed, ĭnordĭnātus
disk, orbis, *m*
dislike, *nn*, ŏdĭum, *n*

dislike, *v.t,* ăbhorrĕo (2) ab (*with abl*); displĭcĕo (2)
dislocate, *v.t,* extorquĕo (2)
dislodge, *v.t,* dēĭcĭo (3), pello (3)
disloyal, infidēlis
dismal, āter, maestus
dismantle, *v.t,* dīrĭpĭo (3)
dismay, *nn,* păvor, *m*
dismay, *v.t,* consterno (1), perturbo (1)
dismiss, *v.t,* dīmitto (3)
dismissal, dīmissĭo, *f*
dismount, *v.i,* ex ĕquo dēscendo (3)
disobedience, *use phr.* with *vb,* pārĕo (obey)
disobedient, măle pārens
disobey, *v.t,* măle pārĕo (*with dat*)
disoblige, *v.t,* offendo (3)
disorder, *nn,* perturbātĭo, *f*
disorderly, *adv,* turbātus; (**crowd**), turbŭlentus
disown, *v.t,* infĭtĭor (1 *dep*)
disparage, *v.t,* dētrăho (3), obtrecto (1)
dispatch, *v.t,* (see **despatch**)
dispel, *v.t,* dĕpcllo (3), discŭtĭo (3)
dispense, *v.t* dispertĭor (4 *dep*) distrĭbŭo (3); (— **with**), dimitto (3)
dispersal, dissĭpātĭo, *f*
disperse, *v.t,* dispergo (3), dissĭpo (1), *v.i,* diffŭgĭo (3)
dispirited, *use adv. phr,* dēmisso ănĭmo
display, *nn,* ostentātĭo, *f*
display, *v.t,* ostento (1)
displease, *v.t,* displĭcĕo (2) (*with dat*)
displeasing, ŏdĭōsus
displeasure, offensĭo, *f*
disposal, ēmissĭo, *f*; (**power**), arbĭtrĭum, *n*
dispose, *v.t,* (**arrange**), constĭtŭo (3), dispōno (3); (**induce**), inclīno (1); (**get rid of**), ēlŭo (3)
disposed, inclīnātus
disposition (**arrangement**), dispŏsĭtĭo, *f*; (**of mind, etc.**), nātūra, *f,* ingĕnĭum, *n*
dispossess, *v.t,* dēturbo (1), dētrūdo (3)
disproportion, dissĭmĭlĭtūdo, *f*; (**of parts, etc.**), inconcinnĭtas, *f*
disprove, *v.t,* rĕfello (3), rĕfūto (1)
dispute, *nn,* contrōversĭa, *f*
dispute, *v.t,* dispŭto (1)
disqualify, *v.t,* (**prevent**), prŏhĭbĕo (2)
disregard, *nn,* neglĕgentĭa, *f*
disregard, *v.t,* neglĕgo (3)
disreputable, infāmis
disrespectful, contŭmax, insŏlens
dissatisfaction, mŏlestĭa, *f*
dissatisfied (**to be** —), *use impers. vb,* paenĭtet (*with acc. of subject and genit. of object*)

dissect, *v.t,* insĕco (1), persĕco (1)
dissemble, *v.i,* dissĭmŭlo (1)
dissension, discordĭa, *f,* dissensĭo, *f*
dissent, *v.i,* dissentĭo (4)
dissimilar, dissĭmĭlis
dissipate, *v.t,* dissĭpo (1)
dissipated, dissŏlūtus, lĭbīdĭnōsus
dissipation, lĭcentĭa, *f*
dissolute, dissŏlūtus, lĭbīdĭnōsus
dissolve, *v.t,* solvo (3), lĭquĕfăcĭo (3), *v.i,* solvor (3 *pass*), lĭquesco (3)
dissuade, *v.t,* dissuādĕo (2) (*with dat*)
distaff, cŏlus, *f*
distance, spătĭum, *n;* (**remoteness**), longinquĭtas, *f;* (**at a** —), *adv,* longē, prŏcul
distant, rĕmōtus, distans; (**to be** —), absum (*irreg*)
distaste, fastīdĭum, *n*
distasteful, iniūcundus
distemper (**malady**), morbus, *m*
distend, *v.t,* tendo (3)
distil, *v.t,* stillo (1)
distinct (**separate**), sēpărātus; (**clear**), clārus, mănĭfestus
distinction (**difference**), discrīmen, *n;* (**mark of honour**), hŏnor, *m,* dĕcus, *n*
distinctive, prŏprĭus
distinguish, *v.t,* distinguo (3); *v.i,* (— **oneself**), clāresco (3), ēmĭnĕo (2)
distinguished, insignis, clārus
distort, *v.t,* detorquĕo (2)
distortion, distortĭo, *f*
distract, *v.t,* distrăho (3)
distracted (**mentally**), āmens, turbātus
distraction (**mental**), āmentĭa, *f*
distress, mĭsĕrĭa, *f,* dŏlor, *m*
distress, *v.t,* sollĭcĭto (1)
distressed, sollĭcĭtus
distribute, *v.t,* distrĭbŭo (3), partĭor (4 *dep*)
distribution, partītĭo, *f*
district, rĕgĭo, *f*
distrust, *nn,* diffīdentĭa, *f*
distrust, *v.t,* diffīdo (3) (*with dat*)
distrustful, diffīdens
disturb, *v.t,* turbo (1)
disturbance, mōtus, *m,* tŭmultus, *m*
disunion, discordĭa, *f*
disunite, *v.t,* sēiungo (3), dissŏcĭo (1)
disused, dēsuētus
ditch, fossa, *f*
ditty, carmen, *n*
divan, lectŭlus, *m*
dive, *v.i,* sē mergĕre (3 *reflex*)
diver, ūrīnātor, *m*
diverge, *v.i,* discēdo (3)
divergence, dēclīnātĭo, *f*

diverse, ălĭus, dīversus

diversion, dērīvātĭo, f; (of thought, etc.), āvŏcātĭo, f

divert, v.t, āverto (3), āvŏco (1); (amuse), oblecto (1), prōlecto (1)

divide, v.t, dīvĭdo (3); (share out), partĭor (4 dep); v.i, sē dīvĭdĕre (3 reflex)

divine, dīvīnus

divine, v.t, dīvīno (1), augŭror (1 dep)

diviner, augur, m

divinity, dīvīnĭtas, f

divisible, dīvĭdŭus

division (act of —), dīvīsĭo, f; (a section), pars, f; (discord), discĭdĭum, n

divorce, dīvortĭum, n

divorce, v.i, dīvortĭum făcĭo (3), cum (and abl)

divulge, v.t, pătĕfăcĭo (3), ăpĕrĭo (4)

dizziness, vertīgo, f

dizzy, vertīgĭnōsus

do, v.t, făcĭo (3), ăgo (3); (to be satisfactory), v.i, sătis esse; (— away with), abŏlĕo (2); (— without), cărĕo (2) (with abl)

docile, făcĭlis, dŏcĭlis

dock, nāvālĭa, n.pl

doctor, mĕdĭcus, m

doctor, v.t, cūro (1)

doctrine, dogma, n, rătĭo, f

document, tăbŭla, f, littĕrae, f. pl

dodge, dŏlus, m

dodge, v.t, (elude), ēlūdo (3)

doe, cerva, f

dog, cănis, c

dog, v.t, insĕquor (3 dep.)

dogged (stubborn), pertĭnax, pervĭcax

dogged (by ill-luck, etc.), ăgĭtātus

dogma, dogma, n

dogmatic, arrŏgans

dole (small allowance), dĭurna, n.pl

dole out, v.t, dīvĭdo (3)

doleful, tristis, maestus

dolefulness, tristĭtĭa, f

doll, pūpa, f

dolphin, delphīnus, m

dolt, caudex, m

dome, thŏlus, m

domestic, dŏmestĭcus, fămĭlĭāris; (animals) villātĭcus

domestic, nn, (servant), fămŭlus, m

domicile, dŏmĭcĭlĭum, n

dominant, pŏtens

dominate, v.t, dŏmĭnor (1 dep)

domination, dŏmĭnātus, m

domineering, impĕrĭōsus

dominion, impĕrĭum, n, regnum, n

donation, dōnum, n

donkey, ăsĭnus, m

doom, fātum, n

doom, v.t, damno (1)

door, iānŭa, f; (out of -s), adv, fŏrīs

doorkeeper, iānĭtor, m

doorpost, postis, f

dormitory, cŭbĭcŭlum, n

dormouse, glīs, m

dot, nn, punctum, n

dotage, sĕnĭum, n

dotard, sĕnex, m

dote upon, v.i, dēpĕrĕo (4)

double, adj, dŭplex, gĕmĭnus

double, v.t, dŭplĭco (1); v.i, dŭplex fĭo (irreg), ingĕmĭno (1)

double-dealing, nn, fraus, f

double-faced fallax

doubt, v.i, dŭbĭto (1)

doubt, nn, dŭbĭum, n, dŭbĭtātĭo, f

doubtful, dŭbĭus, incertus

doubtless, adv, sĭne dŭbĭo, nīmīrum

dough, fărīna, f

dove, cŏlumba, f

dove-coloured, cŏlumbīnus

dove-cot, cŏlumbārĭum, n

dowager, vĭdŭa, f

down, prep, dē (with abl); adv, use dē in a compound verb, e.g. run down, dēcurro (3)

down, nn (feathers, etc.), plūma, f;

down, v.t, (put down), dēpōno (3)

downcast, dēiectus, dēmissus

downfall, occāsus, m, rŭīna, f

down-hearted, adv, dēmisso ănĭmo

downpour, imber, m

downright, dīrectus; (sheer), mĕrus

downward, adj, dēclīvis

downwards, adv, dĕorsum

downy, adj, plūmĕus

dowry, dos, f

doze, v.i, dormīto (1)

dozen (twelve), dŭŏdĕcim

dozing, adj, somnĭcŭlōsus

drab, cĭnĕrĕus (ash-coloured)

drag, v.t, trăho (3)

dragon, drăco, m

drain, nn, clŏāca, f, fossa, f

drain, v.t, (land), sicco (1); (a drink), haurĭo (4)

dram, cўăthus, m

drama, fābŭla, f, scēna, f

dramatic (theatrical), scēnĭcus

dramatist, pŏēta, m

drapery, vēlāmen, n

draught (of air), spīrĭtus, m; (water, etc.) haustus, m; (game of -s), lătruncŭli, m, pl

draw, v.t (pull), trăho (3); (portray), dēscrībo (3); (— a sword), glădĭum stringo (3); (— aside), sēdūco (3); (— water, etc.), haurĭo (4); v.i (—

back), pĕdem rĕfĕro (*irreg*); (—
lots), sortes dūco (3); (— up troops,
etc.), *v.t*, instrŭo (3)
drawback, *nn*, incommŏdum, *n*
drawbridge, pontĭcŭlus, *m*
drawing (picture), pictūra, *f*
drawl, *v.i*, lentē prōnuntĭo (1) (pronounce slowly)
dray, plaustrum, *n*
dread, *nn*, formīdo, *f*, păvor, *m*
dread, *v.t*, tīmĕo (2), formīdo (1)
dreadful, terrĭbĭlis, ătrox
dream, *nn*, somnĭum, *n*
dream, *v.t*, somnĭo (1)
dreamy, somnĭcŭlōsus
dreary, tristis
dregs, faex, *f*
drench, *v.t*, mădĕfăcĭo (3)
dress, *nn*, vestis, *f*, hăbĭtus, *m*
dress, *v.t*, (clothe); vestĭo (4); (—
a wound), cūro (1) (care for)
dressing, *nn*, (of wound), fōmentum, *n*
drift, *nn*, (heap), agger, *m*; (tendency),
use phr. with quōrsus (to what
end?)
drift, *v.i*, dēfĕror (*irreg. pass*)
drill (military), exercĭtātĭo, *f*; (tool),
tĕrĕbra, *f*
drill, *v.t* (pierce), tĕrĕbro (1); (train),
exercĕo (2)
drink, *v.t*, bĭbo (3), pōto (1)
drink, *nn*, pōtĭo, *f*
drinker, pōtător, *m*
drinking, pōtĭo, *f*; (— party), cōmĭs-
sātĭo, *f*
drip, *v.i*, stillo (1)
dripping, *adj*, mădĭdus
drive, *nn* gestātĭo, *f*
drive, *v.t*, ăgo (3); (— away), fŭgo (1)
pello (3); (— back), rĕpello (3); (—
out), expello (3)
drive, *v.i*, (on horse-back, etc.),
vĕhor (3 *pass*)
drivel ĭneptĭae, *f*, *pl*
drivel, *v.i*, dēlīro (1)
driver, aurīga, *c*
drizzle, *v.i*, rōro (1)
droll, rīdĭcŭlus, lĕpĭdus
drollery, făcētĭae, *f*. *pl*
dromedary, drŏmas, *m*
drone, *nn*, (bee), fūcus, *m*; (sound),
murmur, *n*
drone, *v.i*, murmŭro (1)
droop, *v.i*, pendĕo (2), languesco (3)
drooping, *adj*, pendŭlus; (of spirits,
etc.), dēmissus
drop, *nn*, gutta, *f*
drop, *v.t*, dēmitto (3); (leave off),
omitto (3); *v.i*, cădo (3)
dropsy, hydrops, *m*

drought, siccĭtas, *f*
drove (flock), grex, *m*
drown, *v.t*, submergo (3); (of noise)
obstrĕpo (3)
drowsy, somnĭcŭlōsus
drudge, *nn*, servus, *m*
drudge, *v.i*, servĭo (4); (weary oneself), *v.i*, sē fătīgāre (1 *reflex*)
drudgery, lăbor servīlis (servile labour)
drug, *nn*, mĕdĭcāmentum, *n*
drug, *v.t*, mĕdĭco (1)
drum, tympănum, *n*
drunk, *adj*, ēbrĭus
drunkenness, ēbrĭĕtas, *f*
dry, siccus, ārĭdus; (thirsty), sĭtĭens
dry (up), *v.t*, sicco (1); *v.i*, āresco (3)
dryness, siccĭtas, *f*, ārĭdĭtas, *f*
dubious, dŭbĭus
duck, *nn*, ănas, *f*
duck, *v.t*, mergo (3)
duckling, ănătĭcŭla, *f*
duct, förāmen, *n*
due, *adj*, (owed), dēbĭtus; (just),
iustus; (suitable), ĭdōnĕus, aptus
due, *nn*, (a right), ius, *n*; (taxes),
vectīgal, *n*, portōrĭum, *n*
duel, certāmen, *n*
dull (person), hĕbes, obtūsus; (colour),
obscūrus; (blunt), hĕbes; (weather),
subnūbĭlus
dullness (of mind), tardĭtas, *f*
duly, *adv*, (established by precedent),
rĭtē
dumb, mūtus
dumbfound, *v.t*, obstŭpĕfăcĭo (3)
dump, *v.t*, cŏăcervo (1)
dun, fuscus
dunce, hŏmo stŭpĭdus
dung, stercus, *n*
dungeon, carcer, *m*
dupe, *nn*, hŏmo crēdŭlus
dupe, *v.t*, dēcĭpĭo (3)
duplicate, exemplum, *n*
duplicity, fallācĭa, *f*
durability, firmĭtas, *f*
durable, firmus
duration, spătĭum, *n*; (long —),
dĭŭturnĭtas, *f*
during, *prep*, per (*with acc*)
dusk, crĕpuscŭlum, *n*
dusky, fuscus, nĭger
dust, *nn*, pulvis, *m*
dust, *v.t*, dētergĕo (2)
duster, pēnĭcŭlus, *m*
dusty, pulvĕrŭlentus
dutiful, pĭus
dutifulness, pĭĕtas, *f*
duty (moral), offĭcĭum, *n*; (given),
mūnus, *n*; (tax), vectīgal, *n*; (it is
my —), *use vb*. dēbĕo (2) (ought)

For List of Abbreviations used, turn to pages 3, 4

dwarf, pūmĭlĭo, c
dwarfish, pŭsillus
dwell, v.i, hăbĭto (1), incŏlo (3);
(— on a theme), commŏror (1
dep), haerĕo (2) in (with abl)
dweller, incŏla, c
dwelling (place), dŏmĭcĭlĭum, n
dwindle, v.i, dēcresco (3)
dye, nn, fūcus, m
dye, v.t, tingo (3), infĭcĭo (3)
dyer, infector, m
dying, adj, mŏrĭens
dynasty, dŏmus, f
dysentery, dўsentĕrĭa, f
dyspeptic, crūdus

E

each, ūnusquisque; (— of two),
ŭterque; (one —), use distributive
num, singŭli, bīni
eager, cŭpĭdus, ăvĭdus (with genit)
eagerness, cŭpĭdĭtas, f, ăvĭdĭtas, f
eagle, ăquĭla, f
ear, auris, f; (— of corn), spīca, f
early, adj, (in the morning), mātūtīnus; (of time, etc.), mātūrus
early, adv, (in the morning), māne;
(in time, etc.), mātūrē
earn, v.t, mĕrĕo (2), mĕrĕor (2 dep)
earnest, intentus, ācer
earnestly, adv intentē
earth (land), terra, f; (ground), sŏlum,
n; (globe), orbis, (m) terrārum
earthenware, fictĭlĭa, n.pl
earthly, adj, (terrestrial) terrestris
earthquake, terrae mōtus, m, (movement of the earth)
earth-work, agger, m
ease, quĭes, f, ōtĭum, n
ease, v.t, (lighten), lĕvo (1), exŏnĕro (1)
easily, adv, făcĭlē
easiness, făcĭlĭtas, f
east, nn, ŏrĭens, m
eastern, use genit. of ŏrĭens (east)
eastward, adv. phr, ăd ŏrĭentem
easy, făcĭlis
eat, v.t, ĕdo (3); (— away), rōdo (3)
eatable, escŭlentus
eating-house, pŏpīna, f
eaves, prōtectum, n
eaves-dropper, auceps, c
ebb, v.i, rĕcēdo (3)
ebb-tide, rĕcessus aestus (receding
of the tide)
ebony, ĕbĕnus, f
eccentric (of persons), nŏvus
echo, nn, ĭmāgo, f, ēcho, f

echo, v.t, rĕfĕro (irreg), rĕsŏno (1)
echoing, adj, rĕsŏnus
eclipse, nn, dēfectĭo, f
eclipse, v.t, obscūro (1)
economical, parcus, dīlĭgens
economy, parsĭmōnĭa, f, (frugality)
ecstasy, fŭror, m
ecstatic, fŭrens
eddy, vertex, m
edge (of knife, etc.), ăcĭes, f; (margin),
margo, c, ōra, f
edible, escŭlentus
edict, ēdictum, n
edifice, aedĭfĭcĭum, n
edify, v.t, instĭtŭo (3)
edit, v.t, ēdo (3)
edition, ēdĭtĭo, f
educate, v.t, ēdŭco (1)
education, ēdŭcātĭo, f, doctrīna, f
eel, anguilla, f
efface, v.t, dēlĕo (2)
effect, v.t, effĭcĭo (3)
effect, nn, (influence, impression),
vīs, f; (result), effectus, m; (consequence), ēventus, m; (without —),
(adv), nēquīquem
effective (impressive), grăvis; or use
phr. with confĭcĭo (3) (to bring to a
conclusion)
effectual, effĭcax
effeminate, effēmĭnātus
effervescence (of spirit, etc.), fervor, m
efficacy, vīs, f
efficiency, vīs, f
efficient, hăbĭlis, effĭcĭens
effigy, ĭmāgo, f
effort, ŏpĕra, f
effrontery, ōs, n
effulgent, fulgens
effusion, effūsĭo, f
egg, ōvum, n
egg on, v.t, incĭto (1)
egoism, ămor, (m) sŭi (fondness of
oneself)
egoist, ămātor, (m) sŭi
egregious, insignis
egress, exĭtus, m
eight, octo; (— each), octōni; (—
times), adv. octĭens; (— hundred)
octingenti
eighteen, dŭŏdēvīginti
eighteenth, dŭŏdēvīcensimus
eighth, octāvus
eightieth, octōgēsĭmus
eighty, octōginta
either, pron, altĕrŭter; conj, aut
either ... or, aut ... aut, vel ...
vel

ejaculate, *v.t*, ēmitto (3)
ejaculation (cry), vox, *f*, clāmor, *m*
eject, *v.t*, ēĭcĭo (3)
eke out, *v.t*, parco (3) (*with dat*)
elaborate, *adj*, ēlăbōrātus
elaborate, *v.t*, ēlăbōro (1)
elapse, *v.i*, (of time), intercēdo (3)
elate, *v.t*, effĕro (*irreg*)
elated (joyful), laetus
elbow, cŭbĭtum, *n*
elder, *adj*, māior nātu (greater by birth)
elder-tree, sambūcus, *f*
elderly, *adj*, prōvectus aetāte (advanced in age)
elect, *v.t*, crĕo (1), dēlĭgo (3)
elect, *adj*, dēsignātus
election, ēlectĭo, *f*, cŏmĭtĭa, *n.pl*
elector, suffrāgātor, *m*
elegance, ēlĕgantĭa, *f*, vĕnustas, *f*
elegant, ēlĕgans, vĕnustus
elegy, ēlĕgĭa, *f*
element, ēlĕmentum, *n*, prĭncĭpĭa, *n.pl*
elementary, prīmus, simplex
elephant, ēlĕphantus, *m*
elevate, *v.t*, tollo (3)
elevated, ēdĭtus; (mind) ēlātus
elevation, altĭtūdo, *f*, ēlātĭo, *f*
eleven, undĕcim; (— each), undēni
eleventh, undĕcĭmus
elicit, *v.t*, ēlĭcĭo (3)
eligible, ĭdōnĕus, opportūnus
elk, alces, *f*
ell, ulna, *f*
elm, ulmus, *f*
elocution, prōnuntĭātĭo, *f*
elope, *v.i*, aufŭgĭo (3) (run away)
eloquence, ēlŏquentĭa, *f*
eloquent, ēlŏquens, dĭsertus
else, *adj*, ălĭus
else, *adv*, ălĭter
elsewhere, *adv*, ălĭbī
elude, *v.t*, ēlūdo (3)
emaciate, *v.t*, attĕnŭo (1)
emaciated, măcer
emaciation, măcĭes, *f*
emanate, *v.i*, ēmāno (1)
emancipate, *v.t*, lībĕro (1), mănū-mitto (3)
embalm, *v.t*, condĭo (4)
embankment, mōles, *f*
embark, *v.t*, in nāvem impōno (3); *v.i*, nāvem conscendo (3)
embarrass, *v.t*, (entangle), impĕdĭo (4); (confuse), turbo (1)
embarrassment, scrūpŭlus, *m*; (difficulty), diffĭcultas, *f*
embassy (delegation), lēgāti, *m. pl*, (ambassadors)
embedded, sĭtus

embellish, *v.t*, orno (1)
embellishment, ornāmentum, *n*
embers, cĭnis, *m*
embezzle, *v.t*, āverto (3), pĕcŭlor (1 *dep*)
embezzlement, pĕcūlātus, *m*
embezzler, āversor, (*m*) pĕcūnĭae
embitter, *v.t*, exăcerbo (1)
emblem, insigne, *n*, indĭcĭum, *n*
embody, *v.t*, inclūdo (3)
embolden, *v.t*, confirmo (1)
embrace, *nn*, amplexus, *m*, complexus, *m*
embrace, *v.t*, amplector (3 *dep*), complector (3 *dep*); (— an opportunity), arrĭpĭo (3)
embroidered (clothing, etc.), pictus
embroil, *v.t*, (entangle), implĭco (1)
emerald, smăragdus, *c*
emerge, *v.i*, ēmergo (3), prōdĕo (4)
emergency, discrīmen, *n*, tempus, *n*
emigrate, *v.i*, mĭgro (1)
emigration, mĭgrātĭo, *f*
eminence (high ground), tŭmŭlus, *m*; (of rank, etc.), lŏcus amplissĭmus
eminent, ēgrĕgĭus, insignis
emissary, lēgātus, *m*
emit, *v.t*, ēmitto (3)
omolument, lŭcrum, *n*
emotion, mōtus, (*m*,) ănĭmi (movement of the mind)
emperor, impĕrātor, *m*, princeps, *m*
emphasize, *v.t*, prĕmo (3)
emphatic, grăvis
empire, impĕrĭum, *n*
empirical, empĭrĭcus
employ, *v.t*, ūtor (3 *dep*) (*with abl*)
employed (of persons), occŭpātus
employer, conductor, *m*
employment (occupation), quaestus, *m*; (business), nĕgōtĭum, *n*; (using) ūsurpātĭo, *f*
emporium, empŏrĭum, *n*
empower (someone to do ...), *v.i*, pŏtestātem făcĭo (3) (*with dat. of person and genit. of gerund(ive*))
empty, *adj*, văcŭus, ĭnānis
empty, *v.t*, exīnānĭo (4)
emulate, *v.t*, aemŭlor (1 *dep*)
emulous, aemŭlus
enable, *v.t*, făcultātem do (1) (*with dat*)
enact, *v.t*, (law), sancĭo (4), constĭtŭo (3)
enactment lex, *f*
enamoured (to be — of somone), *v.t*, ămo (1)
encamp, *v.i*, castra pōno (3)
enchant, *v.t*, fascĭno (1), dēlecto (1)

enchantment (allurement), blandī-mentum, *n*
encircle, *v.t*, circumdo (1)
enclose, *v.t*, inclūdo (3), saepĭo (4)
enclosure, saeptum, *n*
encounter, *v.t*, incĭdo (3) in (*with acc*); concurro (3), obvĭam ĕo (4) (*irreg*) (*with dat*)
encounter, *nn*, congressus, *m*
encourage, *v.t*, hortor (1 *dep*)
encouragement, hortātus, *m*; con-firmātĭo, *f*, hortātĭo, *f*
encroach upon, *v.t*, occŭpo (1)
encumber, *v.t*, ŏnĕro (1), impĕdĭo (4)
encumbrance, impĕdimentum, *n*
end, finis, *m*; *or use* extrēmus, *adj*, *agreeing with a noun*; *e.g.* at the end of the bridge, in extrēmo ponte
end, *v.t*, confĭcĭo (3), fīnĭo (4); *v.i*, *use phr. with* extrēmum, *n*, (end); (turn out, result), cēdo (3), ēvĕnĭo (4)
endanger, *v.t*, in pĕrīcŭlum addūco (3)
endear, *v.t*, dēvincĭo (4)
endeavour, *nn*, cōnātus, *m*
endeavour, *v.t*, cōnor (1 *dep*)
endless, infīnītus, perpĕtŭus
endorse, *v.t*, confirmo (1)
endow, *v.t*, dōno (1)
endowed, praedītus
endurable, tŏlĕrābĭlis
endurance, pătĭentĭa, *f*
endure, *v.t*, pătĭor (3 *dep*), fĕro (*irreg*); *v.i*, dūro (1)
enemy (public), hostis, *c*; (private), ĭnĭmīcus, *m*
energetic, ācer, strēnŭus, impĭger
energy, vīs, *f*, vĭgor, *m*
enervate, *v.t*, ēnervo (1)
enervation, dēbĭlĭtātĭo, *f*
enfeeble, *v.t*, dēbĭlĭto (1)
enforce, *v.t*, (carry out), exsĕquor (3 *dep*)
enfranchise, *v.t*, (give the right of voting), suffrāgĭum do (1) (*with dat*)
enfranchisement, cīvītātis dōnātĭo, *f*, (granting of citizenship)
engage, *v.t*, (join) iungo (3); (hire), condūco (3); (— in battle); signa conferre (*irreg*); (enter into), ingrĕdĭor (3 *dep*)
engaged, occŭpātus; (betrothed), sponsus
engagement (battle), proelĭum, *n*; (agreement), pactum, *n*; (promise), sponsĭo, *f*
engender, *v.t*, gigno (3), părĭo (3)
engine, māchĭna, *f*; (military —), tormentum, *n*

engineer, făber, *m*
England, Brītannĭa, *f*
English, Brītannus, Brītannĭcus
engrave, *v.t*, scalpo (3)
engraver, scalptor, *m*
engraving, *nn*, scalptūra, *f*
engross, *v.t*, occŭpo (1)
enhance, *v.t*, augĕo (2), orno (1)
enigma, aenigma, *n*, ambāges, *f*, *pl*
enigmatic, ambĭgŭus
enjoin, *v.t*, iūbĕo (2), mando (1)
enjoy, *v.t*, frŭor (3 *dep*) (*with abl*); (possess), ūtor (3 *dep*) (*with abl*)
enjoyment (pleasure), gaudĭum, *n*, lībīdo, *f*
enlarge, *v.t*, augĕo (2), amplĭfĭco (1)
enlargement, prōlātĭo, *f*
enlighten, *v.t*, (instruct), dŏcĕo (2)
enlist, *v.t*, (troops), conscrībo (3); (bring over), concĭlĭo (1); *v.i*, nōmen do (1) (give one's name)
enliven, *v.t*, excĭto (1)
enmity, ĭnĭmīcĭtĭa, *f*
ennoble, *v.t*, (make honourable), hŏnesto (1)
enormity, immānĭtas, *f*; (crime), scĕlus, *n*
enormous, ingens
enough, *nn. and adv*, sătis; (*foll. by genit*), *e.g.* enough water, sătis ăquae
enquire, *v.t*, quaero (3) ab (*with abl*)
enrage, *v.t*, irrīto (1), inflammo (1)
enrapture, *v.t*, oblecto (1)
enrich, *v.t*, lŏcŭplēto (1)
enroll, *v.t*, scrībo (3)
ensign, signum, *n*; (— bearer), signĭfer, *m*
enslave, *v.t*, servĭtūtem iniungo (3) (*with dat*)
ensue, *v.i*, sĕquor (3 *dep*)
entail, *v.t*, affĕro (*irreg*)
entangle, *v.t*, impĕdĭo (4)
enter, *v.i*, *and v.t*, intro (1), ingrĕdĭor (3 *dep*), ĭnĕo (4 *irreg*); *v.t*, (— write in), inscrībo (3)
enterprise (undertaking), inceptum, *n*
enterprising, promptus, strēnŭus
entertain, *v.t*, (people), excĭpĭo (3) (receive); (amuse), oblecto (1); (an idea, etc.) hăbĕo (2)
entertainment (of guests), hospĭtĭum, *n*
enthusiasm, stŭdĭum, *n*, fervor, *m*
enthusiastic, fānātĭcus, stŭdĭōsus
entice, *v.t*, illĭcĭo (3)
entire, tōtus, intĕger
entirely, *adv*, omnīno
entitle, *v.t*, (give the right to), ius do (1) (*with dat*); (name), inscrībo (3)

entitled (to be — to), *v.i*, ius hăbĕo (2)
entrails, viscĕra, *n.pl*
entrance (act of —), ingressĭo, *f*;
(door, etc), ădĭtus, *m*, ostĭum, *n*
entreat, *v.t*, obsĕcro (1), ōro (1)
entreaty, obsĕcrātĭo, *f*
entrust, *v.t*, crēdo (3) (*with dat*)
committo (3) (*with dat*)
enumerate, *v.t*, nŭmĕro (1)
envelop, *v.t*, involvo (3)
envelope, *nn*, invŏlūcrum, *n*
enviable, fortūnātus
envious, invĭdus
envoy, lēgātus, *m*
envy, invĭdĭa, *f*
envy, *v.t*, invĭdĕo (2) (*with dat*)
ephemeral, brĕvis
epic, *adj*, ĕpĭcus
epidemic, pestĭlentĭa, *f*
epigram, ĕpĭgramma, *n*
epigrammatic, ĕpĭgrammătĭcus, a,
um, *adj*
epilepsy, morbus cŏmĭtĭālis, *m*
episode (digression), excursus, *m*; res, *f*
epitaph, ŏlŏgĭum, *n*
epoch, aetas, *f*
equable. aequus
equal, *adj*, aequus, pār
equal, *nn*, use *adj*, pār
equal, *v.i and v.t*, aequo (1)
equality, aequālĭtas, *f*
equanimity, aequus ănĭmus, *m*
equator, aequĭnoctĭālis circŭlus, *m*
equestrian, ĕquester
equilibrium, aequĭlībrĭum, *n*
equinox, aequĭnoctĭum, *n*
equip, *v.t*, orno (1), armo (1)
equipment, arma, *n.pl*, armāmenta,
n.pl
equitable, aequus
equity, aequĭtas, *f*; (justice), iustĭtĭa, *f*
equivalent, *adj*, pār; (to be —),
v.i, *use* vălĕo (2) (to be worth) tanti
equivocal, ambĭgŭus
era, tempus, *n*, aetas, *f*
eradicate, *v.t*, ēvello (3), exstirpo (1)
erase, *v.t*, dēlĕo (2)
ere (before), *conj*, prĭusquam
erect, *v.t*, ērĭgo (3); (build), exstrŭo
(3)
erect, *adj*, rectus
erection (act of —), aedĭfĭcātĭo, *f*;
(a building), aedĭfĭcĭum, *n*
err, *v.i*, erro (1), pecco (1)
errand, mandātum, *n*
erratic, văgus
erroneous, falsus
error, error, *m*
erudite, doctus
eruption, ēruptĭo, *f*

escape, *nn*, fŭga, *f*
escape, *v.i*, *and v.t*, effŭgĭo (3), ēlābor
(3 *dep*)
escarpment, praeruptus lŏcus, *m*
escort, *nn*, comĭtātus, *m*; (protective),
praesĭdĭum, *n*
escort, *v.t*, cŏmĭtor (1 *dep*)
especial, praecĭpŭus
especially, *adv*, praecĭpŭē
espouse, *v.t*, (betroth), spondĕo (2);
(marry), dūco (3), nūbo (3)
essay (attempt), cōnātus, *m*; (composition), lĭbellus, *m*
essence (nature), nātūra, *f*, vīs, *f*
essential (necessary), nĕcessārĭus
establish, *v.t*, constĭtŭo (3), confirmo
(1)
establishment, constĭtūtĭo, *f*
estate (property), rēs, *f*, fundus, *m*
esteem, *nn*, existĭmātĭo, *f*
esteem, *v.t*, (think), aestĭmo (1),
pŭto (1); (think highly of), magni
aestĭmo (1)
estimable, laudātus
estimate, *nn*, aestĭmātĭo, *f*
estimate, *v.t*, aestĭmo (1)
estimation (opinion), ŏpĭnĭo, *f*
estrange, *v.t*, ălĭēno (1)
estrangement, ălĭēnātĭo, *f*
estuary, aestŭārĭum, *n*
eternal, aeternus
eternally, *adv*, *phr*, in aeternum
eternity, aeternĭtas, *f*
ether, aether, *m*
ethereal, aethĕrĭus
ethical (moral), mōrālis
eulogy, laudātĭo, *f*
evacuate, *v.t*, (— troops from a place),
dēdūco (3); *v.i*, (depart from),
excēdo (3), ex (*with abl*)
evade, *v.t*, ēlūdo (3)
evaporate, *v.i*, discŭtĭor (3 *pass*)
evasion, lătĕbra, *f*
evasive, ambĭgŭus
eve (evening), vesper, *m*
even, *adv*, ĕtĭam, *often use emphatic*
pron, *e.g.* even Caesar, Caesar
ipse; (not —), nĕ . . . quĭdem
even, *adj*, (level, equable), aequus;
(— number), pār
even if, *conj*, etsi
evening, vesper, *m*, (in the —), sub
vespĕrum
event (occurrence), rēs, *f*; (outcome),
exĭtus, *m*
eventually, *adv*, ălĭquando
ever, *adv*, (at any time), umquam;
(always), semper; (if —), si quando
evergreen, *adj*, semper vĭrĭdis
everlasting, aeternus

every (all), omnis; **(each),** quisque; (— **day),** *adv,* cottīdiē; (— **one),** omnes, *m.pl;* (— **thing),** omnĭa, *n.pl;* (— **where),** *adv,* ŭbīque

evict, *v.t,* expello (3)

evidence, testĭmōnĭum, *n;* **(factual),** argūmentum, *n*

evident, mănĭfestus, perspĭcŭus; **(it is —),** appāret (2 *impers*)

evil, *adj,* mălus, prāvus

evil, *nn,* mălum, *n*

evil-doer, hŏmo nēfārĭus

evoke, *v.t,* ēvŏco (1)

evolve, *v.t,* ēvolvo (3)

ewe, ŏvis, *f*

exact, *adj,* **(number, etc.),** exactus; **(persons),** dīlĭgens

exact, *v.t,* exĭgo (3)

exactness, subtīlĭtas, *f*

exaggerate, *v.t,* augĕo (2)

exaggeration, sŭperlātĭo, *f*

exalt, *v.t,* tollo (3), augĕo (2)

exalted, celsus

examination (test, etc.), prŏbātĭo, *f;* **(enquiry),** investīgātĭo, *f*

examine, *v.t,* investīgo (1), interrŏgo (1); **(test),** prŏbo (1)

example, exemplum, *n;* **(for —),** verbi causā

exasperate, *v.t,* exăcerbo (1)

excavate, *v.t,* căvo (1)

excavation (cavity), căvum, *n*

exceed, *v.t,* sŭpĕro (1), excēdo (3)

exceedingly, *adv,* admŏdum; *or use superlative of adj, e.g.* (— **large),** maxĭmus

excel, *v.t,* praesto (1) *(with dat)*

excellence, praestantĭa, *f*

excellent, praestans, ēgrĕgĭus

except, *prep,* praeter *(with acc)*

except, *v.t,* excĭpĭo (3)

exception (everyone, without —), omnes ad ūnum; **(take — to)** aegre fĕro *(irreg)*

exceptional, rārus, īnsignis

excess (over-indulgence), intempĕr-antĭa, *f*

excessive, nĭmĭus

exchange, *nn,* permūtātĭo, *f*

exchange, *v.t,* permūto (1)

exchequer, aerārĭum, *n*

excitable, fervĭdus, fĕrox

excite, *v.t,* excĭto (1), incendo (3)

excited, commŏtus, incensus

excitement, commōtĭo, *f*

exclaim, *v.i,* clāmo (1), conclāmo (1)

exclamation, exclāmātĭo, *f*

exclude, *v.t,* exclūdo (3)

exclusion, exclūsĭo, *f*

exclusive (one's own), prŏprĭus

excrescence, tūber, *n*

excruciating (pain, etc.), ācer

excursion, ĭter, *n*

excusable, excūsābĭlis

excuse, *nn,* excūsātĭo, *f*

excuse, *v.t,* excūso (1); **(pardon),** ignosco (3) *(with dat)*

execrable, nēfārĭus

execrate, *v.t,* dētestor (1 *dep*)

execute, *v.t,* **(carry out),** exsĕquor (3 *dep*); **(inflict capital punishment),** nĕco (1)

execution (carrying out), *use vb* exsĕquor; **(capital punishment),** supplĭcĭum, *n*

executioner, carnĭfex, *m*

exemplary, ēgrĕgĭus

exempt, *v.t,* excĭpĭo (3)

exempt, *adj,* immūnis

exemption, immūnĭtas, *f*

exercise, exercĭtātĭo, *f;* **(set task),** ŏpus, *n*

exercise, *v.t,* exercĕo (2)

exert, *v.t,* contendo (3), ūtor (3 *dep*) *(with abl);* **(to — oneself),** *v.i,* nītor (3 *dep*)

exertion, contentĭo, *f,* lăbor, *m*

exhale, *v.t,* exhālo (1)

exhaust, *v.t,* exhaurĭo (4); **(weary),** confĭcĭo (3), dēfătīgo (1)

exhausted (tired out), confectus

exhaustion, vīrĭum dēfectĭo, *f,* **(failing of strength)**

exhibit, *v.t,* expōno (3)

exhibition (spectacle), spectācŭlum, *n*

exhilarate, *v.t,* hĭlăro (1)

exhilaration, hĭlărĭtas, *f*

exhort, *v.t,* hortor (1 *dep*)

exhume, *v.t,* ērŭo (3)

exile, *nn,* **(person),** exsul, *c;* **(banishment),** exsĭlĭum, *n;* **(to be in —),** *v.i,* exsŭlo (1)

exile, *v.t,* in exsĭlĭum pello (3) **(drive into exile)**

exist, *v.i,* sum *(irreg),* exsisto (3)

existence (life), vīta, *f*

exit, exĭtus, *m*

exonerate, *v.t,* lībĕro (1)

exorbitant, nĭmĭus

exotic, externus

expand, *v.t,* extendo (3); *v.i,* extendor (3 *pass*)

expanse, spătĭum, *n*

expatiate (on a theme, etc.), *v.,* permulta dissĕro (3) dē *(with abl.)*

expatriate, *v.t*, ēĭcĭo (3)
expect, *v.t*, exspecto (1)
expectation, exspectātĭo, *f*
expediency, ūtĭlĭtas, *f*
expedient, *adj*, ūtĭlis
expedient, *nn*, rātĭo, *f*
expedite, *v.t*, expĕdĭo (4)
expedition (military, etc.), expĕdītĭo, *f*
expeditious, cĕler
expel, *v.t*, expello (3)
expend, *v.t*, expendo (3)
expenditure, ērŏgātĭo, *f*
expense, impensa, *f*, sumptus, *m*
expensive, sumptŭōsus, prĕtĭōsus
experience, ūsus, *m*, pĕrītĭa, *f*
experience, *v.t*, expĕrĭor (4 *dep*), pātĭor (3 *dep*)
experienced, pĕrītus
experiment, expĕrĭmentum, *n*
expert, *adj*, scĭens
expiate, *v.t*, expĭo (1)
expiation, expĭātĭo, *f*
expiatory, pĭācŭlāris
expiration (breathing out), exspīrātĭo, *f*; (time), *use partic*. confectus (completed)
expire, *v.i*, (persons), exspīro (1); (time), exĕo (4), confĭcĭo (3)
explain, *v.t*, explĭco (1), expōno (3)
explanation, explĭcātĭo, *f*
explicit, ăpertus
explode, *v.i*, dīrumpor (3 *pass*)
explore, *v.t*, explōro (1)
export, *v.t*, exporto (1)
exports, merces, *f*, *pl*
expose, *v.t*, expōno (3), dētĕgo (3), nūdo (1); (— to danger, etc.), offĕro (*irreg*)
exposition (statement), expŏsĭtĭo, *f*
expostulate, *v.i*, expostŭlo (1)
expound, *v.t*, explĭco (1), expōno (3)
express, *v.t*, exprĭmo (3); (— in writing), dēscrĭbo (3)
expression (verbal), vox, *f*, verba, *n.pl*; (facial), vultus, *m*
expressive, *use phr*, multam vim hăbens (having much significance)
expulsion, exactĭo, *f*
expunge, *v.t*, dēlĕo (2)
exquisite, conquīsītus
extant (to be —), *v.i*, exsto (1)
extemporary, extempŏrālis
extemporize, *v.i*, sŭbĭta dīco (3)
extend, *v.t*, extendo (3), distendo (3); *v.i*, pătĕo (2); (— to), pertĭnĕo (2) ad (*with acc*)
extension (act of), porrectĭo, *f*; (of boundaries, etc.), prŏpāgātĭo, *f*
extensive, amplus
extent, spătĭum, *n*

extenuate, *v.t*, lĕvo (1), mītĭgo (1)
exterior, *adj*, externus
exterior, *nn*, spĕcĭes, *f*
exterminate, *v.t*, interfĭcĭo (3), dēlĕo (2)
extermination, internĕcĭo, *f*
external, externus
extinct, exstinctus
extinguish, *v.t*, exstinguo (3)
extirpate, *v.t*, exstirpo (1), excīdo (3)
extol, *v.t*, laudo (1)
extort, *v.t*, (by force), extorquĕo (2)
extortion, res rĕpĕtundae, *f. pl*
extra, *adv*, praetĕrĕā
extract, *nn*, (from a book, etc.), exceptĭo, *f*
extract, *v.t*, extrăho (3), ēvello (3)
extraction (pulling out), ēvulsĭo, *f*
extraordinary, extraordĭnārĭus, insŏlĭtus
extravagance, sumptus, *m*, luxŭrĭa, *f*, intempĕrantĭa, *f*
extravagant, immŏdĭcus, sumptŭōsus
extreme, *adj*, extrēmus, ultĭmus
extremity, extrēmum, *n*; (top), căcūmen, *n*, vertex, *m*; *or use adj*, extrēmus (extreme)
extricate, *v.t*, expĕdĭo (4), solvo (3)
exuberance, luxŭrĭa, *f*
exuberant, luxŭrĭōsus, offūsus
exude, *v.i*, māno (1)
exult, *v.i*, exsulto (1), laetor (1 *dep*)
exultant, laetus, ēlātus
eye, ŏcŭlus, *m*; (— lash), palpĕbrae pĭlus, *m*; (— lid), palpĕbra, *f*; (— sight), ăcĭes, *f*; (— witness), arbĭter, *m*

F

fable, fābŭla, *f*
fabric (woven), textum, *n*; (building), aedĭfĭcĭum, *n*
fabricate, *v.t*, fabrĭcor (1 *dep*)
fabrication, mendācĭum, *n*
fabulous, fictus, falsus
face, făcĭes, *f*, vultus, *m*, ōs, *n*
face, *v.t* (confront), obvĭam ĕo (4) (*with dat*); (look towards), specto (1) ad (*with acc*)
facetious, făcētus
facilitate, *v.t*, făcĭlĭorem reddo (3) (make easier)
facility (possibility), făcultas, *f*; (dexterity), făcĭlĭtas, *f*
facing, *prep*, adversus (*with acc*)
fact, rēs, *f*; (in —, truly), cŏnj, ĕnim; *adv*, vērō
faction, factĭo, *f*
factious, factĭōsus

factory, offĭcĭna, *f*
faculty, făcultas, *f*, vīs, *f*
fade, *v.i*, pallesco (3)
faggot, sarmenta, *n.pl*
fail, *v.i*, cădo (3), dēfĭcĭo (3), dēsum (*irreg*) (*with dat*)
failing, *nn* (defect), vĭtĭum, *n*
failure (of supplies, strength, etc.), dēfectĭo, *f*, *otherwise use* irrĭtus (vain, unsuccessful)
faint, *v.i*, collābor (3 *dep*), languesco (3)
faint, *adj*, (exhausted), dēfessus
faint-hearted, tĭmĭdus, imbellis
faintness (of body), languor, *m*
fair, *nn*, (market), nundĭnae, *f*, *pl* (ninth day)
fair, *adj*, (beautiful), pulcher; (just), aequus; (colour), candĭdus; (weather), sĕrēnus; (wind, etc.), sĕcundus; (fairly good), mĕdĭŏcris
fairly, *adv*, (justly), iustē; (moderately), mĕdĭŏcrĭter
fairness (justice), aequĭtas, *f*; (of complexion, etc.), candor, *m*
faith, fĭdes, *f*; (to keep —), *v.i*, fĭdem servo (1)
faithful, fĭdēlis, fĭdus
faithfulness, fĭdēlĭtas, *f*
faithless, infĭdus, perfĭdus
faithlessness, perfĭdĭa, *f*
falcon, falco, *m*
fall, *nn*, cāsus, *m*, rŭīna, *f*
fall, *v.i*, cădo (3); (— back) rēcĭdo (3); (retreat), pĕdem rĕfĕro (*irreg*); (— headlong), praecĭpĭto (1); (— in love with), ădămo (1); (— off), dēlābor (3 *dep*); (— out, happen), cădo (3); (— upon, attack), *v.t*, invādo (3)
fallacious, fallax, falsus
fallacy, vĭtĭum, *n*
falling off, *nn*, (revolt), dēfectĭo, *f*
fallow, nŏvālis, ĭnărātus
false, falsus; (not genuine), fictus; (person), perfĭdus
falsehood, mendācĭum, *n*
falsify, *v.t*, vĭtĭo (1)
falter, *v.i*, haerĕo (2), haesĭto (1)
faltering, *adj*, haesĭtans
fame, glōrĭa, *f*, fāma, *f*
familiar, nōtus, fămĭlĭāris; (usual), consŭētus, *f*
familiarity, fămĭlĭărĭtas, *f*
familiarize, *v.t*, consŭesco (3)
family, *nn*, fămĭlĭa, *f*, dŏmus, *f*, gens, *f*
family, *adj*, fămĭlĭāris, gentīlis
famine, fămes, *f*
famished, făme confectus (exhausted from hunger)

famous, clārus
fan, flābellum, *n*
fan, *v.t*, ventĭlo (1)
fanatical, fānātĭcus
fanaticism, sŭperstĭtĭo, *f*
fancied (imaginary), fictus
fancy, *nn*, (notion), ŏpīnĭo, *f*; (liking for), lībīdo, *f*
fancy, *v.t*, (imagine), fingo (3); (think), ŏpīnor (1 *dep*); (want) cŭpĭo (3)
fang, dens, *m*
far, *adv*, (of distance), prŏcul, longē; (as — as), *prep*, tĕnus; (with comparatives*, multō, *e.g.* far bigger, multō māior; (how —), quātĕnus; (— and wide), longē lātēque
far-fetched, quaesītus
farce, mīmus, *m*
farcical, mīmĭcus
fare (food), cĭbus, *m*; (charge), vectūra, *f*
farewell!, ăvĕ; (*pl*) ăvete; vălē, vălete; (to bid —), vălēre iŭbĕo (2)
farm, *nn*, fundus, *m*
farm, *v.t*, cŏlo (3)
farmer, agrĭcŏla, *m*, cŏlōnus, *m*
farming, agrĭcultūra, *f*
farther, *adj*, ultĕrĭor
farther, *adv*, longĭus
farthest, *adj*, ultĭmus
farthest, *adv*, longissĭme
fascinate, *v.t*, fascĭno (1)
fascination, fascĭnātĭo, *f*
fashion, *nn*, mōs, *m*
fashion, *v.t*, fingo (3)
fashionable, ēlĕgans
fast, *nn*, iēiūnĭum, *n*
fast, *v.i*, iēiūnus sum (*irreg*) (be hungry)
fast, *adj*, (quick), cĕler; (firm), firmus; (make —), *v.t*, firmo (1), dēlĭgo (1)
fast, *adv*, (quickly), cĕlĕrĭter; (firmly), firme
fasten, *v.t*, fīgo (3), dēlĭgo (1); (doors, etc.), obtūro (1)
fastening, *nn*, vincŭlum, *n*
fastidious, dēlĭcātus
fat, *adj*, pinguis
fat, *nn*, ădeps, *c*
fatal (deadly), pernĭcĭōsus
fatality, cāsus, *m*
fate, fātum, *n*
fated, fātālis
father, păter, *m*; (-in-law), sŏcer, *m*
fatherland, pătrĭa, *f*
fatherless, orbus
fathom, *nn*, ulna, *f*
fatigue, *nn*, dēfătĭgātĭo, *f*
fatigue, *v.t*, fătĭgo (1)
fatigued, fătĭgātus

fatten, *v.t*, săgĭno (1)
fault, culpa, *f*, vĭtĭum, *n*
faultless, intĕger, perfectus
faulty, mendōsus, vĭtĭōsus
favour, *nn*, grātĭa, *f*, făvor, *m*, stŭdĭum, *n*; (a benefit), grātĭa, *f*, bĕnĕfĭcĭum, *n*
favour, *v.t*, făvĕo (2) (*with dat*)
favourable, commŏdus; (of wind),
 sĕcundus
favourite, *nn*, dēlĭcĭae, *f. pl*
favourite, *adj*, grātus
fawn, *nn*, hinnŭlĕus, *m*
fawn upon, *v.t*, ădūlor (1 *dep*)
fear, *nn*, tĭmor, *m*, mĕtus, *m*
fear, *v.t*, tĭmĕo (2), mĕtŭo (3),
 vĕrĕor (2 *dep*)
fearful, *adj*, (afraid), tĭmĭdus; (terrible), terrĭbĭlis
fearless, intrĕpĭdus
fearlessness, audācĭa, *f*
feasible, *use phr. with vbs*, posse (to
 be able) *and* effĭcĕre (to bring about)
feast, *nn*, daps, *f*, ĕpŭlae, *f. pl*; (—
 day), dĭes festus, *m*
feast, *v.i*, ĕpŭlor (1 *dep*); *v.t*, pasco (3)
feat, făcĭnus, *n*
feather, penna, *f*, plūma, *f*
feature (of face, etc.), lĭnĕāmentum,
 n; (peculiarity) *use adj*, prŏprĭus,
 (one's own)
February, Fĕbrŭārĭus (mensis)
fecundity, fēcundĭtas, *f*
federal, foedĕrātus
fee, merces, *f*, hŏnor, *m*
feeble, infirmus, imbēcillus
feebleness, infirmĭtas, *f*
feed, *v.t*, pasco (3), ălo (3); *v.i*,
 vescor (3 *dep*), pascor (3 *dep*)
feel, *v.t*, sentĭo (4); (with the hands),
 tempto (1)
feeler, cornĭcŭlum, *n*
feeling, *nn*, (sensation or emotion),
 sensus, *m*, tactus, *m*; (spirit, etc.),
 ănĭmus, *m*
feign, *v.t*, sĭmŭlo (1)
feigned, sĭmŭlātus
feint, sĭmŭlātĭo, *f*
felicitous, fēlix
felicity, fēlĭcĭtas, *f*
fell, *v.t*, excīdo (3), sterno (3)
fellow (companion), cŏmĕs, *c*; (—
 citizen), cīvis, *c*; (— feeling),
 consensĭo, *f*; (— soldier), commīlĭto, *m*; (worthless —), nēbŭlo, *m*
fellowship (companionship), sŏcĭĕtas,
 f
felt, *nn*, cŏactum, *n*
female, *nn*, fēmĭna, *f*
female, *adj*, mŭlĭĕbris

fen, pălus, *f*
fence, *nn*, saeptum, *n*, cancelli, *m*,
 pl
fence, *v.t*, saepĭo (4); (with swords),
 v.i, băttŭo (3)
fencing (art of —), ars, (*f*) glădĭi
ferment, *nn*, (excitement), aestus, *m*
ferment, *v.i*, fervĕo (2)
fern, fĭlix, *f*
ferocious, saevus, fĕrus
ferocity, saevĭtĭa, *f*
ferry, *nn*, trāiectus, *m*; (— boat),
 cymba, *f*
ferry, *v.t*, trāĭcĭo (3)
fertile, fēcundus, fertĭlis
fertility, fēcundĭtas, *f*
fervent, ardens, fervĭdus
fervour, ardor, *m*, fervor, *m*
festival (holidays), fērĭae, *f. pl*;
 (religious —, etc.), sollemne, *n*
festive (gay), hĭlăris
festivity (gaiety), hĭlărĭtas, *f*
fetch, *v.t*, pĕto (3), affĕro (*irreg*)
fetter, *nn*, vincŭlum, *n*
fetter, *v.t*, vincŭla inĭcĭo (3) (*with
 dat*)
feud (quarrel), sĭmultas, *f*
fever, fĕbris, *f*
feverish, fĕbrĭcŭlōsus; (excited) commōtus
few, *adj*, pauci (*pl*)
fewness, paucĭtas, *f*
fib, mendācĭum, *n*
fibre, fibra, *f*
fickle, inconstans
fickleness, inconstantĭa, *f*
fiction, commentum, *n*, fābŭla, *f*
fictitious, commentĭcĭus
fiddle (instrument), fĭdes, *f. pl*
fidelity, fĭdēlĭtas, *f*
fidgety, inquĭetus
field, ăger, *m*; (plain), campus, *m*;
 (— of battle), lŏcus, (*m*) pugnae;
 (scope), lŏcus, *m*
fiendish, nēfandus
fierce, fĕrox, fĕrus
fierceness, fĕrōcĭtas, *f*
fiery (of temper, etc.), ardens
fifteen, quindĕcim; (— times), *adv*,
 quindĕcĭes
fifteenth, quintus dĕcĭmus
fifth, quintus
fiftieth, quinquāgēsĭmus
fifty, quinquāginta
fig, fig-tree, fĭcus, *f*
fight, *nn*, pugna, *f*
fight, *v.i*, pugno (1)
fighter, pugnātor, *m*
figurative, translātus
figure, fĭgūra, *f*, forma, *f*

FIG 196 FLI

For List of Abbreviations used, turn to pages 3, 4

figure, *v.t*, (imagine), fingo (3)
figured, sĭgillātus
filch, *v.t*, surrĭpĭo (3)
file (tool), scŏbīna, *f*; (rank), ordo, *m*
file, *v.t*, (wood, metal), līmo (1)
filial (dutiful, respectful), pĭus
fill, *v.t*, implĕo (2), complĕo (2); (a post, etc.), fungor (3 *dep*) (*with abl*)
fillet (for the hair), vitta, *f*
film, membrāna, *f*
filter, *v.t*, cōlo (1)
filth, caenum, *n*
filthy, sordĭdus, foedus
fin, pinna, *f*
final, ultĭmus
finally, *adv*, postrēmo, dēnĭque, tandem
finance (of the state), aerārĭum, *n*
find, *v.t*, invĕnĭo (4), rĕpĕrĭo (4); (— out); cognosco (3), compĕrĭo (4); (— fault with), culpo (1); accūso (1)
fine, *v.t*, multo (1)
fine, *nn*, multa, *f*
fine, *adj*, (of texture), subtīlis; (handsome, etc.), praeclārus; (weather), sĕrēnus
finery, mundĭtĭa, *f*
finger, dĭgĭtus, *m*; (fore —), index dĭgĭtus
finger, *v.t*, tango (3)
finish, *nn*, (perfection), perfectĭo, *f*
finish, *v.t*, confĭcĭo (3); (limit), fīnĭo (4)
finished (complete, perfect), perfectus
fir, fir-tree, ăbĭes, *f*
fire, ignis, *m*; (ardour), vīs, *f*, ardor, *m*; (to be on —), *v.i*, ardĕo (2); (to set on —), *v.t*, incendo (3)
fire, *v.t*, incendo (3); (missiles), cōnĭcĭo (3)
fire-brand, fax, *f*
fire-place, fŏcus, *m*
fire-wood, lignum, *n*
firm, firmus; (constant), constans; (to make —), *v.t*, confirmo (1)
first, *adj*, prīmus
first, *adv*, prīmum, prīmō
fish, *nn*, piscis, *m*
fish, *v.i*, piscor (1 *dep*)
fisherman, piscātor, *m*
fishing, *nn*, piscātus, *m*
fishing-boat, hŏrĭŏla, *f*
fishing-net, rēte, *n*
fishmonger, cētārĭus, *m*
fishpond, piscīna, *f*
fissure, rīma, *f*

fist, pugnus, *m*
fit (violent seizure), accessĭo, *f*, impĕtus, *m*
fit, fitted, aptus, ĭdōnĕus, accommŏdātus
fit, *v.t*, accommŏdo (1), apto (1); (— out), exorno (1)
five, quinque; (— each), quīni; (— times), *adv*, quinquĭes
five hundred, quingenti
fix, *v.t*, fīgo (3); (determine), stătŭo (3), constĭtŭo (3)
fixed, certus
flabby, flaccĭdus
flag, vexillum, *n*
flag, *v.i*, (become weak), languesco (3)
flagrant (clear), mănĭfestus; (heinous), nĕfandus
flail, pertĭca, *f*
flame, *nn*, flamma, *f*
flame, *v.i*, flagro (1)
flame-coloured, flammĕus
flank (of army, etc.), lătus, *n*; (of animal), īlĭa, *n. pl*
flap (of dress, etc.), lăcĭnĭa, *f*
flare, *v.i*, flăgro (1)
flash, *nn*, fulgor, *m*
flash, *v.i*, fulgĕo (2)
flask, ampulla, *f*
flat, aequus, plānus
flatness, plānĭties, *f*
flatter, *v.t*, ădūlor (1 *dep*)
flatterer, ădūlātor, *m*
flattering, ădūlans
flattery, ădūlātĭo, *f*
flaunt, *v.t*, iacto (1)
flavour, săpor, *m*
flaw, vĭtĭum, *n*
flawless, ēmendātus
flax, līnum, *n*
flaxen, *adj*, līnĕus
flea, pūlex, *m*
flee, *v.i*, (flee from, *v.t*.), fŭgĭo (3)
fleece, *nn*, vellus, *n*
fleece, *v.t*, (rob), spŏlĭo (1)
fleecy, lānĭger
fleet, *nn*, classis, *f*
fleet, *adj*, cĕler
fleeting, fŭgax
flesh, căro, *f*
flesh-coloured, fleshy, carnōsus
flexibility, făcĭlĭtas, *f*
flexible, flexĭbĭlis
flicker, *v.i*, trĕpĭdo (1), cŏrusco (1)
flickering, trĕpĭdans, trĕmŭlus
flight (flying), vŏlātus, *m*; (escape) fŭga, *f*
flighty, mōbĭlis, lĕvis

fling, *v.t*, cŏnĭcĭo (3)

flint, sĭlex, *m*

flippant, făcētus

flirt, *v.i*, blandĭor (4 *dep*)

flit, *v.i*, vŏlĭto (1); (— in, or upon), inno (1) (*with dat*)

float, *v.i*, năto (1); (in the air), vŏlĭto (1)

flock, grex, *m*, pĕcus, *n*

flock, *v.i*, conflŭo (3), concurro (3)

flog, *v.t*, verbĕro (1)

flogging, verbĕra, *n. pl*

flood, dĭlŭvĭes, *f*, *n*

flood, *v.t*, ĭnundo (1)

floor, sŏlum, *n*; (upper —) contăbŭlātĭo, *f*

florid, flōrĭdus

flotilla, classis, *f*

flounder, *v.i*, vŏlūtor (1 *pass*)

flour, fărīna, *f*

flourish, *v.i*, flōrĕo (2); *v.t*, vĭbro (1)

flourishes (of style), călămistri, *m*, *pl*

flow, *nn*, cursus, *m*, fluxĭo, *f*; (of the tide), accessus, *m*

flow, *v.i*, flŭo (3); (— past), praeterflŭo (3); (— together), conflŭo (3); (trickle), māno (1)

flower, *nn*, flos, *m*

flower, *v.i*, flōrĕo (2)

flowing, flŭens; (hair), fūsus

fluctuate, *v.i*, iacter (1 *pass*); aestŭo (1)

fluctuation, mŭtatĭo, *f*

fluency, vŏlūbĭlĭtas, *f*

fluent, vŏlūbĭlis

fluid, *nn*, hūmor, *m*, lĭquor, *m*

fluid, *adj*, lĭquĭdus

flurry, concĭtatĭo, *f*

flush, *nn*, rŭbor, *m*

flush, *v.i*, ērŭbēsco (3)

fluster, *v.i*, ăgĭto (1)

flute, tībĭa, *f*; (— player), tībĭcen, *m*

flutter, *nn*, trĕpĭdatĭo, *f*

flutter, *v.i*, vŏlĭto (1), (in fear), trĕpĭdo (1)

flux (flow), fluctus, *m*, fluxus, *m*

fly, *nn*, musca, *f*

fly, *v.i*, vŏlo (1)

flying, *adj*, vŏlātĭlis, vŏlŭcer

flying, *nn*, vŏlātus, *m*

foal, ĕquŭlĕus, *m*, pullus, *m*

foam, *nn*, spūma, *f*

foam, *v.i*, spūmo (1)

foaming, foamy, spūmōsus

fodder, pābŭlum, *n*

foe, hostis, *c*

fog, cālīgo, *f*

foggy, cālīgĭnōsus

foil (sword), rŭdis, *f*; (metal leaf), lāmĭna, *f*

foil, *v.t*, (parry a blow, delude), ēlūdo (3)

fold, *nn*, (of garment, etc.), sĭnus, *m*

fold, *v.t*, plĭco (1)

folding-doors, valvae, *f. pl*

foliage, frons, *f*

folk (people), hŏmĭnes, *c. pl*

follow, *v.i. and v.t*, sĕquor (3 *dep*); sector (1 *dep*); (succeed), succēdo (3) (*with dat*)

follower (attendant), assectātor, *m*; or use *adj*, *e.g.* (—of Caesar) Caesărĭānus

following, sĕquens, proxĭmus, sĕcundus

folly, stultĭtĭa, *f*

foment, *v.t*, fŏvĕo (2); (— trouble, etc.), sollĭcĭto (1)

fond, ămans (*with genit*)

fondle, *v.t*, mulcĕo (2)

food, cĭbus, *m*; (fodder), pābŭlum, *n*

fool, hŏmo stultus; (to act the —), *v.i*, dēsĭpĭo (3)

fool, *v.t*, lūdo (3)

foolhardy, tĕmĕrārĭus

foolish, stultus

foot, pes, *m*; (on —), *adj*, pĕdester; (— in length), *adj*, pĕdālis; (bottom of), *use adj*, īmus, *in agreement with noun*, *e.g.* īma quercus (foot of an oak)

footing, status, *m*, *or use vb*, consisto (3), (to stand)

footman, pĕdĭsĕquus, *m*

footpath, sēmĭta, *f*

footprint, vestĭgĭum, *n*

footsoldier, pĕdes, *m*

for, *prep*, (on behalf of), prō (*with abl*); (on account of), propter, ŏb (*with acc*); (during a certain time), *use acc*, *e.g.* for two hours, dŭas hōras, *or* per (*with acc*); (expressing purpose), *use* ad (*with acc.*)

for, *conj*, nam, namque; ĕnim (*second word in clause*); (because), quippe, quod

forage, *nn*, pābŭlum, *n*

forage, *v.i. and v.t*, pābŭlor (1 *dep*)

forbear, *v.i. and v.t*, parco (3)

forbearance, contĭnentĭa, *f*

forbid, *v.t*, vĕto (1)

force, *nn*, vīs, *f*; (military forces), cōpĭae, *f*, *pl*

force, *v.t*, (compel), cōgo (3); (break through), perrumpo (3)

forced (unnatural), quaesītus; (a — march), magnum ĭter *n*

forcible, forcibly, *use adv. phr*, per vim

ford, *nn*, vădum, *n*

ford, *v.i. and v.t*, vădo transĕo (4) (cross by a ford)

forearm, bracchĭum, *n*
forebode, *v.t*, praesāgĭo (4), portendo (3)
foreboding, *nn*, praesensĭo, *f*
forecast, *v.t*, praevĭdĕo (2)
forefather, prŏăvus, *m*; (*pl*) māĭōres *m. pl*
forehead, frons, *f*
foreign, externus, pĕrĕgrīnus
foreigner, pĕrĕgrīnus, *m*
foreman, qui (servis) praeest (who is in charge of (slaves))
foremost, prīmus
forensic, fŏrensis
forerunner, praenuntĭus, *m*
foresee, *v.t*, prōvĭdĕo (2)
foresight, prōvĭdentĭa, *f*
forest, silva, *f*
foretell, *v.t*, praedīco (3)
forethought, prōvĭdentĭa, *f*
forewarn, *v.t*, praemŏnĕo (2)
forefeit, *nn*, poena, *f*
forfeit, *v.t*, āmitto (3)
forge, *nn*, fornax, *f*
forge, *v.t*, făbrĭcor (1 *dep*), excūdo (3); (strike counterfeit coins), nummos ădultĕrīnos cūdo (3); (documents), suppōno (3)
forgery *use phr*. subiectĭo falsārum littĕrārum (substitution of counterfeit letters)
forget, *v.t*, oblīviscor (3 *dep*) (*with genit*)
forgetful, immĕmor
forgetfulness, oblīvĭo, *f*
forgive, *v.t*, ignosco (3) (*with dat of person*)
forgiveness, vĕnĭa,
fork, furca, *f*
forked, bĭfurcus
forlorn, destĭtūtus, perdĭtus
form, forma, *f*, fĭgūra, *f*
form, *v.t*, (shape), formo (1), fingo (3); (— a plan), ĭnĕo (4), căpĭo (3); (troops, etc.), instrŭo (3)
formality, rītus, *m*
formally, *adv*, rītĕ
formation, conformātĭo, *f*
former, prĭor, sŭpĕrĭor; (the — and the latter), ille . . . hic
formerly, *adv*, antĕā, ōlim
formidable, grăvis, mĕtŭendus
formula, formŭla, *f*
forsake, *v.t*, rĕlinquo (3), dēsĕro (3)
forswear, *v.t*, (renounce), abiūro (1); (swear falsely), periūro (1)
fort, castellum, *n*
forth, *adv*, *use compound vb. with* e *or* ex, e.g. exĕo, go forth; (of time), inde
forthwith, *adv*, stătim, extemplo

fortification, mūnītĭo, *f*
fortify, *v.t*, mūnĭo (4)
fortitude, fortĭtūdo, *f*
fortuitous, fortŭĭtus
fortunate, fēlix, fortūnātus
fortune, fortūna, *f*, (property, etc.), rēs, *f*, ŏpes, *f. pl*
fortune-teller, hărĭolŭs, *m*
forty, quădrāginta
forum, fŏrum, *n*
forward, forwards, *adv*, porro, prorsum, ante; *or use compound verb with* pro, e.g. prōdūco, (lead forward)
forward, *adj*, praecox
forward, *v.t*, (send on), perfĕro (*irreg*)
foster, *v.t*, nūtrĭo (4)
foster-brother, collactĕus, *m*; (— child), ălumnus, *m*; (— father), altor, *m*; (— mother), nūtrix, *f*; (— sister), collactĕa, *f*
foul, *adj*, foedus
found, *v.t*, condo (3); (metal), fundo (3)
foundation, fundāmenta, *n*, *pl*
founder, condĭtor, *m*
founder, *v.i*, submergor (3 *pass*)
fountain, fons, *m*
four, quattŭor; (— times), *adv*, quătĕr; (— each), quăterni
fourteen, quattŭordĕcim; (-teenth), quartus dĕcĭmus
fourth, quartus; (— part, quarter), quădrans, *m*
fowl, ăvis, *f* gallīna, *f*
fowler, auceps, *c*
fox, vulpes, *f*
fraction (part) pars, *f*
fractious, diffĭcĭlis
fracture, *nn*, fractūra, *f*
fracture, *v.t*, frango (3)
fragile, frăgĭlis
fragment, fragmentum, *n*
fragrance, dulcis ŏdōr, *m*, (pleasant smell)
fragrant, dulcis, suāvis
frail, frăgĭlis, dēbĭlis
frailty, frăgĭlĭtas, *f*, dēbĭlĭtas
frame, forma, *f*, compāges, *f*; (— of mind), ănĭmus, *m*, affectĭo, *f*
frame, *v.t*, (shape), făbrĭcor (1 *dep*), fingo (3); (form), compōno (3)
franchise (citizenship), cīvĭtas, *f*; (right of voting), suffrāgĭum, *n*
frank, līber, ăpertus
frantic, āmens
fraternal, frāternus
fraternity (association of men), sŏdālĭtas, *f*
fratricide (the person), frātrĭcīda, *m*; (the crime), fraternum parrĭcīdĭum, *n*

fraud, fraus, *f*, dŏlus, *m*

fraudulent, fraudŭlentus, dŏlōsus

fraught, opplētus (filled)

fray, certāmen, *n*, pugna, *f*

freak, (prodigy), prōdĭgĭum, *n*

freckle, lentīgo, *f*

free, līber; (generous), lībĕrālis; (of one's will), sua sponte

free, *v.t*, lībĕro (1), solvo (3)

free-born, ingĕnŭus

freedman, lībertus, *m*

freedom, lībertas, *f*; (— from a burden, tax, etc.), immūnĭtas, *f*

freehold, *nn*, praedĭum lībĕrum, *n*, (free estate)

freely, *adv*, lībĕrē; (generously), mūnĭfĭcē, largē; (of one's own free will), sŭā sponte

free-will, vŏluntas, *f*

freeze, *v.t*, glăcĭo (1); *v.i*, congĕlo (1)

freight, *nn*, ŏnus, *n*

freight, *adj*, ŏnustus

French, *adj*, Gallĭcus; (The French), Galli, *pl*

frenzied, fŭrens, āmens

frenzy, fŭror, *m*, āmentĭa, *f*

frequent, *adj*, crēber, frĕquens

frequent, *v.t*, cĕlĕbro (1)

frequently, *adv*, saepe

fresh, (new), rĕcens, nŏvus; (wind), vĕhĕmens

freshen, *v.t*, rĕcrĕo (1); *v.i*, (of wind), incrēbrescō (3)

freshness, vĭrĭdĭtas, *f*

fret, *v.i*, dŏlĕo (2)

fretful, mōrōsus

fretfulness, mōrōsĭtas, *f*

friction, trītus, *m*

friend, ămīcus, *m*

friendless, inops. ămīcōrum (destitute of friends)

friendliness, cōmĭtas, *f*

friendly, ămīcus, cōmis

friendship, ămīcĭtĭa, *f*

fright, terror, *m*, păvor, *m*; (to take —), *v.i*, păvesco (3)

frighten, *v.t*, terrĕo (2)

frightful, terrĭbĭlis, horrĭbĭlis

frigid, frīgĭdus

frill, segmenta, *n.pl*

fringe, fimbrĭae, *f. pl*

frippery, nūgae, *f. pl*

frisk, *v.i*, lascīvĭo (4)

fritter away, *v.t*, dissĭpo (1)

frivolity, lĕvĭtas, *f*

frivolous, lĕvis; (opinion, etc.), fŭtĭlis

fro (to and —), *adv. phr*, hūc et illūc

frock, stŏla, *f*

frog, rāna, *f*

frolic, *nn*, lūdus, *m*

frolic, *v.i*, lūdo (3)

from, ā, ab, dē, ē, ex (all with abl) (with expressions of place, time and cause)

front, *nn*, frons, *f*, prĭor pars; (in —) ā fronte, or use adj, adversus; (in — of) prep, prō (with abl)

front, *adj*, prĭor

frontage, frons, *f*

frontier, fīnis, *m*

frost, gĕlu, *n*; (— bitten), adj, ambustus

frosty, gĕlĭdus

froth, *nn*, spūma, *f*

froth, *v.i*, spūmo (1)

frown, *nn*, contractĭo, (*f*) frontis (contraction of the forehead)

frown, *v.i*, frontem contrăho (3)

frowsy, incultus

frozen, rĭgĭdus, glăcĭālis

fructify, *v.t*, fēcundo (1)

frugal, frūgi, indool

frugality, parsĭmōnĭa, *f*

fruit, fructus, *m*, pōmum, *n*

fruitful, fēcundus

fruitfulness, fēcundĭtas, *f*

fruition, fructus, *m*

fruitless (without result), irrĭtus

fruit-tree, pōmum, *n*, pōmus, *f*

frustrate, *v.t*, (an undertaking, etc.), ad vānum rĕdĭgo (3)

frustrated (to be —), *v.i*, frustrā esse

frustration, frustrātĭo, *f*

fry, *v.t*, frīgo (3)

frying-pan, sartāgo, *f*

fuel, ligna, *n. pl*

fugitive, *nn*, prŏfŭgus, *m*, fŭgĭtīvus, *m*

fugitive, *adj*, fŭgĭtīvus

fulfil, *v.t*, explĕo (2), exsĕquor (3 dep), fungor (3 dep) (with abl)

full, plēnus, replētus; (with people), frĕquens, crēber

full-grown, ădultus

fulminate, *v.i*, fulmĭno (1), intŏno (1)

fulness (abundance), ūbertas, *f*

fulsome, pūtĭdus

fumble, *v.t*, (handle), tento (1)

fume, *nn*, hālĭtus, *m*

fume, *v.i*, (with anger, etc.), fŭro (3)

fumigate, *v.t*, suffĭo (4)

fun, iŏcus, *m*, lūdus, *m*

function, offĭcĭum, *n*, mūnus, *n*

fund (of knowledge, etc.), cōpĭa, *f*, with nn. in genit.

fundamental, prīmus

funeral, fūnus, *n*, exsĕquĭae, *f*, *pl*

funeral, funereal, *adj*, fūnĕbris

fungus, fungus, *m*

funnel, infundĭbŭlum, *n*

funny, rĭdĭcŭlus

For List of Abbreviations used, turn to pages 3, 4

fur, pĭlus, *m*

furbish, *v.t*, interpŏlo (1)

furious, fŭrens, saevus; **(to be —)**, *v.i*, saevĭo (4), fŭro (3)

furl, *v.t*, contrăho (3), lĕgo (3), subdūco (3)

furlough, commĕātus, *m*

furnace, fornax, *f*

furnish, *v.t*, suppĕdĭto (1), orno (1)

furniture, sŭpellex, *f*

furrow, *nn*, sulcus, *m*

furrow, *v.t*, sulco (1)

further, *adj*, ultĕrĭor; *adv*, ultĕrĭus

further, *v.t*, (help), adiŭvo (1)

furthermore, *adv*, porro, praetĕrĕa

furthest, *adj*, ultĭmus

furtive, furtīvus

fury, fŭror, *m*

fuse, *v.t*, (melt), lĭquĕfācĭo (3); **(— together)**, miscĕo (2)

fuss, *nn*, perturbātĭo, *f*

fussy, nĭmis stŭdĭōsus

fusty, mūcĭdus

futile, vānus, fūtĭlis

futility, fūtĭlĭtas, *f*

future, *adj*, fŭtūrus

future, *nn*, fŭtūra, *n.pl*; **(in —)**, *adv*, in rĕlĭquum tempus

futurity, tempus fŭtūrum, *n*

G

gabble, *v.i*, blătĕro (1)

gabbler, blătĕro, *m*

gable, fastīgĭum, *n*

gad about, *v.i*, văgor (1 *dep*)

gadfly, tăbānus, *m*

gag, *v.t*, ōs obvolvo (3) *(with dat)* (muffle the mouth)

gage, pignus, *n*

gaiety, hĭlărĭtas, *f*

gaily, *adv*, hĭlăre

gain, *nn*, lŭcrum, *n*, quaestus, *m*

gain, *v.t*, (profit, etc.), lŭcror (1 *dep*); (obtain), consĕquor (3 *dep*), pŏtĭor (4 *dep*) *(with abl)*; **(— a victory)**, victōrĭam rĕporto (1) *or* părĭo (3)

gainsay, *v.t*, contrā dīco (3)

gait, incessus, *m*

gaiters, ōcrĕae, *f. pl*

galaxy, *use* vĭa lactĕa, *f*. (milky way)

gale, ventus, *m*, prŏcella, *f*

gall, *nn*, fel, *n*

gall, *v.t*, (chafe), ūro (3); (annoy), sollĭcĭto (1); *or* pĭget (2 *impers*) (it irks)

gallant, fortis

gallant, *nn*, (lover), ămātor, *m*

gallantry, virtus, *f*

gallery, portĭcus, *f*

galley (ship), nāvis, *f*

galling, mordax

gallon, congĭus, *m*

gallop, *v.i*, ĕquo cĭtāto vĕhi (3 *pass*) (to be carried by a swift horse)

gallows, furca, *f*, crux, *f*

gamble, *v.i*, ālĕa lūdo (3) (play with dice)

gambler, ālĕātor, *m*

gambling, *nn*, ālĕa, *f*

gambol, *v.i*, lascīvĭo (4),

game, lūdus, *m*; (wild beasts), fĕrae, *f. pl*

gamester, ālĕātor, *m*

gammon, perna, *f*

gander, anser, *m*

gang, grex, *m*, căterva, *f*

gangrene, gangraena, *f*

gangway, fŏrus, *m*

gaol, carcer, *m*

gaoler, custos, *m*

gap, lăcūna, *f*, hĭātus, *m*

gape, *v.i*, hĭo (1)

gaping, *adj*, hĭans

garb, vestītus, *m*

garbage, quisquĭlĭae, *f, pl*

garden, hortus, *m*

gardening, cūra, (*f*) hortōrum (care of gardens)

gargle, *v.i*, gargărīzo (1)

garland, serta, *n.pl*

garlic, ālĭum, *n*

garment, vestīmentum, *n*

garner, *v.t*, (store), condo (3)

garnish, *v.t*, dĕcŏro (1)

garret, cēnācŭlum, *n*

garrison, praesĭdĭum, *n*

garrison, *v.t*, praesĭdĭum collŏco (1) in *(with abl)*

garrulity, lŏquācĭtas, *f*

garrulous, lŏquax

gas, spīrĭtus, *m*

gash, *nn*, plāga, *f*

gash, *v.t*, percŭtĭo (3)

gasp, *nn*, ănhēlĭtus, *m*

gasp, *v.i*, ănhēlo (1)

gastric, *use genitive* stŏmăchi (of the stomach)

gate, porta, *f*, iānŭa, *f*; **(-keeper)**, iānĭtor, *m*

gather, *v.t*, lĕgo (3), collĭgo (3); (pluck), carpo (3); *v.i*, convĕnĭo (4), congrĕgor (1 *dep*)

gathering, coetus, *m*

gaudy, fūcātus

gauge, *v.t*, mētĭor (4 *dep*)

gauge, *nn*, mŏdŭlus, *m*
gaunt, măcer
gay, hĭlăris
gaze at, *v.t*, tŭĕor (2 *dep*)
gaze, *nn*, obtūtus, *m*
gazelle, dorcas, *f*
gazette, acta dĭurna, *n. pl,* **(daily events)**
gear, appărātus, *m*
geld, *v.t*, castro (1)
gelding, cantērĭus, *m*
gem, gemma, *f*
gender, gĕnus, *n*
geneology (lineage), ŏrĭgo, *f*, gĕnus, *n*
general, *adj*, **(opp. to particular),** gĕnĕrālis; **(common, wide-spread),** vulgāris, commūnis
general, *nn*, dux, *m*, ĭmpĕrator, *m*
generality (majority), plērique
generally (for the most part), *adv*, plērumque
generalship, /ductus, *m*
generate, *v.t*, gĕnĕro (1), gĭgno (3)
generation, saecŭlum, *n*
generosity, bĕnignĭtas, *f*
generous (with money, etc.), lībĕrālis
genial, cōmis
geniality, cōmĭtas, *f*
genius (ability), ĭngĕnĭum, *n*; **(guardian spirit),** gĕnĭus, *m*
genteel, urbānus.
gentle (mild), mītis; **(of birth),** gĕnĕrōsus
gentleman, hŏmo ingĕnŭus
gentlemanly, *adj*, lībĕrālis, hŏnĕstus
gentleness, lēnĭtas, *f*
gently, *adv*, lĕnĭter
gentry, nōbĭles, *m. pl*
genuine, sincērus
geography, gĕōgraphĭa, *f*
geometry, gĕōmĕtrĭa, *f*
germ, germen, *n*
German, Germānus
germane, affĭnis
germinate, *v.i*, germĭno (1)
gesticulate, *v.i*, sĕ Iactāre (1 *reflex*)
gesture, gestus, *m*
get, *v.t*, **(obtain),** ădĭpiscor (3 *dep*), nanciscor (3 *dep*); **(a request),** impĕtro (1); **(become),** *v.i*, fio (*irreg*); **(— about, or spread, etc.),** percrēbesco (3); **(— away),** effŭgĭo (3); **(— back),** *v.t*, rĕcĭpĭo (3); **(— the better of),** sŭpĕro (1); **(— down),** *v.i*, dēscendo (3); **(— out),** exĕo (4); **(— ready),** *v.t*, păro (1); **(— rid of),** āmŏvĕo (2) in *or* ad *(with acc)*; **(— up, rise),** surgo (3)
ghastly, exsanguis,
ghost, mānes, *m. pl*

giant, vir ingenti stătūra **(man of huge stature)**
gibbet, crux, *f*
giddy, vertĭgĭnōsus
gift, dōnum, *n*
gifted (mentally, etc.), ingĕnĭōsus
gigantic, ingens
giggle, *v.i*, *use* rīdĕo (2), **(to laugh)**
gild, *v.t*, ĭnauro (1)
gills (of fish), branchĭae, *f. pl*
gimlet, tĕrĕbra, *f*
gin, pĕdĭca, *f*
giraffe, cămēlŏpardălis, *f*
gird, *v.t*, cingo (3); **(— oneself),** sĕ accingĕre (3 *reflex*)
girder, trabs, *f*
girdle, cingŭlum, *n*
girl, pŭella, *f*, virgo, *f*
girlhood, aetas, *(f)* pŭellăris
girth, ambĭtus, *m*
give, *v.t*, do (1), dŏno (1); **(render),** reddo (3); **(— an opportunity),** făcultātem do (1); **(— back),** reddo (3); **(— in,),** *v.i*, cēdo (3); **(— up, deliver),** trādo (3); **(abandon),** dĭmitto (3); **(— up hope),** *v.i*, dēspēro (1); **(— orders),** iŭbĕo (2)
glad, laetus, hĭlăris
gladden, *v.t*, hĭlăro (1)
glade, nĕmus, *n*, saltus, *m*
gladiator, glădĭātor, *m*
gladness, laetĭtĭa, *f*
glance at, *v.t*, aspĭcĭo (3); **(graze)** strĭngo (3)
glance, *nn*, aspectus, *m*
gland, glans, *f*
glare, *nn*, fulgor, *m*
glare, *v.i*, fulgĕo (2); **(look with stern glance),** torvis ŏcŭlis tŭĕor (2 *dep*)
glaring (conspicuous), mănifestus
glass, *nn*, vĭtrum, *n*; **(drinking —),** pōcŭlum, *n*
glass, *adj*, vĭtrĕus
gleam, *nn*, fulgor, *m*
gleam, *v.i*, fulgĕo (2)
glean, *v.t*, spīcas collĭgo (3) **(collect ears of corn)**
glee, laetĭtĭa, *f*
glen, valles, *f*
glib (of tongue), vŏlūbĭlis
glide, lābor (3 *dep*)
glimmer, *v.i*, sublūcĕo (2)
glimmering, *adj*, sublustris
glimpse (get a — of), *v.t*, dispĭcĭo (3)
glitter, *v.i*, fulgĕo (2)
glittering, *adj*, fulgĭdus, cŏruscus
gloat over, *v.t*, gaudens aspĭcĭo (3)
globe, glŏbus, *m*; **(the earth),** orbis, *m*
gloom, tĕnebrae, *f. pl*, tristĭtĭa, *f*
gloomy, tĕnebrōsus, tristis

glorify, *v.t,* laudo (1), extollo (3)
glorious, praeclārus, illustris
glory, glōrĭa, *f,* dĕcus, *n,* laus, *f*
gloss, *nn,* nĭtor, *m*
gloss over, *v.t,* praetĕrĕo (4)
glossy, nĭtĭdus
gloves, mănĭcae, *f. pl*
glow, *nn,* ardor, *m*
glow, *v.i,* ardĕo (2), candĕo (2)
glue, *nn,* glūten, *n*
glut, *nn,* sătĭĕtas, *f*
glut, *v.t,* explĕo (2), sătĭo (1)
glutton, hellŭo, *m*
gluttonous, ĕdax
gluttony, ĕdācĭtas, *f*
gnarled, nōdōsus
gnash (the teeth), *v.t,* frendĕo (2), (dentibus)
gnat, cŭlex, *m*
gnaw, *v.t,* rōdo (3)
gnawing, *adj,* mordax
go, *v.i,* ĕo (*irreg*), vādo (3); (**depart**), ăbĕo (4), prŏfĭciscor (3 *dep*); (— **abroad**), pĕrĕgre exĕo (4 *irreg*); (— **away**), ăbĕo (4 *irreg*); (— **back**), rĕdĕo (4 *irreg*); (— **by, past**), praetĕrĕo (4 *irreg*); (— **down**), dēscendo (3); (— **in**), ĭnĕo (4 *irreg*); (— **over**), transĕo (4 *irreg*); (— **round**), circumĕo (4 *irreg*) (— **through**), ŏbĕo (4 *irreg*); (— **up**), ascendo (3); (— **without**), cărĕo (2) (*with abl*)
goad, *v.t,* stĭmŭlo (1)
goal, mēta, *f*
goat, căper, *m*
go-between, *nn,* interpres, *c*
goblet, pōcŭlum, *n*
god, dĕus, *m*
goddess, dĕa, *f*
godless, impĭus
godlike, dīvīnus
godly, *adj,* pĭus
gold, aurum, *n*
golden, aurĕus
goldsmith, aurĭfex, *m*
good, *adj,* bŏnus, prŏbus, hŏnestus, aptus, commŏdus
good, *nn,* bŏnum, *n;* (**advantage**), commŏdum, *n;* (**goods, possessions**), bŏna, *n.pl;* (— **for nothing**), *adj,* nēquam; (**to do —**), prōdesse (*irreg*) (*with dat*)
good-bye! vălē! (*pl,* vălete!)
good-humour, cōmĭtas, *f*
good-humoured, cōmis
good-looking, spĕcĭōsus
good-nature, cōmĭtas, *f*
good-natured, cōmis
goodness (virtue), virtus, *f,* prŏbĭtas, *f;* (**excellence**), bŏnĭtas, *f*

good-tempered, mītis
goose, anser, *m*
gore, *nn,* crŭor, *m*
gorge (throat), guttur, *n,* fauces, *f. pl;* (**mountain pass**), angustĭae, *f. pl*
gorge oneself, *v.i,* sē ingurgĭtāre (1 *reflex*)
gorgeous, spĕcĭōsus, splendĭdus
gorgeousness, magnĭfĭcentĭa, *f*
gory, crŭentus
gossip, *v.i,* garrĭo (4)
gossip, *nn,* (**talk**), rūmor, *m;* (**person**), garrŭlus, *m*
gouge, *v.t,* (— **out eyes**), ŏcŭlos ērŭo (3)
gourd, cŭcurbĭta, *f*
gout, morbus, (*m*) artĭcŭlōrum (**disease of the joints**)
gouty, arthrītĭcus
govern, *v.t,* gŭberno (1), impĕro (1), tempĕro (1), mŏdĕror (1 *dep*)
government (act of —), admĭnistrātĭo, *f,* cūra, *f;* (**persons**), *use phr,* ii qui summum impĕrĭum hăbent (**those who hold supreme authority**)
governor (supreme), gŭbernātor, *m;* (**subordinate**), prōcūrātor, *m,* lēgātus, *m*
gown (woman's), stŏla, *f;* (**man's**), tŏga, *f*
grace, grātĭa, *f;* (**pardon**), vĕnĭa, *f;* (**charm**), vĕnustas, *f;* (**to say —**), grātĭas ăgo (3)
grace, *v.t,* (**adorn**), dĕcŏro (1)
graceful, vĕnustus, lĕpĭdus
gracious, prŏpĭtĭus, bĕnignus
grade, grădus, *m*
gradient, clīvus, *m*
gradually, *adv,* paulātim
graft, *v.t,* insĕro (3)
grain, frumentum, *n*
grammar, grammătĭca, *f*
granary, horrĕum, *n*
grand, magnĭfĭcus, grandis
grandchild, nĕpos, *m, f*
granddaughter, neptis, *f*
grandeur, magnĭfĭcentĭa, *f*
grandfather, ăvus, *m*
grandiloquent, grandĭlŏquus
grandmother, ăvĭa, *f*
grandson, nĕpos, *m*
granite, (hard rock), *use* sĭlex, *m,* (**flint stone**)
grant, granting, *nn,* concessĭo, *f*
grant, *v.t,* concēdo (3), do (1)
grape, ăcĭnus, *m,* ūva, *f*
graphic, expressus
grapple, *v.i,* luctor (1 *dep*)
grappling-iron, harpăgo, *m*
grasp, *nn,* mănus, *f;* (**of the mind**), captus, *m*

grasp, *v.t*, prēhendo (3); **(mentally)**, intellĕgo (3); **(snatch at, aim at)**, capto (1)
grass, grāmen, *n*, herba, *f*
grasshopper, gryllus, *m*
grassy, grāmĭnĕus
grate, crātĭcŭla, *f*
grate, *v.t*, tĕro (3); *v.i*, strīdĕo (2)
grateful, grātus
gratification, explētĭo, *f*, vŏluptas, *f*
gratify, *v.t*, grātĭfĭcor (1 *dep*) *(with dat)*
grating, *nn*, **(noise)**, strīdor, *m*
gratitude, grātĭa, *f*, grātus ănĭmus, *m*
gratuitous, grātŭĭtus
gratuity, congĭārĭum, *n*
grave, *nn*, sĕpulcrum, *n*
grave, *adj*, grăvis,
gravel, glārĕa, *f*
gravity, grăvĭtas, *f*
gravy, ius, *n*
gray, *see* grey
grayness, *see* grey, greyness
graze, *v.t*, **(animals)**, pasco (3); *v.i*, pascor (3 *dep*); **(touch lightly)**, *v.i*, stringo (3)
grease, *nn*, ădeps, *c*
grease, *v.t*, ungo (3)
greasy, unctus
great, magnus, grandis, amplus; **(distinguished)**, illustris
greatcoat, lācerna, *f*
great-grandfather, prŏăvus, *m*
great-grandson, prŏnĕpos, *m*
greatness, magnĭtūdo, *f*
greaves, ŏcrĕae, *f. pl*
Greece, Graecia, *f*
greed, ăvārĭtĭa, *f*
greedy, ăvārus
Greek, Graecus
green, *adj*, vĭrĭdis; **(unripe)**, crūdus; **(to become —)**, *v.i*, vĭresco (3)
greet, *v.t*, sălūto (1)
greeting, sălūtātĭo, *f*
gregarious, grĕgālis
grey, caesĭus, rāvus; **(of hair)**, cānus
greyness (of hair), cānĭtĭes, *f*
gridiron, crātĭcŭla, *f*
grief, dŏlor, *m*, luctus, *m*
grievance, quĕrĭmōnĭa, *f*
grieve, *v.i. and v.t*, dŏlĕo (2)
grievous, grăvis, ăcerbus
grim, trux
grin, *v.i*, rīdĕo (2)
grind, *v.t*, contĕro (3); mŏlo (3) **(— down, oppress)**, opprĭmo (3);
grindstone, cōs, *f*
grip, *nn*, *use* mănus, *f*, **(hand)**
grip, *v.t*, arrĭpĭo (3)

gripes, tormĭna, *n.pl*
grisly, horrendus
grist, fărīna, *f*
gristle, cartĭlāgo, *f*
grit, glārĕa, *f*
groan, *nn*, gĕmĭtus, *m*
groan, *v.i*, gĕmo (3)
grocer, tūrārĭus, *m*
groin, inguen, *n*
groom, *nn*, ăgāso, *m*
groom, *v.t*, **(look after)**, cūro (1)
groove, cănālis, *m*
grope, *v.i*, praetento (1)
gross, *adj*, crassus; **(unseemly)**, indĕcōrus
grotto, antrum, *n*
grotesque, monstrŭōsus
ground (earth), hŭmus, *f*, sŏlum, *n*, terra, *f*; **(cause, reason)**, causa, *f*; **(to give —)**, pĕdem rĕfĕro *(irreg)*
ground, *v.i*, **(of ships)**, sido (3)
groundless, vānus
groundwork (basis), fundāmentum, *n*
group, glŏbus, *m*
group, *v.t*, dispōno (3)
grouse, lăgōpŭs, *f*
grove, lūcus, *m*
grovel, *v.i*, serpo (3)
grow, *v.i*, cresco (3), augesco (3); **(— up), (become)**, fīo *(irreg)*; *v.t*, cōlo (3)
growl, *nn*, frĕmĭtus, *m*
growl, *v.i*, frĕmo (3)
growth, incrēmentum, *n*
grub, *nn*, vermĭcŭlus, *m*
grudge, *nn*, sĭmultas, *f*
grudge, *v.t*, invĭdĕo (2) *(with dat)*
grudgingly, *adv, use adj*, invītus
gruel, ptĭsăna, *f*
gruff, asper
grumble, *v.i*, frĕmo (3)
grunt, *nn*, grunnītus, *m*
grunt, *v.i*, grunnĭo (4)
guarantee, *nn*, fĭdes, *f*
guarantee, *v.t*, fĭdem do (1) *(with dat)*
guarantor, vas, *m*
guard (person), custos, *c*; **(defence)**, custōdĭa, *f*, praesĭdĭum, *n*: **(to keep —)**, *v.i*, custōdĭam ăgo (3)
guard, *v.t*, custōdĭo (4)
guarded (cautious), cautus
guardian, custos, *c*; **(of child)**, tūtor, *m*
guardianship, custōdĭa, *f*; **(of child)**, tūtēla, *f*
guess, *nn*, coniectūra, *f*
guess, *v.t*, cōnĭcĭo (3), dīvīno (1)
guest, hospes, *m*, hospĭta, *f*; **(at a party, etc.)**, convīva, *c*
guidance (advice), consĭlĭum, *n*

For List of Abbreviations used, turn to pages 3, 4

guide, *nn,* dux, *c*
guide, *v.t,* dūco (3)
guild, collēgĭum, *n*
guile, dŏlus, *m*
guileful, dŏlōsus
guileless, simplex
guilt, culpa, *f*
guiltless, innŏcens, insons
guilty, sons, nŏcens
guise, hăbĭtus, *m*, spĕcĭes, *f*
gulf (bay), sĭnus, *m*; **(abyss),** gurges, *m*, vŏrāgo, *f*
gullet, guttur, *n*
gullible, crēdŭlus
gully (channel), cănālis, *m*, fossa, *f*
gulp, *v.t,* haurĭo (4)
gum (of the mouth), gingīva, *f*; **(of plants, etc.),** gummi, *n*
gurgle, *v.i,* singulto (1)
gush, *v.i,* prŏfundor (3 *pass*)
gust, flātus, *m*
gut, intestīna, *n.pl*
gutter, fossa, *f,* clŏāca, *f*
guttural, grăvis
gymnasium, gymnăsĭum, *n*
gymnastics, pălaestra, *f*

H

haberdasher, lintĕo, *m*
habit, consŭētūdo, *f,* mōs, *m*
habitable, hăbĭtābĭlis
habitation, dŏmĭcĭlĭum, *n*
habitual, ūsĭtātus
habituate, *v.t,* consŭēfăcĭo (3)
hack, căballus, *m*
hack, *v.t,* concīdo (3)
hackneyed, trītus
haft, mănūbrĭum, *n*
hag, ănus, *f*
haggard, măcĭe corruptus **(marred by leanness)**
haggle, *v.i,* dē prĕtĭo căvillor (1 *dep*) **(to quibble about price)**
hail, *nn,* grando, *f*
hail, *v.i,* **(weather),** grandĭnat *(impers.)*; *v.t,* **(greet),** sălūto (1)
hair, căpillus, *m,* crīnis, *m,* caesărĭes, *f*
hair-dresser, tonsor, *m*
hairless (bald), calvus
hairy, pĭlōsus
halcyon, *adj,* alcўŏnēus
hale (healthy), vălĭdus
half, *nn,* dīmĭdĭum, *n; adj,* dīmĭdĭus; *adv, use prefix* sēmi-, *e.g.*
half-asleep, sēmĭsomnus; **(half-dead),** sēmĭănĭmis, mŏrĭbundus;

(— hour), sēmĭhōra, *f*; **(— moon),** lūna dīmĭdĭāta, *f*; **(— yearly),** sēmestris
hall (of house), ātrĭum, *n*; **(public),** concĭlĭābŭlum, *n*
hallo! heus!
hallow, *v.t,* consĕcro (1)
hallucination, somnĭa, *n.pl*
halo, cŏrōna, *f*
halt, *nn, use vb,* consisto (3)
halt, *v.i,* consisto (3)
halter (horse), căpistrum, *n*; **(noose),** lăquĕus, *m*
halve, *v.t.* ex aequo dīvĭdo (3)
ham, perna, *f*
hamlet, vīcus, *m*
hammer, *nn,* mallĕus, *m*
hammer, *v.t,* contundo (3)
hamper, quălum, *n*
hamper, *v.t,* impĕdĭo (4)
hamstring, *v.t,* poplĭtem succīdo (3) *(with dat)*
hand, mănus, *f*; **(left)** —), mănus sĭnistra; **(right** —), dextra mănus; **(to shake** —s), dextras coniungĕre (3); **(— cuffs),** mănĭcae, *f, pl*; **(— writing),** chīrŏgrăphum, *n*; **(on the one** —, **on the other** —), et ... et, *or* quĭdem *(second word in clause)* ... autem *(second word in clause)*; **(— to— fighting, etc.),** commĭnus, *adv*; **(at hand),** praesto, *adv*
hand, *v.t,* do (1), trādo (3); **(—down or over),** trādo (3)
handful (few), *use adj,* pauci
handicraft, artĭfĭcĭum, *n*
handiwork, ŏpus, *n*
handkerchief, sūdārĭum, *n*
handle, mănūbrĭum, *n*
handle, *v.t,* tracto (1)
handling (treatment), tractātĭo, *f*
handsome, spĕcĭōsus, pulcher
handy (manageable), hăbĭlis
hang, *v.t,* suspendo (3); **(— the head),** dēmitto (3); *v.i,* pendĕo (2); **(— back, hesitate),** dŭbĭto (1); **(over-hang),** impendĕo (2)
hanger-on, assecla, *c*
hanging (death by —), suspendĭum, *n*
hangman, carnĭfex, *m*
hanker after, *v.t,* opto (1)
haphazard, *use adv. phr.* nullo ordĭne **(in no order)**
happen, *v.i,* accĭdo (3), ēvĕnĭo (4)
happiness, fēlĭcĭtas, *f*
happy, fēlix, bĕātus
harangue, *nn,* contĭo, *f*
harangue, *v.t,* contĭōnor (1 *dep.*)

harass, v.t, sollĭcĭto (1)
harbour, portus, m; (— dues), portōrĭum, n
harbour, v.t, (shelter), excĭpĭo (3)
hard, dūrus; (difficult), diffĭcĭlis
hard, adv, (strenuously), strēnŭē
harden, v.t, dūro (1); v.i, dūresco (3)
hard-hearted, dūrus
hardiness, rōbur, n
hardly, adv, vix; (harshly),
  crūdēlĭter
hardness, dūrĭtĭa, f
hardship, lăbor, m
hardware, ferrāmenta, n.pl
hardy, dūrus
hare, lĕpus, m
hark! heus!
harlot, mĕrētrix, f
harm, nn, damnum, n
harm, v.t, nŏcĕo (2) (with dat)
harmful, noxĭus
harmless, innŏcŭus, innŏcens
harmonious, concors
harmonize, v.i, concĭno (3)
harmony, concentus, m, consensus,
  m
harness, nn, ĕquestrĭa arma, n.pl,
  (horse equipment), frēnum, n
harness, v.t, iungo (3)
harp, fĭdes, f. pl; (harpist), fĭdĭcen, m
harrow, nn, irpex, m
harrow, v.t, occo (1)
harrowing, adj, horrendus, terrĭbĭlis
harsh, asper, acerbus
harshness, aspĕrĭtas, f
hart, cervus, m
harvest, messis, f
hasp, fĭbŭla, f
haste, nn, festīnātĭo, f
hasten, v.i, prŏpĕro (1), festīno(1); v.t,
  mātūro (1), accĕlĕro (1)
hastily, adv, prŏpĕrē
hastiness (of temper), īrācundĭa, f
hasty, prŏpĕrus; (of temper), īrācundus
hat, pĕtăsus, m
hatch, v.t, (eggs), exclūdo (3); (plans
  etc.), ĭnĕo (4)
hatchet, sĕcūris, f
hate, nn, ŏdĭum, n
hate, v.t, ōdi (v.defect)
hateful, ŏdĭōsus
haughtiness, sŭperbĭa, f
haughty, sŭperbus, arrŏgans
haul, v.t, trăho (3)
haunt, nn, lătĕbrae, f. pl
haunt, v.t, (visit frequently), cĕlĕbro
  (1); (trouble), sollĭcĭto (1)
have, v.t, hăbĕo (2); or use esse (irreg)
  with dat. of possessor, e.g. I have a
  brother, est mĭhĭ frāter

haven, portus, m
haversack, saccus, m
havoc, strāges, f, vastātĭo,
hawk, nn, accĭpĭter, m,f
hay, faenum, n
hazard, nn, pĕrīcŭlum, n
hazardous, pĕrīcŭlōsus
haze, nĕbŭla, f
hazel, nn, cŏrўlus, f
hazy, nĕbŭlōsus
he, pron, If not emphatic, use 3rd pers.
  of verb; otherwise, ille, hic, is
head, căput, n, vertex, m; (chief),
  prīnceps, m; (to be at the — of)
  praesum (irreg) (with dat)
head, adj, (of wind), adversus
head, v.t, (be in charge), praesum
  (irreg) (with dat)
head-ache, căpĭtis dŏlor, m; (— band),
  vitta, f; (— land), prōmontōrĭum,
  n; (— long), adj, praeceps; (—
  quarters), praetōrĭum, n; (—
  strong), adj, pervĭcax
heal, v.t, sāno (1), mĕdĕor (2 dep)
  (with dat); v.i, consānesco (3)
healing, nn, sānātĭo, f
healing, adj, sălūtāris
health, vălētūdo, f
healthy, sānus, vălĭdus; (of place or
  climate), sălūbris
heap, nn, ăcervus, m
heap, v.t, cŭmŭlo (1), congĕro (3)
hear, v.t, audĭo (4); (learn), cognosco
  (3)
hearer, audītor, m
hearing, nn, (sense of —), audītus, m
hearsay, rūmor, m
heart, cor, n; (interior, use adj, intĭmus (inmost); (feelings, etc.),
  pectus, n, mens, f; (courage),
  ănĭmus, m; (— ache), sollĭcĭtūdo, f;
  (— break), dŏlor, m; (— broken)
  adj. phr, ănĭmo afflictus
hearth, fŏcus, m
heartiness, stŭdĭum, n
heartless, dūrus
heartlessness, crūdēlĭtas, f
hearty, ălăcer
heat, nn, călor, m, ardor, m, aestus,
  m, fervor, m
heat, v.t, călĕfăcĭo (3); (excite), incendo (3)
heath, lŏca obsĭta, n.pl, lŏca inculta,
  n.pl
heave, v.t, tollo (3); v.i, tŭmesco (3)
heaven, caelum, n; (— dwelling) adj,
  caelĭcōla
heavenly, adj, dīvīnus
heaviness, grăvĭtas, f; (— of mind),
  tristĭtĭa, f

heavy, grăvis; (sad), tristis; (air, etc.), crassus
hectic (agitated, confused), turbŭlentus
hedge, saepes, f
hedge in, v.t, saepĭo (4)
hedgehog, ĕchīnus, m
heed, v.t, (obey), pārĕo (2) (with dat); (to take —), v.i, căvĕo (2)
heedless, incautus
heedlessness, neglĕgentĭa, f
heel, calx, f; (take to one's —s), fŭgĭo (3)
heifer, iŭvenca, f
height, altĭtūdo, f; (high ground) sŭpĕrĭor lŏcus, m
heighten, v.t, use augĕo (2) (increase)
heinous, ătrox
heir, heiress, hēres, c
hell, infĕri, m. pl, Orcus, m
hellish, infernus
helm, gŭbernācŭlum, n
helmet, cassis, f, gălĕa, f
helmsman, gŭbernātor, m
help, nn, auxĭlĭum, n
help, v.t, iŭvo (1), subvĕnĭo (4) (with dat); (I cannot help coming), non possum făcĕre quīn vĕnĭam
helper, adiūtor, m
helpful, ūtĭlis
helpless, ĭnops
helplessness, ĭnŏpĭa, f
helpmate, consors, m, f
hem, nn, limbus, m
hem in, v.t, circumsĕdĕo (2), saepĭo (4)
hemisphere, hēmisphaerĭum, n
hemp, cannăbis, f
hen, gallīna, f; (— house), gallīnārĭum, n
hence, adv, (place or cause), hinc; (time), posthāc
henceforth, adv, posthāc
her, pron, adj, eius; (if it refers to the subject of the sentence), sŭus, a, um
herald, praeco, m
herb, herba, f, hŏlus, n
herd, grex, m
herd together, v.i, congrĕgor (1 pass)
herdsman, pastor, m
here, hīc; (hither), hūc; (to be —), v.i, adsum (irreg)
hereafter, adv, posthāc
hereby, adv, ex hōc
hereditary, hērēdĭtārĭus
heredity, gĕnus, n
heretical, prāvus
hereupon, adv, hīc
heritage, hērēdĭtas, f
hermit, hŏmo sōlĭtārĭus
hernia, hernĭa, f

hero, vir fortissĭmus
heroic (brave), fortis
heroine, fēmĭna fortis, f
heroism, virtus, f
heron, ardĕa, f
hers, see her
herself, pron. reflexive, sē; (pron. emphatic), ipsa
hesitancy, hesitation, haesĭtātĭo, f
hesitate, v.i, dŭbĭto (1), haesĭto (1)
hew, v.t, caedo (3)
hey-day (youth), iŭventus, f
hibernate, v.i, condor (3 pass)
hiccough, singultus, m
hidden, occultus
hide, nn, (skin), cŏrĭum, n, pellis, f
hide, v.t, abdo (3), cēlo (1)
hideous, foedus
hideousness, foedĭtas, f
hiding-place, lătĕbrae, f. pl
high, altus, celsus; (of rank), amplus; (of price), magnus, magni; (— born), gĕnĕrōsus; (— handed), impĕrĭōsus; (— lands), montes, m. pl; (— landers), montāni, m. pl; (— spirited), ănĭmōsus; (— treason), māiestas, f; (— way), vĭa, f; (— wayman), lătro, m
hilarity, hĭlărĭtas, f
hill, collis, m
hillock, tŭmŭlus, m
hilly, montŭōsus
hilt, căpŭlus, m
himself, pron. reflexive, sē; pron. emphatic, ipse
hind, adj, postĕrĭor
hinder, v.t, impĕdĭo (4), obsto (1) (with dat)
hindrance, impĕdīmentum, n
hinge, nn, cardo, m
hinge on, v.i, vertor (3 dep), versor (1 dep) in (with abl)
hint, nn, signĭfĭcātĭo, f
hint at, v.t, signĭfĭco (1)
hip, coxendix, f
hippopotamus, hippŏpŏtămus, m
hire (wages), merces, f
hire, v.t, condūco (3)
hired, conductus
his, pron, eius, hūius, illĭus; or sŭus (referring to the subject of the sentence)
hiss, nn, sībĭlus, m
hiss, v.i. and v.t, sībĭlo (1)
historian, scriptor, (m) rērum
historic(al) use nn, histŏrĭa, f, (history)
history, histŏrĭa, f, rēs gestae, f. pl
hit, nn, (blow), plāga, f
hit, v.t, (strike), fĕrĭo (4); (— upon), incĭdo (3)

hitch, impĕdīmentum, *n*
hitch, *v.t*, necto (3)
hither, *adv*, hūc; (— and thither), hūc illūc
hitherto, *adv*, ădhūc
hive, alvĕārĭum, *n*
hoard, *nn*, ăcervus, *m*
hoard, *v.t*, collĭgo (3), condo (3)
hoar-frost, prŭīna, *f*
hoarse, raucus
hoary, cānus
hoax, *nn*, lūdus, *m*
hoax, *v.t*, lūdĭfĭcor (1 *dep*), lūdo (3)
hobble, *v.i*, claudĭco (1)
hobby, stŭdĭum, *n*
hob-nail, clāvus, *m*
hoe, *nn*, sarcŭlum, *n*
hoe, *v.t*, sarrĭo (4)
hog, porcus, *m*
hogshead, dōlĭum, *n*
hoist, *v.t*, tollo (3)
hold, *nn*, (grasp), *use* comprĕhendo (3), *or* mănus, *f*
hold, *v.t*, tĕnĕo (2), obtĭnĕo (2), hăbĕo (2); (— an office), obtĭnĕo (2), fungor (3 *dep*); (— elections, etc.), hăbĕo (2); (— back), *v.i*, cunctor (1 *dep*), *v.t*, rētĭnĕo (2); (— fast), rētĭnĕo (2); (— out), *v.t*, porrĭgo (3); (— endure), sustĭnĕo (4), perfĕro (*irreg*); (— up, lift), tollo (3)
hold-fast, *nn*, fībŭla, *f*
hole, fŏrāmen, *n*, căvum, *n*
holiday, fērĭae, *f. pl*
holiness, sanctĭtas, *f*
hollow, *nn*, căvum, *n*, lăcūna, *f*; (— of the hand), căva mănus, *f*
hollow, *adj*, căvus; (false), vānus
hollow, *v.t*, căvo (1)
holm-oak, īlex, *f*
holy, săcer
homage (respect), observantĭa, *f*
home, *adj*, dŏmestĭcus; (homely), rustĭcus
home, dŏmus, *f*; (at —), dŏmĭ; (homewards), dŏmum; (from —), dŏmo; (— less), cărens tecto (lacking shelter)
homicide (deed), caedes, *f*; (person), hŏmĭcīda, *c*
honest, prŏbus
honesty, prŏbĭtas, *f*, intĕgrĭtas, *f*
honey, mel, *n*
honeycomb, făvus, *m*
honorary, hŏnōrārĭus
honour, hŏnos, *m*; (glory), dĕcus, *n*; (integrity), hŏnestas, *f*, intĕgrĭtas, *f*; (repute), fāma, *f*
honour, *v.t*, cŏlo (3), hŏnesto (1)
honourable, hŏnōrātus, hŏnestus

hood, cŭcullus, *m*
hoof, ungŭla, *f*
hook, hāmus, *m*
hook, *v.t*, hāmo căpĭo (3), (catch by a hook)
hooked, hāmātus
hoop, circŭlus, *m*
hoot, *nn*, cantus, *m*
hoot, *v.i*, căno (3); *v.t*, (hoot at), explōdo (3)
hop, *v.i*, sălĭo (4)
hope, *nn*, spes, *f*
hope, *v.i. and v.t*, spēro (1)
hopeful (promising), *use genit. phr*, bŏnae spĕi
hopefully, *adj, phr*, multa spērans
hopeless (desperate), dēspērātus
hopelessness, dēspērātĭo, *f*
horizon, orbis, (*m*) fīnĭens (limiting circle)
horizontal, lībrātus
horn, cornu, *n*; (made of —), *adj*, cornĕus
hornet, crābro, *m*
horrible, horrĭbĭlis, horrendus, ătrox, foedus
horrid, horrĭbĭlis, horrendus, ătrox, foedus
horrify, *v.t*, (dismay), percello (3), terrĕo (2)
horror, horror, *m*
horse, ĕquus, *m*
horseback (to ride on —), in ĕquo vĕhor (3 *pass*); (to fight on —), ex ĕquo pugno (1)
horse-fly, tābānus, *m*
horse-race, certāmen ĕquestre, *n*
horse-shoe, sŏlĕa, *f*
horse-whip, flăgellum, *n*
horticulture, hortōrum cultus, *m*
hospitable, hospĭtālis
hospital, vălētūdĭnārĭum, *n*
hospitality, hospĭtĭum, *n*
host (one who entertains), hospes, *m*; (innkeeper), caupo, *m*; (large number), multĭtūdo, *f*
hostage, obses, *c*
hostess, hospĭta, *f*
hostile, hostīlis, infestus
hostility, ĭnĭmīcĭtĭa, *f*; (hostilities, war), bellum, *n*
hot, călĭdus, fervens; (of temper), ăcer; (to be —), *v.i*, călĕo (2), fervĕo (2); (to become —), *v.i*, călesco (3); (— headed), *adj*, fervĭdus, fervens; (hotly), *adv*, ardenter
hotel, hospĭtĭum, *n*
hound, cănis, *m*, *f*
hound on, *v.t*, (goad on), instīgo (1), ăgĭto (1)

hour, hōra, *f*
hourly, *adv*, in hōras
hour-glass, hōrārĭum, *n*
house, dŏmus, *f*, aedes, *f*, *pl*; (**family**), gens, *f*; (— **hold**), dŏmus, *f*, fămĭlĭa, *f*; (— **keeper**), prōmus, *m*; (— **maid**), ancĭlla, *f*; (— **wife**), māterfămĭlĭas, *f*
house, *v.t*,(**store**), condo (3), rĕpōno, (3)
hovel, tŭgŭrĭum, *n*, căsa, *f*
hover, *v.i*, vŏlĭto (1), impendĕo (2)
how (**in what way?**), quōmŏdŏ?; *with adj. or adv*, quam?; (— **many**), quot?; (— **often**), qŭotĭes?; (— **great or big**), quantus?
however, *conj*, tămen; *adv*, quamvis; (**how big or great**), quantumvis
howl, *nn*, ŭlŭlātus, *m*
howl, *v.i*, ŭlŭlo (1)
hubbub, tŭmultus, *m*
huddle, *v.i*, (— **together**), congrĕgor (1 *dep*), confĕror (*irreg. pass*)
hue (**colour**), cŏlor, *m*
huff (**to be in a** — **about**), *v.t*, aegrē fĕro (*irreg*)
hug, *nn*, complexus, *m*
hug, *v.t*, amplector (3 *dep*)
huge, ingens, immānis
hull (**of a ship**), alvĕus, *m*
hum, *nn*, frĕmĭtus, *m*
hum, *v.i*, frĕmo (3), strĕpo (3)
human, *adj*, hūmānus; (— **being**), hŏmo, *c*
humane (**compassionate**), mĭsĕrĭcors
humanity, hūmānĭtas, *f*; (**human race**), hŏmĭnes, *c. pl*; (**compassion**), mĭsĕrĭcordĭa, *f*
humble, hŭmĭlis, vĕrēcundus
humble, *v.t*, dēprĭmo (3); (— **in war**), dēbello (1); (— **oneself**), sē summittĕre (3 *reflex*)
humdrum, *adj*, mĕdĭŏcris, tardus
humid, hūmĭdus
humidity, hūmor, *m*
humiliate, *v.t*, dēprĭmo (3)
humility, mŏdestĭa, *f*
humorous, rĭdĭcŭlus
humour, făcētĭae, *f. pl*; (**disposition**), ingĕnĭum, *n*. lībĭdo, *f*; (**to be in the** — **to**), *use* lĭbet (*v*. 2 *impers*) (*with dat. of person*)
humour, *v.t*, obsĕquor (3 *dep*) (*with dat. of person*)
hump, gibber, *m*
humpbacked, *adj*, gibber
hunch, hunchbacked, *see* humpbacked
hundred, *adj*, centum; (— **times**), *adv*, centĭes; (— **fold**), *adj*, centŭplex

hundredth, centēsĭmus
hundredweight, centumpondĭum, *n*
hunger, fămes, *f*
hunger, *v.i*, ēsŭrĭo (4)
hungry, ēsŭrĭens, ăvĭdus (cĭbi)
hunt, *v.t*, vēnor (1 *dep*)
hunt, hunting, *nn*, vēnātĭo, *f*
hunter, vēnātor, *m*
huntress, vēnātrix, *f*
hurdle, crātes, *f. pl*
hurl, *v.t*, iăcŭlor (1 *dep*), cōnĭcĭo (3)
hurricane, tempestas, *f*, prŏcella, *f*
hurried, praeceps
hurriedly, *adv*, raptim
hurry, *v.i*, festīno (1), prŏpĕro (1); *v.t*, răpĭo (3); (**an action, etc.**), mātūro (1)
hurt, *nn*, (**wound**), vulnus, *n*
hurt, *v.t*, laedo (3), nŏcĕo (2) (*with dat*)
hurt, *adj*, (**wounded**), saucĭus
hurtful, nŏcens, noxĭus
husband, vir, *m*, mărītus, *m*
husbandry, agrĭcultūra, *f*
hush! tăcē; *pl*, tăcētĕ (*from* tăcĕo)
hush up, *v.t* (**conceal**), tĕgo (3), cēlo (1)
husk, follĭcŭlus, *m*
husky, fuscus, raucus
hustle, *v.t*, pulso (1), trūdo (3)
hut, căsa, *f*, tŭgŭrĭum, *n*
hutch, căvĕa, *f*
hyacinth, hўăcinthus, *m*
hybrid, hybrĭda, ae, *c*
hymn, carmen, *n*
hyperbole, hўperbŏlē, *f*
hyperchondriac, mĕlanchŏlĭcus
hypocrisy, sĭmŭlātĭo, *f*
hypocrite, sĭmŭlātor, *m*
hypocritical, sĭmŭlātus
hypothesis, coniectūra, *f*, condĭcĭo, *f*
hysteria, āmentĭa, *f*, perturbātĭo, *f*

I

I, *pron*, (**emphatic**), ĕgo; *otherwise use 1st pers. sing. of verb, e.g.* **I love**, ămo
iambic, *adj*, ĭambĕus
ice, glăcĭes, *f*
icicle, stĭrĭa, *f*
icy, gĕlĭdus, glăcĭālis
idea, nōtĭo, *f*, ĭmāgo, *f*, sententĭa, *f*; (**to form an** —) *v.i*, cōgĭtātĭōne fingo (3)
ideal, *adj*, (**perfect**), perfectus, summus, optĭmus
ideal, *nn*, exemplar, *n*
identical, īdem (**the same**)
identify, *v.t*, agnosco (3)

identity (to find the — of), cognosco (3) quis sit . . .

ides, īdūs, *f. pl*

idiocy, fătŭĭtas, *f*

idiom, prŏprĭĕtas, *f.* (linguae) (peculiarity of language)

idiot, fătŭus, *m*

idiotic, fătŭus

idle (unemployed), ōtĭōsus; (lazy), ignāvus; (useless), vānus; (to be —), *v.i*, cesso (1)

idleness, ignāvĭa, *f*, cessātĭo, *f*

idler, cessātor, *m*, cessātrix, *f*

idol (statue), sĭmŭlācrum, *n*; (something loved), dēlĭcĭae, *f. pl*

idolatry, vĕnĕrātĭo, (*f*) sĭmŭlācrōrum (worship of images)

idolize, *v.t*, cŏlo (3)

idyl, īdyllĭum, *n*

if, *conj*, sī; (— not), sīn; (*after a vb. of asking* — whether), num, ŭtrum; (whether . . . or if), sīve . . . sīve; (— only), dummŏdo

ignite, *v.i*, ardesco (3); *v.t*, accendo (3)

ignoble (of birth), ignōbĭlis; (dishonourable), turpis

ignominious, turpis

ignominy, ignōmĭnĭa, *f*, infāmĭa, *f*

ignorance, inscĭentĭa, *f*

ignorant, ignārus, inscĭus

ignore, *v.t*, praetĕrĕo (4)

ill, *adj*, aeger; (evil), mălus; (to be —), *v.i*, aegrōto (1); (to fall —), *v.i*, in morbum incĭdo (3)

ill, *adv*, mălĕ

ill, *nn*, (evil), mălum, *n*

ill-advised (reckless), tĕmĕrārĭus

ill-bred, inhūmānus

ill-disposed, mălĕvŏlus

illegal, illĭcĭtus

illegitimate, non lēgĭtĭmus

ill-favoured, dēformis, turpis

ill-health, vălētūdo, *f*

illicit, illĭcĭtus

illiterate, illittĕrātus

ill-natured, mălĕvŏlus

ill-omened, dīrus

ill-starred, infēlix

ill-temper, īrācundĭa,

illness, morbus, *m*

illogical, absurdus, rĕpugnans

illuminate, *v.t*, illustro (1)

illusion, error, *m*

illusive, vānus

illustrate, *v.t*, illustro (1)

illustration, exemplum, *n*

illustrious, clārus, illustris

image, ĭmāgo, *f*, effĭgĭes, *f*

imaginable, *use phr*, quod concĭpi pŏtest (that can be imagined)

imaginary, commentīcĭus

imagination, cōgĭtātĭo, *f*

imagine, *v.t*, ănĭmo concĭpĭo (3) *or* fingo (3)

imbecile, fătŭus

imbecility, imbēcillĭtas, (*f*) ănĭmi

imbibe, *v.t*, bĭbo (3), haurĭo (4)

imbue, *v.t*, inficĭo (3)

imitate, *v.t*, ĭmĭtor (1 *dep*)

imitation, ĭmĭtātĭo, *f*; (likeness), effĭgĭes, *f*

imitator, ĭmĭtātor, *m*

immaculate, intĕger

immaterial (unimportant), *use phr*, nullo mōmento

immature, immātūrus

immeasurable, immensus

immediate, praesens, proxĭmus

immediately, *adv*, stătim, confestim

immemorial (from time —), ex hŏmĭnum mĕmŏrĭa

immense, immensus, ingens

immensity, immensĭtas, *f*

immerse, *v.t*, immergo (3)

immigrant, advĕna, *m. f*

immigrate, *v.i*, immĭgro (1)

imminent, praesens; (to be —), *v.i*, immĭnĕo (2)

immobility, immōbĭlĭtas, *f*

immoderate, immŏdĕrātus, immŏdĭcus

immodest, impŭdīcus

immodesty, impŭdĭcĭtĭa, *f*

immolate, *v.t*, immŏlo (1)

immoral, prāvus, turpis

immorality, mōres mălĭ, *m. pl*

immortal, immortālis, aeternus

immortality, immortālĭtas, *f*

immovable, immōbĭlis

immunity, immūnĭtas, *f*, văcātĭo, *f*

immutable, immūtābĭlis

impair, *v.t*, mĭnŭo (3)

impale, *v.t*, transfīgo (3)

impart, *v.t*, impertĭo (4)

impartial, aequus, iustus

impartiality, aequĭtas, *f*

impassable, insŭpĕrābĭlis

impassioned, concĭtātus, fervens

impassive, pătĭens

impatience (haste), impătĭentĭa, *f*, festīnātĭo *f*

impatient, ăvĭdus

impeach, *v.t*, accūso (1)

impeachment, accūsātĭo, *f*

impeccable, impeccābĭlis

impede, *v.t*, impĕdĭo (4)

impediment, impĕdīmentum, *n*; (of speech), haesĭtantĭa, *f*

impel, *v.t*, impello (3), incĭto (1)

impend, *v.i*, impendĕo (2), immĭnĕo (2)

impending, fŭtūrus
impenetrable, impĕnĕtrābĭlis
imperfect, imperfectus
imperfection (defect), vĭtĭum, *n*
imperial (kingly), rēgĭus *or use
genit. of* impērĭum, *n*, (empire), *or*
impērātor, *m*, (emperor)
imperil, *v.t*, in pĕrīcŭlum addūco (3)
imperious impĕrĭōsus
impermeable, impervĭus
impersonate, *v.t*, partes sustĭnĕo (2)
(keep up a part)
impertinence, insŏlentĭa, *f*
impertinent, insŏlens
imperturbable, immōtus, immōbĭlis
impetuosity, vīs, *f*
impetuous, vĕhĕmens
impetus, vīs, *f*, impĕtus, *m*
impious, impĭus
implacable, implācābĭlis
implant, *v.t*, insĕro (3)
implement, instrūmentum, *n*
implicate, *v.t*, implĭco (1)
implicit, *adj*, tăcĭtus; (absolute),
· omnis, tōtus
implore, *v.t*, implōro (1), ōro (1)
imply, *v.t*, signĭfĭco (1); (involve),
hăbĕo (2)
impolite, ĭnurbānus
import, *nn*, (meaning), signĭfĭcātĭo, *f*
import, *v.t*, importo (1)
importance, mōmentum, *n*; (of position), amplĭtūdo, *f*
important, grăvis; (people), amplus
importunate, mŏlestus
importune, *v.t*, flāgĭto (1)
impose, *v.t*, impōno (3)
imposition (fraud), fraus, *f*
impossible, *use phr*, quod fĭĕri nōn
pŏtest (which cannot be done)
imposter, fraudātor, *m*
impotence, imbēcillĭtas, *f*
impotent, imbēcillus, infirmus
impoverish, *v.t*, in paupertātem rĕdĭgo (3)
impoverishment, paupertas, *f*
imprecation, exsĕcrātĭo, *f*
impregnable, ĭnexpugnābĭlis
impregnate, *v.t*, ĭnĭcĭo (3)
impress, *v.t*, imprĭmo (3); (the mind),
mŏvĕo (2)
impression (mental), mōtus, (*m*) ănĭmi;
(idea, thought), ŏpīnĭo, *f*, ŏpīnātĭo, *f*;
(mark), vestīgĭum, *n*
impressive, grăvis
imprint, *nn*, signum, *n*; (of a foot),
vestīgĭum, *n*
imprison, *v.t*, in vincŭla cōnĭcĭo (3)
(throw into chains)
imprisonment, vincŭla, *n.pl*

improbable, nōn vĕrĭsĭmĭlis (not
likely)
improper, indĕcōrus
improve, *v.t*, mĕlĭōrem făcĭo (3) *or*
reddo; *v.i*, mĕlĭor fīo (*irreg*)
improvement, ēmendātĭo, *f*
improvident, neglĕgens, imprŏvĭdus
imprudence imprūdentĭa, *f*
imprudent, inconsultus, imprūdens
impudence, impŭdentĭa, *f*
impudent, impŭdens
impulse, impĕtus, *m*, impulsus, *m*
impulsive, vĕhĕmens
impunity (with —), *adv*, impūnĕ
impure, impūrus, foedus
impurity, impūrĭtas, *f*, incestus, *m*
impute, *v.t*, attrĭbŭo (3)
in, *prep*, (place), in (*with abl*.) *or
use locative case if available, e.g.*
Londīnĭi, in London; (time), *use
abl. or* in (*with abl*.)
inability (weakness), imbēcillĭtas, *f*
inaccessible, ĭnaccessus
inaccuracy (fault), error, *m*
inaccurate, (things), falsus
inactive, ĭners
inactivity, cessātĭo, *f*, ĭnertĭa, *f*
inadequate, impar
inadmissible, *use phr*, quod nōn lĭcet
(which is not allowed)
inadvertent, imprūdens
inane, ĭnānis
inanimate, ĭnănĭmus
inappropriate, nōn aptus (not suitable)
inasmuch as, *conj*, quŏnĭam, quandōquĭdem
inattention, neglĕgentĭa, *f*
inattentive, neglĕgens
inaudible, *use phr*, quod audīri nōn
pŏtest (which cannot be heard)
inaugurate, *v.t*, ĭnaugŭro (1)
inauguration, consĕcrātĭo, *f*
inauspicious, infēlix
inborn, insĭtus
incalculable, *use phr*, quod aestĭ-
māri nōn pŏtest (which cannot be
estimated)
incapable, inhăbĭlis
incarcerate, *v.t*, in vincŭla cōnĭcĭo (3)
(throw into chains)
incarnate, spĕcĭe hūmānā ĭndūtus
(clothed with human form)
incautious, incautus
incendiary, incendĭărĭus, *m*
incense, *nn*, tūs, *n*
incense, *v.t*, ad īram mŏvĕo (2)
(arouse to anger)
incentive, stĭmŭlus, *m*
incessant, perpĕtŭus, assĭdŭus
incest, incestum, *n*

inch, uncĭa, *f*
incident, rēs, *f*
incidental (casual), fortŭĭtus
incipient, *use vb*, incĭpĭo (begin)
incision, incīsūra, *f*
incisive, mordax, ācer
incite, *v.t*, incĭto (1)
inclemency, aspĕrĭtas, *f*, sĕvĕrĭtas, *f*
inclement, asper, sĕvērus
inclination (desire), stŭdĭum, *n*, vŏluntas, *f*; (leaning, bias), inclīnātĭo, *f*
incline, *v.t*, inclīno (1); *v.i*, inclīnor (1 *pass*)
incline, *nn*, (slope), acclīvĭtas, *f*
inclined (disposed), prŏpensus
include, *v.t*, rēfĕro (*irreg*), comprĕhendo (3)
including (together with), cum (*with abl*)
incoherent; *use vb. phr. with* nōn *and* cŏhaerĕo (2) (to hold together)
income, fructus, *m*, stīpendĭum, *n*
incomparable, singŭlāris
incompatibility, rĕpugnantĭa, *f*
incompatible, rĕpugnans
incompetent, ĭnhābĭlis
incomplete, imporfootuo
incomprehensible, *use phr*, quod intellĕgi nōn pŏtest
inconceivable, *use phr*, quod ănĭmo fingi nōn pŏtest (that cannot be conceived)
inconclusive (weak), ĭnfirmus
incongruous, rĕpugnans
inconsiderable, parvus
inconsiderate, inconsĭdĕrātus
inconsistency, inconstantĭa, *f*
inconsistent, inconstans; (to be —), *v.i*, rĕpugno (1)
inconsolable, inconsōlābĭlis
inconspicuous, obscūrus
inconstancy, inconstantĭa, *f*
inconstant, inconstans
inconvenience, incommŏdum, *n*
inconvenient, incommŏdus
incorporate, *v.t*, constĭtŭo (3), ĭungo (3)
incorrect, falsus
incorrigible, perdĭtus
incorruptible, incorruptus
increase, *nn*, incrēmentum, *n*
increase, *v.t*, augĕo (2), *v.i*, cresco (1)
incredible, incrēdĭbĭlis
incredulous, incrēdŭlus
incriminate, *v.t*, implĭco (1)
inculcate, *v.t*, inculco (1)
incumbent upon (it is —), ŏportet (*v. 2 impers. with acc. of person*)
incur, *v.t*, sŭbĕo (4)
incurable, insānābĭlis

indebted, obnoxĭus
indecency, turpĭtūdo, *f*
indecent, turpis, obscēnus
indecisive, dŭbĭus, anceps
indeed, *adv*, *emphatic*, prŏfecto; (yes —), vēro; *concessive*; quĭdem
indefatigable, assĭdŭus
indefensible, *use phr*, quod nōn pŏtest făcĭlĕ dēfendi (that cannot be defended easily)
indefinite, incertus
indemnify, *v.t*, damnum rēstĭtŭo (3) (restore a loss)
indentation, lăcūna, *f*
independence, lībertas, *f*
independent, līber
indescribable, ĭnēnarrābĭlis
indestructible (unfailing), pĕrennis
indeterminate, incertus
index, index, *m*
indicate, *v.t*, indĭco (1), signĭfĭco (1)
indication, indĭcĭum, *n*
indict, *v.t*, accūso (1)
indictment, accūsātĭo, *f*
indifference, lentĭtūdo, *f*
indifferent, neglĕgens; (middling), mĕdĭŏcris
indifferently, *adv* (moderately), mĕdĭŏcriter
indigenous, *adj*, indĭgĕna
indigestible, *adj*, grăvis
indigestion, crūdĭtas, *f*
indignant, ĭratus; (to be —), *v.i*, indignor (1 *dep*), īrātus esse
indignation, indignātĭo, *f*, īra, *f*
indignity, contŭmēlĭa, *f*
indirect, oblīquus, (path, etc.), dēvĭus
indiscreet, inconsultus
indiscriminate, prōmiscŭus
indispensable, nĕcessārĭus
indispose, *v.t*, ălĭēno (1)
indisposed (not inclined), āversus; (ill), aegrōtus
indisposition (unwillingness), ănĭmus āversus; (sickness), vălētūdo, *f*
indisputable, certus
indistinct, obscūrus
individual, *nn*, hŏmo, *c*
individual, *adj*, prŏprĭus
indivisible, indīvĭdŭus
indolence, ignāvĭa, *f*
indolent, ignāvus
indomitable, indŏmĭtus
indoor, *adj*, umbrātĭlis (in the shade)
indoors (motion), in tectum
indubitable, certus
induce, *v.t*, addūco (3)
inducement, praemĭum, *n*
indulge, *v.i. and v.t*, indulgĕo (2)
indulgence, indulgentĭa, *f*

indulgent, indulgens
industrious, industrĭus, dīlĭgens
industry (diligence), industrĭa, *f*, dīlĭgentĭa, *f*
inebriated, ēbrĭus
ineffective, ĭnūtĭlis
inefficient, *use phr*, qui rem cĕlĕrĭter confĭcĕre nōn pŏtest (who cannot complete a matter quickly)
inelegant, ĭnēlĕgans
inept, ĭneptus
inequality, dissĭmĭlĭtūdo, *f*
inert, ĭners, segnis
inertly, *adv*, segnĭter
inestimable, ĭnaestĭmābĭlis
inevitable, nĕcessārĭus
inexcusable, *use phr*, quod praeter-mitti nōn pŏtest (that cannot be overlooked)
inexhaustible, infīnītus, sīne fīne
inexorable, ĭnexōrābĭlis
inexperience, impĕrītĭa, *f*, inscĭentĭa, *f*
inexperienced, impĕrītus
inexplicable, ĭnexplĭcābĭlis
inexpressible, ĭnēnarrābĭlis, *or phr*, quod exprĭmi nōn pŏtest (that cannot be expressed)
infallible, qui falli nōn pŏtest (who cannot be mistaken)
infamous, infāmis
infamy, infāmĭa, *f*
infancy, infantĭa, *f*
infant, *adj. and nn*, infans
infantry, pĕdĭtātus, *m*
infatuate, *v.t*, infātŭo (1)
infatuated, dēmens
infect, *v.t*, inficĭo (3)
infection, contāgĭo, *f*
infer, *v.t*, collĭgo (3)
inference, coniectūra, *f*
inferior, *adj*, infĕrĭor, dĕtĕrĭor
infernal, infernus
infested, infestus
infidelity, perfĭdĭa, *f*
infinite, infīnītus
infinity, infīnĭtas, *f*
infirm, invălĭdus, infirmus
infirmity, infirmĭtas, *f*
inflame, *v.t*, accendo (3)
inflammable, *use phr*, quod făcĭlĕ incendi pŏtest (that can be set on fire easily)
inflammation, inflammātĭo, *f*
inflate, *v.t*, inflo (1)
inflexible, rĭgĭdus
inflict, *v.t*, inflīgo (3); (war, etc.), infĕro (*irreg*) (*with dat of person*)
infliction, mălum, *n* (trouble)

influence, *nn*, vīs, *f*, mōmentum, *n*; (authority), auctōrĭtas, *f*; (to have —), *v.i*, vălĕo (2)
influence, *v.t*, mŏvĕo (2)
influential, grăvis
inform, *v.t*, certĭōrem făcĭo (3); (— against someone), nōmen dēfĕro (*irreg*) (*with genit*)
information (news), nuntĭus, *m*
informer, dēlātor, *m*
infrequency, rārĭtas, *f*
infrequent, rārus
infringe, *v.t*, vĭŏlo (1)
infringement, vĭŏlātĭo, *f*
infuriate, *v.t*, effĕro (1)
infuriated, īrā incensus
infuse, *v.t*, infundo (3), inĭcĭo (3)
ingenious, subtīlis
ingenuity, *f*, ars, *f*, callĭdĭtas, *f*
ingenuous, ingĕnŭus
inglorious, inglōrĭus
ingot, lăter, *m*
ingrained, insĭtus
ingratiate oneself with, *v.t*, concĭlĭo (1), sē grātum reddere (*with dat*)
ingratitude, ănĭmus ingrātus, *m*
ingredient, pars, *f*
inhabit, *v.t*, incŏlo (3), hăbĭto (1)
inhabitant, incŏla, *c*
inhale, *v.t*, (spīrĭtum) haurĭo (4)
inherent, insĭtus
inherit, *v.t*, *use phr. with*, hērēs (heir), *and* accĭpĭo (to receive)
inheritance, hērēdĭtas, *f*
inherited, hērēdĭtārĭus
inhibit, *v.t*, interdīco (3)
inhospitable, ĭnhospĭtālis
inhuman, immānis, crūdēlis
inhumanity, immānĭtas, *f*, crūdēlĭtas, *f*
inimitable, nōn ĭmĭtābĭlis
iniquitous, ĭnĭquus, imprŏbus
iniquity, imprŏbĭtas, *f*
initial, *adj*, prīmus
initiate, *v.t*, ĭnĭtĭo (1)
initiative (take the —), *v.i*, occŭpo (1)
inject, *v.t*, ĭnĭcĭo (3)
injudicious, inconsultus
injure, *v.t*, nŏcĕo (2) (*with dat*)
injurious, noxĭus, nŏcens
injury (of the body), vulnus, *n*; (dis-advantage), dētrīmentum, *n*, inĭūrĭa, *f*
injustice, ĭnĭquĭtas, *f*, iniūrĭa, *f*
ink, ātrāmentum, *n*
inland, mĕdĭterrānĕus
inlay, *v.t*, insĕro (3)
inlet, aestŭārĭum, *n*

inn, dēversōrĭum, *n,* caupōna, *f;*
  (keeper), caupo, *m*
innate, insĭtus, innātus
inner, intĕrĭor
innocence, innŏcentĭa, *f*
innocent, innŏcens, insons
innocuous, innŏcŭus
innovate, *v.t,* nŏvo (1)
innumerable, innŭmĕrābĭlis
inobservant, nōn perspĭcax
inoffensive, innŏcens
inopportune, ĭnopportūnus
inordinate, immŏdĕrātus
inquest, quaestĭo, *f*
inquire, *v.i,* quaero (3) ab (*with abl*)
  or dē (*with abl*)
inquiry, interrŏgātĭo, *f;* (official),
  quaestĭo, *f*
inquisitive, cūrĭōsus
inquisitor, quaesītor, *m*
inroad, incursĭo, *f*
insane, insānus, dēmens
insanity, insānĭa, *f,* dēmentĭa, *f*
insatiable, insătĭābĭlis
inscribe, *v.t,* inscrībo (3) in (*with
  abl*)
inscription, inscriptĭo, *f*
inscrutable, obscūrus
insect, bestĭŏla, *f*
insecure, intūtus (unsafe)
insecurity, *use adj,* intūtus
insensible (unfeeling), dūrus
inseparable, *use phr,* quod sēpărāri
  nōn pŏtest (that cannot be separated)
insert, *v.t,* insĕro (3)
inside, *prep,* intrā (*with acc*)
inside, *adv,* intus
inside, *nn,* intĕrĭor pars, *f*
insidious, insĭdĭōsus
insight (understanding), intellĕgentĭa, *f*
insignia, insignĭa, *n.pl*
insignificant, exĭgŭus, nullĭus mōmenti
insincere, sĭmŭlātus
insincerity, fallācĭa, *f,* sĭmŭlātĭo, *f*
insinuate, *v.t,* insĭnŭo (1); (hint),
  signĭfĭco (1)
insinuating (smooth), blandus
insipid, insulsus
insist, *v.i,* insto (1); *v.t,* (— on,
  demand), posco (3), flāgĭto (1)
insolence, contŭmācĭa, *f,* insŏlentĭa, *f*
insolent, contŭmax, insŏlens
insoluble, *use phr,* quod explĭcāri nōn
  pŏtest (that cannot be explained)
insolvent (to be —), *v.i,* nōn esse
  solvendo
inspect, *v.t,* inspĭcĭo (3)

inspection, *use vb,* inspĭcĭo (3), *or*
  lustro (1)
inspector (superintendent), cūrātor,
  m
inspiration (divine, poetic, etc), instinctus, *m,* afflātus, *m*
inspire, *v.t,* inĭcĭo (3) (*with acc. of
  thing inspired and dat. of person*);
  (rouse), accendo (3)
inspired (of persons), incensus
instal, *v.t,* ĭnaugŭro (1)
instalment, pensĭo, *f*
instance (example), exemplum, *n;*
  (for —), verbi grātĭā
instant, *adj,* praesens
instant, *nn,* mōmentum, *n*
instantly (at once), *adv,* stătim
instantaneous, praesens
instead, *adv,* măgis (rather)
instead of, *prep,* prō (*with abl*); *with a
  clause, use* tantum ăbĕrat (ăbest)
  ut ... ut
instigate, *v.t,* instīgo (1)
instill, *v.t,* instillo (1), inĭtĭo (3)
instinct, nātūra, *f*
instinctive, nātūrālis
institute, *v.t,* instĭtŭo (3)
institute, institution, collĕgĭum *n;*
  instĭtūtum, *n*
instruct, *v.t,* dŏcĕo (2), ērŭdĭo (4);
  (order), praecĭpĭo (3)
instruction, dĭscĭplīna, *f,* institutio, *f;*
  (command), mandātum, *n*
instructor, măgister, *m*
instrument, instrūmentum, *n*
instrumental (in doing something),
  ūtĭlis
insubordinate, sēdĭtĭōsus
insufferable, intŏlĕrābĭlis
insufficiency, ĭnŏpĭa, *f*
insufficient, haud sătis (*with genit*)
  (not enough . . .)
insult, *nn,* contŭmēlĭa, *f*
insult, *v.t,* contŭmēlĭam impōno (3)
  (*with dat*)
insulting, contŭmēlĭōsus
insuperable, *use phr,* quod sŭpĕrāri
  nōn pŏtest (that cannot be overcome)
insure against, *v.t,* praecăvĕo (2)
insurgent, rĕbellis, *m*
insurrection, mōtus, *m*
intact, intĕger
integral, nĕcessārĭus (necessary)
integrity, intĕgrĭtas, *f*
intellect, mens, *f,* ingĕnĭum, *n*
intellectual, ingĕnĭōsus
intelligence, ingĕnĭum, *n;* (news),
  nuntĭus, *m*
intelligent, săpĭens, intellĕgens

intelligible, perspĭcŭus

intemperate, intempĕrans

intend, v.t, in ănĭmo hăbĕo (2) (with infinitive)

intense, ācer

intensify, v.t, augĕo (2), incendo (3) (inflame, rouse)

intensity, vīs, f

intent, adj, intentus; (to be — on), ănĭmum intendo (3) in (with acc)

intention, consĭlĭum, n, prŏpŏsĭtum, n

intentionally, adv, consultō

inter, v.t, sĕpĕlĭo (4)

intercede (on behalf of), dēprĕcor (1 dep) pro (with abl)

intercept, v.t, (catch), excĭpĭo (3); (cut off), interclūdo (3)

intercession, dēprēcātĭo, f

interchange, nn, permūtātĭo, f

interchange, v.t, permūto (1)

intercourse, commercĭum, n, ūsus, m

interest, nn, (zeal), stŭdĭum, n; (advantage), commŏdum, n; (it is in the — of), intĕrest (v. impers. with genit); (financial), fēnus, n, ūsūra, f

interest, v.t, tĕnĕo (2), plăcĕo (2); (— oneself in), stŭdĕo (2) (with dat)

interested, attentus

interesting, use vb. to interest

interfere, v.i, sē interpōnĕre (3 reflex)

interim, adv, (in the —), intĕrim

interior, adj, intĕrĭor; nn, pars intĕrĭor, f

interject, v.t, intericĭo (3)

interlude, embŏlĭum, n

intermarriage, connūbĭum, n

intermediate, mĕdĭus

interminable, infīnītus

intermingle, v.t, miscĕo (2); v.i, sē miscēre (2 reflex)

intermission, intermissĭo, f

internal, intestīnus

international, use genit, gentĭum (of nations)

internecine, internĕcīnus

interpose, v.t, interpōno (3)

interpret, v.t, interprĕtor (1 dep)

interpretation, interprĕtātĭo, f

interpreter, interpres, c

interregnum, interregnum, n

interrogate, v.t, interrŏgo (1)

interrupt, v.t, interpello (1), interrumpo (3)

interruption, interpellātĭo, f

intersect, v.t, sĕco (1) (cut)

interval, intervallum, n, spătĭum, n

intervene, v.i, intercēdo (3), sē interpōnĕre (3 reflex) (both with dat)

intervention, intercessĭo, f

interview, collŏquĭum, n

interview, v.t, collŏquor (3 dep) cum (with abl) (speak with)

interweave, v.t, intertexo (3), implĭco (1)

intestines, intestīna, n.pl

intimacy, consŭētūdo, f, fămĭlĭārĭtas, f

intimate, adj, fămĭlĭāris

intimate, v.t, signĭfĭco (1)

intimidate, v.t, dēterrĕo (2)

intimidation, terror, m, mĭnae, f. pl

into, prep, in (with acc)

intolerable, intŏlĕrābĭlis

intolerance, sŭperbĭa, f

intolerant, sŭperbus

intone, v.t, căno (3)

intoxicate, v.t, ēbrĭum reddo (3) (make drunk)

intoxicated, ēbrĭus

intoxication, ēbrĭĕtas, f

intractable, diffĭcĭlis

intrepid, intrĕpĭdus

intricacy (difficulty), diffĭcultas, f

intricate, diffĭcĭlis

intrigue, dŏlus, m

intrigue, v.i, dŏlīs ūtor (3 dep)

introduce, v.t, intrōdūco (3)

introduction, intrōductĭo, f; (letter of —) littĕrae commendātĭcĭae, f. pl

intrude, v.i, sē inculcāre (1 reflex)

intrusive use phr, qui interpellāre sŏlet (who usually disturbs)

intuition, cognĭtĭo, f

inundate, v.t, ĭnundo (1)

inundation, ĭnundātĭo, f

inure, v.t, assŭēfăcĭo (3)

invade, v.t, bellum infĕro (irreg) (with dat), invādo (3) in (with acc)

invader, hostis, c

invalid, nn, aeger, m

invalid, adj, (of no avail), irrĭtus, infirmus

invalidate, v.t, infirmo (1)

invariable, constans

invasion, incursĭo, f

invective, convĭcĭum, n

inveigh against, v.i, invĕhor (3 dep) in (with acc.)

inveigle, v.t, illĭcĭo (3)

invent, v.t, invĕnĭo (4)

invention (faculty), inventĭo, f; (thing invented), inventum, n

inventor, inventor, m

inverse, inversus

invert, v.t, inverto (3)

invest, v.t, (money), collŏco (1); (besiege), obsĭdĕo (2); (— someone with an office), măgistrātum committo (3) (with dat) investigate, *v.t*, exquīro (3), cognosco (3)

investigation, investīgātīo, *f*, cognītīo, *f*

investiture, consĕcrātīo, *f*

inveterate, invĕtĕrātus

invidious (envious, hateful), invĭdĭōsus

invigorate, *v.t*, vīres rĕfĭcĭo (3)

invincible, invictus

inviolability, sanctĭtas, *f* (sacredness)

inviolable, invĭŏlātus

invisible, caecus

invitation, invītātĭo, *f*; (at your —), tŭo invītātu

invite, *v.t*, invīto (1)

inviting, blandus

invoke, *v.t*, invŏco (1)

involuntary, nōn vŏluntārĭus,

involve, *v.t*, involvo (3), illĭgo (1), hăbĕo (2)

invulnerable, *use phr*, quod vulnĕrāri nōn pŏtest (that cannot be wounded)

inward, *adj*, intĕrĭor

inwardly, inwards, *adv*, intus

irascibility, īrācundĭa, *f*

irascible, īrācundus

iris, īris, *f*

irk (it —s), pĭget (*v*. 2 *impers*.) (*with acc. of person*)

irksome, grăvis, mŏlestus

iron, *nn*, ferrum, *n*

iron, *adj*, ferrĕus

ironical, *use nn*, īrōnĭa, *f* (irony)

ironmongery, ferrāmenta, *n.pl*

irony, īrōnĭa, *f*, dissĭmŭlātĭo, *f*

irradiate, *v.t*, illustro (1)

irrational, rătĭōnis expers (devoid of reason)

irreconcilable, rĕpugnans

irrefutable, firmus

irregular (out of the ordinary), ĭnūsĭtātus, extrăordĭnārĭus; (not well regulated), nōn ordĭnātus

irregularity, vĭtĭum, *n*; *otherwise use adjs. above*

irrelevant, ălĭēnus

irreligious, impĭus

irremediable, insānābĭlis

irreparable, *use phr*, quod rĕfĭci nōn pŏtest (that cannot be repaired)

irreproachable, intĕger, invictus

irresistible, invictus

irresolute, dŭbĭus

irretrievable, irrĕpĕrābĭlis

irreverance,, impĭĕtas, *f*

irreverent, impĭus

irrevocable, irrĕvŏcābĭlis

irrigate, *v.t*, irrĭgo (1)

irrigation, irrĭgātĭo, *f*

irritable, stŏmăchōsus

irritate, *v.t*, irrīto (1); (make worse), pēius reddo (3)

irruption, (attack), incursĭo, *f*

island, insŭla, *f*

islander, insŭlānus, *m*

isolate, *v.t*, sēpăro (1)

isolation, sōlĭtūdo, *f*

issue, *nn*, (result), ēventus, *m*; (topic), rēs, *f*; (offspring), prōgĕnĭes, *f*

issue, *v.i*, (proceed), ēgrĕdĭor (3 *dep*); (turn out), ēvĕnĭo (4); *v.t* (give out), ēdo (3); (edicts, etc.) ēdīco (3)

isthmus, isthmus, *m*

it, *pron*, id, hoc, illud; *often expressed by 3rd person sing. of verb, e.g*. it is, est

itch, *nn*, prūrītus, *m*; (disease), scăbĭes, *f*

itch, *v.i*, prūrĭo (4)

item, rēs, *f*

itinerant, circumfŏrānĕus

itinerary, ĭter, *n* (route)

itself, *see* himself

ivory, *nn*, ĕbur, *n*; *adj*, ĕburnĕus.

ivy, hĕdĕra, *f*

J

jab, *v.t*, fŏdĭo (3)

jabber, *v.i*, blătĕro (1)

jackass, ăsĭnus, *m*

jacket, tŭnĭca, *f*

jaded, dēfessus

jagged, asper

jail, carcer, *m*

jailer, custos, *c*

janitor, iānĭtor, *m*

January, Iānŭārĭus (mensis)

jar, olla, *f*, amphŏra, *f*, dōlĭum, *n*

jarring, dissŏnus

jaunt, excursĭo, *f*

javelin, pīlum, *n*

jaws, faucēs, *f. pl*

jealous, invĭdus

jealousy, invĭdĭa, *f*

jeer at, *v.t*, dērīdĕo (2)

jeering, *nn*, irrīsĭo, *f*

jejune, iēiūnus

jeopardize, *v.t*, pĕrīclĭtor (1 *dep*)

jeopardy, pĕrīcŭlum, *n*

jerk, *v.t*, quătĭo (3)

jerkin, tŭnĭca, *f*

jest, *nn*, iŏcus, *m*

jest, *v.i*, iŏcor (1 *dep*)

jester, scurra, *m*

jetty, mōles, *f*

Jew, *nn*, Jūdaeus, *m*

jewel, gemma, *f*

jeweller, gemmārĭus, *m*
jibe, convīcĭum, *n*
jilt, *v.t,* rĕpŭdĭo (1)
jingle, *nn,* tinnītus *m*
jingle, *v.i,* tinnĭo (4)
job, ŏpus, *n*
jockey, ăgāso, *m*
jocose, iŏcōsus
jocular, iŏcŭlāris
jocund, hĭlăris, iūcundus
jog, *v.t,* fŏdĭco (1) **(nudge)**
join, *v.t,* iungo (3); *v.i,* sē coniungĕre
   (3 *reflex*); (— **battle**) committo (3)
joiner, lignārĭus, *m*
joint, commissūra, *f*
joist, tignum transversum, *n*
joke, *nn,* iŏcus, *m*
joke, *v.i,* iŏcor (1 *dep*)
joker, iŏcŭlātor, *m*
jollity, hĭlărĭtas, *f*
jolly, hĭlăris
jolt, *v.t,* concŭtĭo (3)
jostle, *v.t,* pulso (1)
jot, *v.t,* adnŏto (1)
journal, commentārĭi dĭurnĭ, *m. pl*
journey, *nn,* ĭter, *n*
journey, *v.i,* ĭter făcĭo (3)
journey-man, ŏpĭfex, *c*
jovial, hĭlăris
jowl, gĕnae, *f. pl*
joy **(outward),** laetĭtĭa, *f*; **(inner),**
   gaudĭum, *n*
joyful, laetus
joyless, tristis
jubilant, gaudĭo (*or* laetĭtĭā) exsultans **(exultant with joy)**
judge, *nn,* iūdex, *m*
judge, *v.t,* iūdĭco (1), aestĭmo (1)
judgement, iūdĭcĭum, *n*
judicature, iūdĭces, *m. pl*
judicial, iūdĭcĭālis
judicious, săpĭens
judiciously, săpĭenter
judiciousness, prūdentĭa, *f*
jug, urcĕus, *m*
juggling-tricks, praestĭgĭae, *f. pl*
juice, sūcus, *m*
juicy, sūcōsus
July **(before Caesar),** Quintīlis (mensis); **(after Caesar),** Iūlĭus (mensis)
jumble, *nn,* congĕrĭes, *f*
jumble, *v.t,* confundo (3)
jump, *nn,* saltus *m*
jump, *v.i,* sălĭo (4)
junction, coniunctĭo, *f*
juncture, tempus, *n*
June, Iūnĭus (mensis)
junior, mĭnor nātu, iūnĭor

juniper, iūnĭpĕrus, *f*
jurisconsult, iūrisconsultus, *m*
jurisdiction, iūrisdictĭo, *f*
juror, iŭdex, *m*
jury, iŭdĭces, *m. pl*
just, iustus
justice, iustĭtĭa, *f*
justification, sătisfactĭo, *f*
justify, *v.t,* purgo (1), excūso (1)
justly, *adv,* iustē
jut, *v.i,* exsto (1)
juvenile, iūvĕnīlis

K

keel, cărīna *f*
keen, ācer; **(mentally),** perspĭcax
keenness **(eagerness),** stŭdĭum, *n*;
   (sagacity), săgācĭtas, *f*; **(sharpness,**
   etc.), ăcerbĭtas, *f*
keep, *nn,* arx, *f*
keep, *v.t,* **(hold),** tĕnĕo (2), hăbĕo (2);
   (preserve), servo (1); **(store),** condo
   (3); **(support, rear),** ălo (3); (—
   apart), distĭnĕo (2); (— **back),** rĕtĭnĕo (2), dētĭnĕo (2); (— **off),** arcĕo
   (2); *v.i,* **(remain),** mănĕo (2)
keeper, custos, *c*
keeping **(protection),** tūtēla, *f*, custōdĭa, *f*
keg, dōlĭum, *n*, amphŏra, *f*
kennel, stăbŭlum, *n*
kerb **(stone),** crĕpĭdo, *f*
kernel, nŭclĕus, *m*
kettle, lēbes, *m*
key, clāvis, *f*
kick, *nn,* calcĭtrātus, *m*
kick, *v.i,* calcĭtro (1)
kid, haedus, *m*
kidnap, *v.t,* surrĭpĭo (3)
kidney, rēn, *m*
kidney-bean, phăsēlus, *m, f*
kill, *v.t,* nĕco (1), interfĭcĭo (3)
kiln, fornax, *f*
kind, *nn,* gĕnus, *n*; **(of such a —),**
   adj, tālis
kind, *adj,* bĕnignus
kindle, *v.t,* accendo (3), excĭto (1)
kindliness, bĕnignĭtas, *f*
kindness, bĕnĕfĭcĭum, *n*; **(of dis-**
   position), bĕnignĭtas, *f*
kindred **(relatives),** consanguĭnĕi, *m.*
   pl; cognāti, *m. pl*
king, rex, *m*
kingdom, regnum, *n*
kingfisher, alcēdo, *f*
kinsman, nĕcessārĭus, *m*
kiss, *nn,* oscŭlum, *n*

kiss, *v.t*, oscŭlor (1 *dep*)
kitchen, cŭlīna, *f*
kitten, fēlis cătŭlus, *m* (the young of a cat)
knapsack, sarcĭna, *f*
knave, scĕlestus, *m*
knavery, nēquĭtĭa, *f*, imprŏbĭtas, *f*
knavish, nēquam (*indeclinable*); improbus
knead, *v.t*, sŭbĭgo (3)
knee, gĕnu, *n*; (knock-kneed), *adj*, vārus
knee-cap, pătella, *f*
kneel, gĕnu (gĕnĭbus) nītor (3 *dep*) (rest on the knee(s))
knife, culter, *m*
knight, ĕques, *m*
knighthood, dignĭtas ĕquestris, *f*
knit, *v.t*, texo (3); (— the forehead) frontem contrăho (3)
knob, bulla, *f*, nōdus, *m*
knock, *v.t*, pulso (1); (— against), offendo (3); (— down), dēpello (3), dēĭcĭo (3)
knock, knocking pulsus, *m*, pulsātĭo, *f*
knoll, tŭmŭlus, *m*
knot, *nn*, nōdus, *m*
knot, *v.t*, nōdo (1)
knotty, nōdōsus
know, *v.t*, scĭo (4); (get to —), cognosco (3); (person, acquaintance) nosco (3); (not to —), nescĭo (4)
knowing, *adj*, (wise), prūdens
knowingly, *adv*, consultō
knowledge, scĭentĭa, *f*
known, nōtus; (to make —), dēclāro (1)
knuckle, artĭcŭlus, *m*

L

label, tĭtŭlus, *m*, pittācĭum, *n*
laborious, lăbōrĭōsus
labour, lăbor, *m*, ŏpus, *n*; (to be in —), *v.i*, partŭrĭo (4)
labour, *v.i*, lăbōro (1), ēnītor (3 *dep*)
labourer, ŏpĕrārĭus, *m*
labyrinth, lăbўrinthus, *m*
lace, rētĭcŭlāta texta, *n.pl* (net-like fabric)
lacerate, *v.t*, lăcĕro (1)
laceration, lăcĕrātĭo, *f*
lack, *nn*, ĭnŏpĭa, *f*
lack, *v.i*, ĕgĕo (2), cărĕo (*both with abl*)
lackey, pĕdĭsĕquus, *m*
laconic, brĕvis
lad, pŭer, *m*
ladder, scālae, *f. pl*
ladle, trulla, *f*

lady, mātrōna, *f*, dŏmĭna, *f*
lady-like, lībĕrālis (gracious)
lag, *v.i*, cesso (1)
laggard, cessātor, *m*
lagoon, lăcus, *m*
lair, lătĭbŭlum, *n*
lake, lăcus, *m*
lamb, agnus, *m* ; (agna, *f*)
lame, claudus; (argument, etc.), lĕvis; (to be —), *v.i*, claudĭco (1)
lameness, claudĭcātĭo, *f*
lament, lāmentātĭo, *f*, complōrātĭo, *f*, ŭlŭlātus, *m*
lament, *v.i, and v.t*, lāmentor (1 *dep*), dēplōro (1), lūgĕo (2)
lamentable, lāmentābĭlis
lamented, dēplōrātus, flēbĭlis
lamp, lūcerna, *f*
lampoon, carmen rĭdĭcŭlum et fāmōsum (facetious defamatory verse)
lance, lancĕa, *f*, hasta, *f*
lancet, scalpellum, *n*
land (earth, etc.), terra, *f*; (region or country), rĕgĭo, *f*, fīnes, *m. pl*; (native —), pătrĭa, *f*
land, *v.t*, expōno (3); *v.i*, ēgrĕdĭor (3 *dep*)
landing, *nn*, ēgressus, *m*
landlord (innkeeper), caupo, *m*; (owner), dŏmĭnus, *m*
landmark, lăpis, *m*
landslide, lapsus, (*m*) terrae
lane, sēmĭta, *f*,
language, lingua, *f*; (speech, style), ōrātĭo, *f*
languid, languĭdus, rĕmissus
languish, *v.i*, languĕo (2), tābesco (3)
languor, languor, *m*
lank, (hair), prōmissus; (persons), prōcerus
lantern, lanterna, *f*
lap, grĕmĭum, *n*, sĭnus, *m*
lap up, *v.t*, lambo (3)
lapse, *nn*, (mistake), peccātum, *n*; (of time), fŭga, *f*
lapse, *v.i*, (err), pecco (1); (time), praetĕrĕo (4)
larceny, furtum, *n*
larch, lărix, *f*
lard, ădeps, *c*, lārĭdum, *n*
larder, use cella, *f*, (store-room), *or* armārĭum, *n*, (food cupboard)
large, magnus
largeness, magnĭtūdo, *f*
largess, largĭtĭo, *f*
lark, ălauda, *f*
larynx, *use* guttur, *n*, (throat)
lascivious, lībīdĭnōsus
lash (whip), lōrum, *n*, flăgellum, *n*; (eye —), pĭlus, *m*

lash, v.t, (whip), verbĕro (1); (bind), allĭgo (1)

lass, pŭella, f

last, adj, ultĭmus, postrēmus, extrēmus; (most recent), nŏvissĭmus, proxĭmus; (at —), adv, tandem

last, v.i, dūro (1), mănĕo (2)

lasting, adj, diūturnus

lastly, adv, postrēmo, dēnĭque

latch, pessŭlus, m

late, sērus, tardus; (dead), mortŭus; adv, sēro; (— at night) (adv. phr.), multā nocte

lately, adv, nūper

latent, occultus

lathe, tornus, m

Latin, Lătīnus; (— language), lingua Lătīna, f

latitude (freedom, scope), lībertas, f

latter (the —), hic

lattice, cancelli, m. pl

laud, v.t, laudo (1)

laudable, laudābĭlis

laugh, nn, rīsus, m; (loud —), căchinnus, m

laugh, v.i, cachinno (1)

laughing-stock, lūdĭbrĭum, n

launch, v.t, (a ship), dēdūco (3); v.i, (launch out), insĕquor (3 dep)

laurel, laurus, f; adj, laurĕus

lava, massa lĭquĕfacta, f, (molten mass)

lavish, adj, prōdĭgus, prōfūsus

lavish, v.t, prōfundo (3)

law (a law), lex, f; (the law), iūs, n

lawful, lēgĭtĭmus

lawless, nĕfārĭus

lawn, prātum, n

lawsuit, līs, f

lawyer, iūrisconsultus, m

lax, dissŏlūtus

laxness, rēmissĭo, f, neglĕgentĭa, f

laxity, rēmissĭo, f, neglĕgentĭa, f

lay, v.t, pōno (3); (— aside), pōno (3); (— foundations), iăcĭo (3); (— an ambush), insĭdĭas collŏco (1); (— down arms), ab armis discēdo (3); (— eggs), ōva părĭo (3)

layer, cŏrĭum, n, tăbŭlātum, n

laziness, ignāvĭa, f

lazy, ignāvus, pĭger

lead, nn, plumbum, n; adj, plumbĕus

lead, v.t, dūco (3); (— a life, etc.), ăgo (3); (— on, persuade), addūco (3)

leader, dux, c

leadership, ductus, m; or use phr. in abl, e.g. under the — of Brutus, Brūto dŭce (with Brutus leader)

leading, adj, princeps

leaf, frons, f, fŏlĭum, n; (paper) schĕda, f

leafy, frondōsus

league, foedus, n, sŏcĭĕtas, f

league together, v.i, coniūro (1)

leak, nn, rīma, f

leak (let in water), ăquam per rīmas accĭpĭo (3)

leaky, rīmōsus

lean, adj, măcer, exīlis

lean, v.i, innītor (3 dep); v.t, inclīno (1)

leanness, măcĭes, f

leap, nn, saltus, m

leap, v.i, sălĭo (4); (— down) dēsĭlĭo (4)

leap-year, bĭsextĭlis annus, m

learn, v.t, disco (3); (ascertain) cognosco (3)

learned, doctus

learning, doctrīna, f, ērŭdītĭo, f

lease, nn, conductĭo, f

lease, v.t, condūco (3)

leash, cōpŭla, f

least, adj, mĭnĭmus; adv, mĭnĭmē; (at —), adv, saltem

leather, cŏrĭum, n

leave, nn, (permission), pŏtestas, f, permissĭo, f; (— of absence) commĕātus, m

leave, v.i, discēdo (3); v.t, rĕlinquo (3), dēsĕro (3)

leave off, v.i. and v.t, dēsĭno (3)

leavings, nn, rĕlĭquĭae, f. pl

lecture, nn, audĭtĭo, f, (hearing)

lecture, v.i, schŏlas hăbĕo (2)

lecture-room, schŏla, f

ledge, use adj, ēmĭnens (projecting) in agreement with a noun

ledger, cōdex, m

leech, hĭrūdo, f

leek, porrum, n

leering, adj, lĭmus

left, adj, (opp. to right), sĭnister, laevus; (remaining), rĕlĭquus

leg, crus, n

legacy, lēgātum, n

legal, lēgĭtĭmus

legalize, v.t, sancĭo (4)

legate, lēgātus, m

legation, lēgātĭo, f

legend, fābŭla, f

legendary, fābŭlōsus

leggings, ŏcrĕae, f. pl

legible, use phr, făcĭlis ad lĕgendum (easy for reading)

legion, lĕgĭo, f

legislate, v.i, lēges făcĭo (3) (make laws)

legislator, lātor, (m) lēgum (proposer of laws)

legitimate, lēgĭtĭmus

leisure, ōtǐum, *n*; **(to be at —),** *v.i*,
  ōtǐor (1 *dep*)
leisurely, *adj*, lentus
lend, *v.t*, mūtǔum do (1) **(give a loan),**
  commǒdo (1)
length, longǐtūdo, *f*; **(of time),** dǐūtur-
  nǐtas, *f*; **(at —),** *adv*, tandem
lengthen, *v.t*, prōdūco (3), longǐōrem
  reddo (3)
leniency, clēmentǐa, *f*
lenient, mītis, clēmens
lentil, lens, *f*
leper, hǒmo lěprōsus, *m*
leprosy, lěprae, *f. pl*
less, *adj*, mǐnor; *adv*, mǐnus
lessen, *v.i. and v.t*, mǐnǔo (3)
lesson, dǒcǔmentum, *n*
lest, *conj*, nē
let, *v.t*, sǐno (3), permitto (3) *(with dat
  of person)*; **(lease),** lǒco (1);**(— go),**
  dīmitto (3); **(— in),** admitto (3); **(—
  out),** ēmitto (3)
lethal, mortǐfer
lethargic, lentus
letter (of the alphabet), littěra, *f*;
  (epistle), littěrae, *f. pl*, ěpǐstǒla, *f*
lettering, *nn*, littěrae, *f.pl*
letters (learning), littěrae, *f. pl*
lettuce, lactūca, *f*
level, *adj*, plānus; **(— place),** *nn*,
  plānǐtǐes, *f*
level, *v.t*, aequo (1);**(— to the ground),**
  sterno (3)
lever, vectis, *m*
levity, lěvǐtas, *f*
levy, *nn*, dēlectus, *m*
levy, *v.t*, **(troops),** scrībo (3); **(taxes,**
  etc.), impěro (1), ěxǐgo (3)
lewd, incestus, impǔdīcus
lewdness, incestum, *n*
liable, obnoxǐus
liar, hǒmo mendax
libellous, fāmōsus
liberal, līběrālis, largus
liberality, līběrālǐtas, *f*, largǐtas, *f*
liberate, *v.t*, līběro (1)
liberation, līběrātǐo, *f*
liberty, lībertas, *f*
librarian, bibliǒthēcārǐus, *m*
library, bibliǒthēca, *f*
licence, līcentǐa, *f*; **(permission),**
  pǒtestas, *f*
licentious, dissǒlūtus
lick, *v.t*, lambo (3)
lid, ǒpercǔlum, *n*
lie, *nn*, mendācǐum, *n*
lie, *v.i*, **(tell a —),** mentǐor (4 *dep*)
lie, *v.i*, iǎcěo (2); **(rest),** cǔbo (1); **(—
  ill),** iǎcěo (2); **(— in wait),** insǐdǐor
  (1 *dep*)

lieutenant, lēgātus, *m*
life, vīta, *f*, ǎnǐma, *f*; **(vivacity)** vǐgor,
  m; **(— blood),** sanguis, *m*
lifeless, exǎnǐmis, exsanguis
lifelike, *use* sǐmǐlis **(similar)**
lifetime, aetas, *f*
lift, *v.t*, tollo (3)
ligament, lǐgāmentum, *n*
light, *nn*, lux, *f*, lūmen, *n*; **(to bring
  to —),** in mědǐum prōfěro *(irreg)*
light, *adj* **(not dark),** illustris; **(in
  weight),** lěvis; **(— armed),** expědī-
  tus; **(trivial, of opinions, etc.),**
  lěvis
light, *v.t*, **(illuminate),** illustro (1);
  (kindle), accendo (3)
lighten, *v.t*, **(burden, etc.),** lěvo (1);
  v.i, **(of lightning),** fulgěo (2)
lighthouse, phǎrus, *f*
lightly, *adv*, lěvǐter
lightning, fulmen, *n*
like, *v.t*, ǎmo (1)
like, *adj*, sǐmǐlis *(with genit. or dat)*,
  par *(with dat)*
like, *adv*, sǐmǐlǐter; **(just as),** sīcut
likelihood, sǐmǐlǐtūdo, *(f)* věli
likely, sǐmǐlis věri; *often uso future
  participle, e.g.* **likely to come,**
  venturus
liken, *v.t*, compǎro (1)
likeness, sǐmǐlǐtūdo, *f*
likewise, *adv*, ǐtem
liking, *nn*, ǎmor, *m*, lǐbīdo, *f*
lily, lǐlǐum, *n*
limb, membrum, *n*, artus, *m. p*
lime, calx, *f*; **(tree),** tǐlǐa, *f*
limit, *nn*, fīnis, *m*, termǐnus, *m*
limit, *v.t*, fīnǐo (4)
limitation, fīnis, *m*
limited (small), parvus
limitless, infīnītus
limp, *adj*, **(slack),** rěmissus
limp, *v.i*, claudǐco (1)
limping, *adj*, claudus
limpid, limpǐdus
linden-tree, tǐlǐa, *f*
line, līněa, *f*; **(boundary —),** fīnis, *m*;
  (of poetry), versus, *m*; **(of battle),**
  ǎcǐes, *f*; **(front —),** prīma ǎcǐes, *f*;
  (second —), princǐpes, *m.pl*; **(third
  —),** trǐārǐi, *m.pl*; **(— of march),**
  agmen, *n*
line, *v.t*, **(put in —),** instrǔo (3)
lineage, stirps, *f*, gěnus, *n*
linen, *nn*, lintěum, *n*; *adj*, lintěus
linger, *v.i*, mǒror (1 *dep*); cunctor
  (1 *dep*)
lingering, *nn*, mǒra, *f*
link, *nn*, **(of chain),** ānǔlus, *m*
link, *v.t*, coniungo (3)

For List of Abbreviations used, turn to pages 3, 4

lint, līnāmentum, *n*
lintel, līmen sŭpĕrum, *n*
lion, lĕo, *m;* (lioness), lĕaena,,
lip, lābrum, *n*
liquefy, *v.t*, līquĕfăcĭo (3)
liquid, *nn*, līquor, *m*
liquid, *adj*, līquĭdus
liquidate, *v.t*, solvo (3)
liquor, līquor, *m*
lisping, *adj*, blaesus
list, tăbŭla, *f*
listen (to), *v.t*, audĭo (4)
listener, auscultātor, *m*
listless, languĭdus
listlessness, languor, *m*
literal, *use*, prŏprĭus (its own)
literally, *adv. phr*, ad verbum
literary (person), littĕrātus
literature, littĕrae, *f. pl*
lithe, flexĭbĭlis, ăgĭlis
litigation, līs, *f*
litter (of straw, etc.), strāmentum, *n*;
(sedan), lectīca, *f*; (of young), fētus, *m*
little, *adj*, parvus, exĭgŭus; (for a —while), *adv*, părumper, paulisper
little, *adv*, paulum
little, *nn*, paulum, *n*, nonnĭhil, *n*;
(too little), părum, *n*; *with comparatives*, paulo; *e.g.* a little bigger, paulo māior
littleness, exĭgŭĭtas, *f*
live, *v.i*, vīvo (3); (— in or at), hăbĭto (1), incŏlo (3); (— on), vescor (3 *dep*) (*with abl*); (— one's life, etc.), vītam ăgo (3)
live, *adj*, vīvus
livelihood, victus, *m*
liveliness, ălăcrĭtas, *f*
lively, *adj*, ălăcer
liver, iĕcur, *n*
livery, vestītus, *m*
livid, līvĭdus
living, *adj*, vīvus
lizard, lăcerta, *f*
load, ŏnus, *n*
load, *v.t*, ŏnĕro (1)
loaded, ŏnustus
loaf, pānis, *m*
loam, lūtum, *n*
loan, mūtŭum, *n, or use adj*, mūtuus (borrowed, lent)
loathe, *v.t*, ŏdi (*defect*)
loathing, *nn*, ŏdĭum, *n*
loathesome, tēter
lobby, vestībŭlum, *n*
local, *use genit. of* lŏcus (place)
locality, lŏcus, *m*

lock (bolt), claustra, *n.pl*; (hair), crīnis, *m*
lock, *v.t*, obsĕro (1)
locker, capsa, *f*, armārĭum, *n*
locust, lŏcusta, *f*
lodge, *v.i*, dēversor (1 *dep*); (stick fast), adhaerĕo (2) fixus; *v.t* (accommodate temporarily), excĭpĭo (3)
lodger, inquĭlīnus, *m*
lodgings, dēversōrĭum, *n*
loft, cēnācŭlum, *n*
loftiness, altĭtūdo, *f*
lofty, celsus, altus
log, tignum, *n*
logic, dĭălectĭca, *f*
logical, dĭălectĭcus
loin, lumbus, *m*
loiter, *v.i*, cesso (1), cuhctor (1 *dep*)
loiterer, cessātor, *m*
loneliness, sōlĭtūdo, *f*
lonely, *adj*, sōlus
long, *adj*, longus (*with acc. of extent of length*), *e.g.* three feet long, longus tres pĕdes; (a — way), *adv*, prŏcul, longē; (of time), dĭūtĭnus, dĭūturnus; (how —?), quam dĭū? (for a -time), *adv*, dĭū
long, *adv*, (time), dĭū
long for, *v.t*, dēsīdĕro (1), cŭpĭo (3)
longevity, vīvācĭtas, *f*
longing, *nn*, dēsīdĕrĭum, *n*
long-suffering, *adj*, pătĭens
look at, *v.t*, aspĭcĭo (3); (— back), rēspĭcĭo (3); (— down (upon)), dēspĭcĭo (3); (— for), quaero (3); (— round), circumspĭcĭo (3); *v.i* (— towards), specto (1); (seem), vĭdĕor (2 *pass*)
look, *nn*, aspectus, *m*; (appearance), spĕcĭes, *f*; (expression), vultus, *m*
looking-glass, spĕcŭlum, *n*
loom, tēla, *f*
loop (winding), flexus, *m*
loop-hole, fĕnestra, *f*
loose, *adj*, laxus; (at liberty), sŏlūtus; (hair), passus, prōmissus; (dissolute), dissŏlūtus
loose, *v.t*, laxo (1), solvo (3)
loosely, *adv*, sŏlūtē
loot, *nn*, praeda, *f*
loot, *v.t*, praedor (1 *dep*)
lop off, *v.t*, ampŭto (1)
loquacious, lŏquax
loquacity, lŏquăcĭtas, *f*
lord, dŏmĭnus, *m*
lordly, *adv*, rēgālis, sŭperbus
lordship (supreme power), impĕrĭum, *n*

lore, doctrīna, *f*
lose, *v.t*, āmitto (3), perdo (3); (— heart), ănĭmo dēfīcĭo (3)
loss (act of losing), āmissĭo, *f*; (the loss itself), damnum, *n*, dētrĭmentum, *n*; (to be at a —), *v.i*, haerĕo (2)
lost (*adj*) āmissus, perdĭtus
lot (chance), sors, *f*; (to draw —s), sortĭor (4 *dep*); (much), multum, *n*
loth (unwilling), invītus
lottery, sortītĭo, *f*
loud, clārus, magnus
loudness, magnĭtūdo, *f*
lounge, *v.i*, (recline), rĕcŭbo (1)
louse, pĕdīcŭlus, *m*
lousy, pĕdĭcŭlōsus
lout, hŏmo agrestis
love, *nn*, ămor, *m*
love, *v.t*, ămo (1), dīlĭgo (3)
loveliness, vĕnustas, *f*
lovely, vĕnustus
lover, ămātor, *m*, ămans, *c*
loving, *adj*, ămans
low, hŭmĭlis; (sounds), grăvis; (— born), hŭmĭli lŏco nātus; (price), vīlis; (conduct, etc.), sordĭdus; (in spirits), *adv. phr*, ănĭmo dēmisso
low, *v.i*, mūgĭo (4)
lower, *comp. adj*, infĕrĭor
lower, *v.t*, dēmitto (3); (— oneself), sē ăbĭcĕre (3 *reflex*)
lowering, mĭnax
lowest, infĭmus
lowing, mūgītus, *m*
lowlands, lŏca, plāna, *n.pl*
lowness, lowliness, hŭmĭlĭtas, *f*
lowly, hŭmĭlis, obscūrus
loyal, fĭdēlis
loyalty, fĭdes, *f*
lozenge, pastillus, *m*
lubricate, *v.t*, ungo (3)
lucid, lūcĭdus
lucidity, perspĭcŭĭtas, *f*
luck, fortūna, *f*, fors, *f*; (good —), fēlīcĭtas, *f*; (bad —), infēlīcĭtas,
luckily, *adv*, fēlīcĭter
luckless, infēlix
lucky, fēlix, fortūnātus
lucrative, quaestŭōsus
ludicrous, rĭdĭcŭlus
lug, *v.t*, trăho (3)
luggage, impĕdīmenta, *n.pl*
lugubrious, lūgŭbris
lukewarm, tĕpĭdus
lull, *v.t*, sēdo (1); *v.i*, (of wind), sēdor (1 *pass*)
lull, *nn*, *use vb*. intermitto (3)
lumber, scrūta, *n.pl*

luminary, lūmen, *n*
luminous, illustris, lūcĭdus
lump, massa, *f*
lunacy, insānĭa, *f*, ălĭēnātĭo, *f*
lunar, lūnāris
lunatic, hŏmo insānus
lunch, *nn*, prandĭum, *n*
lunch, *v.i*, prandĕo (2)
lung, pulmo, *m*
lurch, *v.i*, ăgĭtor (1 *pass*) (leave in the —), rĕlinquo (3)
lure, *nn*, illex, *c*, illĕcĕbrae, *f. pl*
lure, *v.t*, allĭcĭo (3)
lurid, lūrĭdus
lurk, *v.i*, lătĕo (2)
lurking in wait, *use* insĭdĭor (1 *dep*) (lie in ambush)
luscious, dulcis
lust, *nn*, lĭbīdo, *f*
lust after, *v.t*, concŭpisco (3)
lustful, lĭbīdĭnōsus
lustiness, vĭgor, *m*
lustre, splendor, *m*
lusty, vălĭdus
lute, cĭthăra, *f*
luxuriance, luxŭrĭa, *f*
luxuriant, luxŭrĭōsus
luxurious, luxŭrĭōsus, lautus
luxury, luxus, *m*, luxŭrĭa, *f*
lying, *adj*, (telling lies), mendax
lynx, lynx, *c*
lyre, cĭthăra, *f*, fĭdes, *f, pl*
lyrical, lyrĭcus

M

mace-bearer, lictor, *m*
macerate, *v.t*, mācĕro (1)
machination, dŏlus, *m*
machine, māchĭna, *f*
machinery, māchĭnātĭo, *f*
mackerel, scomber, *m*
mad, insānus, vēcors, fŭrĭōsus; (to be —), *v.i.*, fŭro (3)
madden, *v.t*, mentem ălĭēno (1) (*with dat*); (excite), accendo (3)
maddening, *adj*, fŭrĭōsus
madman, hŏmo vēcors
madness, insānĭa, *f*
magazine, horrĕum, *n*; (arsenal), armāmentārĭum, *n*
maggot, vermĭcŭlus, *m*
magic, *adj*, măgĭcus
magic, *nn*, ars măgĭca, *f*
magician, măgus, *m*
magistracy, măgistrātus, *m*
magistrate, măgistrātus, *m*
magnanimity, magnănĭmĭtas, *f*
magnanimous, magnănĭmus
magnet, lăpis magnes, *m*

magnetic, magnētĭcus
magnificence, magnĭfĭcentĭa, *f*
magnificent, magnĭfĭcus, splendĭdus
magnify, *v.t*, amplĭfĭco (1), exaggĕro (1)
magnitude, magnĭtūdo, *f*
magpie, pīca, *f*
maid, maiden, virgo, *f*; **(servant),** ancilla, *f*
maiden, *adj*, virgĭnālis
mail (letters), littĕrae, *f. pl*, ĕpistŏlae, *f. pl*; **(armour),** lōrīca, *f*
maim, *v.t*, mŭtĭlo (1)
main, *adj*, prīmus, praecĭpŭus
mainland, contĭnens terra, *f*
maintain, *v.t*, servo (1), sustĭnĕo (2); **(with food, etc.),** ălo (3); **(by argument),** affirmo (1)
maintenance, *use vb.* servo (1) **(to maintain)**
majestic, augustus
majesty, māiestas, *f*
major, *nn*, **(officer),** praefectus, *m*
major, *adj*, māior
majority, māior pars, *f*
make, *v.t*, făcĭo (3), effĭcĭo (3), fingo (3), reddo (3); **(compel),** cōgo (3); **(appoint),** crĕo (1); **(— for, seek),** pĕto (3); **(— haste),** *v.i*, festīno (1), accĕlĕro (1); **(— good),** *v.t*, rĕpăro (1), sarcĭo (1); **(— ready),** praepăro (1); **(— up, a total, etc.),** explĕo (2); **(— use of),** ūtor (3 *dep*) *(with abl)*
maker, făbrĭcātor, *m*
maladministration, măla admĭnistrātĭo, *f*
malady, morbus, *m*
malcontent, cŭpĭdus nŏvārum rērum **(eager for innovations)**
male, *adj*, mascŭlus, mās
male, *nn*, mās, *m*
malediction, dīrae, *f.pl*, **(curses)**
malefactor, hŏmo mălĕfĭcus, nŏcens
malevolence, mălĕvŏlentĭa, *f*
malevolent, mălĕvŏlus
malice, mălĕvŏlentĭa, *f*; **(envy),** invĭdĭa, *f*
malicious, mălĕvŏlus
malignant, mălĕvŏlus
maligner, obtrectātor, *m*
malignity, mălĕvŏlentĭa, *f*
malleable, ductĭlis
mallet, mallĕus, *m*
maltreat, *v.t*, vĕxo (1)
maltreatment, vexātĭo, *f*
man (human being), hŏmo, *c*; **(opp. to woman, child),** vĭr, *m*; **(mankind),** hŏmĭnes, *c.pl*; **(chess, etc.),** latruncŭlus, *m*; **(fighting —),** mīles, *c*
man, *v.t*, **(ships, etc.),** complĕo (2)

man-of-war(ship), nāvis longa, *f*
manacle, *nn*, mănĭcae, *f.pl*, vincŭla *n.pl*
manage, *v.t*, admĭnistro (1), cūro (1), gĕro (3)
manageable, tractābĭlis, hăbĭlis
management, cūra, *f*, admĭnistrātĭo, *f*
manager, prōcūrātor, *m*, admĭnistrātor, *m*
mandate, impĕrātum, *n*, mandātum, *n*
mane (of horse), iŭba, *f*
manful, vĭrīlis
manger, praesēpe, *n*
mangle, *v.t*, lăcĕro (1), lănĭo (1)
mangled, truncus
mangy, scăber
manhood, pūbertas, *f*, tŏga vĭrīlis, *f* **(manly dress)**
mania, insānĭa, *f*
maniac, hŏmo vēcors, āmens
manifest, *v.t*, ostendo (3), ăpĕrĭo (4)
manifest, *adj*, mănĭfestus, ăpertus
manifestation, ostentātĭo, *f, or use vbs. above*
manifold, multĭplex
maniple (of a legion), mănĭpŭlus, *m*
manipulate, *v.t*, tracto (1)
mankind, hŏmĭnes, *c.pl*
manliness, virtus, *f*
manly, vĭrīlis
manner (way), mŏdus, *m*, rătĭo, *f*; **(custom),** mos, *m*; **(type),** gĕnus, *n*; **(good manners),** dĕcōrum, *n*
mannerism, gestus prŏprĭus
manoeuvre (military), dēcursus, *m*; **(trick),** dŏlus, *m*
manoeuvre, *v.i*, dēcurro (3)
manor, praedĭum, *n*
manservant, servus, *m*
mansion, dŏmus magna, *f*
manslaughter, hŏmĭcīdĭum, *n*
mantle, palla, *f*, lăcerna, *f*
manual, *adj*, *use* mănus **(hand)**
manual, *nn*, **(book),** lĭbellus, *m*
manufacture, *nn*, făbrĭca, *f*
manufacture, *v.t*, făbrĭcor (1 *dep*)
manufacturer, făbrĭcātor, *m*
manumission, mănūmissĭo, *f*
manure, stercus, *n*
manuscript, lĭber, *m*
many, *adj*, multi *(pl)*; **(very —),** plūrĭmi; **(a good —),** plērīque, complūres; **(as — as),** tŏt . . . quŏt; **(how —?),** quŏt?; **(so —),** tŏt; **(— times),** *adv*, saepĕ
map, tăbŭla, *f*
map (to — out), *v.t*, dēsigno (1)
maple, ăcer, *n*; *adj*, ăcernus
mar, *v.t*, dēformo (1)
marauder, praedātor, *m*

marble, marmor, *n*; *adj*, marmŏrĕus
March, Martĭus (mensis)
march, *nn*, ĭter, *n*; **(forced —),**
  magnum ĭter; **(on the —),** *adv.*
  phr, in ĭtĭnĕre
march, *v.i*, ĭter făcĭo (3); **(— quickly),**
  contendo (3); **(advance),** prōgrĕdĭor (3 *dep*)
mare, ĕqua, *f*
margin, margo, *m,f*
marine, *nn*, mīles classĭcus, *m*
marine, *adj*, mărīnus
mariner, nauta, *m*
maritime, mărĭtĭmus
mark, nŏta, *f*, signum, *n*, vestīgĭum,
  n; **(characteristic),** *use genit. case of*
  nn. with esse; *e.g.* it is the — of a
  wise man, est săpĭentis. . . .
mark, *v.t*, nŏto (1); **(indicate),** dēsigno
  (1); **(notice, observe),** ănĭmădverto
  (3)
market, fŏrum, *n*, măcellum, *n*;
  (cattle —), fŏrum bŏărĭum, *n*
market, *v.t*, nundĭnor (1 *dep*)
market-day, nundĭnae, *f.pl*, **(ninth**
  day)
marketing, *nn*, *use vb.* vendo (3) **(sell)**
market-place, fŏrum, *n*
marriage, conĭŭgĭum, *n*, connūbĭum,
  n, mătrĭmōnĭum, *n*; **(— feast),**
  nuptĭae, *f.pl*; **(— contract),** pactĭo
  nuptĭālis, *f*
marriageable, nūbĭlis
marrow, mĕdulla, *f*
marry, *v.t*, **(— a woman),** dūco (3);
  (— a man), nūbo (3) *(with dat)*
marsh, pălus, *f*
marshal, appărĭtor, *m*
marshal, *v.t*, **(troops, etc.),** dispōno (3)
marshy, păluster
martial, bellĭcōsus; **(court —),**
  castrense iūdĭcĭum, *n*
martyr, martyr, *c*
martyrdom, martўrĭum, *n*
marvel (miracle, etc.), mīrācŭlum, *n*
marvel at, *v.t*, mīror (1 *dep*)
marvellous, mīrus, mīrābĭlis
masculine, vĭrīlis
mash, *nn*, farrāgo, *f*
mash, *v.t*, contundo (3)
mask, *nn*, persōna, *f*; **(disguise),**
  intĕgŭmentum, *n*
mask, *v.t*, **(oneself),** persōnam indŭo
  (3); **(disguise),** dissĭmŭlo (1)
mason, structor, *m*
masonry, structūra, *f*
mass, mōles, *f*; **(of people),** multĭtūdo,
  f
mass, *v.t*, cŭmŭlo (1), ăcervo (1)
massacre, *nn*, caedes, *f*

massacre, *v.t*, trŭcīdo (1), caedo (3)
massive, sōlĭdus; **(huge),** ingens
mast, mālus, *m*
master, dŏmĭnus, *m*; **(— of the house-**
  hold), păterfămĭlĭas, *m*; **(school —),**
  măgister, *m*; **(skilled in . . .),** *use*
  adj. pĕrītus
master, *v.t*, **(subdue),** dŏmo (1);
  (knowledge, etc.), bĕne scĭo (4),
  disco (3)
masterful, impĕrĭōsus
masterly, *adj*, bŏnus; **(plan, etc.),**
  callĭdus
masterpiece, ŏpus summā laude
  dignum **(work worthy of the highest**
  praise)
mastery (rule), dŏmĭnātus, *m*
masticate, *v.t*, mandūco (1)
mastiff, cănis Mŏlossus **(Molossian**
  hound)
mat, stŏrĕa, *f*
mat, *v.t*, implĭco (1)
match (contest), certāmen, *n*; **(equal),**
  adj, pār; **(marriage —),** nuptĭae,
  f. pl
match, *v.t*, **(equal),** aequo (1)
matchless, ēgrĕgĭus
matching, *adj*, **(equal)** pār
mate, sŏcĭus, *m*; **(— in marriage),**
  conlunx, *m,f*.
mate, *v.i*, coniungor (3 *pass*)
material, *nn*, mătĕrĭa, *f*
material, *adj*, corpŏrĕus
materially, *adv*, **(much),** multum
maternal, măternus
maternity, māter, *f*, **(mother)**
mathematician, măthēmătĭcus, *m*
mathematics, măthēmătĭca, *f*
matter (substance), corpus, *n*, mătĕrĭa,
  f; **(affair),** res, *f*; **(what is the —?),**
  quid est?; **(it matters, it is import-**
  ant), rēfert *(v. impers)*
mattress, culcĭta, *f*
mature, *adj*, mātūrus, ădultus
mature, *v.t*, mātūro (1); *v.i*, mātūresco
  (3)
maturity, mātūrĭtas, *f*
maudlin, ĭneptus
maul, *v.t*, mulco (1), lănĭo (1)
maw, inglŭvĭes, *f*
maxim, praeceptum, *n*
maximum, *use adj*, maxĭmus **(bigges**
May, Māius (mensis)
may, *v.* **auxiliary, (having permission**
  to), lĭcet (2 *impers. with dat. of person*
  allowed), e.g. **you may go,** lĭcet tĭbĭ
  īre; **(having ability to),** possum
  (irreg); often expressed by sub-
  junctive mood of verb
maybe (perhaps), *adv*, fortassĕ

For List of Abbreviations used, turn to pages 3, 4

may-day, Kălendae Māiae (first day of May)
mayor, praefectus, *m*
maze, *nn*, lăbÿrinthus, *m*
meadow, prātum, *n*
meagre, măcer, ieiūnus
meagreness, ieiūnĭtas, *f*
meal (flour), fārīna, *f*; (food), cĭbus, *m*
mean, *nn*, mŏdus, *m*
mean, *adj*, (middle, average), mĕdĭus; (of low rank), hŭmĭlis; (miserly), sordĭdus
mean, *v.t*, signĭfĭco (1); (intend), in ănĭmo hăbĕo (2)
meander, *v.i*, (of a river), sĭnŭōso cursu flŭo (3) (flow on a winding course)
meaning, *nn*, signĭfĭcātĭo, *f*
meanness, hŭmĭlĭtas, *f*; (of disposition), sordes, *f. pl*
means (method), mŏdus, *m*; (opportunity), făcultas, *f*; (resources), ŏpes, *f. pl*; (by no —), *adv*, haudquāquam, nullo mŏdo
meantime, meanwhile (in the —), *adv*, intĕrĕā, intĕrim
measure, mensūra, *f*, mŏdus, *m*; (plan), consĭlĭum, *n*; (music), mŏdi, *m, pl*
measure, *v.t*, mētĭor (4 *dep*)
measureless, immensus
meat, căro, *f*
mechanic, făber, *m*, ŏpĭfex, *c*
mechanical, māchĭnālis
mechanism, māchĭnātĭo, *f*
medal, medallion, phălĕrae, ārum, *f. pl*
meddle, *v.i*, sē interpōnĕre (3 *reflex*)
mediate, *v.i*, sē interpōnĕre (3 *reflex*) intervĕnĭo (4)
mediator, dēprēcātor, *m*
medical, mĕdĭcus
medicine (art of —), ars mĕdĭcīna, *f*; (the remedy itself), mĕdĭcāmentum, *n*
mediocre, mĕdĭŏcris
mediocrity, mĕdĭŏcrĭtas, *f*
meditate, *v.t*, cōgĭto (1)
Mediterranean Sea, măre nostrum, *n*, (our sea)
medium, *use adj*, mĕdĭus (middle); (through the — of) per
medley, farrāgo, *f*
meek, mītis
meekness, ănĭmus summissus, *m*
meet, *v.t*, obvĭam fīo (*irreg*) (*with dat*); (go to —, encounter), obvĭam ĕo (*irreg*) (*with dat*); *v.i*, convĕnĭo (4); concurro (3)
meeting, *nn*, conventus, *m*
melancholy, *nn*, tristĭtĭa, *f*

melancholy, *adj*, tristis
mellow, mītis
mellow, *v.i*, mātūresco (3)
melodious, cănōrus
melody, mĕlos, *n*
melon, mēlo, *m*
melt, *v.t*, lĭquĕfăcĭo (3); (people, etc.), mŏvĕo (2); *v.i*, lĭquesco (3)
member (of a society), sŏcĭus, *m*; (of the body), membrum, *n*
membrane, membrāna, *f*
memoirs, commentārii, *m. pl*
memorable, mĕmŏrābĭlis
memorandum, lĭbellus mĕmŏrĭālis
memorial, mŏnŭmentum, *n*
memory, mĕmŏrĭa, *f*
menace, mĭnae, *f. pl*
menace, *v.t* mĭnor (1 *dep*)
menacing, *adj*, mĭnax
mend, *v.t*, rĕfĭcĭo (3), sarcĭo (4); *v.i*, (in health), mĕlĭor fīo (*irreg*) (get better)
mendacious, mendax
mendicant, mendĭcus, *m*
menial, *adj*, servīlis
mensuration, rătĭo, (*f*) mētĭendi; (system of measuring)
mental, *use genitive of* mens, *or* ănĭmus (mind)
mention, *nn*, mentĭo, *f*
mention, *v.t*, mĕmŏro (1), dīco (3)
mercantile, mercātōrum, (of merchants)
mercenary, *adj*, mercēnārĭus
merchandise, merx, *f*
merchant, mercātor, *m*
merchant-ship, nāvis ŏnĕrārĭa, *f*
merciful, mĭsĕrĭcors
merciless, crūdēlis, inclēmens
mercury (quick silver), argentum vīvum, *n*; (god), Mercŭrĭus
mercy, mĭsĕrĭcordĭa, *f*
mere, *adj*, sōlus, *or use emphatic pron*, ipse
merely, *adv*, tantummŏdo
merge, *v.i*, miscĕor (2 *pass*)
meridian, circŭlus mĕrīdĭānus, *m*
meridian, *adj*, mĕrīdĭānus
merit, *nn*, mĕrĭtum, *n*
merit, *v.t*, mĕrĕor (2 *dep*)
meritorious, dignus laude (worthy of praise)
merriment, hĭlărĭtas, *f*
merry, hĭlăris
mesh, măcŭla, *f*
mess (confused state), turba, *f*; (dirt), squālor, *m*
message, nuntĭus, *m*

messenger, nuntĭus, *m*
metal, mĕtallum, *n*
metallic, mĕtallĭcus
metamorphosis, *use vb*, transformo (1)
  (to change in shape)
metaphor, translātĭo, *f*
metaphorical, translātus
meteor, fax, *f*
method, rătĭo, *f*
methodically, ex ordĭne, *or use adv*
  phr, rătĭōne et vĭā (by reckoning
  and method)
metre, nŭmĕrus, *m*
metrical, mĕtrĭcus
metropolis, căpŭt, *n*
mettle, fĕrōcĭtas, *f*
mettlesome, ănĭmōsus, fĕrox
mew, *v.i*, (cat), quĕror (3 *dep*)
mica, phengītes, *m*
mid, *adj*, mĕdĭus
midday, *nn*, mĕrĭdĭes, *m*
midday, *adj*, mĕrĭdĭānus
middle, *adj*, mĕdĭus
middle, *nn, use* mĕdĭus *in agreement
  with noun, e.g.* the middle of the
  river, mĕdĭus flŭvĭus
middling, *adj*, mĕdĭŏcris
midnight, mĕdĭa nox, *f*
midst, *nn, use adj*, mĕdĭus
midsummer, mĕdĭa aestas, *f*
midwife, obstĕtrix, *f*
might (power), vīs, *f*
mighty, fortis, vălĭdus, magnus
migrate, *v.t*, ăbĕo (4)
migratory bird, advĕna ăvis, *f*
mild, mītis, clēmens, lēvis
mildew, rōbīgo, *f*
mildness, lēnĭtas, *f*,
mile, mille passus (*or* passŭum) (a
  thousand paces)
milestone, millĭārĭum, *n*
military, *adj*, mĭlĭtāris; (— service),
  stīpendĭa, *n.pl*.
militate against, *v.t*, făcĭo (3) contrā
  (*with acc*)
milk, lac, *n*
milk, *v.t*, mulgĕo (2)
milky, lactĕus
mill, mŏla, *f*, pistrīnum, *n*
miller, mŏlĭtor, *m*
million, dĕcĭes centēna mīlĭa
mill-stone, mŏla, *f*
mimic, *v.t*, ĭmĭtor (1 *dep*)
mince, *v.t*, concīdo (3)
mincemeat, mĭnūtal, *n*
mind, ănĭmus, *m*, mens, *f*; (intellect),
  ingĕnĭum, *n*; (to make up one's —)
  constĭtŭo (3)
mind, *v.t*, (I — my own business),
  nĕgōtĭum mĕum ăgo (3)

mindful, mĕmor (*with genit*)
mine, *adj*, mĕus
mine, *nn*, mĕtallum, *n*, cŭnīcŭlus, *m*
mine, *v.i*, fŏdĭo (3)
miner, fŏdĭens, *m*
mineral, *nn*, mĕtallum, *n*
mineral, *adj*, mĕtallĭcus
mingle, *v.i*, sē miscĕre (2 *reflex*)
miniature, *nn*, parva tăbella, *f*
minimum, *adj*, mĭnĭmus (smallest)
minister mĭnister, *m*, admĭnister, *m*
ministry (office), mĭnĭstĕrĭum, *n*
minor, *nn*, pūpillus, *m*
minority, mĭnor pars, *f*
minstrel, tībĭcen văgus (wandering—)
mint (plant), menta, *f*; (coinage),
  mŏnēta, *f*
mint, *v.t*, cūdo (3)
minute, *adj*, exĭgŭus, mĭnūtus
minute, *nn*, (of time), mōmentum, (*n*)
  tempŏris
miracle, mīrācŭlum, *n*
miraculous, mīrus
mire, lŭtum, *n*
mirror, spĕcŭlum, *n*
mirth, hĭlărĭtas, *f*
mirthful, hĭlăris
misadventure, cāsus, *m*
misanthropy, *use phr*. ŏdĭum, (*n*) ergā
  hŏmĭnes (hatred towards mankind)
misapply, *v.t*, ăbūtor (3 *dep with abl*)
misbehave, *v.i*, mălĕ sē gĕrĕre (3
  reflex)
miscalculate, *v.i*, fallor (3 *pass*), erro
  (1)
miscalculation, error, *m*
miscarriage (childbirth), ăbortus, *m*;
  (— of justice) error, (*m*) iūdĭcum
miscarry, *v.i*, (child), ăbortum făcĭo
  (3); (fail) frustrā *or* irrĭtum ēvĕnĭo
  (4)
miscellaneous, vărĭus
mischief (injury, wrong) mălĕfĭcĭum,
  n
mischievous, mălĕfĭcus; (playful),
  lascīvus
misconduct, *nn*, dēlictum, *n*
miscreant, hŏmō scĕlestus
misdeed, dēlictum, *n*
misdemeanour, dēlictum, *n*, peccātum, *n*
miser, hŏmō ăvārus
miserable, mĭser, infēlix
miserliness, ăvārĭtĭa, *f*
miserly, *adj*, ăvārus, sordĭdus
misery, mĭsĕrĭa, *f*, angor, *m*
misfortune, rēs adversae, *f*, *pl*
misgiving, praesāgĭum, *n*
misgovern, *v.t*, mălĕ rĕgo (3)
misguided (deceived), dēceptus

misinterpret, *v.t,* mălĕ interprĕtor (1 *dep*)
misjudge, *v.t,* mălĕ iūdĭco (1)
mislay, *v.t,* āmitto (3)
mislead, *v.t,* dēcĭpĭo (3)
misplace, *v.t,* ălĭēno lŏco pōno (3) **(put in an unsuitable place)**
misprint, *nn,* mendum, *n*
misrepresent, *v.t,* verto (3); **(disparage),** obtrecto (1)
misrule, *v.t,* mălĕ rĕgo (3)
miss, *v.i,* **(fail to hit or meet),** ăberro (1), frustrā mittor (3 *pass*); *v.t,* **(want),** dēsīdĕro (1)
misshapen, dēformis
missile, tēlum, *n*
mission (embassy), lēgātĭo, *f*; **(task),** ŏpus, *n*
misspend, *v.t,* perdo (3)
mist, nĕbŭla, *f*
mistake, error, *m*; **(make a —),** *v.i,* erro (1)
mistake, *v.t,* **(for someone else),** crēdĕre ălĭum esse
mistaken, falsus; **(to be —),** *v.i,* erro (1)
mistletoe, viscum, *n*
mistress (of the house, etc.), dŏmĭna, *f*; **(sweetheart),** pŭella, *f*, concŭbīna, *f*
mistrust, *v.t,* diffīdo (3 *semi-dep. with dat*)
misty, nĕbŭlōsus
misunderstand, *v.t,* haud rectē, *or* mălĕ, intellĕgo (3)
misunderstanding, error, *m*
misuse, *v.t,* ăbūtor (3 *dep. with abl*)
mitigate, *v.t,* mītĭgo (1), lēnĭo (4)
mitigation, mītĭgātĭo, *f*
mittens, mănĭcae, *f. pl*
mix, *v.t,* miscĕo (2); **(— up together),** confundo (3); *v.i,* miscĕor (2 *pass*)
mixed, *adj,* mixtus; **(indiscriminate),** prōmiscŭus
mixture, mixtūra, *f*
moan, *nn,* gĕmĭtus, *m*
moan, *v.i,* gĕmo (3)
moat, fossa, *f*
mob, turba, *f,* vulgus, *n*
mobile, mōbĭlis
mock, *v.t,* illūdo (3) *(with dat)*; dērīdĕo (2)
mockery, irrīsus, *m,* lūdĭbrĭum, *n*
mode, mŏdus, *m,* rătĭo, *f*
model, exemplum, *n,* exemplar, *n*
model, *v.t,* fingo (3)
moderate, mŏdĕrātus, mŏdĭcus
moderate, *v.t,* tempĕro (1)
moderation, mŏdus, *m,* mŏdĕrātĭo, *f*
modern, rĕcens, nŏvus

modest, vĕrēcundus
modesty, vĕrēcundĭa, *f,* pŭdor, *m*
modify, *v.t,* immūto (1)
modulate, *v.t,* flecto (3)
moist, hūmĭdus
moisten, *v.t,* hūmecto (1)
moisture, hūmor, *m*
molar, dens gĕnŭīnus
mole (animal), talpa, *f*; **(dam, etc.),** mōles, *f*; **(on the body),** naevus, *m*
molest, *v.t,* vexo (1), sollĭcĭto (1)
mollify, *v.t,* mollĭo (4)
molten, lĭquĕfactus
moment, punctum, *(n)* tempŏris; **(in a —),** *adv,* stătim; **(importance),** mōmentum, *n*
momentary, brĕvis
momentous, magni mōmenti **(of great importance)**
momentum, impĕtus, *m*
monarch, rex, *m*
monarchy, regnum, *n*
monastery, mŏnastērĭum, *n*
money, pĕcūnĭa, *f*; **(coin),** nummus, *m*; **(profit),** quaestus, *m*
money-bag, fiscus, *m*
money-lender, faenĕrātor, *m*
money-making, quaestus, *m*
moneyed, pĕcūnĭōsus
mongrel, *nn,* hibrĭda, *c*
monkey, sīmĭa, *f*
monopolize, *v.i,* use *phr. with* sōlus **(alone),** *and* hăbĕo (2)
monopoly, mŏnŏpōlĭum, *n*
monotonous, use *phr. with* mŏlestus **(laboured),** *or* sĭmĭlis **(similar)**
monster, monstrum, *n*
monstrous (huge), immānis; **(shocking),** infandus
month, mensis, *m*
monthly, *adj,* menstrŭus
monument, mŏnŭmentum, *n*
mood, affectĭo, *(f)* ănĭmi
moody, mōrōsus
moon, lūna, *f*
moonlight, lūmen, *(n)* lūnae; **(by —),** ad lūnam
moonlit, *adj,* illustris lūnā **(lighted up by the moon)**
moor, lŏca dēserta, *n.pl,* **(a lonely place)**
moor, *v.t,* **(ship, etc.),** rĕlĭgo (1)
moorhen, fŭlĭca, *f*
moot (it is a — point), nondum convēnit . . . **(it is not yet decided . . .)**
mop, *nn,* pēnĭcŭlus, *m*
mop, *v.t,* dētergĕo (2)
moral, *adj,* mŏrālis; **(of good character),** hŏnestus
moral, *nn,* **(of a story),** use *phr. with*

significo (1) (**to indicate**), *e.g.* haec
fābŭla significat ... (**this story
indicates ...**)
morale, ănĭmus, *m*
morals, morality, mōres, *m. pl*
moralize, *v.i*, dē mōrĭbus dissĕro (3)
(**discuss conduct**)
morbid, aeger, aegrōtus
more, *nn*, plus, *n*, (*with genit*), *e.g.*
more corn, plus frūmenti; (*adv.
before adjs. or advs*) *use comparative
of adj. or adv*, *e.g.* more quickly,
cĕlĕrĭus; *otherwise use* măgis (**to a
higher degree**) *or* pŏtĭus; (**in
addition**), amplĭus
moreover, *adv*, praetĕrĕā
moribund, mŏrĭbundus
morning, *nn*, tempus mātūtīnum, *n*;
(**in the —**), *adv*, mānĕ
morning, *adj*, mātūtīnus
morose, tristis
morrow (**following day**), postĕrus
dies, *m*
morsel, offa, *f*
mortal, *adj*, mortālis; (**causing death**),
mortĭfer
mortality, mortālĭtas, *f*
mortar, mortārĭum, *n*
mortgage, pignus, *n*
mortgage, *v.t*, oblĭgo (1)
mortification, offensĭo, *f*
mortify, *v.t*, (**vex**) offendo (3)
mosaic, *adj*, tessellātus
mosquito, cŭlex, *m*
moss, muscus, *m*
mossy, muscōsus
most, *adj*, plūrĭmus *or* plūrĭmum, *n*,
with genit, of noun, e.g. most importance, plūrĭmum grăvĭtātis; (**for
the — part**), *adv*, plērumque
most, *adv*, *with adjs. and advs. use
superlative*; **e.g.** most quickly,
cĕlerrĭmē; *with vbs*, maxĭmē
mostly (**usually**), *adv*, plērumque
moth, blatta, *f*
mother, māter, *f*; (**-in-law**), socrus, *f*
motherly, *adj*, māternus
motion (**movement**), mōtus, *m*; (**proposal**), rŏgātĭo, *f*
motion, *v.t*, gestu indĭco (1) (**indicate
by a gesture**)
motionless, immōtus
motive, causa, *f*
mottled, măcŭlōsus
motto, sententĭa, *f*
mould (**soil**), sŏlum, *n*; (**shape**),
forma, *f*
mould, *v.t*, formo (1)
mouldiness, sĭtus, *m*
mouldy, mūcĭdus

moult, *v.i*, plūmas exŭo (3) (**lay down
feathers**)
mound, tŭmŭlus, *m*
mount, *v.t* (**horse, ship, etc.**), conscendo (3); *otherwise*, scando (3)
mounted (**on horseback**), *adj*, ĕquo
vectus
mountain, mons, *m*, iŭgum, *n*
mountaineer, hŏmŏ montānus
mountainous, montŭōsus
mourn, *v.t. and v.i*, lūgĕo (2)
mournful luctŭōsus; (**of sounds, etc.**),
lūgŭbris
mourning, luctus, *m*, maeror, *m*
mouse, mūs, *c*
mouse-trap, muscĭpŭlum, *n*
mouth, ōs, *n*; (**of river**), ostĭum, *n*
mouthful, bucca, *f*, (**filled out cheek**)
mouth-piece interprĕs, *c*, ōrātor, *m*
movable, mōbĭlis
move, *v.t*, mŏvĕo (2); *v.i*, sē mŏvĕre
(*2 reflex*)
movement, mōtus, *m*
moving, *adj*, (**of pity, etc.**), mĭsĕrābĭlis
mow, *v.t*, sĕco (1)
much, *adj*, multus; (**too —**), nĭmĭus
much, *adv*, multum; *with comparative
adj. or adv*, multo, *e.g.* much bigger,
multo māior
muck, stercus, *n*
mucous, *adj*, mucōsus
mud, muddiness, lŭtum, *n*
muddle, *v.t*, confundo (3)
muddle, *nn*, turba, *f*
muddy, lŭtĕus
muffle, *v.t*, obvolvo (3)
mug, pōcŭlum, *n*
muggy, ūmĭdus
mulberry (**tree**), mōrus, *f*; (**fruit**),
mōrum, *n*
mule, mūlus, *m*
mullet, mullus, *m*
multifarious, vărĭus
multiplication, multĭplĭcātĭo,
multiply, *v.t*, multĭplĭco (1)
multitude, multĭtūdo, *f*
multitudinous, plūrĭmus, crēber
mumble, *v.i. and v.t*, murmŭro (1)
munch, *v.t*, mandūco (1)
mundane, *use genit. of* mundus (**world**)
municipal, mūnĭcĭpālis
municipality, mūnĭcĭpĭum, *n*
munificence, mūnĭfĭcentĭa, *f*
munificent, mūnĭfĭcus
munition, appărātus (*m*) belli (**war-
equipment**), arma, *n.pl*
murder, *nn*, caedes, *f*
murder, *v.t*, nĕco (1), interfĭcĭo (3)
murderer, hŏmĭcīda, *c*, sīcārĭus, *m*
murky, cālĭgĭnōsus

For List of Abbreviations used, turn to pages 3, 4

murmur, *nn*, murmur, *n*,
murmur, *v.i*, murmŭro (1)
muscle, tŏrus, *m*, lăcertus, *m*
muscular, lăcertōsus
muse, *nn*, mūsa, *f*
muse, *v.i*, mĕdĭtor (1 *dep*)
museum, mūsēum, *n*
mushroom, fungus, *m*
music, mūsĭca, *f*, cantus, *m*
musical, mūsĭcus; (person), stŭdĭōsus
 mūsĭcōrum (keen on music)
musician, mūsĭcus, *m*
muslin, byssus, *f*
must, *v.i*, (obligation), *use gerundive*:
 e.g. Carthage must be destroyed,
 Carthāgo dēlenda est; (duty),
 ŏportet (2 *impers*) *with acc. of person
 and infinitive, e.g.* we must go,
 nōs ŏportet īre
mustard, sĭnāpi, *n*
muster, *nn*, dēlectus, *m*
muster, *v.t*, convŏco (1), rĕcensĕo (2);
 v.i, convĕnĭo (4)
musty, mūcĭdus
mutable, mūtābĭlis
mute, *adj*, mūtus, tăcĭtus
mutilate, *v.t*, mŭtĭlo (1), trunco (1)
mutilated, mŭtĭlus, truncātus
mutiny, sēdĭtĭo, *f*
mutiny, *v.i*, sēdĭtĭōnem făcĭo (3)
mutter, *v.i. and v.t*, musso (1)
muttering, *nn*, murmur *n*
mutton, ŏvilla căro, *f*, (sheep's flesh)
mutual, mūtŭus
muzzle (for the mouth), fiscella, *f*
my, mĕus
myriad (10,000), dĕcem mīlĭa (*with
 genit*)
myrrh, murra, *f*
myrtle, myrtus, *f*
myself (*emphatic*), ipse; (*reflexive*) mē
mysterious, occultus
mystery, rēs abdĭta, *f*; (religious, etc.),
 mystērĭa, *n.pl*
mystic, mystĭcus
mystification, ambāges, *f*, *pl*
mystify, *use adv. phr*, per ambāges (in
 an obscure way)
myth, fābŭla, *f*
mythology, fābŭlae, *f*, *pl*

N

nab, *v.t*, (catch), apprĕhendo (3)
nag, *nn*, căballus, *m*
nag, *v.t*, incrĕpĭto (1), obiurgo (1)
nail (finger, toe), unguis, *m*; (of
 metal), clāvus, *m*

nail, *v.t*, clāvīs affīgo (3) (fix on with
 nails)
naive, simplex
naked, nūdus
nakedness, *use adj*, nūdus (naked)
name, nōmen, *n*; (personal —, equivalent to our Christian name), praenōmen, *n*; (— of a class of things),
 vŏcābŭlum, *n*; (reputation), existĭmātĭo, *f*
name, *v.t*, nōmĭno (1), appello (1)
nameless, nōmĭnis expers (without a
 name)
namely (I mean to say), dīco (3)
namesake, *use phr*, cui est ĭdem
 nōmen (who has the same name)
nap, *v.i*, (sleep), paulisper dormĭo (4)
napkin, mappa, *f*
narcissus, narcissus, *m*
narcotic, mĕdĭcāmentum somnĭfĕrum,
 n, (sleep-bringing drug)
narrate, narro (1)
narrative, narrātĭo, *f*; *adj, use vb*,
 narro (1) (narrate)
narrator, narrātor, *m*
narrow, angustus
narrow, *v.t*, cŏarto (1); *v.i*, sē cŏartāre
 (1 *reflex*)
narrowly (nearly, scarcely), *adj*, vix
narrow-minded, anĭmi angusti (of
 narrow mind)
narrowness, angustĭae, *f*, *pl*
nasal, nārĭum (of the nose)
nastiness, foedĭtas, *f*
nasty, foedus
natal, nātālis
nation, gens, *f*
national, dŏmestĭcus *or use genit.of* gens
nationality, pŏpŭlus, *m*, cīvĭtas, *f*
native, *adj*, indĭgĕna; (— land),
 pătrĭa, *f*
native, *nn*, indĭgĕna, *c*
nativity (birth), gĕnus, *n*, ortus, *m*
natural, nātūrālis; (inborn), nātīvus,
 innātus; (genuine), sincērus
naturalize, *v.t*, cīvĭtātem do (1) (*with
 dat*) (grant citizenship)
naturally, sĕcundum nātūram (according to nature)
nature, nātūra, *f*; (character of
 persons), ingĕnĭum, *n*
naught, nĭhil, *n*
naughty, imprŏbus, lascīvus
nausea, nausĕa, *f*
nauseate, *v.t*, fastīdĭo (4)
nautical, nāvālis, nautĭcus
navel, umbĭlīcus, *m*
navigable, nāvĭgābĭlis

navigate, *v.i*, nāvĭgo (1)
navigation, nāvĭgātĭo, *f*
navy, classis, *f*
nay (no), nōn
neap-tide, mĭnĭmus aestus, *m*
near, *adv*, prŏpĕ, iuxtā
near, *prep*, *adv*, prŏpĕ
nearly, *adv*, prŏpĕ, fermē
nearness, prŏpinquĭtas, *f*, vīcīnĭtas, *f*
neat, nĭtĭdus, mundus
neatly, *adv*, mundē
neatness, mundĭtĭa, *f*
nebulous, nĕbŭlōsus
necessarily, *adv*, nĕcessārĭo
necessary, nĕcessārĭus, nĕcesse
necessitate, *v.t*, (compel), cōgo (3)
necessity (inevitableness), nĕcessĭtas, *f*; (something indispensable), rēs nĕcessārĭa, *f*
neck, collum, *n*, cervix, *f*
necklace, mŏnīle, *n*
need, *nn*, ŏpus, *n*, (*with abl. of thing needed or infinitive*); (lack), ĭnŏpĭa, *f*
need, *v.t*, ĕgĕo (2) (*with abl*)
needful, nĕcessārĭus, *or use nn*, ŏpus, *n*, (necessity)
needle, acus, *f*
needless, nōn nĕcessārĭus
needy, ĕgens
nefarious, nĕfārĭus
negation, nĕgātĭo, *f*
negative, *adj*, *use* nōn (not), *or* nĕgo (1) (to deny)
neglect, *v.t*, neglĕgo (3), praetermitto (3)
neglect, *nn*, neglĕgentĭa, *f*
negligent, neglĕgens
negotiate, *v.t*, ăgo (3) dē (*with abl. of thing*) cum (*with abl. of person*)
negotiation, *use vb*, ăgo (3), (to negotiate)
negress, Aethĭŏpissa, *f*
negro, Aethĭops, *m*
neigh, *v.i*, hinnĭo (4)
neigh, neighing, hinnītus, *m*
neighbour, vīcīnus, *m*; (of nations), *adj*, finĭtĭmus
neither, *pron*, neuter
neither, *conj*, nĕque, nĕc; neither . . . nor, neque . . . neque, *or* nec . . . nec
nephew, fīlĭus, (*m*) frātris (*or* sŏrōris)
nerve, nervi, *m. pl*
nervous (afraid), tĭmĭdus
nervousness, tĭmĭdĭtas, *f*, formīdo, *f*
nest, nīdus, *m*
nestle, *v.i*, haerĕo (2), ĭaccĕo (2)
nestlings, nīdi, *m*, *pl*
net, rētĕ, *n*
net, *v.t*, plăgīs căpĭo (3) (catch with a net)

nettle, urtīca, *f*
net-work, rētĭcŭlum, *n*
neuter, neuter
neutral, mĕdĭus; (to be or remain —), neutri parti făvĕo (2) (to favour neither side)
neutralize, *v.t*, aequo (1), compenso (1)
never, *adv*, numquam
nevertheless, nĭhĭlōmĭnus, tămen
new, nŏvus; (fresh), rĕcens
new-comer, advĕna, *c*
newly, *adv*, nūper, mŏdo
newness, nŏvĭtas, *f*
news, nuntĭus, *m*
newspaper, acta dĭurna, *n.pl*
newt, lăcertus, *m*
next, *adj*, proxĭmus; (on the — day), *adv*, postrīdĭē
next, *adv*, (of time), dĕinceps, dĕinde; (of place), iuxtā, proxĭmē
nibble, *v.t*, rodo (3)
nice (pleasant), dulcis; (particular), fastīdĭōsus; (precise), subtīlĭs
nicety (subtlety), subtīlĭtas, *f*
niche, aedĭcŭla, *f*
in the nick of time, in ipso artĭcŭlo tempŏris
nickname, agnōmen, *n*, (an additional name)
niece, fīlĭa, (*f*) frātris (*or* sŏrōris)
niggardly, ăvārus, parcus
night, nox, *f*; (by, at —), *adv*, noctu, nocte; (at mid —), mĕdĭā nocte; (at the fall of —), prīmis tĕnĕbris
nightingale, luscĭnĭa, *f*
nimble, ăgĭlis
nine, nŏvem; (— times), *adv*, nŏvĭens; (— each), nŏvēni; (— hundred), nongenti
nineteen, undēvīginti
ninety, nōnāginta
ninth, nōnus
nip, *v.t*, vellīco (1); (with frost), ūro (3)
nipple, păpilla, *f*
no, *adj*, nullus, nĭhĭl (*foll. by genit*)
no, *adv*, nōn, mĭnĭmē; (to say —), *v.i*, nĕgo (1)
nobility, (of birth), nōbĭlĭtas, *f*; (people of noble birth), nōbĭles, *m. pl*
noble (of birth), nōbĭlis; (of birth or character), gĕnĕrōsus
nobody, nēmo, *m*, *f*
nocturnal, nocturnus
nod, *v.i*, nūto (1); (assent), annŭo (3)
nod, *nn*, nūtus, *m*
noise, strĕpĭtus, *m*, sŏnĭtus, *m*; (of shouting), clāmor, *m*; (to make a —), *v.i*, strĕpo (3)

noiseless, tăcĭtus
noisily, *adv*, cum strĕpĭtu
noisy, *use a phr. with* strĕpo **(to make a noise)**
nomadic, văgus
nominal, *use* nōmen **(name)**
nominally, *adv*, nōmĭne
nominate, *v.t*, nōmĭno (1)
nomination, nōmĭnātĭo, *f*
nominee, *use vb.* nōmĭno, **(name)**
nonchalant, aequo ănĭmo **(with un-ruffled mind)**
nondescript, nōn insignis
none, nullus
nonentity, nĭhil, *n*
nonsense, nūgae, *f. pl*, ĭneptĭae, *f. pl*
nonsensical, ĭneptus, absurdus
nook, angŭlus, *m*
noon, mĕrīdĭes, *m*; **(at —)**, *adv*, mĕrīdĭe; *adj*, mĕrīdĭanus
noose, lăquĕus, *m*
nor, *conj*, nĕc, nĕque
normal **(usual)**, ūsĭtātus
north, *nn*, septentrĭōnes, *m. pl*
north, northern, northerly, *adj*, septentrĭōnālis
north-east wind, ăquĭlo, *m*
north-pole, arctos, *f*
northwards, versus ad septentrĭōnes
north wind, ăquĭlo, *m*
nose, nāsus, *m*, nāres, *f. pl* **(nostrils)**
not, nōn, haud; **(— at all)**, *adv*, haudquāquam; **(not even . . .)**, nē . . . quĭdem; **(and not)**, nĕc, nĕque; **(in commands)**, e.g. do not go, nōli īre
notable, insignis, mĕmŏrābĭlis
notary, scrība, *m*
notch, *nn*, incīsūra, *f*
notch, *v.t*, incīdo (3)
note **(explanatory, etc.)**, adnŏtātĭo, *f*; **(mark)**, nŏta, *f*; **(letter)**, littĕrae, *f. pl*
note, *v.t*, **(notice)**, ănĭmadverto (3); **(jot down)**, ēnŏto (1)
note-book, commentārĭi, *m. pl*
noted **(well-known)**, insignis
nothing, nĭhil, *n*; **(good for —)**, nēquam
nothingness, nĭhĭlum, *n*
notice, *v.t*, ănĭmadverto (3)
notice, *nn*, **(act of noticing)**, ănĭmadversĭo, *f*; **(written —)**, prōscriptĭo, *f*
noticeable, insignis
notification, dēnuntĭātĭo, *f*
notify, *v.t*, dēnuntĭo (1)
notion, nŏtĭo, *f*
notoriety, infāmĭa, *f*
notorious, nŏtus, fāmōsus

notwithstanding, *adv*, nĭhĭlōmĭnus, tămen
nought, nĭhil
noun, nōmen, *n*, **(name)**
nourish, *v.t*, ălo (3)
nourishment, ălĭmentum, *n*
novel, *nn*, **(story)**, fābŭla, *f*
novel, *adj*, **(new)**, nŏvus
novelist, fābŭlārum scriptor, *m*, **(writer of stories)**
novelty **(strangeness)**, nŏvĭtas, *f*
November, Nŏvember **(mensis)**
novice, tīro, *m*
now **(at the present time)**, *adv*, nunc; **(at the time of the action)**, iam; **(just —)**, mŏdŏ; **(now . . . now)**, mŏdŏ . . . mŏdŏ; **(— and then)**, ălĭquandŏ
nowadays, *adv*, nunc
nowhere, *adv*, nusquam
noxious, nŏcens
nozzle, nāsus, *m*
nude, nūdus
nudge, *v.t*, fŏdĭco (1)
nuisance, incŏmmŏdum, *n, or use adj*, mŏlestus **(troublesome)**
null, irrĭtus, vānus
nullify, *v.t*, irrĭtum făcĭo (3)
numb, torpens; **(to be —)**, *v.i*, torpĕo (2)
numb, *v.t*, torpĕfăcĭo (3)
number, *nn*, nŭmĕrus, *m*; **(what —, how many?)**, quot?; **(a large —)**, multĭtūdo, *f*
number, *v.t*, nŭmĕro (1)
numbering **(in number)**, ad *(with acc)*
numberless, innŭmĕrābĭlis
numbness, torpor, *m*
numerically, *adv*, nŭmĕro
numerous, plūrĭmi, crēber
nun, mŏnăcha, *f*
nuptial, nuptĭālis, iŭgālis
nuptials, nuptĭae, *f. pl*
nurse, nūtrix, *f*
nurse, *v.t*, **(the sick)**, cūro (1); **(cherish)**, fŏvĕo (2)
nursery **(for plants)**, sēmĭnārĭum, *n*
nurture, ēdŭcātĭo, *f*
nut, nut-tree, nux, *f*
nutriment, ălĭmentum, *n*
nutrition, ălĭmentum, *n*
nutritious, vălens
nutshell, pūtāmen, *n*
nymph, nympha, *f*

O

o! oh! o! oh!; **(Oh that . . .)** ŭtĭnam . . .
oak, quercus, *f*; **(holm —)**, īlex, *f*; **(oak-wood)**, rōbur, *n*

oak, oaken, *adj*, quernus
oakum, stuppa, *f*
oar, rēmus, *m*
oarsmen, rēmĭges, *m. pl*
oats, ăvēna, *f*
oath, iusiūrandum, *n*; (to take an—),
   v.i, iusiūrandum accĭpĭo (3);
   (military —), săcrāmentum, *n*
oatmeal, fărīna ăvēnācĕa, *f*
obdurate, obstĭnātus, dūrus
obedience, ŏbēdĭentĭa, *f*; *or use vb*,
   pārĕo (2) (to obey, *with dat*)
obeisance (to make an —), ădōro (1)
   (reverence)
obelisk, ŏbĕliscus, *m*
obese, ŏbēsus
obey, *v.i. and v.t*, pārĕo (2) (*with dat*),
   ŏbēdĭo (4) (*with dat*)
object, *nn*, (thing), rēs, *f*; (aim), consĭlĭum, *n*. fīnis, *m*; (to be an — of
   hatred), ŏdĭo esse (*irreg*)
object, *v.t*, rĕcūso (1), nōlo (*irreg*)
objection, *use vb*, rĕcūso (1) (object to)
objectionable, ingrātus, *m*
objective *nn*, quod petĭtur (that is
   sought)
obligation (moral), offĭcĭum, *n*; (legal),
   oblĭgātĭo, *f*; (religious —, conscientiousness), rĕlĭgĭo, *f*; (to put
   someone under an —), *v.t*, obstringo
   (3); (to be under an —), *v.i*, dēbĕo (2)
obligatory (it is —), ŏportet (2 *impers*)
   or use gerundive of vb
oblige, *v.t*, obstringo (3); (compel),
   cōgo (3)
obliging, cōmis
oblique (slanting), oblīquus
obliterate, *v.t*, dēlĕo (2)
oblivion, oblīvĭo, *f*
oblivious, immĕmor
oblong, *adj*, oblongus
obloquy, vĭtŭpĕrātĭo, *f*
obnoxious, invīsus, noxĭus
obscene, obscēnus
obscenity, obscēnĭtas, *f*
obscure, obscūrus, caecus, rĕcondĭtus; (of birth, etc.), hŭmĭlis
obscure, *v.t*, obscūro (1)
obscurity, obscūrĭtas, *f*
obsequies, exsĕquĭae, *f. pl*
obsequious, obsĕquens, offĭcĭōsus
observance, observantĭa, *f*, conservātĭo *f*; (practice), rītus, *m*
observant, attentus, dīlĭgens
observation, observātĭo, *f*; (attention),
   ănĭmadversĭo, *f*; (remark), dictum, *n*
observatory, spĕcŭla, *f*
observe, *v.t*, observo (1), ănĭmadverto
   (3); (remark), dīco (3); (maintain),
   conservo (1)

observer, spectātor, *m*
obsolete, obsŏlētus; (to become —),
   v.i, obsŏlesco (3), sĕnesco (3)
obstacle, impĕdīmentum, *n*
obstinacy, pertĭnācĭa, *f*
obstinate, pertĭnax
obstreperous, (noisy), vōcĭfĕrans
obstruct, *v.t*, obstrŭo (3), obsto (1)
   (*with dat*)
obstruction, impĕdīmentum, *n*
obtain, *v.t*, ădĭpiscor (3 *dep*), nanciscor
   (3 *dep*), consĕquor (3 *dep*), (—
   possession of), pŏtĭor (4 *dep. with
   abl*)
obtrude, *v.t*, inculco (1)
obtrusive, mŏlestus
obtuse, hĕbes
obviate, *v.t*, (meet), obvĭam ĕo (4
   irreg) (*with dat*)
obvious, ăpertus, mănĭfestus
occasion (opportunity), occāsĭo, *f*;
   (cause), causa, *f*; (on that —), illo
   tempŏre
occasion, *v.t* mŏvĕo (2), fĕro (*irreg*)
occasionally, *adv*, interdum, rāro
occult, occultus, arcānus
occupancy, possessĭo, *f*
occupant, possessor, *m*
occupation (act of —), *use vb*, occŭpo
   (1); (employment), quaestus, *m*;
   nĕgŏtĭum, *n*
occupy, *v.t*, occŭpo (1), obtĭnĕo (2);
   (to be occupied with something), *v.t*,
   tĕnĕor (2 *pass*)
occur, *v.i*, (take place), accĭdo (3);
   (come into the mind), in mentem
   vĕnĭo (4), sŭbĕo (4) (*with dat*)
occurrence, rēs, *f*
ocean, ōcĕănus, *m*
ochre, ōchra, *f*
octagon, octōgōnum, *n*
October, Octōber (mensis)
oculist, ŏcŭlārĭus mĕdĭcus, *m*
odd (numbers, etc.), impar; (strange),
   nŏvus
odds (to be at — with), *v.i*, dissĭdĕo
   (2) ab (*with abl*)
odious, ŏdĭōsus, invīsus
odium, invĭdĭa, *f*, ŏdĭum, *n*
odorous, ŏdōrātus
odour, ŏdor, *m*
of, *usually the genit. of the noun, e.g.*
   the head of the boy, căput pŭĕri;
   (made —), ex (*with abl*); (about,
   concerning), dē (*with abl*)
off, *adv*, *often expressed by prefix* ab-
   with vb, e.g. to cut off, abscīdo (3);
   (far —), *adv*, prŏcul; (a little way
   —), *prep and adv*, prŏpe
offal (waste), quisquĭlĭae, *f. pl*

For List of Abbreviations used, turn to pages 3, 4

offence, offensĭo, *f*; (crime, etc.), dēlictum, *n*; (to take — at), aegrē fĕro (*irreg.*)

offend, *v.t,* offendo (3), laedo (3); (to be offended), aegrē fĕro (*irreg*) (tolerate with displeasure)

offensive, *adj,* ŏdĭōsus, grăvis

offensive, *nn,* (military), *use phr,* bellum infĕro (*irreg*) (to inflict war)

offer, *nn,* condĭcĭo, *f*

offer, *v.t,* offĕro (*irreg*); (stretch out), porrĭgo (3); (give), do (1)

offering (gift), dōnum, *n*

office (political power), măgĭstrātus, *m*; (duty), offĭcĭum, *n*; (place of business), fŏrum, *n*

officer (military), praefectus, *m*

official, *nn,* măgĭstrātus, *m,* mĭnister, *m*

official, *adj,* (state), pūblĭcus

officiate, *v.i,* (perform), fungor (3 *dep*)

officious, mŏlestus

offing, (in the —), *use* longē (far off), *or* prŏpĕ (near), *acc. to sense*

offshoot, surcŭlus, *m*

offspring, prōgĕnĭes, *f* lībĕri, *m, pl*

often, *adv,* saepĕ; (how —?), quŏtĭes?; (so —), *adv,* tŏtĭes

ogle, *v.t,* ŏcŭlis līmis intŭĕor (2 *dep*) (look at with sidelong glances)

oil, ŏlĕum, *n*

oily, ŏlĕācĕus

ointment, unguentum, *n*

old, vĕtus; (of persons), sĕnex; (so many years —, of persons), nātus (*with acc. of extent of time*), *e.g.* three years old, tres annos nātus; (— age), sĕnectus, *f*; (— man), sĕnex, *m*; (— woman), ănus, *f*

olden, priscus

oldness, vĕtustas, *f*

oligarchy, dŏmĭnātĭo, (*f*) paucōrum (rule of a few)

olive (tree), ŏlĕa, *f*

Olympic, *adj,* Ŏlympĭcus; (— Games), Ŏlympĭa, *n.pl*

omelet, lăgănum, *n*

omen, ōmen, *n*

ominous, infaustus

omission, praetermissĭo, *f*

omit, *v.t,* ŏmitto (3), praetermitto (3)

omnipotent, omnĭpŏtens

on, *prep,* in (*with abl*); (in the direction of, *e.g.* on the right), ā, āb (*with abl*); (— everyside), *adv,* undĭque; (of time), *abl case, e.g.* on the Ides of March, Ĭdĭbus Martĭis; (about a subject), dē (*with abl*)

once, *num. adv,* sĕmel; (— upon a time), ōlim, ălĭquandŏ; (at —, immediately), stătim; (at the same time), sĭmul

one, *num. adj,* ūnus; (in —s, singly), *adv,* singillātim, *adj,* singŭli; (at — time), *adv,* ălĭquandŏ; (one ... another), ălĭus ... ălĭus; (one ... the other), alter ... alter; (a certain), quĭdam; (indefinite), *use* 2nd *pers sing. of the vb*

onerous, grăvis

oneself (*emphatic*) ipsĕ; (*reflexive*), sē

one-sided, inaequālis

onion, caepa, *f*

onlooker, circumstans, *m*

only, *adj,* ūnus, sōlus, ūnĭcus

only, *adv,* sōlum, tantum, mŏdŏ; (not only ...), non mŏdŏ ...

onset, impĕtus, *m*

onwards, *adv,* porro, *often use compound vb. with* pro, *e.g.* prōcēdĕre (3) (to go onwards)

ooze, *nn,* ūlīgo, *f*

ooze, *v.i,* māno (1)

oozy, ūlīgĭnōsus

opal, ŏpălus, *m*

opaque, caecus

open, *v.t,* ăpĕrĭo (4), pătĕfăcĭo (3), pando (3); (inaugurate), consēcro (1); *v.i,* sē ăpĕrīre (4 *reflex*); (gape open), hisco (3)

open, *adj,* ăpertus; (wide —), pătens, hĭans; (to lie, stand or be —), pătĕo (2); (— handed), *adj,* lībĕrālis

opening (dedication), consēcrātĭo, *f*; (hole), fŏrāmen, *n*; (opportunity), occāsĭo, *f*

openly, *adv,* pălam

operate, *v.t,* (set in motion), mŏvĕo (2); *v.i,* (in war), rem gĕro (3)

operation (task), ŏpus, *n*; (military —), rēs bellĭca, *f*; (naval —), rēs mărĭtĭma, *f*

operative, *adj,* effĭcax

opiate, mĕdĭcāmentum somnĭfĕrum, *n,* (sleep-bringing drug)

opinion, sententĭa, *f,* ŏpīnĭo, *f,* existĭmātĭo, *f*

opium, ŏpĭum, *n*

opponent, adversārĭus, *m*

opportune, opportūnus

opportunity, occāsĭo, *f,* cōpĭa, *f,* făcultas, *f*

oppose, *v.t,* oppōno (3); (resist), rĕsisto (3 *with dat*), adversor (1 *dep*)

opposite, *adj,* adversus, contrārĭus, dīversus

opposite (to), *prep*, contrā (*with acc*)
opposition (from people), *use partic*, adversans *or* rĕsistens; (from a party), *use* factĭo, *f*, (party)
oppress, *v.t*, opprĭmo (3)
oppression (tyranny), iniūrĭa, *f*
oppressive, grăvis, mŏlestus
oppressor, tўrannus, *m*
opprobrious, turpis
optical, *adj*, *use genit. case of* ŏcŭlus, *m*, (eye)
option, optĭo, *f*
opulence, ŏpŭlentĭa, *f*, ŏpes, *f*, *pl*
opulent, dīves, lŏcŭples
or, aut, vel; (either . . . or), aut . . . aut, vel . . . vel; (whether . . . or) (*questions*), ŭtrum . . . an; (or not) (*direct questions*), annon, (*indirect questions*), necne
oracle, ōrăcŭlum, *n*
oral, *use* vox (voice)
oration, ōrătĭo, *f*
orator, ōrātor, *m*
oratory, ars ōrātōrĭa, *f*
orb, orbit, orbis, *m*
orchard, pōmārĭum, *n*
orchid, orchis, *f*
ordain, *v.t*, ēdīco (3), stătŭo (3)
ordeal, discrīmen, *n*
order, *nn*, (arrangement), ordo, *m*; (in —), *adv*, ordĭne; (command, direction), iussum, *n*; (class, rank), ordo, *m*; (in — to), ut
order, *v.t*, (command), iŭbĕo (2); (arrange), dispōno (3)
orderly, *adj*, (behaviour), mŏdestus; (arrangement), ordĭnātus dispŏsĭtus
orderly, *nn*, stător, *m*
ordinary, ūsĭtātus, mĕdĭŏcris
ordnance, tormenta, *n.pl*
ore, aes, *n*
organ (of the body), membrum, *n*
organization, dispŏsĭtĭo, *f*
organize, *v.t*, ordĭno (1)
orgies, orgĭa, *n.pl*; (revelry), cōmis-sātĭo, *f*
orient, ŏrĭens, *m*
oriental, *use genit. of* ŏrĭens (orient)
orifice, fŏrāmen, *n*, os, *n*
origin, ŏrīgo, *f*, princĭpĭum, *n*
original, princĭpālis, antīquus, (one's own), prŏprĭus
originally, *adv*, princĭpĭo, ĭnĭtĭo
originate, *v.i*, ŏrĭor (4 *dep*)
originator, auctor, *m*
ornament, *nn*, ornāmentum, *n*
ornament, *v.t*, orno (1)
ornate, *adj*, ornātus, pictus
orphan, orbus, *m*
oscillate, *v.i*, quătĭor (3 *pass*)

oscillation, *nse vb*. quătĭor (*above*)(3 *pass*)
osier, *nn*, vīmen, *n*
osier, *adj*, vīmĭnĕus
osprey, ossĭfrăgus, *m*
ostensible, *use adv. below*
ostensibly, *adv*, per spĕcĭem
ostentation, ostentātĭo, *f*
ostentatious, glōrĭōsus
ostler, ăgāso, *m*
ostracise, *v.t*, vīto (1) (avoid)
ostrich, strūthĭŏcămēlus, *m*
other, *adj*, ălĭus; (the — of two), alter; (the others, the rest), cētĕri
others, *adj*, (belonging to —), ălĭēnus
otherwise, *adv*, (differently), ălĭter; (in other respects also), ălĭŏqui
otter, lūtra, *f*
ought, *v.auxil*, dĕbĕo (2), ŏportet (2 *impers, with acc. of person*), *e.g.* I ought, ŏportet mē
ounce, uncĭa, *f*
our, ours, noster
ourselves (*in apposition to subject*), ipsi; (*reflexive*), nos
out, *adv*, (being out), fŏris; (going out), fŏras
out of, *prep*, ē, ex, dē (*with abl*); extrā (*with acc*); (on account of), propter (*with acc*)
outbid, *v.t*, *use phr*, plūs offĕro quam . . . (offer more than . . .)
outbreak, *use vb*. ŏrĭor (4 *dep*) (to arise); (beginning), ĭnĭtĭum, *n*
outcast, prŏfŭgus, *m*
outcome (result), exĭtus, *m*
outcry, clāmor, *m*
outdo, *v.t*, sŭpĕro (1)
outdoors, *adv*, fŏras
outer, *adj*, extĕrĭor
outfit (equipment), appărātus, *m*
outflank, *v.i*, circŭmĕo (4)
outgrow, *v.t*, *use phr*, magnĭtūdĭne sŭpĕro (1) (surpass in size)
outhouse, tŭgŭrĭum, *n*
outlast, *v.t*, dĭŭturnĭtāte sŭpĕro (surpass in duration)
outlaw, *nn*, prŏscrīptus, *m*
outlaw, *v.t*, prŏscrībo (3)
outlay, *nn*, sumptus, *m*
outlet, exĭtus, *m*
outline, fīnis, *m*, ădumbrātĭo, *f*
outlive, *v.i*, sŭperstĕs sum (*irreg*) (to be a survivor)
outlook (future), fŭtūra, *n.pl*
outnumber, *v.t*, plūres nŭmĕro esse quam . . . (to be more in number than . . .)
outpost, stătĭo, *f*
outrage, *nn*, iniūrĭa, *f*

outrage, *v.t*, vĭŏlo (1)
outrageous, indignus
outright, *adv*, prorsus; (immediately), stătim
outset, ĭnĭtĭum, *n*
outside, *nn*, extĕrna pars, *f*; (on the —), *adv*, extrinsĕcus; (appearance), spĕcĭes, *f*, frons, *f*
outside, *adj*, externus
outside, *adv*, extrā
outside of, *prep*, extrā *(with acc)*
outskirts, *use adj*. sŭburbānus (near the city)
outspoken (frank), līber
outstretched, porrectus
outstrip, *v.t*, sŭpĕro (1)
outward, *adj*, externus
outwardly, *adv*, extrā
outweigh, *v.t*, grăvĭtāte sŭpĕro (1) (surpass in weight)
outwit, *v.t*, dēcĭpĭo (3)
oval, *adj*, ōvātus
oven, furnus, *m*
over, *prep*, (above, across, more than), sŭper *(with acc)*
over, *adv*, (above), sŭper, suprā; (left —), *adj*, rĕlĭquus; (it is —, all up with), actum est; (— and — again), *adv*, ĭdentĭdem
overawe, *v.t*, percello (3)
overbearing, sŭperbus
overboard, *adv*, ex nāvi
overcast (sky), nūbĭlus
overcoat, lăcerna, *f*
overcome, *v.t*, vinco (3), sŭpĕro (1)
overdone, *use adv*, nĭmis (too much)
overdue, *use adv*, dĭūtĭus (too long), and dĭffĕro *(irreg)*, (to put off)
overflow, *v.i*, effundor (3 *pass*); *v.t*, ĭnundo (1)
overgrown, obsĭtus
overhang, *v.i*, immĭnĕo (2), impendĕo (2) *(both with dat)*
overhanging, impendens
overhasty, praeceps
overhaul, *v.t*, (repair), rĕsarcĭo (4)
overhead, *adv*, insŭper
overhear, *v.t*, excĭpĭo (3)
overjoyed, laetĭtĭā ēlātus (elated with joy)
overland, *adv*, terrā, per terram
overlap, *v.t*, (overtake), sŭpervĕnĭo (4)
overlay, *v.t*, indūco (3)
overload, *v.t*, grăvo (1)
overlook, *v.t*, prōspĭcĭo (3); (forgive), ignosco (3) *(with dat)*; (neglect), praetermitto (3)
overmuch, *adv*, nĭmis
overpower, *v.t*, opprĭmo (3)

overrate, *v.t*, plūris aestĭmo (1) (value too highly)
override, *v.t*, praeverto (3)
overrule, *v.t*, vinco (3)
overrun, *v.t*, pervăgor (1 *dep*)
oversee, *v.t*, cūro (1), inspĭcĭo (3)
overseer, cūrātor, *m*
overshadow, *v.t*, offĭcĭo (3) *(with dat)*
oversight (omission), error, *m*, neglĕgentĭa, *f*, *or use vb*, praetermitto (3) (overlook)
overspread, *v.t*, obdūco (3)
overt, ăpertus, plānus
overtake, *v.t*, consĕquor (3 *dep*)
overtax (strength, etc.), *v.t*, nĭmis ūtor (3 *dep*) *(with abl)*
overthrow, *nn*, rŭīna, *f*
overthrow, *v.t*, ēverto (3), opprĭmo (3)
overtop, *v.t*, sŭpĕro (1)
overture (to make —s), *use vb*. instĭtŭo (3) (to begin)
overweening, sŭperbus
overwhelm, *v.t*, opprĭmo (3), obrŭo (3)
overwork, *v.i*, nĭmis lăbōro (1)
overwrought (exhausted), confectus
owe, *v.t*, dēbĕo (2)
owing to, *prep*, (on account of), propter, ob *(both with acc)*
owl, būbo, *m*, strix, *f*
own, *adj*, prŏprĭus; *often expressed by possessive pron*, e.g. my own, mĕus
own, *v.t*, (possess), tĕnĕo (2), possĭdĕo (2); (confess), fătĕor (2 *dep*)
owner, possessor *m*, dŏmĭnus, *m*
ox, bŏs, *c*
oxherd, armentārĭus, *m*
oyster, ostrĕa, *f*

P

pace, *nn*, passus, *m*
pace (step), spătĭor (1 *dep*), grădĭor (3 *dep*)
pacific, pācĭfĭcus
pacification, pācĭfĭcātĭo, *f*
pacify, *v.t*, plāco (1), sēdo (1)
pack (bundle), sarcĭna, *f*; (— of people), turba, *f*
pack, *v.t*, (gather together), collĭgo (3); (— close together), stĭpo (1)
package, sarcĭna, *f*
packet, fascĭcŭlus, *m*
pack-horse, iūmentum, *n*
pact, pactum, *n*, foedus, *n*
padding, *nn*, fartūra, *f*
paddle, *nn*, (oar), rēmus, *m*
paddle, *v.t*, rēmĭgo (1), (to row)
paddock, saeptum, *n*

padlock, sĕra, f
pagan, pāgānus
page (book), pāgĭna, f; (boy), pŭer, m
pageant, spectācŭlum, n, pompa, f
pageantry, spĕcĭes, (f) atque pompa,
   f (display and public procession)
pail, sĭtŭla, f
pain, dŏlor, m; (to be in —), v.i,
   dŏlĕo (2)
pain, v.t, dŏlōre afficĭo (3) (inflict
   pain)
painful, ăcerbus
painless, use adv. phr, sĭne dŏlōre
   (without pain)
pains (endeavour), ŏpĕra, f; (to take
   — over), ŏpĕram do (1) (with dat)
painstaking, ŏpĕrōsus
paint, v.t, pingo (3); (colour), fūco (1)
paint, nn, pigmentum, n
paint-brush, pēnĭcullus, m
painter, pictor, m
painting, pictūra, f
pair, pār, m
pair, v.t, iungo (3); v.i, iungor (3 pass)
palace, rēgĭa, f
palatable, iūcundus
palate, pălātum, n
palatial, rēgĭus
pale, adj, pallĭdus; (to be —), v.i,
   pallĕo (2); (to become —), v.i,
   pallesco (3)
pale, nn, (stake), pālus, m
paleness, pallor, m
palisade, vallum, n
pall, nn, pallĭum, n
pall, v.i, (it —s), taedet (2 impers)
pallet, lectŭlus, m
palliate, v.t, extĕnŭo (1)
palliation, use vb, extĕnŭo (1) (palliate)
palliative, lēnĭmentum, n
pallid, adj pallĭdus
pallor, pallor, m
palm (of hand, tree), palma, f
palm (to — off), v.t, suppōno (3)
palpable (obvious), mănĭfestus
palpitate, v.t, palpĭto (1)
palpitation, palpĭtātĭo, f
palsy, părălўsis, f
paltry, vīlis
pamper, v.t, nĭmĭum indulgĕo (2)
   (with dat) (to be too kind to . . .)
pamphlet, lĭbellus, m
pamphleteer, scriptor, (m) lĭbellorum
pan, pătĭna, f; (frying —), sartāgo, f
panacea, pănăcĕa, f
pancake, lăgānum, n
pander, v.i, lēnōcĭnor (1 dep)
panegyric, laudātĭo, f
panel (of door, etc.), tympănum, n
panelled, lăquĕātus

pang, dŏlor, m
panic, păvor, m
panic-stricken, păvĭdus
pannier, clītellae, f, pl
panorama, prōspectus, m
pant, v.i, ănhēlo (1)
panther, panthēra, f
panting, nn, ănhēlĭtus, m
pantomime, mīmus, m
pantry, cella pĕnarĭa, f
pap (nipple), păpilla, f
paper, charta, f; (sheet of —),
   schĕda, f; (newspaper), acta dĭurna,
   n.pl
papyrus, păpŷrus, m, f
par (on a — with), adj, pār
parable, părăbŏla, f
parade (military), dēcursus, m; (show),
   appărātus, m, pompa, f
parade, v.i, (of troops), dēcurro (3);
   v.t (display), ostento (1)
paradise, Ēlўsĭum, ĭi, n
paragon, spĕcĭmen, n
paragraph, căput, n
parallel, adj, părallēlus; (like),
   sĭmĭlis
paralyse, v.t, dēbĭlĭto (1)
paralysed, dēbĭlis
paralysis, părălўsis, f, dēbĭlĭtas, f
paramount summus
paramour ădulter, m, ămātor, m
parapet, lōrīca, f, mūnītĭo, f
paraphernalla, appărātus, m
parasite, assecla, c
parasol, umbella, f
parcel, fascĭcŭlus, m
parcel out, v.t, partĭor (4 dep)
parch, v.t, torrĕo (2)
parched (dry), ārĭdus; (scorched),
   torrĭdus
parchment, membrāna, f
pardon, nn, vĕnĭa, f
pardon, v.t, ignosco (3) (with dat)
pardonable, use phr, cui ignoscendum
   est (who should be pardoned)
pare, v.t, (circum)sĕco (1) (cut
   around))
parent, părens, m, f
parentage, gĕnus, n
parental, pătrĭus, or use genit pl,
   părentum (of parents)
parenthesis, interpŏsĭtĭo, f
parish, părœcĭa, f
park, horti, m. pl
parley, collŏquĭum, n
parley, v.i, collŏquor (3 dep)
parliament, sĕnātus, m
parliamentary, use genit. case of
   sĕnātus
parlour, conclāve, n

For List of Abbreviations used, turn to pages 3, 4

parody, versus rīdĭcŭli, *m*, *pl*
parole, fĭdes, *f* (promise)
paroxysm, *use* accessus, *m*, (approach)
parricide (person), parrĭcīda, *c*; (act), parrĭcīdĭum, *n*
parrot, psittăcus, *m*
parry, *v.t*, prōpulso (1)
parse, *v.t*, *use phr*, verba singŭlātim percĭpĭo (understand the words one by one)
parsimonious, parcus
parsimony, parsĭmōnĭa, *f*
parsley, āpĭum, *n*
parson (priest), săcerdos, *c*
part, pars, *f*; (in a play), persōna, *f*, partes, *f*, *pl*; (side, faction), partes, *f*, *pl*; (duty), offĭcĭum, *n*; (region), lōca, *n.pl*; (from all —s), *adv*, undĭque; (for the most —), *adv*, plērumque; (to take — in), intersum (*irreg*) (*with dat*)
part, *v.t*, dīvĭdo (3), sēpăro (1); *v.i*, discēdo (3)
partake of, *v.t*, partĭceps sum (*irreg*) (*with genit*); (food), gusto (1)
partaker, partĭceps, *adj*
partial (affecting only a part), *use adv. phr*, ex ălĭquā parte; (unfair), ĭnīquus
partiality, stŭdĭum, *n*
participate, *v.i*, partĭceps sum (*irreg*) (*with genit*)
participation, sŏcĭĕtas, *f*
particle, partĭcŭla, *f*
particular (characteristic), prŏprĭus; (special), singŭlāris; (exacting), dēlĭcātus
particularly (especially), *adv*, praecĭpŭē
parting, *nn*, dīgressus, *m*
partisan, fautor, *m*
partition (act of —), partītĭo, *f*; (wall), părĭes, *m*
partly, *adv*, partim
partner, sŏcĭus, *m* (sŏcĭa, *f*)
partnership, sŏcĭĕtas, *f*
partridge, perdix, *c*
party (political, etc.), factĭo, *f*; (of soldiers), mănus, *f*; (for pleasure), convīvĭum, *n*
pasha, sătrăpes, *m*
pass, *nn* (mountain), angustĭae, *f*. *pl*
pass, *v.t*. (go beyond), praetergrĕdĭor (3 *dep*); (surpass), excēdo (3); (— on, — down), trādo (3); (of time), ăgo (3), tĕro (3); (— over, omit), praetĕrĕo (4); (— a law),

sancĭo (4); (approve), prŏbo (1); *v.i*, praetĕrĕo (4); (of time), transĕo (4); (give satisfaction), sătisfăcĭo (3); (— over, cross over), transĕo (4); (come to —, happen), fīo (*irreg*)
passable (road, etc.), pervĭus
passage (crossing), transĭtus, *m*, trāiectĭo, *f*; (route, way), ĭter, *n*, vĭa, *f*; (in a book), lŏcus, *m*.
passenger, vector, *m*
passion, mōtus, (*m*) ănĭmi (impulse of the mind); (love), ămor, *m*
passionate, fervĭdus, ardens, īrācundus
passive, pătĭens
passivity, pătĭentĭa, *f*
passport, dīplōma, *n*
password, tessĕra, *f*
past, *adj*, praetĕrĭtus; (just —), proxĭmus
past, *nn*, praetĕrĭtum tempus, *n*
past, *prep*, praeter (*with acc*); (on the far side of), ultrā (*with acc*)
past, *adv*, *use compound vb. with* praeter, *e.g.* praetĕrĕo (4) (go past)
paste, fărīna, *f*
paste, *v.t*, glūtĭno (1)
pastime, oblectāmentum, *n*
pastor, pastor, *m*
pastoral pastōrālis
pastry, crustum, *n*
pastry-cook, crustŭlārĭus, *m*
pasture, pascŭum, *n*
pasture, *v.t*, pasco (3)
pat, *v.t*, (caress), permulcĕo (2)
patch, *nn*, pannus, *m*
patch, *v.t*, sarcĭo (4)
patent, *adj*, ăpertus
paternal, păternus
path, sēmĭta, *f*, vĭa, *f*
pathetic, mĭsĕrandus
pathless, invĭus
pathos, *f*; affectĭo, (*f*) ănĭmi
pathway, sēmĭta, *f*
patience, pătĭentĭa, *f*
patient, *adj*, pătĭens
patient, *nn*, *use* aeger (ill)
patiently, *adv*, pătĭenter
patrician, *nn. and adj*, pătrĭcĭus
patrimony, pătrĭmōnĭum, *n*
patriot, *use phr*, qui pătrĭam ămat (who loves his country)
patriotic, ămans pătrĭae
patriotism, ămor (*m*) pătrĭae
patrol, *nn*, *use* custōdes, *m*. *pl*, (guards)
patrol, *v.t*, circŭmĕo (4)

patron, pătrōnus, *m*
patronage, pătrōcĭnĭum, *n*
patronize, *v.t*, făvĕo (2) (*with dat*)
patter, *nn*, crĕpĭtus, *m*
patter, *v.i*, crĕpo (1)
pattern, exemplum, *n*, exemplar, *n*
paucity, paucĭtas, *f*
pauper, pauper *c*, ĕgens (needy)
pause, *nn*, mŏra, *f*
pause, *v.i*, intermitto (3)
pave, *v.t*, sterno (3)
pavement, păvīmentum, *n*
pavilion, *use* praetōrĭum, *n*, (general's tent), *or* tăbcrnācŭlum, *n*, (tent)
paw, *nn*, pes, *m*
paw, *v.t*, pĕdĭbus calco (1) (tread with the feet)
pawn (chess), lătruncŭlus, *m*; (security), pignus, *n*
pawn, *v.t*, pignĕro (1)
pay, *nn*, stīpendĭum, *n*
pay, *v.t*, solvo (3), pendo (3), nŭmĕro (1); *v.i* (— attention), ŏpĕram do (1); (— the penalty), poenas do (1)
pay-master (in army), trĭbūnus aerārĭus, *m*
payment, sŏlūtĭo, *f*
pea, pīsum, *n*, cĭcer, *n*
peace, pax, *f*, ōtĭum, *n*
peaceable, plăcĭdus
peaceful, plăcĭdus, pācātus
peacefulness, tranquillĭtas, *f*
peace-offering, plăcŭlum, *n*
peacock, păvo, *m*
peak, ăpex, *m*; (mountain), căcūmen, *n*
peal (thunder), frăgor, *m*; *otherwise use* sŏnus, *m*, (sound)
peal, *v.i*, sŏno (1)
pear, pŷrum, *n*; (— tree), pŷrus, *f*
pearl, margărīta, *f*
peasant, rustĭcus, *m*, ăgrestis, *m*
peasantry, ăgrestes, *m. pl*
pebble, lăpillus, *m*
peck (measure), mŏdĭus, *m*
peck, *v.t*, vellĭco (1)
peculation, pĕcūlātus, *m*
peculiar (to one person, etc.), prŏprĭus; (remarkable), singŭlāris
peculiarity, prŏprĭĕtas, *f*
pecuniary, pĕcūnĭārĭus
pedagogue, măgister, *m*
pedant, hŏmo ĭneptus
pedantic (affected — of style, etc.), pūtĭdus
peddle, *v.t*, vendĭto (1)
pedestal, băsis, *f*
pedestrian, *nn*, pĕdes, *m*
pedestrian, *adj*, pĕdester

pedigree, stemma, *n*
pedlar, instĭtor, *m*
peel, *nn*, cŭtis, *f*
peel, *v.i*, cŭtem rĕsĕco (1)
peep, *nn*, aspectus, *m*
peep at, *v.t*, inspicio (3); *v.i*, sĕ prōferre (*irreg*)
peer (equal), par, *m*
peer at, *v.t*, rīmor (1 *dep*)
peerless, ūnĭcus
peevish, stŏmăchōsus
peevishness, stŏmăchus, *m*
peg, clāvus, *m*
pelt, *v.t*, *use* intorquĕo (2) (hurl at); *v.i*, (of rain, etc.), *use* plŭit (it rains)
pen, călămus, *m*; (for cattle), saeptum, *n*
pen, *v.t*, (write), scrībo (3)
penal, poenālis
penalty, poena, *f*, damnum, *n*; (to pay the —), poenas do (1)
penance (do —), *use vb*. explo (1) (to make amends)
pencil, pĕnĭcillum, *n*
pending, *prep*, inter, per (*with acc*)
pendulous, pendŭlus
penetrate, *v.i*, *and v.t*, pĕnĕtro (1) pervādo (3)
penetrating, *adj*, ăcūtus, ācer (mentally), săgax
penetration, ăcūmen, *n*
peninsula, paeninsŭla, *f*
penitence, paenĭtentĭa, *f*
penitent, *use vb*, paenĭtet (2 *impers*) (*with acc. of person*), *e.g.* I am penitent, mē paenĭtet
pennant, vexillum, *n*
penny, as, *m*
pension, annŭa, *n.pl*
pensive, multa pŭtans (thinking many things)
penthouse, vĭnĕa, *f*
penultimate, paenultĭmus
penurious, parcus
penury, ĕgestas, *f*, ĭnŏpĭa, *f*
people (community), pŏpŭlus, *m*; (persons), hŏmĭnes, *c. pl*; (the common —), plebs, *f*, vulgus, *n*
people, *v.t*; frĕquento (1); (inhabit), incŏlo (3)
pepper, pĭper, *n*
perambulate, *v.t*, pĕrambŭlo (1)
perceive, *v.t*, sentĭo (4), percĭpĭo (3), ănĭmadverto (3), intellĕgo (3)
percentage, pars, *f*
perception, perspĭcācĭtas, *f*, *or use adj*, perspĭcax (sharp-sighted)
perceptive, perspĭcax
perch, *nn*, pertĭca, *f*; (fish), perca, *f*
perch, *v.i*, insĭdo (3)

perchance, *adv*, fortě
percolate, *v.i*, permāno (1)
percussion, ictus, *m*
perdition, exĭtĭum, *n*
peremptory, *use vb.* obstringo (3) (to put under obligation)
perennial, pĕrennis
perfect, perfectus, absŏlūtus
perfect, *v.t*, perfĭcĭo (3), absolvo (3)
perfection, perfectĭo, *f*, absŏlūtĭo, *f*
perfidious, perfĭdus
perfidy, perfĭdĭa, *f*
perforate, *v.t*, perfŏro (1)
perform, *v.t*, fungor (3 *dep. with abl*); perăgo (3), praesto (1), exsĕquor (3 *dep*)
performance, functĭo, *f*
performer, actor, *m*
perfume, ŏdor, *m*
perfume, *v.t*, ŏdōro (1)
perfunctory, neglĕgens
perhaps, *adv*, fortě, fortassě, forsĭtan
peril, pĕrīcŭlum, *n*
perilous, pĕrīcŭlōsus
period, spătĭum, *n*
periodical, *adj*, stătus
perish, *v.i*, pĕrĕo (4)
perishable, frăgĭlis
perjure, *v.t*, periūro (1)
perjured, periūrus
perjury, periūrĭum, *n*
permanence, stăbĭlĭtas, *f*
permanent, stăbĭlis
permanently, *adv*, perpĕtŭo
permeate, *v.i*, permāno (1)
permissible (it is —), lĭcet (2 *impers*)
permission (to give —), permitto (3) (*with dat*); (without your —), tě invīto
permit, *v.t*, sĭno·(3), permitto (3)
pernicious, pernĭcĭōsus
perpendicular, *adj*, dīrectus
perpetrate, *v.t*, admitto (3)
perpetual, sempĭternus
perpetuate, *v.t*, contĭnŭo (1)
perplex, *v.t*, distrăho (3), sollĭcĭto (1)
perplexed, dŭbĭus
perquisite, pĕcūlĭum, *n*
persecute, *v.t*, insector (1 *dep*)
persecution, insectātĭo, *f*
persecutor, insectātor, *m*
perseverance, persĕvērantĭa, *f*
persevere, *v.i*, persĕvēro (1)
persist, *v.i*, persto (1)
persistence pertĭnācĭa, *f*
person, hŏmo, *c*; (body), corpus, *n*; (in person), *use pron*, ipse (self)
personal (opp. to public), prīvātus
personality, ingĕnĭum, *n*
perspicacious, perspĭcax

perspicacity, perspĭcācĭtas, *f*
perspiration, sūdor, *m*
perspire, *v.i*, sūdo (1)
persuade, *v.t*, persuādĕo (2) (*with dat of person*)
persuasion, persuāsĭo, *f*
persuasive, suāvĭlŏquens
pert, prŏcax
pertain, *v.i*, attĭnĕo (2)
pertinacious, pertĭnax
pertinacity, pertĭnācĭa, *f*
perturb, *v.t*, turbo (1)
perusal, perlectĭo, *f*
peruse, *v.t*, perlĕgo (3)
pervade, *v.t*, permāno (1), perfundo (3)
perverse, perversus
perversion, dēprāvātĭo, *f*
pervert, *v.t*, dēprāvo (1)
pervious, pervĭus
pest, pestis, *f*
pester, *v.t*, sollĭcĭto (1)
pestilence, pestĭlentĭa, *f*
pestilential, pestĭlens
pestle, pistillum, *n*
pet, *nn*, dēlĭcĭae, *f. pl*
pet, *v.t*, in dēlĭcĭīs hăbĕo (2) (regard among one's favourites), indulgĕo (2)
petition, *use vb.* pĕto (3) (seek)
petition, *v.t*, rŏgo (1)
petitioners, pĕtentes, *c.pl*
petrify, *v.t*, (with fear, etc.), terrōrem ĭnĭcĭo (3), (*with dat*)
pettifogging, vīlĭs
petty, mĭnūtus
petulance, pĕtŭlantĭa, *f*
petulant, pĕtŭlans
phantom, sĭmŭlācrum, *n*, ĭmāgo, *f*
phases (alternations), vĭces, *f. pl*
pheasant, āles, (c) Phāsĭdis (bird of Phasis)
phenomenon, rēs, *f*; (remarkable occurrence), rēs mīrābĭlis
phial, lăguncŭla, *f*
philanthropic, hūmānus
philanthropy, hūmānĭtas, *f*
philologist, phĭlŏlŏgus, *m*
philology, phĭlŏlŏgĭa, *f*
philosopher, phĭlŏsŏphus, *m*
philosophical, phĭlŏsŏphus
philosophy, phĭlŏsŏphĭa, *f*
philtre, philtrum, *n*
phlegm, pītuīta, *f*; (of temperament), aequus ănĭmus, *m*
phoenix, phoenix, *m*
phrase, *nn*, lŏcūtĭo, *f*
phraseology, *use* verba, *n.pl*, (words)
phthisis, phthĭsis, *f*
physic, mĕdĭcāmentum, *n*

physical (relating to the body), *use*
nn, corpus, *n*, (body); (natural),
use nātūra, *f*, (nature)
physician, mĕdĭcus, *m*
physics, phўsĭca, *n.pl*
physiology, phўsĭŏlŏgĭa, *f*
pick (axe), dŏlābra, *f*; (choice), *use*
adj, dēlectus (chosen)
pick, *v.t*, (pluck), lĕgo (3), carpo (3);
(choose), ēlĭgo (3); (— up, seize),
răpĭo (3)
picked (chosen), dēlectus
picket, stătĭo, *f*
pickle, mūrĭa, *f*
pickle, *v.t*, condĭo (4)
pickpocket, fūr, *c*
picnic, *use phr*, fŏrīs ĕpŭlor (1 *dep*) (to
eat out of doors)
picture, tăbŭla, *f*
picture, *v.t*, expingo (3)
picturesque, ămocnus
pie, crustum, *n*
piebald, bĭcŏlor
piece (part), pars, *f*; (of food), frustrum, *n*; (to pull or tear to —s),
discerpo (3), dīvello (3); (to fall to
—s), dīlābor (3 *pass*)
piecemeal, *adv*, membrātim
piece together, *v.t*, compōno (3)
pier, mōles, *f*
pierce, *v.t*, perfŏdĭo (3)
piercing, *adj*, ăcūtus
piety, pĭĕtas, *f*
pig, porcus, *m*, sūs, *c*
pigeon, cŏlumba, *f*
pigheaded, obstĭnātus, diffĭcĭlis
pigsty, hăra, *f*
pike, hasta, *f*
pile (heap), ăcervus, *m*; (building),
mōles, *f*; (supporting timber),
sublĭca, *f*
pile, *v.t*, ăcervo (1), congĕro (3)
pilfer, *v.t*, surrĭpĭo (3)
pilfering, *nn*, furtum, *n*
pilgrim, pĕrĕgrīnātor, *m*
pilgrimage, pĕrĕgrīnātĭo, *f*
pill, pĭlŭla, *f*
pillage, *nn*, răpīna, *f*, dīreptĭo, *f*
pillage, *v.t*, praedor (1 *dep*), dīrĭpĭo
(3)
pillar, cŏlumna, *f*
pillory, vincŭla, *n.pl*
pillow, pulvīnus, *m*
pillow, *v.t*, suffulcĭo (4)
pilot, gŭbernātor, *m*
pilot, *v.t*, gŭberno (1)
pimp, lēno, *m*
pimple, pustŭla, *f*
pin, ăcus, *f*
pin, *v.t*, ăcu fīgo (3) (fix with a pin)

pincers, forceps, *m*, *f*
pinch, *nn*, (bite), morsus, *m*
pinch, *v.t*, ūro (3), vellĭco (1);
(squeeze), cŏarto (1)
pine, *nn*, pīnus, *f*; *adj*, pīnĕus
pine, *v.i*, tābesco (3); *v.t*, (—for), dēsĭdĕro (1)
pinion (nail), clāvus, *m*; (bond),
vincŭla, *n.pl*
pinion, *v.t*, rĕvincĭo (4)
pink, rŭbor, *m*
pinnace, lembus, *m*
pinnacle, fastīgĭum, *n*
pint, sextārĭus, *m*
pioneer, explŏrātor, *m*
pious, pĭus
pip (seed), sēmen, *n*, grānum, *n*
pipe, cănālis, *m*; (musical), fistŭla, *f*
pipe, *v.i*, căno (3)
piper, tībīcen, *m*
piquant, ăcerbus
pique, *nn*, offensĭo, *f*
pique, *v.t*, laedo (3)
piracy, lătrōcĭnĭum, *n*
pirate, praedo, *m*, pīrāta, *m*
pit, fŏvĕa, *f*; (arm —), āla, *f*; (theatre),
căvĕa, *f*
pit (— one's wits, etc.), *use* ūtor (3
dep) (to use)
pitch, *nn*, pix, *f*; (in music), sŏnus, *m*
pitch, *v.t*, (camp, tent, etc.), pōno(3);
(throw), cōnĭcĭo (3); (ships), *use*
ăgĭtor (1 *pass*) (to be tossed about)
pitcher, urcĕus, *m*
pitchfork, furca, *f*
piteous, pĭtiable, mĭsĕrābĭlis
pitfall, fŏvĕa, *f*
pith, mĕdulla, *f*
pitiful mĭser, mĭsĕrĭcors
pitifulness, mĭsĕrĭa, *f*
pitiless, immĭsĕrĭcors
pittance (small pay) tips, *f*
pity, *v.t*, mĭsĕret (2 *impers*) (*with acc.
of subject and genit. of object, e.g.* I
pity you; mē mĭsĕret tŭi
pity, *nn*, mĭsĕrĭcordĭa, *f*
pivot, cardo, *m*
placard, inscriptum, *n*
placate, *v.t*, plāco (1)
place, lŏcus, *m*; (in this —), *adv*, hīc;
(in that —), illīc, ĭbī; (in what —?)
ŭbī?; (in the same —), ĭbīdem; (to
this —) hūc; (to that —), illūc;
(to the same —), ĕōdem; (to what
—?), quō; (from this —), hinc;
(from that —), inde; (from the
same —), indĭdem; (from what—?),
unde?; (in the first —), prīmum;
(to take —, happen), *v.i*, accĭdo (3)
place, *v.t*, pōno (3), lŏco (1); (— in

command), praeffcĭo (3); (— **upon**), impŏno (3)

placid, plăcĭdus, tranquillus

plague, *nn*, pestĭlentĭa, *f*, pestĭs, *f*

plague, *v.t*, (trouble), sollĭcĭto (1)

plain, *nn*, campus, *m*, plānĭtĭes, *f*

plain, *adj*, (clear), clārus, plānus; (unadorned), subtīlis, simplex; (frank, candid), sincērus

plainness, perspĭcŭĭtas, *f*, simplĭcĭtas, *f*, sincērĭtas, *f*

plaintiff, pētĭtor, *m*

plaintive, *adj*, mĭsĕrābĭlis

plait, *v.t*, intexo (3)

plan, *nn*, consĭlĭum, *n*; (drawing), dēscriptĭo, *f*; (to **make a —**), consĭlĭum căpĭo (3)

plan, *v.i*, (intend), in ănĭmo hăbĕo (2); *v.t*, (design), dēscrībo (3)

plane, *nn*, (tool), runcīna, *f*; (tree), plătănus, *f*

plane, *v.t*, runcīno (1)

planet, sīdus, (*n*) errans (moving constellation)

plank, tăbŭla, *f*

plant, *nn*, herba, *f*

plant (seeds, etc.), sĕro (3); (otherwise), pōno (3), stătŭo (3)

plantation, plantārĭum, *n*, arbustum, *n*

planter, sător, *m*

planting, *nn*, sătus, *m*

plaster, *nn*, tectōrĭum, *n*; (medical), emplastrum, *n*

plaster, *v.t*, gypso (1)

plasterer, tector, *m*

plate (dish), cătillus, *m*; (thin layer of metal), lāmĭna, *f*; (silver, gold), argentum, *n*

plate, *v.t*, indūco (3)

platform, suggestus, *m*

Platonic, Plătōnĭcus

platoon, dĕcŭrĭa, *f*

plausible, spĕcĭōsus

play, *nn*, lūdus, *m*, lūsus, *m*; (theatre), fābŭla, *f*; (scope), campus, *m*

play, *v.i*, lūdo (3) (*with abl. of game played*); (musical), căno (3); (a **part in a play**), partes ăgo (3); (a **trick**), lūdĭfĭco (1)

player (stage), histrĭo, *m*; (flute —), tībīcen, *m*; (strings —), fĭdĭcen, *m*; (lute, guitar —), cĭthărista, *m*

playful (frolicsome), lascīvus

playfulness, lascīvĭa, *f*

playground, ārĕa, *f*

playwright, fābŭlārum scriptor, *m*

plea (asking), obsĕcrātĭo, *f*; (excuse), excūsātĭo, *f*

plead, *v.t*, ōro (1), ăgo (3); (as an excuse), excūso (1); (beg earnestly), obsĕcro (1); (law), dīco (3)

pleader (in law), ōrātor, *m*

pleasing, pleasant, iūcundus

pleasantness, iūcundĭtas, *f*

please, *v.t*, plăcĕo (2) (*with dat*); (if you —), si vis

pleasurable, iūcundus

pleasure, vŏluptas, *f*; (will), arbĭtrĭum, *n*; (— gardens), horti, *m. pl*

plebeian, plēbēius

pledge, *nn*, pignus, *n*; (to **make a —, promise**), sē obstringĕre (3 *reflex*)

pledge, *v.t*, oblĭgo (1), prōmitto (3)

plenipotentiary, lēgātus, *m*

plenitude, plēnĭtūdo, *f*

plentiful, largus, cōpĭōsus

plenty, cōpĭa, *f*; (enough), sătis (*with genit*)

pleurisy, pleurītis, *f*

pliable, flexĭbĭlis, lentus

plight, angustĭae, *f. pl* (difficulties)

plight, *v.t*, spondĕō (2), oblĭgo (1)

plinth, plinthus, *m, f*

plod, *v.i*, lentē prōcēdo (3)

plot (of ground), ăgellus, *m*; (conspiracy), conĭūrātĭo, *f*; (story), argūmentum, *n*

plot, *v.i*, conĭūro (1)

plough, *nn*, ărātrum, *n*; (— share), vōmer, *m*

plough, *v.t*, ăro (1)

ploughman, ărātor, *m*, bŭbulcus, *m*

pluck, *nn*, fortĭtūdo, *f*, ănĭmus, *m*

pluck, *v.t*, carpo (3); (— up courage), ănĭmum rĕvŏco (1)

plug, *nn*, obtūrāmentum, *n*

plum, prūnum, *n*

plum-tree, prūnus, *f*

plumage, plūmae, *f, pl*

plume, penna, *f*

plumb-line, līnĕa, *f*

plump, pinguis

plumpness, nĭtor, *m*, pinguĭtūdo, *f*

plunder, *nn*, praeda, *f*; (act of plundering), răpīna, *f*, dīreptĭo, *f*

plunder, *v.t*, praedor (1 *dep*), dīrĭpĭo (3)

plunderer, praedātor, *m*

plunge, *v.i*, sē mergĕre (3 *reflex*); *v.t*, mergo (3)

plural, *adj*, plūrālis

plurality, multĭtūdo, *f*

ply, *v.t*, exercĕo (2)

poach, *v.t*, *use* răpĭo (3), (to **seize**); (cook), cŏquo (3)

poacher, fur, *c*, raptor *m*.

pocket, sĭnus, *m*

pocket, *v.t.* (money), āverto (3)
pocket-book, pŭgillāres, *m, pl*
pocket-money, pēcŭlĭum, *n*
pod, sĭlĭqua, *f*
poem, pŏēma, *n,* carmen, *n*
poet, pŏēta, *m*
poetical, pŏētĭcus
poetry, pŏēsis, *f,* carmĭna, *n.pl*
poignant, ācerbus
point, ăcūmen, *n;* (of a sword), mūcro, *m;* (spear), cuspis, *f;* (place), lŏcus, *m;* (issue), res, *f;* (on the — of), *use fut. participle of vb, e.g.* on the point of coming; ventūrus
point, *v.t* (make pointed), praeăcŭo (3); (direct), dīrĭgo (3)
point out *or* **at,** *v.t,* monstro (1)
pointed, praeăcūtus; (witty) salsus
pointer, index, *m, f*
pointless, insulsus
poison, vĕnēnum, *n,* vīrus, *n*
poison, *v.t,* vĕnēno nĕco (1) (kill by poison)
poisoning, *nn,* vĕnēfĭcĭum, *n*
poisonous, vĕnēnātus
poke, *v.t,* fŏdĭco (1)
polar, scptcntrĭōnālĭs
pole (rod, staff), contus, *m,* longŭrĭus, *m;* (earth), pŏlus, *m*
polemics, contrōversĭae, *f. pl*
police (men), vĭgĭles, *m, pl*
policy, rătĭo, *f*
polish, *nn,* (brightness), nĭtor, *m*
polish, *v.t,* pŏlĭo (4)
polished, pŏlītus
polite, cōmis, urbānus
politeness, cōmĭtas, *f,* urbānĭtas, *f*
politic, *adj,* prūdens
political, cīvīlis, pūblĭcus
politician, qui reīpūblĭcae stŭdet (who pursues state affairs)
politics, rēs pūblĭca, *f*
poll (vote), suffrāgĭum, *n*
pollute, *v.t,* inquĭno (1)
pollution, collŭvĭo, *f*
polytheism, *use phr,* crēdĕre multos esse dĕos (believe that there are many gods)
pomade, căpillāre, *n*
pomegranate, mālum grānātum, *n*
pommel, *v.t,* verbĕro (1)
pomp, appărātus, *m*
pompous, magnĭfĭcus
pompousness, magnĭfĭcentĭa, *f*
pond, stagnum, *n;* (fish —), piscīna, *f*
ponder, *v.t,* rĕpŭto (1)
ponderous, grăvis
poniard, pŭgĭo, *m*
pontiff, pontĭfex, *m*
pontoon, pons, *m*

pony, mannus, *m*
pool, lăcūna, *f*
poop, puppis, *f*
poor, pauper, ĭnops; (worthless), vīlĭs; (wretched), mĭser
poorly, *adj,* (sick, ill), aeger
poorly, *adv,* tĕnŭĭter, mălĕ
pop, *v.i,* crĕpo (1)
pope, Pontĭfex Maxĭmus, *m*
poplar, pōpŭlus, *f*
poppy, păpāver, *n*
populace, vulgus, *n,* plebs, *f*
popular, grātĭōsus; (of the people), pŏpŭlāris
popularity, făvor, (*m*) pŏpŭli (good-will of the people)
population, cives, *c. pl*
populous, frēquens
porch, vestĭbŭlum, *n*
porcupine, hystrix, *f*
pore, fŏrāmen, *n*
pore over, *v.i,* ănĭmum intendo (3) (direct the mind)
pork, porcīna, *f*
porker, porcus, *m*
porous, rārus
porpoise, porcŭlus mărīnus, *m*
porridge, puls, *f*
port, portus, *m*
portable, quod portāri pŏtest (that can be carried)
portal, porta, *f,* iānŭa, *f*
portcullis, cătăracta, *f*
portend, *v.t,* portendo (3)
portent, portentum, *n*
portentous, monstrŭōsus
porter (doorkeeper), iānĭtor, *m;* (baggage carrier), bāiŭlus, *m*
portfolio, lĭbellus, *m*
portico, portĭcus, *f*
portion, pars, *f*
portion out, *v.t,* partĭor (4 *dep*)
portrait, ĭmāgo, *f*
portray, *v.t,* dēpingo (3)
pose, *nn,* stătus, *m*
position, lŏcus, *m;* (site), sĭtus, *m*
positive, certus
possess, *v.t,* hăbĕo (2), possĭdĕo (2)
possession, possessĭo, *f;* (to take — of), pŏtĭor (4 *dep. with abl*); (property), *often use possessive pron. e.g.* mĕa (my —s), *or* bŏna *n.pl*
possessor, possessor, *m,* dŏmĭnus, *m*
possibility, *use phr. with* posse; (to be possible)
possible, *use vb,* posse (*irreg*) (to be possible); (as . . . as possible), *use* quam *with superlative, e.g.* as large as possible, quam maxĭmus; (as soon as —), quam prīmum

post, cippus, *m*, pālus, *m*; (military), stătĭo, *f*, lŏcus, *m*; (letter), tăbellārĭi pūblĭci, *m. pl* (state couriers)

post, *v.t*, (in position), lŏco (1); (letter), tăbellārĭo do (1) (give to a courier)

posterior, *nn*, nătes, *f. pl*

posterity, postĕri, *m. pl*

postern, postīcum, *n*

posthumous, *use phr*, post mortem (*with genit*) (after the death of . . .)

postman, tăbellārĭus, *m*

postpone, *v.t*, diffĕro (*irreg*)

postscript, verba subiecta, *n.pl*, (words appended)

posture, stătus, *m*

pot, olla, *f*

potent, pŏtens, effĭcax

potentate, tўrannus, *m*

potion, pōtĭo, *f*

potsherd, testa, *f*

potter, fĭgŭlus, *m*

pottery (articles), fictĭlĭa, *n.pl*

pouch, saccŭlus, *m*

poultice, mălagma, *n*

poultry, ăves. cŏhortāles, *f. pl*

pounce upon, *v.t*, invŏlo (1)

pound, *nn*, (weight), lībra, *f*

pound, *v.t*, tundo (3), tĕro (3)

pour, *v.t*, fundo (3); *v.i*, fundor (3 *pass*)

pouring, *adj*, effūsus

pout, *v.i*, lăbellum extendo (3) (stretch a lip)

poverty, paupertas, *f*, ĕgestas, *f*, ĭnŏpĭa, *f*; (— stricken), *adj*, ĭnops

powder, *nn*, pulvis, *m*

power, vīres, *f. pl*; (dominion), pŏtestas, *f*; (authority), ius, *n*, impĕrĭum, *n*; (unconstitutional —), pŏtentĭa, *f*

powerful, pŏtens; (of body), vălĭdus

powerless, invălĭdus; (to be —), *v.i*, mĭnĭmum posse (*irreg*)

practicable, *use phr*, quod fĭĕri pŏtest (that can be done)

practical (person), făbrĭcae pĕrītus (skilled in practical work)

practically (almost), *adv.*, paene

practice, ūsus, *m*; (custom), mos, *m*, consŭētūdo, *f*

practise, *v.t*, exercĕo (2), factĭto (1)

practitioner (medical), mĕdĭcus, *m*

praetor, praetor, *m*

praetorship, praetūra, *f*

praise, *nn*, laus, *f*

praise, *v.t*, laudo (1)

praiseworthy, laudābĭlis

prance, *v.i*, exsulto (1)

prank, *use* lūdĭfĭcor (1 *dep*) (to make fun of)

prattle, *v.i*, garrĭo (4)

pray, *v.i. and v.t*, ōro (1), prĕcor (1 *dep*)

prayer, prĕces, *f. pl*

preach, *v.t*, contĭōnor (1 *dep*)

preamble, exordĭum, *n*

precarious, incertus

precaution (to take —s (against)), *v.i. and v.t*, praecăvĕo (2)

precede, *v.t*, antĕcēdo (3), antĕĕo (4)

precedence (to give —), *use vb*, cēdo (3); (to take —), prĭor esse (*irreg*)

precedent, exemplum, *n*

preceding, *adj*, prĭor, proxĭmus

precept, praeceptum, *n*

precious (of great price), magnĭ prĕtĭi; (dear), dīlectus

precipice, lŏcus praeceps, *m*

precipitate, *adj*, praeceps

precipitate, *v.t*, praecĭpĭto (1)

precipitous, praeceps

precise, subtīlis

precision, subtīlĭtas, *f*

preclude, *v.t*, prŏhĭbĕo (2)

precocious, praecox

preconceived, praeiūdĭcātus

precursor, praenuntĭus, *m*

predatory, praedātōrĭus

predecessor (my —), *use phr*, quĭ ante me . . . (who before me . . .)

predicament, angustĭae, *f. pl*

predict, *v.t*, praedīco (3)

prediction, praedictĭo, *f*

predilection, stŭdĭum, *n*

predisposed, inclīnātus

predominant, pŏtens

predominate, *v.i*, *use phr*, quĭ in pŏtentĭā sunt (who are in authority)

preeminent, praestans

preface, praefātĭo, *f*

preface, *v.t*, praefor (1 *dep*)

prefer, *v.t*, *with infinitive*, mālo (*irreg*); (put one thing before another), antĕpōno (3); (— a charge), dēfĕro (*irreg*)

preferable, pŏtĭor

preference, (desire), vŏluntas, *f*; (in —), *adv*, pŏtĭus

preferment, hŏnor, *m*

pregnant, praegnans, grăvĭda

prejudge, *v.t*, praeiūdĭco (1)

prejudice, praeiūdĭcāta ŏpīnĭo, *f*

prejudice, *v.t*, (impair), immĭnŭo (3)

prejudicial, noxĭus; (to be — to), obsum (*irreg*) (*with dat*)

prelate, săcerdos, *c*

preliminary, *use compound word with* prae, *e.g.* to make a — announcement, praenuntĭo (1)

prelude, prŏoemĭum, *n*
premature, immātūrus
premeditate, *v.t*, praemědĭtor (1 *dep*)
premeditation, praemědĭtātĭo, *f*
premier, princeps, *m*
premise, prŏpŏsĭtĭo, *f*
premises (buildings), aedĭfĭcĭa, *n.pl*
premium, praemĭum, *n*
premonition, mŏnĭtĭo, *f*
preoccupy (to be — with), stŭdĕo
  (2) (*with dat*)
preparation, compărātĭo, *f*, appărātus, *m*; (to make —s), compăro (1)
prepare, *v.t*, păro (1), compăro (1)
prepossess, *v.t*, commendo (1)
prepossessing, *adj*, suāvĭs, blandus
preposterous, praepostĕrus
prerogative, ĭūs, *n*
presage, praesāgĭum, *n*
presage, *v.t*, portendo (3)
prescribe, *v.t*, praescrībo (3)
presence, praesentĭa, *f*; (in the — of),
  prep, cōram (*with abl*)
present, *nn* (gift), dōnum, *n*; (time),
  praesentĭa, *n.pl*
present, *adj*, praesens; (to be —), *v.i*,
  adsum (*irreg*)
present, *v.t*, offĕro (*irreg*); (give), dōno
  (1) (*with acc. of person and abl. of gift*)
presentation, dōnātĭo, *f*
presentiment, augŭrĭum, *n*
presently, *adv*, (soon), mox
preservation, conservātĭo, *f*
preserve, *v.t*, servo (1)
preserver, servātor, *m*
preside, *v.i*, praesĭdĕo (*with dat*)
presidency, praefectūra, *f*
president, praefectus, *m*
press, *nn*, (machine), prēlum, *n*
press, *v.t*, prēmo (3); (urge), urgĕo (2)
pressure, nīsus, *m*
prestige, fāma, *f*, ŏpīnĭo, *f*
presume, *v.t*, (assume), crēdo (3);
  (dare), *v.i*, audĕo (2)
presumption (conjecture), coniectūra,
  f; (conceitedness), arrŏgantĭa, *f*
presumptuous, arrŏgans
pretence, sĭmŭlātĭo, *f*; (under — of),
  per sĭmŭlātĭōnem
pretend, *v.t*, sĭmŭlo (1)
pretended, *adj*, sĭmŭlātus
pretender (claimant), *use vb*, pĕto (3)
  (aspire to)
pretension postŭlātĭo, *f*
pretext, spĕcĭes, *f*; (on the — of), use
  vb. sĭmŭlo (1) (to pretend)
prettily, *adv*, bellē, vĕnustē
prettiness, concinnĭtas, *f*, vĕnustas, *f*
pretty, *adj*, pulcher

pretty, *adv*, sătis (enough)
prevail, *v.i*, obtĭnĕo (2), sŭpĕrĭor esse
  (*irreg*); (to — upon), *v.t*, persuādĕo
  (2) (*with dat*)
prevalent, vulgātus
prevaricate, *v.t*, tergĭversor (1 *dep*)
prevent, *v.t*, prŏhĭbĕo (2)
prevention, *use vb*, prŏhĭbĕo (prevent)
previous, prōxĭmus
previously, *adv*, antĕā
prey, *nn*, praeda, *f*
prey, *v.t*, praedor (1 *dep*)
price, *nn*, prĕtĭum, *n*; (— of corn),
  annōna, *f*
price, *v.t*, prĕtĭum constĭtŭo (3) (fix
  the price)
priceless, inaestĭmābĭlĭs
prick, *nn*, punctum, *n*
prick, *v.t*, pungo (3); (spur), stĭmŭlo
  (1)
prickly, *adj*, ăcŭlĕātus
pride, sŭperbĭa, *f*; (honourable —),
  spīrĭtus, *m*
priest, săcerdos, *c*
priesthood, săcerdōtĭum, *n*
prim, mōrōsĭor
primarily, *adv*, princĭpĭō
primary, prīmus
prime, *nn*, (of life, etc.), *use vb*,
  flōrĕo (2) (flourish); (best part), flōs,
  m
prime, *adj*, ēgrĕgĭus
primeval, prīmĭgĕnĭus
primitive, prīmĭgĕnĭus
prince (king), rēgŭlus, *m*; (king's son),
  fīlĭus, (*m*) rēgĭs
princess (king's daughter), fīlĭa, (*f*)
  rēgĭs
principal, *adj*, princĭpālĭs, praecĭpŭus
principal, *nn*, măgister, *m*
principality, regnum, *n*
principle, princĭpĭum, *n*; (element),
  ĕlĕmentum, *n*, prīmordĭa, *n.pl*;
  (rule, maxim), praeceptum, *n*
print, *nn*, (mark), nŏta, *f*
print, *v.t*, imprĭmo (3)
prior, *adj*, prĭor
priority, *use adj*, prĭor
prism, prisma, *n*
prison, carcer, *m*
prisoner, captīvus, *m*
privacy, sōlĭtūdo, *f*
private, prīvātus, sēcrētus
private soldier, mīles grĕgārĭus, *m*
privately, *adv*, prīvātim, clam
privation, ĭnŏpĭa, *f*
privet, lĭgustrum, *n*
privilege, ĭūs, *n*
privy, *adj*, (acquainted with), conscĭus; (secret), prīvātus

For List of Abbreviations used, turn to pages 3, 4

privy, *nn*, fŏrĭca, *f*
privy-council, consĭlĭum, *n*
privy-purse, fiscus, *m*
prize, praemĭum, *n*; (booty), praeda, *f*
prize, *v.t*, (value), magni aestĭmo (1)
probability, sĭmĭlĭtūdo, (*f*) vēri
probable, sĭmĭlis vēri
probation, prŏbātĭo, *f*
probe, *v.t*, tento (1)
problem, quaestĭo, *f*
problematical (doubtful), dŭbĭus
procedure, rătĭo, *f*
proceed, *v.i*, (move on), pergo (3); (originate) prŏfĭciscor (3 *dep*); (take legal action against) lītem intendo (3) (*with dat*)
proceedings (legal), actĭo, *f*; (doings), acta, *n.pl*
proceeds, fructus, *m*
process, rătĭo, *f*; (in the — of time), *adv, use phr*, tempŏre praetĕrĕunte (with time going by)
procession, pompa, *f*
proclaim, *v.t*, praedĭco (1), prōnuntĭo (1)
proclamation, prōnuntĭātĭo, *f*, ēdictum, *n*
proconsul, prōconsul, *m*
procrastinate, *v.t*, diffĕro (*irreg*)
procrastination, tardĭtas, *f*, mŏra, *f*
procreate, *v.t*, prōcrĕo (1)
procreation, prōcrĕātĭo, *f*, partus, *m*
procure, *v.t*, compăro (1)
procurer, lēno, *m*
prodigal, *adj*, prōdĭgus
prodigality, effūsĭo, *f*
prodigious, immānis
prodigy, prōdĭgĭum, *n*
produce, *nn*, fructus, *m*
produce, *v.t.* (into view) prōfĕro (*irreg*); (create), părĭo (3); (— an effect), mŏvĕo (2)
product, production, ŏpus, *n*
productive, fĕrax
profanation, vĭŏlātĭo, *f*
profane, impĭus, prŏfānus
profane, *v.t*, vĭŏlo (1)
profanity, impĭĕtas, *f*
profess, *v.t*, prŏfĭtĕor (2 *dep*)
profession (occupation), mūnus, *n*, offĭcĭum, *n*; (avowal), prŏfessĭo, *f*
professor, prŏfessor, *m*
proffer, *v.t*, pollĭcĕor (2 *dep*)
proficient (skilled), pĕrītus
profile, oblīqua fācĭes, *f*
profit, *nn*, ēmŏlŭmentum, *n*, lŭcrum, *n*, quaestus, *m*

profit, *v.t*, (benefit), prōsum (*irreg. with dat*)
profitable, fructŭōsus
profitless, ĭnūtĭlis
profligacy, nēquĭtĭa, *f*
profligate, perdĭtus
profound, altus
profuse, effūsus
profusion, effūsĭo, *f*
progeny, prōgĕnĭes, *f*
prognostic, signum, *n*
programme, lĭbellus, *m*
progress (improvement, etc.), prōgressus, *m*; (to make —), prŏfĭcĭo (3), prōgrĕdĭor (3 *dep*)
progress, *v.i*, prōgrĕdĭor (3 *dep*)
prohibit, *v.t*, vēto (1)
prohibition, interdictum, *n*
project, *nn*, (plan), consĭlĭum, *n*
project, *v.t*, prōĭcĭo (3); *v.i*, ēmĭnĕo (2)
projectile, tēlum *n*,
projecting, ēmĭnens
proletariat, vulgus, *n*
prolific, fēcundus
prolix, verbōsus
prologue, prŏlŏgus, *m*
prolong, *v.t*, prōdūco (3); (— a command), prōrŏgo (1)
prolongation, prōpăgātĭo, *f*
promenade, ambŭlātĭo, *f*
prominence, ēmĭnentĭa, *f*
prominent, ēmĭnens; (person), praeclārus
promiscuous, prōmiscŭus
promise, *nn*, prōmissum, *n*, fĭdes, *f*
promise, *v.i*, prōmitto (3), pollĭcĕor (2 *dep*)
promising, *adj, use adv. phr*, bŏnā spe (of good hope)
promissory note, chīrogrăphum, *n*
promontory, prōmontōrĭum, *n*
promote, *v.t*, prōmŏvĕo (2); (favour, assist), iŭvo (1), prōsum (*irreg*) (*with dat*)
promoter, auctor, *m*
promotion (act of —), *use vb.* prōmŏvĕo (2); (honour), hŏnor, *m*
prompt, *adj*, promptus
prompt, *v.t*, (assist in speaking), sŭbĭcĭo (3) (*with dat. of person*); (incite), incĭto (1)
promptitude, promptness, cĕlĕrĭtas, *f*
promulgate, *v.t*, prōmulgo (1)
prone, prōnus; (inclined to), prōpensus
prong, dens, *m*
pronoun, prōnōmen, *n*
pronounce, *v.t*, prōnuntĭo (1)

pronunciation, appellātĭo, *f*
proof, argūmentum, *n*, dŏcŭmentum *n*, prŏbātĭo, *f*
prop, *nn*, admĭnĭcŭlum, *n*
prop, *v.t*, fulcĭo (4)
propagate, *v.t*, prŏpāgo (1)
propel, *v.t*, prŏpello (3)
propensity, ănĭmus inclīnātus, *m*
proper, dĕcōrus, vērus, aptus
properly, *adv*, (correctly), rectē
property (possessions), bŏna, *n.pl*, rēs, *f*; (characteristic quality), prŏprĭĕtas, *f*
prophecy, praedictĭo, *f*, praedictum, *n*
prophesy, *v.t*, praedīco (3), vātĭcĭnor (1 *dep*)
prophet, vātes, *c*
prophetic, dīvīnus
propitiate, *v.t*, plāco (1)
propitious, prŏpĭtĭus, praesens
proportion, portĭo, *f*; (in —), prŏ portĭōne
proportional, *use adv. phr*, prŏ portĭōne
proposal, condĭcĭo, *f*
propose, *v.t*, fĕro (*irreg*), rŏgo (1)
proposer, lātor, *m*
proposition, condĭcĭo, *f*
proprietor, dŏmĭnus, *m*
propriety (decorum), dĕcōrum, *n*
prorogation, prŏrŏgātĭo, *f*
prosaic (flat), iēiūnus
proscribe, *v.t*, prōscrībo (3)
proscription, prōscriptĭo, *f*
prose, ōrātĭo sŏlūta, *f*
prosecute, *v.t*, (carry through), ex-sĕquor (3 *dep*) ; (take legal proceedings), lītem intendo (3)
prosecution, exsĕcūtĭo, *f*; (legal), accūsātĭo, *f*
prosecutor, accūsātor, *m*
prospect (anticipation), spes fŭtūra, *f*; (view), prospectus, *m*
prospective, fŭtūrus
prosper, *v.i*, flŏrĕo (2)
prosperity, res sĕcundae, *f. pl*
prosperous, sĕcundus
prostitute, *nn*, mĕrĕtrix, *f*
prostitute, *v.t*, vulgo (1)
prostitution, mĕrĕtrīcĭus quaestus, *m*
prostrate (in spirit, etc.), fractus; (lying on the back), sŭpīnus; (lying on the face), prōnus
prostrate, *v.t*, sterno (3), dēĭcĭo (3)
protect, *v.t*, tĕgo (3), tŭĕor (2 *dep*), dēfendo (3)
protection, tūtēla, *f*, praesĭdĭum, *n*
protector, dēfensor, *m*

protest against, *v.t*, intercēdo (3)
prototype, exemplar, *n*
protract, *v.t*, dūco (3)
protrude, *v.t*, prōtrūdo (3); *v.i*, ēmĭnĕo (2)
protuberance, tūber, *n*
proud, sŭperbus
prove, *v.t*, prŏbo (1); (to — oneself) sē praestāre (1 *reflex*); (test), pērĭclītor (1 *dep*); *v.i*, (turn out—of things), fīo (*irreg*), ēvĕnĭo (4)
proverb, prōverbĭum, *n*
proverbial, *use nn*, prōverbĭum, *n*, (proverb)
provide, *v.t*, (supply), păro (1), praebĕo (2); *v.i*, (make provision for), prōvĭdĕo (2); (— against), căvĕo (2) ne (*with vb. in subjunctive*)
provided that, *conj*, dum, dummŏdo
providence, prōvĭdentĭa, *f*
provident, prōvĭdus
province, prōvincĭa, *f*
provincial, prōvincĭālis
provision (to make —), prōvĭdĕo (2)
provisional, *use adv. phr*, ad tempus (for the time being)
provisions, cĭbus, *m*
provocation, use, *vb*, irrīto (1) (to provoke)
provoke, *v.t*, irrīto (1); (stir up), incĭto (1)
prow, prōra, *f*
prowess, virtus, *f*
prowl, *v.i*, văgor (1 *dep*)
proximity, prŏpinquĭtas, *f*
proxy, prōcŭrātor, *m*
prudence, prūdentĭa, *f*
prudent, prūdens
prune, *nn*, prūnum, *n*, (plum)
prune, *v.t*, ampŭto (1)
prurient, lĭbīdĭnōsus
pry, *v.t*, rīmor (1 *dep*)
psalm, carmen, *n*
psychological, *use genit. of* mens, (mind)
puberty, pūbertas, *f*
public, *adj*, pūblĭcus; (of the state), *use nn*, respublĭca, *f*, (state), *or* pŏpŭlus, *m*, (people)
public, *nn*, hŏmĭnes, *c. pl*
publican (innkeeper), caupo, *m*
publication, *use* ēdo (3), (publish)
publicity, cĕlĕbrĭtas, *f*
publicly, *adv*, pălam
publish, *v.t*, effĕro (*irreg*), prōfĕro (*irreg*); (book), ēdo (3)
pucker, *v.t*, corrūgo (1)
puddle, lăcūna, *f*
puerile (silly), ĭneptus

puff, v.i, (pant), ănhēlo (1); v.t, (inflate), inflo (1); **(puffed up),** inflātus

pugilist, pūgil, m

pull, v.t, trăho (3); **(— down, demolish),** dēstrŭo (3)

pulley, trochlĕa, f

pulp, căro, f

pulpit, suggestus, m

pulsate, v.i, palpĭto (1)

pulse, vēnae, f. pl. (veins)

pulverize, v.t, in pulvĕrem contĕro (3) **(pound into dust)**

pumice, pūmex, m

pump, nn, antlĭa, f

pump, v.t, haurĭo (4)

pumpkin, pĕpo, m

pun, făcētĭae, f. pl

punch, ictus, m, pugnus, m

punch, v.t, percŭtĭo (3)

punctilious, mōrōsus

punctual, punctuality, use adv. phr, ad tempus **(at the right time)**

punctuate, v.t, distinguo (3)

punctuation, interpunctĭo, f

puncture, nn, punctum, n

puncture, v.t, pungo (3)

pungency, morsus, m, ăcerbĭtas, f

pungent, ācer

punish, v.t, pūnĭo (4), ănĭmadverto (3) in (with acc), poenas sūmo (3); **(to be —ed),** poenas do (1)

punishment, poena, f, supplĭcĭum, n; **(to undergo —),** poenam sŭbĕo (4)

punitive; use vb, pūnĭo **(punish)**

puny, pŭsillus

pup, puppy, cătŭlus, m

pupil (scholar), discĭpŭlus, m; **(of the eye),** pūpilla, f

puppet, pūpa, f

purchase, nn, emptĭo, f

purchase, v.t, ĕmo (3)

pure, pūrus, mĕrus; **(morally),** intĕger

purgative, use phr. with mĕdĭcāmentum, n, **(medicine)**

purge, nn, use vb, purgo (1)

purge, v.t, purgo (1)

purification, purgātĭo, f

purify, v.t, purgo (1), lustro (1)

purity, castĭtas, f, intĕgrĭtas, f

purloin, v.t, surrĭpĭo (3)

purple, nn, purpŭra, f

purple, adj, purpŭrĕus

purport, nn, (meaning), signĭfĭcātĭo, f

purport, v.t, (mean), signĭfĭco (1)

purpose, nn, prōpŏsĭtum, n, consĭlĭum, n; **(for the — of doing something),** ĕo consĭlĭo ut (with vb in subjunctive); **(on —),** adv, consulto; **(to no —, in vain),** adv, frustrā; **(for what —?),** quārĕ

purpose, v.t, (intend), in ănĭmo hăbĕo (2)

purr, v.i, murmŭro (1)

purse, saccŭlus, m

in pursuance of, ex (with abl)

pursue, v.t, sĕquor (3 dep)

pursuit (chase), use vb, sĕquor **(to pursue); (desire for),** stŭdĭum, n

purvey, v.t, obsōno (1)

purveyor, obsōnātor, m

pus, pūs, n

push, pushing, nn, impulsus, m, impĕtus, m

push, v.t, pello (3), trūdo (3); **(— back),** rĕpello (3); **(— forward),** prōmŏvĕo (2)

pushing, adj, mŏlestus

pusillanimity, ănĭmus hŭmĭllis, m

pusillanimous, hŭmĭlis

pustule, pustŭla, f

put, v.t, (place), pōno (3), do (1), impōno (3); **(— aside),** sēpōno (3); **(— away),** abdo (3), condo (3); **(— back),** rĕpōno (3); **(— down),** dēpōno (3); **(suppress),** exstinguo (3); **(— forward),** praepōno (3), prōfĕro (irreg); **(— in),** immitto (3); **(— into land, port, etc.),** v.i, portum căpĭo (3); **(— off),** v.t, pōno (3); **(delay),** differo (irreg); **(— on),** impōno (3); **(—clothes),** indŭo (3); **(— out),** ēĭcĭo (3); **(quench),** exstinguo (3); **(— to, drive to),** impello (3); **(— together),** colligo (3), confĕro (irreg); **(— under),** sūbĭcĭo (3); **(— up, erect),** stătŭo (3); **(offer),** prōpōno (3); **(put up with, bear),** fĕro (irreg); **(— upon),** impōno (3); **(— to flight)** fŭgo (1)

putrefy, v.i, pūtesco (3)

putrid, pŭtrĭdus

putty, glūten, m or n

puzzle, nn, (riddle), nōdus, m; **(difficulty),** difficultas, f, angustĭae, f, pl

puzzling, adj, perplexus; **(in a — way),** adv. phr, per ambāges

pygmy, nănus, m

pyramid, pýrămis, f

pyre, rŏgus, m

Pyrenees, Montes Pýrēnaei, m. pl

python, pýthon, m

Q

quack, nn, (medicine), pharmăcŏpōla, m

quadrangle, ārĕa, f

quadrant, quădrans, m

quadrilateral, quădrĭlătĕrus

quadruped, quădrŭpes
quadruple, *adj*, quădruplex
quaff, *v.t*, haurĭo (4)
quagmire, pălus, *f*
quail, *nn*, cŏturnix, *f*
quail, *v.i*, trĕpĭdo (1)
quaint, nŏvus
quake, *nn*, trĕmor, *m*
quake, *v.i*, trĕmo (3)
qualification, iūs, *n*; (condition), con- dĭcĭo, *f*
qualified (suitable), aptus, ĭdōnĕus
qualify, *v.t*, (fit someone for something), aptum reddo (3); (restrict), circum- scrībo (3), mītĭgo (1)
quality, nātūra, *f*
qualm (doubt), dŭbĭtātĭo, *f*
quantity, nŭmĕrus, *m*, magnĭtūdo, *f*; (a certain —), ălĭquantum, *n* (*nn*); (a large —) cōpĭa, *f*, multum, *n*; (what —?), *use adj*, quantus (how great)
quarrel, iurgĭum, *n*, rixa, *f*
quarrel, *v.i*, iurgo (1), rixor (1 *dep*)
quarrelsome, lītĭgĭōsus
quarry (stone), lăpĭcīdīnae, *f. pl*; (prey), praeda, *f*
quarry, *v.t*, caedo (3)
quart (measure), dŭo sextārĭī, *m. pl*
quarter, quarta pars, *f*, quădrans, *m*; (district), rĕgĭo, *f*; (surrender), dēdĭtĭo, *f*
quarter, *v.t*, quădrĭfărĭam dīvĭdo (3), (divide into four parts)
quarter-deck, puppis, *f*
quartermaster, quaestor mīlĭtāris, *m*
quarterly, *adj*, trĭmestris
quarters (lodging), hospĭtĭum, *n*; (at close —), *adv*, commĭnus; (to come to close —), signa confĕro (*irreg*)
quash, *v.t*, opprĭmo (3); (sentence, verdict), rēscindo (3)
quaver, *v.i*, trĕpĭdo (1)
quay, crēpīdo, *f*
queen, rēgĭna, *f*
queer, rīdĭcŭlus
queerness, insŏlentĭa, *f*
quell, *v.t*, opprĭmo (3)
quench, *v.t*, exstinguo (3)
quenchless, ĭnexstinctus
querulous, quĕrŭlus
query, quaestĭo, *f*
query, *v.t*, quaero (3)
quest, inquīsītĭo, *f*
question, *nn*, rŏgātĭo, *f*, interrŏgātum, *n*, quaestĭo, *f*; *or use vb*, rŏgo (1) (to ask —s); (doubt), dŭbĭum, *n*
question, *v.t*, rŏgo (1), quaero (3); (doubt), dŭbĭto (1)
questionable, incertus

questioner, interrŏgātor, *m*
quibble, *nn*, captĭo, *f*
quibble, *v.i*, căvillor (1 *dep*)
quick, *adj*, cĕler; (sprightly), ăgĭlis; (— witted), săgax
quickly, *adv*, cĕlĕrĭter, cĭto
quicken, *v.t*, accĕlĕro (1), stĭmŭlo (1); *v.i*, (move quicker), sē incĭtāre (1 *reflex*)
quickness, vēlōcĭtas, *f*; (— of wit), săgācĭtas, *f*
quicksilver, argentum vīvum, *n*
quick-tempered, īrācundus
quiescent, quĭescens
quiet, *nn*, quĭes, *f*
quiet, *adj*, quĭētus, tranquillus
quiet, quieten, *v.t*, sēdo (1)
quietly, *adv*, quĭētē, tranquillē
quill, penna, *f*; (for writing), *use* stĭlus, *m*, (pen)
quilt, *nn*, străgŭlum, *n*
quinquennial, quinquennālis
quinsy, angīna, *f*
quintessence, vis, *f*, flōs, *m*
quip, *nn*, rēsponsum (salsum) ((witty) reply)
quirk, căvillātĭo, *f*
quit, *v.t*, rĕlinquo (3)
quite, *adv*, admŏdum, prorsus; (— enough), sătis
quiver, *nn*, phărĕtra, *f*
quiver, *v.i*, trĕmo (3)
quoit, discus, *m*
quota, răta pars, *f*
quotation, prŏlātĭo, *f*
quote, *v.t*, prŏfĕro (*irreg*)
quotidian, cottīdĭānus

R

rabbit, cŭnīcŭlus, *m*
rabble, turba, *f*
rabid, răbĭdus
race (family), gĕnus, *n*, prōgĕnĭes, *f*; (running), cursus, *m*, certāmen, *n*
race, *v.i*, cursu certo (1) (contend by running)
race-course, stădĭum, *n*, currĭcŭlum, *n*
race-horse, ĕquus cursor, *m*
rack (for torture), ĕquŭlĕus, *m*
rack, *v.t*, (torture), torquĕo (2)
racket (bat), rētĭcŭlum, *n*; (noise), strĕpĭtus, *m*
racy (smart), salsus
radiance, fulgor, *m*
radiant, clārus, fulgens
radiate, *v.i*, fulgĕo (2)
radiation, rădĭātĭo, *f*

For List of Abbreviations used, turn to pages 3, 4

radical (fundamental), tōtus; (original), innātus; (keen on change), cŭpĭdus rērum nŏvārum
radically, *adv*, pĕnĭtus, fundĭtus
radish, rădix
radius, rădĭus, *m*
raffle, ālĕa, *f*
raft, rătis, *f*
rafter, cantērĭus, *m*
rag, pannus, *m*
rage, fŭror, *m*
rage, *v.i*, fŭro (3)
ragged, pannōsus
raging, *adj*, fŭrens
raid, incursĭo, *f*; (to make a —), invādo (3) in (*with acc.*)
rail, longŭrĭus, *m*
rail at (abuse), mălĕdīco (3) (*with dat.*)
railing, cancelli, *m. pl*
raillery, căvillātĭo, *f*
raiment, vestīmenta, *n.pl*
rain, *nn*, plŭvĭa, *f*, imber, *m*
rain, *v.i*, (it rains), plŭit (3 *impers.*)
rainbow, arcus, *m*
rainy, plŭvĭus
raise, *v.t*, (lift), tollo (3); (forces), compăro (1); (rouse), ērĭgo (3); (—a seige), obsĭdĭōnem solvo (3)
raisin, ăcĭnus passus, *m*, (dried berry)
rake, *nn*, (tool), rastellus, *m*; (person), nĕpos, *c*
rake, *v.t*, rādo (3)
rally, *v.t*, (troops), mīlĭtes in ordĭnes rĕvŏco (1), (call back the soldiers to their ranks); *v.i*, se collĭgĕre (3 *reflex.*)
ram (or battering —), ărĭes *m*; (beak of a ship), rostrum, *n*
ram, *v.t*, fistūco (1); (ship) rostro laedo (3)
ramble, *v.i*, erro (1)
rambler, erro, *m*
rammer, fistūca, *f*
rampart, agger, *m*, vallum, *n*
rancid, rancĭdus
rancorous, infestus
rancour, ŏdĭum, *n*
random, *adj*, fortŭĭtus; (at —), *adv*, fortŭĭto
range, ordo, *m*; (— of mountains), iŭga, *n.pl*; (of a missile), iactus, *m*; (scope), campus, *m*
rank, *nn*, ordo, *m*
rank, *v.i*, sĕ hăbĕre (2 *reflex.*)
rank, *adj*, (smell, etc.), fētĭdus
rankle, *v.t*, exulcĕro (1), mordĕo (2)
ransack, *v.t*, dĭrĭpĭo (3)

ransom, *nn*, rĕdemptĭo, *f*; (— money), prĕtĭum, *n*
ransom, *v.t*, rĕdĭmo (3)
rant, *v.t*, dēclāmo (1)
ranting, *nn*, sermo tŭmĭdus, *m*, (bombastic speech)
rap, *nn*, pulsātĭo, *f*
rap, *v.t*, pulso (1)
rapacious, răpax
rapacity, răpācĭtas, *f*
rape, *nn*, raptus, *m*
rapid, răpĭdus, cĕler
rapidity, cĕlĕrĭtas, *f*
rapier, glădĭus, *m*
rapine, răpīna, *f*
rapture, laetĭtĭa, *f*
rapturous, laetus
rare, rārus
rarely, *v.t*, extĕnŭo (1)
rareness, rarity, rārĭtas, *f*
rascal, scĕlestus, *m*
rascality, scĕlĕra, *n.pl*
rase (to the ground), *v.t*, sŏlo aequo (1)
rash, *adj*, tĕmĕrārĭus
rash, *nn*, ēruptĭo, *f*
rashness, tĕmĕrĭtas, *f*
rasp, *nn*, (file), scŏbīna, *f*
rasp, *v.t*, rādo (3)
rat, mūs, *c*
rate (price), prĕtĭum, *n*; (tax), vectĭgal, *n*; (speed), cĕlĕrĭtas, *f*; (at any —), *adv*, ŭtīque
rate, *v.t*, (value), aestĭmo (1); (chide), incrĕpo (1); (tax), censĕo (2)
rather, *adv*, (preferably), pŏtĭus; (somewhat), ălĭquantum; (a little), *with comparatives, e.g.* **rather** (more quickly), paulo (cĕlĕrĭus)
ratification, sanctĭo, *f*
ratify, *v.t*, rătum făcĭo (3)
ratio, portĭo, *f*
ration, *nn*, dēmensum, *n*, cĭbārĭa, *n.pl*
rational (a — being), partĭceps rătĭonis (participant in reason)
rationally, *adv*, rătĭōne
rattle, *nn*, crĕpĭtus, *m*; (toy), crĕpĭtăcŭlum, *m*
rattle, *v.i*, crĕpo (1)
ravage, *v.t*, pŏpŭlor (1 *dep.*)
ravaging, *nn*, pŏpŭlātĭo, *f*
rave, *v.i*, fŭro (3)
raven, corvus, *m*
ravening, ravenous, răpax
ravine, fauces, *f.pl*
raving, *adj*, fŭrens, insānus
raving, *nn*, fŭror, *m*
ravish, *v.t*, răpĭo (3), stŭpro (1)
ravishing, suāvis

raw, crūdus; (inexperienced, un-worked), rŭdis
ray, rădĭus, *m*
razor, nŏvācŭla, *f*
reach, *nn*, (range), iactus, *m*; (space), spătĭum, *n*
reach, *v.i*, (extend), pertĭněo (2), attingo (3); *v.t*, (come to), pervěnĭo (4) ad (*with acc.*)
react, *v.t*, (be influenced), afficĭor (3 *pass.*)
reaction (of feeling), *use vb*, commŏvěo (2) (to make an impression on)
read, *v.t*, lěgo (3); (— aloud), rěcĭto (1)
readable, făcĭlis lectu
reader, lector, *m*
readily, *adv*, (willingly), lĭbenter
readiness (preparedness), *use adj*, părātus (ready); (willingness), ănĭmus lĭbens, *m*
reading, *nn*, lectĭo, *f*, rěcĭtātĭo, *f*
reading-room, bibliŏthēca, *f*
ready, părātus, promptus; (to be —), părātus, praesto esse (*irreg.*); (to make, get —), păro (1)
real, *adj*, vērus
realism, vērĭtas, *f*
reality, rēs, *f*
realization (getting to know), cognĭtĭo, *f*; (completion), confectĭo, *f*
realise, *v.t*, intellĕgo (3); (a project), perficĭo 3), perdūco (3)
really, *adv*, rēvērā; (is it so?), ĭtăne est?
realm, regnum, *n*
reap, *v.t*, měto (3); (gain), compăro (1)
reaper, messor, *m*
reaping-hook, falx, *f*
reappear, *v.i*, rēděo (irreg.)
rear, *nn*, (of a marching column), agmen nŏvissĭmum, *n*; (of an army), ăcĭes nŏvissĭma, *f*; (in the —), *adv*, ā tergo
rear, *v.t*, (bring up), ēdūco (1), ălo (3); *v.i*, (of horses), sē ērĭgěre (3 *reflex.*)
reason (faculty of thinking), mens, *f*; (cause), causa, *f*; (for this —), *adv*, ĭděo, idcirco; (for what —, why?), cur, quārē; (without —, heedlessly), *adv*, těměrē
reason, *v.t*, rătĭōcĭnor (1 *dep.*); (— with), dissěro (3), cum (*with abl.*)
reasonable (fair), aequus, iustus; (in size), mŏdĭcus
reasonableness (fairness), aequĭtas, *f*
reasoning, *nn*, rătĭo, *f*
reassemble, *v.t*, cōgo (3), in ūnum lŏcum collĭgo (3), (collect into one place); *v.i*,rēděo (4)

reassert, *v.t*, rēstĭtŭo (3)
reassure, *v.t*, confirmo (1)
rebel, *nn*, sēdĭtĭōsus, *m*
rebel, *v.i*, rěbello (1), dēfĭcĭo (3)
rebellion, sēdĭtĭo, *f*
rebellious, sēdĭtĭōsus
rebound, *v.i*, rěsĭlĭo (4)
rebuff, *v.t*, rěpello (3)
rebuff, *nn*, rěpulsa, *f*
rebuke, *nn*, rěprěhensĭo, *f*
rebuke, *v.t*, rěprěhendo (3)
recall, *nn*, rěvŏcātĭo, *f*
recall, *v.t*, rěvŏco (1); (— to mind), rěpěto (3)
recapitulate, *v.t*, ēnŭměro (1)
recapitulation, ēnŭměrātĭo, *f*
recapture, *v.t*, rěcĭpĭo (3)
recede, *v.i*, rěcēdo (3)
receipt (act of receiving), acceptĭo, *f*; (document), ăpocha, *f*
receipts (proceeds), rědĭtus, *m*
receive, *v.t*, accĭpĭo (3), excĭpĭo (3)
receiver (of stolen goods), rěceptor, *m*
recent, rěcens
recently, *adv*, nŭper
receptacle, rěceptācŭlum, *n*
reception, ădĭtus, *m*
receptive, dŏcĭlis
recess, rěcessus, *m*; (holidays), fērĭae, *f. pl*
reciprocal, mūtŭus
reciprocate, *v.t*, rěfěro (*irreg.*)
recital, narrātĭo, *f*
recite, *v.t*, rěcĭto (1), prōnuntĭo (1)
reckless, těměrārĭus
recklessness, těměrĭtas, *f*
reckon, *v.t*, (count), nŭměro (1); (— on, rely on), confīdo (3) (*with dat.*); (consider), dūco (3)
reckoning, rătĭo, *f*
reclaim, *v.t*, rěpěto (3)
recline, *v.i*, rěcŭbo (1)
recluse, hŏmo sōlĭtārĭus
recognizable, *use phr*, quod agnosci pŏtest (that can be recognized)
recognize, *v.t*, agnosco (3), cognosco (3); (acknowledge), confĭtěor (2 *dep.*)
recognition, cognĭtĭo, *f*
recoil, *v.i*, rěsĭlĭo (4)
recollect, *v.t*, rěmĭniscor (3 *dep. with genit*)
recollection, měmŏrĭa, *f*
recommence, *v.t*, rědintěgro (1)
recommend, *v.t*, commendo (1)
recommendation, commendātĭo, *f*
recompense, *v.t*, rěmūněror (1 *dep*)
reconcile, *v.t*, rěconcĭlĭo (1)
reconciliation, rěconcĭlĭātĭo, *f*
reconnoitre, *v.t*, explōro (1)
reconsider, *v.t*, rěpŭto (1)

record, *v.t*, in tăbŭlas rĕfĕro (*irreg*)
records, tăbŭlae, *f. pl*, fasti, *m. pl*
recount, *v.t.* (expound), ēnarro (1)
recourse (to have — to), *v.i*, confŭgĭo (3) ad (*with acc*)
recover, *v.t*, rĕcŭpĕro (1), rĕcĭpĭo (3); *v.i*, (from illness, etc.), rĕvălesco (3), rĕfĭcĭor (3 *pass*), sē collĭgĕre (3 *reflex*)
recovery, rĕcŭpĕrātĭo, *f*; (from illness), sălus, *f*
recreate, *v.t*, rĕcrĕo (1)
recreation, rĕmissĭo, *f*
recruit, *nn*, tīro, *m*
recruit, *v.t*, (enrol), conscrībo (3)
recruiting, *nn*, dēlectus, *m*
rectify, *v.i*, corrĭgo.(3)
rectitude, prŏbĭtas, *f*
recumbent, rĕcŭbans
recur, *v.i*, rĕdĕo (4)
red, rŭber, rūfus; (redhanded), *adj*, mănĭfestus
redden, *v.t*, rŭbĕfăcĭo (3); *v.i*, rŭbesco (3)
redeem, *v.t*, rĕdĭmo (3)
redeemer, lībĕrātor, *m*
redemption, rĕdemptĭo, *f*
red-lead, mĭnĭum, *n*
redness, rŭbor, *m*
redouble, *v.t*, ingĕmĭno (1)
redound, rĕdundo (1)
redress, *v.t*, rĕstĭtŭo (3)
reduce, *v.t*, rĕdĭgo (3)
reduction, dēmĭnūtĭo, *f*; (taking by storm), expugnātĭo, *f*
redundancy, rĕdundantĭa, *f*
redundant, sŭpervăcŭus
re-echo, *v.i*, rĕsŏno (1)
reed, ărundo, *f*
reef, saxa, *n.pl*
reek, *v.i*, fūmo (1)
reel, *v.i*, (totter), văcillo (1)
re-elect, *v.t*, rĕcrĕo (1)
re-establish, *v.t*, rĕstĭtŭo (3)
refectory, cēnăcŭlum, *n*
refer, *v.t*, rĕfĕro *or* dēfĕro (*irreg*) ad (*with acc*); (to — to), perstringo (3), specto (1) ad (*with acc*)
referee, arbĭter, *m*
reference, rătĭo, *f*
refill, *v.t*, rĕplĕo (2)
refine, *v.t*, (polish), expŏlĭo (4)
refined, pŏlītus, hūmānus
refinement, hūmānĭtas, *f*
refinery, officīna, *f*
reflect, *v.t*, rĕpercŭtĭo (3); *v.i*, (ponder), rĕpŭto (1) (ănĭmo) (in the mind)
reflection (image), ĭmāgo, *f*; (thought), cōgĭtātĭo, *f*

reform, ēmendātĭo, *f*
reform, *v.t*, rĕstĭtŭo (3); (correct), corrĭgo (3); *v.i*, sē corrĭgĕre (3 *reflex*)
reformer, ēmendātor, *m*
refract, *v.t*, infringo (3)
refractory, contŭmax
refrain from, *v.i*, sē contĭnēre (2 *reflex*) ab (*with abl*)
refresh, *v.t*, rĕcrĕo (1), rĕfĭcĭo (3)
refreshment (food), cĭbus, *m*
refuge, perfŭgĭum, *n*; (to take —), *v.i*, confŭgĭo (3) ad (*with acc*)
refugee, *adj*, prŏfŭgus
refulgent, splendĭdus
refund, *v.t*, reddo (3)
refusal, rĕcūsātĭo, *f*
refuse, *nn*, purgāmentum, *n*
refuse, *v.t*, rĕcūso (1); (to — to do) nōlo (*irreg*) (*with infin*); (say no), nĕgo (1)
refute, *v.t*, rĕfello (3)
regain, *v.t*, rĕcĭpĭo (3)
regal, rēgālis
regale, *v.t*, excĭpĭo (3)
regalia, insignĭa, *n.pl*
regard, *nn*, (esteem),studĭum,*n*,hŏnor, *m*; (consideration), rēspectus, *m*
regard, *v.t*, (look at), intŭĕor (2 *dep*); (consider), hăbĕo (2); (esteem), aestĭmo (1)
regardless, neglĕgens
regency, interregnum, *n*
regent, interrex, *m*
regicide, caedes, (*f*) rēgis (killing of a king)
regiment, lĕgĭo, *f*
region, rĕgĭo, *f*, tractus, *m*
register, tăbŭlae, *f.pl*
register, *v.t*, perscrībo (3)
registrar, tăbŭlārĭus, *m*
regret, *nn*, dŏlor, *m*
regret, *v.t*, (repent of), *use* paenĭtet (2 *impers*) (*with acc. of subject*), *e.g.* I repent of, mē paenĭtet (*with genit*)
regular (correctly arranged), ordĭnātus, compŏsĭtus; (customary), sollémnis
regularity, ordo, *m*
regularly, *adv*, (in order), ordĭne; (customarily), sollemnĭter
regulate, *v.t*, ordĭno (1)
regulation (order), iussum, *n*; (rule), praeceptum, *n*
rehabilitate, *v.t*, rĕstĭtŭo (3)
rehearsal (practice), exercĭtātĭo, *f*
rehearse, *v.t*, (premeditate), praemĕdĭtor (1 *dep*)
reign, *nn*, regnum, *n*
reign, *v.i*, regno (1)

reimburse, *v.t*, rĕpendo (3)
rein, *nn*, hăbēna, *f*
rein, *v.t*, (curb), frēno (1)
reinforce, *v.t*, confirmo (1)
reinforcement (help), auxĭlĭum, *n*
reinstate, *v.t*, rēstĭtŭo (3)
reiterate, *v.t*, ĭtĕro (1)
reject, *v.t*, rēĭcĭo (3)
rejection, rēiectĭo, *f*
rejoice, *v.i*, gaudĕo (2)
rejoicing, *nn*, laetĭtĭa, *f*
rejoin, *v.i*, rĕdĕo (4)
relapse, *v.i*, rĕcĭdo (3)
relate, *v.t*, (tell), narro (1), expōno (3); *v.i*, pertĭnĕo (2)
related (by birth), cognātus; (by marriage), affīnis; (by blood), consanguĭnĕus; (near), prŏpinquus
relation (relative), cognātus *m*, affīnis *m*; (connection), rătĭo, *f*
relationship, cognātĭo, *f*, affīnĭtas, *f*
relative, *nn*, cognātus, *m*, affīnis, *m*
relative, *adj*, compărātus (compared)
relax, *v.t*, rĕmitto (3); *v.i*, rĕlanguesco (3)
relaxation, rĕmissĭo, *f*
relay, *v.t*, (send), mitto (3)
relays of horses, ĕqui dispŏsĭti, *m.pl* (horses methodically arranged)
release, *nn*, lībĕrātĭo *f*
release, *v.t*, exsolvo (3) lībĕro (1)
relent, *v.t*, rĕmitto (3)
relentless, immĭsērĭcors
relevant, *use vb*, pertĭnĕo (2) (to concern)
reliance, fīdūcĭa, *f*
relic, rēlĭquĭae, *f*, *pl*
relief (alleviation), lĕvātĭo, *f*; (help), auxĭlĭum, *n*
relieve, *v.t*, lĕvo (1), rĕmitto (3); (help), subvĕnĭo (4) (*with dat*); (of command, etc.), succĕdo (3) (*followed by in with acc. or by dat*)
religion, rĕlĭgĭo, *f*, săcra, *n.pl*
religious, rĕlĭgĭōsus, pĭus
relinquish, *v.t*, rĕlinquo (3)
relish, *nn*, stŭdĭum, *n*, săpor, *m*
relish, *v.t*, frŭor (3 *dep. with abl*)
reluctance, *use adj*, invītus (unwilling)
reluctant, invītus
rely on, *v.t*, confīdo (3) (*with dat. of person or abl. of thing*)
relying on, *adj*, frētus (*with abl*)
remain, *v.i*, mănĕo (2); (be left over), sŭpersum (*irreg*)
remainder, rĕlĭquum, *n*
remaining, *adj*, rĕlĭquus
remains, rēlĭquĭae, *f*, *pl*
remand, *v.t*, amplĭo (1)
remark, *nn*, dictum, *n*

remark, *v.t*, (say), dīco (3); (observe), observo (1)
remarkable, insignis
remedy, rĕmĕdĭum, *n*, mĕdĭcāmentum, *n*
remedy, *v.t*, sāno (1); (correct), corrĭgo (3)
remember, *v.i*, mĕmĭni (*v.defect. with genit*), rĕcordor (1 *dep. with acc*)
remembrance, rĕcordātĭo, *f*, mĕmŏrĭa, *f*
remind, *v.t*, mŏnĕo (2)
reminiscence, rĕcordātĭo, *f*
remiss, neglēgens
remission (forgiveness), vĕnĭa, *f*; (release), sŏlūtĭo, *f*
remit, *v.t*, rĕmitto (3)
remittance, pĕcūnĭa, *f*
remnant, rĕlĭquĭae, *f*. *pl*
remonstrate, *v.i*, rĕclāmo (1) (*with dat*)
remorse, conscĭentĭa, *f*
remorseless, immĭsĕrĭcors, dūrus
remote, rĕmōtus
remoteness, longinquĭtas, *f*
removal (driving away), āmōtĭo, *f*; (sending away), rĕlēgātĭo, *f*; (— by force), raptus, *m*
remove, *v.t*, rĕmŏvĕo (2); (send away), rĕlēgo (1); *v.i*, migro (1)
remunerate, *v.t*, rĕmūnĕror (1 *dep*)
remuneration, rĕmūnĕrātĭo, *f*
rend, *v.t*, scindo (3)
render, *v.t*, reddo (3)
rendezvous (to fix a —), lŏcum (et dĭem) constĭtŭo (3), (place and day)
rending (severing), discĭdĭum, *n*
renegade (deserter), transfŭga, *c*
renew, *v.t*, rĕnŏvo (1), rĕdintĕgro (1)
renewal, rĕnŏvātĭo, *f*
renounce, *v.t*, rĕnuntĭo (1), rĕmitto (3)
renovate, *v.t*, rĕnŏvo (1)
renovation, rĕstĭtūtĭo, *f*
renown, fāma, *f*, glōrĭa, *f*
renowned, clārus
rent, *nn*, scissūra, *f*; (of houses, etc.), merces, *f*
rent, *v.t*, (let), lŏco (1); (hire), condūco (3)
renunciation, rĕpŭdĭātĭo, *f*
repair, *v.t*, rĕfĭcĭo (3), sarcĭo (4)
repaired, sartus
reparation, sătisfactĭo, *f*
repast, cĭbus, *m*
repay, *v.t*, (grātĭam) rĕfĕro (*irreg*)
repayment, sŏlūtĭo, *f*
repeal, *nn*, abrŏgātĭo, *f*
repeal, *v.t*, abrŏgo (1), rĕscindo (3)
repeat, *v.t*, ĭtĕro (1), reddo (3)

For List of Abbreviations used, turn to pages 3, 4

repeatedly, *adv,* ĭdentĭdem
repel, *v.t,* rĕpello (3)
repent, *v.i,* paenĭtet (2 *impers*) (*with acc. of person and genit. of cause*), *e.g.* **I repent of this deed,** mē paenĭtet huius facti
repentance, paenĭtentĭa, *f*
repentant, paenĭtens
repetition, ĭtĕrātĭo, *f*
replace, *v.t,* rĕpōno (3); **(substitute),** substĭtŭo (3)
replenish, *v.t,* rĕplĕo (2)
replete, rĕplētus
reply, *nn,* rēsponsum, *n*
reply, *v.i,* rēspondĕo (2)
report, *nn,* nuntĭus, *m;* **(rumour),** fāma, *f;* **(bang),** crĕpĭtus, *m*
report, *v.t,* rĕfĕro (*irreg*), nuntĭo (1)
repose, *nn,* quĭes, *f*
repose, *v.i,* **(rest),** quĭesco (3)
repository, rĕceptācŭlum, *n*
reprehend, *v.t,* rĕprĕhendo (3)
reprehensible, culpandus
represent, *v.t,* exprĭmo (3), fingo (3); **(take the place of),** persōnam gĕro (3)
representation, ĭmāgo, *f*
representative (deputy), prōcūrātor, *m*
repress, *v.t,* cŏhĭbĕo (2)
reprieve, *nn,* **(respite),** mŏra, *f*
reprieve, *v.t,* **(put off),** diffĕro (*irreg*)
reprimand, *nn,* rĕprĕhensĭo, *f*
reprimand, *v.t,* rĕprĕhendo (3)
reprisal, *use* poena, *f,* **(punishment)**
reproach, *nn,* exprŏbrātĭo, *f,* opprŏbrĭum, *n*
reproach, *v.t,* exprŏbro (1), ŏbĭcĭo (3) (*both with acc. of thing and dat. of person*)
reproachful, obiurgātōrĭus
reprobate, *nn,* perdĭtus, *m,* nēbŭlo, *m*
reproduce, *v.t,* rĕcrĕo (1)
reproof, rĕprĕhensĭo, *f,* obiurgātĭo, *f,* vĭtŭpĕrātĭo, *f*
reprove, *v.t,* rĕprĕhendo (3), obiurgo (1), vĭtŭpĕro (1)
reptile, serpens, *f*
republic, respublĭca, *f*
republican, *adj,* pŏpŭlāris
repudiate, *v.t,* rĕpŭdĭo (1)
repudiation, rĕpŭdĭātĭo, *f*
repugnance, ŏdĭum, *n*
repugnant, āversus; **(it is — to me, I hate it),** *use phr,* ŏdĭo esse **(to be hateful),** *with dat. of person*
repulse, *v.t,* rĕpello (3)
repulsive, foedus, ŏdĭōsus
reputable, hŏnestus

reputation, repute, fāma, *f;* **(good —),** existĭmātĭo, *f;* **(bad —),** infāmĭa, *f*
request, *nn,* rŏgātĭo, *f*
request, *v.t,* rŏgo (1), prĕcor (1 *dep*)
require, *v.t,* **(demand),** postŭlo (1); **(need),** ĕgĕo (2) (*with abl*)
requirement (demand), postŭlātĭo, *f;* *or use adj,* nĕcessārĭus
requisite, *adj,* nĕcessārĭus
requisition, postŭlātĭo, *f*
requite, *v.t,* rĕpōno (3)
rescind, *v.t,* rēscindo (3)
rescue, *v.t,* ērĭpĭo (3)
rescue, *nn,* lībĕrātĭo, *f*
research, investĭgātĭo, *f*
resemblance, sĭmĭlĭtūdo, *f*
resemble, *v.t,* rĕfĕro (*irreg*), sĭmĭlis esse (*irreg*) (*with genit. or dat*)
resembling, *adj,* sĭmĭlis
resent, *v.t,* aegrē fĕro (*irreg*) **(tolerate with displeasure)**
resentful, īrācundus
resentment, īra, *f*
reservation (restriction), exceptĭo, *f*
reserve, *nn,* **(military),** subsĭdĭum, *n;* **(of disposition),** grăvĭtas, *f*
reserve, *v.t,* servo (1); **(put aside),** sēpōno (3)
reserved (of disposition), grăvis
reservoir, lăcus, *m*
reside, *v.i,* hăbĭto (1)
residence, sēdes, *f. pl,* dŏmĭcĭlĭum, *n*
resident, incŏla, *c*
resign, *v.i, and v.t,* concēdo (3); **(to — oneself to),** sē committĕre (3 *reflex. with* in *and* acc)
resignation (of office, etc.), abdĭcātĭo, *f;* **(of mind)** aequus ănĭmus, *m*
resin, rēsīna, *f*
resist, *v.t,* rĕsisto (3) (*with dat*)
resistance, rĕpugnantĭa, *f, or use vb,* rĕsisto (3) **(to resist)**
resolute, firmus, fortis
resolution, obstĭnātĭo, *f,* constantĭa, *f;* **(decision),** *use vb,* plăcet **(it is resolved)**
resolve, *v.t,* **(determine),** stătŭo (3); **(solve),** dissolvo (3)
resort to, *v.t* **(a place),** cĕlĕbro (1); **(have recourse to),** confŭgĭo (3) ad (*with acc*)
resort, *nn,* **(plan),** consĭlĭum, *n;* **(last —),** extrēma, *n.pl*
resound, *v.i,* rĕsŏno (1)
resource (help), auxĭlĭum, *n;* **(wealth, means),** ŏpes, *f, pl*
respect, *nn,* **(esteem),** observantĭa, *f;* **(in all —s),** omnĭbus partĭbus; **(in**

— of), *use abl. case, e.g.* **stronger in respect of number,** sŭpĕrĭor nŭmĕro
respect, *v.t,* (esteem), observo (1); (reverence), suspĭcĭo (3)
respectability, hŏnestas, *f*
respectable, hŏnestus
respectful, observans
respecting, *prep,* dē (*with abl*)
respective, *use* quisque (each) *with* sŭus (his own)
respiration, respĭrātĭo, *f*
respite (delay), mŏra, *f*
resplendent, splendĭdus
respond, *v.i,* rēspondĕo (2)
response, rēsponsum, *n*
responsibility (duty, function), offĭcĭum, *n*; *or use imp. vb,* ŏportet (it behoves)
responsible, (to be — for), praesto (1)
rest, *nn,* (repose), quĭes, *f,* ōtĭum, *n*; (remainder), *use adj,* rēlĭquus, *e.g.* the — of one's life, rēlĭqua vĭta, *f*
rest, *v.i,* quĭesco (3); (— on, depend on), nītor (3 *dep*)
resting-place, cŭbĭle, *n*
restitution (to make —), *v.t,* rēstĭtŭo (3)
restive, *use phr,* qui nōn făcĭle dŏmāri pŏtest (that cannot easily be subdued)
restless, inquĭetus
restlessness, ĭnquĭes, *f*
restoration, rēstĭtūtĭo, *f*
restore, *v.t,* rēstĭtŭo (3)
restrain, *v.t,* cŏercĕo (2), rēprĭmo (3), cŏhĭbĕo (2)
restraint, mŏdĕrātĭo, *f*
restrict, *v.t,* circumscrĭbo (3)
restriction (bound), mŏdus, *m*
result, *nn,* ēventus, *m*
result, *v.i,* ēvĕnĭo (4)
resume, *v.t,* rĕpĕto (3)
resurrection, rēsurrectĭo, *f*
resuscitate, *v.t,* rēsuscĭto (1)
retail, *v.t,* dīvendo (3)
retailer, caupo, *m*
retain, *v.t,* rĕtĭnĕo (2)
retainer, sătelles, *c*; (*pl*) soldŭrĭi, *m. pl*
retake, *v.t,* rĕcĭpĭo (3)
retaliate, *v.t,* ulciscor (3 *dep*)
retaliation, ultĭo, *f*
retard, *v.t,* mŏror (1 *dep*)
reticent, tăcĭturnus
retinue (companions), cŏmĭtes, *c.pl*
retire, *v.i,* (go away), rĕcēdo (3), ăbĕo (4); (from a post, etc.), dēcēdo (3); (retreat), sē rĕcĭpĕre (3 *reflex*)
retired, rĕmōtus
retirement (act of —), rĕcessus, *m*; (leisure), ōtĭum, *n*

retiring, *adj,* vĕrēcundus
retort, *v.t,* rĕfĕro (*irreg*)
retrace, *v.t,* rĕpĕto (3)
retract, *v.t,* rĕnuntĭo (1)
retreat, *nn,* rĕceptus, *m*; (place of refuge), rĕfŭgĭum, *n*
retreat, *v.i,* sē rĕcĭpĕre (3 *reflex*)
retrench, *v.t,* mĭnŭo (3)
retribution, poena, *f*
retrieve, *v.t,* rĕcŭpĕro (1)
retrograde, *adj, use comp. adj,* pēior (worse)
retrogression, rĕgressus, *m*
retrospect, *use vb,* rĕspĭcĭo (3) (to look back)
return, *nn,* (coming back), rĕdĭtus, *m*; (giving back), rēstĭtūtĭo, *f*; (profit), quaestus, *m*
return, *v.t,* (give back), reddo (3), rĕfĕro (*irreg*); *v.i,* (go back), rĕdĕo (4)
reunite, *v.t,* rĕconcĭlĭo (1)
reveal, *v.t,* pătĕfăcĭo (3)
revel, *nn,* cōmissātĭo, *f*
revel, *v.i,* cōmissor (1 *dep*)
revelation, pătĕfactĭo, *f*
revenge, *nn,* ultĭo, *f*
revenge oneself on, *v.t,* ulciscor (3 *dep*)
revengeful, cŭpĭdus ulciscendi (keen on revenge)
revenue, vectīgal, *n*
reverberate, *v.i,* rĕsŏno (1)
revere, reverence, *v.t,* vĕnĕror (1 *dep*)
reverence, vĕnĕrātĭo, *f*
revered, vĕnĕrābĭlis
reverend, vĕnĕrābĭlis
reverent, rĕvĕrens
reverse (contrary), *adj,* contrārĭus (opposite); (defeat), clādes, *f*
reverse, *v.t,* inverto (3)
revert, *v.i,* rĕdĕo (4)
review, *nn,* rĕcognĭtĭo, *f,* rĕcensĭo, *f*
review, *v.t,* rĕcensĕo (2)
revile, *v.t,* mălĕdīco (3) (*with dat*)
reviling, *nn,* mălĕdictĭo, *f*
revise, *v.t,* ēmendo (1)
revision, ēmendātĭo, *f*
revisit, *v.t,* rĕvīso (3)
revival, rĕnŏvātĭo, *f*
revive, *v.t,* rĕcrĕo (1), excĭto (1); *v.i,* rĕvīvisco (3)
revocable, rĕvŏcābĭlis
revoke, *v.t,* abrŏgo (1)
revolt, *nn,* dēfectĭo, *f,* sēdĭtĭo, *f*
revolt, *v.i,* dēfĭcĭo (3)
revolting, *adj,* (disgusting), foedus
revolution (turning round), conversĭo, *f*; (political), nŏvae res, *f. pl*
revolutionize, *v.t,* nŏvo (1)
revolutionary, sēdĭtĭōsus

revolve, *v.i*, sē volvĕre (3 *reflex*)
reward, *nn*, praemĭum, *n*
reward, *v.t*, rĕmunĕror (1 *dep*)
rewrite, *v.t*, rēscrībo (3)
rhetoric, rhētŏrĭca, *f*
rhetorical, rhētŏrĭcus
Rhine, Rhēnus, *m*
rhinoceros, rhīnŏcĕros, *m*
rhubarb, rādix Pontĭca, *f* (Black Sea root)
rhyme (verse), versus, *m*
rhythm, nŭmĕrus, *m*
rhythmical, nŭmĕrōsus
rib, costa, *f*
ribald, obscēnus
ribbon, taenĭa, *f*
rice, ŏrȳza, *f*
rich, dīves, lŏcŭples; (fertile), pinguis
riches, dīvĭtĭae, *f. pl*
richness, ūbertas, *f*
rick (heap), ăcervus, *m*
rid, *v.t* lībĕro (1); (to get — of), dēpōno (3), dēpello (3)
riddle, aenigma, *n*; (in —s), per ambāges
riddle, *v.t*, (sift), cerno (3); (— with holes), confōdĭo (3)
ride, *v.i*, vĕhor (3 *dep*); (— at anchor), ·consisto (3)
rider (horseman), ĕquĕs, *m*
ridge (mountain —), iŭgum, *n*
ridicule, *nn*, rīdĭcŭlum, *n*
ridicule, *v.t*, irrīdĕo (2)
ridiculous, rīdĭcŭlus
riding, *nn*, ĕquĭtātĭo, *f*
rife, frĕquens, crēber
rifle, *v.t*, praedor (1 *dep*.)
rift, rīma, *f*
rig, *v.t*, armo (1)
rigging, armāmentum, *n.pl*
right, *adj*, (direction), dexter; (true), rectus, vērus; (correct), rectus; (fit), ĭdōnĕus; (—hand), dextra (manus)
right, *nn*, (moral), fas, *n*; (legal), iūs, *n*
rightly, *adv*, rectē, vērē
right, *v.t*, rēstĭtŭo (3)
righteous, iustus
righteousness, prŏbĭtas, *f*
rightful, iustus
rigid, rīgĭdus, dūrus
rigorous, dūrus
rigour, dūrĭtĭa, *f*
rill, rīvŭlus, *m*
rim, ōra, *f*, lābrum, *n*
rime, prŭīna, *f*
rind, crusta, *f*
ring (finger, etc.), ānŭlus, *m*; (circle), orbis, *m*

ring, *v.i*, tinnĭo (4); (surround) circŭmĕo (4)
ringing, *nn*, tinnītus, *m*
ringing, *adj*, tinnŭlus
ringleader, auctor, *m*
ringlet, cincinnus, *m*
rinse, *v.t*, collŭo (3)
riot, turba, *f*, tŭmultus, *m*; (to make a —), tŭmultum făcĭo (3)
riotous, turbŭlentus; (extravagent), luxŭrĭōsus
rip, *v.t*, scindo (3)
ripe, mātūrus
ripen, *v.i*, mātūresco (3); *v.t*, mātūro (1)
ripeness, mātūrĭtas, *f*
ripple, *v.i.* (tremble), trĕpĭdo (1)
rise, *nn*, (of sun, etc., *or* origin), ortus, *m*,
rise, *v.i*, surgo (3); (of sun, etc.), ŏrĭor (4 *dep*); (in rank), cresco (3); (in rebellion), consurgo (3)
rising, *nn*, ortus, *m*; (in rebellion), mōtus, *m*
rising (ground), *nn*, clīvus, *m*
risk, *nn*, pĕrīcŭlum, *n*
risk, *v.t*, pĕrīclītor (1 *dep*)
ritual, rītus, *m*
rival, *nn*, aemŭlus, *m*, rīvālis, *c*
rival, *v.t*, aemŭlor (1 *dep*)
rivalry, aemŭlātĭo, *f*
river, *nn*, flūmen, *n*, flŭvĭus, *m*
river-bank, rīpa, *f*
river-bed, alvĕus, *m*
rivet, clāvus, *m*
rivulet, rīvŭlus, *m*
road, vĭa, *f*, ĭter, *n*; (to make a —), vĭam mūnĭo (4)
road-making, mūnītĭo, (*f*) vĭārum
roadstead (for ships), stătĭo, *f*
roam, *v.i*, văgor (1 *dep*), erro (1)
roaming, *adj*, văgus
roar, *nn*, frĕmĭtus, *m*
roar, *v.i*, frĕmo (3)
roast, *v.t*, torrĕo (2)
roasted, assus
rob, *v.t*, spŏlĭo (1) (*with acc. of person robbed, abl. of thing taken*)
robber, lătro, *m*
robbery, lătrōcĭnĭum, *n*
robe, vestis, *f*, vestīmentum, *n*; (woman's —), stŏla, *f*; (— of state), trăbĕa, *f*; (— of kings), purpŭra, *f*
robe, *v.t*, vestĭo (4), indŭo (3)
robust, rōbustus
rock, rūpes, *f*
rock, *v.t*, ăgĭto (1)
rocky, scŏpŭlōsus
rod, virga, *f*; (fishing —), ărundo, *f*
roe, căprĕa, *f*; (of fish), ōva, *n.pl* (eggs)

rogue, scĕlestus, *m*
roguery, nēquĭtĭa, *f*
roll, *nn*, (something rolled up), vŏlūmen, *n*; (names), album, *n*
roll, *v.t*, volvo (3); *v.i*, volvor (3 *pass*)
roller, cўlindrus, *m*
rolling, *adj*, vŏlūbĭlis
Roman, Rōmānus
romance (story), fābŭla, *f*
romance, *v.i*, fābŭlor (1 *dep*)
romantic (fabulous), commentĭcĭus
Rome, Rōma, *f*
romp, *v.i*, lūdo (3)
romp, *nn*, lūsus, *m*
roof, *v.t*, tĕgo (3)
roof, *nn*, tectum, *n*
rook (raven), corvus, *m*
room, conclāve, *n*; (space), spătĭum, *n*; (bed —), cŭbĭcŭlum, *n*; (dining —), trīclīnĭum, *n*
roomy, căpax
roost, *nn*, pertĭca, *f*
root, rādix, *f*; (to strike —s, become rooted), rādīces ăgo (3); (—ed to the spot), dēfixus
rope, fūnis, *m*, restis, *f*, rŭdens, *m*
rosary (garden), rŏsārĭum, *n*
rose, rŏsa, *f*
rosemary, ros mărīnus, *m*
rostrum, rostra, *n.pl*
rosy, rŏsĕus
rot, *nn*, tābes, *f*
rot, *v.i*, putesco (3)
rotate, *v.i*, sē volvĕre (3 *reflex*)
rotation, turbo, *m*
rotten, pŭtrĭdus
rotundity, rŏtundĭtas, *f*
rouge, *nn*, fūcus, *m*
rouge, *v.t*, fūco (1)
rough, asper; (weather), ătrox; (of sea), turbĭdus; (of manner), incultus
roughness, aspĕrĭtas, *f*
round, *adj*, rŏtundus
round, *adv*, circum
round, *prep*, circum (*with acc*)
round, *v.t*, (to make —), rŏtundo (1), curvo (1); (to — off), conclūdo (3); *v.i*, (to go —), circumăgor (3 *pass*)
roundabout, *adj*, dēvĭus
rouse, *v.t*, excĭto (1)
rout, *nn*, (flight, defeat), fŭga, *f*
rout, *v.t*, fŭgo (1)
route, ĭter, *n*
routine, ūsus, *m*
rove, *v.i*, văgor (1 *dep*)
roving, *nn*, văgătĭo, *f*
row (line), ordo, *m*; (quarrel), rixa, *f*; (noise), strĕpĭtus, *m*
row, *v.i*, rēmĭgo (1)

rowing, *nn*, rēmĭgĭum, *n*
royal, rēgĭus
royalty, regnum, *n*
rub, *v.t*, tĕro (3), frĭco (1); (— out), dēlĕo (2)
rubbish, quisquĭlĭae, *f. pl*
rubicund, rŭbĭcundus
ruby, *nn*, carbuncŭlus, *m*
ruby, *adj*, purpŭrĕus
rudder, gŭbernācŭlum, *n*
ruddy, rŭbĭcundus
rude (person), asper, ĭnurbānus
rudeness, ĭnhūmānĭtas, *f*
rudimentary, incŏhātus (incomplete)
rudiments, ĕlĕmenta, *n.pl*
rue, *nn*, rūta, *f*
rueful, maestus
ruff, torquis, *m. or f*
ruffian, perdĭtus, *m*, lătro, *m*
ruffianly, *adj*, scĕlestus
ruffle, *v.t*, ăgĭto (1)
rug, strāgŭlum, *n*
rugged, asper
ruin, exĭtĭum, *n*, rŭīna, *f*; (building), părĭĕtīnae, *f. pl*
ruin, *v.t*, perdo (3)
ruinous, exĭtĭōsus, damnōsus
rule, *nn*, (law), lex, *f*; (precept), praeceptum, *n*; (pattern), norma, *f*; (for measuring), rēgŭla, *f*; (government), impĕrĭum, *n*
rule, *v.t*, rēgo (3); *v.i*, regno (1)
ruler (person), dŏmĭnus, *m*; (measurement), rēgŭla, *f*
rumble, *nn*, murmur, *n*
rumble, *v.i*, murmŭro (1), mūgĭo (4)
ruminate, *v.i*, cŏgĭto (1)
rummage, *v.t*, rīmor (1 *dep*)
rumour, *nn*, rūmor, *m*, fāma, *f*
rump, clūnes, *f. pl*
rumple, *v.t*, corrūgo (1)
run, *v.i*, curro (3); (— about), hūc illūc curro (3); (— after), persĕquor (3 *dep*); (— away), fūgio (3); (— aground), impingor (3 *pass*), inflĭgor (3 *pass*); (— back), rĕcurro (3); (— down), dē curro (3); (— forward), prōcurro (3); (— into), incurro (3); (— out), excurro (3); (— over, with vehicle etc.), obtĕro (3); (— through), percurro (3)
runaway, *adj*, fŭgĭtīvus
runner, cursor, *m*
running, *nn*, cursus, *m*
running, *adj*, (water), vīvus
rupture (disease), hernĭa, *f*
rupture, *v.t*, rumpo (3)
rural, rustĭcus
rush, *nn*, (plant), iuncus, *m*; (rushing, running), impĕtus, *m*

For List of Abbreviations used, turn to pages 3, 4

rush, v.i, rŭo (3); (— forward), sē prōrĭpĕre (3 reflex); (— into), irrŭo (3); (— out), sē effundĕre (3 reflex)
rusk, crustum, n
russet, rūfus
rust, nn, rōbīgo, f
rustic, adj, rustĭcus
rusticate, v.i, rustĭcor (1 dep); v.t, rēlēgo (1)
rusticity, rustĭcĭtas, f
rustle, v.i, crĕpo (1)
rustle, rustling, nn, sŭsurrus, m
rusty, rōbīgĭnōsus
rut, orbĭta, f
ruthless, immītis, sēvērus
rye, sēcāle, n

S

Sabbath, sabbăta, n.pl
sable, adj, (black), āter
sabre, glădĭus, m
sack (bag), saccus, m; (pillage), dīreptĭo, f
sack, v.t, (pillage), dīrĭpĭo (3)
sackcloth, saccus, m
sacrament, săcrāmentum, n
sacred, săcer, sanctus
sacredness, sanctĭtas, f
sacrifice, săcrĭfĭcĭum, n; (the victim), hostĭa, f
sacrifice, v.i, săcrĭfĭco (1); v.t, im-mŏlo (1)
sacrificial, săcrĭfĭcus
sacrilege, săcrĭlĕgĭum, n; or use vb, dīrĭpĭo (3) (to plunder)
sad, tristis
sadden, v.t, tristĭtĭā affĭcĭo (3) (affect with sadness)
saddle, nn, ĕphippĭum, n
saddle, v.t, sterno (3); (impose), impōno (3)
sadness, tristĭtĭa, f
safe (free from danger), tūtus; (having escaped from danger), incŏlŭmis
safe-conduct, fīdes, f
safeguard (act of —), cautĭo, f; (defence), prōpugnācŭlum, n
safely, adv, tūtō
safety, sălus, f
saffron, nn, crŏcus, m
saffron, adj, crŏcĕus
sagacious, prūdens, săgax
sagacity, prūdentĭa, f, săgācĭtas, f
sage (wise man), săpĭens, m; (plant), salvĭa, f

sail, nn, vēlum, n; (to set —), vēla do (1)
sail, v.i, nāvĭgo (1), vĕhor (3 pass); (to go by means of sails), vēla făcĭo (3)
sailing, nn, nāvĭgātĭo, f
sailor, nauta, m
saint, sanctus, m
saintly, sanctus
sake (for the — of), prep, causā (with genit); (on behalf of), prō (with abl), ŏb, propter (with acc)
salad, ăcētārĭa, n.pl
salary, merces, f
sale, vendĭtĭo, f; (auction), hasta, f
salient, adj, prīmus (first)
saline, salsus
saliva, sălīva, f
sallow, pallĭdus
sally, nn, ēruptĭo, f
sally, v.i, ēruptĭōnem făcĭo (3)
salmon, salmo, m
saloon, ātrĭum, n
salt, nn, sal, m
salt, adj, salsus
salt, v.t, săle condĭo (4) (season with salt)
salt-cellar, sălīnum, n
salt-mines, sălīnae, f. pl
salubrious, sălūbris
salutary, sălūtāris; (useful), ūtĭlis
salutation, sălūtātĭo, f
salute, v.t, sălūto (1)
salvation, sălus, f
salve, unguentum, n
salver, scŭtella, f, pătella, f
same, prep, īdem; (the same as), īdem qui, īdem atque; (in the — place), adv, ĭbīdem (at the — time), sĭmŭl; (fixed, constant), constans
sample, exemplum, n
sanctification, sanctĭfĭcātĭo, f
sanctify, v.t, consĕcro (1)
sanction, auctōrĭtas, f; (penalty) poena, f
sanction, v.t, rătum făcĭo (3)
sanctity, sanctĭtas, f
sanctuary, fānum, n, templum, n: (refuge), rĕfŭgĭum, n
sand, hărēna, f
sandal, sŏlĕa, f
sandstone, tōfus, m
sandy, hărēnōsus
sane, sānus
sanguinary, crŭentus, sanguĭnārĭus
sanguine, use spēs, f, (hope)
sanity, mens sāna, f

sap, *nn*, sūcus, *m*
sap, *v.t*, subrŭo (3)
sapient, *adj*, săpĭens
sapless, ārĭdus
sapling, arbor nŏvella,
sappers (military), mūnītōres, *m. pl*
sapphire, sapphīrus, *f*
sarcasm, căvillātĭo, *f*, (scoffing)
sarcastic, ăcerbus
sarcophagus, sarcŏphăgus, *m*
sash, cingŭlum, *n*
satanic, nĕfandus
satchel, lŏcŭlus, *m*
satellite (star), stella, *f*; (attendant),
    sătelles, *c*
satiate, *v.t*, sătĭo (1)
satiety, sătĭĕtas, *f*
satire, sătūra, *f*
satirical (bitter), ăcerbus
satirize, *v.t*, perstringo (3)
satirist, scrīptor sătīrĭcus, *m*
satisfaction (inner), vŏluptas, *f*;
    (compensation, punishment), poena,
    f
satisfactorily, *adv*, ex sententĭā
satisfactory, īdōnĕus, *or* sătis (enough)
satisfied, contentus
satisfy, *v.t*, (a need), explĕo (2), (*with
    dat*); (convince), persuādĕo (2)
satrap, sătrăpes, *m*
saturate, *v.t*, sătŭro (1)
satyr, sătyrus, *m*
sauce, condīmentum, *n*
saucepan, cācăbus, *m*, cortīna, *c*
saucer, pătella, *f*
saucy, pĕtŭlans
saunter, *v.i*, văgor (1 *dep*)
sausage, farcīmen, *n*
savage, *adj*, fĕrus, ătrox, effĕrātus
savageness, savagery fĕrĭtas, *f*,
    saevĭtĭa, *f*
save, *v.t*, servo (1); (defend), tŭĕor (2
    dep); (lay by), rĕservo (1)
save, *prep*, praeter (*with acc*)
saving, *nn*, conservātĭo, *f*
savings, pĕcūlĭum, *n*
saviour, servātor, *m*
savour, *nn*, săpor, *m*
savour, *v.t*, săpĭo (3)
savoury, *adj*, condītus
saw serra, *f*
saw, *v.t*, serrā sĕco (1) (cut with a saw)
sawdust, scŏbis, *f*
say, *v.t*, dīco (3), lŏquor (3 *dep*); (to
    — that something will *not* . . .),
    use nĕgo (1) (to deny); (it is said),
    fertur
saying, *nn*, dictum, *n*
scab, crusta, *f*
scabbard, văgīna, *f*

scabby, scăber
scaffold (frame), măchĭna, *f*; (execu-
    tion), supplĭcĭum, *n*
scald, *nn*, ădusta, *n.pl*
scale (pair of —s), lībra, *f*; (of fish),
    squāma, *f*; (gradation), grădus, *m*
scale, *v.t*, (climb with ladders),
    scālis ascendo (3)
scaling-ladders, scālae, *f. pl*
scallop, pecten, *n*
scalp, cŭtis, *f*, (skin)
scalpel, scalpellum, *n*
scamp, scĕlestus, *m*
scamper, *v.i*, fŭgĭo (3)
scan, *v.t*, contemplor (1 *dep*)
scandal, opprŏbrĭum, *n*; (disparage-
    ment) obtrectātĭo, *f*
scandalous, infāmis
scanty, exĭgŭus
scantiness, exĭgŭĭtas, *f*
scapegrace, nĕbŭlo, *m*
scar, cīcātrix, *f*
scarce, rārus
scarcely, *adv*, vix, aegrē
scarcity (of supplies, etc.), ĭnŏpĭa, *f*
scare, *v.t*, terrĕo (2)
scarecrow, formīdo, *f*
scarf, chlămys, *f*
scarlet, *nn*, coccum, *n*
scarlet, *adj*, coccĭnĕus
scathing, ăcerbus
scatter, *v.t*, spargo (3); *v.i*, sē spargĕre
    (3 *reflex*)
scene (of play), scēna, *f*; (spectacle),
    spectācŭlum, *n*
scenery (natural —), *use* rĕgĭo, *f*,
    (region)
scent (sense of smell), ŏdōrātus, *m*;
    (the smell itself), ŏdor, *m*
scent, *v.t*, (discern by smell), ŏdōror (1
    dep);
scented, ŏdōrātus
sceptical, dŭbĭtans
sceptre, sceptrum, *n*
schedule, tăbŭla, *f*
scheme, *nn*, consĭlĭum, *n*
scheme, *v.t*, consĭlĭum căpĭo (3)
    (make a plan)
scholar (pupil), discĭpŭlus, *m*; (learned
    man), doctus, *m*
scholarly, doctus
scholarship, littĕrae, *f. pl*
school, lūdus, *m*, schŏla, *f*
school, *v.t*, ĕrŭdĭo (4)
school-master, măgister, *m*
school-mistress, măgistra, *f*
schooner, phăsēlus, *m*
sciatica, ischĭas, *f*
science, scĭentĭa, *f*, discĭplīna, *f*,
    rătĭo, *f*

scientific, *use genit. of nouns above*
scimitar, ăcīnăces, *m*
scintillate, *v.i*, scintillo (1)
scion, prōles, *f*
scissors, forfĭces, *f. pl*
scoff at, *v.t*, irrīdĕo (2)
scoffer, irrīsor, *m*
scoffing, *nn*, irrīsĭo, *f*
scold, *v.t*, objurgo (1), incrĕpo (1)
scoop out, *v.t*, căvo (1)
scoop, *nn*, trulla, *f*
scope (room), campus, *m*
scorch, *v.t*, ambūro (3)
scorched, torrĭdus
scorching, torrĭdus
score (total), summa, *f*; (account, reckoning), rătĭo, *f*; (mark), nŏta, *f*
score, *v.t*, (note, mark), nŏto (1); (— a victory), victōrĭam rĕporto (1)
scorn, *nn*, contemptus, *m*
scorn, *v.t*, sperno (3), contemno (3)
scornful, sŭperbus
scorpion, scorpĭo, *m*
scoundrel, nĕbŭlo, *m*
scour, *v.t*, (clean), tergĕo (2); (run over) percurro (3)
scourge, *nn*, (whip), flăgellum, *n*; (pest), pestis, *f*, pernĭcĭes, *f*
scourge, *v.t*, verbĕro (1)
scourging, *nn*, verbĕra, *n.pl*
scout, explōrātor, *m*
scout, *v.t*, (spy out), spĕcŭlor (1 *dep*)
scowl, *nn*, frontis contractĭo, *f*
scowl, *v.i*, frontem contrăho (3), (contract the brow)
scramble for, *v.t*, *use phr*, inter sē certāre (struggle among themselves)
scrap, frustrum, *n*
scrape, *v.t*, rādo (3)
scraper, strĭgĭlis, *f*
scratch, *v.t*, rādo (3), scalpo (3)
scream, *nn*, vōcĭfĕrātĭo, *f*
scream, *v.i*, vōcĭfĕror (1 *dep*)
screech-owl, ŭlŭla, *f*
screen, tĕgĭmen, *n*
screen, *v.t*, tĕgo (3)
screw, *nn*, clāvus, *m*
scribble, *v.t*, scrībo (3)
scribe, scrība, *m*
Scripture, Scriptūra, *f*
scroll, vŏlūmen, *n*
scrub, *v.t*, tergĕo (2)
scruple (religious, etc.), rĕlĭgĭo, *f*
scrupulous, rĕlĭgĭōsus, dīlĭgens
scrutinize, *v.t*, scrūtor (1 *dep*)
scrutiny, scrūtātĭo, *f*
scuffle, *nn*, rixa, *f*
scull (oar), rēmus, *m*; (*v.i*, rēmĭgo (1)
sculptor, sculptor, *m*

sculpture (art of —), sculptūra, *f*; (the work itself), ŏpus, *n*
scum, spūma, *f*
scurf, furfur, *m*
scurrility, prōcācĭtas, *f*
scurrilous, scurrīlis, prōcax
scurvy, foedus
scuttle, *v.t*, (a ship), *use phr*, nāvem ultro dēprĭmo (3) (sink the ship of their own accord)
scythe, falx, *f*
sea, măre, *n*, (to be at —), nāvĭgo (1)
sea, *adj*, mărītĭmus, mărīnus
sea-coast, ōra mărītĭma, *f*
sea-faring, *adj*, mărītĭmus
sea-fight, pugna nāvālis, *f*
sea-gull, lărus, *m*
seal, *nn*, (of letter), signum, *n*; (animal), phōca, *f*
seal, *v.t*, (letter), signo (1); (close up), comprĭmo (3)
sealing-wax, cēra, *f*
seam, sūtūra, *f*
seaman, nauta, *m*
sear, *v.t*, ădūro (3)
search for, *v.t*, quaero (3); (explore), rīmor (1 dep)
search, *nn*, investīgātĭo, *f*
seasick, *adj*, nausĕābundus; (to be —), *v.i*, nausĕo (1)
seasickness, nausĕa, *f*
season, tempus, *n*, tempestas, *f*; (right time), tempus, *n*
season, *v.t*, condĭo (4)
seasonable, tempestivus
seasoned (flavoured), condītus; (hardened), dūrātus
seasoning, *nn*, condīmentum, *n*
seat, sēdes, *f*, sĕdīle, *n*, sella, *f*; (home), dŏmĭcĭlĭum, *n*: *v.t*. collŏco (1)
sea-weed, alga, *f*
secede, *v.i*, dēcēdo (3)
secession, dēfectĭo, *f*
secluded, sēcrētus
seclusion, sōlĭtūdo, *f*
second, *adj*, sĕcundus; (— of two), alter; (for the — time), *adv*, ĭtĕrum; (—ly), *adv*, de inde
second, *nn*, (time), mōmentum, *n*
second, *v.t*, adĭŭvo (1)
secondary, inférĭor
second-hand, ūsu trītus (worn with usage)
secrecy, sēcrētum, *n*
secret, arcāna, *n.pl*
secret, *adj*, occultus, arcānus; (hidden), clandestīnus; (to keep something —), *v.t*, cēlo (1)
secretary, scrība, *m*

secrete, *v.t*, cēlo (1), abdo (3)
secretly, *adv*, clam
sect, secta, *f*
section, pars, *f*
secular (not sacred), prŏfānus
secure, *v.t*, mūnĭo (4), firmo (1), līgo (1) (tie up)
secure, *adj*, tūtus
security, sălus, *f*; (guarantee), pignus, *n*; (to give —), căvĕo (2)
sedate, grăvis
sedative, mĕdĭcāmentum sŏpōrĭfĕrum
sedentary, sĕdentārĭus
sedge, ulva, *f*
sediment, faex, *f*
sedition, sēdītĭo, *f*
seditious, sēdĭtĭōsus
seduce, *v.t*, tento (1), sollĭcĭto (1)
seducer, corruptor, *m*
seduction, corruptēla, *f*
sedulous, assĭdŭus
see, *v.t*, vĭdĕo (2), cerno (3), aspĭcĭo (3); (to — to it that . . .), cūro (1) ad (*with gerund phr*); (understand), intellĕgo (3)
seed, sēmen, *n* (literal and metaphorical)
seedling, arbor nŏvella, *f*
seedy, grānōsus
seeing that, *conj*, cum
seek, *v.t*, quaero (3), pĕto (3), affecto (1)
seem, *v.i*, vĭdĕor (2 *pass.*)
seeming, *nn*, spĕcĭes, *f*
seemly, *adj*, dĕcōrus, (it is —), dĕcet (2 *impers*)
soor, vātes, *c*
seethe, *v.i*, fervĕo (2)
segment, segmentum, *n*
segregate, *v.t*, sēcerno (3)
seize, *v.t*, răpĭo (3), corrĭpĭo (3), prendo (3), occŭpo (1); (of illness, passion, etc.), affĭcĭo (3)
seizure, comprĕhensĭo, *f*
seldom, *adv*, rārŏ
select, *v.t*, lĕgo (3)
select, *adj*, lectus
selection, dēlectus, *m*
self, *pron*, (emphatic), ipse; (reflexive), sē
self-confident, confīdens
self-satisfied, contentus
selfish, selfishness, (to be —), sē ămāre (1 *reflex*)
sell, *v.t*, vendo (3)
seller, vendĭtor, *m*
semblance, ĭmāgo, *f*
semicircle, hēmĭcyclĭum, *n*
senate, sĕnātus, *m*
senate-house, cūrĭa, *f*

senator, sĕnātor, *m*
send, *v.t*, mitto (3); (— away), dīmitto (3); (— back), rĕmitto (3); (— for), arcesso (3); (— forward), praemitto (3); (— in), immitto (3)
senile, sĕnīlis
senior, (in age) nātu maior
sensation (feeling), sensus, *m*; mōtus (*m*) ănĭmi (impulse)
sensational, nŏtābĭlis
sense (feeling), sensus, *m*; (understanding), prūdentĭa, *f*; (meaning), sententĭa, *f*
senseless (unconscious), *use adv. phr*, sensu ablāto (with feeling withdrawn); (stupid), sōcors
sensible, prūdens
sensitive, sensĭlis
sensitiveness, mollĭtĭa, *f*
sensual, lĭbīdĭnōsus
sensuality, lĭbīdo, *f*
sentence (criminal), iūdĭcĭum, *n*; (writing, etc.), sententĭa, *f*
sentence, *v.t*, damno (1)
sententious, sententĭōsus
sentiment (feeling), sensus, *m*; (opinion), ŏpīnĭo, *f*
sentimental, mollis
sentimentality, mollĭtĭa, *f*
sentinel, vĭgil, *m*; (to be on — duty), in stătĭōne esse (*irreg*)
separable, dīvĭdŭus
separate, *v.t*, sēpăro (1), dīvĭdo(3), sēiungo (3), sēcerno (3)
separate, *adj*, sēpărātus, sēcrētus
separately, *adv*, sēpărātim
separation, sēpărātĭo, *f*
September, September (*mensis*)
sepulchre, sĕpulcrum, *n*
sequel (outcome), exĭtus, *m*
sequence, ordo, *m*
serene, tranquillus
serf, servus, *m*
series, sĕrĭes, *f*
serious, grăvis
seriousness, grăvĭtas, *f*
sermon, ōrātĭo, *f*
serpent, serpens, *f*
serried, confertus
servant, mĭnister, *m*, fămŭlus, *m*, servus, *m*
serve, *v.t*, servĭo (4), (*with dat*); (at table, etc.), mĭnistro (1); (in the army), stĭpendĭa mĕrĕor (2 *dep*); (to — as), esse (*irreg*) (*with* prŏ *and abl*)
service, mĭnistĕrĭum, *n*, ŏpĕra, *f*; (military), mĭlĭtĭa, *f*
serviceable, ūtĭlis
servile, servīlis

For List of Abbreviations used, turn to pages 3, 4

servitude, servĭtus, *f*

session (assembly), conventus, *m*

set, *nn*, (of people), glŏbus, *m*

set, *adj*, stătus

set, *v.t*, (place), stătŭo (3); pōno (3); *v.i*, (of the sun), occĭdo (3); (— about, begin), incĭpĭo (3); (— aside), *v.t*, sēpōno (3); (— down in writing), nŏto (1); (— free), lībĕro (1); (set off or out), *v.i*, prŏfĭciscor (3 *dep*); (— up), *v.t*, stătŭo (3)

settee, lectŭlus, *m*

setting (of sun), occāsus, *m*

settle, *v.t*, constĭtŭo (3); (a dispute), compōno (3); (debt), solvo (3); *v.i* (in a home, etc.), consīdo (3)

settled, certus

settlement (colony), cŏlōnĭa, *f*; (— of an affair), compŏsĭtĭo, *f*

settler, cŏlōnus, *m*

seven, septem; (— hundred), septingenti; (— times), *adv*, septĭes

seventeen, septendĕcim

seventeenth, septĭmus dĕcĭmus

seventh, septĭmus

seventieth, septŭāgēsĭmus

seventy, septŭāginta

sever, *v.t*, sēpăro (1); sēiungo (3)

several, complūres, ălĭquot

severe, sĕvērus, dūrus

severity, sĕvērĭtas, *f*, ăcerbĭtas, *f*

sew, *v.t*, sŭo (3)

sewer (drain), clŏāca, *f*

sex, sexus, *m*

sexagenarian, sexāgēnārĭus, *m*

sexual, *use nn.* sexus, *m*, (sex)

shabbiness, sordes, *f. pl*

shabby, sordĭdus

shackle, *v.t*, vincŭlis constringo (3) (bind with chains)

shackle(s), *nn*, vincŭla, *n.pl*

shade, *nn*, umbra, *f*; (the —s of the dead), mānes, *m. pl*

shade, *v.t*, ŏpāco (1)

shadow, umbra, *f*

shadowy, ŏpācus, ĭnānis

shady, ŏpācus

shaft (of a weapon), hastīle, *n*; (an arrow), săgitta, *f*; (of a mine), pŭtĕus, *m*

shaggy, hirtus, hirsūtus

shake, *v.t*, quătĭo (3), ăgĭto (1) lăbĕfăcĭo (3); *v.i*, trĕmo (3), trĕpĭdo (1); (— hands), dextras iungo (3) (join right hands)

shaking, *nn*, quassătĭo, *f*

shallow, *adj*, (sea), vădōsus, brĕvis

shallows, *nn*, văda, *n.pl*

sham, *adj*, sĭmŭlātus

sham, *nn*, sĭmŭlātĭo, *f* (pretence)

sham, *v.t*, sĭmŭlo (1)

shambles, *use* turba, *f*

shame, *nn*, (feeling), pŭdor, *m*; (disgrace), dēdĕcus, *n*

shame, *v.t*, rŭbōrem incŭtĭo (3) (*with dat*)

shamefaced, vĕrēcundus

shameful, turpis

shamefulness, turpĭtūdo, *f*

shameless, impŭdens

shamelessness, impŭdentĭa, *f*

shamrock, trĭfŏlĭum, *n*

shank, crus, *n*

shape, *nn*, forma, *f*

shape, *v.t*, formo (1)

shapeless, informis

shapely, formōsus

share (part), pars, *f*; (plough —), vōmer, *m*

share, *v.t*, partĭor (4 *dep*)

sharer, particeps, *c*

shark, pistrix, *f*

sharp, ăcūtus, ācer

sharp-sighted, perspĭcax

sharp-witted, ăcūtus

sharpen, *v.t*, ăcŭo (3)

sharply, *adv*, ăcūte, ācrĭter

sharpness (of tongue), aspĕrĭtas, *f*; (mental), ăcūmen, *n*

shatter, *v.t*, frango (3)

shave, *v.t*, rādo (3)

shawl, ămĭcŭlum, *n*

she, *pron*, illa, ĕa, haec, ista

sheaf, mănĭpŭlus, *m*

shear, *v.t*, tondĕo (2)

shearing, *nn*, tonsūra, *f*

shears, forfex, *f*

sheath, vāgīna, *f*

sheathe, *v.t*, in vāgīnam rĕcondo (3) (put back into the sheath)

shed, *nn*, tŭgŭrĭum, *n*

shed, *v.t*, fundo (3)

sheen, fulgor, *m*

sheep, ŏvis, *f*

sheep-fold, saeptum, *n*

sheep-skin, pellis ŏvilla, *f*

sheepish, sōcors, *or use adv. phr*, dēmisso vultu (with downcast face)

sheer (steep), abruptus; (pure, absolute), mĕrus

sheet (cloth), lintĕum, *n*; (paper), schĕda, *f*; (— of a sail), pes, *m*

shelf, plŭtĕus, *m*

shell, concha, *f*, crusta, *f*

shell-fish, conchȳlĭum, *n*

shelter, *nn*, perfŭgĭum, *n*, tectum, *n*
shelter, *v.t*, tĕgo (3); *v.i*, *use phr*, ad perfŭgĭum sē conferre (*irreg*) (betake oneself to shelter)
shelving, *adj*, dēclīvis
shepherd, pastor, *m*
shield, *nn*, scūtum, *n*
shield, *v.t*, tĕgo (3); dēfendo (3)
shift (change), vĭcissĭtūdo, *F*.
shift, *v.t*, mūto (1); *v.i*, mūtor (1 *pass*)
shifty, versūtus
shin, crūs, *n*
shine, *v.i*, lūcĕo (2), fulgĕo (2)
ship, *nn*, nāvis, *f*; (war —), nāvis longa, *f*; (transport —), nāvis ŏnĕrārĭa, *f*
ship, *v.t*, (put on board), in nāvem impōno (3); (transport), nāvĕ transporto (1)
ship-owner, nāvĭcŭlārĭus, *m*
shipping, nāvĭgĭa, *n.pl*
shipwreck, naufrăgĭum, *n*
shipwrecked, naufrăgus
shirt, sŭbūcŭla, *f*
shiver, *v.i*, horrĕo (2)
shivering, *nn*, horror, *m*
shoal (water), vădum, *n*; (fish), exāmen, *n*
shock, offensĭo, *f*, ictus, *m*; (of battle), concursus, *m*
shock, *v.t*, offendo (3), percŭtĭo (3)
shocking, *adj*, ătrox
shoe, *nn*, calcĕus, *m*
shoe, *v.t*, calcĕo (1)
shoe-maker, sūtor, *m*
shoot, *nn*, (sprout), surcŭlus, *m*
shoot, *v.t*, (a missile), mitto (3); *v.i*, (— along, across), vŏlo (1)
shooting-star, fax caelestis, *f*
shop, tăberna, *f*
shop-keeper, tăbernārĭus, *m* (*pl. only*)
shore, lītus, *n*, ōra, *f*
shore-up, *v.t*, fulcĭo (4)
short, brĕvis, ĕxĭgŭus; (— cut), vĭa compendĭārĭa, *f*; (in —), *adv*, dēnīque
shortage, ĭnŏpĭa, *f* (lack)
shortcoming, dēlictum, *n*
shorten, *v.t*, contrăho (3)
shortly, *adv*, (of time), brĕvi; (briefly), brĕvĭter
shortness, brĕvĭtas, *f*
shot (firing), ictus, *m*
shoulder, hŭmĕrus, *m*; (— blade), scăpŭlae, *f. pl*
shoulder, *v.t*, fĕro (*irreg*) (to bear)
shout, *nn*, clāmor, *m*
shout, *v.i*, clāmo (1)
shove, *v.t*, trūdo (3)

shovel, pāla, *f*
show, *nn*, (appearance), spĕcĭes, *f*; (spectacle), spectācŭlum, *n*; (procession, etc.), pompa, *f*
show, *v.t*, monstro (1), praebĕo (2), ostendo (3); (— off), *v.t*, ostento (1); *v.i*, sē ostentare (1 *reflex*)
shower, imber, *m*
shower, *v.t*, fundo (3)
showery, plŭvĭus
showy, spĕcĭōsus
shred, pannus, *m*
shrew, fēmĭna prŏcax
shrewd, ăcūtus, săgax
shrewdness, săgācĭtas, *f*
shriek, *nn*, ŭlŭlātus, *m*
shriek, *v.i*, ŭlŭlo (1)
shrill, ăcūtus, ācer
shrine, dēlūbrum, *n*
shrink, *v.t*, contrăho (3); *v.i*, (— from), ăbhorrĕo (2)
shrinking, *nn*, contractĭo, *f*
shrivel, *v.t*, corrūgo (1)
shrivelled, rūgōsus
shroud, *use* lintĕum, *n*, (cloth)
shroud, *v.t*, involvo (3)
shrub, frŭtex, *m*
shrubbery, frŭtĭcētum
shudder, *v.i*, horrĕo (2)
shudder, *nn*, horror, *m*
shuffle, *v.t*, miscĕo (2); *v.i*, *use phr*, lentē ambŭlo (1) (walk slowly)
shun, *v.t*, fŭgĭo (3), vīto (1)
shut, *v.t*, claudo (3); (— in or up), inclūdo (3); (— out), exclūdo (3)
shutters, fŏrĭcŭlae, *f. pl*
shuttle, rădĭus, *m*
shy, vĕrēcundus
shy, *v.i*, (of horses), consternor (1 *pass*)
shyness, vĕrēcundĭa, *f*
sick, aeger; (to be —), *v.i*, aegrōto (1); (vomit), *v.i*, *and v.t*, vŏmo (3)
sicken, *v.t*, fastīdĭum mŏvĕo (2); *v.i*, aeger fīo (*irreg*)
sickle, falx, *f*
sickly, infirmus
sickness morbus, *m*
side (of the body), lătus, *n*; (part, region), pars, *f*; (party, faction), pars, *f*; (from (or on) all —s), *adv*, undīque; (on both —s), ŭtrimque; (on this —), hinc; (on that —), illinc; (on this — of), *prep*, citra (*with acc*); (on that — of), ūltra
side, *adj*, (sidelong), oblīquus
sideboard, ăbăcus, *m*
sideways, *adv*, oblīquē
siege, *nn*, obsĭdĭo, *f*
siege-works, ŏpĕra, *n.pl*
sieve, crībrum, *n*

sift, *v.t*, crībro (1); (— evidence, etc.),
  scrūtor (1 *dep*)
sigh, *nn*, suspīrium, *n*
sigh, *v.i*, suspīro (1)
sight (sense or act), vīsus, *m*; (view),
  conspectus, *m*; (spectacle), spectācŭlum, *n*
sight, *v.t*, conspĭcor (1 *dep*)
sightly, formōsus, vĕnustus
sign, *nn*, signum, *n*; (mark), nŏta, *f*;
  (trace, footprint), vestīgĭum, *n*;
  (portent), portentum, *n*
sign, *v.t*, subscrībo (3); (give a —),
  v.i, signum do (1)
signal, signum, *n*
signal, *v.i*, signum do (1)
signature, nōmen, *n*
signet, signum, *n*
significance, signĭfĭcātĭo, *f*
significant, signĭfĭcans
signify, *v.t*, signĭfĭco (1)
silence, sĭlentĭum, *n*
silent, tăcĭtus, (to be —), *v.i*, tăcĕo
  (2), sĭlĕo (2)
silk, *nn*, bombyx, *m*
silk, silken, *adj*, sērĭcus
silk-worm, bombyx, *m*
silky, mollis
sill, līmen, *n*
silliness, stultĭtĭa, *f*
silly, stultus
silt, *nn*, līmus, *m*, sentīna, *f*
silver, *nn*, argentum, *n*
silver, *adj*, argentĕus
silver-mine, argentārium metallum
similar, sĭmĭlis (*with genit. or dat*)
similarity, sĭmĭlĭtūdo, *f*
similarly, *adv*, sĭmĭlĭter
simmer, *v.i*, lentē fervĕo (3) (boil
  slowly)
simper, *v.i*, subrīdĕo (2)
simple, simplex; (weak-minded), ĭneptus
simpleton, stultus, *m*
simplicity, simplĭcĭtas, *f*
simplify, *v.t*, făcĭlem reddo (3)
simulation, sĭmŭlātĭo, *f*
simultaneous, *use adv*, sĭmul (at the
  same time)
sin, *nn*, peccātum, *n*
sin, *v.i*, pecco (1)
since, *conj*, cum (*foll. by vb. in subjunctive*); (temporal) postquam
since, *adv*, ăbhinc
since, *prep*, ē, ex, ā, ăb (*with ăbl*)
sincere, sincērus, simplex
sincerity, sincērĭtas, *f*, simplĭcĭtas, *f*
sinew, nervus, *m*
sinful, impĭus,
sinfulness, impĭĕtas, *f*

sing, *v.i. and v.t*, căno (3)
singe, *v.t*, ădūro (3)
singer, cantātor, *m*
singing, *nn*, cantus, *m*
single, *adj*, (one, sole), ūnus, sōlus;
  (unmarried), caelebs
single out, *v.t*, ēlĭgo (3)
singly, *adv*, singŭlātim
singular, (one), singŭlāris; (strange),
  nŏvus
singularly, *adv*, ūnĭcē
sinister, sĭnister
sink, *v.t*, mergo (3); *v.i*, sīdo (3),
  consīdo (1)
sinner, peccātor, *m*
sinuous, sĭnŭōsus
sip, *v.t*, dēgusto (1), lībo (1)
sir (respectful address), bŏne vir
sire, păter, *m*
siren, sīrēn, *f*
sister, sŏror, *f*
sit, *v.i*, sĕdĕo (2); (— down), consīdo
  (3); (— up, stay awake), vĭgĭlo (1)
site, sĭtus, *m*
sitting, *nn*, sessĭo, *f*
situated, sĭtus
situation sĭtus, *m*
six, sex; (— each), sēni; (— times),
  adv, sexĭens
sixteen, sēdĕcim
sixteenth, sextus dĕcĭmus
sixth, sextus
sixtieth, sexāgēsĭmus
sixty, sexāginta
size, magnĭtūdo, *f*; (of great —), *adj*,
  magnus; (of small —), parvus; (of
  what —?), quantus?
skeleton, ossa, *n.pl*, (bones)
sketch, *nn*, ădumbrātĭo, *f*
sketch, *v.t*, ădumbro (1)
skewer, vērŭcŭlum, *n*
skiff, scăpha, *f*
skilful, skilled, pĕrītus
skilfulness, skill, pĕrītĭa, *f*
skim, *v.t*, (— off), dēspūmo (1); (—
  over), percurro (3)
skin, cŭtis, *f*, pellis, *f*
skin, *v.t*, pellem dīrĭpĭo (3) (tear away
  the skin)
skip, *v.i*, exsulto (1); (— over), *v.i. and
  v.t*, praetĕrĕo (4)
skipper, nauarchus, *m*
skirmish, *nn*, lĕve certāmen, *n*
skirmish, *v.i*, parvŭlis proelĭis contendo (3) (fight in small engage-
  ments)
skirmisher, vēlĕs, *m*
skirt, *nn*, limbus, *m*
skirt, *v.t*, (scrape past), rādo (3)
skittish, lascīvus

skulk, v.i, lătĕo (2)
skull, calvārĭa, f
sky, caelum, n
sky-blue, caerŭlĕus
sky-lark, ălauda, f
slab (of stone), ăbăcus, m
slack, rĕmissus
slacken, v.t, rĕmitto (3); v.i, rĕmittor (3 pass)
slackness, rĕmissĭo, f; (idleness), pĭgrĭtĭa, f
slake (thirst), v.t, (sĭtim) exstinguo (3)
slander, nn, călumnĭa, f
slander, v.t, călumnĭor (1 dep)
slanderer, obtrectātor, m
slanderous, fāmōsus
slanting, adj, oblīquus
slap, nn, ălăpa, f
slap, v.t, fĕrĭo (4)
slash, nn, (blow), ictus, m
slash, v.t, caedo (3)
slate (roofing), tēgŭlae, f. pl.
slate, v.t, rĕprĕhendo (3)
slaughter, nn, caedes, f, strāges, f
slaughter, v.t, caedo (3)
slaughter-house, use lānĭĕna, f (butcher's stall)
slave, servus, m
slave-dealer, vēnālĭcĭus, m
slavery, servĭtus, f
slave-trade, vēnālĭcĭum, n
slavish, servīlis
slay, v.t, interfĭcĭo (3)
slayer, interfector, m
slaying, nn, trŭcĭdātĭo, f
sledge, trăhĕa, f
sleek, nĭtĭdus
sleep, nn, somnus, m
sleep, v.i, dormĭo (4), quĭesco (3); (to go to —), obdormisco (3)
sleepless, insomnis
sleeplessness, insomnĭa, f
sleepy, somnĭcŭlōsus
sleeve, mănĭca, f. pl
sleigh, trăhĕa, f
sleight-of-hand, praestĭgĭae, f. pl
slender, grăcĭlis
slenderness, grăcĭlĭtas, f
slice, segmentum, n, frustum, n
slice, v.t, concĭdo (3)
slide, v.i, lābor (3 dep)
slight, adj, lĕvis, exĭgŭus
slight, v.t, neglĕgo (3)
slim, grăcĭlis
slime, līmus, m
slimy, līmōsus
sling, nn, (for throwing), funda, f; (bandage), mĭtella, f
sling, v.t, mitto (3)

slinger, fundĭtor, m
slip, v.i, lābor (3 dep); (— away), sē subdūcĕre (3 reflex); (— out from), ēlābor (3 dep)
slip, nn, lapsus, m; (mistake), error, m
slipper, sŏlĕa, f
slippery, lūbrĭcus
slipshod, neglĕgens
slit, nn, scissūra, f
slit, v.t, incīdo (3)
sloop, nāvis longa, f
slope, nn, clīvus, m
slope, v.i, sē dēmittĕre (3 reflex), vergo (3)
sloping, adj, (down), dēclīvis; (up), acclivis
sloth, segnĭtĭa, f, ignāvĭa, f
slothful, segnis
slough (mire), pălus, f
slovenliness, cultus neglectus (neglected dress)
slow, tardus, lentus
slowly, adv, tardē, lentē
slowness, tardĭtas, f
slug, limax, f
sluggish, pĭger, segnis
sluggishness, pĭgrĭtĭa, f
sluice, ductus, (m) ăquārum (bringing of water)
slumber, nn, somnus, m
slumber, v.i, dormĭo (4)
slur, nn, măcŭla, f
sly, astūtus, callĭdus
smack, nn, (blow), ălăpa, f; (taste), săpor, m
smack, v.t, (slap), verbĕro (1)
small, parvus, exĭgŭus
smallness, exĭgŭĭtas, f
smart, adj, ācer; (clothes, etc.), nĭtĭdus; (witty), făcĕtus
smart, nn, dŏlor, m
smart, v.i, dŏlĕo (2), ūror (3 pass)
smartness (alertness), ălăcrĭtas, f
smash, nn, fractūra, f
smash, v.t, confringo (3)
smattering, lĕvis cognĭtĭo, f, (slight knowledge)
smear, v.t, līno (3)
smell, nn, (sense of —), ŏdōrātus, m; (scent), ŏdor, m
smell, v.t, olfăcĭo (3); v.i, ŏlĕo (2)
smelt, v.t, cŏquo (3)
smile, nn, rīsus, m
smile, v.i, subrīdĕo (2)
smirk, nn, rīsus, m
smite, v.t, fĕrĭo (4)
smith, făber, m
smithy, făbrĭca, f
smock, indūsĭum, n
smoke, nn, fūmus, m

For List of Abbreviations used, turn to pages 3, 4

smoke, *v.i*, fūmo (1)
smoky, fūmōsus
smooth, lĕvis, (**of the sea**), plăcĭdus; (**of temper**), aequus
smooth, *v.t*, lēvo (1)
smoothness, lēvĭtas, *f*, lēnĭtas, *f*
smother, *v.t*, suffōco (1), opprĭmo (3)
smoulder, *v.i*, fūmo (1)
smudge, *nn*, lābes, *f*
smuggle, *v.t*, furtim importo (1) (**bring in secretly**)
snack, cēnŭla, *f*
snail, cochlĕa, *f*
snake, anguis, *m*, *f*
snaky, vīpĕrĕus
snap, *v.t*, rumpo (3); (— **the fingers**), *v.i*, concrĕpo (1); (— **up**), *v.t*, corrĭpĭo (3)
snare, lăquĕus, *m*
snarl, *nn*, gannītus, *m*
snarl, *v.i*, gannĭo (4)
snatch, *v.t*, răpĭo (3)
sneak, *v.i* corrēpo (3)
sneer, *nn*, obtrectātĭo, *f*
sneer at, *v.t*, dērīdĕo (2)
sneeze, *v.i*, sternŭo (3)
sneezing, sternūmentum, *n*
sniff at (**smell at**), *v.t*, ŏdōror (1 *dep*)
snip, *v.t*, (**cut off**), ampŭto (1)
snob, nŏvus hŏmo (**upstart**)
snore, *v.i*, sterto (3)
snore, snoring, *nn*, rhonchus, *m*
snort, *v.i*, frĕmo (3)
snorting, *nn*, frĕmĭtus, *m*
snout, rostrum, *n*
snow, *nn*, nix, *f*
snow (**it** —**s**), ningit (*v. impers*)
snowy, nĭvĕus
snub, *v.t*, rĕprĕhendo (3)
snub-nosed, sīlus
snuff, *v.t*, (**extinguish**), exstinguo (3)
snug, commŏdus
so, *adv*, (**in such a way**), sīc, ĭtă; (**to such an extent**), ădĕo; (*with adj and adv*) tam, *e.g.* **so quickly**, tam cĕlērĭter; (*with a purpose or consecutive clause*, **so that** . . .) ut; (— **big**, — **great**), tāntus; (— **many**), tot; (— **much**), tantum; (— **often**), tŏtĭes
soak, *v.t*, mădĕfăcĭo (3)
soaking, mădens; (**of rain**), largus
soap, *nn*, sāpo, *m*
soar, *v.i*, sublīme fĕror (*irreg pass*) (**be borne aloft**)
sob, *nn*, singultus, *m*
sob, *v.i*, singulto (1)
sober, sōbrĭus

sobriety, sōbrĭĕtas, *f*, mŏdĕrātĭo, *f*
sociability, făcĭlĭtas, *f*
sociable, făcĭlis
social, commūnis
society (**in general**), sŏcĭĕtas, *f*; (**companionship**), sŏdālĭtas, *f*
sock, tībĭāle, *n*
sod, caespes, *m*
soda, nītrum, *n*
sodden, mădĭdus
sofa, lectŭlus, *m*
soft, mollis
soften, *v.t*, mollĭo (4); *v.i*, mollĭor (4 *pass*)
softness, mollĭtĭa, *f*
soil, sŏlum, *n*
soil, *v.t*, inquĭno (1)
sojourn, *nn*, commŏrātĭo, *f*
sojourn, *v.i*, commŏror (1 *dep*)
solace, *nn*, sōlātĭum, *n*
solace, *v.t*, consōlor (1 *dep*)
solar, *use genit. case of* sōl, *m*, (**sun**)
solder, *nn*, ferrūmen, *n*
solder, *v.t*, ferrūmĭno (1)
soldier, mīles, *c*; (**foot** —), pĕdes, *m*; (**cavalry** —), ĕques, *m*; *v.i*, (**serve as a** —), stipendĭa mĕrĕor (2 *dep*)
soldierly, *adj*, mīlĭtāris
sole, *adj*, sōlus
sole, *nn*, sŏlum, *n*; (**fish**), sōlĕa, *f*
solely, *adv*, sōlum
solemn (**serious**), grăvis; (**festivals**, **etc.**), sollemnis
solemnity, grăvĭtas, *f*; (**religious** —), sollemne, *n.*
solemnize, *v.t*, cĕlĕbro (1)
solicit, *v.t*, pĕto (3), obsĕcro (1), sollĭcĭto (1)
solicitation, flāgĭtātĭo, *f*
solicitor, advŏcātus, *m*
solicitude, anxĭĕtas, *f*
solid, *adj* sŏlĭdus
solid, *nn*, sŏlĭdum, *n*
solidity, sŏlĭdĭtas, *f*
soliloquize, *v.i*, sēcum lŏquor (3 *dep*) (**speak with oneself**)
solitary, sōlus, sōlĭtārĭus; (**places**), dēsertus
solitude, sōlĭtūdo, *f*
solstice (**summer** —), solstĭtĭum, *n*; (**winter** —), brūma, *f*
solution, *use vb.* solvo (3) (**to solve**), *or nn*, explĭcātĭo, *f*
solve, *v.t*, explĭco (1)
solvent (**to be** —), solvendo esse (*irreg*)
sombre, obscūrus
some, *adj*, ălĭquis, nonnullus; (**a certain**), quidam

somebody, someone, *pron,* ălĭquis, nonnullus; **(a certain one),** quĭdam; **(— or other),** nescĭo quis; **(some . . . others),** ălĭi . . . ălĭi

somehow, *adv,* nescĭŏ quŏmŏdŏ

something, *pron,* ălĭquid

sometime, *adv,* ălĭquandŏ

sometimes *adv,* ălĭquandŏ, interdum; **(occasionally),** sŭbinde; **(sometimes . . . sometimes . . .),** mŏdŏ . . . mŏdŏ . . .

somewhat, *adv,* ălĭquantum

somewhere, *adv,* ălĭcŭbi; **(to —),** ălĭquo

somnolent, sēmĭsomnus

son, fīlĭus, *m;* **(— in-law),** gĕner, *m*

song, carmen, *n*

sonorous, sŏnōrus,

soon, *adv,* mox; **(as — as),** sĭmul ac, sĭmŭl atque, cum prīmum; **(as— as possible),** quam prīmum

sooner (earlier), mātūrĭus; **(rather),** pŏtĭus

soot, fūlīgo, *f*

soothe, *v.t,* mulcĕo (2), lēnĭo (4)

soothing, *adj,* lēnis

soothsayer, auspex, *c,* hăruspex, *m*

sooty, fūlĭgĭnōsus

sop, offa, *f*

sophist, sŏphistes, *m*

soporific, sŏpōrĭfer

sorcerer, vĕnēfĭcus, *m*

sorcery, vĕnēfĭcĭa, *n.pl*

sordid, sordĭdus

sore, ăcerbus

sore, *nn,* ulcus, *n*

sorrel, lăpăthus, *f*

sorrow, *nn,* dŏlor, *m,* maeror, *m*

sorrow, *v.i,* dŏlĕo (2)

sorrowful, maestus, tristis

sorry (to be —), mĭsĕret (2 *impers*) **(*with acc. of subject and genit. of object*),** *e.g.* I am sorry for you, me mĭsĕret tŭi

sort, gĕnus, *n;* **(what — of?),** quālis?

sort, *v.t,* dīgĕro (3)

sot, pōtātor, *m*

soul, ănĭma, *f,* ănĭmus, *m,* spīrĭtus, *m*

sound, *nn,* sŏnus, *m,* sŏnĭtus, *m*

sound, *adj,* sānus; **(of sleep),** artus; **(of arguments),** firmus

sound, *v.i,* sŏno (1); *v.t,* inflo (1); **(— the trumpet),** būcĭnam inflo (1), căno (3)

soundness, sānĭtas, *f,* intĕgrĭtas, *f*

soup, iūs, *n*

sour, ăcerbus, ācer, ămārus

source, fons, *m,* căput, *n*

sourness, ăcerbĭtas, *f*

south, *nn,* mĕrīdĭes, *m*

south, southern, *adj,* mĕrīdĭānus

southwards, *adv. phr,* in mĕrīdĭem

sovereign, *nn,* princeps, *m,* rex, *m* tўrannus, *m*

sovereign (independent), *adj, use phr* sŭi iūris **(of one's own authority)**

sovereignty, impĕrĭum, *n*

sow, *nn,* sūs, *f*

sow, *v.t,* sĕro (3)

sower, sător, *m*

space, spătĭum, *n;* **(— of time),** spătĭum, **(*n*)** tempŏris

spacious, amplus

spaciousness, amplĭtūdo, *f*

spade, pāla, *f*

span palmus, *m*

span, *v.t,* **(river, etc.),** *use vb,* iungo (3) **(join)**

spangled, distinctus

Spanish, Hispānus

spar (of timber), asser, *m*

spare, *adj,* exīlis **(thin)**

spare, *v.t,* parco (3) **(*with dat*)**

sparing, *adj,* **(frugal),** parcus

spark, *nn,* scintilla, *f*

sparkle, *v.i,* scintillo (1)

sparkling, *adj,* scintillans

sparrow, passer, *m*

sparse, rārus

spasm, spasmus, *m*

spatter, *v.t,* aspergo (3)

spawn, *nn,* ōva, *n.pl*

spawn, *v.i,* ōva gigno (3) **(produce eggs)**

speak, *v.t,* lŏquor (3 *dep*), dīco (3); **(— out),** ēlŏquor (3 *dep*); **(— to),** allŏquor (3 *dep*)

speaker, ōrātor, *m*

spear, hasta, *f*

special (one in particular), pĕcūlĭāris; **(one's own),** prŏprĭus; **(outstanding),** praecĭpŭus

speciality, *use adj,* prŏprĭus **(one's own)**

specially, *adv,* praecĭpŭē, praesertim .

species, gĕnus, *n*

specific, dīsertus; *or use emphatic pron,* ipse

specify, *v.t,* ēnŭmĕro (1)

specimen, exemplum, *n*

specious, prōbābĭlis

speck, măcŭla, *f*

spectacle, spectācŭlum, *n*

spectator, spectātor, *m*

spectre, īmāgo, *f*

spectrum, spectrum, *n*

speculate, *v.i,* cōgĭto (1); **(guess),** cōnĭcĭo (3)

speculation, cōgĭtātĭo, *f;* **(guess),** coniectūra, *f* speech, ōrātĭo, *f*

speechless (literally so), mūtus; (struck with fear, etc.), stŭpĕfactus

speed, cĕlĕrĭtas, *f*

speed, *v.t*, mātūro (1); *v.i*, festīno (1)

speedy, cĕler, cĭtus

spell (charm), carmen, *n*

spell, *v.t, use phr. with* littĕra, *f*, (letter)

spellbound, obstŭpĕfactus

spend, *v.t*, (money), impendo (3), insūmo (3); (time), ăgo (3)

spendthrift, nĕpos, *m, f*

spew, *v.t*, vŏmo (3)

sphere, glŏbus, *m*; (— of responsibility, etc.), prōvincĭa, *f*

spherical, glŏbōsus

sphinx, sphinx, *f*

spice, condīmentum, *n*

spice, *v.t*, condĭo (4)

spicy, condītus

spider, ărănĕa, *f*

spider's web, ărănĕa, *f*

spike, clāvus, *m*

spill, *v.t*, effundo (3)

spin, *v.t*, (thread, etc.), nĕo (2); (turn rapidly), verso (1); *v.i*, versor (1 *pass*)

spinster, virgo, *f*

spiral, *nn*, cochlĕa, *f*

spiral, *adj*, invŏlūtus

spire, turris, *f*

spirit (breath of life), ănĭma, *f*; (mind, soul), ănĭmus, *m*; (disposition), ingĕnĭum, *n*; (character), mōres, *m. pl*; (courage), ănĭmus, *m*; (departed —), mānes, *m. pl*

spirited, ănĭmōsus

spiritual (of the mind), *use* ănĭmus, *m*

spit, *nn*, (for roasting), vĕru, *n*

spit, *v.t*, spŭo (3)

spite, mălĕvŏlentĭa, *f*; (in — of), *often use abl. phr. with* obstans (standing in the way)

spiteful, mălignus

spittle, spūtum, *n*

splash, *v.t*, aspergo (3)

spleen, lĭēn, *m*; (vexation), stŏmăchus, *m*

splendid, splendĭdus

splendour, splendor, *m*

splint, fĕrŭlae, *f. pl*

splinter, fragmentum, *n*

split, *v.t*, findo (3); *v.i*, findor (3 *pass*)

split, *nn*, fissūra, *f*

splutter, *v.i*, balbūtĭo (4)

spoil, *nn*, praeda, *f*, spŏlĭa, *n.pl*

spoil, *v.t*, corrumpo (3), vĭtĭo (1)

spokesman, ōrātor, *m*

sponge, *nn*, spongĭa, *f*

spongy, spongĭōsus

sponsor auctor, *c*

spontaneous, *use adv. phr*, sŭā (mĕā), sponte (of his (my) own accord)

spoon, coclĕar, *n*

sporadic, rārus

sport, *nn*, lūdus, *m*, lūsus, *m*; (ridicule), lūdĭbrĭum, *n*

sport, *v.i*, lūdo (3)

sportive (playful), lascīvus

sportsman, vēnātor, *m*

spot, *nn*, (stain), măcŭla, *f*; (place), lŏcus, *m*

spot, *v.t*, (look at), aspĭcĭo (3); (stain), măcŭlo (1)

spotless (of character, etc.), intĕger, pūrus

spotted, măcŭlōsus

spouse, coniunx, *c*

spout, *nn*, ōs, *n*

spout, *v.i*, ēmĭco (1); *v.t*, (pour out), effundo (3)

sprain, *v.t*, intorquĕo (2)

sprawl, *v.i*, fundor (3 *pass*)

spray, *nn*, aspergo, *f*

spread, *v.t*, extendo (3), pando (3), diffundo (3); (— about, publish), diffĕro (*irreg*) dīvulgo (1); *v.i*, diffundor (3 *pass*), incrēbresco (3)

sprightly, ălăcer

spring, *nn*, (season), vēr, *n*; (leap), saltus, *m*; (fountain), fons, *m*

spring, *adj*, vernus

spring, *v.i*, (leap), sălĭo (4); (— from, proceed from), ŏrĭor (4 *dep*) (— upon, assault), ădŏrĭor (4 *dep*)

sprinkle, *v.t*, spargo (3)

sprout, *nn*, surcŭlus, *m*

sprout, *v.i*, pullŭlo (1)

spruce, *adj*, nĭtĭdus

spruce, *nn*, (fir), pīnus, *f*

spur, *nn*, calcar, *n*

spur, *v.t*, concĭto (1)

spurious, ădultĕrīnus

spurn, *v.t*, aspernor (1 *dep*)

spurt, *v.i*, ēmĭco (1)

spy, *nn*, explōrātor, *m*, dēlātor, *m*

spy, *v.t*, spĕcŭlor (1 *dep*)

squabble, *nn*, rixa, *f*

squabble, *v.i*, rixor (1 *dep*)

squadron (of cavalry), turma, *f*; (of ships), classis, *f*

squalid, sordĭdus

squall (storm), prŏcella, *f*

squall, *v.i*, (cry), vāgĭo (4)

squalor, sordes, *f. pl*

squander, effundo (3)

squanderer, nĕpos, *m, f*

square, *adj*, quădrātus; *nn*, quădrātum, *n*

square, *v.t*, quădro (1); (accounts, etc.), subdūco (3), constĭtŭo (3)
squash, *v.t*, contĕro (3)
squat, *v.i*, subsīdo (3)
squat, *adj*, (of figure), brĕvis
squeak, *nn*, strīdor, *m*
squeak, *v.i*, strīdĕo (2)
squeamish, fastīdĭōsus
squeeze, *v.t*, prĕmo (3)
squint, *v.i*, străbō esse (*irreg*)
squirrel, sciūrus, *m*
squirt, *v.t*, ēĭcĭo (3); *v.i*, ēmĭco (1)
stab, *v.t*, fŏdĭo (3)
stab, *nn*, ictus, *m*
stability, stăbĭlĭtas, *f*
stable, *adj*, stăbĭlis
stable, *nn*, stăbŭlum, *n*
stack, *nn*, ăcervus, *m*
stack, *v.t*, cŏăcervo (1)
staff, băcŭlum, *n*; (advisers), consĭlĭārĭī, *m. pl*
stag, cervus, *m*
stage (theatre), proscaenĭum, *n*; (step), grădus, *m*
stagger, *v.i*, văcillo (1); *v.t*, concŭtĭo (3), commŏvĕo (2)
stagnant, stagnans
stagnate, *v.i*, stagno (1)
staid, grăvis
stain, *nn*, măcŭla, *f*
stain, *v.t*, măcŭlo (1)
stainless, pūrus, intĕger
stairs, scalae, *f. pl*
stake (post, etc), pālus, *m*, sŭdis, *f*, stīpes, *m*; (pledge, wager), pignus, *n*
stake, *v.t*, (wager), dēpōno (3)
stale, vĕtus
stalk, stirps, *f*
stalk, *v.i*, incēdo (3); (game, etc), *use phr*, cautē sĕquor (3 *dep*) (follow cautiously)
stall (cattle), stăbŭlum, *n*; (shop, etc.), tăberna, *f*
stallion, admissārĭus, *m*
stalwart, *adj*, fortis
stamina, vīres, *f. pl*
stammer, *nn*, haesĭtantĭa (*f*) linguae (hesitation of speech)
stammer, *v.i*, balbūtĭo (4)
stamp (mark), nŏta, *f*; (with a ring, etc.), signum, *n*
stamp, *v.t*, (mark), signo (1); (— with the foot), supplōdo (3)
stand, *nn* (halt), mŏra, *f*; (to make a —) consisto (3) rĕsisto (3), (*with dat.*); (platform), suggestus, *m*; (stall), mensa, *f*
stand, *v.i*, sto (1), consisto (3); (— back), rĕcēdo (3), (— by, help), adsum (*irreg with dat*); (— for,

seek a position), *v.t*, pĕto (3); (endure), pătĭor (3 *dep*); (— out, project) exsto (1); (— up), surgo (3)
standard, signum, *n*; (of the legion), ăquĭla, *f*; (measure), norma, *f*; (— bearer), signĭfer, *m*
standing, *nn*, (position), stătus, *m*
staple products, merces, *f, pl*
star, stella, *f*, sīdus, *n*
starboard, *use adj*, dexter (right)
starch, *nn*, ămўlum, *n*
stare, *nn*, obtūtus, *m*
stare, *v.t*, (— at), intŭĕor (2 *dep*)
stark (stiff), rĭgĭdus; (— naked), nūdus; (—mad) āmens
starling, sturnus, *m*
start, *nn*, (movement), trĕmor, *m*; (beginning), ĭnĭtĭum, *n*; (setting out), prŏfectĭo, *f*; (starting point), carcĕres, *m. pl*
start, *v.i*, (make a sudden movement), trĕmo (3), horrĕo (2); (— out), prŏfĭciscor (3 *dep*); *v.t* (establish), instĭtŭo (3)
startle, *v.t*, terrĕo (2)
startling, *adj*, terrĭbĭlis
starvation, fămes, *f*
starve, *v.t*, făme nĕco (1) (kill by starvation); *v.i*, făme nĕcor (1 *pass*)
state (condition), stătus, *m*, condĭcĭo, *f*; (the —), respublĭca, *f*, cīvĭtas, *f*
state, *v.t*, prŏfĭtĕor (2 *dep*)
stately, magnĭfĭcus, cĕlĕber
statement, dictum, *n*
statesman, *use phr. with* respublĭca (state), *and* admĭnistro · (1), (to manage)
station (standing), stătus, *m*; (occupied place), stătĭo, *f*
station, *v.t*, lŏco (1)
stationary, *adj*, immōtus
stationer, bĭblĭŏpōla, *m*
statistics, census, *m*
statue, stătŭa, *f*
stature, stătūra, *f*
status, stătus, *m*
statute, lex, *f*
staunch, *adj*, firmus
stave off, *v.t*, arcĕo (2)
stay, *nn*, (prop), firmāmentum, *n*; (rest, etc), mansĭo, *f*, commŏrātĭo, *f*
stay, *v.i*, mănĕo (2), mŏror (1 *dep*); *v.t*, (obstruct, stop), mŏror (1 *dep*)
steadfast, firmus, stăbĭlis
steady, firmus, stăbĭlis
steadfastness, stăbĭlĭtas, *f*
steadiness, stăbĭlĭtas, *f*
steak, offa, *f*

For List of Abbreviations used, turn to pages 3, 4

steal, *v.t,* fūror (1 *dep*); *v.i,* (— **upon),** surrēpo (3)(*with dat*)
stealing, *nn,* (theft), furtum, *n*
stealth, (by —), (*adv*) furtim
stealthy, furtīvus
steam, văpor, *m*
steam, *v.i,* exhālo (1)
steed, ĕquus, *m*
steel, chălybs, *m*; (iron, sword, etc.), ferrum, *n*
steel, *v.t,* (strengthen), confirmo (1)
steep, praeruptus
steep, *v.t,* (soak), mădĕfăcĭo (3)
steeple, turris, *f*
steer, *nn,* iŭvencus, *m*
steer, *v.t,* gŭberno (1)
steersman, gŭbernător, *m*
stem, stirps, *f,* (— *literal and metaphorical*)
stem, *v.t,* (check), sisto (3), rĕsisto (3) (*with dat*)
stench, fētor, *m*
step, *nn,* grădus, *m,* passus, *m*; (foot —), vestīgĭum, *n*; (— by —), pĕdĕtentim; (steps, stairs), scālae, *f.pl*
step, *v.i,* grădĭor (3 *dep*); (— forward); prōgrĕdĭor (3 *dep*)
step-brother (father's side), fīlĭus vītrīci; (mother's side), fīlĭus nŏvercae; (— daughter), prīvigna, *f*; (— father) vītrīcus, *m*; (— mother), nŏverca, *f*; (— sister), fīlĭa vītrīci *or* nŏvercae; (— son), prīvignus, *m*
sterile, stĕrĭlis
sterility, stĕrĭlĭtas, *f*
sterling, *adj,* (genuine), vērus
stern, *nn,* puppis, *f*
stern, *adj,* dūrus
sternness, sĕvērĭtas, *f*
stew, *v.t,* cŏquo (3)
steward, vīlĭcus, *m*
stick, *nn,* băcŭlum, *n*
stick, *v.t,* (fix), fīgo (3); *v.i,* haerĕo (2)
sticky, *adj,* tĕnax
stiff, rĭgĭdus; (to be —), *v.i,* rĭgĕo (2)
stiffen, *v.i,* rĭgĕo (2); *v.t,* rĭgĭdum făcĭo (3)
stiffness, rĭgor, *m*
stifle, *v.t,* suffōco (1); (suppress), opprĭmo (3)
stigma, stigma, *n*
stigmatize, *v.t,* nŏto (1)
still, *adj,* immōtus, tranquillus
still, *adv,* (nevertheless), tămen; (up to this time), ădhuc; (even), ĕtĭam
still, *v.t,* sēdo (1)
stillness, quĭes, *f*

stilts, grallae, *f. pl*
stimulant (incentive), stĭmŭlus, *m*
stimulus (incentive), stĭmŭlus, *m*
stimulate, *v.t,* stĭmŭlo (1)
sting, *nn,* ăcŭlĕus, *m*
sting, *v.t,* pungo (3)
stinging, *adj,* mordax
stingy, sordĭdus
stink, *nn,* fētor, *m*
stink, *v.i,* fētĕo (2)
stipend, merces, *f*
stipulate, *v.i,* stĭpŭlor (1 *dep*)
stir, *nn,* mōtus, *m*
stir, *v.t,* mŏvĕo (2); *v.i,* mŏvĕor (2 *pass*)
stitch, *v.t,* sŭo (3)
stock (of tree, family, etc.), stirps, *f*; (amount), vīs, *f*
stock, *v.t,* complĕo (2)
stockbroker, argentărĭus, *m*
stocking, tībĭāle, *n*
stoic, *nn. and adj,* stōĭcus
stoical, dūrus
stoicism, rătĭo Stōĭca, *f*
stolen, furtīvus
stomach, stŏmăchus, *m*
stomach, *v.t,* (put up with), perfĕro (*irreg*)
stone, lăpis, *m*; (precious —), gemma, *f*; (fruit —), nūclĕus, *m*
stone, *adj,* lăpĭdĕus
stone, *v.t,* (— to death), lăpĭdĭbus cŏŏpĕrĭo (4) (overwhelm with stones)
stone-quarry, lăpĭcīdīnae, *f. pl*
stony, lăpĭdōsus; (of heart), asper
stool, scăbellum, *n*
stoop, *v.i,* sē dēmittĕre (3 *reflex*); (condescend), dēscendo (3)
stop, *nn,* intermissĭo, *f*
stop, *v.t,* sisto (3); (— up a hole, etc.), obtūro (1); *v.i,* (pause), sisto (3); (desist), dēsĭno (3); (remain), mănĕo (2)
stoppage (hindrance), impĕdīmentum, *n*
stopper, obtūrāmentum, *n*
store (supply), cōpĭa, *f*; (place), rĕceptăcŭlum, *n*
store, *v.t,* condo (3)
storey, tăbŭlātum, *n*
stork, cĭcōnĭa, *f*
storm, *nn,* tempestas, *f*
storm, *v.t,* (attack), expugno (1)
storming, *nn,* expugnātĭo, *f*
stormy (weather), turbĭdus
story, fābŭla, *f*
story-teller, narrător, *m*

stout, (fat), pinguis; (strong), vălĭdus;
(— hearted), fortis
stove, fŏcus, *m*
stow, *v.t*, rĕpōno (3)
straddle, *v.i*, vārĭco (1)
straggle, *v.i*, văgor (1 *dep*)
straight, *adj*, rectus
straight, *adv*, rectā
straight away, *adv*, stătim
straighten, *v.t*, corrĭgo (3)
straightforward, simplex
strain, *nn*, contentĭo, *f*
strain, *v.t*, (stretch), tendo (3); (liquids, etc.), cōlo (3); *v.i*, (strive), nītor (3 *dep*)
strait, *adj*, angustus
strait, *nn*, (a narrow place or a difficulty), angustĭae, *f. pl* (sea) frētum *n.*
strand (shore), lītus, *n*
stranded, rĕlictus
strange, insŏlĭtus, nŏvus
strangeness, insŏlentĭa, *f*
stranger, hospes, *m*
strangle, *v.t*, strangŭlo (1)
strap, *nn*, lōrum, *n*
stratagem, dŏlus, *m*
strategist, *use phr. with* pĕrītus (skilled in), *with phr. below*
strategy, ars, (*f*) bellandi (the art of making war)
straw, strāmentum, *n*
strawberry, frăgum, *n*
stray, *v.i*, erro (1)
stray, *adj*, errābundus
streak, *nn*, līnĕa, *f*
streak, *v.t*, līnĕis vărĭo (1), (variegate with streaks)
streaky, virgātus
stream, *nn*, flūmen, *n*
stream, *v.i*, effundor (3 *pass*)
street, vĭa, *f*
strength, vīres, *f. pl*, rōbur, *n*
strengthen, *v.t*, firmo (1)
strenuous, impĭger
stress (importance), mōmentum, *n*
stretch, *nn*, (extent), spătĭum, *n*
stretch, *v.t*, tendo (3); (— out), extendo (3); *v.i*, sē tendĕre (3 *reflex*)
stretcher, lectīca, *f*
strew, *v.t*, sterno (3)
strict (severe), dūrus; (careful), dīlĭgens
strictness, sĕvĕrĭtas, *f*
stricture, rĕprĕhensĭo, *f*
stride, *nn*, passus, *m*
strife, certāmen, *n*, discordĭa, *f*
strike, *v.t*, fĕrĭo (4), percŭtĭo (3), pulso (1); (— the mind, occur to), subvĕnĭo (4)

striking, *adj*, insignis
string, līnĕa, *f*; (of bow or instrument), nervus, *m*
stringent, sĕvērus
strip, *v.t*, spŏlĭo (1), nūdo (1)
strip, *nn*, (flap, edge), lăcĭnĭa, *f*
stripe, līmes, *m*; (blow), verber, *n*
stripling, ădŏlescentŭlus, *m*
strive, *v.i*, nītor (3 *dep*), contendo (3)
striving, *nn*, contentĭo, *f*
stroke, *nn*, verber, *n*, ictus, *m*; (line), līnĕa, *f*
stroke, *v.t*, mulcĕo (2)
stroll, *nn*, ambŭlātĭo, *f*
stroll, *v.i*, ambŭlo (1)
strong, vălĭdus, firmus; (powerful), fortis; (to be —), *v.i*, vălĕo (2)
stronghold, arx, *f*
structure (building), aedĭfĭcĭum, *n*
struggle, *nn*, certāmen, *n*
struggle, *v.i*, luctor (1 *dep*), nītor (3 *dep*)
strumpet, mĕrĕtrix, *f*
strut, *v.i*, incēdo (3)
stubble, stĭpŭla, *f*
stubborn, pertĭnax
stucco, tectōrĭum, *n*
stud, clāvus, *m*; (horses), ĕquārĭa, *f*
stud, *v.t*, insēro (3)
student, *use adj*, stŭdĭōsus (devoted to), *with a suitable noun*
studied, mĕdĭtātus
studious, stŭdĭōsus
study, *nn*, stŭdĭum, *n*; (room, library), bĭblĭŏthēca, *f*
study, *v.t*, stŭdĕo (2) (*with dat*)
stuff (material), mătĕrĭa, *f*; (woven-), textĭle, *n*
stuff, *v.t*, farcĭo (4)
stuffing, *nn*, fartum, *n*
stumble, *nn*, (fall), lapsus, *m*
stumble, *v.i*, offendo (3)
stumbling-block, impĕdīmentum, *n.*
stump (post), stīpes, *m*
stun, *v.t*, obstŭpĕfăcĭo (3)
stupefaction, stŭpor, *m*
stupefy, *v.t*, obstŭpĕfăcĭo (3)
stupendous, mīrābĭlis
stupid, stŏlĭdus, stultus
stupidity, stultĭtĭa, *f*
stupor, stŭpor, *m*
sturdiness, firmĭtas, *f*
sturdy, firmus, vălĭdus
sturgeon, ăcĭpenser, *m*
stutter, *v.i*, balbŭtĭo (4)
sty, hăra, *f*; (in the eye), hordĕŏlus, *m*
style, gĕnus, *n*
style, *v.t* (name), appello (1)
stylish, spĕcĭōsus
suave, suāvis

subaltern, subcentŭrĭo, *m*
subdivide, *v.t*, dīvĭdo (3)
subdue, *v.t*, sŭbĭcĭo (3)
subject, *adj*, subiectus
subject, *nn*, (of a state, etc), cīvis, *c*; (matter), rēs, *f*
subject, *v.t*, sŭbĭcĭo (3)
subjection (slavery), servĭtus, *f*
subjoin, *v.t*, subiungo (3)
subjugate, *v.t*, sŭbīgo (3)
sublime, ēlātus
sublimity, ēlātĭo, *f*
submerge, *v.t*, submergo (3)
submission (compliance), obsĕquĭum, *n*
submissive, ŏbēdĭens
submit, *v.t*, sŭbĭcĭo (3); (present), rĕfĕro (*irreg*); *v.i*, (yield), cēdo (3)
subordinate, *adj*, subiectus
subordination (obedience), obsĕquĭum, *n*
subscribe, *v.t*, (give money, etc.), confĕro (*irreg*); (signature), subscrībo (3)
subscription (of money, etc.), collātĭo, *f*
subsequent, sĕquens
subsequently, *adv*, postĕā
subservient, obsĕquens
subside, *v.i*, rēsĭdo (3)
subsidize, *v.t*, pĕcūnĭam suppĕdĭto (1), (furnish with money)
subsidy, subsĭdĭum, *n*
subsist, *v.i*, consto (1)
subsistence, victus, *m*
substance (essence), nātūra, *f*; (being), rēs, *f*; (goods), bŏna, *n.pl*
substantial (real), vērus; (important), grăvis
substitute, *nn*, vĭcārĭus, *m*
substitute, *v.t*, suppōno (3)
subterfuge, lătĕbra, *f*
subterranean, subterrānĕus
subtle (crafty), astūtus; (refined), subtīlis
subtlety (craftiness), astūtĭa, *f*; (fineness), subtīlĭtas, *f*
subtract, *v.t*, dēdūco (3)
subtraction, dētractĭo, *f*
suburb, sŭburbĭum, *n*
suburban, sŭburbānus
subvert, *v.t*, ēverto (3)
succeed, *v.t*, (in, do well), bĕnĕ effĭcĭo (3); (of things), *v.i*, prospĕrē ēvĕnĭo (4); *v.t*, (follow), sĕquor (3 *dep*); (to an office), succēdo (3)
success, res sĕcundae, *f.pl*
successful (persons), fēlix; (things), prospĕrus
succession (to an office, etc.), successĭo, *f*; (series), contĭnŭātĭo, *f*

successive, contĭnŭus
successor, successor, *m*
succinct, brĕvis
succour, *nn*, auxĭlĭum, *n*
succour, *v.t*, succurro (3) (*with dat*)
succulent, sūcōsus
succumb, *v.i*, cēdo (3)
such, *adj*, tālis, hūius mŏdi (of this kind)
suck, *v.t*, sūgo (3)
sucker, planta, *f*
suckle, *v.t*, ūbĕra do (1) (*with dat*)
suction, suctus, *m*
sudden, sŭbĭtus
suddenly, *adv*, sŭbĭto, rĕpentē
sue, *v.t*, (in law), in ius vŏco (1); (— for, beg for), rŏgo (1)
suet, sēbum, *n*
suffer, *v.t*, pătĭor (3 *dep*), fĕro (*irreg*); (permit), permitto (3) (*with dat*); *v.i*, affĭcĭor (3 pass)
sufferance, pătĭentĭa, *f*
sufferer (of illness), aeger, *m*
suffering, *nn*, dŏlor, *m*
suffice, *v.i*, sătis esse (*irreg*)
sufficiency, *use adv*, sătis (enough)
sufficient, *use* sătis, *adv*, (*with genit. of noun*)
suffocate, *v.t*, suffŏco (1)
suffrage, suffrāgĭum, *n*
sugar, sacchăron, *n*
suggest, *v.t*, sŭbĭcĭo (3) (*with acc. of thing and dat. of person*)
suggestion, admŏnĭtus, *m*
suicide, mors vŏluntārĭa, *f*; (to commit —), sĭbĭ mortem conscisco (3) (inflict death upon oneself)
suit (law —), līs, *f*; (clothes), vestīmenta, *n.pl*
suit, *v.i*, convĕnĭo (4); *or use impers. vb*, dĕcet (it —s)
suitable, aptus, ĭdōnĕus
suite (retinue), cŏmĭtes, *c, pl*
suitor, prŏcus, *m*
sulky, mōrōsus
sullen, torvus
sully, *v.t*, inquĭno (1)
sulphur, sulfur, *n*
sultry, aestŭōsus
sum (total), summa, *f*; (— of money), pĕcūnĭa, *f*
sum up, *v.t*, compŭto (1); (speak briefly), summātim dīco (3)
summarily, *adv*, (immediately), sĭne mŏrā
summary, *nn*, ĕpĭtŏme, *f*
summary, *adj*, (hasty), sŭbĭtus
summer, *nn*, aestas, *f*; *adj*, aestīvus
summit, căcūmen, *n*, *or use adj*, summus (top of)

summon, *v.t*, arcesso (3)
summon up, *v.t*, excĭto (1)
summons, vŏcātĭo, *f*, accītu (*abl. case only*: at the — of)
sumptuous, sumptŭōsus
sumptuousness, appărātus, *m*
sun, sōl, *m*
sun, *v.i*, (— oneself), ăprīcor (1 *dep*)
sunbeam, rădĭus, (*m*) sōlis
sunburnt, ădustus
sundial, sōlārĭum, *n*
sunny, aprīcus
sunrise, ortus, (*m*) sōlis
sunset, occāsus, (*m*) sōlis
sunshine, sōl, *m*
sup, *v.i*, cēno (1)
superabound, *v.i*, sŭpersum (*irreg*)
superb, magnĭfĭcus
supercilious, sŭpcrbus
superficial, lĕvis
superfluous, sŭpervăcănĕus
superhuman, dīvīnus
superintend, *v.t*, prōcūro (1)
superintendent, cūrātor, *m*, praefectus, *m*
superior, sŭpĕrĭor; (to be —), *v.i*, sŭpĕro (1)
superiority, *use adj*, sŭpĕrĭor
superlative, exīmĭus
supernatural, dīvīnus
supernumerary, ascriptīvus
superscription, tĭtŭlus, *m*
supersede, *v.t*, succēdo (3) (*with dat*)
superstition, sŭperstĭtĭo, *f*
superstitious, sŭperstĭtĭōsus
supervise, *v.i*, prōcūro (1)
supper, cēna, *f*
supplant, *v.t*. (surpass), praeverto (3)
supple, flexĭbĭlis
supplement, supplēmentum, *n*
suppliant, supplex, *c*
supplication, obsĕcrātĭo, *f*
supply, *nn*, cōpĭa, *f*; (supplies, esp. military), commĕātus, *m*
supply, *v.t*, suppĕdĭto (1); afferŏ(*irreg*)
support, *nn*, (bearing), firmāmentum, *n*; (military), subsĭdĭa, *n.pl*; (sustenance), ălīmentum, *n*
support, *v.t*, sustĭnĕo (2); (aid), adiŭvo (1); (nourish), ălo (3)
supportable, tŏlĕrābĭlis
supporter, adiŭtor, *m*
suppose, *v.t*, pŭto (1), ŏpīnor (1 *pass*)
supposition, ŏpīnĭo, *f*
suppress, *v.t*, opprĭmo (3)
suppurate, *v.i*, suppūro (1)
supremacy, impĕrĭum, *n*
supreme, sŭprēmus
sure, certus; (reliable), fĭdēlis; (I am —), compertum hăbĕo (2)

surely, *adv*, prŏfecto; (no doubt), nīmīrum; (*in questions*; *if an affirmative answer is expected*) nonne; (*if a negative answer*), num
surety, vas, *m*, sponsor, *m*
surf, fluctus, *m*
surface, sŭperfĭcĭes, *f*
surge, *v.i*, surgo (3)
surgeon, chīrurgus, *m*
surgery, chīrurgĭa, *f*
surly, mōrōsus
surmise, *nn*, coniectūra, *f*
surmise, *v.t*, suspĭcor (1 *dep*)
surmount, *v.t*, sŭpĕro (1)
surname, cognōmen, *n*
surpass, *v.t*, sŭpĕro (1)
surplus, rĕlĭquum, *n*
surprise, *nn*, mīrātĭo, *f*
surprise, *v.t*, admīrātĭōnem mŏvĕo (2) (*with dat*); (to attack), ădŏrĭor (4 *dep*)
surrender, *nn*, dēdĭtĭo, *f*
surrender, *v.t*, dēdo (3), trādo (3); *v.i*, sē dēdĕre (3 *reflex*)
surround, *v.t*, cingo (3), circumdo (1)
survey, *v.t*, contemplor (1 *dep*); (land), mētĭor (4 *dep*)
surveyor, fīnĭtor, *m*
survive, *v.i*, sŭpersum (*irreg*)
survivor, sŭperstes, *m*, *f*
susceptibility, mollĭtĭa, *f*
susceptible, mollis
suspect, *v.t*, suspĭcor (1 *dep*)
suspend, *v.t*, suspendo (3); (interrupt), intermitto (3); (— from office), dēmŏvĕo (2)
suspense, dŭbĭtātĭo, *f*
suspension (interruption), intermissĭo, *f*
suspicion, suspĭcĭo, *f*
suspicious, suspĭcĭōsus
sustain, *v.t*, sustĭnĕo (2)
sustenance, ălīmentum, *n*
swaddling-clothes, incūnābŭla, *n.pl*
swagger, *v.i*, sē iactăre (1 *reflex*)
swallow, *nn*, hĭrundo, *f*
swallow, *v.t*, gluttĭo (4), sorbĕo (2)
swamp, *nn*, pălus, *f*
swamp, *v.t*, opprĭmo (3)
swampy, pălūdōsus
swan, cycnus, *m*
swarm (people), turba, *f*; (bees), exāmen, *n*
swarm, *v.i*, glŏmĕror (1 *pass*)
swarthy, fuscus
swathe, *v.t*, collĭgo (1)
sway, *nn*, impĕrĭum, *n*
sway, *v.t*, (rule), rĕgo (3); *v.i* (— to and fro), văcillo (1)

swear, *v.i,* iūro (1); (— allegiance to), iūro in nōmen *(with genit. of person)*
sweat, *nn,* sūdor, *m*
sweat, *v.i,* sūdo (1)
sweep, *v.t,* verro (3)
sweet, dulcis
sweeten, *v.t,* dulcem reddo (3) **(make sweet)**
sweetheart, dēlīcĭae, *f. pl*
sweetness, dulcĭtūdo, *f*
swell, *nn,* **(wave),** fluctus, *m*
swell, *v.i,* tŭmĕo (2); *v.t,* augĕo (2)
swelling, tŭmor, *m*
swerve, *v.i,* dēclīno (1)
swift, *adj,* cĕler
swiftness, cĕlĕrĭtas, *f*
swill, *v.t,* **(drink),** pōto (1)
swim, *v.i,* năto (1)
swimmer, nătātor, *m*
swimming, *nn,* nătātĭo, *f*
swindle, *nn,* fraus, *f*
swindle, *v.t,* fraudo (1)
swindler, fraudātor, *m*
swine, sūs, *m, f*
swineherd, sŭbulcus, *m*
swing, *nn,* oscillātĭo, *f*
swing, *v.t,* ăgĭto (1); *v.i,* pendĕo (2)
switch, (cane), virga, *f*
switch, *v.t,* mūto (1)
swollen, tŭmĭdus
swoon, *v.i, use phr,* ănĭmus rĕlinquit . . . **(sensibility leaves . . .)**
swoop, *nn, use vb.* advŏlo (1)
swoop on, *v.i,* advŏlo (1)
sword, glădĭus, *m*
sword-edge, ăcĭes, *f*
swordfish, xĭphĭas, *m*
sworn (treaty, etc.), confirmātus iūrĕiūrando **(confirmed by swearing)**
sycamore, sȳcămōrus, *f*
sycophant, sȳcŏphanta, *m*
syllable, syllăba, *f*
symbol, signum, *n*
symmetrical, congrŭens
symmetry, convĕnĭentĭa, *f*
sympathetic, mĭsĕrĭcors
sympathize, *v.t,* consentĭo (4)
sympathy, consensus, *m*
symphony, symphōnĭa, *f*
symptom, signum, *n*
synagogue, sȳnăgōga, *f*
syndicate, sŏcĭĕtas, *f*
synonym, verbum ĭdem signĭfĭcans **(word expressing the same thing)**
synopsis, ēpĭtŏma, *f*
syntax, syntaxis, *f*
syringe, sīpho, *m*

syringe, *v.t,* aspergo (3) **(sprinkle)**
system, formŭla, *f,* rătĭo, *f*
systematic, ordĭnātus

T

table, mensa, *f,* tăbŭla, *f;* **(list),** index, *m*
tablecloth, mantēle, *n*
tablet, tăbŭla, *f*
tacit, tăcĭtus
taciturn, tăcĭturnus
tack, clāvŭlus, *m*
tack, *v.t,* **(fix),** fīgo (3); *v.i,*(**ships),** rēcĭprŏcor (1 *pass*)
tackle (fittings), armāmenta, *n.pl*
tact, dextĕrĭtas, *f,* urbānĭtas, *f*
tactician, pĕrītus, *(m)* rĕi mĭlĭtāris
tactics (military), rătĭo, *(f)* bellandi **(method of making war)**
tadpole, rānuncŭlus, *m*
tag, *v.t, use* fīgo (3) **(fix)**
tail, cauda, *f*
tailor, vestītor, *m*
taint, *nn,* contāgĭo, *f*
taint, *v.t,* infĭcĭo (3)
take, *v.t,* căpĭo (3); **(grasp),** prĕhendo (3); **(receive),** accĭpĭo (3); **(seize),** răpĭo (3); **(take possession of),** occŭpo (1); (— **by storm),** expugno (1); (— **away),** aufĕro *(irreg)* ădĭmo (3); (— **in),** excĭpĭo (3); (— **off),** dēmo (3); (— **on),** suscĭpĭo (3); (— **up),** sūmo (3)
taking (capture of a city), expugnātĭo, *f*
tale, fābŭla, *f*
talent (ability), ingĕnĭum, *n;* **(money),** tălentum, *n*
talk, *nn,* sermo, *m*
talk, *v.i,* lŏquor (3 *dep*)
talkative, lŏquax
tall, prōcērus
tallness, prōcērĭtas, *f*
tallow, sēbum, *n*
tally, *v.i,* convĕnĭo (4)
talon, unguis, *m*
tamable, dŏmābĭlis
tame, *v.t,* dŏmo (1), mansŭēfăcĭo (3)
tame, *adj,* mansŭēfactus, dŏmĭtus
tameness, mansŭētūdo, *f*
tamer, dŏmĭtor, *m*
tamper with, *v.t,* tempto (1)
tan, *v.t,* **(leather, etc.),** confĭcĭo (3)
tangent, *use* līnĕa, *f,* **(line)**
tangible, tractābĭlis
tangle, *nn,* implĭcātĭo, *f*

tangle, *v.t*, implĭco (1)
tank, lăcus, *m*
tanner, cŏrĭārĭus, *m*
tantalize, *v.t*, (torment), fătīgo (1)
tap, *nn*, (blow), ictus, *m*
tap, *v.t*, (hit), fĕrĭo (4), pulso (1); *with* lĕvĭter (lightly)
tape, taenĭa, *f*
taper, cērĕus, *m*
taper, *v.i*, fastīgor (1 *pass*)
tapestry, *use* vēlum, *n*, (curtain)
tar, pix līquĭda, *f*
tardiness, tardĭtas, *f*
tardy, tardus
tare, lŏlĭum, *n*
target, scŏpus, *m*
tarnish, *v.i*, hĕbesco (3); *v.t*, inquĭno (1)
tarry, *v.i*, mŏror (1 *dep*)
tart, *nn*, crustŭlum, *n*
tart, *adj*, ăcĭdus
task, ŏpus, *n*
taste, *nn*, (sense of —), gustātus, *m*; (flavour), săpor, *m*; (judgement), iūdĭcĭum, *n*
taste, *v.t*, gusto (1); *v.i* (have a flavour), săpĭo (3)
tasteful (elegant), ēlĕgans
tasteless, insulsus
tasty, săpĭdus
tattered, pannōsus
tatters, pannus, *m*
tattle, *v.i*, garrĭo (4)
taunt, *nn*, convĭcĭum, *n*
taunt, *v.t*, ŏbĭcĭo (3) *(dat. of person and acc. of thing)*
taunting, *adj*, contŭmēlĭōsus
tavern, caupōna, *f*
tavern-keeper, caupo, *m*
tawdry, fūcōsus
tawny, fulvus
tax, *nn*, vectīgal, *n*
tax, *v.t*, (impose —), vectīgal impōno (3) *(with dat)*
taxable, vectīgālis
tax-collector, exactor, *m*, pūblĭcānus, *m*
teach, *v.t*, dŏcĕo (2) *(with acc. of person and acc. of thing)*
teacher, doctor, *m*, măgister, *m*
teaching, *nn*, doctrīna, *f*
team (— of horses), iŭgum, *n*
tear, *nn*, lăcrĭma, *f*; (to shed —s), lăcrĭmas fundo (3); (rent), scissūra, *f*
tear, *v.t*, scindo (3); (— away), abscindo (3); (— down, open), rēscindo (3); (— up, in pieces), distrăho (3)
tearful, flēbĭlis

tease, *v.t*, obtundo (3)
teat, mamma, *f*
technical, *use phr*, prŏprĭus artis (particular to a skill)
tedious, lentus
teem with, *v.i*, scătĕo (2)
teethe, *v.i*, dentĭo (4)
teething, *nn*, dentĭtĭo, *f*
tell, *v.t*, (give information), dīco (3); narro (1) *(with acc. of thing said and dat. of person told)*, certĭōrem făcĭo (3) *(acc. of person told, foll. by* dē *with abl. of thing said)*; (order), iŭbĕo (2)
teller (counter), nŭmĕrātor, *m*
temerity, tĕmĕrĭtas, *f*
temper (of mind), ănĭmus, *m*; (bad —), īrācundĭa, *f*
temper, *v.t*, tempĕro (1)
temperament, nātūra, *f*, ingĕnĭum, *n*
temperance, tempĕrantĭa, *f*
temperate, tempĕrātus
temperate climate, tĕmpĕrĭes, *f*
temperateness, mŏdĕrātĭo, *f*
tempest, tempestas, *f*
tempestuous, prŏcellōsus
temple, templum, *n*, aedes, *f*; (of the head), tempus, *n*
temporal, hūmānus
temporary, *use adv. phr*, ad tempus (for the time being)
tempt, *v.t*, tento (1)
temptation (allurement), ĭllĕcĕbra, *f*
tempter, tentātor, *m*
tempting, *adj*, illĕcĕbrōsus
ten, dĕcem; (— each), dēni; (— times), *adv*, dĕcĭes
tenacious, tĕnax
tenacity, tĕnācĭtas, *f*
tenant, inquĭlīnus, *m*
tend, *v.t*, (care for), cōlo (3); *v.i*, (go, direct oneself), tendo (3); (incline to), inclīno (1); (be accustomed), consŭesco (3)
tendency, inclīnātĭo, *f*
tender, *adj*, tĕner, mollis
tender, *v.t*, (offer), dēfĕro *(irreg)*
tenderness, mollĭtĭa, *f*, indulgentĭa, *f*
tenement, conductum, *n*
tenour (course), tĕnor, *m*, cursus, *m*
tense, *adj*, tentus, intentus
tense, *nn*, tempus, *n*
tension, intentĭo, *f*
tent, tăbernācŭlum, *n*; (general's —), praetōrĭum, *n*
tentacle, cornĭcŭlum, *n*
tenth, dĕcĭmus
tepid, ēgĕlĭdus, tĕpĭdus; (to be —), *v.i*, tĕpĕo (2)

term (period of time), spătĭum, n;
(limit), fĭnis, m; (word), verbum, n;
(condition), condĭcĭo, f
term, v.t, vŏco (1)
terminate, v.t, termĭno (1)
termination, fĭnis, m
terrace, sōlārĭum, n
terrestrial, terrestris
terrible, terrĭbĭlis
terrify, v.t, terrĕo (2)
territory, fĭnes, m. pl, ăger, m
terror, terror, m, păvor, m
terse, brĕvis
terseness, brĕvĭtas, f
test, nn, expĕrīmentum, n
test, v.t, expĕrĭor (4 dep)
testament, testāmentum, n
testator, testātor, m
testify, v.t, testĭfĭcor (1 dep)
testimony, testĭmōnĭum, n
testy, stŏmăchōsus
text, scriptum, n
textile, textĭle, n
texture, textus, m
than, conj, quam
thank, v.t, grātĭas ăgo (3) (with dat. of
person)
thankfulness, grātus ănĭmus, m
thankless, ingrātus
thanks, grātĭae, f. pl
thanksgiving, actĭo, (f) grātĭārum
that, demonstrative pron, ille, is, iste
that, relative pron, qui, quae, quad
that, conj, (with purpose or consecutive clauses) ut (ne if negative);
(after vbs introducing statements)
no separate word, but rendered by
the expression itself: e.g. he said that
the king was coming, rēgem vēnīre
dixit
thatch, strāmentum, n
thaw, v.t, solvo (3); v.i, sē rĕsolvĕre (3
reflex)
the, no equivalent in Latin
theatre, thĕātrum, n
theatrical, thĕātrālis
theft, furtum, n
their, reflexive, sŭus; otherwise ĕōrum,
(f, ĕārum)
them, use appropriate case of pron, is,
ille, iste
theme, prŏpŏsĭtĭo, f
themselves, reflexive pron, sē; (emphatic), ipsi, ae, a
then, adv. of (time), tum (therefore),
ĭgĭtur
thence, adv, inde, illinc
theologian, thĕŏlŏgus, m
theology, thĕŏlŏgĭa, f
theorem, thĕōrēma, n

theoretical, rătĭōnālis
theory, rătĭo, f
there (in or at that place), ĭbĭ; (to that
place), ĕō; (— is), est; (— are),
sunt (from esse)
thereabouts, adv, circā
thereafter, adv, dĕinde
therefore, adv, ĭgĭtur, ergo
thereupon, adv, sŭbinde
thesis, prōpŏsĭtum, n
they, as subject of vb. usually not
rendered; otherwise use ĭi, illi, isti.
thick, crassus, densus, confertus
thicken, v.t, denso (1); v.i, concresco
(3)
thicket, dūmētum, n
thick-headed, crassus
thickness, crassĭtūdo, f
thick-set (of body), compactus
thick-skinned, (indifferent), neglĕgens
thief, fur, c
thieve, v.t, fūror (1 dep)
thieving, nn, (theft), furtum, n
thigh, fĕmur, n
thin, tĕnŭis, grăcĭlis
thin, v.t, tĕnŭo (1)
thing, rēs, f
think, v.t, cōgĭto (1); (believe, suppose), crēdo (3), arbĭtror (1 dep),
pŭto (1), existĭmo (1)
thinker, phĭlŏsŏphus, m
thinness, tĕnŭĭtas, f
third, adj, tertĭus; (a — part), tertĭa
pars, f; (thirdly), adv, tertĭo
thirst, v.i, sĭtĭo (4)
thirst, nn, sĭtis, f
thirsty, sĭtĭens
thirteen, trēdĕcim
thirteenth, tertĭus dĕcĭmus
thirtieth, trīgēsĭmus
thirty, trīginta
this, demonstrative pron, hīc, haec,
hōc
thistle, cardŭus, m
thither, adv, ĕō, illūc; (hither and —),
hūc atque illūc
thong, lōrum, n
thorn, sentis, m, spīna, f
thorn-bush, vĕpres, m
thorny, spīnōsus
thorough, perfectus; (exact), subtīlis
thoroughbred, gĕnĕrōsus
thoroughfare, pervĭum, n
those, demonstrative pron, illi
though, conj, etsi
thought (act or faculty of thinking),
cōgĭtātĭo, f; (opinion), cōgĭtātum,
n; (plan, intention), consĭlĭum, n
thoughtful (careful), prŏvĭdus; (deep
in thought), multa pŭtans

thoughtfulness, cūra, *f*, cōgǐtātǐo, *f*
thoughtless, těměrārǐus, inconsultus
thoughtlessness, něglegentǐa, *f*, těměrǐtas, *f*
thousand, mille (*indeclinable adj*); in *pl*, milǐa (*n.pl, nn*)
thrash, *v.t*, tundo (3); (**corn**), těro (3)
thrashing, *nn*, trītūra, *f*; (**chastisement**), verběrātǐo, *f*
thrashing-floor, ārěa, *f*
thread, filum, *n*
thread, *v.t*, (— **one's way**), sē insǐnǔāre (1 *reflex*)
threadbare, obsǒlētus
threat, mǐnae, *f. pl*
threaten, *v.t*, mǐnor (1 *dep*) (*with acc. of thing and dat. of person*); *v.i*, (impend), immǐněo (2)
threatening, *adj*, mǐnax
three, tres; (— **each**), terni; (— **times**), *adv*, ter
threefold (triple), trǐplex
threehundred, trěcenti
threehundredth, trěcentensǐmus
thresh, *v.t*, těro (3)
threshold, limen, *n*
thrice, *adj*, ter
thrift, frūgālǐtas, *f*
thrifty, parous
thrill, *v.t, use* afficǐo (3) (**affect**)
thrill (of pleasure), hǐlărǐtas, *f*; (a shock), stringor, *m*
thrilling, *adj, use vb*, afficǐo (3) (to affect)
thrive, *v.i*, vǐgěo (2)
throat, fauces, *f. pl*
throb, *v.i*, palpǐto (1)
throbbing, *nn*, palpǐtātǐo, *f*
throne, sǒlǐum, *n*; (**regal, imperial power**), regnum, *n*
throng, *nn*, multǐtūdo, *f*
throng, *v.t*, cělěbro (1)
throttle, *v.t*, strangǔlo (1)
through, *prep*, per (*with acc*); (on account of), propter (*with acc*)
through, *adv, often expressed by a compound vb, with* per: e.g. perfěro (carry through)
throughout, *prep*, per; *adv*, pěnǐtus (entirely, wholly)
throw, *nn*, iactus, *m*
throw, *v.t*, iǎcǐo (3), cōnǐcǐo (3) (— **away**), ǎbǐcǐo (3); (— **back**), rēǐcǐo (3); (— **down**), dēǐcǐo (3); (— **oneself at the feet of**), se prōǐcěre ad pědes (*with genit. of person*); (— **out**), ēǐcǐo (3)
thrush, turdus, *m*
thrust, *nn*, pětǐtǐo, *f*

thrust, *v.t*, trūdo (3); (— **forward**), prōtrūdo (3)
thumb, pollex, *m*
thump, *nn*, cōlǎphus, *m*
thump, *v.t*, tundo (3)
thunder, *nn*, tǒnǐtrus, *m*; (— **bolt**), fulmen, *n*
thunder, *v.i*, tǒno (1)
thunderstruck, attǒnǐtus
thus, *adv*, īta, sīc
thwart, *nn*, (seat), transtrum, *n*
thwart, *v.t*, obsto (1) (*with dat. of person*), impědǐo (4)
tiara, tǐāra, *f*
ticket, tessěra, *f*
tickle, *v.t*, tǐtillo (1)
tickling, *nn*, tǐtillātǐo, *f*
ticklish, lūbrǐcus
tide, aestus, *m*
tidiness, mundǐtǐa, *f*
tidings, nuntǐus, *m*
tidy, mundus
tie, *nn*, vincǔlum, *n*
tie, *v.t*, lǐgo (1), nōdo (1)
tier, ordo, *m*
tiger, tigris, *c*
tight, strictus
tighten, *v.t*, stringo (3)
tile, tēgǔla, *f*
till, *prep*, usque ad (*with acc*)
till, *conj*, dum, dōněc
till, *nn*, arca, *f*
till, *v.t*, cōlo (3)
tillage, tilling, *nn*, cultus, *m*
tiller (boat), clāvus, (*m*) gǔbernācǔli (handle of the rudder)
till, *v.t*, (bend), dēclīno (1)
timber, mātěrǐa, *f*
time, tempus, *n*; (period, space of —), intervallum, *n*, spǎtǐum, *n*; (generation, age), aetas, *f*; (— **of day**), hōra, *f*; (at the right —), *adv. phr*, ad tempus; (at —s), *adv*, interdum; (once upon a —), *adv*, ōlim; (at the same —), *adv*, sǐmǔl; (at that —), *adv*, tum
timely, *adj*, opportūnus
timid, tǐmǐdus
timidity, tǐmǐdǐtas, *f*
tin, plumbum album, *n*
tincture, cǒlor, *m*
tinder, fōmes, *m*
tinge, *v.t*, tingo (3)
tingle, *v.i*, prūrǐo (4)
tinker, fǎber, *m*, (artificer)
tinkle, *v.i*, tinnǐo (4)
tiny, exǐgǔus, parvǔlus
tip, cǎcūmen, *n*
tip, *v.t*, (put a point on), praefǐgo (3); (tip over), verto (3)

For List of Abbreviations used, turn to pages 3, 4

tire, *v.t*, fătĭgo (1); *v.i*, dēfătĭgor (1 *dep*)
tired, fessus
tiresome, mŏlestus
tissue, textus, *m*
tit-bits, cūpēdĭa, *n.pl*
tithe, dĕcŭma, *f*
title, tĭtŭlus, *m*
titled (of nobility), nōbĭlis
titter, *nn*, rīsus, *m*
to, *prep*, (*motion towards a place, and expressions of time*), ad (*with acc*); (*sometimes, e.g. names of towns, acc. of nn. alone*); *often dat. case can be used, e.g. indirect object after vb. to give; (before a clause expressing purpose*), ut; (*sometimes indicates the infinitive of a vb*), *e.g.* **to love**, ămāre
toad, būfo, *m*
toast, *v.t*, torrĕo (2); (**a person's health**), prŏpīno (1) (*with dat.·of person*)
today, *adv*, hŏdĭē
toe, dĭgĭtus, *m*
together, *adv*, sĭmŭl, ūnā
toil, *nn*, lăbor, *m*
toil, *v.i*, lăbōro (1)
toilet (care of person, etc.), cultus, *m*
token, signum, *n*
tolerable, tŏlĕrābĭlis
tolerance, tŏlĕrantĭa, *f*
tolerate, *v.t*, tŏlĕro (1)
toll, *nn*, vectīgal, *n*
tomb, sĕpulcrum, *n*, tŭmŭlus, *m*
tombstone, lăpis, *m*
tomorrow, *adv*, crās
tomorrow, *nn*, crastīnus dĭes, *m*
tone, sŏnus, *m*
tongs, forceps, *m*
tongue, lingua, *f*
tonight, *adv*, hŏdĭē nocte
tonsils, tonsillae, *f. pl*
too (also), ĕtĭam; (— **little**), părum; (— **much**), nĭmis; *comparative adj. or adv. can be used, e.g.* **too far**, longĭus
tool, instrūmentum, *n*
tooth, dens, *m*
toothache, dŏlor (*m*) dentĭum
toothed, dentātus
toothless, ēdentŭlus
toothpick, dentiscalpĭum, *n*
top, *use adj*, summus *in agreement with nn, e.g.* **the top of the rock**, summum saxum, *n*; (**summit**), căcūmen, *n*

top, *v.t*, sŭpĕro (1)
topic, rēs, *f*
topmost, summus
topography, *use phr*, nătūra (*f*) lŏci (**nature of the land**)
torch, fax, *f*
torment, *nn*, crŭcĭātus, *m*
torment, *v.t*, crŭcĭo (1)
tornado, turbo, *m*
torpid, torpens, pĭger
torpor, torpor, *m*
torrent, torrens, *m*
tortoise, testūdo, *f*
tortuous, sĭnŭōsus
torture, *nn*, crŭcĭātus, *m*
torture, *v.t*, crŭcĭo (1)
torturer, carnĭfex, *m*
toss, *nn*, iactus, *m*
toss, *v.t*, iacto (1)
total, *nn*, summa, *f*
total, *adj*, tōtus
totally, *adv*, omnīno
totter, *v.i*, lābo (1)
touch, *nn*, tactus, *m*; (**contact**), contāgĭo, *f*
touch, *v.t*, tango (3), attingo (3); (**move**), mŏvĕo (2)
touchy, stŏmăchōsus
tough, *adj*, lentus
toughness, dūrĭtĭa, *f*
tour, pĕrĕgrīnātĭo, *f*, ĭter, *n*
tourist, pĕrĕgrīnātor, *m*
tournament, *use* certāmen, *n*, (**contest**)
tow, *v.t*, trăho (3)
tow, *nn*, (**hemp**), stuppa, *f*
towards, *prep*, (**of direction, position**) ad (*with acc*); (**of time**), sub (*with acc*); (**emotions**), ergā, in (*with acc*); (**with names of towns**), versus (*placed after the noun*)
towel, mantēle, *n*
tower, *nn*, turris, *f*
tower, *v.i*, exsto (1)
town, urbs, *f*, oppĭdum, *n*
townsman, oppĭdānus, *m*
toy (child's rattle), crĕpundĭa, *n.pl*
toy with, *v.i*, illūdo (3)
trace, *nn*, vestīgĭum, *n*, signum, *n*
trace, *v.t*, sĕquendo invĕnĭo (4) (**find by following**)
track, *nn*, (**path**), callis, *m*; (**footsteps, etc.**), vestīgĭum, *n*
track, *v.t* (— **down**), investīgo (1); (**pursue**), sĕquor (3 *dep*)
trackless, āvĭus
tract (region), rĕgĭo, *f*; (**booklet**), lĭbellus, *m*
tractable, dŏcĭlis

trade, mercātūra, *f*; (a particular —),
  ars, *f*
trade, *v.i*, mercātūram făcĭo (3)
trader, mercător, *m*
tradition, mĕmŏrĭa, *f*
traditional, *use phr*, trādĭtus ā
  māĭŏrĭbus (handed down from our
  ancestors)ₑ
traffic (trade, etc.), commercĭum, *n*;
  (streets, etc.), *use phr*. with frĕquento (1) (to crowd)
tragedy, trăgoedĭa, *f*
tragic, trăgĭcus; (unhappy), tristis
trail (path), callis, *m*
train, ordo, *m*; (procession), pompa, *f*.
  pl; (of a dress), pēnĭcŭlāmentum, *n*
train, *v.t*, instĭtŭo (3), exercĕo (2)
trainer, exercĭtor, *m*
training, *nn*, disciplīna, *f*
traitor, prōdĭtor, *m*
traitorous, perfĭdus
tramp, *v.i*, ambŭlo (1)
trample on, *v.t*, obtĕro (3)
trance (elation, exaltation), ēlātĭo, *f*
tranquil, tranquillus, plăcĭdus
transact, *v.t*, ăgo (3)
transaction, rēs, *f*, nĕgōtĭum, *n*
transcend, *v.t*, sŭpĕro (1)
transcribe, *v.t*, transcrībo (3)
transfer, *nn*, (of property), mancĭpĭum,
  n
transfer, *v.t*, transfĕro (*irreg*)
transfix, *v.t*, transfīgo (3)
transform, *v.t*, mūto (1)
transgress, *v.t*, vĭŏlo (1); *v.i*, pecco (1)
transgression (fault), dēlictum, *n*
transit, transĭtus, *m*
transitory, cădūcus
translate, *v.t*, verto (3)
translation (a work), ŏpus translātum,
  n; (act), translātĭo, *f*
translator, interpres, *c*
transmigrate, *v.i*, transmĭgro (1)
transmit, *v.t*, transmitto (3)
transparent, perlūcĭdus
transpire, *v.i*. (get about), vulgor (1
  pass)
transplant, *v.t*, transfĕro (*irreg*)
transport, *nn*, *use vb. below*; (joy),
  laetĭtĭa, *f*, exsultātĭo, *f*
transport, *v.t*, transporto (1), trăĭcĭo (3)
trap, *nn*, insĭdĭae, *f*. *pl*; (for animals),
  lăquĕus, *m*
trap, *v.t*, *use phr*, illĭcĭo (3) in
  insĭdĭas (entice into a trap)
trappings, insignĭa, *n.pl*
trash, scrūta, *n.pl*, nūgae, *f. pl*
travel, *nn*, ĭter, *n*
travel, *v.i*, ĭter făcĭo (3) .
traveller, vĭātor, *m*

traverse, *v.t*, ŏbĕo (4)
travesty (mockery), lūdĭbrĭum, *n*
tray, fercŭlum, *n*
treacherous, perfĭdus
treachery, perfĭdĭa, *f*, fraus, *f*
tread, *nn*, grădus, *m*
tread, *v.i*, ingrĕdĭor (3 *dep*); *v.t* (— on),
  calco (1)
treason, māiestas, *f*
treasure, ŏpes *f*. *pl*; (hoard,
  treasure-house), thēsaurus, *m*
treasure, *v.t*, (regard highly), magni
  aestĭmo (1); (store up), rĕcondo (3)
treasurer, praefectus, (*m*) aerārĭi
  (director of the treasury)
treasury, aerārĭum, *n*
treat, *nn*, dēlectātĭo, *f*
treat, *v.t*, (deal with, behave towards),
  hăbĕo (2); (medically), cūro (1);
  (discuss), ăgo (3)
treatise, lĭber, *m*
treatment, tractātĭo, *f*; (cure), cūrātĭo,
  f
treaty, foedus, *n*
treble, *adj*, trĭplex
treble, *v.t*, trĭplĭco (1)
tree, arbor, *f*
trellis, cancelli, *m*. *pl*
tremble, *v.i*, trĕmo (3)
trembling, *nn*, trŏmor, *m*
tremendous, ingens
tremulous, trĕmŭlus
trench, fossa, *f*
trepidation, trĕpĭdātĭo, *f*
trespass (crime), dēlictum, *n*
trespass, *v.i*, *use phr. with* ingrĕdi (to
  enter), *and* tē (me, *etc*.), invīto
  (without your (my) permission)
tress (hair), grădus, *m*
trial (legal), iūdĭcĭum, *n*; (experiment),
  expĕrientĭa, *f*
triangle, trĭangŭlum, *n*
triangular, trĭangŭlus
tribe (Roman), trĭbus, *f*; (other),
  pŏpŭlus, *m*
tribunal, iūdĭcĭum, *n*
tribune, trĭbūnus, *m*
tributary, *adj*, (paying tribute), vectīgālis
tributary, *nn*, (river), *use phr*, qui in
  flūmen influit (which flows into a
  river)
tribute, trĭbūtum, *n*, vectīgal, *n*
trick, *nn*, dŏlus, *m*, fraus, *f*
trick, *v.t*, dēcĭpĭo (3)
trickery, dŏlus, *m*
trickle, *v.i*, māno (1)
trickster, hŏmo dŏlōsus, fallax
tricky (dangerous), pĕrīcŭlōsus
trident, trĭdens, *m*

tried (well —), prŏbātus

trifle, *nn*, rēs parva, *f*, nūgae, *f. pl*

trifle, *v.i*, lūdo (3)

trifling, *adj*, lěvis

trim, *adj*, nītĭdus

trim, *v.t*, pŭto (1)

trinkets, mundus, *m*

trip, *nn*, (journey), ĭter, *n*

trip, *v.t*, supplanto (1); *v.i* (stumble), offendo (3), lābor (3 dep)

tripe, ŏmāsum, *n*

triple, trĭplex

tripod, trĭpūs, *m*

trite, trītus

triumph (Roman celebration of victory), trĭumphus, *m*; (victory), victōrĭa, *f*

triumph, *v.i, and v.t*, trĭumpho (1)

triumphant, victor

triumvirate, trĭumvĭrātus, *m*

trivial, lěvis, vīlis

troop (band), mănus, *f*; (— of cavalry), turma, *f*; (—s), cōpĭae, *f*, *pl*

troop, *v.i*, conflŭo (3)

trooper, ĕques, *m*

trophy, trŏpaeum, *n*

trot, *nn*, lentus cursus, *m*

trot, *v.i*, lento cursu ěo (4); (proceed on a slow course)

trouble, *nn*, (disadvantage), incommŏdum, *n*; (exertion), ŏpěra, *f*; (commotion), tŭmultus, *m*; (annoyance), mŏlestĭa, *f*

trouble, *v.t*, (disturb), sollĭcĭto (1); (harass), vexo (1); (— oneself about), cŭro (1)

troublesome, mŏlestus

trough, alvěus, *m*

trousers, brācae, *f. pl*

trowel, trulla, *f*

truant, *nn, use phr*, qui consultō ăbest (who is absent deliberately)

truce, indūtĭae, *f. pl*

truck, plaustrum, *n*

truculent (grim), trux

trudge, *v.i, use phr*, aegrē ambŭlo (1) (walk with difficulty)

true, vērus; (faithful), fīdus

truffle, tūber, *n*

truly, *adv*, vērē, prŏfectō

trumpery, scrūta, *n.pl*

trumpet, *nn*, tūba, *f*, būcĭna, *f*

trumpeter, tŭbĭcen, *m*

truncheon, fustis, *m*

trundle, *v.t*, volvo (3)

trunk, truncus, *m*; (of elephant) prŏboscis, *f*; (box), arca, *f*

truss, fascĭa, *f*

trust, *nn*, fīdes, *f*

trust, *v.t*, confīdo (3 *semi-dep*) (with *dat. of person*), crēdo (3); (commit to), commĭtto (3)

trustworthy, trusty certus, fīdus

truth, vērĭtas, *f*; (true things), věra, *n.pl*; (in —), *adv*, vēro

truthful, věrax

truthfulness, vērĭtas, *f*

try, *v.i*, (attempt), cōnor (1 *dep*); *v.t*, (put to the test), tento (1); (— in court), iūdĭco (1)

trying, *adj*, mŏlestus

tub, lābrum, *n*

tube, tŭbŭlus, *m*

tuber, tūber, *n*

tubular, tŭbŭlātus

tuck up, *v.t*, succingo (3)

tuft, crīnis, *m*

tug, *v.t*, trăho (3)

tuition, instĭtūtĭo, *f*

tumble, *nn*, cāsus, *m* ·

tumble, *v.i*, cădo (3)

tumbler (beaker), pōcŭlum, *n*

tumour, tŭmor, *m*

tumult, tŭmultus, *m*

tumultuous, tŭmultŭōsus

tun (cask), dōlĭum, *n*

tune (melody), cantus, *m*; (out of —), *adj*, absŏnus

tune, *v.t*, (stringed instrument), tendo (3)

tuneful, cănōrus

tunic, tŭnĭca, *f*

tunnel, cănālis, *m*, cŭnĭcŭlus, *m*

tunny fish, thunnus, *m*

turban, mĭtra, *f*

turbid, turbĭdus

turbot, rhombus, *m*

turbulence, tŭmultus, *m*

turbulent, turbŭlentus

turf, caespes, *m*

turgid, turgĭdus

turmoil, turba, *f*, tŭmultus, *m*

turn (movement), conversĭo, *f*; (bending), flexus, *m*; (change), commūtātĭo, *f*; (by —s, in —), *adv*, invĭcem, per vĭces; (a good —), offĭcĭum, *n*

turn, *v.t*, verto (3); (bend), flecto (3); (— aside), dēflecto (3); *v.i*, sē dēclīnāre (1 *reflex*); (— away), āverto (3); (— the back), *v.i*, tergum verto (3); (change), *v.i*, mŭtor (1 *pass*); (— back), *v.i*, rěvertor (3 *pass*); (— out), *v.t*, ēĭcĭo (3); *v.i*, ēvěnĭo (4); (— round), *v.t*, circumăgo (3); *v.i*, circumăgor (3 *pass*)

turning, *nn*, flexus, *m*

turnip, răpum, *n*

turpitude, turpǐtūdo, *f*
turret, turris, *f*
turtle-dove, turtur, *m*
tusk, dens, *m*
tutelage, tūtēla, *f*
tutor, mǎgister, *m*
twang, *nn*, sǒnǐtus, *m*
twang, *v.i*, sǒno (1)
tweak, *v.t*, vellǐco (1)
tweezers, volsella, *f*
twelfth, dǔǒdĕcǐmus
twelve, dǔǒdĕcim; (— each), duodeni
twentieth, vīcēsǐmus
twenty, vīgǐnti
twice, *adj*, bis
twig, rāmǔlus, *m*
twilight, crĕpuscŭlum, *n*
twin, *nn and adj*, gĕmǐnus
twine, *nn*, līnum, *n*
twine, *v.t*, circumplǐco (1); *v.i*, circumplector (3 *dep*)
twinge, *nn*, dǒlor, *m*
twinkle, *v.i*, mǐco (1)
twirl, *v.t*, verso (1)
twist, *v.t*, torquĕo (2); *v.i*, sē torquēre (2 *reflex*)
twit, *v.t*, ōbǐcǐo(3) (*acc. of thing and dat, of person*)
twitch, *v.i*, vellǐco (1)
twitter, *v.i*, (chirp), pīpǐlo (1)
two, dǔǒ; (— each), bīni
two-fold, dǔplex
two-footed, bǐpes
two hundred, dǔcenti
type (class, sort), gĕnus, *n*; (example), exemplar, *n*
typical, *use adj*, ǒsǐtālǐus (familiar)
tyrannical, tўrannǐcus, sǔperbus
tyrannize, *v.i*, dǒmǐnor (1 *dep*)
tyranny, dǒmǐnātǐo, *f*
tyrant, tўrannus, *m*

U

ubiquitous, praesens (**present**)
udder, ūbcr, *n*
ugliness, dēformǐtas, *f*
ugly, dēformis
ulcer, vǒmǐca, *f*
ulcerate, *v.i*, suppūro (1)
ulceration, ulcĕrātǐo, *f*
ulcerous, ulcĕrōsus
ulterior, ultĕrǐor
ultimate, ultǐmus
ultimatum (to present —) ultǐmam condǐcǐōnem ferre (*irreg*)
umbrage (to take — at), *v.t*, aegrē fĕro (*irreg*)
umbrella, umbella, *f*
umpire, arbǐter, *m*

un-, *prefix, often* nōn, haud, *can be used*
unabashed, intrĕpǐdus; (**brazen**), impǔdens
unabated, immǐnūtus
unable, *use vb. phr. with* non posse (**to be unable**)
unacceptable, ingrātus
unaccompanied, incǒmǐtātus
unaccomplished, infectus
unaccountable, inexplǐcābǐlis
unaccustomed, insǒlǐtus
unacquainted, ignārus
unadorned, ǐnornātus
unadulterated, sincērus
unadvisable (foolhardy), audax
unadvised, inconsǐdĕrātus
unaffected (natural), simplex; (**untouched**), intĕgĕr
unaided, *use adv. phr*, sǐne auxǐlǐo (**without help**)
unalloyed, pūrus
unalterable, immūtābǐlis
unambitious, hǔmǐlis,
unanimity, ūnǎnǐmǐtas, *f*
unanimous, ūnǐversus (**all together**)
unanimously, *adv*, ūnā vōce
unanswerable, non rĕvincendus
unanswered, *use vb*. rĕspondĕo (2) (**to answer**)
unappeased, implācātus
unapproachable, nōn ādĕundus
unarmed, ǐnermis
unassailable, ǐnexpugnābǐlis
unassailed, intactus
unassuming, mǒdestus
unattainable, *use phr. with vb*. attǐngo (3) (**to reach**)
unattempted, ǐnexpertus
unauthorized, illǐcǐtus
unavailing, fūtǐlis
unavoidable, ǐnēvǐtābǐlis
unaware, inscǐus
unawares, *adv*, dē imprōvīso
unbar, *v.t*, rĕsĕro (1)
unbearable, intǒlĕrābǐlis
unbecoming, indĕcōrus
unbelieving, incrēdǔlus
unbend, *v.t*, rĕmitto (3)
unbending, rǐgǐdus
unbiassed, intĕger
unbidden, iniussus
unbind, *v.t*, solvo (3)
unblemished, pūrus
unbound, sǒlūtus
unbounded, infinǐtus
unbreakable, *use phr*, quod frangi non pǒtest (**that cannot be broken**)
unbridled, effrēnātus
unbroken, intĕger, perpĕtǔus

For List of Abbreviations used, turn to pages 3, 4

unbuckle, *v.t*, diffībŭlo (1)
unburden, *v.t*, exŏnĕro (1)
unburied, ĭnhŭmātus
uncared for, neglectus
unceasing, perpĕtŭus
uncertain, incertus, dŭbĭus; (to be —),
  v.i, dŭbĭto (1)
uncertainty, dŭbĭtātĭo, *f*
unchangeable, immūtābĭlis
unchanged, constans; (to remain —),
  v.i, permănĕo (2)
uncharitable, inhūmānus
uncivil, ĭnurbānus
uncivilized, incultus
uncle (father's side), pătrŭus, *m*;
  (mother's side), ăvuncŭlus, *m*
unclean, inquĭnātus
unclouded, sĕrēnus
uncoil, *v.t*, ēvolvo (3); *v.i*, se ēvolvĕre
  (3 *reflex*)
uncombed, incomptus
uncomfortable, mŏlestus
uncommon, rārus, insŏlĭtus
uncompleted, imperfectus
unconcerned, sēcūrus
unconditional, simplex; (to surrender -ly), mănus do (1)
uncongenial, ingrātus
unconnected, disiunctus
unconquerable, invictus
unconquered, invictus
unconscious (unaware), inscĭus; (insensible), *use phr*, sensu ablāto (with
  feeling withdrawn)
unconstitutional, non lēgĭtĭmus
uncontaminated, incontāmĭnātus
uncontested, *use phr*, quod in con-
  tentĭōnem non vēnit (that has not
  come into dispute)
uncontrollable, impŏtens
uncontrolled, līber
uncooked, incoctus
uncouth, incultus
uncover, *v.t*, dētĕgo (3)
unction, unctĭo, *f*
uncultivated, incultus; (person),
  ăgrestis
uncut (hair), intonsus, prōmissus
undamaged, intĕger
undaunted, fortis
undeceive, *v.t*, errōrem ērĭpĭo (3)
undecided, incertus; (of a battle),
  anceps
undefended, nūdus, indēfensus
undeniable, certus
under, *prep*, sub (*with abl. to denote
  rest, and acc. to denote motion*);
  infra (*with acc*); (— the leadership

of), *use abl. phr*, *e.g.* tŭ dūce (—
  your leadership)
underclothes, sūbūcŭla, *f*
under-current, flŭentum subterlābens,
  n
underestimate, *v.t*, mĭnōris aestĭmo (1)
undergo, *v.t*, sŭbĕo (3), fĕro (*irreg*)
underground, *adj*, subterrānĕus
undergrowth, virgulta, *n.pl*
underhand, *adj*, clandestīnus
underlying (lying hidden), lătens
undermine, *v.t*, subrŭo (3)
undermost, *adj*, infĭmus
underneath, *adv*, infrā
underrate, *v.t*, mĭnōris aestĭmo (1)
understand, *v.t*, intellĕgo (3), comprĕhendo (3)
understanding, *nn*, mens, *f*; (agreement), conventum, *n*
undertake, *v.t*, suscĭpĭo (3); (put in
  hand), incĭpĭo (3)
undertaker, vespillo, *m*
undertaking, *nn*, inceptum, *n*
undervalue, *v.t*, mĭnōris aestĭmo (1)
undeserved, immĕrĭtus
undeserving, indignus
undesirable, *use phr. with* nōn *and*
  cŭpĭo (3) *or* expĕto (3) (to desire)
undetected, tectus
undeveloped, immātūrus
undigested, crūdus
undiminished, immĭnūtus
undisciplined, ĭnexercĭtātus
undisguised, non dissĭmŭlātus
undistinguished, ignōbĭlis
undisturbed, stăbĭlis, immōtus
undo, *v.t*, solvo (3); (render ineffec-
  tual), irrĭtum făcĭo (3)
undone, infectus
undoubted, certus
undoubtedly, *adv*, sĭne dŭbĭo
undress, *v.t*, vestem dētrăho (3) (*with
  dat. of person*)
undressed, *adj*, nūdus
undue, nĭmĭus
undulate, *v.i*, fluctŭo (1)
unduly, *adv*, (excessively), nĭmĭum
undying, immortālis
unearth, *v.t*, dētĕgo (3)
unearthly, *adv*, *use* terrĭbĭlis (frightful)
uneasiness, anxĭĕtas, *f*
uneasy, anxĭus
uneducated, indoctus
unemployed, ōtĭōsus
unending, aeternus, infīnītus
unenterprising, ĭners, ĭnaudax
unequal, impar, ĭnīquus
unequalled, singŭlāris

unequivocal, non dŭbĭus
unerring, certus
uneven, ĭnaequālis; (of ground), ĭnīquus
unevenness, ĭnīquĭtas, f
unexampled, ĭnaudītus, ūnĭcus
unexpected, ĭnŏpīnātus
unexpectedly, adv, ex (or dē) imprōvīso
unexplored, ĭnexplōrātus
unfailing, pĕrennis
unfair, ĭnīquus, iniustus
unfairness, ĭnīquĭtas, f
unfaithful, infĭdēlis, perfĭdus
unfaithfulness, infĭdēlĭtas,
unfamiliar, insŭētus
unfashionable, use phr. with extrā consŭētūdĭnem (outside of custom)
unfasten, v.t, solvo (3), rĕfīgo (3)
unfathomable, infīnītus
unfavourable, ĭnīquus; (omen), sĭnister, infēlix
unfeeling, dūrus
unfeigned, sincērus, sĭmplex
unfinished, imperfectus; (task) infectus
unfit, incommŏdus
unfitness, ĭnūtĭlĭtas, f
unfitting, indĕcōrus
unfix, v.t, rĕfīgo (3)
unfold, v.t, explĭco (1)
unforeseen, imprōvīsus
unforgiving, implācābĭlis
unforgotten, use phr. with mĕmor, adj, (remembering)
unfortified, immūnītus
unfortunate, infēlix
unfounded (groundless), vānus
unfriendliness, ĭnĭmīcĭtĭa,
unfriendly, ĭnĭmīcus
unfulfilled, irrĭtus, ĭnānis
unfurl, v.t, pando (3)
unfurnished nūdus
ungainly, rŭdis
ungentlemanly, illĭbĕrālis
ungodly, incestus
ungovernable, impŏtens, indŏmĭtus
ungraceful, ĭnēlĕgans
ungrateful, ingrātus
unguarded, incustōdītus; (speech or action), incautus
unhappiness, mĭsērĭa, f
unhappy, mĭser, infēlix
unharmed, incŏlŭmis
unhealthiness, vălētūdo, f; (of place, etc.), grăvĭtas, f
unheard (of), ĭnaudītus
unheeded, neglectus
unhesitating, confĭdens
unhindered, expĕdītus
unhoped for, inspērātus

unhorse, v.t, ĕquo dēĭcĭo (3) (throw down from a horse)
unicorn, mŏnŏcĕros, m
uniform, nn, (military —), hăbĭtus mīlĭtāris, m
uniform, adj, aequābĭlis
unimaginable, use phr, quod mente concĭpi non pŏtest (that cannot be conceived in the mind)
unimpaired, intĕger
unimportant, lĕvis
uninhabitable, ĭnhăbĭtābĭlis
uninhabited, dēsertus
uninitiated, prŏfānus
uninjured, incŏlŭmis
unintelligible, obscūrus
unintentional, non praemĕdĭtātus
uninteresting (flat, insipid), frīgĭdus
uninterrupted, contĭnŭus
uninvited, invŏcātus
union (act of joining), iunctĭo, f; (— of states), cīvĭtates foedĕrātae, f.pl; (agreement), consensus, m
unique, ūnĭcus
unit (one), ūnus
unite, v.t, coniungo (3), consŏcĭo (1); v.i, sē consŏcĭāre (r reflex), sē coniungĕre (3 reflex)
united, consŏcĭātus
unity (one), ūnus; (agreement), concordĭa, f
universal, ūnĭversus
universe, mundus, m
university, ăcădēmĭa, f
unjust, iniustus
unjustifiable, use phr, quod excūsāri non pŏtest (that cannot be excused)
unkind, ĭnhūmānus
unkindness, ĭnhūmānĭtas, f
unknowingly, adj. imprūdens
unknown, ignōtus, incognĭtus
unlawful (forbidden), vĕtĭtus
unlearned, indoctus
unless, conj, nĭsi
unlettered, indoctus, illittĕrātus
unlike, dissĭmĭlis (foll. by dat. or genit)
unlikely, non vēri sĭmĭlis (not like the truth)
unlimited, infīnītus
unload, v.t, exŏnĕro (1); (goods, etc.), expōno (3)
unlock, v.t, rĕsĕro (1)
unlooked for, ĭnexpectātus
unloose, v.t, solvo (3)
unlucky, infēlix
unmanageable, impŏtens; (things), ĭnhābĭlis
unmanly, mollis
unmarried, caelebs
unmask, v.t, (plans, etc.), ăpĕrĭo (4)

unmerciful, ĭmmĭsĕrĭcors
unmindful, immĕmor
unmistakable, certus
unmitigated, mĕrus
unmolested, intĕger
unmoved, immōtus
unnatural, monstrŭōsus; (far-fetched), arcessītus
unnavigable, innāvĭgābĭlis
unnecessary, non nĕcessārĭus, sŭper-văcănĕus
unnoticed, *use vb*, lătĕo (2) (to lie hidden)
unnumbered, innŭmĕrābĭlis
unoccupied (at leisure), ōtĭōsus; (of land), ăpertus
unoffending, innŏcens
unopposed (militarily), *use phr*, nullo hoste prŏhĭbente (with no enemy impeding)
unpack, *v.t*, exŏnĕro (1)
unpaid, *use* rēlĭquus (remaining)
unparalleled, ūnĭcus
unpitied, ĭmmĭsĕrābĭlis
unpleasant, iniūcundus
unpleasantness (trouble), mŏlestĭa, *f*
unpolished, impŏlītus
unpolluted, intactus
unpopular, invĭdĭōsus,
unpopularity, invĭdĭa, *f*
unprecedented, nŏvus
unprejudiced, intĕger
unpremeditated, sŭbĭtus
unprepared, impărātus
unpretentious, hŭmĭlis
unprincipled (good for nothing), nēquam
unproductive, infēcundus
unprofitable, non quaestŭōsus
unprotected, indēfensus
unprovoked, illăcessītus
unpunished, impūnītus
unqualified, nōn aptus; (unlimited), infīnītus
unquestionable, certus
unravel, *v.t*, rĕtexo (3); (a problem, etc.), explĭco (1)
unreasonable, ĭnīquus
unrelenting, ĭnexōrābĭlis
unremitting, assĭdŭus
unreserved, līber
unrestrained, effrēnātus
unrewarded, ĭnhŏnōrātus
unrighteous, iniustus
unripe, immātūrus
unrivalled, praestantissĭmus
unroll, *v.t*, ēvolvo (3)
unruffled, immōtus
unruly, effrēnātus, impŏtens
unsafe, intūtus

unsatisfactory, nōn aptus
unscrupulous (wicked), mălus
unseal, *v.t*, rēsigno (1)
unseasonable, intempestīvus
unseemly, indĕcōrus
unseen, invīsus
unselfish (persons), innŏcens; (actions), grātŭītus
unselfishness, innŏcentĭa, *f*
unserviceable, ĭnūtĭlis
unsettle, *v.t*, turbo (1)
unsettled, incertus, dŭbĭus
unshaken, immōtus
unshaved, intonsus
unsheath, *v.t*, stringo (3)
unship, *v.t*, expōno (3)
unsightly, foedus
unskilful, impĕrītus
unskilfulness, impĕrītĭa, *f*
unslaked (thirst), nōn explētus
unsociable, diffĭcĭlis
unsophisticated, simplex
unsound (of health or opinions), infirmus; (of mind), insānus
unsoundness, infirmĭtas, *f*, insānĭtas, *f*
unsparing (severe), sĕvērus; (lavish), prōdĭgus; (effort, etc.), non rēmissus
unspeakable, infandus
unspoiled, intĕger
unstained, pūrus
unsteadiness, mōbĭlĭtas, *f*
unsteady, instăbĭlis, vărĭus
unstring, rĕtendo (3)
unsuccessful, irrĭtus; (person), infaustus
unsuitable, incommŏdus
unsuitableness, incommŏdĭtas, *f*
unsuspected, non suspectus
unsuspecting, incautus
untameable, impŏtens
untamed, indŏmĭtus
untaught, indoctus
unteachable, indŏcĭlis
untenable (position), *use phr*, quod tĕnēri non pŏtest (that cannot be held)
unthankful, ingrātus
unthinking (inconsiderate), inconsīdĕrātus
untie, *v.t*, solvo (3)
until, *conj*, dum, dōnec
until, *prep*, ad, (with *acc*)
untilled, incultus
untimely, *adj*, immātūrus
untiring, assĭdŭus
untold (numbers), innŭmĕrābĭlis
untouched, intĕger
untried, ĭnexpertus
untroubled, sēcūrus
untrue, falsus
untruth, mendācĭum, *n*

unused (of persons), insŏlĭtus; (things) intĕger

unusual, insŏlĭtus, ĭnŭsĭtātus

unutterable, infandus

unveil, v.t, dĕtĕgo (3)

unwarily, adv, incautē

unwarlike, imbellis

unwarrantable, ĭnīquus

unwary, incautus

unwavering, constans

unwearied, indēfessus

unwelcome, ingrātus

unwell, aeger

unwholesome, grăvis

unwieldy, ĭnhăbĭlis

unwilling, invītus; (to be —), v.i, nolle (irreg)

unwillingly, unwillingness, use adj, invītus (unwilling)

unwind, v.t, rĕtexo (3), rĕvolvo (3)

unwise, stultus, imprŭdens

unworthiness, indignĭtas, f

unworthy, indignus, immĕrĭtus

unwrap, v.t, explĭco (1)

unyielding, firmus, inflexĭbĭlis

unyoke, v.t, disiungo (3)

up, prep, (— stream or hill), adversus (in agreement with noun); (— to), tĕnus (with abl)

up, adv, sursum; (— and down), sursum dĕorsum

upbraid, v.t, obiurgo (1)

upbraiding, nn, exprŏbrātĭo, f

uphill, adv, phr, adverso colle

uphold, v.t, sustĭnĕo (2)

uplift, v.t, tollo (3)

upon, prep, sŭper (with acc); (on), in (with abl)

upper, adj, sŭpĕrĭor; (to get the — hand), sŭpĕrĭor esse (irreg)

uppermost, adj, summus

upright, rectus; (of morals), prŏbus

uprightness, prŏbĭtas, f

uproar, clāmor, m

uproarious, tŭmultŭōsus

uproot, ēvello (3)

upset, v.t, ēverto (3)

upset, adj, mōtus; (troubled), anxĭus

upshot, exĭtus, m

upside down, (to turn —), use vb. verto (3) (to overturn) or miscĕo (2) (throw into confusion)

upstart, nŏvus hŏmo

upwards, adv, sursum; (of number, — of), amplĭus quam

urbane, urbānus

urbanity, urbānĭtas, f

urchin, pūsĭo, m

urge, v.t, urgĕo (2); (persuade), suādĕo (2) (with dat. of person)

urgency, grăvĭtas, f

urgent, grăvis

urine, ūrīna, f

urn, urna, f

us, obj. pron, nos

usage, mos, m

use, ūsus, m; (advantage), commŏdum, n

use, v.t, ūtor (3 dep. with abl)

useful, ūtĭlis

usefulness, ūtĭlĭtas, f

useless, ĭnūtĭlis

uselessness, ĭnūtĭlĭtas, f

usher in, v.t, intrōdūco (3)

usual, ūsĭtātus, sŏlĭtus

usually, adv, plērumque, fĕrē

usurer, fēnĕrātor, m

usurious, fēnĕrātōrĭus

usurp, v.t, occŭpo (1); (seize), răpĭo (3)

usury, fēnĕrātĭo, f, ūsūra, f

utensils, vāsa, n.pl

utilize, v.t, ūtor (3 dep. with abl)

utility, ūtĭlĭtas, f

utmost, extrēmus, summus

utter, adj, tōtus

utter, v.t, dīco (3)

utterance, dictum, n

utterly, adv, omnīno

V

vacancy, (empty post), lŏcus văcŭus, m

vacant, adj, văcŭus, ĭnānis

vacate, v.t, rĕlinquo (3) (a post), ējūro (1)

vacation, fērĭae, f.pl

vacillate, v.i, văcillo (1)

vacillation, văcillātĭo, f

vacuum, ĭnāne, n

vagabond, erro, m

vagabond, adj, văgus

vagary, lībīdo, f

vagrant, adj, văgus

vague, ĭncertus

vagueness, obscūrĭtas, f

vain, vānus; (boastful, etc.), glōrĭōsus; (in —), adv, frustrā

vainglorious, glōrĭōsus

vainglory, glōrĭa, f

vale, valles, f

valet, cŭbĭcŭlārĭus, m

valetudinarian, vălētūdĭnārĭus, m

valiant, fortis

valid, firmus, vălĭdus

validity, grăvĭtas, f

valise, capsa, f

valley, valles, f

valorous, fortis

For List of Abbreviations used, turn to pages 3, 4

valour, virtus, *f*
valuable, prětiōsus
valuation, aestǐmātǐo, *f*
value, *nn*, prětǐum, *n*
value, *v.t*, aestǐmo (1); (— **highly**), magni dūco (3) (— **little**), parvi dūco
valueless, vīlis
valve, ěpistǒmǐum, *n*
van (**vanguard**), prīmum agmen, *n*
vanish, *v.i*, vānesco (3), dīlābor (3 *dep*)
vanity, vānǐtas, *f*, iactātǐo, *f*
vanquish, *v.t*, vinco (3)
vanquisher, victor, *m*
vantage-point, lǒcus sǔpěrǐor, *m*
vapid, vǎpǐdus
vapour, vǎpor, *m*,
variability, mūtābǐlǐtas, *f*
variable, vǎrǐus, mūtābǐlis
variance, dissensǐo, *f*; (**to be at —** **with**), dissǐděo (2) ab (*with abl*)
variation, vǎrǐětas, *f*
varicose, vǎrǐcōsus; (**a — vein**), vǎrix, *c*
variegated, vǎrǐus
variety, vǎrǐětas, *f*, dīversǐtas, *f*
various, vǎrǐus, dīversus
varnish, *nn*, ātrāmentum, *n*
vary, *v.i and v.t*, vǎrǐo (1)
vase, vās, *n*
vassal, clǐens, *m*, *f*
vast, vastus, ingens
vastness, immensǐtas, *f*
vat, cūpa, *f*
vault, fornix, *m*
vault, *v.i*, sǎlǐo (4)
vaunt, *v.t*, iacto (1); *v.i*, glōrǐor (1 *dep*)
vaunting, *nn*, iactātǐo, *f*
veal, vǐtūlǐna cǎro, *f*, (**calf's flesh**)
veer, *v.i*, sē vertěre (3 *reflex*)
vegetable, hǒlus, *n*
vehemence, vīs, *f*
vehement, věhěmens, ācer
vehicle, věhǐcǔlum, *n*
veil, *v.t*, vēlo (1), těgo (3)
veil, *nn*, rīca, *f*; (**bridal —**), flamměum, *n*; (**disguise**), intěgūmentum, *n*
vein, věna, *f*
velocity, vēlōcǐtas, *f*
venal, vēnālis
venality, vēnālǐtas, *f*
vendor, vendǐtor, *m*
veneer, *nn*, *use* cortex, *m*, (**bark, shell**)
venerable, věněrābǐlis
venerate, *v.t*, cǒlo (3), věněror (1 *dep*)
veneration, cultus, *m*
venereal, věněrěus

vengeance, ultǐo, *f*; (**to take —**), ulciscor (3 *dep*)
venial, *use phr*, cui ignosci pǒtest (**that can be pardoned**)
venison, fěrīna cǎro, *f*
venom, věnēnum, *n*
venemous, věnēnātus
vent, *nn*, spīrāmentum, *n*
vent, *v.t*, (**pour out**), effundo (3)
ventilate, *v.t*, ventǐlo (1); (**discuss**, etc.), *use vb*, prōfěro (*irreg*) (**to bring out**)
ventilator, spīrāmentum, *n*
ventricle, ventrǐcǔlus, *m*
venture, *nn*, (**undertaking**), rēs, *f*, inceptum, *n*
venture, *v.t*, pērīclǐtor (1 *dep*)
venturous, audax
veracious, vērus
veracity, vērǐtas, *f*
veranda, pǒdǐum, *n*
verb, verbum, *n*
verbal, *nn*, *see adv*, **verbally**
verbally, per verba (**by means of words**)
verbatim, *adv*, tǒtǐdem verbis (**with the same number of words**)
verbose, verbōsus
verdant, vǐrǐdis
verdict (**of a person or jury**), sententǐa, *f*; (**of a court**), iūdǐcǐum, *n*
verdigris, aerūgo, *f*
verge, *nn*, ōra, *f*, margo, *c*; (**on the —** **of**) *use phr*. minimum abest quin .. (**it is very little wanting that . . .**)
verge, *v.i*, vergo (3)
verger, appārǐtor, *m*
verification, prōbātǐo, *f*
verify, *v.t*, prǒbo (1)
veritable, vērus
vermilion, mǐnǐum, *n*
versatile, vǎrǐus
versatility, ǎgǐlǐtas, *f*
verse, versus, *m*
versed in, *adj*, exercǐtātus
versify, *v.i*, versus fǎcǐo (3)
version, *use vb*, converto (3) (**turn**)
vertebra, vertěbra, *f*
vertical, rectus
vertigo, vertǐgo, *f*
very, *adj*, *use emphatic pron*, ipse
very, *adv*, *use superlative of adj. or adv*, *e.g.* **—beautiful**, pulcherrǐmus; **—quickly**, cělerrǐme; *otherwise* maxǐmē, valdē, admǒdum
vessel (**receptacle**), vās, *n*; (**ship**), nāvis, *f*
vest, tǔnǐca, *f*

vest, *v.t*, (invest, impart), do (1)
vestal virgin, vestālis virgo, *f*
vestibule, vestĭbŭlum, *n*
vestige, vestīgĭum, *n*; (mark), nŏta, *f*, indĭcĭum, *n*
vestry, aedĭcŭla, *f*
veteran, *adj*, vĕtĕrānus; (— soldier), vĕtĕrānus mĭles, *m*
veterinary, vĕtĕrīnārĭus
veto, *nn*, intercessĭo, *f*
veto, *v.i*, intercēdo (3) (*with dat*)
vex, *v.t*, vexo (1), sollĭcĭto (1)
vexation, indignātĭo, *f*, dŏlor, *m*
vexatious, mŏlestus
vial, lăgēna, *f*
viands, cĭbus, *m*
viaticum, vĭātĭcum, *n*
vibrate, *v.i.* and *v.t*, vībro (1)
vibration, ăgĭtātĭo, *f*
vicarious, vĭcārĭus
vice, turpĭtūdo, *f*
viceroy, lēgātus, *m*
vicinity, vīcīnĭtas, *f*
vicious, vĭtĭōsus; (fierce), fĕrus
vicissitude, vĭces, *f. pl*, vĭcissĭtūdo, *f*
victim, hostĭa, *f*, victĭma, *f*
victor, victor, *m*, victrix, *f*
victorious, victor
victory, victōrĭa, *f*
victual, *v.t*, *use phr*, rem frūmentārĭam prōvĭdĕo (2) (to look after the supply of provisions)
victuals, cĭbus, *m*
vie with, *v.i*, certo (1) cum (*with abl*)
view, *nn*, aspectus, *m*, conspectus, *m*; (opinion), sententĭa, *f*
view, *v.t*, conspĭcĭo (3); (consider), *use* sentĭo (4) (to feel)
vigil, pervĭgĭlātĭo, *f*
vigilance, vĭgĭlantĭa, *f*
vigilant, vĭgĭlans
vigorous, impĭger
vigour, vīs, *f*, vĭgor, *m*
vile, turpis
vileness, turpĭtūdo, *f*
vilify, *v.t*, infāmo (1), dētrăho (3)
villa, villa, *f*
village, pāgus, *m*
villager, pāgānus, *m*
villain, hŏmo scĕlĕrātus
villainy, prāvĭtas, *f*, scĕlus, *n*
vindicate, *v.t*, vindĭco (1); (justify), purgo (1)
vindication, purgātĭo, *f*
vindictive, *use phr*, ăvĭdus iniūrĭae ulciscendae (eager to avenge a wrong)
vine, vītis, *f*
vine-grower, cultor, (*m*) vītis
vinegar, ăcētum, *n*

vineyard, vīnĕa, *f*
vintage, *nn*, vindēmĭa, *f*
vintner, vīnārĭus, *m*
violate, *v.t*, vĭŏlo (1)
violation, vĭŏlātĭo, *f*
violator, vĭŏlātor, *m*
violence, vīs, *f*, vĭŏlentĭa, *f*, impĕtus, *m*
violent, vĭŏlentus, impŏtens
violet, *nn*, vĭŏla, *f*
violet, *adj* (— colour), ĭanthĭnus
viper, vīpĕra, *f*; *adj*, vīpĕrīnus
virago, vīrāgo, *f*
virgin, *nn*, virgo, *f*
virgin, *adj*, virgĭnālis
virginity, virgĭnĭtas, *f*
virile, vĭrīlis
virtually, *adv* re ipsā
virtue, virtus, *f*, hŏnestas, *f*; (by — of), *use abl. case of noun alone, or use* pcr (*with acc*)
virtuous, hŏnestus
virulent, ăcerbus
viscous, lentus
visible (noticeable), mănĭfestus; *or use nn.* conspectus, *m* (view)
vision, visus, *m*; (phantom, apparition), ĭmāgo, *f*, spĕcĭes, *f*
visionary, vānus
visit, *nn*, (call), sălūtātĭo, *f*; (stay), commŏrātĭo, *f*
visit, *v.t* vīso (3)
visitor, sălūtātor, *m*, hospes, *m*
visor, buccŭla, *f*
vista, prospectus, *m*
visual, *use phr. with* ŏcŭlus, *m*, (eye)
vital, vītālis; (important), grăvĭs
vitality, vīs, *f*, vīvācĭtas, *f*
vitiate, *v.t*, vĭtĭo (1), corrumpo (3)
vitreous, vĭtrĕus
vituperation, vĭtŭpĕrātĭo, *f*
vituperate, *v.t*, vĭtŭpĕro (1)
vivacious, ălăcer
vivacity, ălăcrĭtas, *f*
vivid, vīvus
vivify, *v.t*, ănĭmo (1)
vixen, vulpes, *f*
vocabulary, verba, *n.pl*
vocal, vōcālis
vocation, offĭcĭum, *n*
vociferate, *v.i*, clāmo (1)
vociferous, clāmōsus
vociferously, *adv*, magno clāmōre
vogue, mos, *m*, (custom)
voice, vox, *f*
voice, *v.t*, dīco (3)
void, *nn*, ĭnāne, *n*
void, *adj*, ĭnānis; (— of), văcŭus (*with abl*)
volatile, lĕvis

volcano, mons qui ēructat flammas (a
    mountain which 'emits flames)
volition, vŏluntas, f; (of his own —),
    sŭā sponte
volley (of javelins), tēla missa, n.pl
volubility, vŏlūbĭlĭtas, f
voluble, vŏlūbĭlis
volume (book), lĭber, m; (of noise),
    magnĭtūdo, f
voluminous, cōpĭōsus
voluntarily, adv, sponte (of one's own
    accord) with appropriate pron, mĕā,
    tŭā, sŭā
voluntary, vŏluntārĭus
volunteer, nn, mīles vŏluntārĭus, m
volunteer, v.i, (of soldiers), use phr,
    ultro nōmen dāre (enlist voluntarily)
voluptuous, vŏluptārĭus
voluptuousness, luxŭrĭa, f
vomit, nn, vŏmĭtĭo, f
vomit, v.i. and v.t, vŏmo (3)
voracious, ĕdax, vŏrax
voracity, ĕdācĭtas, f
vortex, vertex, m
vote, suffrāgĭum, n, sententĭa, f
vote, v.i, suffrāgĭum fĕro (irreg);
    (to — in favour of), in sententĭam
    īre (irreg) (with genit)
voter, suffrāgātor, m
voting-tablet (ballot-paper), tăbella, f
vouch for, v.t praesto (1), testor (1
    dep), testĭfĭcor (1 dep.)
voucher (authority), auctōrĭtas, f
vow, vōtum, n; (promise), fĭdes, f
vow, v.t. prōmitto (3), vŏvĕo (2)
vowel, vōcālis littĕra, f
voyage, nn, nāvĭgātĭo, f
voyage, v.i, nāvĭgo (1)
voyager, pĕrĕgrīnātor, m
vulgar, vulgāris, plēbĕius, sordĭdus
vulgarity (of manner, etc.), use phr,
    mōres sordĭdi, m.pl
vulgarize, v.t, pervulgo (1)
vulnerable, ăpertus
vulture, vultur, m

W

wadding, use lānūgo, f, (woolly down)
wade, v.i, use phr, per văda īre (irreg)
    (to go through the shallows)
wafer, crustŭlum (pastry)
waft, v.t, fĕro (irreg)
wag, nn, (jester), iŏcŭlātor, m
wag, v.t, quasso (1)
wage (war), v.t, gĕro (3) (bellum)
wager, nn, sponsĭo, f
wager, v.i, sponsĭōnem făcĭo (3)
wages, merces, f
waggish, făcētus

waggon, plaustrum, n
wagtail, mōtăcilla, f
wail, wailing, nn, plōrātus, m, flētus, m
wail, v.i, plōro (1) flĕo (2)
waist, mĕdĭum corpus, n
waistcoat, sŭbūcŭla, f, (undergarment)
wait, v.i, mănĕo (2); v.t, (to — for),
    exspecto (1); (serve), fămŭlor (1
    dep.); (— in ambush), insĭdĭas făcĭo
    (3) (with dat)
wait, nn, mŏra, f
waiter, fămŭlus, m
waiting, exspectātĭo, f, mansĭo, f
waive, v.t, rēmitto (3)
wake, v.t, excĭto (1); v.i, expergīscor
    (3 dep.)
wakeful, vĭgil
wakefulness, vĭgĭlantĭa, f, insomnĭa, f
walk, nn, ambŭlātĭo, f; (gait), in-
    cessus, m; (— of life, occupation),
    quaestus, m
walk, v.i, ambŭlo (1), grădĭor (3 dep.),
    incēdo (3)
walker, pēdes, m
walking, nn, ambŭlātĭo, f
wall, mūrus, m; (ramparts), moenĭa,
    n.pl; (inner —), părĭes, m
wall, v.t, mūnĭo (4) (fortify)
wallet, saccŭlus, m
wallow, v.i, vŏlūtor (1 pass)
walnut (tree and nut), iūglans, f
wan, adj, pallĭdus
wand, virga, f, cādūcĕus, m
wander, v.i, erro (1), văgor (1 dep.)
wanderer, erro, m
wandering, nn, error, m
wane, v.i, dēcresco (3)
want, nn, (lack), ĭnōpĭa, f, pēnūrĭa, f;
    (longing for), dēsīdĕrĭum, n; (fail-
    ing), dēfectĭo, f; (in —), adj, ĭnops
want, v.i, (wish), vŏlo (irreg); v.t, (to
    lack), cărĕo (2), ĕgĕo (2) (with abl);
    (long for), dēsīdĕro (1); (desire),
    cŭpĭo (3)
wanting (to be —, to fail), v.i, dēsum
    (irreg)
wanton, adj, lascīvus, lĭbĭdĭnōsus
wantoness, lascīvĭa, f
war, bellum, n; (civil —), bellum
    cīvīle, n; (in —), adv, bello; (to
    make — on), bellum infĕro (irreg,
    with dat); (to declare — on), bellum
    indīco (3) (with dat); (to wage —),
    bellum gĕro (3)
warble, v.i, căno (3)
war-cry, clāmor, m
ward, pūpillus, m, pūpilla, f; (district),
    rĕgĭo, f
ward off, v.t, arcĕo (2)
warden, cūrātor, m

warder, custos, *c*
wardrobe, vestiārĭum, *n*
warehouse, horrĕum, *n*
wares, merx, *f*
warfare, mīlĭtĭa, *f*
warily, *adv,* cautē
wariness, cautĭo, *f*
warlike, *adj,* bellĭcōsus, mīlĭtārĭs
warm, călĭdus; (to be —), *v.i,* călĕo (2)
warm, *v.t,* călĕfăcĭo (3)
warmly (eagerly), *adv,* vĕhementer
warmth, călor, *m*
warn, *v.t,* mŏnĕo (2)
warning, *nn,* (act of —), mŏnĭtĭo, *f;* (the warning itself), mŏnĭtum, *n*
warp, *nn,* stāmen, *n*
warp, *v.t,* (distort, of mind, etc.), dēprāvo (1)
warrant, *nn,* mandātum, *n;* (authority), auctōrĭtas, *f*
warrant, *v.t,* (guarantee), firmo (1), praesto (1)
warranty, sătisdătĭo, *f*
warren, lĕpŏrārĭum, *n*
warrior, mīles, *c,* bellātor, *m*
wart, verrūca, *f*
wary, prōvĭdus, prūdens
wash, *v.t,* lăvo (1); *v.i,* lăvor (1 *pass*)
wash, washing, *nn,* lăvātĭo, *f*
wash-basin, ăquālĭs, *c*
wasp, vespa, *f*
waspish, ăcerbus
waste, *nn,* damnum, *n;* (careless throwing away), effūsĭo, *f;* (—land), vastĭtas, *f*
waste, *adj,* vastus, dēsertus
waste, *v.t,* consūmo (3), perdo (3); (— time), tempus tĕro (3); *v.i,* (— away), tābesco (3)
wasteful, prōfūsus
wastefulness, prōfūsĭo, *f*
watch (a — of the night), vĭgĭlĭa, *f;* (watching on guard), excŭbĭae, *f.pl*
watch, *v.t,* (observe), specto (1); (guard), custōdĭo (4); *v.i,* (not to sleep), excŭbo (1)
watchful, vĭgĭlans
watchfulness, vĭgĭlantĭa, *f*
watchman, custos, *m*
watchword, tessĕra, *f*
water, ăqua, *f;* (fresh —), ăqua dulcĭs, *f;* (salt —), ăqua salsa, *f*
water, *v.t,* rĭgo (1), irrĭgo (1)
water-carrier, ăquārĭus, *m*
water-closet, lātrīna, *f*
waterfall, ăqua dēsĭlĭens, *f,* (water leaping down)
watering-place, ăquātĭo, *f;* (resort), ăquae, *f.pl*
water-snake, hydrus, *m*

waterworks, ăquaeductus, *m*
watery, ăquātĭcus
wattle, crātĭs, *f*
wave, *nn,* unda, *f,* fluctus, *m*
wave, *v.i,* undo (1), fluctŭo (1); *v.t,* ăgĭto (1)
waver, *v.i,* fluctŭo (1) dŭbĭto (1)
wavering, *adj,* dŭbĭus
wavering, *nn,* dŭbĭtātĭo, *f*
wavy (of hair), crispus
wax, *nn,* cēra, *f; adj,* cērĕus
wax, *v.i,* cresco (3)
way, vĭa, *f;* (journey), ĭter, *n;* (pathway), sēmĭta, *f;* (course), cursus, *m;* (manner), mŏdus, *m;* (habit), mos, *m;* (system), rătĭo, *f;* (in the —), *adj,* obvĭus; (in this —), *adv,* ĭta, sīc; (out of the —), *adj,* āvĭus; (to give or to make —), *v.i,* cēdo (3); (to get one's own —), vinco (3)
wayfarer, vĭātor, *m*
waylay, *v.t,* insĭdĭor (1 *dep.*) (*with dat*)
wayward, pertĭnax
we, *pron,* nos; *often expressed by 1st person plural of vb, e.g.* **we are,** sumus
weak, infirmus, dēbĭlĭs; (overcome), confectus; (of arguments, etc.), lēvĭs
weaken, *v.t,* infirmo (1), dēbĭlĭto (1); *v.i,* languesco (3), dēfĭcĭo (3)
weak-hearted, pŭsĭllĭ ănĭmĭ (of weak heart)
weakness, infirmĭtas, *f,* dēbĭlĭtas, *f,* lēvĭtas, *f*
weal (the common —), bŏnum pūblĭcum, *n;* (on skin), vibex, *f*
wealth, dīvĭtĭae, *f.pl,* ŏpes, *f.pl;* (large supply), cōpĭa, *f*
wealthy, dīves, lŏcŭples
wean, *v.t,* lacte dēpello (3) (remove from the milk)
weapon, tēlum, *n;* (*pl*) arma, *n.pl*
wear, *v.t,* (rub), tĕro (3); (— out), contĕro (3); (— a garment), gĕro (3); *v.i,* (last), dūro (1)
weariness, lassĭtūdo, *f*
wearisome, lăbōrĭōsus
weary, *adj,* fessus, fătĭgātus
weary, *v.t,* fătĭgo (1); *v.i,* (grow —), dēfătĭgor (1 *pass*)
weasel, mustēla, *f*
weather, tempestas, *f*
weather, *v.t,* (endure, bear), perfĕro (*irreg*)
weave, *v.t,* texo (3)
weaver, textor, *m*
web, tēla, *f*
wed, *v.t,* (of the husband), dūco (3); (of the wife), nūbo (3) (*with dat*)

wedding, *nn,* nuptĭae, *f.pl;* (— **day**), dĭes (*m*) nuptĭārum

wedge, *nn,* cŭnĕus, *m*

wedlock, mātrĭmōnĭum, *n*

weed, *nn,* herba ĭnūtĭlis, *f* (**harmful plant**)

weed, *v.t,* runco (1)

week, *use phr,* spătĭum septem dĭērum (**a space of seven days**)

weep, *v.i,* lăcrĭmo (1)

weeping, *nn,* flētus, *m*

weeping-willow, sălix, *f*

weevil, curcūlĭo, *m*

weigh, *v.t,* pendo (3), penso (1); (**consider**), pondĕro (1); (— **down**), grăvo (1)

weight, pondus, *n;* (**a** —), lībrāmentum, *n;* (**influence, etc.**), *use adj.* grăvis (**important**)

weightiness, grăvĭtas, *f*

weighty, grăvis

weir (**dam**), mōles, *f*

welcome, *adj,* grātus, acceptus

welcome, *nn,* sălūtātĭo, *f*

welcome! salve! (*pl.* salvēte!)

welcome, *v.t,* excĭpĭo (3)

weld, *v.t,* ferrūmĭno (1)

welfare, bŏnum, *n,* sălus, *f*

well, *adv,* bĕnĕ; (**very** —), optĭmē

well, *nn,* pŭtĕus, *m*

well, *adj,* (**safe**), salvus; (**healthy**), sānus, vălens; (**to be** —), *v.i,* vălĕo (2)

well-being, *nn,* sălus, *f*

well-born, nōbĭlis

well-disposed, bĕnĕvŏlus

well-favoured, pulcher

well-known, nōtus

well-wisher, *use adj,* bĕnĕvŏlus (**well-disposed**)

welter, *v.i,* vŏlūtor (1 *pass*)

wench, pŭella, *f*

west, *nn,* occĭdens, *m*

west, *adj,* occĭdentālis

westward, *adv,* ad occĭdentem (sōlem)

wet, *adj,* hūmĭdus, mădĭdus

wet, *v.t,* mădĕfăcĭo (3)

wether, vervex, *m*

wet-nurse, nūtrix, *f*

whale, bālaena, *f*

wharf, nāvāle, *n*

what, *interrog. pron,* quid? *interrog. adj,* qui, quae, quod; *relative pron,* quod, *pl,* quae; (— **for, wherefore, why**), quārē; (— **sort**), quālis?

whatever, *pron,* quodcumque; *adj,* quīcumque

wheat, trītĭcum, *n*

wheel, rŏta, *f*

wheel, *v.t,* circŭmăgo (3)

wheelbarrow, păbo, *m*

wheeling, *adj,* circumflectens

whelp, *nn,* cătŭlus, *m*

when? *interrog,* quando? (*temporal*), cum (*with vb, in indicative or subjunctive mood*), ŭbĭ (*vb. in indicative*)

whence, *adv,* undĕ

whenever, *adv,* quandōcumque

where? *interrog,* ŭbĭ?; (*relative*), quā; (— **from**), undĕ; (— **to**), quō; (**anywhere, everywhere**), *adv,* ŭbĭque

whereas, *adv,* quŏnĭam

wherever, quācumque

wherefore, *adv,* quārē

whereupon, *use phr,* quo facto (**with which having been done**)

whet, *v.t.* (**sharpen**), ăcŭo (3)

whether, *conj.* (*in a single question*), num, nĕ; (*in a double question,* **whether . . . or**), ūtrum . . . an; (*in a conditional sentence*), sīve . . . sīve

whetstone, cōs, *f*

whey, sĕrum, *n*

which, *interrog,* quis, quid; (*relative*), qui, quae, quod; (**which of two**), ūter

while, *conj,* dum (*often foll. by. vb. in present tense indicative*)

while, *nn,* tempus, *n,* spătĭum, *n;* (**for a little** —), *adv,* părumper; (**in a little** —), brĕvi (tempŏre)

while away, *v.t,* fallo (3), tĕro (3)

whim, lĭbĭdo, *f*

whimper, *v.i,* vāgĭo (4)

whimsical, rĭdĭcŭlus

whine, *v.i,* vāgĭo (4)

whinny, *v.i,* hinnĭo (4)

whip, *nn,* flăgellum, *n*

whip, *v.t,* verbĕro (1), flăgello (1)

whirl, *v.t,* torquĕo (2); *v.i,* torquĕor (2 *pass*)

whirlpool, *m,* gurges, *m*

whirlwind, turbo, *m*

whirr, *nn,* strīdor, *m*

whirr, *v.i,* strīdĕo (2)

whiskers, *use* barba, *f,* (**beard**)

whisper, *nn,* sŭsurrus, *m*

whisper, *v.i,* sŭsurro (1)

whispering, *adj,* sŭsurrus

whistle, whistling, *nn,* sībĭlus, *m*

whistle, *v.i,* sībĭlo (1)

white, *adj,* albus; (**shining** —), candĭdus

white, *nn,* album, *n*

whiten, *v.t,* dĕalbo (1); *v.i,* albesco (3)

whiteness, candor, *m*

whitewash, *nn,* albārĭum, *n*
white-wash, *v.t,* dēalbo (1)
whither, *(interrog. and relative),* quo
whiz, *v.i,* strīdĕo (2)
whiz, whizzing, *nn,* strīdor, *m*
who, *interrog,* quis? *(relative),* qui, quae
whoever, *pron,* quĭcunque
whole, *adj,* tōtus; **(untouched),** intĕger
whole, *nn,* tōtum, *n,* ūnĭversĭtas, *f, or use adj,* tōtus, *e.g.* **the — of the army,** tōtus exercĭtus, *m.*
wholesale trader, mercātor, *m*
wholesale trading, mercātūra,*f*
wholesome, sălūbris
wholly, *adv,* omnīno
whoop, *nn,* ŭlŭlātus, *m*
whom, *acc. case of rel. pron,* quem, quam; *pl,* quos, quas
whore, mērētrix, *f*
whose, *genit. case of rel. pron,* cŭius; *pl,* quōrum, quārum
why, *adv,* cur, quārē
wick, ellychnĭum, *n*
wicked, scĕlestus, mălus, imprŏbus
wickedness, scĕlus, *n,* imprŏbĭtas, *f*
wicker, vīmĭnĕus
wide, lātus; **(— open),** pătens
widen, *v.t,* dĭlāto (1); *v.i,* sē dĭlātāre (1 *reflex*)
widow, vĭdŭa, *f*
widower, vĭdŭus vir, *m*
widowhood, vĭdŭĭtas, *f*
width, lātĭtūdo, *f*
wield, *v.t,* tracto (1)
wife, uxor, *f*
wig, căpillāmentum, *n*
wild, indŏmĭtus, fĕrus; **(uncultivated),** incultus; **(mad),** āmens
wilderness, dēserta lŏca, *n.pl*
wildness, fĕrĭtas, *f*
wile, dŏlus, *m*
wilful, pervĭcax
wilfully, *adv,* pervĭcācĭter; **(deliberately),** consultō
wilfulness, pervĭcācĭa, *f*
wiliness, callĭdĭtas, *f*
will (desire), vŏluntas, *f*; **(purpose),** consĭlĭum, *n*; **(pleasure),** lĭbīdo, *f*; **(decision, authority),** arbĭtrĭum, *n*; **(legal),** testāmentum, *n*
will, *v.t,* **(bequeath),** lēgo (1)
willing, *adj,* lĭbens
willingly, *adv,* lĭbenter
willingness, vŏluntas, *f*
willow, sălix, *f*
wily, callĭdus, văfer
win, *v.i,* vinco (3); *v.t,* consĕquor (3 *dep*), ădĭpiscor (3 *dep*)

wind, ventus, *m*; **(breeze),** aura, *f*
wind, *v.t,* volvo (3)
winding, *nn,* flexus, *m*
winding, *adj,* flexŭōsus
windlass, sŭcŭla, *f*
window, fĕnestra, *f*
windward, *use phr,* conversus ad ventum **(turned towards the wind)**
windy, ventōsus
wine, vīnum, *n*
wine-cask, dōlĭum, *n*
wine-cellar, ăpŏthēca, *f*
wine-cup, pōcŭlum, *n*
wine-merchant, vīnārĭus, *m*
wing, āla, *f*; **(of army, etc.),** cornu, *n*
winged, pennĭger
wink, *nn,* nictātĭo, *f*
wink, *v.i,* nicto (1); **(overlook),** cōnīvĕo (2)
winner, victor, *m*
winning, *adj,* **(of manner),** blandus
winnow, *v.t,* ventĭlo (1)
winter, *nn,* hĭems, *f*
winter, *adj,* hĭĕmālis
winter, *v.i,* hĭĕmo (1)
wintry, hĭĕmālis
wipe, *v.t,* tergĕo (2)
wire, fīlum, *n,* **(thread)**
wisdom, săpĭentĭa, *f,* prūdentĭa, *f*
wise, *adj,* săpĭens, prūdens
wisely, *adv,* săpĭenter, prūdenter
wish, *nn,* **(desire),** vŏluntas, *f*; **(the wish itself),** optātum, *n*; **(longing),** dēsīdĕrĭum, *n*
wish, *v.t,* vŏlo *(irreg),* cŭpĭo (3), opto (1); **(long for),** dēsīdĕro (1)
wishing, *nn,* optātĭo, *f*
wisp, mănĭpŭlus, *m*
wistful, cŭpĭdus **(longing for); (dejected),** tristis
wit, ingĕnĭum, *n*; **(humour),** făcētĭae, *f. pl*; **(out of one's — s),** *adj,* āmens
witch, săga, *f*
witchcraft, ars măgĭca, *f*
with, *prep,* cum *(with abl, but when denoting the instrument, use abl. case, alone);* **(among, at the house of),** ăpud *(with acc)*
withdraw, *v.i,* cēdo (3), sē rĕcĭpĕre (3 *reflex*); *v.t,* dēdūco (3), rĕmŏvĕo (2)
withdrawal, regressus, *m*
wither, *v.i,* languesco (3); *v.t,* **(parch),** torrĕo (2)
withered, flaccĭdus
withhold, *v.t,* rĕtĭnĕo (2)
within, *adv,* intus
within, *prep,* **(time and space),** intrā *(with acc);* **(time),** *use abl. case alone, e.g.* **within three days,** trĭbus dĭēbus

without, *prep,* sĭne (*with abl*); (outside of), extrā (*with acc*); *when* without *is followed by a gerund* (e.g. I returned without seeing him) *use a clause introduced by* nēque, quĭn, ĭta . . . ut: *e.g.* rĕgressus sum, nēque ĕum vīdi

without, *adv,* extrā

withstand, *v.t,* rĕsisto (3) (*with dat*)

witness, *nn,* (person), testis, *c;* (testimony), testĭmōnĭum, *n*

witness, *v.t,* testor (1 *dep*), testĭfĭcor (1 *dep*); (to see), vĭdĕo (2)

witticism, fācĕtĭae, *f. pl*

witty, fācētus; (sharp), salsus

wizard, măgus, *m*

woad, vĭtrum, *n*

woe, dŏlor, *m,* luctus, *m*

woeful, tristis

wolf, lŭpus, *m*

wolfish (greedy, rapacious), răpax

woman, fēmĭna, *f,* mŭlĭer, *f;* (young —), pŭella, *f;* (old —), ănus, *f*

womanish, womanly, mŭlĭĕbris

womb, ŭtĕrus, *m*

wonder, mīrātĭo, *f;* (a marvel) mīrācŭlum, *n*

wonder, *v.i. and v.t,* mīror (1 *dep*)

wonderful, mīrus, mīrābĭlis

wont, wonted, *adj,* sŭētus

wont, *nn,* mos, *m*

woo, *v.t,* pĕto (3), ămo (1)

wood (material), mātĕrĭa, *f;* (forest), silva, *f*

wood-collector, lignātor, *m*

wooded, silvestris

wooden, lignĕus

woodland, silvae, *f. pl*

woodpecker, pīcus, *m*

wooer, prŏcus, *m*

wool, lāna, *f*

woollen, lānĕus

word, verbum, *n;* (promise), fĭdes, *f;* (information), nuntĭus, *m;* send word, *v.t,* nuntĭo (1)

wordy, verbōsus

work, *nn,* ŏpus, *n;* (labour), lăbor, *m*

work, *v.i,* ŏpĕror (1 *dep*)

work, *v.t,* exercĕo (2); (handle, manipulate), tracto (1); (bring about), effĭcĭo (3)

worker, ŏpĭfex, *c,* ŏpĕrārĭus, *m*

workman, ŏpĭfex, *c,* ŏpĕrārĭus, *m*

workmanship, ars, *f*

workshop, offĭcīna, *f*

world, mundus, *m,* orbis (*m*) terrārum; (people), hŏmĭnes, *c. pl*

worldliness, *use phr,* stŭdĭum rērum prŏfānārum (fondness for common matters)

worm, vermis, *m*

worm-eaten, vermĭnōsus

worm (one's way), *v.i,* sē insĭnŭāre (1 *reflex*)

wormwood, absinthĭum, *n*

worn (— out), *adj,* trītus; (as clothes), gestus

worry, *nn,* anxĭĕtas, *f*

worry, *v.t,* vexo (1); *v.i,* cūrā affĭci (3 *pass*) (to be affected by worry)

worse, *adj,* pēior.

worse, *adv,* pēius

worship, *v.t,* vĕnĕror (1 *dep*), cŏlo (3)

worship, *nn,* vĕnĕrātĭo, *f,* cultus, *m*

worshipper, cultor, *m*

worst, *adj,* pessĭmus

worst, *adv,* pessĭmē

worst, *v.t,* vinco (3)

worth, *nn,* (price), prĕtĭum, *n;* (valuation), aestĭmātĭo, *f;* (worthiness), virtus, *f,* dignĭtas, *f;* (— nothing), nĭhĭli; (to be — much), *v.i,* multum vălĕo (2); (*adj*) dignus

worthiness, dignĭtas, *f*

worthless, vīlis

worthy (*with noun*), dignus (*with abl*); (*with phr*) dignus qui (ut)(*with vb. in subjunctive*); (man), prŏbus

wound, *nn,* vulnus, *n*

wound, *v.t,* vulnĕro (1), saucĭo (1)

wounded, vulnĕrātus, saucĭus

wrangle, *v.i,* rixor (1 *dep*)

wrangle, wrangling, *nn,* rixa, *f*

wrap, *v.t,* involvo (3)

wrapper, invŏlūcrum, *n*

wrath, īra, *f*

wrathful, īrātus

wreak vengeance on, *v.t,* ulciscor (3 *dep*)

wreath, *nn,* serta, *n.pl*

wreathe, *v.t,* torquĕo (2)

wreck, *nn,* naufrăgĭum, *n*

wreck, *v.t,* frango (3)

wrecked, naufrăgus

wren, rēgŭlus, *m*

wrench away, wrest, *v.t,* extorquĕo (2)

wrestle, *v.i,* luctor (1 *dep*)

wrestler, luctātor, *m*

wrestling, *nn,* luctātĭo, *f*

wretch, perdĭtus, *m*

wretched, mĭser

wretchedness, mĭsĕrĭa, *f*

wriggle, *v.i,* torquĕor (2 *pass*)

wring, *v.t,* torquĕo (2)

wrinkle, rūga, *f*

wrinkled, rūgōsus

wrist, *use* bracchĭum, *n,* (forearm)

writ (legal —), mandātum, *n*

write, *v.t,* scrībo (3)

writer, scriptor, *m;* (author), auctor, *c*

writhe, *v.i,* torquĕor (2 *pass*)

writing, scriptĭo, *f*; (something written), scriptum, *n*, ŏpus, *n*
wrong, *adj*, falsus; (improper, bad), prăvus; (to be —), *v.i*, erro (1)
wrong, *nn*, nĕfas, *n*, peccātum *n*; (a —), iniūrĭa, *f*
wrongly *adv*, (badly), măle; (in error), falso
wrong, *v.t*, fraudo (1), iniūrĭam infĕro (*irreg*) (*with dat*)
wrongful, iniustus
wroth, īrātus
wrought, confectus
wry, distortus

Y

yacht, cĕlox, *f*
yard (measurement), *often* passus, *m*, (five feet approx.) (court —), ārĕa, *f*
yarn (thread), fīlum, *n*; (story), fābŭla, *f*
yawn, *nn*, oscĭtātĭo, *f*
yawn, *v.i*, oscĭto (1)
year, annus, *m*; (a half —), sēmestre spătĭum, *n*, (space of six months)
yearly, *adj*, (throughout a year), annŭus; (every year), *adv*, quŏtannis
yearn for, *v.t*, dēsĭdĕro (1)
yearning, dēsĭdĕrĭum, *n*
yeast, fermentum, *n*
yell, clāmor, *m*, ŭlŭlātus, *m*
yell, *v.i*, magnā vōce clāmo (1)
yellow, flāvus
yellowish, subflāvus
yelp, *v.i*, gannĭo (4)
yelping, *nn*, gannītus, *m*
yeoman, cŏlōnus, *m*
yes, *adv*, ĭta
yesterday, *adv*, hĕrī; *nn*, hesternus dĭes, *m*
yet, *adv*, (nevertheless), tămen; (*with comparatives*) ĕtĭam, *e.g.* yet bigger, ĕtĭam māior; (of time; still), ădhuo

yew, taxus, *f*
yield, *v.i*, cēdo (3) (*with dat*); (surrender), sē dēdĕre (*3 reflex*)
yielding, *nn*, concessĭo, *f*
yielding, *adj*, (soft), mollis
yoke, *nn*, iŭgum, *n*
yoke, *v.t*, iungo (3)
yoked, iŭgālis; (— pair), iŭgum, *n*
yolk, vĭtellus, *m*
yonder, *adv*, illic
yore, *adv*, ōlim (once, in time past)
you, *pron*, *often not expressed*, *e.g.* you come, vĕnis; *pl*, vĕnītis; *otherwise use appropriate case of* tu; *pl*, vos
young, *adj*, iŭvĕnis, parvus; (child), infans; (— person), ădŏlescens
young, *nn*, (offspring), partus, *m*
younger, iūnĭor, mĭnor nātu (less in age)
young man, iŭvĕnis, *m*.
youngster, iŭvĕnis, *c*
your, yours (*singular*), tŭus; (*of more than one*), vester
yourself (*emphatic*), *use* ipse *in agreement with pron*; (*reflexive*), te; *pl*, vos
youth (time of —), iŭventus, *f*, ădŏlescentĭa, *f*; (young man), ădŏlescens, iŭvĕnis, *c*; (body of young persons), iŭventus, *f*
youthful, iŭvĕnīlis

Z

zeal, stŭdĭum, *n*
zealous, stŭdĭōsus
zenith, *use* summus, *adj*, (top of)
zephyr, Zĕphўrus, *m*, Făvōnĭus, *m*
zero (nothing), nĭhil
zest, ălăcrĭtas, *f*
zodiac, signĭfer orbis, *m*, (sign-bearing orb)
zone, lŏcus, *m*

LIST OF PROPER NAMES

With Classical equivalents

Adriatic, Măre Sŭpĕrum, *n*
Aegean, Măre Aegaeum, *n*
Africa, Afrĭca, ae, *f*
African, *adj*, Afrĭcānus, a, um
Alps, Alpes, ĭum, *f. pl*
Antioch, Antĭŏchĭa, ae, *f*
Anthony, Antōnĭus
Apennines, Mons Ăpennīnus, *m*
Ardennes, Ardŭenna, ae, *f*
Athens, Athēnae, ārum, *f. pl*
Athenian, *adj*, Athēnĭensis, e
Aventine, Ăventīnus, i, *m*
Babylon, Băbўlōn, ōnis, *f*
Bath, Ăquae, (*f. pl*,) Sulis
Belgium, Gallia Belgĭca, *f*
The Belgians, Belgae, *m. pl*
Black Sea, Pontus Euxīnus, *m*
Britain, Brĭtannĭa, ae, *f*
British, *adj*, Brĭtannĭcus, a, um
Caerleon, Isca, ae, *f*
Capri, Caprĕae, ārum, *f. pl*
Cyprus, Cўprus, i, *f*
Damascus, Dămascus, i, *f*
Danube (lower part), Hister, tri, *m*; (upper), Dānŭvĭus, ii, *m*
Ebro, IIIbĕrus, i, *m*
Egypt, Aegyptus, i, *m*
Egyptian, *adj*., Aegyptĭus
Etna, Aetna, ae, *f*
Europe, Eurōpa, ae, *f*
France, Gallĭa, ae, *f*
Gaul, Gallĭa, ae, *f*
Geneva (Lake —), lacus Lĕmannus, *m*
German, *adj*, Germānus, a, um
Germany, Germānĭa, ae, *f*

Gloucester, Glevum, i, *n*
Greece, Graecĭa, ae, *f*
Greek, *adj*, Graecus, a, um
Helen, Hĕlĕna, ae, *f*
Horace, Hŏrātĭus
Ireland, Hībernĭa, *f*
Italy, Itălĭa, ae, *f*
Jerusalem, Hĭĕrŏsŏlўma, ōrum, *n.pl*
Kent, Cantĭum, i, *n*
Lincoln, Lindum, *n*
Loire, Lĭger, ĕris, *m*
London, Londīnĭum, i, *n*
Lyons, Lugdūnum, i, *n*
Majorca, Băliāris Māior, *f*
Malta, Mĕlĭta, ae, *f*
Marseilles, Massilĭa, ae, *f*
Messina, Messāna, ae, *f*
Mediterranean, măre nostrum, *n*
Provence, Prŏvincĭa, ae, *f*
Pyrenees, Pўrēnaei Montes, *m. pl*
Rhine, Rhēnus, i, *m*
Rhodes, Rhŏdos, i, *f*
Rhone, Rhŏdănus, i, *m*
Roman, Rōmānus, a, um,
Rome, Rōma, ae, *f*
Scotland, Cālēdŏnĭa, ae, *f*
Severn, Săbrĭna, ae, *f*
Sicily, Sĭcilĭa, ae, *f*
Spain, Hispānĭa, ae, *f*
St. Albans, Vērŭlamĭum, i, *n*
Syracuse, Sўrăcūsae, ārum, *f. pl*
Thames, Tămĕsis, is, *m*
Tiber, Tĭbĕris, is, *m*
Tuscany, Ĕtrūrĭa, ae, *f*
Isle of Wight, Vectis, is, *f*

Names of the Winds

North, Bŏrĕas, ae, *m*
North-east, Ăquĭlo, ōnis, *m*
East, Eurus, i, *m*
South-east, Vulturnus, i, *m*
South, Auster, tri, *m*, Nŏtus, i, *m*

South-west, Afrĭcus, i, *m*
West, Făvōnĭus, i, *n*
　　Zĕphўrus, i, *m*
North-west, Cōrus, i, *m*

CONCISE GRAMMAR
ALPHABET

The Latin alphabet contained twenty-three letters:

A B C D E F G H I K L M N O P Q R S T V X Y Z

Pronunciation

Although there is not complete agreement about the way in which the Romans spoke Latin, this is one method of pronunciation which many people believe to have been used by the Romans.

Vowels

ă (short a) as in "fat"; ā (long a) as in "father".
ĕ (short e) as in "net"; ē (long e) as in "they".
ĭ (short i) as in "pin"; ī (long i) as in "police".
ŏ (short o) as in "not"; ō (long o) as in "note".
ŭ (short u) as "oo" in "wood"; ū (long u) as "oo" in "mood".

Long vowels only are marked in this section. Other vowels are short, unless they are made long by two consonants or *x* immediately following them.

Diphthongs

Two vowels pronounced together to form one sound are called Diphthongs, e.g. ae, au, oe, and are pronounced as follows.

ae, as "ai" in "aisle".
au, as "ow" in "cow".
oe, as "oi" in "oil".

Consonants

These are mostly pronounced as in English, but note:

c is always hard, as in "cat".
g is always hard, as in "get".
i, when it is used as a consonant, is always pronounced as y in "yellow" e.g. *iam*, "yam".
s is always pronounced as in "son".
t is always pronounced as in "top".
v is pronounced as "w" in "wall", e.g. *servi*, pronounced "serwee".
th is pronounced as "t" and *ch* as "k".

NOUNS

Latin is a language of "endings", or, as they are sometimes called "inflections". It is usually by the ending of a noun in Latin that we can tell what its relationship is to the other words in the sentence. Nouns which have the same sets of endings are grouped together in what is known as a Declension. There are five of these in Latin, and each one is distinguished by the way in which the nouns belonging to it form their genitive singular case, e.g.

First Declension—*ae*—insul*ae*
Second Declension—*i*—mur*i*
Third Declension—*is*—reg*is*
Fourth Declension—*us*—exercit*us*
Fifth Declension—*ei*—di*ei*

The genitive is one of the six cases which each noun in Latin has. These are:

Nominative: This is used when the noun is the *subject* of the sentence, e.g. *The sailor* loves the queen.

Vocative: This is the case of the person *addressed*, e.g. *Sailor*, where are you going?

Accusative: This is used when the noun is the *object* of the sentence, e.g. The queen loves *the sailor*.

Genitive: This case denotes *possession*, and translates the English word "of", e.g. The dog *of the sailor*, or, *The sailor's* dog.

Dative: This is used when the noun is the *indirect object* of the sentence, and usually translates the English words "to" and "for", e.g. He gives money *to the sailor*.

Ablative: This translates the English words "by", "with", "from", "on", and "in".

These cases have different endings when they are used in the singular and in the plural.

First Declension

Most nouns of the First Declension end in "a" and are feminine, e.g *insula*, f . . . an island.

	Singular	Plural
Nom.	*insula*	*insulae*
Voc.	*insula*	*insulae*
Acc.	*insulam*	*insulās*
Gen.	*insulae*	*insulārum*
Dat.	*insulae*	*insulīs*
Abl.	*insulā*	*insulis*

Second Declension

Some nouns in this declension are masculine, and end in "*us*" or "*er*", e.g. *mūrus*, m . . . a wall, and *ager*, m . . . a field.

	Singular	Plural	Singular	Plural
Nom.	*mūrus*	*mūrī*	*ager*	*agrī*
Voc.	*mūre*	*mūrī*	*ager*	*agrī*
Acc.	*mūrum*	*mūrōs*	*agrum*	*agrōs*
Gen.	*mūrī*	*mūrōrum*	*agrī*	*agrōrum*
Dat.	*mūrō*	*mūrīs*	*agrō*	*agrīs*
Abl.	*mūrō*	*mūrīs*	*agrō*	*agrīs*

Some nouns in this declension are neuter, and end in "*um*", e.g. *bellum*, n . . . war.

	Singular	Plural
Nom.	*bellum*	*bella*
Voc.	*bellum*	*bella*
Acc.	*bellum*	*bella*
Gen.	*bellī*	*bellōrum*
Dat.	*bellō*	*bellīs*
Abl.	*bellō*	*bellīs*

Third Declension

In this declension are nouns of all three genders, masculine, feminine, and neuter.

(*a*) Masculine and feminine nouns are usually declined like *rex*, m . . . a king, or *civis*, m . . . a citizen.

	Singular	Plural	Singular	Plural
Nom.	*rex*	*rēgēs*	*cīvis*	*cīvēs*
Voc.	*rex*	*rēgēs*	*cīvis*	*cīvēs*
Acc.	*rēgem*	*rēgēs*	*cīvem*	*cīvēs*
Gen.	*rēgis*	*rēgum*	*cīvis*	*cīvium*
Dat.	*rēgī*	*rēgibus*	*cīvī*	*cīvibus*
Abl.	*rēge*	*rēgibus*	*cīve*	*cīvibus*

Parisyllabic nouns (i.e. with the same number of syllables in nominative and genitive singular) e.g. *nāvis* (nom.), *nāvis* (gen.) are declined like *cīvis*, except the following "family" nouns:

pater, m, father	*senex*, m, old man
māter, f, mother	*iuvenis*, m, young man
frāter, m, brother	*canis*, m, dog

These nouns have the same genitive plural ending as *rex*.

Imparisyllabic nouns (i.e. with more syllables in genitive than in the nominative singular case) e.g. *ōrātor* (nom.), *ōrātōris* (gen.) are declined like *rex*, except those which are monosyllabic and whose stem ends in two consonants e.g. *urbs*, *urbis*—city; *mens*, *mentis*—mind.

They have the same genitive plural ending as *cīvis*.

(*b*) Neuter nouns are declined like *mare*, n . . . the sea, or *tempus*, n . . . time.

	Singular	Plural	Singular	Plural
Nom.	*mare*	*maria*	*tempus*	*tempora*
Voc.	*mare*	*maria*	*tempus*	*tempora*
Acc.	*mare*	*maria*	*tempus*	*tempora*
Gen.	*maris*	*marium*	*temporis*	*temporum*
Dat.	*marī*	*maribus*	*temporī*	*temporibus*
Abl.	*marī*	*maribus*	*tempore*	*temporibus*

The nouns whose stems end in *ar*, *al*, *il*, are declined like *mare*, others like *tempus*.

Fourth Declension

In this declension, masculine and feminine nouns end in "*us*", e.g. *exercitus*, m . . . an army, *manus*, f . . . a hand, and neuter nouns in "*u*", e.g. *cornū*, n . . . horn.

	Singular	Plural	Singular	Plural
Nom.	*exercitus*	*exercitūs*	*cornū*	*cornua*
Voc.	*exercitus*	*exercitūs*	*cornū*	*cornua*
Acc.	*exercitum*	*exercitūs*	*cornū*	*cornua*
Gen.	*exercitūs*	*exercituum*	*cornūs*	*cornuum*
Dat.	*exercituī*	*exercitibus*	*cornū*	*cornibus*
Abl.	*exercitū*	*exercitibus*	*cornū*	*cornibus*

Fifth Declension

The nouns in this declension are all declined like *diēs*, m, or f . . . a day, or *rēs*, f . . . a thing.

	Singular	Plural	Singular	Plural
Nom.	*diēs*	*diēs*	*rēs*	*rēs*
Voc.	*diēs*	*diēs*	*rēs*	*rēs*
Acc.	*diem*	*diēs*	*rem*	*rēs*
Gen.	*diēī*	*diērum*	*reī*	*rērum*
Dat.	*diēī*	*diēbus*	*reī*	*rēbus*
Abl.	*diē*	*diēbus*	*rē*	*rēbus*

Irregular Nouns·

A few of the commoner nouns which contain irregularities of inflexion are given below:

domus, f . . . house, home; *vīs*, f . . . force; *bos*, c . . . ox; *Iuppiter*, m . . . Juppiter

	Singular	Plural	Singular	Plural
Nom. Voc.	*domus*	*domūs*	*vīs*	*vīrēs*
Acc.	*domum*	*domūs (domōs)*	*vim*	*vīrēs*
Gen.	*domūs* (or *domī*)	*domōrum*	—	*vīrium*
Dat.	*domuī (domō)*	*domibus*	—	*vīribus*
Abl.	*domū (domō)*	*domibus*	*vī*	*vīribus*

	Singular	Plural	Singular
Nom. Voc.	*bos*	*bovēs*	*Iuppiter*
Acc.	*bovem*	*bovēs*	*Iovem*
Gen.	*bovis*	*boum*	*Iovis*
Dat.	*bovī*	*bōbus (būbus)*	*Iovī*
Abl.	*bove*	*bōbus (būbus)*	*Iove*

ADJECTIVES

In Latin, adjectives, like nouns, have different "endings", or inflections. If an adjective describes a singular masculine noun it has one set of endings, if it describes a singular feminine noun it has another set. All adjectives must agree with the noun they describe in three respects:

(*a*) Number, i.e. Singular or Plural
(*b*) Gender, i.e. Masculine, Feminine or Neuter
(*c*) Case, whichever case the noun is in.

Therefore each adjective must have three different sets of endings, in singular and plural, in order to be able to agree with masculine, feminine, and neuter nouns.

There are two main classes of adjectives in Latin.

Class I

In this class, adjectives have the endings of First and Second Declension nouns and are declined either like *bonus, -a, -um* . . . good; *asper, aspera, asperum* . . . rough; or *āter, ātra, ātrum* . . . black.

	Singular			Plural		
	MASC.	FEM.	NEUT.	MASC.	FEM.	NEUT.
Nom.	*bonus*	*-a*	*-um*	*bonī*	*-ae*	*-a*
Voc.	*bone*	*-a*	*-um*	*bonī*	*-ae*	*-a*
Acc.	*bonum*	*-am*	*-um*	*bonōs*	*-ās*	*-a*
Gen.	*bonī*	*-ae*	*-ī*	*bonōrum*	*-ārum*	*-ōrum*
Dat.	*bonō*	*-ae*	*-ō*	*bonīs*	*-īs*	*-īs*
Abl.	*bonō*	*-ā*	*-ō*	*bonīs*	*-īs*	*-īs*
Nom. Voc.	*asper*	*aspera*	*asperum*	*asperī*	*-ae*	*-a*
Acc.	*asperum*	*-am*	*-um*	*asperōs*	*-ās*	*-a*
Gen.	*asperī*	*-ae*	*-ī*	*asperōrum*	*-ārum*	*-ōrum*
Dat.	*asperō*	*-ae*	*-ō*	*asperīs*	*-īs*	*-īs*
Abl.	*asperō*	*-ā*	*-ō*	*asperīs*	*-īs*	*-īs*
Nom. Voc.	*āter*	*ātra*	*ātrum*	*ātrī*	*-ae*	*-a*
Acc.	*ātrum*	*-am*	*-um*	*ātrōs*	*-ās*	*-a*
Gen.	*ātrī*	*-ae*	*-ī*	*ātrōrum*	*-ārum*	*-ōrum*
Dat.	*ātrō*	*-ae*	*-ō*	*ātrīs*	*-īs*	*-īs*
Abl.	*ātro*	*-ā*	*-ō*	*ātrīs*	*-īs*	*-īs*

Class II

These adjectives are declined like nouns of the Third Declension. If the nominative ends in *is* (*omnis* ... all), *er* (*ācer* ... keen), *x* (*fēlix* ... happy), *ens* (*ingens* ... huge), they are declined as follows:

	Singular		Plural	
	MASC. AND FEM.	NEUT.	MASC. AND FEM.	NEUT.
Nom. Voc.	omnis	omne	omnēs	-ia
Acc.	omnem	-e	omnēs	-ia
Gen.	omnis	-is	omnium	-ium
Dat.	omnī	-ī	omnibus	-ibus
Abl.	omnī	-ī	omnibus	-ibus

	MASC.	FEM.	NEUT.	MASC. AND FEM.	NEUT.
Nom. Voc.	ācer	ācris	ācre	ācrēs	-ia
Acc.	ācrem	-em	-e	ācrēs	-ia
Gen.	ācris	-is	-is	ācrium	-ium
Dat.	ācrī	-ī	-ī	ācribus	-ibus
Abl.	ācrī	-ī	-ī	ācribus	-ibus

	MASC. AND FEM.	NEUT.	MASC. AND FEM.	NEUT.
Nom. Voc.	fēlix	-ix	fēlīcēs	-ia
Acc.	fēlicem	-ix	fēlīcēs	-ia
Gen.	fēlīcis	-is	fēlīcium	-ium
Dat.	fēlīcī	-ī	fēlīcibus	-ibus
Abl.	fēlīcī	-ī	fēlīcibus	-ibus

	MASC. AND FEM.	NEUT.	MASC. AND FEM.	NEUT.
Nom. Voc.	ingens	-ens	ingentēs	-ia
Acc.	ingentem	-ens	ingentēs	-ia
Gen.	ingentis	-is	ingentium	-ium
Dat.	ingentī	-ī	ingentibus	-ibus
Abl.	ingentī	-ī	ingentibus	-ibus

Other adjectives of the Class II are declined like *melior* ... better, or *vetus* ... old.

	MASC. AND FEM.	NEUT.	MASC. AND FEM.	NEUT.
Nom. Voc.	melior	-ius	meliōrēs	-a
Acc.	meliōrem	-ius	meliōrēs	-a
Gen.	meliōris	-is	meliōrum	-um
Dat.	meliōrī	-ī	meliōribus	-ibus
Abl.	meliōre	-e	meliōribus	-ibus

	MASC. AND FEM.	NEUT.	MASC. AND FEM.	NEUT.
Nom. Voc.	vetus	-us	veterēs	-a
Acc.	veterem	-us	veterēs	-a
Gen.	veteris	-is	veterum	-um
Dat.	veterī	-ī	veteribus	-ibus
Abl.	vetere	-e	veteribus	-ibus

Adjectives with ... ius in the Genitive Singular and ... i in the Dative Singular

There is also a class of adjectives which, from the endings of the nominative singular, one would expect to belong to Class I. They are in fact exactly the same in declension as adjectives of Class I, except in the genitive and dative singular. The genitive has the ending *-ius* in all genders, and the dative—*ī*. These adjectives are *sōlus* (alone); *tōtus* (whole); *ūnus* (one); *ullus* (any); *nullus* (not any, no one); *alius* (other, another); *alter* (one of two); *uter?* (which of two?); *neuter* (neither of two).

Singular

	MASC.	FEM.	NEUT.
Nom.	*sōlus*	*-a*	*-um*
Acc.	*sōlum*	*-am*	*-um*
Gen.	*sōlīus*	*-īus*	*-īus*
Dat.	*sōlī*	*-ī*	*-ī*
Abl.	*sōlō*	*-ā*	*-ō*

The plural is quite regular, like *bonus*.

COMPARISON OF ADJECTIVES

In English we talk of one thing being "hard", of another being "harder" and of a third thing being "hardest" of all. These are called different "degrees" of the adjective, the first being called the Positive Degree, the second the Comparative Degree, the third the Superlative Degree. In English we usually form the comparative and superlative by adding -er and -est to the adjective, e.g. harder, hardest. In Latin we add *-ior* and *-issimus* to the *stem* of the adjective. (The stem is the genitive singular without its ending). Thus positive *dūrus*—hard, genitive *dūrī*, gives comparative *dūrior*, (harder) and superlative "*dūrissimus*", (hardest). Comparative adjectives are declined like *melior* (P. 298) and superlative adjectives like *bonus* (P. 297).

Besides "harder", *dūrior* can mean "too hard", and besides "hardest", *dūrissimus* can mean "very hard".

N.B. Adjectives which end in *-er* form the superlative by doubling the "*r*" and adding *-imus*, e.g.

> *asper*—*asperrimus*, *niger*—*nigerrimus*
> *ācer*—*ācerrimus*, *celer*—*celerrimus*

Six adjectives form the superlative by doubling the "*l*" and adding *-imus*. They are:

facilis, (easy)—*facillimus*	*difficilis*, (difficult)—*difficillimus*
similis, (like)—*simillimus*	*dissimilis*, (unlike)—*dissimillimus*
gracilis, (slender)—*gracillimus*	*humilis*, (low)—*humillimus*

Irregular Comparisons

bonus, good	*melior*, better	*optimus*, best
malus, bad	*pēior*, worse	*pessimus*, worst
magnus, great	*māior*, greater	*maximus*, greatest
parvus, small	*minor*, smaller	*minimus*, smallest
multus, much	*plūs*, more	*plūrimus*, most
senex, old	*nātū māior*, older	*nātū maximus*, oldest
iuvenis, young	*nātū minor*, younger	*nātū minimus*, youngest

When two things are compared after the comparative one may use *quam* (than), and put the two things in the same case, or omit the *quam* and put the second thing in the ablative case:

Illud est dūrius quam hoc (nom. sing. neut.). That is harder than this.
Illud est hoc (abl. sing. neut.) *dūrius*. That is harder than this.

VERBS

In Latin, when the subject of a verb is a pronoun, I, you, he, etc., it is represented by the ending or inflection only. Further, different inflections show differences of tense, e.g. Present, I am loving, *am-ō*; Future, I shall love, *am-ābō*. Verbs which have a similar set of endings are classed together into what is known as a Conjugation. There are four of these in Latin. All verbs, except irregular ones, fall into one of these conjugations, according to the termination of their present infinitive. To love, to advise, to rule, to hear, are present infinitives in English. *Am-āre, mon-ēre, reg-ĕre, aud-īre* are the corresponding infinitives in Latin. So, verbs with infinitives ending in *-āre* belong to the First Conjugation. Verbs with infinitives ending in *-ēre* belong to the Second Conjugation. Verbs with infinitives ending in *-ĕre* belong to the Third Conjugation. Verbs with infinitives ending in *-īre* belong to the Fourth Conjugation.

TABLES OF THE REGULAR VERBS

Active Voice

First Conjugation. Example, *Amō*, I love.
(From Present Stem *Am-*)

INDICATIVE MOOD	SUBJUNCTIVE MOOD
Present	*Present*
Am-ō, I love, I am loving	*Am-em*
Am-ās, you love, you are loving	*Am-ēs*
Am-at, he, she, it loves; he, she, it is loving	*Am-et*
Am-āmus, we love, we are loving	*Am-ēmus*
Am-ātis, you love, you are loving	*Am-ētis*
Am-ant, they love, they are loving	*Am-ent*

Imperfect	*Imperfect*
Am-ābam, I was loving, I used to love	*Am-ārem*
Am-ābās, you were loving, you used to love	*Am-ārēs*
Am-ābat, he, she, it was loving, he, she, it used to love	*Am-āret*
Am-ābāmus, we were loving, we used to love	*Am-ārēmus*
Am-ābātis, you were loving, you used to love	*Am-ārētis*
Am-ābant, they were loving, they used to love	*Am-ārent*

Future	
Am-ābō, I shall love	**Present Participle**
Am-ābis, you will love	*Am-ans*, loving
Am-ābit, he, she, it will love	**Present Infinitive**
Am-ābimus, we shall love	*Am-āre*, to love
Am-ābitis, you will love	Gerund
Am-ābunt, they will love	*Am-andum-ī*, loving (noun)

IMPERATIVE MOOD

Am-ā, love thou	*Am-āte*, love ye	*Am-ātō*, thou shalt love
Am-ātōte, ye shall love	*Am-ātō*, he shall love	*Am-antō*, they shall love

(From Perfect Stem *Amāv-*)

INDICATIVE MOOD	SUBJUNCTIVE MOOD
Perfect	*Perfect*
Amāv-ī, I loved, I did love, I have loved	*Amāv-erim*
Amāv-istī, you loved, etc.	*Amāv-erīs*
Amāv-it, he, she, it loved, etc.	*Amāv-erit*
Amāv-imus, we loved, etc.	*Amāv-erīmus*
Amāv-istis, you loved, etc.	*Amāv-erītis*
Amāv-ērunt, or *-ēre*, they loved, *etc*	*Amāv-erint*

INDICATIVE MOOD	SUBJUNCTIVE MOOD
Pluperfect	*Pluperfect*

Amāv-eram, I had loved	*Amāv-issem*
Amāv-erās, you had loved	*Amāv-issēs*
Amāv-erat, he, she, it had loved	*Amāv-isset*
Amāv-erāmus, we had loved	*Amāv-issēmus*
Amāv-erātis, you had loved	*Amāv-issētis*
Amāv-erant, they had loved	*Amāv-issent*

Future Perfect

Amāv-erō, I shall have loved	Perfect Infinitive
Amāv-eris, you will have loved	*Amāv-isse,* to have
Amāv-erit, he, she, it will have loved	loved
Amāv-erimus, we shall have loved	
Amāv-eritis, you shall have loved	
Amāv-erint, they will have loved	

(From Supine Stem *Amāt-*)
First Supine, *Amāt-um*   Second Supine, *Amāt-ū*

Future Participle, *Amāt-ūrus, -a, -um,* about to love
Future Infinitive = Future Participle + *esse* = *Amātūrus esse,* to be about to love.

Second Conjugation. Example, *Moneō,* I warn.
(From Present Stem *Mon-*)

INDICATIVE MOOD		SUBJUNCTIVE MOOD	
Present		*Present*	
Mon-eō	*Mon-ēmus*	*Mon-eam*	*Mon-eāmus*
Mon-ēs	*Mon-ētis*	*Mon-eas*	*Mon-eātis*
Mon-et	*Mon-ent*	*Mon-eat*	*Mon-eant*
Imperfect		*Imperfect*	
Mon-ēbam	*Mon-ēbāmus*	*Mon-ērem*	*Mon-ērēmus*
Mon-ēbās	*Mon-ēbātis*	*Mon-ērēs*	*Mon-ērētis*
Mon-ēbat	*Mon-ēbant*	*Mon-ēret*	*Mon-ērent*
Future			
Mon-ēbō	*Mon-ēbimus*	Present Participle.	*Mon-ens*
Mon-ēbis	*Mon-ēbitis*	Present Infinitive.	*Mon-ēre*
Mon-ēbit	*Mon-ēbunt*	Gerund.	*Mon-endum, -ī.*

IMPERATIVE MOOD

Mon-ē warn thou	*Mon-ēte* warn ye	*Mon-ētō* thou shalt warn
Mon-ētōte ye shall warn	*Mon-ētō* he shall warn	*Mon-ento* they shall warn

(From Perfect Stem *Monu-*)

INDICATIVE MOOD		SUBJUNCTIVE MOOD	
Perfect		*Perfect*	
Monu-ī	*Monu-imus*	*Monu-erim*	*Monu-erīmus*
Monu-istī	*Monu-istis*	*Monu-erīs*	*Monu-erītis*
Monu-it	*Monu-ērunt* or *-ēre*	*Monu-erit*	*Monu-erint*

INDICATIVE MOOD		SUBJUNCTIVE MOOD	
Pluperfect		*Pluperfect*	
Monu-eram	*Monu-erāmus*	*Monu-issem*	*Monu-issēmus*
Monu-erās	*Monu-erātis*	*Monu-issēs*	*Monu-issētis*
Monu-erat	*Monu-erant*	*Monu-isset*	*Monu-issent*

Future Perfect		
Monu-erō	*Monu-erimus*	Perfect Infinitive, *Monu-isse,*
Monu-eris	*Monu-eritis*	
Monu-erit	*Monu-erint*	

(From Supine Stem *Monit-*)

First Supine, *Monit-um*   Second Supine, *Monit-ū*

Future Participle, *Monit-ūrus, -a, -um*
Future Infinitive = Future Participle + *esse* = *Monitūrus esse*

Third Conjugation. Example, *Regō*, I rule.
(From Present Stem *Reg-*.)

INDICATIVE MOOD		SUBJUNCTIVE MOOD	
Present		*Present*	
Reg-ō	*Reg-imus*	*Reg-am*	*Reg-āmus*
Reg-is	*Reg-itis*	*Reg-ās*	*Reg-ātis*
Reg-it	*Reg-unt*	*Reg-at*	*Reg-ant*

Imperfect		*Imperfect*	
Reg-ēbam	*Reg-ēbāmus*	*Reg-erem*	*Reg-erēmus*
Reg-ēbās	*Reg-ēbātis*	*Reg-erēs*	*Reg-erētis*
Reg-ēbat	*Reg-ēbant*	*Reg-eret*	*Reg-erent*

Future		
Reg-am	*Reg-ēmus*	Present Participle. *Reg-ens*
Reg-ēs	*Reg-ētis*	Present Infinitive. *Reg-ere*
Reg-et	*Reg-ent*	Gerund. *Reg-endum, -ī*

IMPERATIVE MOOD

Rege, rule thou	*Regite*, rule ye	*Regito*, thou shalt rule
Regitōte, ye shall rule	*Regitō*, he shall rule	*Reguntō*, they shall rule

(From Perfect Stem *Rex-*)

INDICATIVE MOOD		SUBJUNCTIVE MOOD	
Perfect		*Perfect*	
Rex-ī	*Rex-imus*	*Rex-erim*	*Rex-erīmus*
Rex-istī	*Rex-istis*	*Rex-eris*	*Rex-eritis*
Rex-it	*Rex-ērunt* or *-ēre*	*Rex-erit*	*Rex-erint*

Pluperfect		*Pluperfect*	
Rex-eram	*Rex-erāmus*	*Rex-issem*	*Rex-issēmus*
Rex-erās	*Rex-erātis*	*Rex-issēs*	*Rex-issētis*
Rex-erat	*Rex-erant*	*Rex-isset*	*Rex-issent*

Future Perfect		
Rex-erō	*Rex-erimus*	Perfect Infinitive, *Rex-isse*
Rex-eris	*Rex-eritis*	
Rex-erit	*Rex-erint*	

(From Supine Stem Rect-)

First Supine, Rect-um Second Supine, Rect-û

Future Participle, Rect-ūrus, -a, -um

Future Infinitive = Future Participle + esse = Rectūrus esse

Fourth Conjugation. Example, Audiō, I hear.

(From Present Stem Aud-)

INDICATIVE MOOD		SUBJUNCTIVE MOOD	
Present		*Present*	
Aud-iō	*Aud-īmus*	*Aud-iam*	*Aud-iāmus*
Aud-īs	*Aud-ītis*	*Aud-iās*	*Aud-iātis*
Aud-it	*Aud-iunt*	*Aud-iat*	*Aud-iant*
Imperfect		*Imperfect*	
Aud-iēbam	*Aud-iōbāmus*	*Aud-īrem*	*Aud-īrēmus*
Aud-iēbās	*Aud-iēbātis*	*Aud-īrēs*	*Aud-īrētis*
Aud-iēbat	*Aud iōbant*	*Aud-iret*	*Aud-īrent*

Future			
Aud-iam	*Aud-iēmus*	Present Participle.	*Aud-iens*
Aud-iēs	*Aud-iētis*	Present Infinitive.	*Aud-īre*
Aud-iet	*Aud-ient*	Gerund.	*Aud-iendum, -ī*

IMPERATIVE MOOD

Aud-ī, hear thou *Aud-īte*, hear ye *Aud-ītō*, thou shalt hear
Aud-ītōte, ye shall hear *Aud-ītō*, he shall hear *Aud-iuntó*, they shall hear

(From Perfect Stem Audīv-)

INDICATIVE MOOD		SUBJUNCTIVE MOOD	
Perfect		*Perfect*	
Audīv-ī	*Audīv-īmus*	*Audīv-erim*	*Audīv-erimus*
Audīv-istī	*Audīv-istis*	*Audīv-eris*	*Audīv-eritis*
Audīv-it	*Audīv-ērunt* or *-ēre*	*Audīv-erit*	*Audīv-erint*
Pluperfect		*Pluperfect*	
Audīv-eram	*Audīv-erāmus*	*Audīv-issem*	*Audīv-issēmus*
Audīv-erās	*Audīv-erātis*	*Audīv-issēs*	*Audīv-issētis*
Audīv-erat	*Audīv-erant*	*Audīv-isset*	*Audīv-issent*

Future Perfect			
Audīv-erō	*Audīv-erimus*		
Audīv-eris	*Audīv-eritis*	Perfect Infinitive, *Audīv-isse*	
Audīv-erit	*Audīv-erint*		

(From Supine Stem Audīt-)

First Supine *Audīt-um* Second Supine, *Audīt-û*

Future Participle, *Audīt-ūrus, -a, um*, about to hear

Future Infinitive = Future Participle + *esse* = *Audīturus esse*

Passive Voice
First Conjugation. *Amor*, I am loved.

(From Present Stem *Am-*)

INDICATIVE MOOD	SUBJUNCTIVE MOOD
Present	*Present*

Am-or, I am being loved   *Am-er*
Am-āris (-āre), you are being loved   *Am-ēris (ēre)*
Am-ātur, he is being loved   *Am-ētur*
Am-āmur, we are being loved   *Am-ēmur*
Am-āminī, you are being loved   *Am-ēminī*
Am-antur, they are being loved   *Am-entur*

Imperfect	*Imperfect*

Am-ābar, I was being loved   *Am-ārer*
Am-ābāris (-ābāre), you were being loved   *Am-ārēris (-ārēre)*
Am-ābātur, he was being loved   *Am-ārētur*
Am-ābāmur, we were being loved   *Am-ārēmur*
Am-ābāminī, you were being loved   *Am-ārēminī*
Am-ābantur, they were being loved   *Am-ārentur*

Future	

Am-ābor, I shall be loved   Present Participle
Am-āberis (-ābere), you will be loved   —
Am-ābitur, he will be loved   Present Infinitive
Am-ābimur we shall be loved   *Amārī,* to be loved
Am-ābiminī, you shall be loved   Gerundive
Am-ābuntur, they will be loved   *Amandus, -a, -um,* fit to be loved

IMPERATIVE MOOD

Am-āre } be thou loved   *Am-āminī,* be ye loved
Am-ātor }   *Am-ātor,* let him be loved
Am-antor, let them be loved

Perfect Tenses

INDICATIVE MOOD	SUBJUNCTIVE MOOD
Perfect	*Perfect*

Amātus, a, um, I have been loved   *Amātus,* etc., *sim*
Amātus, etc., *es,* you have been loved   *Amātus,* etc., *sīs*
Amātus, etc., *est,* he has been loved   *Amātus,* etc., *sit*
Amātī, etc., *sumus,* we have been loved   *Amātī,* etc., *sīmus*
Amātī, etc., *estis,* you have been loved   *Amātī,* etc., *sītis*
Amātī, etc., *sunt,* they have been loved   *Amātī,* etc., *sint*

Pluperfect	*Pluperfect*

Amātus eram, I had been loved   *Amātus essem*
Amātus erās, you had been loved   *Amātus essēs*
Amātus erat, he had been loved   *Amātus esset*
Amātī erāmus, we had been loved   *Amātī essēmus*
Amātī erātis, you had been loved   *Amātī essētis*
Amātī erant, they had been loved   *Amātī essent*

Future Perfect	

Amātus erō, I shall have been loved   Perfect Infinitive
Amātus eris, you will have been loved   *Amātus esse,* to have been loved
Amātus erit, he will have been loved
Amātī erimus, we shall have been loved
Amātī eritis, you will have been loved
Amātī erunt, they will have been loved

(From Supine Stem *Amāt-*)
Past Participle Passive, *Amātus, -a, -um.* Future Infinitive Passive,
Amātum iri, to be` about to be loved.

Second Conjugation. *Moneor,* I am warned.

(From Present Stem *Mon-*)

INDICATIVE MOOD		SUBJUNCTIVE MOOD	
Present		*Present*	
Mon-eor	*Mon-ēmur*	*Mon-ear*	*Mon-eāmur*
Mon-ēris	*Mon-ēminī*	*Mon-eāris*	*Mon-eāminī*
(or *-ēre*)		(or *-eāre*)	
Mon-ētur	*Mon-entur*	*Mon-eātur*	*Mon-eantur*
Imperfect		*Imperfect*	
Mon-ēbar	*Mon-ēbāmur*	*Mon-ērer*	*Mon-ērēmur*
Mon-ēbāris	*Mon-ēbāminī*	*Mon-ērēris*	*Mon-ērēminī*
(or *-ēbāre*)		(or *ērēre*)	
Mon-ēbātur	*Mon-ēbantur*	*Mon-ērētur*	*Mon-ērentur*
Future			
Mon-ēbor	*Mon-ēbimur*	Present Participle, —	
Mon-ēberis (or *-ēbere*)	*Mon-ēbiminī*	Present Infinitive, *Mon-ērī*	
Mon-ēbitur	*Mon-ēbuntur*	Gerundive, *Mon-endus, -a, -um*	

IMPERATIVE MOOD			
Mon-ēre	*Mon-ēminī*	*Mon-ētor*	
		Mon-ētor	*Mon-entor*

Perfect Tenses

INDICATIVE MOOD		SUBJUNCTIVE MOOD	
Perfect		*Perfect*	
Monitus sum	*Monitī sumus*	*Monitus sim*	*Monitī sīmus*
Monitus es	*Monitī estis*	*Monitus sīs*	*Monitī sītis*
Monitus est	*Monitī sunt*	*Monitus sit*	*Monitī sint*
Pluperfect		*Pluperfect*	
Monitus eram	*Monitī erāmus*	*Monitus essem*	*Monitī essēmus*
Monitus erās	*Monitī erātis*	*Monitus essēs*	*Monitī essētis*
Monitus erat	*Monitī erant*	*Monitus esset*	*Monitī essent*
Future Perfect		Perfect Infinitive, *Monitus esse*	
Monitus erō	*Monitī erimus*		
Monitus eris	*Monitī eritis*		
Monitus erit	*Monitī erunt*		

(From Supine Stem *Monit*)
Past Participle Passive, *Monitus, -a, -um*
Future Infinitive Passive, *Monitum iri*

Third Conjugation. *Regor,* I am ruled.
(From Present Stem *Reg-*)

INDICATIVE MOOD		SUBJUNCTIVE MOOD	
Present		*Present*	
Reg-or	*Reg-imur*	*Reg-ar*	*Reg-āmur*
Reg-eris (-ere)	*Reg-iminī*	*Reg-āris (-āre)*	*Reg-āminī*
Reg-itur	*Reg-untur*	*Reg-ātur*	*Reg-antur*

INDICATIVE MOOD		SUBJUNCTIVE MOOD	
Imperfect		*Imperfect*	
Reg-ēbar	Reg-ēbāmur	Reg-erer	Reg-erēmur
Reg-ēbāris	Reg-ēbāminī	Reg-erēris	Reg-erēminī
(-ēbāre)		(-erēre)	
Reg-ēbātur	Reg-ēbantur	Reg-erētur	Reg-erentur

Future		
Reg-ar	Reg-ēmur	Present Participle, —
Reg-ēris (-ēre)	Reg-ēminī	Present Infinitive, *Reg-i*
Reg-ētur	Reg-entur	Gerundive, *Reg-endus, -a, -um*

IMPERATIVE MOOD

Reg-ere	Reg-iminī	Reg-itor	
		Reg-itor	Reg-untor

Perfect Tenses

INDICATIVE MOOD		SUBJUNCTIVE MOOD	
Perfect		*Perfect*	
Rectus sum	Rectī sumus	Rectus sim	Rectī sīmus
Rectus es	Rectī estis	Rectus sīs	Rectī sītis
Rectus est	Rectī sunt	Rectus sit	Rectī sint

Pluperfect		*Pluperfect*	
Rectus eram	Rectī erāmus	Rectus essem	Rectī essēmus
Rectus erās	Rectī erātis	Rectus essēs	Rectī essētis
Rectus erat	Rectī erant	Rectus esset	Rectī essent

Future Perfect		
Rectus erō	Rectī erimus	Perfect Infinitive, *Rectus esse*
Rectus eris	Rectī eritis	
Rectus·erit	Recti erunt	

(From Supine Stem *Rect-*)
Past Participle Passive, *Rectus, -a, -um*
Future Infinitive Passive, *Rectum īrī.*

Fourth Conjugation. *Audior,* I am heard.

(From Present Stem *Aud-*)

INDICATIVE MOOD		SUBJUNCTIVE MOOD	
Present		*Present*	
Aud-ior	Aud-īmur	Aud-iar	Aud-iāmur
Aud-īris (-īre)	Aud-īminī	Aud-iāris	Aud-iāminī
		(-iāre)	
Aud-ītur	Aud-iuntur	Aud-iātur	Aud-iantur

Imperfect		*Imperfect*	
Aud-iēbār	Aud-iēbāmur	Aud-īrer	Aud-īrēmur
Aud-iēbāris	Aud-iēbāminī	Aud-īrēris	Aud-īrēminī
(-iēbāre)		(-īrēre)	
Aud-iēbātur	Aud-iēbantur	Aud-īrētur	Aud-īrentur

Future		
Aud-iar	Aud-iēmur	Present Participle, —
Aud-iēris	Aud-iēminī	Present Infinitive, *Aud-īrī*
(-iēre)		Gerundive, *Aud-iendus, -a, -um*
Aud-iētur	Aud-ientur	

Aud-īre   *Aud-īminī*

IMPERATIVE MOOD

     Aud-ītor
     Aud-ītor   *·Aud-iuntor*

Perfect Tenses

INDICATIVE MOOD		SUBJUNCTIVE MOOD	
Perfect		**Perfect**	
Audītus sum	*Audītī sumus*	*Audītus sim*	*Audītī sīmus*
Audītus es	*Audītī estis*	*Audītus sīs*	*Audītī sītis*
Audītus est	*Audītī sunt*	*Audītus sit*	*Audītī sint*
Pluperfect		**Pluperfect**	
Audītus eram	*Audītī erāmus*	*Audītus essem*	*Audītī essēmus*
Audītus erās	*Audītī erātis*	*Audītus essēs*	*Audītī essētis*
Audītus erat	*Audītī erant*	*Audītus esset*	*Audītī essent*

Future Perfect		
Audītus erō	*Audītī erimus*	Perfect Infinitive, *Audītus esse*
Audītus eris	*Audītī eritis*	
Audītus erit	*Audītī erunt*	

(From Supine Stem *Audīt-*)
Past Participle Passive, *Audītus, -a, -um*
Future Infinitive Passive, *Audītum īrī.*

IRREGULAR VERBS

Verb *Sum*, I am

(Tenses from the Present Stems)

INDICATIVE	SUBJUNCTIVE
Present	*Present*
sum, I am	*sim*
es, you are	*sīs*
est, he is	*sit*
sumus, we are	*sīmus*
estis, you are	*sītis*
sunt, they are	*sint*
Imperfect	*Imperfect*
eram, I was	*essem*
erās, you were	*essēs*
erat, he was	*esset*
erāmus, we were	*essēmus*
erātis, you were	*essētis*
erant, they were	*essent*
Future	
erō, I shall be	Present Infinitive
eris, you will be	*Esse*, to be
erit, he will be	
erimus, we shall be	
eritis, you will be	
erunt, they will be	

IMPERATIVE

Es, be (thou)	*Estō*, you shall be
Este, be (ye)	*Estōte*, you shall be
	Estō, he shall be
	Suntō, they shall be

(From Perfect Stem *Fu-*)

INDICATIVE	SUBJUNCTIVE
Perfect	*Perfect*

Fu-ī, I have been or I was	*Fu-erim*
Fu-istī, you have been or you were	*Fu-eris*
Fu-it, he has been or he was	*Fu-erit*
Fu-imus, we have been or we were	*Fu-erīmus*
Fu-istis, you have been or you were	*Fu-erītis*
Fu-ērunt or *-ēre*, they have been or they were	*Fu-erint*

Pluperfect	*Pluperfect*
Fu-eram, I had been	*Fu-issem*
Fu-erās, you had been	*Fu-issēs*
Fu-erat, he had been	*Fu-isset*
Fu-erāmus, we had been	*Fu-issēmus*
Fu-erātis, you had been	*Fu-issētis*
Fu-erant, they had been	*Fu-issent*

Future Perfect	
Fu-erō, I shall have been	Perfect Infinitive,
Fu-eris, you will have been	*Fu-isse*, to have been
Fu-erit, he will have been	
Fu-erimus, we shall have been	
Fu-eritis, you will have been	
Fu-erint, they will have been	

(From Supine Stem *Fut-*)

First Supine, wanting. Second Supine, wanting
Future Participle, *Futūrus, -a, -um*, about to be
Future Infinitive, *Futūrus esse*, to be about to be

Tables of the commoner irregular verbs are given below:

Possum	*posse*	*potuī*	—	to be able
Volō	*velle*	*voluī*	—	to wish
Nōlō	*nolle*	*nōluī*	—	to be unwilling
Ferō	*ferre*	*tulī*	*lātum*	to bear, bring
Fīō	*fierī*	*factus sum*		to become, be made
Eō	*īre*	*iī*	*itum*	to go

Ferre, (to bear) and *īre*, (to go) have many compounds which are conjugated like the basic verb given below:

Active

INDICATIVE

Present	Singular			Plural		
Pos-sum	*pot-es*	*pot-est*		*pos-sumus*	*pot-estis*	*pos-sunt*
Volō	*vīs*	*vult*		*volumus*	*vultis*	*volunt*
Nōlō	*nōnvīs*	*nōnvult*		*nōlumus*	*nōnvultis*	*nōlunt*
Mālō	*māvīs*	*māvult*		*mālumus*	*māvultis*	*mālunt*
Ferō	*fers*	*fert*		*ferimus*	*fertis*	*ferunt*
Fīō	*fīs*	*fit*		—	—	*fīunt*
Eō	*īs*	*it*		*īmus*	*ītis*	*eunt*

Imperfect

| Pot-eram | -erās | -erat | -erāmus | -erātis | -erant |

| Volĕ-
Nōlĕ-
Mālĕ-
Ferĕ-
Fīĕ-
Ī- }bam | -bās | -bat | -bāmus | -bātis | -bant |

Future

| Pot-erō | -eris | -erit | -erimus | -eritis | -erun |

| Vol-
Nōl-
Māl-
Fer-
Fī- }am | -ēs | -et | -ēmus | -ētis | -ent |
| Īb-ō | -is | -it | -imus | -itis | -unt |

Perfect, Pluperfect, Future Perfect Tenses are formed regularly from
the Perfect Stem.

PARTICIPLE	INFINITIVE	GERUND
	posse	
Vol- Nōl- Māl- Fer- Ī— }ens Gen. *euntis*	*velle* *nolle* *malle* *ferre* *fieri* *ire*	vol- nōl- māl- fer- }endum, -ī e-undum

SUBJUNCTIVE

	Singular			Plural	

Present

| Pos-sim | pos-sīs | pos-sit | pos-sīmus | pos-sītis | pos-sint |

| Vel-
Nōl-
Māl- }im | -īs | -it | -īmus | -ītis | -int |

| Fer-
Fī-
E- }am | -ās | -at | -āmus | -ātis | -ant |

	Singular			Plural	

Imperfect

| Poss-
Vell-
Noll-
Mall-
Ferr-
Fier-
Ir- }-em | -ēs | -et | -ēmus | -ētis | -ent |

IMPERATIVE

	Singular		Plural	
Nōl-ī, nōl-ītō	nōl-ītō	nōl-īte, nōl-ītōte	nōl-untō
Fer, fer-tō	fer-tō	fer-te, fer-tōte	fer-untō
Fī		fī-te	
Ī, ī-tō	ī-tō	ī-te, ī-tōte	e-untō

Passive

INDICATIVE

	Singular			Plura		
Present						
Fer-or	*fer-ris*	*fer-tur*	*fer-imur*	*fer-iminī*	*fer-untur*	
Imperfect						
Fer-ēbar	*fer-ēbāris*	*fer-ēbātur*	*fer-ēbāmur*	*fer-ēbāminī*	*fer-ēbāntur*	
Future						
Fer-ar	*Fer-ēris*	*er-ētur*	*fer-ēmur*	*fer-ēminī*	*fer-entur*	

SUBJUNCTIVE

Present						
Fer-ar	*fer-āris*	*fer-ātur*	*fer-āmur*	*fer-āminī*	*fer-antur*	
Imperfect						
Ferr-er	*ferr-ēris*	*ferrētur*	*ferr-ēmur*	*ferr-ēminī*	*ferr-entur*	

IMPERATIVE

Fer-re, fer-tor	*fer-tor*	*fer-iminī*	*fer-untor*

Gerundive: *Fer-endus*   Present Infinitive: *Ferr-ī*

DEPONENT VERBS

Many Latin verbs are passive in form but active in meaning, e.g. *hortor* "I exhort"; *hortātus sum*, "I have exhorted"; *hortārī*, "to exhort". They are conjugated like ordinary passive verbs, but of course they have no passive meanings themselves. *Hortor* means "I exhort". If you want to say in Latin "I am exhorted", you have to use a different verb.

There are, however, two exceptions to the above rule.

1. Most deponent verbs still keep their active voice forms for the present and future participle, future infinitive and gerund, e.g. *morior*, "I die"; *moriens*, "dying"; *moritūrus*, "about to die"; *moritūrus esse*, "to be about to die"; *moriendum* (gerund) "dying".

2. Their gerundives are passive both in form and meaning. E.g. *hortandus*, "fit to be exhorted".

N.B. The past participle is passive in form, but active in meaning, e.g. *veritus*, "having feared".

Here is a list of some of the commoner deponent verbs:

	Present Tense	*Infinitive*	*Perfect Tense*	*Meaning*
1st conjugation	*cōnor*	*cōnārī*	*cōnātus sum*	to try
	hortor	*hortārī*	*hortātus sum*	to exhort
	vēnor	*vēnārī*	*vēnātus sum*	to hunt
2nd conjugation	*vereor*	*verērī*	*veritus sum*	to fear
	polliceor	*pollicērī*	*pollicitus sum*	to promise
3rd conjugation	*patior*	*patī*	*passus sum*	to suffer
	ūtor	*ūtī*	*ūsus sum*	to use
	morior	*morī*	*mortuus sum*	to die
	aggredior	*aggredī*	*agressus sum*	to attack
	prōgredior	*prōgredī*	*prōgressus sum*	to set out
	ingredior	*ingredī*	*ingressus sum*	to enter
	regredior	*regredī*	*regressus sum*	to return
	loquor	*loquī*	*locūtus sum*	to speak
	proficiscor	*proficiscī*	*profectus sum*	to set out
4th conjugation	*partior*	*partīrī*	*partītus sum*	to share
	orior	*orīrī*	*ortus sum*	to rise

IMPERSONAL VERBS

There are certain verbs in Latin which can only be used in the third person singular and in the infinitive. They never have a personal subject but always the pronoun "it": hence they are called Impersonal Verbs. These verbs have only the third person singular *of each tense*, an infinitive, and a gerund. They may be divided into four types.

(*a*) Verbs which have an accusative of the person and a genitive of the cause:

Present	Perfect	Infinitive	Meaning
Miseret	*miseruit*	*miserēre*	it pities
Paenitet	*paenituit*	*paenitēre*	it repents
Pudet	*puduit*	*pudēre*	it shames
Taedet	*taeduit*	*taedēre*	it wearies
Piget	*piguit*	*pigēre*	it annoys, vexes

Example:
Pudet me huius facti, I am ashamed of this deed.

(*b*) In this class are two verbs which take a genitive of person, unless a personal pronoun is used, in which case they take the feminine ablative singular of the possessive pronoun. These verbs are *interest* (from *inter-sum*) and *rēfert* (from *re-fero*), both meaning "it matters", "it is important", "it is in the interests of—".

Example:
Interest civium regem bene regere. It is in the interest of the citizens that the king should rule well.
Quid id refert tua? What does it matter to you?

(*c*) Verbs taking the accusative and infinitive:
Oportet me, it behoves me; I ought
Decet me, it becomes me
Dēdecet me, it does not become me
Iuvat me, it delights me, I delight.

Example:
Oportet me hoc facere, I ought to do this
Oportuit me hoc facere, I ought to have done this.

(*d*) Verbs taking the dative and infinitive:
Licet mihi, it is permitted to me, I may
Accidit tibi, it happens to you
Libet } *eis*, it is pleasing to them, they are pleased.
Placet

Example:
Tibi abesse licet, you may be absent.

DEFECTIVE VERBS

There are a number of verbs in Latin which lack a considerable number of parts. The commonest of them are:

Coepī, I have begun

Perfect	Fut. Perfect	Pluperfect	Infinitive	Perf. Subj.	Pluperf. Subj
Coepī	*coeperō*	*coeperam*	*coepisse*	*coeperim*	*coepissem*

Odī, I hate

Ōdī	*ōderō*	*ōderam*	*ōdisse*	*ōderim*	*ōdissem*

Meminī, I remember

Meminī	*meminerō*	*memineram*	*meminisse*	*meminerim*	*meminissem*

Nōvī, I have got to know, I know

Nōvī	*nōverō*	*nōveram*	*nōvisse*	*nōverim*	*nōvissem*

Inquam, I say

Pres. tense	*Inquam*,	*inquis*	*inquit*	*inquimus*	*inquitis*	*inquiunt*
Imperfect	—	—	*inquiēbat*	—	—	*inquiēbant*
Future	—	—	*inquiet*	—	—	—
Perfect	—	*inquistī*	*inquit*	—	—	—

Fārī, to speak

Pres. tense	—	—	*fātur*	—	—	—
Future	*Fābor*	—	*fābitur*	—	—	—

Present Participle, acc. *Fantem*; Perfect, *Fātus*.
Gerund, *Fandī, fando*; Gerundive, *Fandus*.

Note that *memini* and *odi* are perfect in form, but present in meaning. The tenses which are missing from these verbs can often be supplied by other verbs with the same meaning, e.g. *incipio* (begin) can supply present, future, and imperfect tenses meaning I begin, I shall begin, etc.

PRONOUNS

1. *Personal Pronouns.* Latin has pronouns to translate our English "I" and "you", but they are employed in the nominative cases, only when very emphatic.

	Singular			Plural	
Nom.	*ego*	I	*nōs*		we
Acc.	*mē*	me	*nōs*		us
Gen.	*meī*	of me	*nostrum, nostrī*[1]		of us
Dat.	*mihī*	to, for me	*nōbīs*		to, for us
Abl.	*mē*	from me	*nōbīs*		from us
Nom.	*tū*	you	*vōs*		you
Acc.	*tē*	you	*vōs*		you
Gen.	*tuī*	of you	*vestrum, vestrī*[1]		of you
Dat.	*tibī*	to, for you	*vōbīs*		to, for you
Abl.	*tē*	from you	*vōbīs*		from you

[1] *Nostrum* and *vestrum* are partitive genitives, e.g. *Unus vestrum*, one of you. *Nostri* and *vestri* are objective genitives, e.g. *memor vestri*, mindful of you.

2. *Reflexive Pronouns*. This pronoun is used when the subject of the verb is denoted as acting on itself, e.g. The enemy are slaying themselves. *Hostes se interficiunt.*

Acc.   *sē* (or *sēsē*), himself, herself, itself, themselves.
Gen.   *suī*, of himself, etc.
Dat.   *sibī*, to, for himself, etc.
Abl.   *sē* (or *sēsē*), by, with, from himself, etc.

3. *Demonstrative Pronouns*. There are two common demonstrative pronouns in Latin which mean that; *is* and *ille*. They can also mean "he", "she" or "it". *Ille* has a stronger demonstrative force than *is*, meaning "that" (over there, near him). Declined exactly like *ille* is *iste*, meaning "that over there, near you".

	Singular			*Plura*		
	Masc.	Fem.	Neut.	Masc.	Fem.	Neut.
Nom.	*is*	*ea*	*id*	*eī (iī)*	*eae*	*ea*
Acc.	*eum*	*eam*	*id*	*eōs*	*eās*	*ea*
Gen.	*eius*	*eius*	*eius*	*eōrum*	*eārum*	*eōrum*
Dat.	*eī*	*eī*	*eī*	*eīs (īīs)*	*eīs*	*eīs*
Abl.	*eō*	*eā*	*eō*	*eīs*	*eīs*	*eīs*
Nom.	*ille*	*illa*	*illud*	*illī*	*illae*	*illa*
Acc.	*illum*	*illam*	*illud*	*illōs*	*illās*	*illa*
Gen.	*illīus*	*illīus*	*illīus*	*illōrum*	*illārum*	*illōrum*
Dat.	*illī*	*illī*	*illī*	*illīs*	*illīs*	*illīs*
Abl.	*illō*	*illā*	*illō*	*illīs*	*illīs*	*illīs*

The pronoun meaning "this" is *hic, haec, hoc.*

	Masc.	Fem.	Neut.	Masc.	Fem.	Neut.
Nom.	*hic*	*haec*	*hōc*	*hī*	*hae*	*haec*
Acc.	*hunc*	*hanc*	*hōc*	*hōs*	*hās*	*haec*
Gen.	*huius*	*huius*	*huius*	*hōrum*	*hārum*	*hōrum*
Dat.	*huic*	*huic*	*huic*	*his*	*his*	*his*
Abl.	*hōc*	*hāc*	*hōc*	*his*	*his*	*hic*

The pronoun meaning "the same" is *idem.*

	Singular			*Plural*		
	Masc.	Fem.	Neut.	Masc.	Fem.	Neut.
Nom.	*īdem*	*eadem*	*idem*	*eīdem*	*eaedem*	*eadem*
Acc.	*eundem*	*eandem*	*idem*	*eōsdem*	*eāsdem*	*eadem*
Gen.	*eiusdem*	*eiusdem*	*eiusdem*	*eōrundem*	*eārundem*	*eōrundem*
Dat.	*eīdem*	*eīdem*	*eīdem*	*eīsdem*	*eīsdem*	*eīsdem*
				(or *īsdem*)		
Abl.	*eōdem*	*eādem*	*eōdem*	*eīsdem*	*eīsdem*	*eīsdem*

4. *Emphatic Pronoun*. *Ipse*, a pronoun meaning "— self", simply emphasizes the noun or pronoun to which it refers, e.g. *Puer ipse cantat.* The boy himself sings.

	Singular			*Plural*		
	Masc.	Fem.	Neut.	Masc.	Fem.	Neut.
Nom.	*ipse*	*ipsa*	*ipsum*	*ipsī*	*ipsae*	*ipsa*
Acc.	*ipsum*	*ipsam*	*ipsum*	*ipsōs*	*ipsās*	*ipsa*
Gen.	*ipsīus*	*ipsīus*	*ipsīus*	*ipsōrum*	*ipsārum*	*ipsōrum*
Dat.	*ipsī*	*ipsī*	*ipsī*	*ipsīs*	*ipsīs*	*ipsīs*
Abl.	*ipsō*	*ipsā*	*ipsō*	*ipsīs*	*ipsīs*	*ipsīs*

5. *Relative Pronouns.* The relative pronoun, "who", "which", is *qui, quae, quod*. In Latin this pronoun takes its number (singular or plural) and its gender (masc., fem., or neut.) from the word in the main clause of the sentence to which it refers (its antecedent). But its case is determined by its own clause, i.e. depending on whether it is the subject or object, etc., of the verb. The pronoun is declined as follows.

	Singular			*Plural*		
	Masc.	Fem.	Neut.	Masc.	Fem.	Neut.
Nom.	qui	quae	quod	qui	quae	quae
Acc.	quem	quam	quod	quōs	quās	quae
Gen.	cuius	cuius	cuius	quōrum	quārum	quōrum
Dat.	cui	cui	cui	quibus	quibus	quibus
Abl.	quō	quā	quō	quibus	quibus	quibus

6. *Interrogative Pronoun.* *Quis,* who? what? is declined in all cases except the nominative and accusative in the same way as the relative pronoun.

	Singular		
	Masc.	Fem.	Neut.
Nom.	quis	quis	quid
Acc.	quem	quam	quid

7. *Other Pronouns.* A list of other pronouns in common use is given below:

Masc.	Fem.	Neut.	Meaning
quīdam	quaedam	quoddam	a certain (person) (thing)
aliquis	aliqua	aliquid	someone, something
quivis	quaevis	quodvis }	anyone you like
quilibet	quaelibet	quodlibet }	
quisque	quaeque	quodque	each
quicumque	quaecumque	quodcumque }	whosoever, whatsoever
quisquis	quisquis	quidquid }	
quisquam	quaequam	quidquam	anyone

PREPOSITIONS

In Latin prepositions help the inflections or endings of nouns, adjectives, and pronouns to show the relations between them and other words in a sentence. They are also compounded with verbs, to change the meaning of the original verb, e.g. *eo,* I go; *abeo,* I go away.

The following is a list of the prepositions used with the ablative case:
ā, ab, cum, dē, cōram, palam, ē, ex, sine, tenus, prō, prae
Nearly all other prepositions are used with the accusative case.

The following prepositions take the accusative when "motion towards" is meant, and the ablative when "place where" is meant.

in	in, on, into	*super*	upon, over
sub	under, up to	*subter*	under

CONJUNCTIONS

Conjunctions are words which join together words or sentences. The commonest of them are given, with their meanings, and in alphabetical order, below.

after	*postquam.* (with verb in indicative)
and	*et, atque, āc, -que* (joined to a word)
and . . . lest	*neu, nēve* (with verb in subjunctive)
and . . . not	*nec, neque*
although	*quamquam* (with factual concessive clause); *quamvis* (hypothetical)
as	*ut* (with verb in indicative)
as if	*quasi*
as soon as	*cum prīmum, ut prīmum, simul āc (atque)*
because	*quod, quia, quoniam, cum*
before	*antequam, priusquam* (with indicative when purely temporal; subjunctive when there is an additional idea of intention)
both . . . and	*et . . . et*
but	*sed, autem* (second word)
but . . . not	*neque . . . vēro*
either . . . or	*aut . . . aut, vel . . . vel*
for	*nam, namque, enim* (second word)
for . . . not	*neque . . . enim*
however	*tamen, autem*
if	*sī* (with indicative or subjunctive, depending on the type of conditional sentence)
if not	*nisi, sī . . . non*
just as if	*tamquam si* (with verb in subjunctive)
neither	*nec, neque*
neither . . . nor	*neque . . . neque, nec . . . nec*
nevertheless	*tamen*
or	*aut, vel;* (in questions) *an*
questions are introduced by	*ne* (joined to the first word in the sentence) *nonne* (introducing a question expecting the answer "yes") *num* (introducing a question expecting the answer "no")
since	*cum, quoniam*
so (in such a way) . . . that	*ita . . . ut*
so that (purpose)	*ut*
so that . . . never	*ut numquam* (consecutive); *nē umquam* (purpose)
so that . . . not	*ut nōn* (consecutive); *nē* (purpose)
so that . . . no-one	*ut nēmo* (consecutive); *nē quis* (purpose)
so that . . . nowhere	*ut nusquam* (consecutive); *nē usquam* (purpose)
therefore	*itaque, igitur*
until	*dum, dōnec* (with verb in indicative when purely temporal, subjunctive when there is an additional idea of purpose)
when	*cum, ubĭ* (temporal); *quandō* (interrogative)
where	*ubĭ* (relative and interrogative)
whether	*num* (introducing single indirect questions); *ŭtrum* (introducing alternative indirect questions); *sīve, seu* (introducing alternative conditional sentences)
while	*dum* (usually with verb in indicative)
whither	*quō* (relative and interrogative)
why	*cur, quārē*

ADVERBS

In Latin it is easy to make adverbs from adjectives. With adjectives of Class I, simply add -e to the stem of the adjective to form the adverb, e.g. *benignus* (kind), genitive singular, *benigni*, adverb, *benignē* (kindly); *liber* (free), genitive singular, *liberi*, adverb, *liberē* (freely). Note these common exceptions to this rule, *subitus* (sudden), gives *subitō*; *falsus* (false), gives *falsō*; *necessārius* (necessary), gives *necessāriō*.

In adjectives of the second class, add -*iter* to the stem, e.g. *ferox*, (fierce,) genitive singular, *ferōc-is*, adverb, *ferōciter*. Note that adjectives like *prūdens* (prudent), simply add -*er* to the stem, *prūdenter*, (prudently).

Common Irregular Adverbs

bene, well	*diū*, for a long time
multum, much	*saepe*, often
magnoperē, greatly	*tandem*, at length

Comparison of Adverbs

The comparative of an adverb is simply the neuter singular of the comparative adjective. The superlative is obtained from the superlative of the adjective by changing the -*us* ending into -*e*, e.g.

	Positive	Comparative	Superlative
Adjective	*liber*, free	*liberior*	*liberrimus*
Adverb	*liberē*, freely	*liberius*	*liberrimē*
Adjective	*prūdens*, prudent	*prūdentior*	*prūdentissimus*
Adverb	*prūdenter*, prudently	*prūdentius*	*prūdentissimē*

A few adverbs are compared irregularly:

bene (*bonus*), well	*melius*, better	*optimē*, best
male (*malus*), badly	*pēius*, worse	*pessimē*, worst
multum (*multus*), much	*plūs*, more	*plūrimum*, most
magnoperē (*magnus*), greatly	*magis*, more	*maximē*, most
paulum (*parvus*), little	*minus*, less	*minimē*, least
diū, for a long time	*diūtius*, longer	*diūtissimē*, longest
saepe, often	*saepius*, oftener	*saepissimē*, oftenest

NUMERALS

	CARDINAL	ORDINAL
1	*Ūn-us, -a, -um*, one	*Prīm-us, -a, -um*, first
2	*Du-o, -ae, -o*, two	*Secund-us, -a, -um, (alter)*, second
3	*Trēs, tria*, three	*Terti-us, -a, -um*, third
4	*Quattuor*, four	*Quart-us, -a, -um*, fourth
5	*Quinque*	*Quint-us, -a, -um,*
6	*Sex*	*Sext-us, -a, -um*
7	*Septem*	*Septim-us, -a, -um*
8	*Octō*	*Octāv-us, -a, -um*
9	*Novem*	*Nōn-us, -a, -um*
10	*Decem*	*Decim-us, -a, -um*
11	*Undecim*	*Undecim-us, -a, -um*
12	*Duodecim*	*Duodecim-us, -a, -um*
13	*Trēdecim*	*Tertius decim-us, -a, -um*, etc.
14	*Quattuordecim*	*Quart-us decim-us*, etc.
15	*Quindecim*	*Quint-us decim-us*, etc.
16	*Sēdecim*	*Sext-us decim-us*, etc.

17	Septendecim	Septim-us decim-us, etc.
18	Duodēvīgintī	Duodēvīcēsim-us, etc.
19	Undēvīgint	Undēvīcēsim-us, etc.
20	Vīgintī	Vīcēsim-us, etc.
30	Trīgintā	Trīcēsim-us, etc.
40	Quădrāgintā	Quădrāgēsim-us, etc.
50	Quinquāgintā	Quinquāgēsim-us, etc.
60	Sexāgintā	Sexāgēsim-us, etc.
70	Septuāgintā	Septuāgēsim-us, etc.
80	Octōgintā	Octōgēsim-us, etc.
90	Nōnāgintā	Nōnāgēsim-us, etc.
100	Centum	Centēsim-us, etc.
200	Ducent-ī, -ae, -a	Ducentēsim-us, etc.
300	Trecent-ī, -ae, -a	Trecentēsim-us, etc.
400	Quădringent-ī, -ae, -a	Quădringentēsim-us, etc.
500	Quingent-ī, -ae, -a	Quingentēsimus
600	Sescent-ī, -ae, -a	Sexcentēsim-us, etc.
700	Septingent-ī, -ae, -a	Septingentēsim-us, etc.
800	Octingent-ī, -ae, -a	Octingentēsim-us, etc.
900	Nongent-ī, -ae, -a	Nongentēsim-us, etc.
1,000	Mīlle (indeclinable)	Millēsim-us, etc.
2,000	Duo mīlia (followed by genitive case)	Bis millēsim-us, etc.
100,000	Centum mīlia	Centiēs millēsim-us, etc.
1,000,000	Deciēs centēna mīlia	Deciēs centiēs millēsim-us, etc.

	DISTRIBUTIVE	NUMERAL ADVERBS
1	Singul-ī, -ae, -a, one each	Semel, once
2	Bīn-ī, -ae, -a, two each	Bis, twice
3	Tern-ī (trīn-ī), -ae, -a, three each	Ter, thrice
4	Quatern-ī, -ae, -a, four each	Quater, four times
5	Quīn-ī, -ae, -a	Quinquiēs
6	Sēn-ī, -ae, -a	Sexiēs
7	Septēn-ī, -ae, -a	Septiēs
8	Octōn-ī, -ae, -a	Octiēs
9	Novēn-ī, -ae, -a	Noviēs
10	Dēn-ī, -ae, -a	Deciēs
11	Undēn-ī, -ae, -a	Undeciēs
12	Duodēn-ī, -ae, -a	Duodeciēs
13	Tern-ī dēn-ī, -ae, -a	Ter deciēs
14	Quatern-ī dēn-ī, -ae, -a	Quater deciēs
15	Quīn-ī dēn-ī, -ae, -a	Quinquiēs deciēs
16	Sēn-ī dēn-ī, -ae, -a	Sexiēs deciēs
17	Septēn-ī dēn-ī, -ae, -a	Septiēs deciēs
18	Duodēvīcēn-ī, -ae, -a	Duodēvīciēs
19	Undēvīcēn-ī, -ae, -a	Undēvīciēs
20	Vīcēn-ī, -ae, -a	Vīciēs
30	Trīcēn-ī, -ae, -a	Trīciēs
40	Quădrāgēn-ī, -ae, -a	Quădrāgiēs
50	Quinquāgēn-ī, -ae, -a	Quinquāgiēs
60	Sexāgēn-ī, -ae, -a	Sexāgiēs
70	Septuāgēn-ī, -ae, -a	Septuāgiēs
80	Octōgēn-ī, -ae, -a	Octōgiēs
90	Nōnāgēn-ī, -ae, -a	Nōnāgiēs
100	Centēn-ī, -ae, -a	Centiēs
200	Ducēn-ī, -ae, -a	Ducentiēs
300	Trecēn-ī, -ae, -a	Trecentiēs
400	Quădringēn-ī, -ae, -a	Quădringentiēs

500	Quingēn-ī, -ae, -a	Quingentiēs
600	Sescēn-ī, -ae, -a	Sexcentiēs
700	Septingēn-ī, -ae, -a	Septingentiēs
800	Octingēn-ī, -ae, -a	Octingentiēs
900	Nōngēn-ī, -ae, -a	Nongentiēs
1,000	Singula mīlia	Mīliēs
2,000	Bīna mīlia	Bis mīliēs
100,000	Centēna mīlia	Centiēs mīliēs
1,000,000	Deciēs centēna mīlia	Deciēs centiēs mīliēs

Ūnus, *duo*, and *trēs* are declined as follows. The cardinals from *quattuor* to *centum* are indeclinable. *Ducentī*, *trecentī*, etc., are declined as the plural of *bonus*.

	Singular			Plural		
	Masc.	Fem.	Neut.	Masc.	Fem.	Neut.
Nom.	ūnus	ūna	ūnum	ūnī	ūnae	ūna
Acc.	ūnum	ūnam	ūnum	ūnōs	ūnās	ūna
Gen.	ūnīus	ūnīus	ūnīus	ūnōrum	ūnārum	ūnōrum
Dat.	ūnī	ūnī	ūnī	ūnīs	ūnīs	ūnīs
Abl.	ūnō	ūnā	ūnō	ūnīs	ūnīs	ūnīs

	Plural			Plural		
	Masc.	Fem.	Neut.	Masc.	Fem.	Neut.
Nom.	duo	duae	duo	trēs	trēs	tria
Acc.	duōs, (duo)	duās	duo	trēs	trēs	tria
Gen.	duōrum	duārum	duōrum	trium	trium	trium
Dat.	duōbus	duābus	duōbus	tribus	tribus	tribus
Abl.	duōbus	duābus	duōbus	tribus	tribus	tribus

ROMAN CALENDAR

There were twelve months in the Roman year. The Latin word for month is *mensis*, m., and the names of the months are given as adjectives, agreeing with *mensis* (understood).

Thus:

Jānuārius	January	*Jūlius* (or *Quintīlis*)	July
Februārius	February	*Augustus* (or *Sextīlis*)	August
Martius	March	*September*	September
Aprīlis	April	*Octōber*	October
Māius	May	*November*	November
Jūnius	June	*December*	December

There were three chief days in each month:

- 1st = *Kalendae* (Calends)
- 5th = *Nōnae* (Nones)
- 13th = *Īdus* (Ides)

but "in March, July, October, May the Nones fall on the 7th day," and the Ides 8 days later, on the 15th.

Dating

(a) For one of the chief days, e.g. on the first of January, use the ablative case (point of time) with the name of the month in agreement, *Kalendīs Januariis*; 13th November, *Idibus Novembribus*.

(b) For the day before one of the chief days, e.g. on the 4th of January; use the word *prīdiē* (on the day before) with the chief day and the name of the month in the accusative case, *pridie Nonas Januarias*; 30th September, *pridie Kalendas Octobres.*

(c) For any other day, e.g. 3rd January, reckon backwards from the next chief day, in this case the *Nonae* (5th), but do so "inclusively", counting in the days at both ends. So, for days before the *Nonae*, or the *Idus*, subtract the day you require from the day on which the next chief day falls, and increase by one. For days before the *Kalendae* subtract the day you require from the number of days in the month, and increase by two. Then use the following formula: *ante diem* (ordinal number), *important day* (acc.), *name of month* (acc.).

Examples: 3rd January—*ante diem* tertium *Nonas Januarias*
26th September: *ante diem* sextum *Kalendas Octobres.*

MONEY, WEIGHTS, MEASURES

I. *Roman Money* (1)

Bronze or Copper Coinage
As—originally a bar of bronze, 1 lb in weight, later 2 ounces

Sēmis	one-half *as*
Triens	one-third *as*
Quādruns	one-quarter *as*
Sextans	one-sixth *as*
Uncia	one-twelfth *as, as* one ounce.

(2) Silver Coinage

Dēnārius	10 *asses,* later 16
Quīnārius	5 *asses,* later 8
Sestertius	2½ *asses,* later 4; this was the ordinary coin of the Romans, used in the reckoning of even the largest sums. Its symbol was HS.

Sestertium = 1,000 *Sestertii.*

(3) Gold Coinage

Denarius aureus (or simply *"aureus"*) was the standard gold coin of the Romans, equivalent in value to 25 silver *denarii,* or 100 *sestertii.*

II. *Weights*

Libra. This was the unit of weight, the Roman pound.
Uncia. The *libra* (pound) was divided into 12 *unciae* (ounces).

III. *Measures*

Length: *Pes.* This was the unit of length, equivalent to our "foot".
Uncia. This *pes* (foot) was divided into 12 *unciae* (inches).
Passus. This was equivalent to 5 *pedes* (5 feet).
Mille Passus (pl. *milia passuum*) was one Roman mile (1,620 yards).

Area: *iugerum,* equivalent to five-eighths of an acre.

Capacity:
coclear	= a "spoonful"	
cyathus	= one-twelfth sextarius	= 0·08 of a pint
sextārius	= 0·96 of a pint	
modius	= 16 sextarii	= 15 pints
amphora	= 48 sextarii	= 5 gallons 6 pints.

TIME, PLACE, SPACE

Time

(a) Point of time, or the time *at which* something happens, is expressed in Latin by the ablative case, e.g.

Auctumno folia sunt rubra.
In autumn the leaves are red.

(b) Duration of time, or the time *during which* something happens, is expressed in Latin by the accusative case, e.g.

Viginti annos Poeni cum Romanis bellabant.
During twenty years the Carthaginians waged war with the Romans.

(c) The time *within which* something happens (usually denoted by the word "in" or "within" in the English) is expressed in Latin by the ablative case, e.g.

Tribus mensibus redibit.
He will return *within three months.*

Place

(a) *Motion towards* a place is expressed in Latin by a preposition (*in, ad*) with the accusative case, except where names of towns or small islands, *domus* (house), and *rus* (countryside) are concerned. With these use the accusative case without a preposition, e.g.

Ad villam eò, I go to the country-house.
Romam eo, I go to Rome.

(b) *Motion from* a place is expressed in Latin by a preposition (*a, ab, e, ex*) with the ablative case, except where the names of towns or small islands, *domus* (house) and *rus* (countryside) are concerned. With these use the ablative case without a preposition, e.g.

Ab Africa navigavit, he sailed from Africa.
Rure venit, he comes from the country.

(c) *Place where, Rest in* a place is expressed in Latin by the preposition *in* with the ablative case, except where the names of towns or small islands, *domus* (house) and *rus* (countryside) are concerned. With these use the locative case, which in a singular noun of the First or Second Declension is like the genitive case, e.g. *Romae* (at Rome), *Londinii* (in London), and in all other nouns is like the ablative case, e.g. *Carthagine* (at Carthage), *Athenis* (in Athens).

N.B. at home, *domi*; in the countryside, *ruri.*

Space

Extent of space is expressed in Latin by the accusative case, e.g.

Tria milia passuum progressus est.
He advanced three miles.

Space which is the *amount of difference* between two points is expressed in Latin by the ablative case. (There is usually a comparative adjective in such a phrase.) e.g. This wall is three feet higher than that one. *Altior illo hic murus est tribus pedibus.*

LATIN

A Complete Course

GAVIN BETTS

A comprehensive introduction, enriched with authentic Latin poetry and prose passages, to help the beginner approach Latin translation and reading with confidence.

This lively and clearly structured course progresses in easily assimilated stages and assumes no prior knowledge of Latin or of grammatical terms. Each of the units has two sections, the first utilising well-chosen examples to explain new grammar, the second containing carefully graded Latin sentences and passages. Where appropriate, a third section is included, either to introduce the reader to a topic of interest for Latin or Roman studies, or to give additional reading which introduces some of the most famous Roman authors. Revision exercises are provided after every third unit.

Grammatical tables, a key to all exercises, an extensive Latin–English vocabulary and an index are provided at the end of the book.

TEACH YOURSELF BOOKS

ANCIENT GREEK
A Complete Course

GAVIN BETTS and ALAN HENRY

An introduction to the language of the people who began Western civilisation.

This book presents the Ancient Greek language clearly and precisely, without academic stuffiness or unnecessary detail. Each of the 25 units contains grammar practice and a reading exercise, with a revision section provided at the end of the book. Additional information on topics such as the history of the Greek language is included to broaden the reader's interest. Simple extracts from Plato, Euripides and Homer are used from the start, and the reader will soon begin to find the study of Ancient Greek a richly rewarding experience.

TEACH YOURSELF BOOKS